Emily Dickinson's Reception in the 1890s

Emily Dickinson's Reception in the 1890s

A DOCUMENTARY HISTORY

Edited by Willis J. Buckingham

UNIVERSITY OF PITTSBURGH PRESS

Published by the University of Pittsburgh Press, Pittsburgh, Pa. 15260
Copyright © 1989, University of Pittsburgh Press
Baker & Taylor International, London
Manufactured in the United States of America

Library of Congress Cataloging in Publication Data

Emily Dickinson's reception in the 1890s: a documentary
    history / edited by Willis J. Buckingham.
        p.   cm.
    Includes indexes.
    ISBN 0-8229-3604-6
    1. Dickinson, Emily, 1830–1886 — Criticism and interpretation.
    2. Dickinson, Emily, 1830–1886 — Bibliography.   I. Buckingham,
Willis J.
PS1541.Z5E44   1989
811'.4 — dc19   88-19816
                                                                    CIP

The frontispiece is reproduced by permission of the Trustees of Amherst College. The following photographs are also reprinted with
permission: pictures of Mabel Loomis Todd and Thomas Niles, courtesy of the Todd-Bingham Picture Collection, Manuscripts and Ar-
chives, Yale University Library; the juvenile portrait of Emily Dickinson, courtesy of Houghton Library of Harvard University Library;
the binding for the first printing of *Poems* (1890), courtesy of Joel
Myerson.

To
JOCELYN *and* DAVID
And especially to
DEBBIE

Fame is a bee.
  It has a song—
It has a sting—
  Ah, too, it has a wing.

  —*Emily Dickinson*

Contents

Acknowledgments

M A N Y have helped with this volume. It is a pleasure to thank staff members at the following libraries: American Antiquarian Society (Worcester, Mass.), Amherst College, Arizona State University (Hayden Library), Boston Public Library, British Library (London and Colindale), Chicago Public Library, Columbia University, Free Library of Philadelphia, Harvard University (Houghton and Widener Libraries), Indiana University, Jones Library, Library of Congress, Newberry Library, New England Deposit Library, New York Historical Society, New York Public Library, Northampton Public Library, Oxford University (Bodleian Library), Pennsylvania Historical Society, San Francisco Public Library, Springfield (Mass.) City Library, Union Theological Seminary, University of California at Berkeley and Los Angeles, University of London, Yale University (Beincke and Stirling Libraries).

I am grateful also to the kind assistance of Robin Pittman, Harold J. Flavin, Daniel Brink, Martin Orzeck, Kathryn Blatt, and Mark Olsen, and for the collegial expertise and encouragement of Jonathan Morse, Edwin H. Cady, Carlton Lowenberg, Joel Myerson, Bert Bender, and Barton Levi St. Armand. Jane Flanders of the University of Pittsburgh Press has done much to make this work more accurate and consistent. I have received crucial support from Wilfred Ferrell, Marvin Fisher, and Nicholas Salerno, Chairs of the Department of English, Arizona State University as well as financial assistance from the A.S.U. College of Liberal Arts and Sciences.

As noted in the Introduction, this volume builds on the review scrapbooks assembled by Mabel Loomis Todd. I wish to thank Yale University Library, where the albums are deposited among the Mabel Loomis Todd Papers, for granting permission to draw upon the scrapbooks and to quote from Mabel Todd's marginal comments in them. The Robert Frost Library, Amherst College, allowed generous access to its Higginson and Todd collections. I am indebted as well to the scholarship of others who have worked with these reviews, especially Klaus Lubbers and Virginia Terris.

The patience and encouragement of my wife, Debra Kessinger Buckingham, has been indispensable.

Art is the expression of a unique personality; yet there is no literature, not even the wildest Prophetic Books of Blake, that is not, in some measure, the joint production of author and public.
                                    —Albert Guerard, *Literature and Society* (1935)

Introduction

*"But then, Miss Dickinson was evidently born
to be the despair of reviewers."* [no. 319]

L AT E in 1890, in time for the Christmas trade, Roberts Brothers of
Boston issued a delicately pretty book of poems by a deceased and unknown writer named Emily Dickinson. As notices began to appear, the
volume's editors, Thomas Wentworth Higginson and Mabel Loomis
Todd, undertook to collect and preserve the reviews in clipping scrapbooks. Higginson added to his album only rarely, but Todd, as if understanding from the start its importance, brought to her work of compilation much of the same resolution and assiduity she gave to her editing
of the poems. She saved even the briefest notices that fell into her hand
and hired a press clipping service to extend her reach outside Amherst
and the circle of her friends. She assembled these clippings in chronologically ordered and meticulously arranged album pages, with handwritten notations identifying unlocated items and anonymous authors.
For each Dickinson volume she edited in the nineties—they included
two additional books of poems and an edition of the poet's letters—
Todd began a new scrapbook.

Mrs. Todd's daughter, Millicent Todd Bingham, appended to *Ancestors' Brocades* (Harper, 1945), a history of her mother's editing of Emily
Dickinson, a list of some 125 reviews drawn from the albums. Only
when the Todd scrapbooks were given to Yale University's Stirling Library after Mrs. Bingham's death in 1968 did it become apparent that her
clipping albums contained another nearly two hundred reviews not recorded in *Ancestors' Brocades.* Although Mabel Todd's collection is almost doubled in the present volume, it is to her vision and effort that
credit for its comprehensiveness must largely fall.

These documents allow a perspective of rarely achieved breadth on
American verse criticism and book publishing in the nineties. They
make it possible, for example, to learn more about the role of religious
family weeklies in contributing to the popular literary taste of the pe-

riod. As for Dickinson herself, the nineties reviewers were her contemporaries or near contemporaries, and their horizon of expectations could not have been wholly unpresupposed by her. Whether she shared or rejected those literary attitudes, they shaped her projection of an ideal reader. Moreover, these documents illustrate the interaction between readers, texts, and norms of valuation by which literary meaning is established and disestablished. They also offer a perspective on the modern championship of Dickinson which, so long preoccupied with recovering her work from genteel distortion, continues to risk separating her from the literary and historical contexts in which she wrote. Twentieth-century Dickinson criticism, in many ways, has been a history of mischaracterizing the nineteenth-century reception (as mostly unfavorable) for the purpose of writing against it. On the other hand, also revealed to literary excavation is the instability of end-of-the-century criticism compared to literary opinion when Dickinson began writing. She was published at the moment when the nineteenth century could feel, and take pleasure in, the alien force of her voice. These documents reveal how quickly and fundamentally Dickinson's first audience delighted in her "strangeness." Finally, the power of Dickinson's words to take on the inflections of succeeding generations lends intrinsic interest to the privileged responses of her first readers—their impressions unrepeatably exempt from the heft of major reputation.

The materials gathered here confirm Klaus Lubbers's thoughtful, well-researched chapters on the poet's early reception in his *Emily Dickinson: The Critical Revolution* (Univ. of Michigan, 1968). As he points out, Dickinson's early acclaim—surprising to all but the poet's sister—can be credited in part to Higginson's expertly promotional preface (item no. 10), his anonymous defense of her from the respected pages of the *Nation* (no. 28), and a *Harper's* review by William Dean Howells that described her first volume as "a distinctive addition to the literature of the world" (no. 64). Roberts Brothers did their part as well, binding the book with an eye toward Christmas and wedding sales and getting review copies into the right hands with notable efficiency. The number of reviews Dickinson's book elicited, in their quantity alone, suggests that it received a push from shore of unusual firmness for a first volume by an unknown poet.

But the nineties was a time of literary crazes and the immense amount of attention given Dickinson began to seem to some an unmerited excitement. Andrew Lang, a British critic well known in America, savaged Howells's Dickinson essay immediately (no. 72). American reviewers, who noted his remarks primarily for their contentious tone, were not ready to recant. There were adverse reviews and others that attempted to balance praise with blame, as the initial response continued, but the first important downward revaluation did not appear until the March 1891 issue of *Scribner's Monthly*. With blandishing evenness of tone, the anonymous critic undermined the often-remarked mainstay of Higginson's defense of Dickinson, that "when a thought takes one's breath away, a lesson on grammar seems an impertinence." "One thing is very certain," said *Scribner's*, "neglect of form involves the sacrifice of an element of positive attractiveness as well as offending positively by perverseness and eccentricity" (no. 123). The reviewer, by seeming reluctant to diminish Higginson's chivalrous apologetics with fair-minded criticism, only made his argument more persuasive.

Scribner's partially counterbalanced Howells's *Harper's* essay, while the *Century*, the other high-circulation arbiter of literary opinion, continued its conspicuous silence on Dickinson (as it would throughout the nineties), when the "Second Series" of her poems appeared a year after the first. The new collection was first met, much as was the earlier volume, with journalistic expressions of enthusiasm and longer critical articles rehashing the issue of form versus thought.

Partly to promote the "Second Series," Higginson had published in the *Atlantic* some of Dickinson's letters (no. 221). Whatever positive effect his article had, its contribution to the poet's critical acceptance was largely effaced by excoriating comment on her that appeared a few months later in the same journal (no. 325). Everyone knew the piece to have been written by New England's own Thomas Bailey Aldrich, a nationally prominent poet and critic and recent editor of the *Atlantic*, the region's august literary voice. His withering tone suggested that his silence on this latest Boston fad had been broken only because he could no longer countenance the lingering international embarrassment to New England literary culture that Dickinson's middlebrow enthusiasts had provoked. In New York, Aldrich's review was instantly noted and approvingly reprinted by Richard Henry Stoddard, another eminent genteel critic of the day (no. 333).

From this time forward (January 1892), the Dickinson rage was largely over. Higginson continued to speak well of her in the *Nation*, but the leading national literary monthlies declined to notice her 1894 volumes of letters and the 1896 "Third Series" of poems. Consistently friendly weeklies like the *Critic* and *Christian Union* changed their tone (nos. 316, 366). Even the loyal *Springfield Republican* cautioned that two books of Dickinson's verse were probably enough (no. 306). Aldrich's assessment insured that the decade's response to Dickinson would remain three-tiered: high-minded silence from the elite and largely New York critics (Aldrich, R. H. Stoddard, E. C. Stedman, Bayard Taylor, G. H. Boker, Brander Matthews, George Woodberry), a middle level of critical estimate treating Dickinson as troublesome but interesting, and a widespread noncritical enthusiasm for her work. Among the second and third groups of reviewers, only the latter maintained the unstinting appreciation struck by Howells and Higginson. The two-volume *Letters* was well received but notices of the poems declined in spiritedness and quantity and sales dipped sharply. *Poems,* "Second Series" (1891) found only slightly more than half the 10,000 buyers of the first; the *Letters* (1894) and *Poems* "Third Series" (1896) sold about two thousand copies each (see Appendix D).

At the point when an elitist aesthetic standard, over against the consensus standard, had nearly put Dickinson into eclipse, scattered younger critics took up her cause. They believed Dickinson would outlive her detractors. For Francis H. Stoddard, Dickinson's poems were not formless but "worded to so fine and subtle a device that they seem formless" (no. 334). For the younger Stoddard, Bliss Carman (nos. 557, 587), Harry Lyman Koopman (no. 560), Grace Musser (no. 526), and most acute and far-sighted of all, Rupert Hughes, only twenty-four years old, Dickinson was to be ranked where Howells had originally placed her, among America's permanent and most original contributors to the world's poetry (no. 553). Hughes believed that Dickinson's artistry had simply not been able to get through to the "orthodox worthies," so diverted were they with their own trivial etiquettes. A Chicago German-language paper looked back, in 1898, on her first reception as another example of that peculiarly American condition, the "tyranny of the majority" set over against genuine individual vitality (no. 581). With this flash of self-awareness, her first reception ended; the poet was to remain a footnote in literary history for another quarter century.

The decade's reviewing of Dickinson is marked by several characteristics. Two have been noted: a tendency to follow the leader and an inclination among younger critics to be less submissive to formalist preoccupations than their older colleagues. Readers of this volume will also discover a bias according to gender, women reviewers being more sympathetic, on average, than men. Regional differences become apparent as well. Some New York and western publications warned against Dickinson as a "Boston fad" (nos. 479, 522), the enervated exemplar of a waning New England school of letters (no. 530). One California paper, early on, suggested that her popularity was the self-serving creation of a "New England clique" (no. 140). The British were similarly disinclined to place themselves in Boston's orbit. Finally, notices may be grouped to some extent by the type of periodical in which they appeared. Newspapers often were friendlier than periodicals, just as the family, society and religious weeklies tended to be less critical than their more strictly literary counterparts.

From the vantage point of a century later, Dickinson's first reception prompts two questions: Why was she liked so well? Why was she liked so little? That is, given her supposed modernity, and the decade's vitiated formalism, how could Dickinson, on first hearing, have found even a modest audience, much less wide acclaim? On the other hand, how could an entire literary community have known her work and yet have understood it so poorly that she was to earn only the transitory success of the popular writer, the favorite of a day? Although this is not the place for exhaustive consideration of these questions, a few observations may be helpful. As to how Dickinson could have made such a stir in the lifeless literary milieu she seems now to so deftly subvert, it should be remembered that of all her qualities, the nineties liked best her originality, strangeness, and force. Arlo Bates, at the beginning, called her "delightfully pagan" (no. 21). For many reviewers in the nineties, the world already had as many "excellent formalists" as it needed (no. 216).

Dickinson's unusual verse did not constitute, universally, an affront. Whitman had opened the door to critical valuation of "incoherence and formlessness" (no. 337). Browning had written poems that were not easily understood (no. 571). To an extent, perhaps, that we cannot now hear, Dickinson's verse had the ring of the nineties in it. As Virginia Terris has suggested in her dissertation, "Emily Dickinson and the Genteel Critics" (New York Univ., 1973), Dickinson's poetry portrayed New England life and landscape, often employing native diction and humor. In addition, it was pleasingly quotable, spiritual, didactic, and "intensely ethical" (no. 27), expressing various calls to self-denial and duty, as in such poems as the widely noted "If I can stop one heart from breaking." It drew upon popular themes in female verse, such as womanhood, home, human relationships, melancholy, and death. It seemed founded on approved literary sources, Emerson above all. The poet's outward life met the decade's severest canons of female and literary respectability. There was nothing in Dickinson's eccentricities comparable to Amy Lowell's cigar.

The poems chosen for publication in the nineties are among her least difficult. Her editors knew there was little enthusiasm at the time for poems as riddles. "Because a plain matter is put in obscure words," said the *New York Commercial Advertiser*, "it is not, therefore, poetry" (no. 545). The editors also did what they could to reduce the oddity of the poems they did choose, making changes in fifty of the one hundred fifteen poems published in the first volume. They further conventionalized the manuscripts by adding generalizing titles of a type used in the decade, such as "Reticence" and "Disenchantment." The editors' topical divisions, sectioning all three volumes into categories headed "Life," "Love," "Nature," and "Time and Eternity," brought the architecture of Dickinson's books into conformity with others of the period.

Another reason Dickinson found so much acceptance is that her work was experienced as fulfilling many of the common reader's religious and sentimental expectations for poetry. If it is surprising to learn that two of Dickinson's erotic poems were chosen for the first and second editions, "My river runs to thee" and "Wild nights, wild nights," it is not astonishing that each was mentioned, among hundreds of reviews, only once. Also unnoticed were many of her most powerful poems of spiritual dereliction and despair, among them "There's a certain slant of light," "I felt a funeral in my brain," "Essential oils are wrung," and "They say that 'time assuages.'" When a despair poem *was* discussed, as was "The heart asks pleasure first," reviewers understood it to refer only to the suffering of certain people (nos. 13, 26), read it to imply an acceptance of fate "without any sign of pessimism" (no. 581), or believed it traced "the course of the weak pleasure-seeker, who is without aspiration or hope except to avoid the results of his folly" (no. 151). These poems were not ignored or misread because of their themes, for many poets of the period expressed pain and despair. Rather the modern age perceives in Dickinson a depth of psychic derangement, and an evocative power in her fractured poetics, that the nineties was unprepared to discover. At the last moment in history when it was still thought possible to see things steadily and whole, it is a mark not only of the poet's camouflage, but of stretching of the cultural seams, that her fleeting verses received the recognition they did. Had she published while in mid-career during the sixties, it is likely that her linguistic freedoms would have received even less acceptance than they did in the nineties. As Barton Levi St. Armand has suggested, and as evidence in this volume will roundly support, the decade tolerated her as well as it did partly because "there was a renewed vogue for New England 'antiquities' of all kinds [during the nineties], and so Dickinson was hailed as the last fading flower of American Puritanism."[1] In addition, Dickinson made her appearance when genteel criticism was in decline. Her seeming disregard for "rules" accorded with a changing literary ethos. In the words of a San Francisco reviewer, "If Emily Dickinson had written to-day, she would have found herself in the full sweep of the art movement, which contends for originality and freshness of expression, at the sacrifice of every art form — instead of the hackneyed, which is powerless to really express" (no. 526).

The parallel question, why Dickinson could be both well known and not better understood, finds a parallel explanation. Modernism, nascent in the nineties, had to reach fuller self-understanding before it could find its expression in Dickinson. Readers still liked euphony and concord in poetry; they liked rhymes. Dickinson's poetics denied them accus-

1. Barton Levi St. Armand, *Emily Dickinson and Her Culture: The Soul's Society* (Cambridge: Cambridge Univ. Press, 1984), p. 3.

tomed pleasures. But stylistic aberrations alone do not account for the unease of her first readers. In her worst reviews, for example, literary rivalries played a part. Had Andrew Lang not enjoyed a longstanding enmity with Howells and Higginson, he probably would not have bothered with an American village recluse. The *New York Tribune's* punishing notices reflect that paper's loathing for the *New York Post,* whose parent company also owned the *Nation,* both associated with Higginson. Furthermore, though there was nothing untoward about the poet's life, it was hard for the nineties to view her as a figure of national importance because of the limited poetic range it supposed available to a woman who chose such a cloistered life. Higginson prefaced his invitation to her to attend some literary gatherings in Boston with the comment, "It is hard [for me] to understand how you can live so alone, with thoughts of such a quality coming up in you" (*L* 2:461). The nineties also felt that however appropriate it was for a woman to write in the lyric and other less weighty poetic modes, Dickinson's verses were too fractional to qualify as serious art. In the language of a reviewer who means to be appreciative, "The verses at their best have also an indefinable charm of will-o' the wisp-ness, leading you to feel that the poet is just about to reach a higher height of solid greatness, and will attain next time, and making it impossible for you not to turn the page to see" (no. 552).

Dickinson's much proclaimed "originality" was another asset that under the surface was a liability as well. When Higginson pointed out that she drew on recognized literary models, Emerson and Blake, for example, while others mentioned Browning, the decade's darling, it was all to her favor. But when one considers that the nineties compared or contrasted her to no fewer than ninety-five other writers, clearly critics found it difficult to discover a secure niche for her in literary history. Their uncertainty was not just an inconvenience; it was the index of her willful aberrancy. The year Dickinson died, George Woodberry argued in the *Nation* that literature is only useful when it communicates shared experience.[2] Dickinson, by contrast, was literature's "odd child" (no. 119). As an individual talent with no tradition, it is remarkable that she came as close as she did to major status among her earliest readers.

We know from her bold, self-effacing first letters to Higginson, that Emily Dickinson was concerned about how she might be understood by her contemporaries. The documents that follow reveal the meanings her words would have for persons close to her in time and place—with one caution. Readers and reviewers cannot be equated, for the latter may reflect what they believe their readers *ought* to appreciate rather than what they honestly enjoy themselves. Yet, as Cathy Davidson has

2. George Woodberry, "Mr. Lowell's New Volume," *Nation* 43 (1886): 525–27.

pointed out, the ordinary reader, as consumer, increasingly "replaced the socially prominent critic as the primary arbiter of nineteenth-century taste."[3] The marketplace demanded that those who produced and promoted books cater to the preferences of their widest potential readership. The effort represented by Aldrich to push Dickinson out of the canon demonstrates a late effort of elite readers to retain a measure of control over literary culture. The more apparently prescriptive the review, the more clearly does it divulge the standards and opinions it was written to raise. This collection strives to minimize bias against the common reader by bringing together all published comment on Dickinson, rather than drawing selectively from "high-culture" critics. Access to Dickinson's specifically private as opposed to public readership is provided by Appendix B, a list of nineties diaries and letters referring to her that were not published until the twentieth century.

This question of which literary standard applied to Dickinson, the privileged or common, took ironic twists during the first decade of her publication. She was announced and initially portrayed as a quality writer who would appeal mainly to "the few"—to the more intelligent and thoughtful members of the reading public (nos. 13, 21, 22, 24, 37, among others). People who might pick up a book of poems "while they wait for the dinner bell or the carriage" could hardly be expected to enjoy the Emersonian epigrams of a recluse genius (no. 86). But when it became evident that booksellers couldn't keep the new poet on their shelves, Dickinson's popularity was charged against her. Parnassian critics like Lang and Aldrich could argue that when the public's thirst for novelty wore off, and the ineluctable touchstones of art and even of grammar were applied to her poems, her "versicles" would slip into oblivion. Critics like Elisha Edwards replied, "The great public does not mind if a poem is ungrammatical or is not a well of English undefiled, provided it only touches something in the human heart" (no. 335), but in this and similar statements Dickinson's defenders began to sound like apologists for a Philistine poetics. They had lost the high ground.

Had Dickinson been Whitman, help might have arrived from a vigorous new group of realist and naturalist critics in revolt against the criterion of beauty as espoused by the whole panoply of genteel, formalist, idealist, and aesthetic movements of the nineties. They sought to elevate truth above aesthetics, but the truths they wished to raise were to be sane and wholesome. Dickinson was not socially uplifting. She may have been, as Howells and others suggested, a type of her race, but for some this type was old-fashioned—"girly-girly" (no. 479). Without mentioning Dickinson by name, one critic may well have had her

3. Cathy Davidson, *Revolution and the Word: The Rise of the Novel in America* (New York: Oxford Univ. Press, 1986), p. 53.

in mind when in 1891 he deplored the rise of a "brain-sickly" school of literature marked by "morbid despair" wherein "acuteness of feeling is in excess of clearness of vision."[4] By the end of the century the last hope for edging Dickinson into the canon lay with those like Francis Stoddard and Rupert Hughes who, as mentioned above, rested their case on the subtlety of her art. She ended the decade as she began, a highbrow poet.

Dickinson's first recognition reveals how literature has been read and judged. Does it also have interpretive value? Whether one is speaking of the literary milieu of her true contemporaries, or that of the nineties, Dickinson, like Whitman, "stood in and out of the game." Her end-of-the-century audience can tell us little with certainty about the creative self-awareness of the artist herself. The light that reflects back so tellingly on her readers in these reviews, glances off their ostensible subject. Interpretation of Dickinson will nevertheless continue to need the countering push of all we can know about her time and place. It is revealing of our impatience with the nineteenth century that Susan Dickinson's obituary of her sister-in-law received its only modern reprinting with the following sentences deleted (see Appendix A):

One can only speak of "duties beautifully done"; of her gentle tillage of the rare flowers filling her conservatory, into which, as into the heavenly Paradise, entered nothing that could defile, and which was ever abloom in frost or sunshine, so well she knew her chemistries; of her tenderness to all in the home circle; her gentlewoman's grace and courtesy to all who served in house and grounds; her quick and rich response to all who rejoiced or suffered at home; or among her wide circle of friends the world over. This side of her nature was to her the real entity in which she rested, so simple and strong was her instinct that a woman's hearthstone is her shrine.

Talk of shrines, duties, and rare flowers probably did not occasion the same uneasiness for the poet as it does for readers one hundred years later. In this sense, the nineties readership might well poke a collective finger at their modern counterparts, questioning their readiness to read.

The value of the nineties response for the modern reader lies also in its capacity to teach the lesson of indeterminacy, "the resistance of art to the meanings it provokes."[5] These documents provide a laboratory perspective on how a generation's determination to make a poet its own

4. F. O. Eggleston, "Brain-sickly Literature," *Unitarian Review* 35 (1891): 477.
5. Geoffrey Hartman, *Criticism in the Wilderness: The Study of Literature Today* (New Haven, Conn.: Yale Univ. Press, 1980), p. 269.

was at every moment undermined by the texts themselves. As a reading community, the nineties kept alive the "strangeness" of Dickinson's verse but could not achieve the necessary distance from its own synthesizing and consistency-building activity to see how the poems slipped away from their attempts to master them. For a modern reader, these reviews powerfully manifest the openness and resistant power of Dickinson's poems.

Some may also find that this collection has value in teaching one to read as a nineties reader. Learning to "read as a woman," for example, has and is earning its place as a productive strategy for experiencing Dickinson's poems. It furnishes clues and affiliations, however, rather than a unifying or all-sufficient perspective, for there are many ways of reading as a woman (i.e., as a reader empathetic with feminine experience): reading as a nineteenth-century woman, a modern woman, an anorexic woman, a woman reading other women, and so on.[6] While not giving up hope for a critical lens that someday will bring all the poems into a single satisfying circumference, Dickinson readers in the meantime appear to enjoy reading playfully, eclectically, and individually. They engage the poems through various adoptive sympathies—existentialism, Christianity, transcendentalism (to name at random a few of the most easily labeled)—appropriating each as it seems revelatory. To read as a nineties reader carries the advantage of reading with some of the pieties Susan Dickinson speaks of still in place. The fullest promise of these reviews will finally lie in the capacity of new generations of readers to discover in them—and to compose out of them—yet another valued constituent of their own patient questioning of Dickinson's words.

The chief function of the present volume is rendered not so much in adding bibliographically to the first chapter of Dickinson's literary life as in making the documents which reveal that history fully accessible. To date, the most extensive reprinting of nineties material is a gathering of sixteen items in *The Recognition of Emily Dickinson*, an anthology of selected criticism from 1890 to 1960 edited by Caesar R. Blake and Carlton F. Wells (Univ. of Michigan, 1964). Most of the early reviews assembled there are from journals such as *Scribner's* and *The Atlantic*, whose back numbers are still readily available. But the great bulk of comment from the nineties lies in the crumbling pages of such periodicals as *The Housekeeper's Weekly*, now retrievable only at a few depositories. The near unavailability of this primary material has allowed even accomplished students of the period to generalize on too little in-

---

6. For discussion of "reading as a woman" as an example of the nature of the reading experience and of the consequences of reading, see Jonathan Culler, *On Deconstruction: Theory and Criticism after Structuralism* (Ithaca, N.Y.: Cornell Univ. Press, 1982), pp. 43–64.

formation; it has been suggested, for example, that "the public's initial reaction" to Dickinson was to view her "as a culturally impoverished literary freak."[7] The present volume seeks, in brushing away the dust, to ensure full knowledge of a remarkable poetic debut. Among the exhibits are bits of biographical remains, such as the affair of the nicked plate, which appear to have eluded modern research (see no. 348; also Index and Finding List, *s.v.* reminiscences).

This volume reprints all comment on Dickinson published in the nineties known to the editor (to whom additions and corrections are most welcome). Nine items added after entry numbering was established — they are given an "A" extension to an existing number — bring the total entries to 600. Coverage is inclusive for brief mention and such ephemera as poems in tribute. Annotations preceding each item are usually confined to matters of publication and attribution; readers may locate information about periodicals and authors in the Index and Finding List. In the case of serials, for example, this index notes place of publication, frequency of issue, subject interests, and estimated circulation. British places of publication appear in heading citations so that English and American reviewing can be broadly distinguished without consulting the index. To avoid annotative duplication, the names of persons, works, and obscure references within the texts of the reviews are identified in the index rather than in footnotes. Subject headings of a more general nature appear in the main index as well. It cites those notices which give significant attention to Dickinson's use of rhyme, for example, or which contain parodies of the poet. The Index and Finding List is followed by a separate enumeration, by first line, of poems discussed or quoted in the reviews. The first appendix reprints the full text of the poet's obituary. Appendix B brings together references to Dickinson from diaries and letters of the period not published until the twentieth century. Appendix C registers unverifiable and probably erroneous citations of nineties material found in other studies. Sales of Dickinson's books are delineated by individual printing in Appendix D. Appendix E collects reviews that followed a 1905 London reissue of Dickinson's first volume.

The separate publication of Dickinson in periodicals, newspapers, and anthologies, when unaccompanied by comment, is not represented here. Those interested in this component of her reception may consult several sources: (a) an appendix listing poems which first appeared in nineties periodicals published in Thomas H. Johnson's variorum, *The Poems of Emily Dickinson* (Harvard, 1955) 3:1207–08; (b) a list of four-

---

7. Thomas Woodson, "'Oblivion Lingers in the Neighborhood': The Loss and Recovery of 19th-Century American Literature," *Bulletin of the Midwest Modern Language Association* 7 (1974): 35.

teen anthologies of the decade that include Dickinson poems in Klaus
Lubbers's *Emily Dickinson: The Critical Revolution*, pp. 273–74; (c) discussions and summary listings of poems reprinted in the nineties contained in Virginia Terris's thesis, "Emily Dickinson and the Genteel
Critics" (New York Univ., 1973), *passim*. The extent to which individual
poems were mentioned or quoted in nineties reviews can be determined
from the index to first lines in this volume.

Roberts Brothers advertisements are listed only when they add to the
critical record by including comment about a Dickinson volume they
announce. For example, during the nineties Dickinson books appear in
thirty ads placed by Roberts Brothers in *Publishers' Weekly*. Twenty-
six contain only routine author-title information and are not collected
here; the four that add a blurb are nos. 130, 160, 346, 511. These and other
promotional use of reviews may be located in the Index and Finding List,
s.v. advertisements.

The documents that follow are arranged chronologically. Within days,
items appear alphabetically by author's last name, and by journal or book
title. Those lacking a source of publication are placed last on the date
of their publication when it is known. Loose clippings, bereft of date
or source, are filed according to their probable time of publication. When
more than one anonymous item appeared in the same issue of a journal,
the sequence of original publication is followed. In addressing problems
of identification, the headnotes use "unlocated" to mean that no search
for the item was carried out because its presumed source was either
unknown or unavailable. "Unverified" indicates that the item's cited
source was located and examined without result.

The reviews assembled here, with certain exceptions, are neither abbreviated nor corrected. Routine publication data for a Dickinson book
under review is deleted. Clear typographical errors are silently amended
both in the reviews themselves and in their quotation from Dickinson.
Alterations to quoted poems, when they constitute a meaningful tex-
tual change that may have been deliberate, are allowed to stand. Original language from the nineties Dickinson editions is bracketed next to
the changed passages where they occur in the review. Repunctuations
of the poems are carefully retained, but because they occur so often
readers will have to compare the review versons with the Todd-Higginson
originals themselves. To have marked each deviation here would have
led to printing half of the poems twice.

Normally, when the reviews address a variety of subjects, only that
portion relating to Dickinson is reproduced. Broader inclusiveness is
adopted for survey articles that place or rank Dickinson's books in relation to other current publications. In some of these cases the entire essay
is included to reveal the proportion of comment accorded Dickinson
and to convey the nature and flavor of her competition in the literary

marketplace. Reprintings within the decade are given separate entry status, with cross-referencing to first publication. Unless otherwise specified, square brackets in the texts of the reviews enclose the present editor's own interpolation. Reviewers' deletion marks have here been standardized as ellipsis points and asterisks have been added to indicate the end of one poem or part of poem and the beginning of another when not clearly distinguished in the original.

The word *edition* was more loosely used in the nineties than it is today. The advertisement, reprinted as item 307, illustrates the difficulty: reissues were then commonly described as editions. In the notices that follow, *edition* usually refers to Roberts Brothers' reissue of a Dickinson volume to meet unanticipated demand—a new printing order, merely, with or without a binding change. Much less often in these reviews, and normally clear from context, *edition* signifies a new collection of Dickinson's poems.

Reviews and Notices
of Emily Dickinson,
1890–1899

Abbreviations

The following abbreviations are used throughout:

AB   *Ancestors' Brocades*, by Millicent Todd Bingham. New York and London: Harper & Brothers, 1945.

CR   *Emily Dickinson: The Critical Revolution*, by Klaus Lubbers. Ann Arbor: University of Michigan Press, 1968.

DB   *Emily Dickinson: A Descriptive Bibliography*, by Joel Myerson. Pittsburgh, Pa.: University of Pittsburgh Press, 1984.

GC   "Emily Dickinson and the Genteel Critics," by Virginia Rinaldy Terris. Ph.D. diss., New York University, 1973. 384 pp. Facsimile issued on demand by University Microfilms, Ann Arbor, Michigan. Diss. no. 73-19,976.

Home   *Emily Dickinson's Home*, by Millicent Todd Bingham. New York: Harper & Brothers, 1955.

L   *The Letters of Emily Dickinson*, ed. Thomas H. Johnson and Theodora Ward. 3 vols. Cambridge, Mass.: The Belknap Press of Harvard University Press, 1958.

Life   *The Life of Emily Dickinson*, by Richard B. Sewall. 2 vols. New York: Farrar, Straus and Giroux, 1974.

YH   *The Years and Hours of Emily Dickinson*, by Jay Leyda. 2 vols. New Haven, Conn.: Yale University Press, 1960.

1   Alexander Young. "Boston Letter." *Critic*, n.s. 14 (August 2, 1890), 60. In promoting Dickinson's book, Roberts Brothers made frequent use of its contact with the Boston correspondent for the *Critic*, New York's leading literary weekly.

A volume of "Poems," which the same firm will bring out in the autumn, is by the late Emily Dickinson, an intimate friend of Helen Hunt, who was a warm admirer of her poetry. She was a woman of vigorous intellect, and her verse demands and repays careful study. Her cast of mind is analytical, and she sounds the depths of poetic insight into the philosophy of things. One of her poems called "Success" was written for that anonymous publication "A Masque of Poets," and the August *Scribner's* has another, entitled "Renunciation." The volume is edited by Col. Higginson, who contributes a preface to it.

2   Thomas Wentworth Higginson. "An Open Portfolio." *Christian Union* 42 (September 25, 1890), 392–93. This essay seeks to prepare an audience for the volume of Dickinson's verse edited by Higginson and Todd that was to appear in November. Higginson's preface to that volume (see no. 10) bears great similarity to this article, though here he provides numerous illustrations from the poet's work. His argument, particularly his stress on the poet's seclusion and on the primitive, Blake-like quality of her verse, became standard points of reference for reviewers throughout the decade. Higginson prepared this article early in July, having in hand the manuscript Roberts would use as the copytext for *Poems*, 1890. Some differences between the article and book versions of the poems seem intended; others are likely copying errors, Higginson's or the *Christian Union's*. The full Latin motto by which he titles Dickinson's "Departed to the Judgment" is "Astra castra, numen, lumen munimen" (The stars are my camp, the Deity is my light and guard).

Emerson said, many years since, in the "Dial," that the most interesting department of poetry would hereafter be found in what might be called "The Poetry of the Portfolio"; the work, that is, of persons who wrote for the relief of their own minds, and without thought of publication. Such poetry, when accumulated for years, will have at least the merit of perfect freedom; accompanied, of course, by whatever drawback follows from the habitual absence of criticism. Thought will have its full strength and uplifting, but without the proper control and chastening of literary expression; there will be wonderful strokes and felicities, and yet an incomplete and unsatisfactory whole. If we believe, with Ruskin, that "no beauty of execution can outweigh one grain or fragment of thought," then we may often gain by the seclusion of the portfolio, which rests content with a first stroke and does not over-refine and prune away afterwards. Such a sheaf of unpublished verse lies before me, the life-work of a woman so secluded that she lived literally indoors by choice for many years, and within the limits of her father's estate for many more — who shrank even from the tranquil society of a New England college town, and yet loved her few friends with profound devotedness, and divided her life between them and her flowers. It absolutely startles one to find among the memorials of this secluded inland life a picture so vividly objective as this:

BY THE SEA.

Glee! the great storm is over!
    Four have recovered the land;
Forty gone down together
    Into the boiling sand.

Ring! for the scant salvation!
    Toll! for the bonnie souls,
Neighbor and friend and bridegroom,
    Spinning upon the shoals.

How they will tell the shipwreck
    When winter shakes the door,
Till the children ask, "But the forty?
    Did they come back no more?"

Then a silence suffuses the story
    And a softness the teller's eye,
And the children no further question;
    And only the waves reply.

Celia Thaxter on her rocky island, Jean Ingelow by her English cliffs, never drew a sea picture in stronger lines than this secluded woman in her inland village, who writes elsewhere, as tersely:

I never saw a moor,
    I never saw the sea,
Yet know I how the heather looks
    And what the billows be.   [what a wave must be

I never spoke with God
    Nor visited in heaven,
Yet certain am I of the spot,
    As if the chart were given.

See now with what corresponding vigor she draws the mightier storms and shipwrecks of the soul; the title being here, as elsewhere, my own, for she herself never prefixes any:

ROUGE ET NOIR.

Soul, wilt thou toss again?
By just such a hazard
Hundreds have lost, indeed,
But tens have won an all.

Angels' breathless ballot
Lingers to record thee;
Imps in eager caucus
Raffle for my soul!

Was ever the concentrated contest of a lifetime, the very issue between good
and evil, put into fewer words? Then comes another, which might fairly be linked
with it, and might be called

ROUGE GAGNE!

'Tis so much joy! 'Tis so much joy!
If I should fail, what poverty!
    And yet as poor as I
Have ventured all upon a throw;
Have gained! Yes! Hesitated so
    This side the victory.

Life is but life, and death but death!
Bliss is but bliss, and breath but breath!
    And if indeed I fail,
At least, to know the worst is sweet!
Defeat means nothing but defeat,
    No drearier can prevail.

And if I gain! O sun at sea!   [gun
O bells! that in the steeple be,   [steeples
    At first, repeat it slow!
For heaven is a different thing
Conjectured and worked sudden in,   [waked
    And might o'erwhelm me so.

Many of these poems are, as might be expected, drawn from the aspects of
Nature, but always with some insight or image of their own; as in the following,
which might be called

THE SEA OF SUNSET.

This is the land the sunset washes,
    These are the banks of the yellow sea;
Where it rose, or whither it rushes,
    These are the western mystery.

Night after night, her purple traffic
    Strews the landing with opal bales,
Merchantmen poise upon horizons,
    Dip and vanish with airy sails.   [fairy

Or this:

THE WIND.

Of all the sounds despatched abroad
   There's not a charge to me
Like that old measure in the boughs,
   That phraseless melody
The wind makes, working like a hand   [wind does,
   Whose fingers brush the sky,
Then quiver down, with tufts of tune,
   Permitted gods—and me.

I crave him grace of summer boughs
   If such an outcast be
Who never heard that fleshless chant
   Rise solemn in the tree;
As if some caravan of sound
   On deserts in the sky
Had broken rank, then knit, and passed
   In seamless company.

This last image needs no praise, and in dealing with Nature she often seems to possess—as was said of her fellow townswoman, Helen Jackson ("H. H.")—a sixth sense. But most of her poems grapple at first hand—the more audaciously the better—with the very mysteries of life and death, as in the following:

TWO KINSMEN.

I died for Beauty, but was scarce
   Adjusted in the tomb
When one who died for Truth was lain
   In an adjoining room.

He questioned softly, why I failed?
   "For Beauty," I replied;
"And I for Truth—the two are one—
   We brethren are," he said.

And so, as kinsmen, met a night,
   We talked between the rooms
Until the moss had reached our lips
And covered up our names.

The conception is weird enough for William Blake, and one can no more criticize a faulty rhyme here and there than a defect of drawing in one of Blake's pictures. When a thought takes one's breath away, who cares to count the syllables? The same iron strength shows itself, merging into tenderness, in this brief dirge for one of the nameless Marthas, cumbered about many things:

REQUIESCAT.

How many times these low feet staggered
   Only the soldered month can tell;   [mouth
Try! can you stir the awful rivet?
   Try! can you lift the hasps of steel?

Stroke the cool forehead, hot so often;
   Lift, if you can, the listless hair;

Handle the adamantine fingers
  Never a thimble more shall wear.

Buzz the dull flies on the chamber window;
  Brave shines the sun through the freckled pane;
Fearless the cobweb swings from the ceiling;
  Indolent housewife! in daisies lain.

The unutterable dignity of death seems to have forced itself again and again upon this lonely woman, and she has several times touched it with her accustomed terse strength, as in these verses:

One dignity delays for all,
  One mitred afternoon.
None can avoid this purple;
  None can evade this crown.

Coach it insures, and footmen,
  Chamber and state and throng,
Bells also, in the village,
  As we ride grand along.

What dignified attendants!
  What service when we pause!
How loyally, at parting,
  Their hundred hats they raise!

What pomp surpassing ermine
  When simple you and I
Present our meek escutcheon
  And claim the rank to die!

Then, approaching the great change from time to eternity at a different angle, she gives two verses of superb concentration, like the following, which might be christened, after the medieval motto,

ASTRA CASTRA.

Departed to the Judgment
  A mighty afternoon;
Great clouds, like ushers, leaning
  Creation looking on.

The flesh surrendered, canceled,
  The bodiless begun;
Two worlds, like audiences, disperse,
  And leave the soul alone.

She shrinks from no concomitant of death; all is ennobled in her imagination:

Safe in their alabaster chambers,
  Untouched by morning and untouched by noon,
Sleep the meek members of the resurrection;
  Rafter of satin and roof of stone.

Light laughs the breeze in her castle above them;   [castle of sunshine
  Babbles the bee in a stolid ear;
Pipe the sweet birds in ignorant cadence—
  Ah! what sagacity perished here!

This is the form in which she finally left these lines, but as she sent them to me, years ago, the following took the place of the second verse, and it seems to me that, with all its too daring condensation, it strikes a note too fine to be lost:

> Grand go the years in the crescent above them,
>> Worlds scoop their arcs, and firmaments row;
> Diadems drop, and Doges surrender,
>> Soundless as dots on a disk of snow.

But with these mighty visions of death and eternity, there are such touches of tender individual sympathy as we find in this, which may be called

TOO LATE.

> Delayed till she had ceased to know!
> Delayed till in its vest of snow
>> Her loving bosom lay.
> An hour behind the fleeting breath!
> Later by just an hour than Death!
>> O! lagging yesterday!
>
> Could she have guessed that it would be;
> Could but a crier of the glee
>> Have climbed the distant hill;
> Had not the bliss so slow a pace,
> Who knows but this surrendered face
>> Were undefeated still?
>
> O! if there may departing be
> Any forgot by victory
>> In her imperial sound,   [round
> Show them this meek-appareled thing,
> That could not stop to be a king,
>> Doubtful if it be crowned!

Almost all these poems are strangely impersonal, but here and there we have a glimpse of experiences too intense to be more plainly intimated, as in the following:

> I shall know why, when time is over
>> And I have ceased to wonder why;
> Christ will explain each separate anguish
>> In the fair schoolroom of the sky.
>
> He will tell me what Peter promised,
>> And I, for wonder at his woe,
> I shall forget the drop of anguish
>> That scalds me now—that scalds me now!

Surely this is as if woven out of the heart's own atoms, and will endear the name of Emily Dickinson, in some hour of trial, to those who never before encountered that name, and who will seek it vainly in the cyclopedias. Her verses are in most cases like poetry plucked up by the roots; we have them with earth, stones, and dew adhering, and must accept them as they are. Wayward and unconventional in the last degree; defiant of form, measure, rhyme, and even grammar; she yet had an exacting standard of her own, and would wait many days for a word that satisfied. Asked again and again for verses to be published, she scarcely ever yielded, even to a friend so tried and dear as the late Mr. Bowles, of the Springfield "Republican"; but she sent her poems with gifts of flowers or—as in my own case—to correspondents whom she had never seen. It is with some misgiving, and almost with a sense of questionable publicity, that it has at last been decided by her surviving sister and her friends to print a small selection from these poems, which will be issued by Roberts Brothers, Boston. The only hint found among her papers of any possible contact with a wider public is found in these few lines, which—although probably the utterance of a passing mood only—have been selected as the prelude to the forthcoming volume:

> This is my letter to the world
>   That never wrote to me;
> The simple news that nature told
>   With tender majesty.
>
> Her message is committed
>   To hands I cannot see;
> For love of her, sweet countrymen,
>   Judge tenderly of me!

3   Alexander Young. "Boston Letter." *Critic*, n.s. 14 (October 11, 1890), 183–84.

The volume of "Poems" by the late Emily Dickinson, which Roberts Bros. are to publish next month and which is edited by two of her friends, Mabel Loomis Todd and T. W. Higginson, is of a quality so fine that the wonder is that she had hardly given anything to the world in her lifetime. Having read the advance-sheets I can bear witness to the originality and strength of these poems, their union of profound insight into nature and life with a remarkable vividness of description. They are compact with thought and imagination and have a quaint directness that is emphasized by the neglect of the attractions of form which some of them betray. But the rough diamonds in the collection have a value beyond that of many polished gems of poetry. Col. Higginson in his discriminating preface remarks that the quality of these poems is more suggestive of the poetry of William Blake than of any other author, and he gives an interesting picture of the secluded life of Miss Dickinson, who "habitually concealed her mind like her person from all but a very few friends, and it was with great difficulty that she was persuaded to print during her lifetime three or four poems." Although Col. Higginson had corresponded with her for many years he saw her but twice face to face, and "brought away the impression of something as unique and remote as Undine or Mignon or Thekla."

4   "Jottings." *Boston Transcript*, October 13, 1890, p. 4.

. . . . Here are two charming stanzas on autumn from the advance sheets of the book of poems by Emily Dickinson of Amherst, who lived and died a recluse in her native town:

> The morns are meeker than they were,
>   The nuts are getting brown;
> The berry's cheek is plumper,
>   The rose is out of town.

> The maple wears a gayer scarf,
>   The field a scarlet gown.
> Lest I should be old-fashioned
>   I'll put a trinket on.

5   "Jottings." *Boston Transcript,* October 14, 1890, p. 4.

. . . . "H. H." was a great admirer of the poetry of Emily Dickinson, whose work is soon to be published, with an appreciative memoir by Mrs. Mabel Loomis Todd and Colonel T. W. Higginson. She often used to praise these unpublished poems to her friends, particularly to Mr. Niles, but Miss Dickinson did not wish to see them in print during her lifetime. "Suspense" is one of these lovely fragments:

> Elysium is as far to   [as far as to
> The very nearest room,
> If in that room a friend await
> Felicity or doom.
>
> What fortitude the soul contains,
> That it can so endure
> The accent of a coming foot,
> The opening of a door!

6   "Literary Notes." *Independent* 42 (October 30, 1890), 1533.

. . . . Poems by Emily Dickinson, edited by her friends, Mabel Loomis Todd and Col. T. W. Higginson, are just published by Roberts Brothers, Boston. Miss Dickinson lived in voluntary retirement, but possessed a deep poetic nature which makes us anxious to see this volume of her modest verses of which we can see in advance that they will be piquant, spirited, and cast in no conventional mold.

7   Mabel Loomis Todd. "Bright Bits From Bright Books." *Home Magazine*
       3 (November 1890), 13. Her position as book columnist for a Washington,
       D.C., women's monthly allowed Mrs. Todd this opportunity to pro-
       mote the forthcoming Dickinson volume. It is remarkable the extent to
       which even Mrs. Todd sought to create an initial interest in the poet by
       reference to the poets' singular life; she appears here, at least, to believe
       that such an approach will secure a strong, sympathetic response from
       women.

I open my article this month with a book which is perhaps one of the most re-markable collections of recently printed verse.

In the literature of the hour we are so accustomed to reading verses in good form, to be sure, with proper rhyme and rhythm, but filled with platitudes of thought—worn-out ideas re-dressed, re-arranged and re-served—that coming upon anything like the present volume is hardly less than a shock. Careless of form, scarcely thinking of the rhyme, knowing or caring nothing of ancient and accepted laws and customs in verse-making, Emily Dickinson has yet never written a line which is not replete with some deep thought, stimulating or satisfying, as the case may be, thoroughly her own, startlingly original, and often appalling in the im-mense fields which it opens of deathless conjecture and desire.

In many of her poems the meaning is so veiled that only the most sympathetic will apprehend the hidden reality. Sometimes but a glimpse is given — and then we may grope in vain for another clue. But the strength and the strangeness of these verses are equally haunting.

The life of their author was intensely picturesque, and at the same time perfectly simple. She merely lived out her own ideas — a thing for which most of us have not the courage. For more than fifty years her home was in Amherst, Massachusetts, yet few of the present residents in the beautiful little town have seen or spoken with her. Only those whose memories go back to her youth can tell of ordinary personal relations with her. But no one was better known.

Finding as her life went on that society grew more distasteful, that the hollowness and insincerity of its forms hampered and annoyed her more than anything it bestowed could compensate, she withdrew more and more into herself. The fine old family mansion, built by her grandfather, and still occupied by his descendants, offered, with its beautiful grounds, ample breathing-space for a recluse. And such she increasingly became. At first, seeing only those who called, she at length abandoned even her loved work among her flowers, and while shutting herself entirely indoors, saw fewer and fewer of those who still sought the time-honored hospitality of the well-known homestead.

During her father's life she still occasionally met some friends for his sake. He was the leading lawyer of the region, Treasurer of Amherst College, and for some time member of Congress. His relations with the world at large were wide and varied, but after his death her seclusion became almost entire.

Dressed always in white, her graceful passing about the house seemed rather the coming and going of some gentle spirit than any mere earthly presence. With her growing distaste at meeting her friends seemed to come a corresponding increase in her spiritual fondness for them, which found its vent in charming courtesies. Into how many homes have her dainty boxes of cut flowers found their cheering way! Or were more substantial remembrance in order, an endless variety of delicate dishes fit for the gods, and fashioned by her own hands, met cordial welcome.

To sick beds, to coming or departing friends, for congratulation or condolence, her thoughtful grace was never lacking; and the poems or the notes accompanying were unfailingly unique or pertinent.

She wrote all her life, but never voluntarily printed a line. It was not until after her death in 1886 that upwards of a thousand unnamed poems were found. The little volume just published contains only one hundred and fifteen. Of the others, some were too obscure to submit to the public, others were so lacking in form that even the brilliant thought could not save them in the minds of an age too given to mechanism to endure its absence. But there are scores as worthy of preservation as those given.

Of these it is difficult to select the best for quotation. One which might well be called "The Riddle," reads thus:

> Some things that fly there be,
> Birds, hours, the bumble-bee.
> Of these no elegy.
>
> Some things that stay there be,
> Grief, hills, eternity;
> Nor this behooveth me.

> There are that resting rise.
> Can I expound the skies?
> How still the riddle lies!

Another in quite a different vein I cannot resist giving.

> I taste a liquor never brewed,
>   From tankards scooped in pearl.
> Not all the vats upon the Rhine
>   Yield such an alcohol.

> Inebriate of air am I,
>   And debauchee of dew,
> Reeling, through endless summer days,
>   From inns of molten blue.

> When landlords turn the drunken bee,
>   Out of the foxglove's door,
> When butterflies renounce their drams,
>   I shall but drink the more:

> Till seraphs swing their snowy hats,
>   And saints to windows run,
> To see the little tippler
>   Leaning against the sun.

The poems pertaining to death and eternity are the most weird and characteristic. Such a one begins

> Because I could not stop for Death,
>   He kindly stopped for me.
> The carriage held but just ourselves
>   And immortality.

And

> I died for Beauty, but was scarce
>   Adjusted in the tomb,
> When one who died for Truth was lain
>   In an adjoining room.

is but the opening stanza of a poem spectral in its suggestiveness. But they all reveal the fearless working of a mind that stopped at no conventional barriers.

These slight tastes are hardly fair. Only in reading the entire volume can any idea be gained of the remarkable method of mind in this gifted woman.

8   *Hinsdale* [N.H.] *Valley Record.* Unlocated. Dated November 1890 in the Todd scrapbook. "Saxe Holm" was the pen name of Helen Hunt Jackson; see no. 79.

The mysterious "Saxe Holm," whose stories excited so much interest some years ago, and are still widely read, was a Miss Emily Dickinson, now deceased, daughter of an Amherst lawyer. A book of her poems is just issued by a Boston house, with an introduction by Col. Higginson.

9 "Notes in Season." *Publishers' Weekly* 38 (November 8, 1890), 665. The Dickinson volume was also entered in the "Weekly Record of New Publications" column of this issue (p. 667) and, due to a price correction— $1.50 instead of $1.25—entered again the following week (p. 695). The first announcement of the book (without a price) appeared in at least two trade periodicals (*PW* and *Literary World*) as early as September 27, 1890.

ROBERTS BROTHERS will publish on the 12th inst. "Poems," by Emily Dickinson, a townswoman and intimate friend of "H. H.," edited by her friends Mabel L. Todd and T. W. Higginson; "Nanon" (one of the most delightful of George Sand's later works, giving the best view of the French Revolution from the rustic's point of view), translated by Elizabeth Wormeley Latimer. Also "News from Nowhere; or an epoch of rest, being some chapters from a Utopian Romance," by William Morris, author of "The Earthly Paradise," etc., a charming socialistic novel, depicting the future of England under favored conditions of human equality, with the lower Thames lined with homes and gardens instead of factories, and workingmen clad in aesthetic costume. Labor is glorified; hospitality is ennobled; education idealized. The frontispiece of the book is called Labor May Day, and represents a globe inscribed "Solidarity of Labor," and its countries united by fraternity, freedom and equality.

10 Thomas Wentworth Higginson. "Preface" to *Poems by Emily Dickinson*, edited by Mabel Loomis Todd and Thomas Wentworth Higginson. Boston: Roberts Brothers, pp. [iii]–vi. Published November 12, 1890. This preface was well adapted to nineties reviewing because it could be read quickly and lent itself to quotation. No other comment on Dickinson was more often repeated during the decade.

The verses of Emily Dickinson belong emphatically to what Emerson long since called "the Poetry of the Portfolio,"—something produced absolutely without the thought of publication, and solely by way of expression of the writer's own mind. Such verse must inevitably forfeit whatever advantage lies in the discipline of public criticism and the enforced conformity to accepted ways. On the other hand, it may often gain something through the habit of freedom and the unconventional utterance of daring thoughts. In the case of the present author, there was absolutely no choice in the matter; she must write thus, or not at all. A recluse by temperament and habit, literally spending years without setting her foot beyond the doorstep, and many more years during which her walks were strictly limited to her father's grounds, she habitually concealed her mind, like her person, from all but a very few friends; and it was with great difficulty that she was persuaded to print, during her lifetime, three or four poems. Yet she wrote verses in great abundance; and though curiously indifferent to all conventional rules, had yet a rigorous literary standard of her own, and often altered a word many times to suit an ear which had its own tenacious fastidiousness.

Miss Dickinson was born in Amherst, Mass., Dec. 10, 1830, and died there May 15, 1886. Her father, Hon. Edward Dickinson, was the leading lawyer of Amherst, and was treasurer of the well-known college there situated. It was his custom once a year to hold a large reception at his house, attended by all the families connected with the institution and by the leading people of the town. On these occasions his daughter Emily emerged from her wonted retirement and did her part as gracious hostess; nor would any one have known from her manner,

I have been told, that this was not a daily occurrence. The annual occasion once past, she withdrew again into her seclusion, and except for a very few friends was as invisible to the world as if she had dwelt in a nunnery. For myself, although I had corresponded with her for many years, I saw her but twice face to face, and brought away the impression of something as unique and remote as Undine or Mignon or Thekla.

This selection from her poems is published to meet the desire of her personal friends, and especially of her surviving sister. It is believed that the thoughtful reader will find in these pages a quality more suggestive of the poetry of William Blake than of anything to be elsewhere found, — flashes of wholly original and profound insight into nature and life; words and phrases exhibiting an extraordinary vividness of descriptive and imaginative power, yet often set in a seemingly whimsical or even rugged frame. They are here published as they were written, with very few and superficial changes; although it is fair to say that the titles have been assigned, almost invariably, by the editors. In many cases these verses will seem to the reader like poetry torn up by the roots, with rain and dew and earth still clinging to them, giving a freshness and a fragrance not otherwise to be conveyed. In other cases, as in the few poems of shipwreck or of mental conflict, we can only wonder at the gift of vivid imagination by which this recluse woman can delineate, by a few touches, the very crises of physical or mental conflict. And sometimes again we catch glimpses of a lyric strain, sustained perhaps but for a line or two at a time, and making the reader regret its sudden cessation. But the main quality of these poems is that of extraordinary grasp and insight, uttered with an uneven vigor sometimes exasperating, seemingly wayward, but really unsought and inevitable. After all, when a thought takes one's breath away, a lesson on grammar seems an impertinence. As Ruskin wrote in his earlier and better days, "No weight nor mass nor beauty of execution can outweigh one grain or fragment of thought."

11 "Literary Notes." *Chicago Inter-Ocean*, November 15, 1890, p. 10.

Roberts Brothers will publish on the 12th inst. "Poems," by Emily Dickinson, a townswoman and intimate friend of "H. H.," edited by her friends, Mabel L. Todd and T. W. Higginson.

12 Identical publication notices, November 15, 1890: *New York Times*, p. 5; *New York Tribune*, p. 8. Routine publication information (title, author, editors, size, binding, price) is followed by an unattributed excerpt from Higginson's "Preface":

"It is believed that the thoughtful reader will find in these pages a quality more suggestive of the poetry of William Blake than of anything to be elsewhere found—flashes of wholly original and profound insight into nature and life; words and phrases exhibiting an extraordinary vividness of descriptive and imaginative power."

13 [Charles Goodrich Whiting.] "The Literary Wayside." *Springfield Republican*, November 16, 1890, p. 4. Attributed to Whiting in the Todd scrapbook and in *AB*, pp. 73, 83. Bingham says of this review that it "had particular importance in Amherst since [the *Republican*] molded opinion throughout western Massachusetts" (*AB*, 72). Whiting correctly recalls the last stanza of "The Snake" ("A narrow Fellow in the Grass"), a poem that was published anonymously in the *Republican* in 1866 and not printed again until the second, 1891 volume of her verse. The other *Republican* item he refers to, an 1878 piece suggesting that Dickinson may have written the "Saxe Holm" stories, was reprinted in its pages January 7, 1891; see no. 79. Whiting's familiarity with the poetry, the longstanding friendship of the Dickinson family with the *Republican*'s former owner and editor, Samuel Bowles, and the normal operation of regional bias, serve to make favorable treatment from this paper unsurprising. Structurally, Whiting's essay adopts the paradigm that became almost inevitable for reviewers presented with this volume: initial attention to the poet's unusual life followed by discussion, with illustrations, of the poems' themes as they had been organized into chapters by the book's editors. In his discerning selection of poems, his understanding of Dickinson's humor and of her affinities with transcendentalism, and in his avoidance of his contemporaries' obsessive hand-wringings over faulty technique, Whiting creditably begins the critical record.

A selection from the poems of the late Emily Dickinson of Amherst is published in a pretty volume by Roberts Bros. of Boston, with a preface by T. W. Higginson, who relates as much, perhaps, as ever has been related concerning the singular life of the writer, — excepting only in the notable article published a good many years ago in The Republican, wherein the attempt was made to identify Miss Dickinson with the mysterious Saxe Holm. Emily Dickinson was a recluse, as Col. Higginson says, "by temperament and habit, literally spending years without setting her foot beyond the doorstep, and many more years during which her walks were strictly limited to her father's grounds." She possessed a sensibility so delicate, so immediately and painfully affected by the rudenesses of life, that she shrank more and more from contact with the world, and presently withdrew herself in the way her friend has described. She was a daughter of Edward Dickinson, the leading lawyer of the town, and treasurer of Amherst college. At the yearly reception he was wont to give to the principal citizens and the college families and trustees, says Col. Higginson, "his daughter Emily emerged from her wonted retirement and did her part as gracious hostess; nor would any one have known from her manner, I have been told, that this was not a daily occurrence." Except for this occasion, she was "as invisible to the world as if she had dwelt in a nunnery. For myself, although I had corresponded with her for many years, I saw her but twice face to face, and brought away the impression of something as unique and remote as Undine or Mignon or Thekla."

In her seclusion Emily Dickinson grew to have many a peculiar way of her own, as to her dress, for instance, and so many of these were recalled in the Saxe Holm story of "Draxy Miller's Dowry," that it is perhaps not to be wondered at that these coincidences led to a suspicion of the identity of the writer masquerading under that title and the secluded genius of whom the story indicated so close knowledge. But this utilizing of her own very nature would have been simply impossible to Emily Dickinson, and the coincidences, such as they were, were attributable to the intimate acquaintance of "H. H." That remarkable woman knew her as well as any one could, and it was due to H. H. that a few of her poems saw print, as the lines on "Success," which appeared in "A Masque of Poets" in the No Name series of books. "H. H." sought her collaboration in a novel for that series, and yet she had no more to do with Mercy Philbrick than with Draxy Miller, though in that book also some of her friends thought they detected her hand, and many of the literary public were led to believe that she was its author.

The Republican was never deceived in either matter, and at no time saw reason to vary from its opinion that only "H. H." could account for "Saxe Holm."

From such a cloistered life as hers—though it was a life full of generous and gracious deeds withal, and of rare friendships—there must have come a sole and individual voice, for her mind was ever active, and she seemed to have at times the spiritual insight that was accredited to the Pythian priestess. This book will for the first time tell the reading world what it lost by the constant seclusion of such a soul,—and yet, it would not have gained this had it not been for that seclusion. Literary form, as used by others, she regarded little, but in her own sight she was rigorously bent to express herself just as she did, having her own standard of rhythm, or perhaps we should say of music, and her own choice of words. Her poems in their apparent wilfulness of intonation often recall Emerson's, but also as much by the character of their thought, for she was a transcendentalist by native essence, and her intuitions were her reasons. So that one sometimes thinks also of Ellery Channing in his highest moments as he reads these legacies; yet there are also subtle sympathies that bring up the magic name of Heine, that most pathetic of mockers. These resemblances are to our mind full as insistent as the suggestions of William Blake which Mr. Higginson perceives most clearly in the quality of the poems—"flashes of wholly original and profound insight into nature and life." These are the intuitions of the transcendentalist, and they abound in these poems.

The volume is bound in a cover whose device is that strange blanched blossom, the Indian Pipe, the flower of shade and silence. It is divided into four books, which are entitled "Life," "Love," "Nature," "Time and Eternity." The poem contributed to "A Masque of Poets" is the first of these:

> Success is counted sweetest
> By those who ne'er succeed.
> To comprehend a nectar
> Requires sorest need.
>
> Not one of all the purple host
> Who took the flag to-day
> Can tell the definition,
> So clear, of victory,
>
> As he, defeated, dying,
> On whose forbidden ear
> The distant strains of triumph
> Break, agonized and clear.

This is fine, but more remarkable is this condensation of life's constant experience for thousands:—

> The heart asks pleasure first,
> And then, excuse from pain;
> And then, those little anodyne   [anodynes
> That deaden suffering.
>
> And then, to go to sleep;
> And then, if it should be
> The will of its Inquisitor,
> The liberty to die.

These, from several poems, are marvelous brevities;—

> The soul selects her own society,
> Then shuts the door;
> On her divine majority
> Obtrude no more.

>   *   *   *   *   *

> When night is almost done
> And sunrise grows so near
> That we can touch the spaces,
> It's time to smooth the hair
> And get the dimples ready,
> And wonder we could care
> For that old faded midnight
> That frightened but an hour.

>   *   *   *   *   *

> Pain has an element of blank;
> It cannot recollect
> When it began, or if there were
> A day when it was not.
> It has no future but itself,
> Its infinite realms contain
> Its past, enlightened to perceive
> New periods of pain.

And now we quote a poem which Emerson's "Humble Bee" may have had some share in and which in its childlike quaintnesses recalls Blake, but also many a rhymer of even greater simplicity:—

> I taste a liquor never brewed
>   From tankards scooped in pearl;
> Not all the vats upon the Rhine
>   Yield such an alcohol!

> Inebriate of air am I,
>   And debauchee of dew,
> Reeling, through endless summer days,
>   From inns of molten blue.

> When landlords turn the drunken bee
>   Out of the fox-glove's door,
> When butterflies renounce their dreams   [drams
>   I shall but drink the more.

> Till seraphs swing their snowy hats,
>   And saints to windows run,
> To see the little tippler
>   Leaning against the sun!

What Emily Dickinson says of love has a peculiar interest, and it can hardly be forbidden that the reader should wonder what experience of her own she might have had to produce so exceptionally personal utterances as some of these voices of imagination seem to be. We may not enlighten the reader, but when one reads such a song as this—which is worthy of Browning—one feels that passion should have throbbed to speak so:—

> Alter? When the hills do.
>   Falter? When the sun
> Question if his glory
>   Be the perfect one!
>
> Surfeit? When the daffodil
>   Doth of the dew;
> Even as herself, O friend!
>   I will of you!

Is not that most exquisite? And just on the opposite page is the counterpart:—

> You left me, sweet, two legacies,—
>   A legacy of love
> A heavenly Father would content
>   Had he the offer of;
>
> You left me boundaries of pain
>   Capacious as the sea,
> Between eternity and time,
>   Your consciousness and me.

And what shall be said as to these lines on "Suspense"?—

> Elysium is as far as to
> The very nearest room,
> If in that room a friend await
> Felicity or doom.
>
> What fortitude the soul contains,
> That it can so endure
> The accent of a coming foot,
> The opening of a door!

These verses are so intense that behind their quiet phrases lie "whole argosies of pain." And still more charged with pain, the pain of renunciation, is the poem "In Vain," of which we choose a few stanzas:—

> I cannot live with you,
> It would be life,
> And life is over there
> Behind the shelf
>
> The sexton keeps the key to,
> Putting up
> Our life, his porcelain,
> Like a cup
>
> Discarded of the housewife
> Quaint or broken;
> A newer Sèvres pleases,
> Old ones crack.
>
> I could not die with you,
> For one must wait

To shut the other's gaze down—
You could not.

. . . .

And were you lost, I would be.
Though my name
Rang loudest
On the heavenly fame.

And were you saved
And I condemned to be
Where you were not,
That self were hell to me.

So we must keep apart;
You there, I here,
With just the door ajar
That oceans are,
And prayer,
And that sole sustenance
Despair!

When we reach the division entitled "Nature," we come upon those brilliant shinings of beauty's inspiration that fairly convict us of blindness and deafness to the loveliness and magnetic grace and sweet speech of the spirit of creation. Who has ever felt the charm of Nature more intimately than this poet, who can express its mystery in this charming indefiniteness?—

The murmur of a bee
A witchcraft yieldeth me.
If any ask me why,
'Twere easier to die
Than tell.

The red upon the hill
Taketh away my will;
If anybody sneer,
Take care, for God is here,—
That's all.

And here are two magical stanzas on "The Sea of Sunset":—

This is the land the sunset washes,
    These are the banks of the Yellow Sea;
Where it rose, or whither it rushes,
    These are the western mystery.

Night after night her purple traffic
    Strews the landing with opal bales;
Merchantmen poise upon horizons,
    Dip, and vanish with fairy sails.

That poem is an example of what lyric elegance this writer might have accomplished had she chosen so to do. There are also melodious settings for the red clover (there is no "purple" clover, as the editor has mistakenly called it in the title) and the bee; here, too, is a rhythmic delicacy:—

I'll tell you how the sun rose, —
    A ribbon at a time.
The steeples swam in amethyst,
    The news like squirrels ran.

The hills untied their bonnets,
    The bobolinks begun.
Then I said softly to myself,
    "That must have been the sun!"

But how he set, I know not.
    There seemed a purple stile
Where little yellow boys and girls
    Were climbing all the while

Till where they reached the other side   [Till when
    A dominie in gray
Put gently up the evening bars
    And led the flock away.

There are some lines on "Indian Summer" which ought to be quoted, as follows: —

These are the days when birds come back,
A very few, a bird or two,
To take a backward look.

These are the days when skies put on
The old, old sophistries of June, —
A blue and gold mistake.

Oh, fraud that cannot cheat the bee!
Almost thy plausibility
Induces my belief,

Till ranks of seeds their witness bear,
And softly through the altered air
Hurries a timid leaf!

Oh, sacrament of summer days,
Oh, last communion in the haze,
Permit a child to join,

Thy sacred emblems to partake,
Thy consecrated bread to break,
Taste thine immortal wine!

A touch of humor will have been noticed rarely in these verses, and certainly Emily Dickinson had not a little of this quality in her nature. A verse of hers published in The Republican many years ago concerning "the snake" was an illustration thereof. We can but imperfectly recall it to memory, but it concluded with these lines: —

I never met this fellow   [But never
Attended or alone,
Without a tighter breathing
And zero at the bone.

For an analogy of human life, take this verse "From the Chrysalis": —

My cocoon tightens, colors tease.
    I'm feeling for the air,
A dim capacity for wings
    Degrades the dress I wear.

A power of butterfly must be
    The aptitude to fly,
Meadows of majesty concedes,
    And easy sweeps of sky.

So I must baffle at the hint
    And cipher at the sign,
And make much blunder, if at last
    I take the clew divine.

This is among the poems on "Time and Eternity," in which the writer is much struck with the pomp of death, which makes so much of those who in their lives were of small consequence. Several pieces of verse relate to this grim contradiction, and of them we choose this:—

That short, potential stir
That each can make but once,
That bustle so illustrious
'Tis Almost consequence,

Is the éclat of death.
Oh, the unknown renown   [thou unknown
That not a beggar would accept
Had he the power to spurn!

But we must now close this survey of an uncommon book. It is the special and serious revelation of a soul apart, by its own choice, but yet vividly sympathetic with its kind, and cognizant of human experience by its intuitive revelations. That it should have a large public is not to be expected. Those who are fit will read and know themselves divined. For farewell, let this one poem be quoted:—

DYING.

The sun kept setting, setting still;
No hue of afternoon
Upon the village I perceived,—
From house to house 'twas noon.

The dusk kept dropping, dropping still;
No dew upon the grass,
But only on my forehead stopped,
And wandered on my face.   [wandered in

My feet kept drowsing, drowsing still,
My fingers were awake;
Yet why so little sound myself
Unto my seeming make?

How well I knew the light before!
I could not see it now.
'Tis dying, I am doing; but
I'm not afraid to know.

14   "Local News." *Amherst Record*, November 19, 1890, p. 4.

—Roberts Bros. of Boston have published a volume of selections from the poems of the late Emily Dickinson of Amherst.

15   "Literary." *Hartford Courant*, November 21, 1890, p. 3.

We have some rather striking books from Messrs. Roberts Brothers this week. The poems of Emily Dickinson, of which there were reports in literary circles, have at last found the light of print under the auspices of Colonel Higginson. Colonel Higginson suggests that they remind of William Blake, but perhaps Emerson will be more in the thought of the general reader, or William Ellery Channing, of a portion of these in this vicinity. They are the work that might be expected of one who lived the life of a recluse as did Miss Dickinson for over fifty years, and who had a genius that was unique in its manifestation. Miss Dickinson was a daughter of one of the old whig magnates of Western Massachusetts. Edward Dickinson of Amherst was the squire of his town, the treasurer of its college, the choice of his party to many offices, though he was defeated, if I remember rightly, as its candidate for Congress. This daughter appears to have been under the dominion of pure intellect, perhaps partly because of frail health. Her book, which is beautifully bound, with an ornament of the Indian pipe upon the cover, a typical flower in this case, is a curiosity.

16   "Books and Authors." *Boston Home Journal*, n.s. 4 (November 22, 1890), 10.

The very beautiful volume of "Poems by Emily Dickinson" will become a cherished companion to thousands of lovers of poetry who never even heard of the name of this lady, but who will at once recognize the richness of the mind of her who was wont to sing from a heart overflowing with love for nature and humanity, and who penned her poetic inspirations simply for her own gratification and pleasure, with no thought of seeking poetical fame in print. Emily Dickinson was born in Amherst, Mass., in 1830, and died there in 1886. Her father, Hon. Edward Dickinson, was the leading lawyer of Amherst, and was treasurer of Amherst College. She was of a retiring disposition, caring little for society, but when occasion required her to preside at her father's receptions, she was a gracious and charming hostess. Her poems were produced absolutely without the thought of publication; they were solely the writer's way of expressing her own mind, and only two or three of them ever got into print during her life, and those by the earnest persuasion of loving friends. This fact puts the poems beyond the critic's province and will make them still more dear to a sympathetic public. While the thought of criticism might have been a discipline in enforcing conformity to accepted ways, no thought of the critic ever having access to her poems imparted to her "the habit of freedom and the unconventional utterance of daring thought." Her own family were astonished to discover, after her death, the extent of her poetical labors, and at the earnest request of many personal friends, and especially her surviving sister, this volume was prepared under the editorship of two of her friends, Mabel Loomis Todd and Thomas W. Higginson. Col. Higginson says in his preface: "It is believed that the thoughtful reader will find in these pages a quality more suggestive of the poetry of William Blake than of anything to be elsewhere found—flashes of wholly original and profound insight into nature and life; words and phrases exhibiting an extraordinary vividness of descriptive and imaginative power, yet often set in a seemingly whimsical or even rugged frame." There is an extraordinary grasp and insight revealed in these poems that make any little violation of poetic rule seem of no account.

17   A. T. "An Edition of the Poems of Emily Dickinson." *Boston Daily Traveller*, November 22, 1890, p. ii.

It is a rare thing in these days of universal print to find a poet who is averse to seeing his or her work before the public, subject alike to its critical judgment and its admiring praise. "The Poems of Emily Dickinson," edited by two of her friends, Mary Loomis Todd and T. W. Higginson, published by Roberts Bros., Boston, belong wholly to what Emerson called "the poetry of the portfolio"— verses written without the thought of publication, and only to express the thoughts of the writer's mind.

Mr. Higginson speaks of this in his preface, and says: "Such verse must inevitably forfeit whatever advantage lies in the discipline of public criticism and the enforced conformity to accepted ways. On the other hand, it may often gain something through the habit of freedom and the unconventional utterance of daring thoughts. In the case of the present author there was absolutely no choice in the matter: she must write thus, or not at all. A recluse by temperament and habit, literally spending years without setting her foot beyond the doorstep, and many more years during which her walks were strictly limited to her father's grounds, she habitually concealed her mind, like her person, from all but a very few friends; and it was with great difficulty that she was persuaded to print, during her lifetime, three or four poems. Yet she wrote verses in great abundance, and though curiously indifferent to all conventional rules, had yet a vigorous literary standard of her own, and often altered a word many times to suit an ear which had its own tenacious fastidiousness. This selection from her poems is published to meet the desire of her personal friends and especially of her surviving sister. It is believed that the thoughtful reader will find in these pages a quality more suggestive of the poetry of William Blake than of anything to be elsewhere found,— flashes of wholly original and profound insight into nature and life; words and phrases exhibiting an extraordinary vividness of descriptive and imaginative power, yet often set in a seemingly whimsical or even rugged frame. They are here published as they were written, with very few and superficial changes. But the main quality of these poems is that of extraordinary grasp and insight, uttered with an uneven vigor, seemingly wayward, but really unsought and inevitable. After all, when a thought takes one's breath away, a lesson on grammar seems an impertinence. As Ruskin wrote in his earlier days, 'No weight nor mass nor beauty of execution can outweigh one grain or fragment of thought.'"

The freedom and fullness of verse written only as the expression of the inward thought, without heed of criticism or regard for praise, has a charm as indefinable as the song of a wild bird that sings out of the fullness of its heart. There is no fear of discord. Whatever a poet may gain through "the discipline of public criticism and the enforced conformity to accepted ways," it is of small value compared to any loss or lack in the musical quality of the verse, or "one grain or fragment of thought." The following poem is one of the few ever published by Miss Dickinson. It appeared in "A Masque of Poets," at the request of H. H., the author's fellow-townswoman and friend:

SUCCESS.

Success is counted sweetest
  By those who ne'er succeed.
To comprehend a nectar
  Requires sorest need.

Not one of all the purple host
  Who took the flag today,
Can tell the definition
  So clear, of victory,

As he, defeated, dying,
  On whose forbidden ear
The distant strain of triumph   [strains
  Breaks, agonized and clear.   [Break,

Mr. Higginson, in the preface, suggests a resemblance to the verse of William
Blake, a similarity to the verse of Landor will doubtless suggest itself to many
readers. There are many bits of unconnected verse perfect in themselves. Like
Landor, even the short form of the sonnet is too long for the perfect expression
of her vivid thought:

The pedigree of honey
  Does not concern the bee;
A clover, any time, to him
  Is aristocracy.

In these four lines there is a fullness and perfectness of form that fits the
thought and gives it to the reader in the most ideal form. It is not for every poet
that circumstances conspire so happily. Writing with no outside interests to irri-
tate or confuse, to please only her own perfect taste, and without fear of publication, Miss Dickinson's verse could be but the expression of the ideal in poetry.
Her poems, too, are introduced to the world by her friends, by two people who
knew and appreciated her genius, and who have selected and arranged her verse
with much critical, as well as with loving, judgment. The cover and binding of
this little volume are well fitted to its contents. The design of flowers in silver
upon a white ground, with the letters at the top in gold, is in the best possible
taste.

Emily Dickinson was born in Amherst, Mass., Dec. 10, 1830, and died there
May 15, 1886. Her father, Hon. Edward Dickinson, was the leading lawyer of
Amherst, and treasurer of the well-known college there. Emily was naturally of
a retiring nature, and except for a very few friends, was as invisible to the world
as if she had dwelt in a nunnery. It was the custom of her father to hold a large
reception at his house once a year, attended by all the families connected with
the institution and by the leading families of the town. On these occasions his
daughter Emily emerged from her wonted retirement and did her part as a gracious hostess, with as much grace of manner as though this were a daily occurrence. Many of her poems show a fullness of the appreciation of life that is markedly in contrast with the quiet of her life. In "Rouge Gagne" this feeling finds its
most noticeable expression:

ROUGE GAGNE.

'Tis so much joy! 'Tis so much joy!
If I should fail, what poverty!

And yet, as poor as I
Have ventured all upon a throw;
Have gained! Yes! Hesitated so
This side the victory.

Life is but life, and death but death!
Bliss is but bliss, and breath but breath!
And if, indeed, I fail,
At least to know the worst is sweet.
Defeat means nothing but defeat,
No drearier can prevail!

And if I gain, — oh, gun at sea,
Oh, bells that in the steeples be,
At first repeat it slow!
For heaven is a different thing
Conjectured, and waked sudden in,
And might o'erwhelm me so!

This collection of verse will find many appreciative readers. It is a book of rare charm from the clearness of thought displayed, and from the completeness and variety of method, if the word method can be used in connection with a work of so much grace and originality.

18 "The World of New Books." *Philadelphia Press*, November 22, 1890, p. 11. This reviewer makes Dickinson an invalid, takes 20 years off her life, and shows no evidence of having read beyond the first poem.

Mr. T. W. Higginson, who, with Mabel Loomis Todd, has edited the very dainty volume of "Poems by Emily Dickinson," says truly in his preface that these verses belong to what Emerson called "the poetry of the portfolio" — something produced absolutely without the thought of publication, and solely by way of expression of the writer's own mind. Miss Dickinson, daughter of the Hon. Edward Dickinson, of Amherst, Mass., died in 1886 at the age of 36. She was an invalid who seldom emerged from the retirement of her home; not oftener than once a year. She shows in these bits of verse as a woman of rare qualities of mind, genuine poetic feeling and power of expression. Her poetry is cast, for the most part, in a single mould; but that is wholly original and of a fine rugged beauty. The influence of Emerson is apparent in it. We quote this first selection, entitled "Success" as representative of the volume's contents: —

Success is counted sweetest
By those who ne'er succeed.
To comprehend a nectar
Requires sorest need.

Not one of all the purple host
Who took the flag to-day,
Can tell the definition,
So clear, of victory.

As he, defeated, dying,
On whose forbidden ear
The distant strains of triumph
Break, agonized and clear.

19   "From the Book Store." *St. Joseph* [Mo.] *Daily News*, November 22, 1890,
p. 9.

In the depth of sentiment and sweetness of note that characterizes the majority
of these poems one forgets entirely whatever may be lacking of the rhyme and
metre that conventionality has stamped as the signia of poesy. The true poet, we
know, need not of necessity give his or her feelings vent at all, so they are but felt;
and true poetry breathes from each of these verses. The originality of these verses
lies mostly in their daring expression, their insight into life, love and nature. Written, not for publication, but as the outpouring of a somewhat lonely, meditative
mind, they have all the imprint of personality that such work must naturally acquire. The verses are carefully edited and arranged by Mabel Loomis Todd and
Thomas Wentworth Higginson, the well-known essayist. The latter also in his
preface, gives a beautiful estimate of Miss Dickinson's work when he quotes
Ruskin's saying: "No weight, nor mass, nor beauty of execution can outweigh one
fragment or grain of thought." In the face of the subject matter of the verse, a criticism on matters of poetic formula, grammar or such details would be out of place.
When the author says:

> If I can stop one heart from breaking,
> I shall not live in vain;
> If I can ease one life the aching,
> Or cool one pain,
> Or help one fainting robin
> Unto his nest again,
> I shall not live in vain.

She sums the mission of her volume. The volume is daintily bound and beautifully printed, making a handsome gift book.

20   [Lilian Whiting.] "Literature." *Boston Budget*, November 23, 1890. Unlocated. Attributed to Whiting in Mrs. Todd's scrapbook and *AB*, p. 75.
Time and familiarity only augmented the note of generous admiration
taken in this, the author's first of many reviews of Dickinson. The reprinting of "Success is counted sweetest" mentioned here immediately
preceded this review. Dickinson, as Higginson correctly noted, died on
May 15, 1886.

Col. Higginson, in his preface to the "Poems by Emily Dickinson," makes a particularly felicitous quotation from Ruskin in the words, "No weight nor mass nor
beauty of execution can outweigh one grain or fragment of thought." The sentiment is especially applicable to these poems — quaint, original and individual of
diction — profound in thought and full of almost startling divination and insight.
Emily Dickinson was born in Amherst, in December of 1830, Col. Higginson tells
us, and died there on May 1, 1886. She was the daughter of Hon. Edward Dickinson, the leading lawyer of the town and treasurer of the college. Miss Dickinson
lived the life of a recluse, save that once a year, when her father held a large reception, she emerged from seclusion and did her part as hostess with the grace of one
accustomed to daily social life. "For myself," Col. Higginson says, "although I had
corresponded with her for many years, I saw her but twice face to face, and
brought away the impression of something as unique and remote as Undine, or
Mignon, or Thekla." Col. Higginson proceeds further to say that he believes the

Thomas Wentworth Higginson (1823–1911): "When a thought takes one's breath away, who cares to count the syllables?" (No. 9)

Mabel Loomis Todd (1856–1932): ". . . startlingly original, and often appalling in the immense fields which it opens of deathless conjecture and desire." (No. 7)

Lilian Whiting (1847–1942): "The reader will find himself pursuing almost a new language." (No. 20)

Arlo Bates (1850–1918): "A new species of art." (No. 21)

Poems (1890), first printing. Reviewers took considerable interest in Roberts Brothers' choice of bindings for the Dickinson volumes. (No. 10)

Roberts Brothers began advertising for the *Poems* in late September 1890. In time, the firm occasionally gave prominence to editions of Dickinson's poems and letters in its advertisements, especially in Boston-area periodicals. (No. 9)

(Left) Robert Bridges (1858–1941): "Poetry of importance." (No. 27)

(Right) Louise Chandler Moulton (1835–1908): "With every page I turn and return I grow more and more in love." (No. 23)

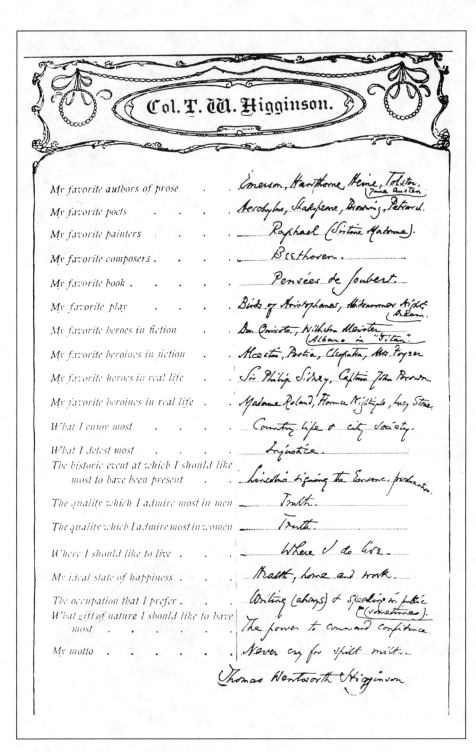

In March 1893 the *Book Buyer* published replies from several authors to this questionnaire. Alone among them, Higginson pointedly resisted the questionnaire's invitation to make gender distinctions. (No. 28)

reader will find in this collection of her verse "a quality more suggestive of William Blake than of anything to be elsewhere found—flashes of wholly original and profound insight into nature and life, words and phrases exhibiting an extraordinary vividness of descriptive and imaginative power, yet often set in a seemingly whimsical or even rugged frame." The poem called "Success," that forms the heading to the literary reviews of today, was a favorite of the author's friend and townswoman, Helen Hunt. Among the fine insights into life is this, entitled "Almost":

> Within my reach!
> I could have touched!
>   I might have chanced that way!
> Soft sauntered through the village,
>   Sauntered as soft away!
> So unsuspected violets
>   Within the fields lie low,
> Too late for striving fingers
>   That passed an hour ago.

Or this:

> To fight aloud is very brave,
>   But gallanter, I know,
> Who charge within the bosom
>   The cavalry of woe.
>
> Who win, and nations do not see,
>   Who fall, and none observe,
> Whose dying eyes no country
>   Regards with patriot love.
>
> We trust, in plumed procession,
>   For such the angels go,
> Rank after rank, with even feet,
>   And uniforms of snow.

Here is the very essence and soul of the purpose of a book condensed into eight lines:

> He ate and drank the precious words,
>   His spirit grew robust,
> He knew no more that he was poor
>   Nor that his frame was dust.
> He danced along the dingy days,
>   And this bequest of wings
> Was but a look. What liberty   [but a book
> A loosened spirit brings!

And what an intense feeling is shown in this:

> Belshazzar had a letter—
> He never had but one;
> Belshazzar's correspondent
> Concluded and begun
> In that immortal copy,
> The conscience of us all

    Can read without its glasses
On revelation's wall.

  Another, in the series of love poems, is this:

    Alter? When the hills do.
Falter? When the sun
Question if his glory
Be the perfect one.

    Surfeit? When the daffodil
Doth of the dew;
Even as herself, O friend!
I will of you!

And this stanza:

    That I shall love alway
I offer thee,
That love is life
And life hath immortality.

And what a picture is in "The Sea of Sunset":

    This is the land the sunset washes,
      These are the banks of the Yellow Sea;
Where it rose or whither it rushes,
      These are the Western mystery!

    Night after night her purple traffic
      Strews the landing with opal bales;
Merchantmen poise upon horizons,
      Dip, and vanish with fairy sails.

    The poems are edited by Mabel Loomis Todd and Col. T. W. Higginson, and are beautifully bound in white with silver lilies on the cover, the volume put up in a white embossed box. They are poems of such extraordinary intensity, insight and vividness, and an almost equally startling disregard of poetic laws, that the reader will find himself pursuing almost a new language, and perhaps speculating curiously as to what results would have been insured had the author subjected herself to careful study of poetic ideals, —had she learned to chip and polish the marble. It might be that such work as hers would lose in strength rather than gain in melody by such revision.

21   [Arlo Bates.] "Books and Authors." *Boston Sunday Courier* 96 (November 23, 1890), 2. Attributed to Bates in Todd's scrapbook and *AB*, pp. 73–74. The latter also prints Todd's diary impression of Bates as a person and critic ("he shows his limitations"). New England literati would have recognized the importance of this review, for Bates was well known in the area as a poet, novelist, and critic—and as literary editor of the *Sunday Courier*. Indeed, before deciding to go ahead with Dickinson's poems, Roberts Brothers had referred them to Bates for an appraisal. This review might well be read as a reply to William Dean Howells's forthcoming appreciative essay on Dickinson which Bates, judging by his concluding reference to the "Editor's Study," seems already to have read (see no. 64). Howells had forwarded proofs of his review to Mrs.

Todd by this time—see *AB*, p. 74; copies were evidently sent to Bates and perhaps others as well. Bates might have taken a somewhat more positive tone had he not felt it necessary to caution against Howells's attempt to excuse Dickinson's technical irregularities and to affirm the lasting interest of her verse. In his own ambivalent and ultimately reductive estimate, Bates typifies male establishment critics. He is distinctive, though, as the only reviewer of the decade to reprint Dickinson's two most sexual poems, "My River runs to thee—" and "Come slowly—Eden!"

It is seldom that the reviewer is called upon to notice a book so remarkable as the "Poems" of Miss Emily Dickinson, which are published posthumously under the editorship of Mrs. Mabel Loomis Todd and Colonel Thomas Wentworth Higginson. The work which it contains has to be treated as so far outside of the ordinary groove, it is so wholly without the pale of conventional criticism, that it is necessary at the start to declare the grounds upon which it is to be judged as if it were a new species of art.

For, in the first place, there is hardly a line in the entire volume, and certainly not a stanza, which cannot be objected to upon the score of technical imperfection. The author was as unlearned in the technical side of art as if she had written when the forms of verse had not yet been invented. She is not so much disdainful of conventions as she seems to be insensible to them. Her ear had certainly not been susceptible of training to the appreciation of form and melody, or it is inconceivable that she should have written as she did. There is on every page ground for the feeling that she was one of those strangely constituted creatures who experience a pleasure from metrical forms, yet who are so insensible to them as to be unable to understand that their own work lacks in that which moves them dimly in the poetry of others. There is evidence that Miss Dickinson was not without some vague feeling for metre and rhythm, yet she was apparently entirely unconscious that her own lines often had neither and constantly violated the canons of both.

There is hardly a line of her work, however, which fails to throw out some gleam of genuine original power, of imagination, and of real emotional thought. There is a real poetic motive here. The high muse has been with her in very truth, passing by to come to her many who have well and painfully learned the secrets of the technique of their art. That the muse was erratic in her choice may be allowed; but it is vain to attempt to deny that it was herself and no other who inspired Miss Dickinson's songs.

There is a certain rude and half barbaric naivete in many of the poems. They show the insight of the civilized adult combined with the simplicity of the savage child. There is a barbaric flavor often discernible, as if this gentle poet had the blood of some gentle and simple Indian ancestress in her veins still in an unadulterated current.

> Angels in the early morning
> May be seen the dews among,
> Stooping, plucking, smiling, flying;
> Do the buds to them belong?

Is not this the voice of a child?

> Some keep the Sabbath going to church;
> I keep it staying at home,

With a bobolink for a chorister,
   And an orchard for a dome.
. . . .

God preaches—a noted clergyman—
   And the sermon is never long;
So instead of getting to heaven at last,
   I'm going all along!

Could anything be more delightfully pagan, or worse in workmanship?
   These two show how near she could come at times to a bit of good workmanship, and how inevitably she spoiled it.

AUTUMN.

The morns are meeker than they were,
   The nuts are getting brown;
The berry's cheek is plumper,
   The rose is out of town.

The maple wears a gayer scarf,
   The field a scarlet gown.
Lest I should be old-fashioned,
   I'll put a trinket on.

BECLOUDED.

The sky is low, the clouds are mean,
   A traveling flake of snow
Across a barn or through a rut
   Debates if it will go.
A narrow wind complains all day
   How some one treated him;
Nature, like us, is sometimes caught
   Without her diadem.

The touch of humor at the end of the former of these is in a way delightful, but it is not enough to justify the place it holds. The first four lines of the second give a picture with a vividness and grace that could hardly be bettered, but the rest does not please us.
   Of the poems dealing with nature this seems to us one of the best.

THE SEA OF SUNSET.

This is the land the sunset washes,
   These are the banks of the Yellow Sea;
Where it rose, or whither it rushes,
   These are the Western mystery.

Night after night her purple traffic
   Strews the landing with purple bales;
Merchantmen poise upon horizons,
   Dip and vanish with fairy sails.

It is not in her poems dealing with nature, however, that Miss Dickinson seems to us most interesting. These are often marked with much felicity of phrase, and they are apt to be less irregular in form than some of the rest, but there is in her poems upon life and ethical themes far more depth and originality. Take, for example, these two:

> The heart asks pleasure first,
>   And then, excuse from pain;
> And then, those little anodynes
>   That deaden suffering;
>
> And then to go to sleep;
>   And then, if it should be
> The will of its Inquisitor,
>   The liberty to die.

THE MYSTERY OF PAIN.

> Pain has an element of blank;
>   It cannot recollect
> When it began, or if there were
>   A day when it was not.
>
> It has no future but itself,
>   Its infinite realms contain
> Its past, enlightened to perceive
>   New periods of pain.

Here is genuine, emotional insight into life, united with no small power of feeling, and, too of expressing. What, too, need be more charming and touching than the spirit of these love songs?

WITH A FLOWER.

> I hide myself within my flower,
>   That wearing on your breast,
> You, unsuspecting, wear me too —
>   And angels know the rest.
>
> I hide myself within my flower,
>   That fading from your vase,
> You, unsuspecting, feel for me
>   Almost a loneliness.

THE OUTLET

> My river runs to thee;
> Blue sea, wilt welcome me?
>
> My river waits reply.
> Oh, sea, look graciously!
>
> I'll fetch thee brooks
> From spotted nooks, —
>
> Say, sea, take me!

A little rhyme which is eminently characteristic in its breaks and technical faults.

TRANSPLANTED.

As if some little Arctic flower,
Upon the polar hem,
Went wandering down the latitudes,
Until it puzzled came
To continents of summer,
To firmaments of sun,
To strange bright crowds of flowers,
And birds of foreign tongues?   [tongue!
I say, as if this little flower
To Eden wandered in—
What then? Why, nothing,
Only your inference therefrom!

The religious poems are distinguished by a singularly frank fearlessness which is most easily described in Mrs. Browning's phrase as an

—infantine,
Familiar clasp of things divine.

Her spiritual life was evidently so much a part of her existence that it never occurred to her that there was a difference made in the manner of treating one serious feeling because it is a fashion of the conventional world so to treat it. She was always reverent because she could not have been irreverent, but she was reverent toward nature, man and God in the same way. Her theology is of a sort to puzzle metaphysicians, and yet one finds it often most suggestive and stimulating. The strangeness of some of the mixtures which she offers may be seen from this bit:

I reason that in Heaven
Somehow it will be even,
Some new equation given;
     But what of that?

Perhaps there is nothing in the volume which is better than the poem which the editors have called "Apotheosis," and which they have placed among the love poems instead of the religious, perhaps rightly, since Miss Dickinson is more fervid in her expressions concerning love than concerning religion.

APOTHEOSIS.

Come slowly, Eden!
     Lips unused to thee,
Bashful, sip thy jasmines,
     As the fainting bee,
Reaching late his flower,
     'Round her chamber hums,
Counts his nectars—enters,
     And is lost in balms!

There is little of the imitative in the book. Such a suggestion of Browning as one may find in this last poem or Emerson in some of the poems to nature there is now and then, but it is not enough to interfere with the feeling of untrammeled freshness with which one reads. We have quoted thus largely because of the charm of this work for us, and because, the poems having never been published before, are sure to be fresh to the reader. It is necessary to lay aside all fondness for technical perfection, and to give one's self up to the spirit, but this being done, the lover of the poetical will find the book a rare delight. There will be those, indeed, who will contend that the book is better for having disregarded technical form, or at least no worse. It is not wholly impossible that in the Editor's Study something looking in this direction will some day see the light. The truth, however, is not so. Had Miss Dickinson possessed the aptitude and the will to learn technical skill, she would have enriched the language with lyrics which would have endured to the end of time, it well might be. As it is, she has put upon paper things which will delight the few, but which will hold their place on sufferance, and as showing what she might have been rather than for what she was. The book gives us keen delight, but it is delight mingled with regret equally keen for what it fails to be.

22   "New Publications." *Boston Saturday Evening Gazette* 78 (November 23, 1890), 4. The apparently erroneous date, falling it does on a Sunday, finds its explanation in the *Gazette*'s Sunday morning publication during the nineties.

Poems by Emily Dickinson, edited by two of her former friends, Mabel Loomis Todd and T. W. Higginson, is a volume that is full of original thought, often crudely expressed and without any great regard to literary form, but frequently showing an insight that is as rare as it is refreshing. The verses were not intended for publication, and are the outcome of the genius of an accomplished woman, who led practically the life of a recluse, and who was not hampered or helped by criticism in putting her conceptions on paper. She was born in Amherst, Mass., Dec. 30 [sic], 1830, and died there May 15, 1886. She was the daughter of the Hon. Edward Dickinson, an eminent lawyer, and treasurer of Amherst College. The poems in the volume were selected from her writings, at the request of her surviving sister and many personal friends, and the intelligent reading public will no doubt derive much pleasure and profit from the unconventional utterances. We select, almost at random, the following from the numerous short poems in the volume, which, however, does not convey as forcibly as some others might, the imaginative power of the poet:

I had no time to hate, because
  The grave would hinder me,
And life was not so ample, I
  Could finish enmity.

Nor had I time to love; but since
  Some industry must be,
The little toil of love, I thought,
  Was large enough for me.

Those who desire to experience a new literary sensation should by all means read this unhackneyed book of verse.

23   Louise Chandler Moulton. "A Very Remarkable Book." *Boston Sunday Herald*, November 23, 1890, p. 24. Few American women were more widely known as writers, and none was so conspicuous and active as a literary hostess, both at home and in England, as Louise Chandler Moulton. Living in each city for half the year, she presided over notable weekly salons in Boston and London for several decades. She knew everyone, from Longfellow and Emerson to Ezra Pound. Her poems, travel sketches, and literary letters, were widely admired. Her own verse was superficially like Dickinson's in being highly personal, brief, and frequently concerned with unfulfilled love and the transience of life. In its graceful, faded diction and utterly conventional pressed-rose melancholy, her verse was eminently suited to the popular taste.

Among the books I have been reading since I came to Boston, the one that has moved me to most enthusiasm is the "Poems" of Emily Dickinson, edited by Mabel Loomis Todd and Col. T. W. Higginson, and published by Roberts Bros. And yet, if one were to judge the book by the theories of poetic art, one would hardly call most of its contents poems at all. Madder rhymes one has seldom seen—scornful disregard of poetic technique could hardly go farther—and yet there is about the book a fascination, a power, a vision that enthralls you, and draws you back to it again and again. Not to have published it would have been a serious loss to the world, and of how few volumes, alas, could this be said in these days when of making many books there is no end.

Miss Dickinson, in her lifetime, was known to singularly few people. She was the daughter of Edward Dickinson, who was treasurer of Amherst College, and was also a lawyer of much distinction. Her father's position compelled him to give a large reception at least once a year, and on these occasions Miss Dickinson came out from her retirement and was as gracious and charming a hostess as if her whole life were devoted to society; but when the last guest had said good night, she would thankfully return to the conditions of her ordinary life, an existence scarcely less secluded from the world than if she had been shut up in a nunnery. A few select souls only were admitted to her intimacy, and these few cherished her all the more dearly because they were not compelled to share her regard with an intrusive and engrossing world.

Emily Dickinson died in 1886, in her 56th year. Her surviving sister rescued these poems—her unique life work—from the destruction that so often awaits the papers of the dead; and it is due to the wishes of this sister and a few near friends that the present volume has been given to the public.

Col. Higginson, in his preface, says, very happily, that "in many cases these verses will seem to the reader like poetry torn up by the roots, with rain and dew and earth still clinging to them, giving a freshness and a fragrance not otherwise to be conveyed."

Miss Dickinson, during all her life, was singularly averse to print, and was with difficulty persuaded to publish three or four of her poems. Still, the "Prelude," which prefaces the "Poems," suggests to me that, like Marie Bashkirtseff, she meant that these leaves torn from her heart should be her legacy to the world when she herself had passed beyond its reach. Read the lines and judge if I am right:

> This is my letter to the world,
>   That never wrote to me,
> The simple news that Nature told,
>   With tender majesty.
>
> Her message is committed
>   To hands I cannot see;
> For love of her, sweet countrymen,
>   Judge tenderly of me!

I have read this book twice through already. I foresee that I shall read it scores of times more. It enthralls me, and will not let me go. For sheer love of my HERALD readers, I should like to give them all of it—as you gave them, last Sunday, all of "The World's Desire"—but at least you will read some of my especial favorites among these poems, more individual and often more subtle than anything I can recall in the whole range of recent verse. Is there one of us who cannot remember the lost opportunity of our lives? and was it not, by some mysterious telepathy, our own mocking memory of this fatal miscarriage which found expression in

ALMOST.

Within my reach!
I could have touched!
I might have chanced that way!
Soft sauntered through the village,
Sauntered as soft away!
So unsuspected violets
Within the fields lie low,
Too late for striving fingers
That passed, an hour ago.

And here, on page 36, you have, in eight lines, the secret of life and love:

I had no time to hate, because
    The grave would hinder me,
And life was not so ample I
    Could finish enmity.

Nor had I time to love; but since
    Some industry must be,
The little toil of love, I thought,
    Was large enough for me.

In many of these poems (as in one I am about to quote) the absence of even the slightest and most evident technique is amazing. Mrs. Browning's rhymes were often amazing; but Mrs. Browning herself would hardly have rhymed tent with stint, can with own, and the rest; but has even Mrs. Browning expressed with such strong yet simple passion a woman's

SURRENDER.

Doubt me, my dim companion!
    Why, God would be content
With but a fraction of the love
    Poured thee without a stint.
The whole of me, forever,
    What more the woman can,—
Say quick, that I may dower thee
    With last delight I own!

It cannot be my spirit,
    For that was thine before;
I ceded all of dust I knew—
    What opulence the more

> Had I, a humble maiden,
>   Whose farthest of degree
> Was that she might, some distant heaven,
>   Dwell timidly with thee!

Some of the poems on different aspects of nature would have delighted Ralph Waldo Emerson. They are akin to him in spirit—such as his feminine counterpart might have written. Read, for instance, what is perhaps, from an artistic point of view, the most polished of these gems:

THE SEA OF SUNSET.

> This is the land the sunset washes,
>   These are the banks of the Yellow Sea;
> Where it rose, or whither it rushes,
>   These are the western mystery!
>
> Night after night her purple traffic
>   Strews the landing with opal bales;
> Merchantmen poise upon horizons,
>   Dip and vanish with fairy sails.

And here is an octave, the spirit of which especially reminded me of Emerson:

> The bee is not afraid of me,
>   I know the butterfly;
> The pretty people in the woods
>   Receive me cordially.
>
> The brooks laugh louder when I come,
>   The breezes madder play—
> Wherefore, mine eyes, thy silver mists?
>   Wherefore, O summer's day?

But Emily Dickinson felt the pitilessness of nature, as, I think, Emerson never felt it; and it is the theme of many of these singular and compelling poems. Read, for instance, her

DEATH AND LIFE.

> Apparently with no surprise
> To any happy flower,
> The frost beheads it, at its play,
> In accidental power.
> The blond assassin passes on,
> The sun proceeds unmoved
> To measure off another day
> For an approving God.

I turn these wonderful pages, full of the secrets of life and love and death. I read of the solstice of the soul; of the pensive spring; the troubadour upon the elm; the grass that "so little has to do,"

> With only butterflies to brood,
> And bees to entertain;

of that "purple democrat," the clover; of the sophistries of June—of death, the one dignity that delays for all, and insures for each of us "one mitred afternoon," and with every page I turn and return I grow more and more in love. I am half tempted to wish that while Emily Dickinson lived she had given more of herself to the world, but after all, if she had been one of the many, perhaps the finest essence of her thought would have been lost, and the subtlety of her perceptions dulled, and all that makes this book so unique and so adorable would have suffered change.

24 Lilian Whiting. "Boston Life." *Chicago Inter-Ocean*, November 23, 1890, p. 29. Whiting's letter of correspondence, dated Nov. 20, begins by describing a reception to which T. W. Higginson and a number of literary women were invited, among them Julia Ward Howe, Elinor Mead (Mrs. William Dean) Howells, and Louise Chandler Moulton. During this gathering, Whiting writes, she was asked whether she had yet read the "Poems" of Emily Dickinson.

One whom they had held spell-bound the day before might, indeed, reply in the affirmative, and hereby hangs a tale which THE INTER OCEAN will be so kind as to let me tell. It may not be amiss to fancy that the name of Emily Dickinson is new to a large proportion of readers. It certainly was unknown to me until recently. Miss Dickinson was the daughter of the Hon. Edward Dickinson, the leading lawyer of Amherst and the treasurer of the college, and was born in that town in 1830 and died in 1886. She lived the life of a recluse, and wrote the poems now collected in a volume as the expression, and, perhaps, solace, of her intense individuality. The volume is edited by Mabel Loomis Todd and T. W. Higginson, and in a brief biographical preface Colonel Higginson says of the author:
"A recluse by temperament and habit literally spending years without setting her foot beyond the door-step, and many more years during which her walks were strictly limited to her father's grounds, she habitually concealed her mind like her person from all save a very few friends, and it was with great difficulty that she was persuaded to print during her life-time three or four poems, yet she wrote verses in great abundance; and though curiously indifferent to all conventional rules, had yet a vigorous literary standard of her own, and often altered a word many times to suit an ear which had its own tenacious fastidiousness. . . . Nor myself, although I had corresponded with her for many years, I saw her but twice face to face, and brought away the impression of something as unique and remote as Undine or Mignon or Thekla." One of the poems I beg to quote is

SUCCESS.

Success is counted sweetest
  By those who ne'er succeed;
To comprehend a nectar
  Requires sorest need.

Not one of all the purple host
  Who took the flag to-day
Can tell the definition,
  So clear, of victory —

As he, defeated, dying,
  On whose forbidden ear
The distant strains of triumph
  Break, agonized and clear.

Another lyric of two stanzas is this:

> I had no time to hate because
>   The grave would hinder me,
> And life was not so ample I
>   Could finish enmity.
>
> Nor had I time to love, but since
>   Some industry must be,
> The little toil of love, I thought
>   Was large enough for me.

And what an intensity of feeling is in this:

> Alter? When the hills do.
>   Falter? When the sun
> Question of his glory   [if
>   Be the perfect one.
>
> Surfeit? When the daffodil
>   Doth of the dew;
> Even as herself, O friend!
>   I will of you!

No criticism on these points can equal that of Colonel Higginson's when he says that one finds in these "poems" a quality more suggestive of the poetry of William Blake than of anything to be elsewhere found—flashes of wholly original and profound insight into nature and life, word and phrases exhibiting an extraordinary vividness of descriptive and imaginative power, yet often set in a seemingly whimsical or even rugged frame. . . . But the main quality of these poems is that of extraordinary grasp and insight, uttered with an uneven vigor, sometimes exasperating, seemingly wayward, but really unsought and inevitable."

These poems will hardly inspire a popular interest but they will deeply interest a certain proportion of the more thoughtful readers.

25 "Book Notices." *Pittsburgh Post*, November 24, 1890, p. 5. "To fight aloud" is reprinted without its middle stanza.

A recluse as well as poet; for the first time the world is allowed to look into the soul of Emily Dickinson. Her thoughts as shown in her poems were always original; sometimes great, sometimes beautiful. Thomas Wentworth Higginson, in a preface he has written for the collected verses of the dead singer, says: "The main quality of these poems is that of extraordinary grasp and insight uttered with an uneven vigor sometimes exasperating, seemingly wayward, but really unsought and inevitable. The following verses give a fair idea of many of her poems:

> To fight aloud is very brave,
>   But gallanter, I know,
> Who charge within the bosom
>   The cavalry of woe.
>
> We trust, in plumed procession,
>   For such the angels go,
> Rank after rank, with even feet
>   And uniforms of snow.

26 "New Books." *Boston Post*, November 27, 1890, p. 2.

The little volume containing few more than a hundred poems by Emily Dickinson, edited by her friends, Mabel Loomis Todd and T. W. Higginson, will prove interesting to those who study human temperaments and emotions and who believe in the frank expression of thought even when simple or capricious. The peculiar habits of Miss Dickinson when living have been given some publicity, and are of importance in reading her verses. A voluntary recluse, controlling in a rare degree her environment both personal and material; living in obedience to her sentiments, her emotions and her tastes: valuing the dignity of self and seclusion, courting the simple influences of nature, she shows in these verses at once the motive and the effect of such a life. Perhaps the following four lines give the best exposition of her mental attitude:

> The soul selects her own society,
> Then shuts the door:
> On her divine majority
> Obtrude no more.

But behind that door is a kindliness which finds expression as follows:

> If I can stop one heart from breaking,
> I shall not live in vain;
> If I can ease one life the aching,
> Or cool one pain,
> Or help one fainting robin
> Unto his nest again,
> I shall not live in vain.

The poem of "Success," printed in "A Masque of Poets," is well known and is one of the best in the volume. The simplicity of these verses is not the simplicity of happiness or ignorance, and few lines trace more fully the curve of a suffering life than these:

> The heart asks pleasure first
> And then, excuse from pain;
> And then, those little anodynes
> That deaden suffering;
>
> And then, to go to sleep;
> And then, if it should be
> The will of its Inquisitor,
> The liberty to die.

In a somewhat similar vein are several poems which in introspection and analysis of feeling and somewhat in structure recall Browning.

There is a winsome playfulness and a sympathy with the trivial chills and flushes of nature, which find expression in fantastic form and almost suggest the capricious feeling of a child. It is not possible here to quote extensively. Yet, throughout the book are found exquisite bits of verse which repay the search. In literary form and structure the verses follow sweet laws of their own and should not meet criticism. There are none so lofty as to be heroic or great or controlling, and the book will not reach a wide audience. Nevertheless, it contains gems which will give great pleasure to those who will find them, and we heartily commend the book to all who enjoy the wild blossoms and field flowers of poesy.

27   [Robert Bridges.] Droch (pseud.). "Bookishness." *Life* 16 (November 27, 1890), 304. The *New Yorker* of the nineties, this satirical weekly was the most elegant and cultivated magazine of its type in America. It did not always view literary events in Boston with deference.

In a recent bit of criticism Henry James said: "However many traps life may lay for us, tolerably firm ground, at any rate, is to be found in perfect art,"—which is a neat modern way of saying *ars longa, vita brevis*. A rather cynical observer of many phases of life once remarked that a good, vigorous religion was the only thing which could give to the mass of people that grace and dignity of ideal living which the persistent and enthusiastic devotion to some form of art gives to the chosen few. And he added that the devotees of religion were more charitable and humane than the devotees of art. There are two sides of the very old discussion about Art and Morals, and Mr. Woodberry (whom we recently quoted), stands between the two with the proposition that the highest art is of necessity ethical.

If this middle ground is tenable, then the "Poems by Emily Dickinson" edited by her friends Mabel L. Todd and T. W. Higginson, are to be classed with poetry of importance—for they are intensely ethical. The editors tell us that the author (who died four years ago at the age of fifty-six), was "a recluse by temperament and habit"—a refined and gentle woman, who wrote these verses with absolutely no thought of publication, but simply to give expression to her deepest feelings. They are, therefore, introspective with outlooks on Life, Love and Nature, which are most unreal as to their externals but deeply true in essentials.

Those who like philosophy in verse will easily find it here, but they will probably overlook what is a finer thing—the original fancy which compresses striking images into a few words, or catches a strange melody in most irregular measures. One of these delicate fancies is the poem to "The Bee":—

> Like trains of cars on tracks of plush
> I hear the level bee;
> A jar across the flower goes,   [flowers
> Their velvet masonry
> Withstands, until the sweet assault
> Their chivalry consumes,
> While he, victorious, tilts away,
> To vanquish other blooms.

Then, in a vein entirely different from her other verses, is the vivid picture of "some lonely houses, off the road, a robber'd like the look of—" which is a bit of poetic melodrama that Poe would have liked.

The love poems are written in the attitude of a worshipper and not of a lover—and the exaggeration is often of a kind that is saved from being absurd by its sincerity. It is not passion, but fervid loyalty that is depicted—and the chill of intellectual monasticism is in it. There are, however, one or two of the love poems that are more human and feminine in feeling, of which we may quote what is perhaps the best:

> I'm wife; I've finished that,
> That other state;
> I'm Czar; I'm woman now;
> It's safer so.
> How odd the girl's life looks
> Behind this soft eclipse;

I think the earth seems so
To those in heaven now.
This being comfort then,
That other kind was pain:
But why compare?
I'm wife! stop there!

The volume will delight thoughtful people as the poetic expression of a rare and shy intelligence.

28 [Thomas Wentworth Higginson.] "Recent Poetry." *Nation* 51 (November 27, 1890), 422–23. As the regular, though anonymous, poetry critic for the *Nation*, Higginson used his column to promote Dickinson's work. Evidence confirming that this review is his may be found in *AB*, pp. 65 and 83. For his *Nation* comment on *Poems*, Second and Third Series, see nos. 246 and 543.

It is a curious fact that the two most interesting and altogether important poetic collections lately published, respectively in England and America, should both be by dead authors. Here, however, the resemblance ends, as the 'Poetical Works' of Thomas Lovell Beddoes were partially reprinted more than forty years ago; while the 'Poems' by Emily Dickinson bear a name that was previously unknown except to a very few friends. The contrast in other respects is as complete; Beddoes being in the last degree objective and dramatic, and Miss Dickinson introspective and subjective — just as his whole life was wandering and wayward, and hers so secluded as to be more than nunlike. They have absolutely nothing in common but the quality of genius, and it is only because that gift does not abound, just now, upon the critic's table, that they are here linked together at all. It may be added, however, that a certain transfusion of blood appears in each; Beddoes being distinctly the last of the Elizabethans, and Emily Dickinson holding distinctly, though unconsciously, to the school of William Blake — if indeed he had any other scholar. . . .

The poems of Emily Dickinson are not so seriously weighed down by their editors — Mrs. Mabel Loomis Todd and Mr. T. W. Higginson — since they leave her mainly to speak for herself. We learn that she was born in 1830 and died in 1886, living almost always in extreme seclusion in the college town of Amherst, Mass., where her father, a lawyer, held also the responsible position of college treasurer. She resolutely refused to publish her verses, showing them only to a very few friends. As a consequence, she had almost no criticism, and was absolutely untrammelled; so that the verses are sometimes almost formless, while at other times they show great capacity for delicate and sweet melody, suggesting the chance strains of an Aeolian harp. But in compass of thought, grasp of feeling, and vigor of epithet, they are simply extraordinary, and strike notes, very often, like those of some deep-toned organ. Take, for instance, this, which fully sustains the Blake-like quality suggested by the editors in their preface (p. 119):

I died for beauty, but was scarce
Adjusted in the tomb,
When one who died for truth was lain
In an adjoining room.

He questioned softly why I failed?
"For beauty," I replied.

"And I for truth,—the two are one;
We brethren are," he said.

And so, as kinsmen met a night,
We talked between the rooms,
Until the moss had reached our lips,
And covered up our names.

The extraordinary terseness and vigor of that weird conclusion runs through all the poems; in this case it so grasps the ear that you hardly notice the defect in the rhyme. Little cared she for that, provided she uttered her thought. Yet at times she reached with the same sudden grasp a completeness of utterance that was nothing less than lyric—as in the two verses on the opposite page to the above (p. 118):

A train went through a burial gate,
    A bird broke forth and sang,
And trilled, and quivered, and shook his throat
    Till all the churchyard rang;

And then adjusted his little notes,
    And bowed and sang again.
Doubtless, he thought it meet of him
    To say good-bye to men.

With all its inequalities and even oddities on its face, there is power enough on many a page of this little book to set up whole volumes of average poetry; and the public will inevitably demand to know more of the thoughts and mental processes of Emily Dickinson. . . .

Among recent volumes by living Americans, Edith Thomas of course takes the lead, holding as she clearly does, with Gilder, the headship of our younger poets. Her new volume, "The Inverted Torch," is a requiem like "In Memoriam," but cannot claim, like that, to have absolutely escaped the peril of monotony; yet it has her accustomed elevation and her invariable fineness of perception. She does not touch an emotion with the single and irresistible needle-touch of Emily Dickinson, but her thoughts are always her own, and are uniformly noble. Who, for instance, has surpassed, upon its own ground, this lofty dirge, embodying the successive experience of every human generation as its elders pass away? (p. 23):

Time takes no toll of thee,
Age spares the soul of thee.
            They vex thee no more
            Besieging thy door;
            Nor without nor within
            Shall the advantage win.

The long years are fled from thee,
The winters are shed from thee
            As the snows retire
            For Spring's hidden fire,
            And the grass of the fields
            To the young green yields.

The long years descend on me,
The winters bend on me

Their gathering might
As when dwindles the light,
And the grave of the fields
To the white drift yields.

This takes rank with Blake's delineation of the Soul and the Body, the old man descending feebly into the tomb, while the freed youth stands in fresh nobleness upon the other side.

29 "Book Notes." *Boston Journal*, November 28, 1890, p. 4.

In a preface introducing the "Poems by Emily Dickinson," the explanation is made by T. W. Higginson, who with another friend of the author, Mabel Loomis Todd, undertook the task of editing, that the verses were produced by a recluse without the thought of publication, and are issued now after her death to meet the desire of her sister and personal friends. Such a volume has more the character of a private edition than of one published for criticism and public inspection. Indeed, criticism seems out of place before these outpourings of a quiet soul. The poems are all brief, some only one stanza, and are quite unconventional in form. They are fresh, spontaneous and original, without a trace of artificiality.

30 Lilian Whiting. "Boston Life." *Chicago Inter-Ocean*, November 29, 1890, p. 12. At the end of her weekly correspondence from Boston—this letter is dated Nov. 26—Lilian Whiting adds a postscript to her notice of Dickinson a week earlier (see no. 24). Whiting remarks that she has just returned from a literary reception at the home of Louise Chandler Moulton. Among those attending were others who had or would soon publish reviews of Dickinson: Howells, Mrs. Moulton, Nathan Haskell Dole, James Jeffrey Roche, and Arlo Bates. Whiting appears to suggest here that Howells spoke of Dickinson to the entire gathering. In any case he would warmly praise the poet to Mrs. Todd at another social occasion only a few days later; see *AB*, p. 74. Though Howells's only published comment on Dickinson was not to appear until January, it is clear that his high regard was from the beginning a powerful influence on the poet's behalf among Boston reviewers.

However malapropos, I beg to add that Mr. Howells today spoke most enthusiastically on the poems of Emily Dickinson (of which I wrote in my last) as poems of the most wonderful insight and vitality. If I did not, in the preceding letter, quote "The Sea of Sunset" I must beg to do so, and if I did—well, it will bear reprinting.

This is the land the sunset washes,
    These are the banks of the Yellow Sea;
Where it rose, or whither it rushes,
    These are the Western mystery!

Night after night her purple traffic
    Strews the landing with opal bales;
Merchantmen poise upon horizons,
    Dip, and vanish with fairy sails.

31　Noah Brooks. "Books of the Christmas Season." *Book Buyer* 7 (December 1890), 521. Brooks, who at the time of this writing was near retirement, had become well known nationally as a journalist and author (largely of boys' books on American western expansion). He is misinformed, of course, about Dickinson's publisher.

Two of the friends of the late Emily Dickinson—Mabel Loomis Todd and Thomas W. Higginson, have edited her poetical literary remains, and the poems now issued by Houghton, Mifflin & Co. bear witness to the erraticism of their author. These verses are largely fragmentary: they bespeak an unregulated fancy, an intense nature, and a powerful imagination. Many of her figures are startlingly original, as, for instance, in her "Indian Summer."

> These are the days when skies put on
> The old, old sophistries of June—
> 　A blue and gold mistake.

32　Nathan Haskell Dole. "Literary Topics in Boston." *Book Buyer* 7 (December 1890), 546. Still in his thirties, Dole would in the nineties publish poetry and fiction that establish his literary reputation in Massachusetts. There is some evidence his judgment was already particularly valued, as Roberts Brothers had sent him unbound sheets of the poems for review as early as October 8th; see *AB*, p. 68. Dole could not have given close attention to the poems, however, for he mistakes the forty numbered verses of the final section of the book for the total number in the volume as a whole (there were in fact 116). All of the anonymous contributors to *A Masque of Poets*, and the volume's printing history and reception, are discussed by Aubrey H. Starke in "An Omnibus of Poets," *Colophon* 4:16 (March 1934), [12 unnumbered pages].

Speaking of Delphic utterances, such may be found in the poems of Emily Dickinson, edited by Mrs. Mabel Loomis Todd and Colonel Higginson. Miss Dickinson was born in Amherst, Mass., in 1830, and died there four years ago, her life having been that of a recluse. Colonel Higginson says that though he had corresponded with her for many years, yet he saw her but twice face to face, "and brought away the impression of something as unique and remote as Undine or Mignon or Thekla." He forestalls the critics and reviewers by saying that "the thoughtful reader will find in the poems a quality more suggestive of the poetry of William Blake than of anything to be elsewhere found—flashes of wholly original and profound insight into nature and life; words and phrases exhibiting an extraordinary vividness of descriptive and imaginative power, yet often set in a seemingly whimsical or even rugged frame." It is not only William Blake that one finds in these quaint and curious stanzas; it is to me like a mixture of Blake, Emerson, and Heine—especially the last.

There are only about forty of these poems, many of them not exceeding eight lines. Though they are reckless of rhyme, they show a quite remarkable sensitiveness to music, and there are several that startle by their depth of poetic insight. Miss Dickinson was from earliest childhood a friend of the late Mrs. Helen Hunt Jackson ("H. H."), who, with other of her friends, tried in vain to persuade her to publish her verses during her lifetime. Mrs. Jackson obtained from her one short poem entitled "Success," which was printed in the "Masque of Poets," published by Roberts Brothers in 1878.

I wonder, by the way, if the complete list of contributors to that little volume has ever been published? It was a notable list, including, among others, the late George H. Boker, Violet Fane, A. E. Francillon, Celia Thaxter, J. J. Piatt and Mrs. Piatt, Christina Rossetti, Theodore Marzials, Lord Houghton, "H. H.," Edgar Fawcett, Mrs. Dodge, Bayard Taylor, Philip Bourke Marston, Mrs. Moulton, Austin Dobson, William Allingham, Mr. and Mrs. James T. Fields, Mr. and Mrs. Lathrop, and James Russell Lowell. Mr. Lowell, indeed, had two in it (those on pages 142 and 153). The long novelette in verse which filled a large part of the volume was rightly attributed, shortly after its appearance, to Mr. James T. Trowbridge.

33 *Springfield Bulletin,* December 1890. Unlocated. The clipping is so identified by hand in Todd's scrapbook. The width of its column is that of a weekly or monthly, but the existence of a publication by this title could not be confirmed.

Miss Dickinson was born in Amherst, Mass., December 10, 1830, and died there May 15, 1886. Her father, Hon. Edward Dickinson, was the leading lawyer of Amherst, and treasurer of the well-known college there situated. Miss D. was a recluse by temperament and habit. Her poems were all written without thought of publication. Only two or three of them were printed during her lifetime. Mr. Thomas Wentworth Higginson, who furnishes an introduction, says of the collection here offered: "It is believed that the thoughtful reader will find in these pages a quality more suggestive of the poetry of William Blake than of anything to be elsewhere found—flashes of wholly original and profound insight into nature and life; words and phrases exhibiting an extraordinary vividness of descriptive and imaginative power, yet often set in a seemingly whimsical or even rugged frame." Bound in gray and white, with ornamental design in silver.

34 "News and Notes." *The Writer* 4 (December 1890), 285.

Notwithstanding newspaper reports, Colonel Higginson is in robust health, and hard at work. He has just brought out three delightful books; one is a revised edition of his "Epictetus," the text of which was so fascinating that even the young lady who read the proof at the University Press almost forgot her corrections in her interest in the text. The second is a choice collection of "American Sonnets," with a delightful little essay on the sonnet, published by Houghton, Mifflin, & Company. Roberts Brothers have published the "Poems" of Emily Dickinson, edited by Colonel Higginson and Mabel Loomis Todd. The best judges are singularly enthusiastic over the poems of this shy, sensitive woman and imaginative poet.

35 Unlocated clipping in Higginson's scrapbook, ca. December 1890, carrying the handwritten initials "W. J." Search of the *Woman's Journal* for the period proved unproductive.

These brief, quaint, sententious poems are flashes of spontaneous utterance which defy analysis and disarm criticism. Not one of them is without imperfection, and not one without a subtle charm. Take at random this:

Alter?—When the hills do.
 Falter?—When the sun

Questions if his glory
  Be the perfect one.

Surfeit? When the daffodil
  Doth of the dew:
Even as herself, O friend,
  I will of you!

36   "What the Critics Say About Emily Dickinson's Poems." *Amherst Record*, December 3, 1890, p. 4. These excerpts were no doubt given to the *Amherst Record* by Mrs. Todd. The review from which they derive, as numbered in this volume, is supplied in brackets following each quotation. The authors of the last two quotations are Mrs. Todd and Mr. Higginson. The *Record* indicated ellipses with asterisks.

"The very beautiful volume of 'Poems by Emily Dickinson' will become a cherished companion to thousands of lovers of poetry who never even heard of the name of this lady, but who will at once recognize the richness of the mind of her who was wont to sing from a heart overflowing with love for nature and humanity."—*Boston Home Journal.* [16]

"It is seldom that the reviewer is called upon to notice a book so remarkable as the 'Poems' of Miss Emily Dickinson."— *Boston Courier.* [21]

"The poems are introduced to the world by her friends, by two people who knew and appreciated her genius, and who have selected and arranged her verse with much critical, as well as with loving judgment."—*Boston Traveller.* [17]

"The rough diamonds in the collection have a value beyond that of many polished gems of poetry."—*The Critic.* [3]

"She often seems to possess—as was said of her fellow-townswoman, Helen Jackson ("H. H.")—a sixth sense."—*T. W. Higginson in Christian Union.* [2]

"It contains gems which will give great pleasure to those who will find them, and we heartily commend the book to all who enjoy the wild blossoms and field flowers of poesy."—*Boston Post.* [26]

"When we reach the division entitled 'Nature,' we come upon those brilliant shinings of beauty's inspiration that fairly convict us of blindness and deafness to the loveliness and magnetic grace and sweet speech of the spirit of creation. . . . An uncommon book."—*Sunday Republican.* [13]

"Among the books I have been reading since I came to Boston, the one that has moved me to most enthusiasm is the 'Poems' by Emily Dickinson. . . . It enthralls me, and will not let me go."—*Louise Chandler Moulton, in the Boston Sunday Herald.* [23]

"Only in reading the entire volume can any idea be gained of the remarkable method of mind in this gifted woman."—*Mrs. Logan's Home Magazine, Washington.* [7]

"In compass of thought, grasp of feeling, and vigor of epithet, they are simply extraordinary, and strike notes, very often, like those of some deep toned organ. . . . There is power enough on many a page of this little book to set up whole volumes of average poetry; and the public will inevitably demand to know more of the thoughts and mental processes of Emily Dickinson."—*N.Y. Nation.* [28]

37   "Conspicuous Books of 1890." *Congregationalist* 75 (December 4, 1890), 426.

—The posthumous *Poems* of Emily Dickinson, published in dainty form by Roberts Bros., will give pleasure to the limited circle for whom they are designed. Col. T. W. Higginson, who, with Mabel L. Todd, has edited them, in a graceful introduction states that they are printed chiefly "to meet the desire of her personal friends, especially of her surviving sister."—

38   "Holiday Books and Reprints." *Churchman* 62 (December 6, 1890), 740.

The same publishers issue a pretty edition of Poems by Emily Dickinson, poems which Thomas Wentworth Higginson in his preface to the volume says are "of extraordinary grasp and insight." We agree with this verdict, and are not severe upon the form, *e.g.*, in such things as the following:

> The bustle in a house
> The morning after death,
> Is solemnest of industries
> Enacted upon earth.
>
> The sweeping up the heart,
> And putting love away
> We shall not want to use again
> Until eternity.

39   Alexander Young. "Boston Letter." *Critic*, n.s. 14 (December 6, 1890), 297. The first reprinting would not in fact occur until December 11th. Sales of the volume seem to have been greatly stimulated by the Christmas gift book trade, as two additional reprintings were ordered during the month; see Appendix D. Reprinted: *Book News* 9 (January 1891), 191.

I hear that the "Poems" of Emily Dickinson, lately published by Roberts Bros., have passed to a second edition. It is seldom that an author who gave to the world so little during her life wins such instant and hearty recognition by her posthumous work.

40   "Emily Dickinson's Poems." *Literary World* 21 (December 6, 1890), 466. If it was inevitable that the sudden fuss over Dickinson would soon prompt strenuous critical reassessment, it is also notable that the first fusillade comes from the pages of a journal as sensitive to New England critical opinion, the center of Dickinson's support, as Boston's *Literary World*. Arlo Bates had had his reservations (see no. 21), but this notice, in its crushing condescension, is the first to carry the note of authoritative refutation and counterstatement. It is of interest as well in its effort to portray the poet as so perilously overwrought as to be all but insane. Indeed, in that respect this review is entirely of a piece with the views of such critics as T. B. Aldrich and Andrew Lang whose judgments would nearly obliterate Dickinson's fame by the turn of the cen-

tury. Laura Bridgman, widely known as the first deaf-mute to be educated, had died in 1889. On the "Saxe Holm" controversy, see no. 79.

It is a somewhat doubtful kindness to the deceased author of these verses to
draw them forth from her portfolio into full daylight, to meet the eyes of readers who can have no clew to their creation. These records of a nature curiously
secluded and secretive must be as dear to the intimate friends of the author as
they are difficult of assimilation by the world at large. Miss Dickinson was surely
a woman possessing, and possessed by, a share of genius. Extraordinary crises of
insight, and strenuous phrases that seem extorted by hard pressure of emotion
attest the presence of the god. Yet few fine minds have been more debarred from
expression. Whatever may have been the cause, whether natural bias or long
custom, Miss Dickinson was a Laura Bridgman, her avenues of spiritual communication being closed or deficient. Even the imperfections and errors of her
rhymes prove how silent she must have been; her verse has almost no vocal quality, as if she never sang it, or even said it, to herself. Yet in the rare cases where
it has not this pathetic dumbness, there is heard a sweet note that is pitifully lost
in jangling harshness or in silence. There is vision in her verse, but it seems to
flash and dazzle and be blotted out. Nothing in recent literature is more painful
than the pent and paralyzed inspiration of this truly gifted mind, incapable of
mastery of its art or of itself. It is a case of arrested development for which another life seems to offer the only consolation in delayed opportunity.

Some of these verses strike the same notes, morbid, wrong in their excess, yet
uplifting, that were heard in the Saxe Holm stories and their incidental poetry.
Had Miss Dickinson something to do, perhaps, with that complex little mystery,
so well kept that people lost interest in guessing longer? Mrs. Helen Hunt had
part in the affair, no doubt; but was not her personality also a screen for Miss
Dickinson's collaboration? We would commend this strange book of verse—with
its sober, old-maidenly binding, on which is a silver Indian pipe, half fungus, half
flower—to pitying and kindly regard. Here, surely, is the record of a soul that
suffered from isolation and the stress of dumb emotion and the desire to make
itself understood by means of a voice so long unused that the sound was strange
even to her own ears.

41 [James Jeffrey Roche.] "Books and Bookmakers." *Pilot* 53 (December 6,
1890), 6. Dickinson's almost uniformly favorable treatment in the large
circulation religious weeklies had much to do with her popular success.
Roche, newly installed as editor of *The Pilot*, a leading and notably
literary Catholic paper, may have heard the Amherst poet discussed at
Mrs. Moulton's reception a week earlier; see no. 30. Author attribution
is by hand in the Todd scrapbook.

Col. Thomas Wentworth Higginson tells in the preface to this handsome volume some facts about the life of the strange poet whose verses he edits in con-
junction with Mrs. Mabel Loomis Todd. Emily Dickinson was born in Amherst,
Mass., Dec. 10, 1830, and died there on May 15, 1886. Her fifty-six years of life were
spent in the seclusion of a recluse. She avoided society, and had nothing of the
poet's yearning for fame or praise. The human side of her poetry is sad, almost
pessimistic, seldom hopeful. There is something pagan in her love of nature. Thus
she introduces herself to her reader: —

This is my letter to the world,
  That never wrote to me,
The simple news that Nature told,
  With tender majesty.

Her message is committed
  To hands I cannot see;
For love of her, sweet countrymen,
  Judge tenderly of me!

"Life," "Love," "Nature," "Time" and "Eternity" are the themes of her muse. Success is understood best by those who lose it. No victor comprehends it so clearly

As he, defeated, dying,
  On whose forbidden ear
The distant strains of triumph
  Break, agonized and clear.

And this is the sum of earthly hopes, in her philosophy: —

The heart asks pleasure first,
And then, excuse from pain;
And then, those little anodynes
That deaden suffering.

And then, to go to sleep;
And then, if it should be,
The will of its Inquisitor,
The liberty to die.

Emerson's terseness, with more than Emerson's contempt of poetical laws, is apparent throughout the work. There are hardly a hundred perfect rhymes in all her poems: "true" is made to mate with "throe," "tell" with "steel," "eye" with "me," etc.; while such enormities as the pairing of "feign" and "strung," "rooms" and "names," "begun" and "alone," grate on the ear in every page. We are better pleased when she boldly discards all semblance of melody, and sets "find" to rhyme with "ashamed," or "morn" with "again"; for then we do not look for rhyme, but reason, and forget the dress in the thought. Here, for instance, is a short poem: —

REAL.

I like a look of agony,
  Because I know it's true;
Men do not sham convulsion,
  Nor simulate a throe.

The eyes glaze once, and that is death,
  Impossible to feign,
The beads upon the forehead
  By hourly anguish strung.   [homely

But *is* this "Real"? Do men never sham agony and "simulate a throe"? Is not nearly all the shamming of the world that of pain, and not of pleasure? Realists preach that only the hard and cold and unlovely things are natural; but we know better. There is more philosophy in her poem of one who "died for beauty," and found his next neighbor one who died for truth—

—"the two are one: we brethren are,"

he said. And there is a better, the best, philosophy in this:—

> I never saw a moor,
>   I never saw the sea;
> Yet know I how the heather looks,
>   And what a wave must be.

> I never spoke with God,
>   Nor visited in heaven:
> Yet certain am I of the spot
>   As if the chart were given.

Altogether, this is a remarkable book of poems, and will be remembered long after more finely finished verses are dead and forgotten, for, as Col. Higginson says, they are "like poetry torn up by the roots, with rain and dew and earth still clinging to them, giving a freshness and a fragrance not otherwise to be conveyed.

42   "Poems and Holiday Books." *San Francisco Evening Bulletin,* December 6, 1890, p. 5.

T. W. Higginson furnishes a preface in which this statement is made: "The main quality of these poems is that of extraordinary grasp and insight uttered with an uneven vigor and sometimes exasperating, seemingly wayward, but really unsought and inevitable." The lines here quoted will more than justify this estimate. These are printed under the head of "The Secret":

> Some things that fly there be—
> Birds, hours, the bumble-bee:
> Of these no elegy.

> Some things that stay there be—
> Grief, hills, eternity:
> Nor this behooveth me.

> There are, that resting, rise.
> Can I expound the skies?
> How still the riddle lies.

There are some admirable qualities in these poems, subtleties of meaning, vividness of description and flashes which half reveal and half obscure the thought. Was ever a better reason given against indulgence in hatred than this?

> I had no time to hate, because the grave would hinder me,
> And life was not so ample I could finish enmity.

What a quaint conceit of the "Mountain" is this:

> The mountain sat upon the plain
> In his eternal chair,
> His observation omnifold,
> His inquest everywhere.

> The seasons prayed around his knee,
> Like children, 'round a sire;
> Grandfather of the days is he,
> Of dawn the ancestor.

And this, at last, for us all:

> One dignity delays for all,
> One mitred afternoon.
> None can avoid the purple,   [this purple
> Nor evade the crown.   [None evade this
> . . . .
>
> How pomp surpassing ermine,
> When simple you and I,
> Present our meek escutcheon,
> And claim the rank to die.

The book is handsomely printed and bound in imitation vellum.

43 "Recent Publications." *Providence Sunday Journal*, December 7, 1890, p. 13. Reprinted: *Literary News* 12 (January 1891), 19.

Emily Dickinson was born in Amherst, Mass., Dec. 10, 1830, and died there May 15, 1886. Her father, Hon. Edward Dickinson, was the leading lawyer of Amherst and Treasurer of the college. Miss Dickinson lived the life of a recluse in her father's house, only emerging from her seclusion when, each year, her father gave a general reception, and she performed dutifully her part as the gracious hostess of the occasion. She wrote an abundance of verses, to give utterance to her fancies and employment for her leisure hours. They were written without a thought of publication and belong emphatically to what Emerson called "The Poetry of the Portfolio." The selection from her poems in the volume now issued was made at the request of her sister and her personal friends. The poems are edited by two of her appreciative friends, Mabel Loomis Todd and T. W. Higginson. They overflow with originality, give evidence of an inherent insight into nature and life, and abound in descriptive and imaginative power. Critical taste will condemn their crudeness and want of conformity to literary form. The circumstances of publication, however, disarm criticism, and win a tribute of admiration for the freshness, strength and naturalness in which the poet found expression for her fancies. We make a selection of two short poems, by no means the best, as an illustration of Miss Dickinson's manner of treatment:

> If I can stop one heart from breaking,
>   I shall not live in vain;
> If I can ease one life the aching
>   Or cool one pain,
> Or help one fainting robin
>   Unto his nest again,
>   I shall not live in vain.

A BOOK.

> He ate and drank the precious words,
>   His spirit grew robust;
> He knew no more that he was poor,
>   Nor that his frame was dust.
> He danced along the dingy days,
>   And this bequest of wings
> Was but a book. What liberty
>   A loosened spirit brings!

44 [Kinsley Twining and William Hayes Ward.] "Poems by Emily Dickinson." *Independent* 42 (December 11, 1890), 1759. The authors are identified in a letter to Mrs. Todd from Ward of December 20, 1890, published in *AB*, pp. 112–13. This notice was particularly influential because of the national standing of the *Independent* as a leading opinion weekly and because the review was thought to have been written by Maurice Thompson, a widely respected critic (see *AB*, p. 77). Thompson's estimate, published a few weeks later, was in fact much less enthusiastic (see no. 81). Indeed, Twining and Ward are among only a small company of Dickinson's earliest readers to bring to her work fresh observation and an understanding of her achievement that anticipates twentieth-century views. Their concluding remarks about misprints, however, are off the mark; see *AB*, pp. 77–79, 83–84.

Whatever may be said as to the merits or demerits of these poems, they bear the stamp of original genius. Making allowance for a certain Emersonian diction, there is nothing like these poems in the language, unless Mr. Higginson's fancy that they resemble William Blake's will hold. "H. H." was the poet's chosen and admiring friend, so far as we know the only literary intimate she had; but we detect no traces of "H. H." in these poems. If there are such they wholly fade in the torrent of original passion which could move in no channel but its own. It would be extravagant to say that they are written in a language of their own; but so far as technical execution is concerned, the author invented her poetic idiom. In her eager passion for direct expression, her thought crowds on in fierce impatience of the restraints and limitations of grammar or rhyme. The poetic substance comes to her mind in broad masses, like a painting of the French school, and takes form on her canvas without the minutiae of pen and pencil details. The poems do not take effect on the reader at once; and if they captivate him at all, will do so slowly. Speaking for all but the hopeless conventional ones, we should say they are sure to win him at last. The poems, though numerous, are desultory and brief. They make no attempt at long flight or sustained power. They shoot up high into the sky and drop thence a few notes of uncommon melody, and the song ends, sometimes broken, generally, too soon. Mr. Higginson, in his fascinating Preface, calls them flashes; but they are flashes that combine into visions. The portrait he draws of the author and his picture of her life is tender, beautiful and strong as a poem; but it was a life which needed for its interpretation to be seen through these poems. In them the witchery of genius throws its charm and its fascination over what without it would strike the eye as bare singularity. Never did a Puritan maiden weave her bower in such silence and solitude as this lady of Amherst chose for herself. Stranger yet was the passion that swept her breast. Where did she learn that delirium that burst into song in the little poem "Rouge Gagne"?

> 'Tis so much joy! 'Tis so much joy!
> If I should fail what poverty!
> And yet, as poor as I
> Have ventured all upon a throw;
> Have gained! Yes! Hesitated so,
> This side the victory!
>
> Life is but life, and death but death:
> Bliss is but bliss, and breath but breath!
> And if, indeed, I fail,

At least to know the worse is sweet.
Defeat means nothing but defeat,
No drearier can prevail!

And if I gain—oh, gun at sea,
Oh, bells that in the steeple be,
At first repeat it slow!
For heaven is a different thing
Conjectured, and waked sudden in,
And might o'erwhelm me so!

There is plenty more of the same delirium in the book; but it is the delirium of a sane mind poised on a very serious basis of living and thinking. She was in this the child of Puritan New England as the poems on "Time and Eternity" show. Through all we have glimpses of a deep and holy tenderness which no vestal virgin ever had, but only the mother-heart of womanhood. Read for example this:

'Twas such a little, little boat
That toddled down the bay;
'Twas such a gallant, gallant sea
That beckoned it away!

'Twas such a greedy, greedy wave
That licked it from the coast;
Nor ever guessed the stately sails
My little craft was lost!

Burns's "A man's a man for a' that," is hardly better than this fragment:

The pedigree of honey
    Does not concern the bee,
A clover any time to him
    Is aristocracy.

The very heart of womanhood is in the poem "Love's Baptism":

I'm ceded, I stopped being theirs;
The name they dropped upon my face
With water in a country church,
Is finished using now,
And they can put it with my dolls,
My childhood and the string of spools
I've finished threading, too.

Baptized before without the choice,
But this time consciously, of grace,
Unto supremest name.
Called to my full, a crescent dropped,
Existence's whole arc filled up
With one small diadem.

My second rank, too small the first.
Crowned, crowing on my father's breast,
A half-unconscious queen.
But this time, adequate, erect,
With will to choose and to reject,
And I choose—just a throne.

How much this poem means and how deeply it discloses the woman heart is seen in the repetition of the theme in another poem in the volume which gives yet more passionate expression to the same idea. When we consider the voluntary isolation and seclusion of the poet, it awakens wonder that her verse is so free from morbid elements. Once, in a little wail, she seems to ask permission to die, but the real spirit of the poems and of the woman is in "The Book of Martyrs."

> Read, sweet, how others strove
> Till we are stouter;
> What they renounced
> Till we are less afraid;
> How many times they bore
> The faithful witness,
> Till we are helped
> As if a kingdom cared.

She loved books and those who loved books, and found company in them; and when we ask why she chose her hidden life, the reply is ready in one of her own poems:

> The soul selects her own society,
>   Then shuts the door:
> On her divine majority
>   Obtrude no more.

The best example of Miss Dickinson's characteristic qualities as a poet, her audacity, the illusiveness of her thought, the essential melody of her verse in spite of the contempt of technical construction is number xx on page 34. To aid our readers in catching the clue to this piece of lyric delirium we suggest that the "tankards scooped in pearl" are the vault of heaven; that the emphasis in the next verse falls on *summer*; the third verse applies to the fresh autumnal air; and that in the following verse the "snowy hats" are the sign of winter, and that the "windows" to which the saints run are those of the "inns of molten blue" of the second verse.

> I taste a liquor never brewed,
>   From tankards scooped in pearl;
> Not all the vats upon the Rhine
>   Yield such an alcohol.
>
> Inebriate of air am I,
>   And debauchee of dew,
> Reeling, through endless summer days,
>   From inns of molten blue.
>
> When landlords turn the drunken bee
>   Out of the foxglove's door,
> When butterflies renounce their drams,
>   I shall but drink the more!
>
> Till seraphs swing their snowy hats,
>   And saints to windows run,
> To see the little tippler
>   Leaning against the sun!

To show how near the author at her best could approach lyric perfection and to what height her imagination carried her we give this. How many lyrics have been written in this century to surpass it?

> Have you got a brook in your little heart
> Where bashful flowers blow,
> And blushing birds go down to drink,
> And shadows tremble so?
>
> And noboby knows, so still it flows,
> That any brook is there:
> And yet your little draught of life
> Is daily drunken there.
>
> Then look out for the little brook in March,
> When the rivers overflow,
> And the snows come hurrying from the hills,
> And the bridges often go.
>
> And later, in August it may be,
> When the meadows parching lie,
> Beware, lest this little brook of life
> Some burning noon go dry!

There are a few serious misprints in the volume. On page 49 read *sate* for *state*; on page 105 for *satin* read *Latin*, and (probably) *tunneled* for *funneled*.

45 [Lilian Whiting]. "Emily Dickinson's Poems." *Boston Beacon*, December 13, 1890, p. 2. The author attribution, noted by hand in Todd's scrapbook, was apparently prompted by Higginson's remark that Whiting was "probably" the writer of this notice; see *AB*, p. 85.

It is refreshing amid the huddle of current verse with its pretty ways of saying pretty nothings to come upon a book so inspired by real insight and imagination as are the *Poems by Emily Dickinson*, which, four years after the author's death, are now for the first time given to the world by two of her friends, Mabel Loomis Todd and T. W. Higginson. By temperament and habit a recluse, Miss Dickinson was endowed with unique mental gifts, and she set down her emotions and ideas with a freedom from conventional modes of expression that was not due to ignorance or carelessness, but to the evident feeling that in this manner only could she make her true thoughts and visions known. The result is, as Mr. Higginson vividly declares, verses which "will seem to the reader like poetry torn up by the roots, with rain and dew and earth still clinging to them." Even those which at first glance seem to be most crude and rough, having the saving grace of originality, grow upon the fancy, and one soon forgets the roughness of the form in contemplating the beautiful idea enshrined like a diamond in its shattered matrix of discolored quartz. "After all," to quote Mr. Higginson once more, "when a thought takes one's breath away, a lesson on grammar seems an impertinence." No amount of reasoning about the laws of metre, the limitations of syntax or the requirements of rhyme will avail to do away with the fact that Emily Dickinson was a genuine poet—one who saw life and nature with clear, wide-open eyes, and who had the power of interpreting what she saw and felt with an imagery all her own. Mr. Higginson finds in these poems suggestions of William Blake, and the comparison is not unjust, for while Miss Dickinson had not the imaginative range of the English artist-poet, she had something of his weird manner. The following, for instance, might have been written by Blake himself:—

> The clouds their backs together laid,
> The North began to push,   [begun
> The forests galloped till they fell,
> The lightnings skipped like mice;
> The thunder crumbled like a stuff—
> How good to be safe in tombs,
> Where nature's temper cannot reach,
> Nor vengeance ever comes!

The philosophy of human existence is summed up in these two stanzas:

> Our share of night to bear,
> Our share of morning,
> Our blank in bliss to fill,
> Our blank in scorning.

> Here a star and there a star,
> Some lose their way.
> Here a mist, and there a mist,
> Afterwards—day!

Sometimes there is a lyric strain of almost unalloyed melody:—

> Alter? When the hills do.
> Falter? When the sun
> Question if his glory
> Be the perfect one.

> Surfeit? When the daffodil
> Doth of the dew:
> Even as herself, O friend,
> I will of you!

The poems classed under the head of "Nature" include several of exquisite suggestiveness. Here is one:—

THE SEA OF SUNSET.

> This is the land the sunset washes,
> These are the banks of the Yellow Sea;
> Where it rose or whither it rushes,
> There are the western mystery;   [These

> Night after night her purple traffic
> Strews the landing with opal bales;
> Merchantmen poise upon horizons,
> Dip, and vanish with fairy sails.

Altogether one may safely say that in the small bulk of contemporary American verse which will survive the lapse of a generation the *Poems* of Emily Dickinson must have an honored place.

46   "The Poems of Emily Dickinson." *Critic*, n.s. 14 (December 13, 1890), 305–06. In the Todd scrapbook three names are penciled close to this review: James H. Morse, Alice W. Rollins, and Jeannette Gilder. The latter, with her brother, Joseph Gilder, was a co-founder and publisher of this respected New York literary weekly. In a letter to Mrs. Todd, Higginson mentions Morse and Rollins as frequent reviewers for the *Critic*, "both of whom," he says, "are appreciative & not truculent" (see *AB*, p. 65). An unbound review copy had been sent to Jeannette Gilder in mid-October 1890 (*AB*, p. 68).

Here is a volume of striking and original poems by a writer who, during the fifty years of her life, wrote much and published almost nothing. The name of Emily Dickinson is a new name in our literature, but whoever reads the striking verses in this book which her two friends, Mabel Loomis Todd and Col. T. W. Higginson, have edited, will agree that its place is established and sure to remain, associated with a collection of poems whose main quality, as is pointed out in an admirable preface, is an extraordinary grasp and insight. So clearly are the characteristics of these verses defined and so exactly does our opinion of them agree with the writer's, that we are almost tempted to quote him literally; but there are some features which he has left for others to describe—namely, the similarity between these poems and some of Emerson's (a similarity both of thought and manner of expression), and, in the poems of love, the absence of much that is essential to poems of this kind—sensuousness and symmetry and melody. It is in the other poems that the rare genius of Miss Dickinson is best seen—in those of Life, Nature, Time and Eternity. Here, for instance, is an example chosen from the verses on Life, which will show, too, what we call the Emersonian influence. The poem appeared first in "A Masque of Poets," published at the request of the author's friend "H. H.," who had often urged her to print a volume. It is called "Success."

> Success is counted sweetest
> By those who ne'er succeed.
> To comprehend a nectar
> Requires sorest need.
>
> Not one of all the purple host
> Who took the flag to-day
> Can tell the definition,
> So clear, of victory,
>
> As he, defeated, dying,
> On whose forbidden ear
> The distant strains of triumph
> Break, agonized and clear.

We venture to give some of the things which have most impressed us. Many of the poems are untitled, but the first of the following is called "The Secret":—

> Some things that fly there be,—
> Birds, hours, the bumble-bee:
> Of these no elegy.
>
> Some things that stay there be,—
> Grief, hills, eternity:
> Not this behooveth me.   [Nor
>
> There are, that resting, rise.
> Can I expound the skies?
> How still the riddle lies!

It is of Nature that the poet writes best. Of the thirty-one poems under this heading, it is hard to find favorites, they are all so fine. We select the two following: —

New feet within my garden go,
New fingers stir the sod;
A troubadour upon the elm
Betrays the solitude.

New children play upon the green,
New weary sleep below;
And still the pensive spring returns,
And still the punctual snow!

———————

Like trains of cars on tracks of plush
I hear the level bee:
A jar across the flowers goes,
Their velvet masonry
Withstands until the sweet assault
Their chivalry consumes,
While he, victorious, tilts away
To vanquish other blooms.
  . . . .
His labor is a chant,
His idleness a tune;
Oh, for a bee's experience
Of clovers and of noon!

We must make room for this one of the poems on Life and Eternity: —

If I shouldn't be alive
When the robins come,
Give the one in red cravat
A memorial crumb.

If I couldn't thank you,
Being just asleep,
You will know I'm trying
With my granite lip!

Miss Dickinson's poems, though rough and rugged, are surprisingly individual and genuinely inspired.

47   Francis A. Nichols. "Some Powerful Poems by Emily Dickinson." *Boston Sunday Globe*, December 14, 1890, p. 25.

The life of thought that Emily Dickinson passed in her solitary way, at her home in Amherst, Mass., dealt with some of the most intricate problems that come to the philosopher, and sought surcease of sorrow and of pain through knowledge of the Infinite.

If I can stop one heart from breaking,
  I shall not live in vain;

If I can ease one life the aching,
    Or cool the pain,
Or help one fainting robin
    Unto his nest again
I shall not live in vain.

But there is never a doubt of destiny, and the duties it implies.

Morn is supposed to be
By people of degree
The breaking of the day.

Morning has not occurred.
That shall aurora be
East of eternity.

In the following lines, she ridicules doubt.

Of resurrection? Is the East
Afraid to trust the morn
With her fastidious forehead?
As soon impeach my crown!

And she is happy in her loneliness with nature and life. With nature, all the intensity of her love of being gets its fill.

Inebriate of air am I
And debauchee of dew,
Reeling through endless summer days,
From inns of molten blue.

When landlords turn the drunken bee
    Out of the foxglove's door,
When butterflies renounce their dreams,   [drams
    I shall but drink the more.

Till seraphs swing their snowy hats
    And saints to windows run,
To see the Little tippler
    Leaning her life against the sun!   [leaning against

But the poems suggest that the human, as well as the divine in her nature, at sometime asserted itself in love to the degree of self-sacrifice in worship. Love makes these lines sympathetically quiver with the intensity of her feeling. She cannot live or die with the loved one, she reasons.

I could not die with you,
    For one must wait
To shut the other's gaze down —
    You could not.

And I, could I stand by
    And see you freeze,
Without my right of frost,
    Death's privilege?

Nor could I rise with you,
    Because your face

Would put out Jesus',
    That new grace.

The retirement in which she lived, in self-communion, or communion with nature, has left no trace of the bitterness that it most always brings. Alone by herself, she was able to round out life, in sentiment and feeling, as experience does not enable many others to do, and to crown it with almost inspired wisdom regarding its meaning to the present, and the future.

The poems of Miss Dickinson are remarkable in their conception, which illustrates seer-like insight, and, in their style, which, with its oracular and penetrative manner, fits becomingly its sometimes startling revelation of truths. Like the poems of Ralph Waldo Emerson, which they suggest, in the quality of their thought, they open visions to the mind undreamed of, in its yearning for more light on spiritual things.

It has white and gray covers.

48   "The Poems of Emily Dickinson." *Boston Evening Transcript,* December 15, 1890, p. 6. Charles Edwin Hurd, literary editor of the *Transcript* in the nineties, may have written this and other notices of Dickinson appearing in that paper during the decade. In Mrs. Todd's scrapbook copy of this review the word "on" in the second line of "There's a certain slant of light" has been crossed out and a proofreader's deletion mark placed to the left of the line, indicating knowledge that although the word was supplied by the editors in the published *Poems,* it did not appear there in Dickinson's manuscript version of the poem. The editorial change may have been Mr. Higginson's, and not Mrs. Todd's, idea.

The name of Emily Dickinson, unknown to the reading world six months ago, is now familiar to it as that of the writer of poems unique in sort and of permanent worth. During her life, which ended four years ago, very few of these poems were published. A brief but very remarkable one of these, was that which, under the title "Success," appeared in "A Masque of Poets," and was, at the time, almost universally attributed to Emerson. Many other poems, for the most part as brief and in some instances as remarkable, were found among her papers, after her death; and selections from these edited by her friends Mabel L. Todd and T. W. Higginson, make up the present volume. In his very sympathetic introduction, Mr. Higginson happily qualifies these verses as "poetry torn up by the roots, with rain and dew and earth still clinging to them, giving a freshness and a fragrance not otherwise to be conveyed." It is not alone in the matter of freshness and fragrance that the editor's original metaphor holds good; the verses "torn up by the roots" have all the disconnectedness from their natural sources and associations, all the marks of rude and careless handling, that the phrase suggests. Scarcely one of them, with the exception of "Success," already alluded to, bears any sign of artistic revision; and that we note, on comparison, was judiciously trained a bit into form before its publication in the "Masque." The verses, as a whole, give an impression which the trained mind will involuntarily resent of wilful whimsicality and scorn of finish and form; an eccentricity which seriously detracts from the value and interest of any literary work in which it may be indulged, though, perhaps, giving to it, as Mr. Higginson points out, a certain impression of freshness, as of the reception of thought at first hand. Of the originality and value of the thought itself, however, there can scarcely be two opinions. Every subject of the writer's musings — the editors have divided her verses into groups on Life,

Love, Nature, Time and Eternity—is approached with a candor, a naivete of mental attitude which for the moment makes one forget every convention of intellect
and religion, and face world-old perplexities as for the first time. And this momentary emancipation from conventions is the best gift Miss Dickinson's readers
will win from her book. For the rest, her verse has frequent, though as it seems,
involuntary felicities of phrase, and an almost elfin, unhuman intimacy with nature, which she seems less to study than to gossip about, with the privilege of
close and long familiarity of acquaintance. Her poems on nature are immensely
the best in the book; full of a strange magic of meaning so ethereal that one must
apprehend rather than comprehend it. It is a quality to be illustrated merely, not
explained; it is at its height in the two poems we quote, but dare not coarsen by
any praise:

BECLOUDED.

The sky is low, the clouds are mean,
　　A travelling flake of snow
Across a barn or through a rut
　　Debates if it will go.

A narrow wind complains all day
　　How some one treated him;
Nature, like us, is sometimes caught
　　Without her diadem.

XXXI.

There's a certain slant of light
　　On winter afternoons
That oppresses, like the weight
　　Of cathedral tunes.

Heavenly hurt it gives us.
　　We can find no scar,
But internal difference
　　Where the meanings are.

None may teach it anything,
　　'Tis the seal, despair,—
An imperial affliction
　　Sent us of the air.

When it comes, the landscape listens,
　　Shadows hold their breath;
When it goes, 'tis like the distance
　　On the face of Death.

49　"Other Publications." *Hartford Times*, December 16, 1890, p. 4.

　　The poems of Emily Dickinson, of Amherst, Mass., are published to meet the
desire of her personal friends. They are edited by Mabel Loomis Todd and T. W.
Higginson, who believe that the thoughtful reader will find in the verses a quality suggestive of the poetry of William Blake, and flashes of wholly original and
profound insight into nature and life; words and phrases exhibiting an extraor-

dinary vividness of descriptive and imaginative power, yet often set in a seemingly whimsical or even rugged frame.

50   "Books and Authors." *Boston Daily Advertiser*, December 18, 1890, p. 5.

The wonderfully strong and impressive poems by Emily Dickinson, also published by Roberts Bros., come in a dainty and tastefully bound little volume.

51   J[ohn] W[hite] C[hadwick]. "Poems by Emily Dickenson" [*sic*]. *Christian Register* 69 (December 18, 1890), 828. Lavinia Dickinson's particular enthusiasm for this review prompted Mrs. Todd to correspond with its author and to learn that Chadwick in turn had been in correspondence with Higginson about Dickinson even before writing this review; see *AB*, pp. 93–94. In January, Chadwick published another spirited appraisal in a religious weekly; see no. 95. See also the *Register's* editorial defense of Dickinson, no. 145. Aside from a mention of the poem by Mrs. Todd (7), this review makes the first critical reference to Dickinson's "Because I could not stop for Death" ("The Chariot"). Roberts Brothers used Chadwick's first two sentences in its advertising; see no. 73.

Seldom have "precious things discovered late" a greater preciousness than these. They seem an argument for immortality. Only three or four of them were published by their author while she lived. And now it seems as if she ought to know — as if she must — what echoes there will be in minds that until now have not known that so strange and beautiful a spirit has been among them on the earth. We say in her own words, —

> Could she have guessed that it would be;
> Could but a crier of the glee
>   Have climbed the distant hill;
> Had not the bliss so slow a pace, —
> Who knows but this surrendered face
>   Were undefeated still?

Or did she only love her work and care no whit for praise? It would seem as if she must have known that she could have it any time by scattering abroad these gems and pearls she hoarded till the end. Let us be glad that loving hands have scattered them at last. Mr. Higginson has, in a brief introduction, told the story of the poet's simple life, — simple and uneventful save as once a year she came out of her seclusion to be hostess in her father's house to those whom he, as treasurer of Amherst College, had invited, discharged her duty with much grace and sweetness, and then withdrew into her loneliness. We are not told that she was an invalid, but only that for years she did not go out of doors, and for many more did not overpass the limits of her father's grounds. But she touches the subject of pain so feelingly that it would seem her knowledge of it must have been direct. She was born in Amherst, Dec. 10, 1830, and died there May 15, 1886, her father being the leading lawyer of the town.

In reading her book, — each little poem with a whole page to itself, as it deserves, — we have found ourselves thinking how Emerson would have enjoyed many of the verses, and how Thoreau might have coveted some of their *naïve* and daring liberties with the deep things of God and with his awful name, as where she writes, —

> I never spoke with God
>> Nor visited in heaven,
> Yet certain am I of the spot
>> As if the chart were given.

But there is no offensive other-worldliness; rather, a very sweet and wholesome satisfaction with the life that now is, as in "The First Lesson": —

> Not in this world to see his face
> Sounds long, until I read the place
> Where this is said to be
> But just the primer to a life
> Unopened, rare, upon the shelf,
> Clasped yet to him and me.

> And yet my primer suits me so
> I would not choose a book to know
> Than that, be sweeter wise;
> Might some one else so learned be,
> And leave me just my A, B, C,
> Himself could have the skies.

Of three or four poems that were printed in her lifetime, we recognize only the first, which came out in "A Masque of Poets," behind which many a good discovery has been made, and "A Service of Song," which appeared in the short-lived *Round Table*, with certain differences from the form given here, unless our memory fails.

Mr. Higginson suggests a likeness to William Blake's in the quality of these poems, but the likeness never in any place impeaches their originality. They are like Blake's only because they are so fresh, so daring, so quaint, so imaginative. There is a great and often startling felicity of word and phrase. The poems have generally a noble, and often subtle, rhythm, which does occasionally halt. To rhyme she is much more indifferent, liking it well enough if it comes handy, but, if it does not, letting it go with easy nonchalance. And we are much mistaken if she does not prove that the adjunct of rhyme is not so necessary to the pleasure of verse as many have believed. Thus: —

> How excellent the heaven,
> When earth cannot be had!
> How hospitable, then, the face
> Of our old neighbor, God!

We should like to quote a score of things, but the reader's pleasure should not be forestalled. There are words "so full of subtle flame," phrases so packed with strangeness, force, suggestion, poems so tremulous with tenderness or so bent under the burden of their mystery, that they shock us with almost intolerable delight or awe. "The Chariot" is one of several poems that have in them an abundance of that wonder of life passing into death, death into life, which had for Michel Angelo a boundless fascination. There is realism here as firm as Mr. Howells can desire, but a profound idealism by which his standards are abashed. In a few instances the riddle is too hard to guess; the symbol baffles us. There are degrees of excellence, but not a poem in the one hundred and fifteen that we would gladly spare. In words that make a poem by themselves, Mr. Higginson has said, and nothing could be truer, "In many cases, these poems will seem to the

reader like poetry torn up by the roots, with rain and dew and earth still clinging to them, giving a freshness and a fragrance not otherwise to be conveyed."

52   "Recent Verse and Poetry." *Hartford Courant,* December 18, 1890, p. 3.

But we find more of that indefinable thing called genius in *Poems* by Emily
Dickinson than in any book yet mentioned. And this quality runs through work
painfully deficient in artistic finish or polish in proportion, in much that poetry
demands; a fact explained when it is said that this verse was written by a recluse,
was not intended for publication, and only now after the author's death, is given
to the public. Edited by Miss Dickinson's friends, T. W. Higginson and Mabel L.
Todd, the volume is prefaced by the former, who claims that readers will discover
in her something akin to the English poet, Blake; and we heartily agree with Mr.
Higginson. On almost every page, intermingled with much that makes us smile
by its naïveté, boldness or even absurdity, one meets with a strength, beauty,
originality, purity and grandeur of conception which fairly startle at the same time
that they charm and compel admiration. Emily Dickinson, child of a well-known
Amherst family, and so much of an invalid that she rarely left the limits of her
father's house, practically out of the world before death actually removed her
from it, has left in these poems a precious legacy, not only for her friends, but for
a wide world of poetry-lovers. Already a second edition of this remarkable book,
published not a month ago as we write, is demanded, and it is evident that appreciation will be general. We quote one characteristic piece: *Setting Sail.*

> Exultation is the going
>   Of an inland soul to sea—
> Past the houses, past the headlands,
>   Into deep eternity!
>
> Bred as we, among the mountains,
>   Can the sailor understand
> The divine intoxication
>   Of the first league out from land?

53   *Commercial Gazette,* December 20, 1890. Unlocated. Although it has
       proved impossible to verify Todd's handwritten identification of this
       scrapbook clipping, a weekly newspaper with this title was published in
       New York City during the nineties.

The Poems of Emily Dickinson, edited by two of her friends, Mabel Loomis
Todd and T. W. Higginson, lately published, have attracted far more than an ordinary share of attention. Miss Dickinson was a New England recluse, who died
in 1886, at the age of fifty-six. Her poems are very terse, the lines short, and the
stanzas few. But they have an Emersonian quality and insight. They may be rugged and whimsical at times, but they are poetry, and of a lofty order.

54   "The Week." *Speaker* [London] 2 (December 20, 1890), 687. This, the ear-
       liest published British notice of Dickinson, was unknown to Mrs. Todd.
       The *Nation* review that provoked it is no. 28. *The Speaker* was soon to
       carry Andrew Lang's sportive dissection of the poet; see no. 102. For
       other British comment, see the index, s.v. Great Britain.

The American *Nation* announces a new poet, Emily Dickinson, whose works have been issued posthumously by Messrs. Roberts Bros., Boston. This lady was born in 1830, and died in 1886. Her life was spent in seclusion in the college town of Amherst, and she resolutely refused to publish her verses, showing them only to a very few friends. She is said to belong distinctly but unconsciously to the school of Blake—"if, indeed, he had any other scholar." The following poem has certainly a sound as of Blake singing in the grave:—

> I died for beauty, but was scarce
> Adjusted in the tomb,
> When one who died for truth was laid   [lain
> In an adjoining room.
>
> He questioned softly why I failed?
> "For beauty," I replied.
> "And I, for truth: the two are one;
> We brethren are," he said.
>
> And so as kinsmen met a-night,
> We talked between the rooms,
> Until the moss had reached our lips
> And covered up our names.

"The extraordinary terseness and vigour of that weird conclusion," says the enthusiastic reviewer in the *Nation*, "runs through all the poems."

———

But why should Emily Dickinson be a scholar of Blake's? No evidence is given that she had even read him. Other English poets, such as Wordsworth and Coleridge in the past, and Mr. Bridges and Miss Rossetti to-day, have struck this note of terseness, have woven verses which have the very ring of Blake; verses combined of strength, sweetness, and simplicity, the qualities usually accompanying originality in poetry. The truth is that the comparative study of literature is at the best a necessary evil; and many people remember with much satisfaction the moment when they shook themselves free of literary primers, and said to themselves, "No more comparing of Virgil with Homer. It was good enough as a bladder, all that assaying and balancing; but now for a free plunge into books!" To think one's own thought, not another's; to like and to hate, not by rule, but at pleasure, is the only way to get anything worth having out of books, as out of dinners. Some people in America, holding a different opinion, started recently "Poet-Lore: a Monthly Magazine devoted to Shakespeare, Browning, and the Comparative Study of Literature." Duxes and prize-takers naturally exaggerate the value of the work in which they have excelled; and it is not astonishing that they try to perpetuate it after they have left school. They, in their turn, must not wonder when the dunces, who are unhappily in a large majority, refuse to be interested in the duxes' ideas of what Browning meant in "Childe Roland to the Dark Tower came."

55 "Local News." *Amherst Record*, December 24, 1890, p. 4.

—The book of poems by the late Emily Dickinson is having a large sale in Amherst.

56   Alexander Young. "Boston Letter." *Critic*, n.s. 14 (December 27, 1890),
         340. This note was slightly recast and reprinted in the *Chicago Post*,
         January 2, 1891. The "third edition" had been printed December 23rd. The
         likely Boston source for the *Critic*'s correspondent was either Higginson
         or Thomas Niles of Roberts Brothers. Plans for these new volumes
         proved premature when the poet's sister refused to give her consent; see
         no. 106.

I hear that two more volumes, one of poetry and one of prose, from the pen of
the late Emily Dickinson, are contemplated by the editors of her recently published volume of poems, Mrs. Mabel Loomis Todd and Col. T. W. Higginson. The
fact that this volume has passed to a third edition is encouraging for the success
of the undertaking, and it will be interesting to see whether Miss Dickinson's
prose has the elements of profound insight into nature and life and vivid imaginative power which are exhibited in her poetry.

57   "The Best Five Books of the Decade." *Critic*, n.s. 14 (December 27, 1890),
         338–39. Of the 18 writers and scholars asked by the *Critic* to name the
         best five books of the previous decade, both Louise Chandler Moulton
         and Sarah C. Woolsey included Dickinson's poems in their list. Their
         other titles are Oliver Wendell Holmes's *Over the Teacups* (1890), *The
         Correspondence of John Lothrop Motley*, ed. George W. Curtis (1889),
         Helen Hunt Jackson's *Ramona* (1884), the initial volumes of John Bach
         McMaster's *A History of the People of the United States*, 8 vols. (1883–
         1919), and sketches of Russian life by George Kennan appearing as ar-
         ticles in the *Century*, 1888–91. Among others responding were Noah
         Brooks, Kate Field, George W. Cable, H. H. Furness, Lucy Larcom,
         Brander Matthews, Francis Parkman, Agnes Repplier, and Moses Coit
         Tyler. Both Moulton and Brooks had recently reviewed Dickinson.

We have obtained from a number of writers lists of the best five American
books published during the past ten years—the *Critic*'s first decade, the century's
ninth. . . .
Mrs. Louise Chandler Moulton "cannot venture to give an opinion about the
best American books of 1890, because she has been absent from the country for
nearly eight months of the time, and is in consequence quite ignorant of a very
large proportion of the past year's issues." She is, however, very sure she would
include "Over the Teacups" and also the posthumous "Poems" of Miss Emily Dickinson, but would not feel justified in any further choice. . . .
Miss Sarah C. Woolsey ("Susan Coolidge") protests that her opinion is not
very valuable, and that she lacks the facilities for forming it in Newport just at
this moment; "but I should say—just speaking from the top of my mind and
memory—that the best biographical book of the last decade in American letters
was, perhaps, Motley's Life and Letters; the most noteworthy novel, 'Ramona';
the most sterling work in history, McMaster's History of the United States; the
most striking travels, George Kennan's Russian papers; and, among poems, that
Emily Dickinson's, just published, are the most distinctly original. This is rather
an impression than an opinion."

58   "Harper's Magazine." *Boston Budget*, December 28, 1890. Unlocated.
         Attribution derives from the Todd scrapbook where this item was

placed directly under the reprinting of a Dickinson poem which in turn appears beneath the separately clipped masthead of the *Budget* for this date. A frequent contributor of editorials and book reviews for the *Budget* during this period was its editor, Lilian Whiting. The Howells review is no. 64.

William Dean Howells reviews some new books, and makes a few remarks on the difficulty of keeping enemies. Charles Dudley Warner gives expression to a train of thought suggested by the recurrence of "the time of year for reforming the world." Mr. Howells's review of the poems of Emily Dickinson is very interesting in its psychological analysis of her strange life that expressed itself in these lyrics. So far, however, as the art of keeping enemies goes, Mr. Howells's testimony is entitled only to the limited consideration given a special pleader. Of course, Mr. Howells cannot keep an enemy—as well expect the snows of January to perpetuate themselves under the sunshine of July—but then all the people who practice the gentle art of making enemies are not so full of the irresistible charm of sweetness and exaltation of nature as is Mr. Howells.

59 "Scraps of Verse from the Pen of Emily Dickinson." *Boston Herald*, December 29, 1890, p. 6. Roberts Brothers used the words "Such a writer is a literary force" from this review in some of their advertisements; see no. 130.

To turn over the pages of the small volume containing the poems of Emily Dickinson is to feel as if committing an intrusion, so direct and so forcible are many of its utterances, so very evidently not meant for the prying public eye. The form is not always perfect, but its faults are not the flagrant indifference of conceit, or the intentional roughness of affectation, but were evidently allowed to remain because, having expressed her thought, the writer did not care to carve and retouch, but pressed forward, intent upon fresh meditation, and after a few pages form is forgotten, except when some monstrous rhyme arouses the reader from the spell of the poet. There is a peculiarly penetrating quality about these scraps of verse, something which imprints them upon the memory as firmly as those haunting scraps of doggerel chanted by the street boy, but these tranquilize instead of irritating, and fill one with the delight of a new possession. Quotation will prove this better than assertion:

> The pedigree of honey
>   Does not concern the bee;
> A clover, any time to him,
>   Is aristocracy.

> *   *   *   *   *

> To fight aloud is very brave,
>   But gallantry, I know,   [gallanter
> Who charge within the bosom
>   The cavalry of woe,

> Who win, and nations do not see,
>   Who fall, and none observe,
> Whose dying eyes no country
>   Regards with patriot love.

We trust in plumed procession
  For such the angels go,
Rank after rank, with even feet,
  And uniforms of snow.

*   *   *   *   *

Glee! the great storm is over
  Four have recovered the land.
Forty have gone down together   [Forty gone
  Into the boiling sand.

Ring for the scant salvation!
  Toll for the bonnie souls,
Neighbor, friend and bridegroom,   [Neighbor and
  Spinning upon the shoals!

How they will tell the shipwreck
  When winter shakes the door,
Till the children ask, "But the forty?
  Did they come back no more?"

Then a silence suffuses the story,
  And a softness the teller's eye;
And the children no further question,
  And only the waves reply.

It is impossible to read these twice and not remember them, and it would require little effort to make the whole little volume one's very own, and readers of leisure will be sorely tempted to do it. The poems are divided into four books— "Life," "Love," "Nature" and "Time and Eternity"—and of these the second and fourth are the most remarkable for vividness and impressiveness; but, in reading all, one can but regret that the world was not given the privilege of thanking the author for her work, instead of not being permitted to see it until after her death. Such a writer is a literary force, not only by the direct influence of her work, but by silencing the frivolous and the trivial, and it would have been pleasant to see her in her proper place during her lifetime. But as her will was otherwise, nothing remains but to read with gratitude to the friends who have prepared the verses for publication and permitted the world to know how true a singer lived in it unknown.

60   C[aroline] G[ray] L[ingle]. "My Study and My Books." *Kate Field's Washington* 2 (December 31, 1890), 447.

"Poems," by Emily Dickinson, sets one to thinking of the definitions of poetry. If we adhere to one of the best—"the exquisite expression of exquisite impressions"—we shall find the author of this little volume only half a poet. The exquisite impressions are here in abundance. There is the divine ability to discern something fresh and new in love and nature and death which has and always will mark the poet. With all this, there is a deliberate carelessness of poetic forms which justifies the comment of Mr. T. W. Higginson, the editor, that these verses "seem like poetry torn up by the roots." This is the more irritating to the fastidious reader, since there is abundant evidence that the author was sometimes mistress of very pleasing and perfect expression. What lover of books has done anything better than this?

He ate and drank the precious words,
   His spirit grew robust;
He knew no more that he was poor,
   Nor that his frame was dust.
He danced along the dingy days,
   And this bequest of wings
Was but a book. What liberty
   A loosened spirit brings!

In no case are the happiest thoughts coupled with the best words, and some of the daintiest of the love poems are marred by their hysterical form. But, to quote again from the editor of the volume, "When a thought takes one's breath away, a lesson on grammar is an impertinence"; and, though critics may deny Miss Dickinson the bay leaf, they cannot deny that she had in her thoughts a great deal of the material out of which poetry is woven.

61 "Note" in *Out of the Heart: Poems for Lovers Young and Old*, selected by John White Chadwick and Annie Hathaway Chadwick (N.Y.: Nims and Knight, 1891) [unpaged leaf preceding "Index of Authors"]. According to *Publishers' Weekly* (40:736–37), *Out of the Heart* was published during the second week of November, 1891. When this note was written—it is signed "Brooklyn, May 5, 1891"—Rev. Chadwick had already written admiringly of Dickinson in two reviews (nos. 51, 95). The Chadwicks imply here that among all Roberts Brothers' poets, Dickinson looms largest in their minds. They reprint five poems: "Have you got a Brook in your little Heart" (p. 51), "If you were coming in the Fall" (p. 69), "I had no time to Hate" (p. 99), "Not in this world to see his face" (p. 114), "The Daisy follows soft the Sun" (p. 180). The same poems, carrying the 1891 Nims and Knight copyright and same pagination (though on larger sheets), appeared in the Chadwick's *The Lovers' Treasury of Verse* (Boston: L.C. Page, 1906). The following sentence of acknowledgment concludes the one-page "Note" in which the editors explain that they have chosen somewhat lesser-known lyrics in their effort not to duplicate such standard verse compilations as Palgrave's *Golden Treasury*.

Our gratitude is due, and is hereby expressed, for the kindness of many authors and publishers in allowing us the use of their poems and their publications: to Charles Scribner's Sons for the poems of Eugene Field and Mrs. Mary Mapes Dodge; to Roberts Brothers for Emily Dickinson's and many others; and especially to Houghton, Mifflin, & Co., on whose editions of various poets, both American and English, we have drawn with no illiberal hand.

62 "Comment on New Books." *Atlantic Monthly* 67 (January 1891), 128–29. Horace E. Scudder, editor of the *Atlantic*, may have written this notice, as Lubbers suggests (*CR*, p. 259, n. 11). Scudder contributed frequently to the "New Books" column during these years, but his responsibility for this item could not be verified.

Lovers of poetry in the making will find exceeding interest in Poems by Emily Dickinson, edited by two of her friends, Mabel Loomis Todd and T. W. Higginson. The brief prose preface tells in choice phrase of the isolation of the remarkable spirit whose poetic, we do not say literary, labor was interrupted by

death. Whether or no Miss Dickinson ever would have struck out a lyric satisfying to soul and ear we have not the temerity to say; but the impression made upon
the reader, who interprets her life by her verse and her verse by her life, is that
there could not well be any poetic wholes in her work. Nevertheless, such is the
fragmentary richness that one who enters upon the book at any point, and discovers, as he surely will, a phrase which is not to be called felicitous, but rather
a shaft of light sunk instantaneously into the dark abysm, will inevitably search
the book through eagerly for the perfect poem which seems just beyond his grasp.
Words, lines, even stanzas, will reward him, and he will turn the leaf over and
over, to make sure he has missed nothing.

62A "Notes." *Book News* 9 (January 1891), 191. A reprinting; see no. 39.

63   "Talk About New Books." *Catholic World* 52 (January 1891), 600–04.
This review is notable for its depth of treatment and for its last
paragraph, which delicately raises the question of Dickinson's religious
propriety. The first paragraph was used in a Roberts Brothers advertisement (no. 118). Italics in the final lines of "The grass so little has to do"
and "No rack can torture me" had no warrant in *Poems* (1890).

The unique book of the year just ended, and, from the poetical point of view,
the most worthy as well as the most uncommon, is the collection of Miss Emily
Dickinson's Poems lately brought out by Roberts Brothers (Boston). Compared
with the better-known verses of the day, or even with most of those which have
borne the test applied by generations of English-speaking readers, these posthumous poems are like strange orchids among a mass of gay, sweet-smelling, highly
cultivated, but not rare or unfamiliar flowers. Considered merely as rhymed and
metrical compositions they are over-full of apparently wilful sins against rule and
convention; but, like the fantastic blooms to which we have compared them,
these deviations from common standards justify themselves by appeal to a law
not made for chrysanthemums and roses; not binding in the school-room nor in
the editorial rooms of popular magazines.
    Mr. T. W. Higginson, who writes a preface to the volume, remarks that verses
like these, which were produced absolutely without thought of publication, and
solely by way of expressing the author's mind, must "inevitably forfeit whatever
advantage lies in the discipline of public criticism and the enforced conformity
to settled ways," but "may often gain something through the habit of freedom and
the unconventional utterance of daring thoughts." Miss Dickinson's thought,
while individual and rare, does not strike us as happily characterized by the word
"daring"; but her expression of it certainly owes an immense debt to the habit of
freedom. Public criticism would probably have had no appreciable effect on
either—certainly none that her reading, her quick eye and delicate ear might not
be trusted to produce had she so willed. Now and then there is a line, and again
what seems a perverse failure to use a rhyme that was almost inevitable and
would have been appropriate, concerning which one finds it for a moment not
so easy to restrain the pedagogic instinct; but, on the whole, here is poet who
knew so well a mind so well worth knowing, and one ends by accepting her expression of it as it stands, and being grateful to the editorial wisdom that left it
unamended.
    Miss Dickinson died four years ago, at the age of fifty-six, after a life spent in
singular seclusion. For years she never set foot outside her father's door, and for

other years her walks were restricted entirely to the limit of his grounds. She wrote a great deal of verse, but, during her life-time, only three or four of her poems were published, and these only at the urgent solicitation of a few personal friends. Mr. Higginson says that though he was for many years in correspondence with her, he never met her face to face but twice, and then "brought away the impression of something as unique and remote as Undine or Mignon or Thekla." "She was a recluse by temperament and habit, and except for a very few friends was as invisible to the world as if she had dwelt in a nunnery."

Her poems have been divided by their present editors into four books, entitled "Life," "Love," "Nature," and "Time and Eternity." Each of them has striking passages which one dallies over and longs to transcribe for readers to whom the volume itself may be inaccessible. But, as a rule, the best poems are to be found in the two latter books, and we give to them what we can spare of space. Miss Dickinson never named her poems, but this one has been called "Day" by her editors:

> I'll tell you how the sun rose, —
> A ribbon at a time,
> The steeples swam in amethyst,
> The news like squirrels ran.
>
> The hills untied their bonnets,
> The bobolinks begun.
> Then I said softly to myself,
> "That must have been the sun!"
>
> But how he set I know not.
> There seemed a purple stile
> Which little yellow boys and girls
> Were climbing all the while
>
> 'Till, when they reached the other side,
> A dominie in gray
> Put gently up the evening bars,
> And led the flock away.

Here are two stanzas from a charming little poem called "The Grass":

> The grass so little has to do,
> A sphere of simple green,
> With only butterflies to brood,
> And bees to entertain,
>
> And stir all day to pretty tunes
> The breezes fetch along;
> *And hold the sunshine in its lap*
> *And bow to everything.*

Other delightful poems in the "Nature" section are the stately lines called "Summer's Armies"; "The Hemlock"; "The Mountain," "Purple Clover"; and "The Sea of Sunset," which runs thus:

> This is the land the sunset washes,
> These are the banks of the Yellow Sea;
> Where it rose, or whither it rushes,
> These are the western mystery!

> Night after night her purple traffic
> Strews the landing with opal bales;
> Merchantmen poise upon horizons,
> Dip, and vanish with fairy sails.

Our selections from "Time and Eternity" are made chiefly from the untitled poems:

> I never saw a moor,
> I never saw the sea;
> Yet know I how the heather looks,
> And what a wave must be.
>
> I never spoke with God,
> Nor visited in heaven;
> Yet certain am I of the spot
> As if the chart were given.

> *   *   *   *   *

> Death is a dialogue between
> The Spirit and the dust.
> "Dissolve," says Death. The Spirit, "Sir:
> I have another trust."
>
> Death doubts it, argues from the ground,
> The Spirit turns away,
> Just laying off, for evidence,
> An overcoat of clay.

This one is called "The Chariot":

> Because I could not stop for Death,
> He kindly stopped for me:
> The carriage held but just ourselves
> And Immortality.
>
> We slowly drove, he knew no haste,
> And I had put away
> My labor, and my leisure too,
> For his civility.
>
> We passed the school where children played,
> Their lessons scarcely done;
> We passed the fields of gazing grain,
> We passed the setting sun.
>
> We paused before a house that seemed
> A swelling of the ground;
> The roof was scarcely visible,
> The cornice but a mound.
>
> Since then 'tis centuries; but each
> Feels shorter than the day
> I first surmised the horses' heads
> Were toward Eternity.

It is hard to stop quoting, but the poem called "Emancipation" marks our limit:

No rack can torture me,
My soul's at liberty.
Behind this mortal bone
There knits a bolder one

You cannot prick with saw,
Nor rend with scimitar.
Two bodies therefore be;
Bind one, and one will flee.

The eagle of his nest
No easier divest
And gain the sky,
Than mayest thou,

Except thyself may be
Thine enemy;
Captivity is consciousness,
So's liberty.

In the poems ranged under the heading "Love," Miss Dickinson struck a note more intimate and personal, but not so welcome. Here, if anywhere — and in writing so individual as this, and so little meant to reach strange eyes, one looks instinctively to find it here — the clue to her proud seclusion may be sought. Now and then one's hand is almost on it. The jar in her music is now inward, and not, as elsewhere, simply a matter of rhyme and rhythm. It recurs again and again, faint, strange, remote, like a phrase half-remembered from some angelic melody, but beaten back and made dissonant by perverse limits when it would rise to its true altitude. It sounds, haughty and full, in these lines which close a poem on the soul's exclusiveness:

I've known her from an ample nation
Choose one;
Then close the valves of her attention
Like stone.

It degrades to a natural level the assurance of immortality, often so wonderfully expressed and so proudly felt; and in the poem called "In Vain" it ranges the God, the Christ, the heaven that she believes in and pays homage to, as, after all, but accessories, necessary indeed, but ancillary, to merely human love — the love of man and woman at its natural best. The note is false. It strikes into the true melody from below, and makes a discord, but one strangely powerful in seductive charm. What the real theme is, one may learn who studies it in Mr. Coventry Patmore's poems; more especially in the volume called "The Unknown Eros."

64   [William Dean Howells.] "Editor's Study." *Harper's New Monthly Magazine* 82 (January 1891), 318–21. Howells had promised to review the 1890 volume when Mrs. Todd sent him, in the summer of that year, some of the soon to be published poems (*AB*, pp. 64, 74). He obtained an unbound copy of the *Poems* in mid-October and by the end of the month had sent galleys of his forthcoming review to a warmly appreciative Mabel Todd, who in turn showed it to the equally approving Lavinia and Austin Dickinson (*AB*, pp. 74, 96). When the volume was published in November, Higginson wrote to Todd that Howells was "doing missionary work in private" on its behalf (*AB*, p. 72). That promotion may have included talks on the poet at small gatherings; see headnote to no. 30. Howells's family apparently shared his enthusiasm, for his daughter Mildred told Higginson her favorite Dickinson poem was "I died for beauty." Howells's review was widely influential during the first year of the poet's reception.

The strange *Poems of Emily Dickinson* we think will form something like an intrinsic experience with the understanding reader of them. They have been edited by Mrs. Mabel Loomis Todd, who was a personal friend of the poet, and by Colonel T. W. Higginson, who was long her epistolary and literary acquaintance, but only met her twice. Few people met her so often, as the reader will learn from Colonel Higginson's interesting preface, for her life was mainly spent in her father's house at Amherst, Massachusetts; she seldom passed its doors, and never, for many years, passed the gates of its grounds. There is no hint of what turned her life in upon itself, and probably this was its natural evolution, or involution, from tendencies inherent in the New England, or the Puritan, spirit. We are told that once a year she met the local world at a reception in her father's house; we do not know that there is any harm in adding, that she did not always literally meet it, but sometimes sat with her face averted from the company in another room. One of her few friends was Helen Hunt Jackson, whom she suffered to send one of her poems to be included in the volume of anonymous pieces which Messrs. Roberts Brothers once published with the title of *A Masque of Poets*. Whether the anonymity flattered her love of obscurity or not, it is certain that her darkling presence in this book was the occasion of her holding for many years a correspondence with its publishers. She wrote them, as the fancy took her, comments on their new books, and always enclosed a scrap of her verse, though without making any reference to it. She never intended or allowed anything more from her pen to be printed in her lifetime; but it was evident that she wished her poetry finally to meet the eyes of that world which she had herself always shrunk from. She could not have made such poetry without knowing its rarity, its singular worth; and no doubt it was a radiant happiness in the twilight of her hidden, silent life.

The editors have discharged their delicate duty toward it with unimpeachable discretion, and Colonel Higginson has said so many apt things of her work in his introduction, that one who cannot differ with him must be vexed a little to be left so little to say. He speaks of her "curious indifference to all conventional rules of verse," but he adds that "when a thought takes one's breath away, a lesson on grammar seems an impertinence." He notes "the quality suggestive of the poetry of William Blake" in her, but he leaves us the chance to say that it is a Blake who had read Emerson who had read Blake. The fantasy is as often Blakian as the philosophy is Emersonian; but after feeling this again and again, one is ready to declare that the utterance of this most singular and authentic spirit would have been the same if there had never been an Emerson or a Blake in the world. She sometimes suggests Heine as much as either of these; all three in fact are spiritually present in some of the pieces; yet it is hardly probable that she had read Heine, or if she had, would not have abhorred him.

Here is something that seems compact of both Emerson and Blake, with a touch of Heine too:

> I taste a liquor never brewed,
> From tankards scooped in pearl;

Not all the vats upon the Rhine
Yield such an alcohol!

Inebriate of air am I,
And debauchee of dew,
Reeling, through endless summer days,
From inns of molten blue.

When landlords turn the drunken bee
Out of the foxglove's door,
When butterflies renounce their drams,
I shall but drink the more!

Till seraphs swing their snowy hats,
And saints to windows run,
To see the little tippler
Leaning against the sun!

But we believe it is only seeming; we believe these things are as wholly her own as this:

The bustle in a house
The morning after death
Is solemnest of industries
Enacted upon earth, —

The sweeping up the heart,
And putting love away
We shall not want to use again
Until eternity.

Such things could have come only from a woman's heart to which the experiences in a New England town have brought more knowledge of death than of life. Terribly unsparing many of these strange poems are, but true as the grave and certain as mortality. The associations of house-keeping in the following poem have a force that drags us almost into the presence of the poor, cold, quiet thing:

"TROUBLED ABOUT MANY THINGS."

How many times these low feet staggered,
Only the soldered mouth can tell;
Try! can you stir the awful rivet?
Try! can you lift the hasps of steel?

Stroke the cool forehead, hot so often,
Lift, if you can, the listless hair;
Handle the adamantine fingers
Never a thimble more shall wear.

Buzz the dull flies on the chamber window;
Brave shines the sun through the freckled pane;
Fearless the cobweb swings from the ceiling—
Indolent housewife, in daisies lain!

Then in this, which has no name—how could any phrase nominate its weird witchery aright?—there is the flight of an eerie fancy that leaves all experience behind:

I died for beauty, but was scarce
Adjusted in the tomb,
When one who died for truth was lain
In an adjoining room.

He questioned softly why I failed.
"For beauty," I replied.
"And I for truth,—the two are one;
We brethren are," he said.

And so, as kinsmen met a night,
We talked between the rooms,
Until the moss had reached our lips,
And covered up our names.

All that Puritan longing for sincerity, for veracious conduct, which in some good New England women's natures is almost a hysterical shriek, makes its exultant grim assertion in these lines:

REAL.

I like a look of agony,
Because I know it's true;
Men do not sham convulsion,
Nor simulate a throe.

The eyes glaze once, and that is death.
Impossible to feign
The beads upon the forehead
By homely anguish strung.

These mortuary pieces have a fascination above any others in the book; but in the stanzas below there is a still, solemn, rapt movement of the thought and music together that is of exquisite charm:

New feet within my garden go,
New fingers stir the sod;
A troubadour upon the elm
Betrays the solitude.

New children play upon the green,
New weary sleep below;
And still the pensive spring returns,
And still the punctual snow!

This is a song that sings itself; and this is another such, but thrilling with the music of a different passion:

SUSPENSE.

Elysium is as far as to
The very nearest room,
If in that room a friend await
Felicity or doom.

What fortitude the soul contains,
That it can so endure
The accent of a coming foot,
The opening of a door!

The last poem is from the group which the editors have named "Love"; the other groups from which we have been quoting are "Nature," and "Time and Eternity"; but the love poems are of the same piercingly introspective cast as those differently named. The same force of imagination is in them; in them, as in the rest, touch often becomes clutch. In them love walks on heights he seldom treads, and it is the heart of full womanhood that speaks in the words of this nun-like New England life.

Few of the poems in the book are long, but none of the short, quick impulses of intense feeling or poignant thought can be called fragments. They are each a compassed whole, a sharply finished point, and there is evidence, circumstantial and direct, that the author spared no pains in the perfect expression of her ideals. Nothing, for example, could be added that would say more than she has said in four lines:

> Presentiment is that long shadow on the lawn
> Indicative that suns go down;
> The notice to the startled grass
> That darkness is about to pass.

Occasionally, the outside of the poem, so to speak, is left so rough, so rude, that the art seems to have faltered. But there is apparent to reflection the fact that the artist meant just this harsh exterior to remain, and that no grace of smoothness could have imparted her intention as it does. It is the soul of an abrupt, exalted New England woman that speaks in such brokenness. The range of all the poems is of the loftiest; and sometimes there is a kind of swelling lift, an almost boastful rise of feeling, which is really the spring of faith in them:

> I never saw a moor,
> I never saw the sea;
> Yet know I how the heather looks,
> And what a wave must be.
>
> I never spoke with God,
> Nor visited in heaven;
> Yet certain am I of the spot
> As if the chart were given.

There is a noble tenderness, too, in some of the pieces; a quaintness that does not discord with the highest solemnity:

> I shall know why, when time is over,
> And I have ceased to wonder why;
> Christ will explain each separate anguish
> In the fair school-room of the sky.
>
> He will tell me what Peter promised,
> And I, for wonder at his woe,
> I shall forget the drop of anguish
> That scalds me now, that scalds me now.

The companionship of human nature with inanimate nature is very close in certain of the poems; and we have never known the invisible and intangible ties binding all creation in one, so nearly touched as in them.

*   *   *   *   *

If nothing else had come out of our life but this strange poetry we should feel that in the work of Emily Dickinson America, or New England rather, had made a distinctive addition to the literature of the world, and could not be left out of any record of it; and the interesting and important thing is that this poetry is as characteristic of our life as our business enterprise, our political turmoil, our demagogism, our millionarism. "Listen!" says Mr. James McNeill Whistler in that "Ten o'Clock" lecture of his which must have made his hearers feel very much lectured indeed, not to say browbeaten,—"Listen! There never was an artistic period. There never was an art-loving nation." But there were moments and there were persons to whom art was dear, and Emily Dickinson was one of these persons, one of these moments in a national life, and she could as well happen in Amherst, Mass., as in Athens, Att.

65   "Poems of Emily Dickinson." *Literary News* 12 (January 1891), 19. This notice is reprinted verbatim from the *Providence Sunday Journal*, December 7, 1890; see no. 43.

66   Unlocated clipping, ca. January 1891. Pasted immediately above it in Todd's scrapbook is the printed heading, "Survey of Current Literature," but whether that is the title of a column or a magazine is unclear. No periodical by this name is listed in standard directories.

Miss Dickinson was born in Amherst, Mass., Dec. 10, 1830, and died there May 15, 1886. Her father, Hon. Edward Dickinson, was the leading lawyer of Amherst, and treasurer of the well-known college there situated. Miss D. was a recluse by temperament and habit. Her poems were all written without thought of publication. Only two or three of them were printed during her lifetime. Mr. Thomas Wentworth Higginson, who furnishes an introduction, says of the collection here offered: "It is believed that the thoughtful reader will find in these pages a quality more suggestive of the poetry of William Blake than of anything to be elsewhere found—flashes of wholly original and profound insight into nature and life; words and phrases exhibiting an extraordinary vividness of descriptive and imaginative power, yet often set in a seemingly whimsical or even rugged frame." Bound in gray and white, with ornamental design in silver.

67   "Poetry." *Golden Rule,* n.s. 5 (January 1, 1891), 221. This item appears in Mrs. Todd's scrapbook without identification.

These verses have been well styled "The Poetry of the Portfolio," as they were written with no thought of publication. They have a delightful unconsciousness of the public, and are the simple, sweet breathing of a poetic soul. Here are found poems of "Life," "Love," "Nature," "Time," and "Eternity." One is glad to find in its appropriate place the poem "Success" published in "A Masque of Poets" at the request of "H.H.," the author's townswoman and friend.

> Success is counted sweetest
> By those who ne'er succeed.

The book is bound most tastefully. It will be highly prized by persons of elegant taste.

68   "Literary Notes." *Independent* 43 (January 1, 1891), 20. The review this note refers to was published December 11, 1890; see no. 4.

The posthumous poems of Emily Dickinson, which we reviewed at length a few weeks ago, have during the six weeks since they first appeared gone into a third edition. There are several hundred other poems of Miss Dickinson's, left in manuscript, and Mrs. Professor Todd, of Amherst, is examining them carefully with reference to a possible second volume.

69 "Books and Authors." *Boston Daily Advertiser*, January 2, 1891, p. 5. In their separate scrapbooks, Todd attributes this clipping to "Thomas L. Reed," Higginson to an "H. L. Reed," though the first initial is apparently corrected by a superscribed "M."

It is long since poems as striking as those of Emily Dickinson have been given to the world. Their quaintness, their vigor, their incisiveness show that they came from a remarkable mind. Col. Higginson in his preface to the volume containing them, well says "In many cases these verses will seem to the reader like poetry torn up by the roots, with rain and dew and earth still clinging to them, giving a freshness and a fragrance not otherwise to be conveyed." These little poems were written with no view to publication.

Many of them contain only six or eight lines, few of them exceed 12. Their author gave them no titles; it has, therefore, devolved on the editors both to classify and to name them. "Life," "Love," "Nature," "Time and Eternity," are the four books in which they are grouped. In an age when verse writers are thinking more of the form and polish of their verse than of the thought therein expressed, Miss Dickinson's poems come as a cool and bracing bath to recall them to their senses. Mere beauty of form shrinks into nothingness before strength of thought. Although rugged, Miss Dickinson's lines are, however, not harsh; their chief technical defect is a rather wide license in the use of rhyme. Mentality is the characteristic of the majority of them, but in the poems grouped under Nature close observation of the outer world is shown. The "Psalm of the Day" abounds in vivid figures.

> A something in a summer's day,
> As slow her flambeaux burn away,
> Which solemnizes me.
>
> A something in a summer's noon, —
> An azure depth, a wordless tune,
> Transcending ecstasy.

There are lines and stanzas of Miss Dickinson that are destined to be among the best known and most highly valued quotations of our language; they express so forcibly what many have thought but few have said: —

> Success is counted sweetest
> By those who ne'er succeed.
>
> *   *   *   *   *
>
> Mirth is the mail of anguish.
>
> *   *   *   *   *
>
> The heart asks pleasure first,
> And then excuse from pain,
> And then those little anodynes
> That deaden suffering.
>
> *   *   *   *   *

How excellent the heaven
When earth cannot be had;
How hospitable, then, the face
Of our old neighbor, God!

70   "Books, Made and Making." *Chicago Post*, January 2, 1891, p. 4. This note derives from one appearing in the *Critic* several days earlier; see no. 56.

Two more volumes, one of poetry and one of prose, from the pen of the late Emily Dickinson, are contemplated by the editors of her recently published volume of poems—Mrs. Mabel Loomis Todd and Colonel T. W. Higginson. The fact that this volume has passed to a third edition is encouraging for the success of the undertaking, and it will be interesting to see whether Miss Dickinson's prose has the elements of profound insight into nature and life and vivid imaginative power which are exhibited in her poetry.

71   *Concord* [N.H.] *People and Patriot*, January 2, 1891. Unverified. Dated by hand in Higginson's scrapbook. "February 2, 1891" is penciled beside Todd's identical item with the note "Have not been able to check this date." "F[rances] M[atilda] Abbott" and a Concord, N.H., street address in Todd's handwriting follows her clipping, but whether her unusual addition of a specific address indicates the supplier rather than the author of this review, if the two are not the same, is unclear.

Readers of that delightful critical commentary, the Editor's Table in Harper's Monthly, will remember that in the January number Mr. Howells devoted considerable space to the remarkable poems of Emily Dickinson. He quotes enough from the volume to make every reader of poetic sensibilities desire the whole. The book is prefaced by an introduction from Col. Higginson who tells of the author's recluse life at Amherst, Mass., where she died in 1886. He speaks of her work with an exquisite perception of its qualities that leaves her greatest admirer nothing more to say. "In many cases these verses will seem to the reader like poetry torn up by the roots with rain and dew and earth still clinging to them," writes Col. Higginson. These poems are so entirely out of the common that they must be judged by their own rules. The author has no regard for the conventional concordance of rhymes, she hardly observed rhythm in the ordinary sense, yet the reader must feel that she somehow satisfied the inner soul of harmony. To her own ear these poems must have been melodious, and that is the impression they leave on the sensitive mind, despite their deviation from common critical standards. As for the thought, Miss Dickinson is compared to Blake and Emerson. Her ideas are like lightning flashes, connecting earth and sky. Though her New England environment shows in nearly every line, yet a dweller on Olympus could not have a deeper spiritual insight into the nature of things.

72   [Andrew Lang.] "The Newest Poet." *Daily News* [London], January 2, 1891, p. 5. Well known as the prolific leading reviewer for the *Daily News*, Lang had conducted more than one transatlantic skirmish with Howells and Higginson. This piece reveals that its author was acquainted with Dickinson only insofar as he had read Howells's review of her in the current *Harper's* (no. 64) and it is clear that Lang here is jousting not so much with the poet as with her admiring American

William Dean Howells (1837–1920): "If nothing else had come out of our life but this strange poetry we should feel that in the work of Emily Dickinson America, or New England rather, had made a distinctive addition to the literature of the world." (No. 64)

John White Chadwick (1840–1904): "And we are much mistaken if she does not prove that the adjunct of rhyme is not so necessary to the pleasure of verse as many have believed." (No. 51)

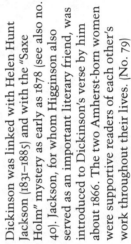

Maurice Thompson (1844–1901): "What a heavy ear for accord!" (No. 81)

Dickinson was linked with Helen Hunt Jackson (1831–1885) and with the "Saxe Holm" mystery as early as 1878 (see also no. 40). Jackson, for whom Higginson also served as an important literary friend, was introduced to Dickinson's verse by him about 1866. The two Amherst-born women were supportive readers of each other's work throughout their lives. (No. 79)

Andrew Lang (1844–1912): "Miss Dickinson reminds us of no sane or educated writer." (No. 72) critic. Nevertheless, Lang's remarks were not kindly taken in Amherst; see *AB*, pp. 100–02. Klaus Lubbers provides helpful comment on Lang's various discussions of Dickinson in *CR*, pp. 36–44. Andrew Lang characteristically underestimated the best writers of his own age; see Harold Orel, *Victorian Literary Critics* (London: Macmillan, 1984), pp. 124–50. Penciled notes near this clipping in the Todd scrapbook read "Andrew Lang" and "also Oct. 3, '91." If Mrs. Todd meant to suggest that the later *Daily News* review for that date (see no. 232) was sufficiently alike in tone and interests to implicate a pen held by the same hand, her observation is amply justified. On Lang's reference to "the Poet Close," see index, *s.v.* John Close.

"If nothing else had come out of her life but this strange poetry," says Mr. W. D. Howells in *Harper's Magazine*, "we should feel that in the work of Emily Dickinson, America, or New England rather, had made a distinctive addition to the literature of the world." Much more Mr. Howells has to say in favour of the newest poetry and the newest poet. Mr. Howells is a critic not always easy to please, and the world cannot but be interested in hearing what the strains of the Tenth Muse are like. As Mr. Howells justly says, "they will form something like an intrinsic experience with the understanding reader of them." This is exactly right. No experience in literature can be more intrinsic than this. The verses remind Mr. Howells of what might be written by "a Blake who had read Emerson who had read Blake," a statement so intrinsic that it quite takes the breath away. What is a Blake who had read Emerson who had read Blake? Is it at all like a Howells who had read Dickinson who had read Howells? Miss Dickinson "sometimes suggests Heine" as much as either Blake or Emerson. To other critics Miss Dickinson's numbers "suggest" a Walt Whitman who had read the Poet Close and attempted a blend with the German Hebrew. For example, here is a piece which Mr. Howells regards as a compound of Emerson, Heine, and Blake. Here it is:

> I taste a liquor never brewed
>   From tankards scooped in pearl;
> Not all the vats upon the Rhine
>   Yield such an alcohol.

"Alcohol" does not rhyme to pearl, but Miss Dickinson is not to be regarded as responsible for mere rhymes. Nor for grammar! It is literally impossible to understand whether she means that she tastes a liquor never brewed at all, or a liquor never brewed "from" tankards scooped in pearl. By "from" she may mean "in." Let us give her the benefit of the doubt, and she still writes utter nonsense. It is clearly impossible to scoop a tankard from pearl. The material is inadequate. Now, neither Blake, nor Mr. Emerson, nor Heine was an idiot. Miss Dickinson must bear her own poetic sins; she reminds us of no sane nor educated writer. Indeed, Mr. Howells himself repents and says, "these things are as wholly her own" as another masterpiece which follows. They are, indeed, and we apologise to the Poet Close.

Here is another example of the Newest Poetry from New England:

> How many times those low feet staggered   [these
> Only the soldered mouth can tell.
> Try! can you stir the awful rivet?
> Try! can you lift the hasps of steel?

We could perhaps if we tried, but we cannot make sense out of balderdash. What are "low feet?" The words are meaningless. This remarkable composition ends thus:

> Indolent housewife in daisies lain!

This is no more English than it is Coptic. "In Daisy's lane" might have a meaning. There might be a lane called after a lady whose *petit nom* was Daisy. But the conjectural emendation rests on a belief that the poet was as ignorant of spelling as of sense and grammar. If the poet meant "in daisies laid"—buried in daisies or under daisies—why not say so? "Laid" rhymes to "pane" (and a rhyme was wanted) quite as well as "pearl" rhymes to "alcohol." But Mr. Howells has been captivated by a minstrel who subdues grammar to rhyme, and puts even grammar before sense. "In the stanzas below," says Mr. Howells, "there is a still, solemn, rapt movement of the thought and music together that is of exquisite charm." Here are "the verses below," or a few of them; they are assuredly below contempt:

> New feet within my garden go,
> New fingers stir the sod,
> A troubadour upon an elm   [the elm
> Betrays the solitude.

What in the world has a troubadour to do in New England? And why did he climb a tree? Or was he a bird? And how can solitude be betrayed by a troubadour, somewhere near Boston, in the foliage of an elm? "Touch often becomes clutch" in these poems, exclaims the admiring critic. Touch would be very welcome to become, not only, "clutch," but sense, rhyme, and grammar, if it could. Mr. Howells admires

> The notice to the startled grass
> That darkness is about to pass.

This is mere maundering. The grass would not be startled in the least, even if it was informed that darkness was not only "about to pass," but about to take high honours. According to the poet, a sacred Person whom we cannot name here

> will explain each separate anguish
> In the fair school room of the sky.

It were enough if Mr. Howells would explain each separate stanza. Of course the idea occurs that Mr. Howells is only bantering; that he cannot really mean to praise this farrago of illiterate and uneducated sentiment. It is as far below the level of the Poet's Corner in a country newspaper as that is usually below Shakespeare. There are no words that can say how bad poetry may be when it is divorced from meaning, from music, from grammar, from rhyme; in brief, from articulate and intelligible speech. And Mr. Howells solemnly avers that this drivel is characteristic of American life!

The unlucky lady who produced these lines only once printed a poem while she was alive. "She never intended or allowed anything more from her pen to be printed in her lifetime." She did well, and far from regretting her resolution every person of sense will admire it. Many uneducated and incompetent persons get pleasure out of scribbling incoherences. These vaguely correspond to vague sentiments and vague emotions. There is no harm in the exercise, but there is a good deal of harm in publicly praising as excellent and typical poetry, the trash which every editor of a magazine receives in bales. If poetry exists it is by virtue of original, or at least of agreeable thought, musically and magically expressed. Poetry has been defined as "the best thought in the best words." The verses adored by Mr. Howells are conspicuously in the worst possible words, and the thought, as far as any thought can be detected, is usually either commonplace or absurd. The thoughts, "take Colonel Higginson's breath away," Colonel Higginson being the editor of the poems. But where is the novelty of thought in

> Stroke the cool forehead, hot so often,
> Lift, if you can, the listless hair,
> Handle the adamantine fingers
> Never a thimble more shall wear.

Any reader of Byron's "he who hath bent him o'er the dead" will be familiar enough with such thought as this piece contains, and will be familiar with it in grammar. The pathos of the absence of thimble in mortality is perfectly legitimate, but not so novel as to warrant raptures. It is, in itself, a touching thing that a lady of extremely solitary habits should have solaced herself by writing a kind of verses; but to proclaim that such verses as we have quoted are poetry, and good poetry, is to be guilty of "the pathetic fallacy" in an original manner, and is to encourage many impossible poets.

73   Advertisement. *Chicago Inter-Ocean*, January 3, 1891, p. 10. For the full text of J.W. Chadwick's review, see no. 51.

THIRD EDITION. "Seldom have 'precious things discovered late' a greater preciousness than these. They seem an argument for immortality," says J.W.C. in the Christian Register, of EMILY DICKINSON'S POEMS. The third edition ready this day. Price $1.50. Roberts Brothers, Publishers, Boston.

74   "The Week." *Speaker* [London] 3 (January 3, 1891), 17. For the *Speaker's* earlier comment on Dickinson, see no. 54. Reprinted: *Boston Evening Transcript*, January 16, 1891, p. 3.

What would a woman's drinking-song be like? — not such a drinking-song as George Meredith might write for the lover of Lassalle, or Robert Browning might have written for Ottima; we mean a drinking-song written by a woman. Mrs. Browning gave us something of the kind in "Wine of Cyprus," but for an actual song, as full of lyrical impulse as "Willie Brewed a Peck o' Maut," although as far removed from it in sentiment as day is from night, how will this do? —

> Inebriate of air am I,
>   And debauchee of dew,
> Reeling, through endless summer days,
>   From inns of molten blue.
>
> When landlords turn the drunken bee
>   Out of the foxglove's door,
> When butterflies renounce their drams,
>   I shall but drink the more!
>
> Till seraphs swing their snowy hats,
>   And saints to windows run,
> To see the little tippler
>   Leaning against the sun!

That is by Emily Dickinson, one of whose poems we quoted a fortnight ago. There ought to be an English edition of her works at once.

75   Unverified clipping, January 3, 1891. The likely source is a British news-paper. My search did not confirm Mrs. Todd's scrapbook attribution of it to the *New York Times*.

Although the expectation of an approaching international copyright might be expected to exert a soothing influence, the acerbities of international criti-cism seem to have grown more marked. Andrew Lang, in a leader in yesterday's *Daily News*, takes up Mr. Howells's panegyric on Emily Dickinson in the Janu-ary *Harper* and hurls right and left such amiable expressions as "idiot," "drivel," "balderdash," "ignorant maundering," and "a farrago of illiterate and uneducated sentiment."

76   "News of the Magazines." *Chicago Tribune*, January 4, 1891, p. 29.

Introspection and heartache go hand in hand in the poems of Emily Dickin-son, which Howells sympathetically reviews in the "Study." These are in strange contrast:

> The bustle in a house
> The morning after death
> Is solemnest of industries
> Enacted upon earth —
>
> The sweeping up the heart,
> And putting love away
> We shall not want to use again
> Until eternity.
>
>   *   *   *   *   *
>
> I never saw a moor,
> I never saw the sea;
> Yet know I how the heather looks,
> And what a wave must be.
>
> I never spoke with God,
> Nor visited in Heaven;
> Yet certain am I of the spot
> As if the chart were given.

77   "Literary Notes." *New York Tribune*, January 4, 1891, sec. 2, p. 14. Re-printed: *Chicago Tribune*, January 10, 1891, p. 12. Though George Fred-eric Parsons of the *New York Tribune* had been sent a prepublication review copy in mid-October (*AB*, p. 68), this and another brief notice, no. 128, constitute his paper's entire response to the first volume of Dickinson's poems. This neglect may have been in part due to the *Tribune*'s longstanding rivalry with the New York *Nation*, a weekly with which Higginson was affiliated as its leading poetry reviewer.

More of the work — both in verse and prose — left by the late Emily Dickin-son, will probably appear by-and-by. Interesting as it is and marked by real genius, it is little less than exasperating to a reader who possesses the least feeling for the art of authorship. Phrases and characterizations so felicitous that they shine in splendor are followed by lines so crude and dull and commonplace that they could only be worthy of a schoolgirl. This woman certainly had genius; — but it was an uncurbed vine, whose roots sometimes touched sunless and unprofitable regions of thought and study.

78 "Grim Slumber Songs." *New York Commercial Advertiser*, January 6, 1891, p. 4. The anonymity of this notice is regrettable, for it is keenly observant. The reviewer particularly notes, with a pleasure rare for the decade, Dickinson's ferocity, extravagance, and playfulness.

With the side-saddle on, to paraphrase an American authoress, Pegasus makes straight for the cemetery. But never before, we venture to say, has he been driven there at a more mad, clattering, cavalry gallop than to the music of these two stanzas:

Glee! the great storm is over!
    Four have recovered the land;
Forty gone down together
    Into the boiling sand.

Ring, for the scant salvation!
    Toll, for the bonnie souls, —
Neighbor and friend and bridegroom,
    Spinning upon the shoals.

These words we quote from the posthumous poems of Miss Emily Dickinson, who, strangely enough, was never known to stir from her native inland town — a town fully as quiet as the ordinary New England villages round about it. Of all its villagers she was the quietest. "A recluse of temperament and habit, literally spending years without setting her foot beyond the doorstep, and many more years during which her walks were strictly limited to her father's grounds, she habitually concealed her mind, like her person, from all but a very few friends." Except for these, she "was as invisible to the world as if she had dwelt in a nunnery."

Her poetry is the passionate appeal of one self-imprisoned. Impetuous in spirit, ungovernable in form, at times abnormal, even morbid, in its power, it has forced itself out through compressed lips.

The author's uncontrolled emotion seems due quite as much to the undue sensitiveness of the author as to the greatness of her inspiration. She raves not so much because of the greatness of the oracle as because of the susceptibility of her woman nature. Extreme hunger often causes strange visions. That this hermitess never satisfied, perhaps never could satisfy, her craving for human companionship, may have first brought her into her strangely visionary state. Upon the theme of human love she becomes absurdly, if not blasphemously intemperate, as in these lines to a lover:

Nor could I rise with you,
Because your face
Would put out Jesus,

In the same spirit every renunciation of love is a "Calvary." These sentimental crucifixes she erects at every turn. Isolated from humanity, she cannot turn the current of her thoughts toward it except in intermittent galvanic shocks.

With nature she is more at ease. It furnishes a substitute for companionship with man. Like an unmated child she is driven to her garden for her friends. She finds it a refuge, though still not her haven. She makes of it, rather than finds it, a home. Bee and butterfly and flower she allegorizes into human fellows. She plays with nature as many a poet has done before her. In these poems she is no longer abnormal. She strikes familiar chords. Their form is still exceptional, but their sentiment is not distinctive. They are at times suggestive, but suggestive because they are fragmentary. They are fanciful, picturesque, nature-scented, irregular, incomplete, impossible of completion. "In many cases," says Mr. Higginson, "they will seem to the reader like poetry torn up by the roots, with rain and dew and earth still clinging to them, giving a freshness and a fragrance not otherwise to be conveyed." In their irregularity lies their individuality and erratic power.

But with neither nature nor human nature was Miss Dickinson at her best. Her most characteristic themes were the mystery, the "quiet nonchalance," the grim interest, the impartial dignity which death bestows. Her best poem on nature describes the "fleshless chant" the wind makes in the trees. So her best poetry throughout deals with the weirdly fleshless. Of this disembodiment of spirit she spoke from every point of view, bitterly, grimly, quaintly, exultantly, metaphysically. We quote to illustrate:

I.

Apparently with no surprise
To any happy flower,
The frost beheads it at its play
In accidental power.
The blond assassin passes on,
The sun proceeds unmoved
To measure off another day
For an approving God.

II.

One dignity delays for all,
One mitred afternoon,
None can avoid this purple,
None evade this crown.

Coach it insures, and footmen,
Chamber and state and throng;
. . . .
How pomp surpassing ermine,
When simple you and I
Present our meek escutcheon,
And claim the rank to die!

III.

I died for beauty, but was scarce
Adjusted in the tomb,
When one who died for truth was lain
In an adjoining room.
. . . .

And so, as kinsmen, met a-night,
We talked between the rooms,
Until the moss had reached our lips,
And covered up our names.

IV.

How many times these low feet staggered,
Only the soldered mouth can tell;
Try! can you stir the awful rivet?
Try! can you lift the hasps of steel?
. . . .
Buzz the dull flies on the chamber window;
Brave shines the sun through the freckled pane;
Fearless the cobweb swings from the ceiling—
Indolent housewife, in daisies lain!

V.

Death is a dialogue between
The spirit and the dust.
"Dissolve," says Death. The Spirit, "Sir,
I have another trust."

Death doubts it, argues from the ground.
The Spirit turns away,
Just laying off, for evidence,
An overcoat of clay.

Mr. Higginson notes in Miss Dickinson's work a quality suggestive of William Blake, to which Mr. Howells adds, "It is a Blake who had read Emerson who had read Blake." She resembles Blake in her daring unconventionality, in her love of weirdness, in the homeliness of her vernacular, in her crudity. Towards God she manifests an Emersonian self-possession. Only toward Him, however, does she display any of the Concord philosopher's serenity of manner. Her fever bears no other resemblance to Emerson's blandness. Nor are her differences from Blake less marked. Her "boundedness" is more noticeable when compared with his wild boundlessness. He dashed fearlessly through the dark; she gropes desperately after him. He spoke with a lisping naturalness; she purses her lips to an earnest but unspontaneous expression. He broke out into oddities; she forces herself into conceits. He was often infantile; she is frequently commonplace. Both Blake and Emerson are unique elements in literature. She is a unique composition of familiar elements. Her poetry, fusion though it is, is authentic, individual, idiosyncratic. It is the poet in quintessence. In common with all great poetry, with most good poetry, with no poor poetry, it bears a seal of vitality, an individuality self-expressed.

79 "Emily Dickinson Was Not 'Saxe Holm.'" *Amherst Record*, January 7, 1891, p. 2. The "not" in the *Record*'s title while demonstrably true and widely accepted by 1891, curiously misrepresents the reprinted article it headlines, whose author, in 1878, plainly argued in the pages of the *Springfield Republican* that "Saxe Holm," a popular pseudonymous writer of the day, *was* Emily Dickinson rather than Helen Hunt. (Mrs. Todd placed "Xs" through "not" in the printed heading of her scrapbook copy of this article.) For information on this identification controversy, see *Life* 1:223. If Emily Dickinson had read the original *Republican* article, as seems likely, she might have found shadowed forth within it a near mirror image of the critical tone and portraiture that was largely to prevail during her early reception.

The interest in the *Poems* of Emily Dickinson exhibited in the eulogistic notices of them in the leading literary papers and magazines, and in the fact that the demand for them has necessitated a third edition within six weeks of their first appearance, has again attracted attention to the discussion of some years ago, pointing to her as the author of the "Saxe Holm" stories. For the benefit of the curious over this conundrum, we re-publish the study of it which appeared in the *Springfield Republican* for July 25th, 1878.

There is no calculating the amount of harm produced by Walter Scott in denying the authorship of the Waverlys, and afterward putting in printed form a rule of morality justifying it. The whole world of letters has seized upon the gospel of the new literary dispensation and circulated fibs with the most saintly confidence. It is this principle, no doubt, which has led our critics to believe that Helen Hunt could be Saxe Holm and deny it and be a very excellent woman all in the same moment. In fact, it has come to such a pass that denials of this sort are of no account whatever in the eyes of the reviewers. The world says "Helen Hunt lived in Amherst, Mass., once upon a time; now Saxe Holm describes Amherst scenes; therefore, Saxe Holm is Helen Hunt." To turn this syllogism into a game of consequences, Helen Hunt says, "I am not Saxe Holm"; the world says "We know better"; and the confidence is general infidelity.

M. Taine, in his history of English literature, as everybody knows, adopts the plan of evolving the literature of that people, as it must necessarily be, with its conditions of climate, temperament and political history; very kindly, for a man of his eminence, leaving the English people to supply the names and dates. We feel inclined to try the virtue of his philosophy and to apply it to the Saxe Holm problem.

Can Saxe Holm be evolved?

Passing over for the present the similarities which people have discovered in the styles of those two writers, let us note their antagonistic elements. Helen Hunt, although open to the charge of sentimentality, is emphatically a woman of every-day life. She deals in practical home and society questions. No one who has read critically her "Bits of Talk" and "Bits of Travel" could for a moment charge them upon Saxe Holm. The questions which the latter propounds are of a subtle, mysterious, wayside, we had almost said underground sort, so much do they smack of the cellar, questions which she gropes about with for some time and then abandons, leaving an uneasy conviction in the mind of the reader of something wrong. Helen Hunt's pages are crowded with children. She understands them, sympathizes with them, loves and enjoys them. Saxe Holm knows nothing whatever of little folks, except ideally. She lives with people grown up, very much grown-up subjects. Does anyone remember a real child in her stories? One waif there is, the central figure in "My Tourmaline," a child more weird, more unnatural, more grown up than Hester Prynne's Little Pearl—a child who talks with stones and through them learns Nature's secrets,—a child so spiritual that she feels when anything unusual is to happen and consequently is never taken by surprise,—a child who develops into a "superb woman" in stature and intellect at fourteen. How different is this child nature from Helen Hunt's troop of little ones! The latter may be at times morbid; Saxe Holm is always morbid, and morbid to the last degree. The morbidness of her prose is, however, the ideal element of her poetry pushed to its extremity. Saxe Holm is essentially a poet. Her stories are weird and improbable; her poems are like strains of solemn music floating at night from some wayside church. Each thought is complete and rare, solemn with a solemnity of intense conviction and calm with the calm of the deep-toned vibrating church bell. In comparing the verses of the two, we find in each the same swinging, easy-flowing lines, the same exquisite thoughts, but in one we recognize the form that dwells by

Ebon shades and low-browed rocks.

What can be more exquisite and at the same time more heart-rending than her "Pomegranate Blossoms," in which she represents herself plucking one of the blossoms to send to her lover, before her death: —

Pomegranate blossom! heart of fire,
   I dare to be thy death,
To slay thee while the summer sun
   Is quickening thy breath,
To rob the autumn of thy wine,
Next year of all ripe seeds of thine,
That thou mayest bear one kiss of mine
   To my dear love before my death.
For, heart of fire! I, too, am robbed,
   Like thee, like thee, I die;
While yet my summer sun of love
   Is near and warm and high.
The autumn will run red with wine,
The autumn fruits will swing and shine,
But in that little grave of mine
   I shall not see them where I lie.

And, again, where can be found a poem that can rival the solemn beauty and unity of her

THREE KISSES OF FAREWELL.

Three, only three, my darling,
   Separate, solemn, slow;
Not like the swift and joyous ones
   We used to know,
When we kissed because we loved each other
   Simply to taste love's sweets,
And lavished our kisses as summer
   Lavishes heats;
But as they kiss whose hearts are wrung
   When hope and fear are spent,
And nothing is left to give, except
   A sacrament!

First of the three, my darling,
   Is sacred unto pain;
We have hurt each other often,
   We shall again;

When we pine because we miss each other;
    And do not understand
How the written words are so much colder
    Than eye and hand.
I kiss thee, dear, for all such pain
    Which we may give or take;
Buried, forgiven, before it comes,
    For our love's sake.

The second kiss, my darling,
    Is full of joy's sweet thrill;
We have blessed each other always,
    We always will.
We shall reach until we feel each other
    Past all of time and space;

We shall listen till we hear each other
    In every place.
The earth is full of messengers
    Which Love sends to and fro;
I kiss thee, darling, for all joy
    Which we shall know!

The last kiss, oh, my darling,
    My love—I cannot see
Through my tears, as I remember
    What it may be.
We may die and never see each other,
    Die with no time to give
Any sign that our hearts are faithful
    To die, as live.
Token of what they will not see
    Who see our parting breath,
This one last kiss, my darling
    Seals the seal of death.

To emphasize the similarity and dissimilarity between this writer and Helen
Hunt we add the following from the "Refrain" of the latter:—

"Now name me a thought
    To make life so sweet,
A thought of such joy
    Its fain to repeat."
Oh! Foolish to ask me. Ever, ever
    Who loves believes;
    But telleth never.
It might be a name, just a name—not said;
But in every thought, like a golden thread
    Which the shuttle weaves
In and out on a fabric red,
    Till it glows all through
    With a golden hue.
Oh! of all the sweet lives,
    Who can tell how sweet

Is the life which one name
In refrain doth repeat?

In these quotations we see the characteristics of each distinctly marked. Helen Hunt is sweet; Saxe Holm is intense; Helen Hunt feels; the soul of Saxe Holm is shaken to its very depths; Helen Hunt is religious; Saxe Holm is reverent with the reverence of one stricken with admiration and awe. From the Puritanical religion of New England's daughters, and especially from its cant, she is singularly free. Her stories have not a religious tone, and, strange as it may seem, neither have her poems. Her feelings in these, as in her other poetic flights, are strained to their utmost, as she somewhere says, "One heart-beat more in a moment, and I shall die;" but it is not wholly a religious throb. In one of her stories these words occur: "I would rather at this moment, dear, lay my cheek on your hands and sit at my old place by your knee and feel myself the woman you have made me, than know all that God knows and makes the universe." No living author but Saxe Holm could have written those lines, certainly Helen Hunt could not. This extreme expression was not from the intensity of the woman's feeling toward her lover.

Now from this it is not hazardous to affirm that Saxe Holm is not Helen Hunt and also that there is a new writer in the field. And having concluded who she is not, let us evolve one step further and discover what, if not who, she is. First, there is in the writings of Saxe Holm what distinguishes her from many writers, a noticeable lack of incident and confinement to quiet, household affairs. Her scenes are mostly in-door scenes, of domestic life in the parlor, kitchen and the garden. Of busy streets and natural scenery she says almost nothing. They seem to be entirely out of her sphere; and this last is the most noticeable from the fact that she seems to feel a kinship to the natural world, is as exquisitely sensitive to feelings produced by birds and flowers and is as familiar with their ways and language as if she were, indeed, one of them. Flowers are her inspiration, and seem as necessary to her as were the two or three bronze trinkets always on Mr. Dickens's desk to him. In variety of incident her resources are limited; in the growth and experiences of the inner life they never are. Her nature is appreciative, her feelings quick, delicate and intense, her imagination rare; but the field of her vision is narrow. She has nothing great to tell; always subtle, secret, small. She can portray vividly the feelings excited by the smallest flower, but she never describes the incidents of a walk. If the progress of the story requires her to take a journey to Europe, she goes in one sentence and returns in the next. Only once has she described a journey, and that with the minuteness of detail and with the fresh, eager enjoyment of one in whose life such an experience is a rare event. She tells a story like one who stands at one side of life and looks on. Her incidents are, many of them, like those gathered by "seeing the passing." Even when she introduces herself into her stories, she unconsciously slips into the background and assumes the character of the spectator. Her career seems not to have been an "anecdotal one," in the words of George Eliot, but rich in internal experiences.

Again, her pages are peculiarly devoid of sunshine. Though sometimes less morbid than at others, she never allows but one sunbeam to peep in at a time, and that is often at loggerheads with the curtains. Draxy Miller, the sunshiniest character in one of the sunshiniest of her stories, expresses this when she says, "Oh, does joy always bring pain in this world?" The joy which her creations experience is of the speechless sort, so intense and silent that they seem to create around them a churchy atmosphere, to use her own words, "with everywhere golden silence." If they are ever gay, it is with the spritelike, fitful, childish gaiety of Annie Ware. In a word, the creatures of her imagination are pale and unhealthy, with a smile, of Mother Superiors, as if they had lived in a darkened room and needed air.

She seems chary of introducing happiness, and the very presence of pleasure she eyes with suspicion. In her lines "The Angel of Pain," she speaks like one accustomed to its "close-clinging friendship" that too much joy overpowers her. She must have it in small doses. This abiding sense of suffering in Saxe Holm is akin to that which pervades the poems of Elizabeth Stuart Phelps, than to the easy, pleasant sentiment of Helen Hunt. Dora Maynard in the "One Legged Dancers," one of the few characters to whom she has chosen to give a happy earthly lot, says: "The only thing that troubles me is that I have no sorrow. It seems dangerous. Dear Mat, although he has all he ever hoped for, need not fear being too happy, because he has the ever-present pain to make him earnest and keep him ready for more pain." That our author can conceive of no life without its over hanging cloud, we see in the legend to "Draxy Miller's Dowry." She cannot feel content to leave poor Draxy with the sun pouring with that rate into her little home. Down comes the curtains! Bang goes the shutters—Draxy Miller's husband is dead. And notice, also, the want of humor and wit in Saxe Holm. She seems not to understand that on life's stage there is a good deal of merriment going on between the heavy scenes.

The next characteristic which we note is the extremeness of her views. Saxe Holm's are superlative truths, often bordering in their application on the improbable. After "Draxy's" husband dies she shuts herself up for a season and when she again appears, her hair is as white as the driven snow and so is her dress. Reuben noticed that she was dressed in white, he touched her gown and looked inquiringly. "Yes, father dear," said she, "always," and, truly, henceforth through all the years of her ministry when, a white-robed priestess, she addressed her husband's people, as their chosen pastor, until the day of her death she "walks in white." She has a beautiful theory of her own as to wearing mourning for friends. "They knew Draxy's deep-rooted belief that to associate gloom with the memory of the dead was alike disloyal to them and to Christ, and so warmly had she imbued most of the people with her sentiment that the dismal black garb of so-called mourning rarely was seen in the village." Another example of improbability and also extravagance of feeling, is seen in the case of a man who with a bullet-hole in both lungs—one large enough for a man to put his fist in—after dragging through Libby prison life, is at last brought to health again, all by the influence of a four leaf clover,—a cure momentous enough to found a new school for medicine. That, after this frail omen of good luck had brought him a wife and home, he should have the design wrought into a wedding ring, is but natural; but that he should cause the little battered talisman to be elegantly framed and hung upon the wall, that the design should occur over and over again in all the carving of the house, that no design was considered complete without its four-leaf clover—carries the thing beyond the power of endurance, and makes him little better than a fanatic. Again, it is highly improbable that a business man of fifty years of age should, as in "Esther Wynne's Love Letters," feel such an intense and all absorbing interest in a package of old letters found in the cellar that he should sit up until morning reading and talking about them, although they be, as those were, of surprising beauty and interest and although they remind him of letters he had received in his youth. Saxe Holm would have done it, but not a busy man of the world.

Her expressions are often quaint and old-fashioned. She makes one of her heroes address his mother-in-law, or would-be mother-in-law, as "sweet mother of Annie," in common conversation, after the manner of the chivalric age, and the love of all her heroes is effeminate and so absolutely without let-up that it wearies. In the story "Whose Wife Was She?" the narrator makes herself the intimate girl friend of the heroine, but her love for her friend is not the affection of a girl, even of a sensitively organized girl. She speaks of her friend as a "beautiful young being" and of her with her lover as "the children." If girls ever have such a friendship for each other, it is not a friendship of the present day. It has the form and flavor of the past. With all the quaintness there is an accompanying timidity and shrinking. Saxe Holm often draws her characters, and always herself, when she appears in the story, with a body so sensitively organized that at the most trifling shock it immediately succumbs. She "trembles from head to foot" at the slightest touch of excitement, and "has more than once fainted at a sudden noise." This sensitiveness is one with a shrinking and retiring nature, and the gems of thought and felicitous expressions which one continually stumbles upon are not so much the flashes of genius as the products of long, quiet thinking, which have, to use her own expression, "never stepped into the glare, the contention of profaner air."

Saxe Holm has a wonderful subtle insight into and perception of character. In the story "How One Woman Kept Her Husband," the only case in which she has completely stepped out of her own sphere and given a natural, rational and acceptable story, she betrays a power of character-drawing worthy of Mrs. Lewes herself. What could be better than her analysis of the characters of John Gray and his wife? "He had a singular mixture of the faults of opposite temperaments. He had the reticent, dreamy, procrastinating inertia of the bilious, melancholic man, side by side with the impressionable sensuousness of the most sanguine, nervous type. There is a great fascination in such a combination, especially to persons of a keen, alert nature. My sister was earnest, wise, resolute; John Gray was nonchalant, shrewd, vacillating. My sister was exact, methodical, ready; John Gray careless, spasmodic, dilatory. My sister had affectionateness; he had tenderness. She was religious of soul; he had a sort of transcendental perceptivity, so to speak, which kept him more alive to the comforts of religion than to the obligations. My sister would have gone to the stake rather than tell a lie; he would tell a lie unhesitatingly rather than give anybody pain. My sister lived earnestly, truly, actively in each moment of the present; it never seemed quite clear whether he was thinking of today, yesterday or tomorrow. She was upright because she could not help it; he was upright when he *was* upright because of custom, taste and fitness of things." Of Mrs. Long she says, "Plain, sharp and self-asserting at 22, she had become magnetic and winning, full of tact and almost beautiful at 35. We see such surprising developments continually; it seems that nature does her best to give every woman one period of triumph and conquest. Perhaps only they know its full sweetness to whom it comes in mature life."

Now, by the light of these discoveries, we have the following qualities: A very subtle analysis upon a very few truths, pushed to their extreme application; a morbidness, improbability, quaintness and shrinking which would result from a lack of the sun's ripening influence, like a lily grown in a cellar. All these lead us to the conclusion that the author may be a person long shut out from the world and living in a world of her own; that perhaps she is a recluse. Her stories are such as might emanate from one who has been for years and years shut up within herself and whose narrowed sphere of observation and constant ponderings over its subtle problems have made life to her an unfathomable mystery; to whom love is not a real, possible thing, but something supernatural, too holy, too tender to know or speak of, except under one's breath. A person accustomed to the constant living over and thinking of the same rounds of thought and experience, without introducing fresh supplies will unavoidably grow over-strained and dull. That she is so, we know, and that theoretically she is not, is but another straw in our bundle of evidence. This is her creed: "That life could be dull to a human being was a mystery to her. Every new discovery in science and art was a stimulus and a delight. The simplest everyday fact had a significance and a beauty to her." Then why do we ever find her "wondering, as lonely people have hours of wondering, why, since the world is thronged with its millions, there need be one lonely man or woman"? Her theory is great and beautiful, but it is too great for any mortal to carry out without the aid of other mortals. No woman can shut herself out from the world, with no companions but her own thoughts, and expect never to be dull. "The simple everyday facts," among which she is compelled to live, grow to have an undue significance. She must have companions. She finds these in the elements. She communes with the winds and sunbeams; she understands the song of birds, and converses with flowers. And what is the result? Exactly what we have found in the author of the Saxe Holm stories.

If we felt inclined to elaborate and unite our separate ideals into something more complete, we may imagine her to be a member of one of those "sleepy and dignified" New England families whom she so vividly described; of a timid nature; separated from the outside world; devoted to literature and flowers. We cannot refrain, also, from picturing her robed in white, like Draxy Miller, whether it be mourning for a friend, a religious notion like that of Hawthorne's Hilda, or, perchance, the result of some decree of fate. We think Saxe Holm a woman capable of making her life the expression of one idea.

The universal conclusion that Helen Hunt is the writer of the Saxe Holm stories, from the fact that they each describe the same scenes is but natural; still, it may be stated in a general way that two persons capable of literary expression may have lived in the same town, and, therefore, we suggest that we take "H. H." at her word and *hunt up her neighbors.*

80   "Literary Notes." *America* 5 (January 8, 1891), 430.

The posthumous poems of Emily Dickinson, reviewed at length in this week's *America,* have, during the six weeks since they first appeared, gone into a third edition. There are several hundred other poems of Miss Dickinson's left in manuscript, and Mrs. Prof. Todd of Amherst is examining them carefully with reference to a possible second volume.

81   Maurice Thompson. "Miss Dickinson's Poems." *America* 5 (January 8, 1891), 425. A nationally known poet and critic, Thompson frequently reviewed for the *Independent;* when that journal's Dickinson notice appeared (see no. 44), Higginson wrote Thompson regarding it. In his reply, dated Dec. 27, Thompson disclaimed authorship but went on to confess that had he been asked to evaluate the poems, "I should not have probably appraised them as highly as did the writer of the notice. . . . Pardon me for saying that Miss Dickinson's verse suggests to me a superb brain that has suffered some obscure lesion which now and again prevents the filling out of a thought—as if a cog slipped in some fine wheel just at the point of consummation. I admit to the fascination of the defect, but I cannot make it out to be equal to the beautiful grace of genius" (*AB,* pp. 79–80). The *Springfield Republican* reacted sharply to Thompson's "mechanical stringency" (no. 98).

In the "Poems of Miss Emily Dickinson" just published under the editorial care of Mabel Loomis Todd and T. W. Higginson, there is a strange mixture of rare individuality and originality; moreover, the touch of surprise here and there excites a novel reaction and sends a tingle through the imagination. Perhaps it ought to satisfy the critic when frequent draughts of genuine refreshment are to be had from a small volume of verses. Certainly there comes a dewy fragrant drop, if not a draught, at short intervals, while we read Miss Dickinson's curiously fragmental poetry. Here is song that has a clastic suggestiveness, as of a strange fortunate deposit wherein precious jewels, gold and crystals water-clear, are jumbled with worthless clay and fragments of coarse rock. I am aware that the comparison may appear strained, but it will be found strikingly apt. Something primitive and rude set over against the subtlest refinement of culture makes Miss Dickinson's verse still more forcibly remind us of the haphazard arrangement of nature's mines. We might change the view so that we could compare these curious flowers of poesy with the fossils of ancient plants pressed in the grip of cold stone, save that the flowers live and wane and exhale delicate perfume and flaunt a whole rainbow of colors.

Col. Higginson has written a most appreciative preface to the volume. He classes the poems with "The Poetry of the Portfolio"—the verse written for the satisfaction of the poet's own desire to write. This is another way of avoiding outright criticism, or it is a lack of insight. Miss Dickinson was a highly educated and exceptionally studious woman, the daughter of a "leading lawyer of Amherst," who was also the treasurer of Amherst College. Her limitations show plainly in her work and much study of Emerson has colored and shaped her vision; it has also cramped her methods of expression. It will not do to say that the "discipline of public criticism and the enforced conformity to accepted ways" could have broadened Miss Dickinson to the stature of a first-class poetical genius. Her lack was intrinsic and constitutional. Mere functional derangement of the organ of expression is curable; but here was organic lesion of the most unmistakable type. Her vision was clear and surprisingly accurate, but her touch was erratic and at frequent intervals nerveless, while her sense of completeness was singularly dull. She exaggerated the faults of Emerson's verse-style into absurdity. She rhymes *tell* and *still, book* and *think, own* and *young, denied* and *smiled, gate* and *mat, care* and *hour,* and so on into hundreds of the like, perhaps, with the singular misfortune of failing often just at the point where a perfect rhyme is absolutely necessary to complete the turn of grace or the point of lyrical surprise.

Here are two examples of the former:

I taste a liquor never brewed,
    From tankards scooped in pearl;
Not all the vats upon the Rhine
    Yield such an alcohol!

*   *   *   *   *

What fortitude the soul contains,
    That it can so endure
The accent of a coming foot,
    The opening of a door!

The rhyming of *pearl* with *alcohol* is ludicrous; but the syllable *dure* when set to match *door* cannot be received by any ear that is not hopelessly defective. The identical rhyme in the following stanzas is preferable:

> And nobody knows, so still it flows
>> That any brook is there;
> And yet your daily draught of life   [little draught
>> Is daily drunken there.

Here is a striking example of a beautiful conceit marred almost to destruction by slip-shod rhyme:

> As if some little Arctic flower,
>> Upon the polar hem,
> Went wandering down the latitudes,
>> Until it puzzled came
> To continents of summer,
>> To firmaments of sun,
> To strange, bright crowds of flowers,
>> And birds of foreign tongue!

It gives one a thrill of vexation to be trifled with just on the horizon of what appears about to turn out a fine lyrical discovery. Look over the stanza last quoted and observe what a glimpse of paleontology it flashes and what a promise it makes of a memorable lyric setting for the migration of the flowers during the coming on of the great ice age. Not that the poet had this foremost in mind; but the suggestion had come out of geological reading and had been modernized and narrowed to suit the sudden flash of poetic vision. We see the conceit struggling for expression until it is almost strangled amidst such rhymes as *hem* with *came* and *sun* with *tongue*. The poet's sight is perfect; she sees a lyric limpid as a brook and prismatic as a bubble, but her modeling is almost fatally defective. What a heavy ear for accord! She seems to wander through a wilderness of phrase-possibilities only to choose with droll indiscretion at the critical moment. But even this faltering and halting expression has its fascination arising out of its utter freedom from affectation. Whatever else may be said of Miss Dickinson's verse there is not room for doubting the sincerity of its origin. Let me quote three stanzas of the poem "Renunciation;" they will show the extremes of blunder and felicity:

> The sun, as common, went abroad.
> The flowers, accustomed, blew,
> As if no soul the solstice passed
> That maketh all things new.

> The time was scarce profaned by speech;
> The symbol of a word
> Was needless, as at sacrament
> The wardrobe of our Lord.

> Each was to each the sealed church,
> Permitted to commune this time,
> Lest we too awkward show
> At supper of the Lamb.

The first and second of these stanzas are very near the line of absolute expression; the third has nothing in it to make it worthy of print. The surprise that the former led us to expect proves to be a sort of absurdity such as some person utterly without imagination or a feeling for music might treat us to. In a certain way these unaccountable discords serve to accentuate the beautiful snatches of melody with which they are so often associated. Occasionally the happy strokes follow the unhappy ones so as to give the effect of art. Thus:

New feet within my garden go,
    New fingers stir the sod;
A troubadour upon the elm
    Betrays the solitude.

New children play upon the green,
    New weary sleep below;
And still the pensive spring returns,
    And still the punctual snow!

How suggestive the two closing verses of each stanza! I have heard New England folk pronounce *Emma* as if it were written *Emmar* and *saw* like *sor;* can this account for the matching of *door* with *draw* in the following:

Until the daffodil
Unties her yellow bonnet
    Beneath the village door,
Until the bees, from clover rows,
    Their hock and sherry draw.

I have called attention to these defects, and the book teems with them, for the purpose of showing that it was not mere lack of public criticism that caused Miss Dickinson to write such curious stuff as this, for example—

One dignity delays for all,
    One mitred afternoon;
None can avoid this purple
    None evade this crown.

        *   *   *   *   *

Departed to the judgment,
    A mighty afternoon;
Great clouds like ushers leaning,
    Creation looking on.

        *   *   *   *   *

On this long storm the rainbow rose,
    On this late morn the sun;
The clouds, like listless elephants,
    Horizons straggled down. . . .

Why could she not feel the inaptitude that forced her to murder art thus:

I lost a world the other day,
    Has anybody found?
You'll know it by the row of stars
    Around its forehead bound.
A rich man might not notice it,
    Yet to my frugal eye
Of more esteem than ducals.   [ducats
    Oh, find it, sir, for me!

Here the first four lines are notably strong in the qualities of terseness, vigor and originality of thought and expression; and if the others had kept up the momentum the culmination must have been a strong shock of true poetic energy. Instead of doing this they drop below the commonplace. It is so all through the book; and yet no lover of poetry can read it without frequent starts of glad surprise and many lingerings over lines, phrases, stanzas, of the richest and most exquisitely original overflow from a nature incomparably individual and independent. To me it is like nothing else so much as it is like a crude translation of some freshly discovered Greek lyrical fragments, the spirit of which, not the art, has been perfectly caught by the translator. Miss Dickinson was a poet who (as Baudelaire described one), like an albatross, could not walk because her wings tripped her feet. If she held up the wing of thought, the wing of expression was sure to drag. Look at this curious conceit:

> I asked no other thing,
>   No other was denied.
> I offered being for it;
>   The mighty merchant smiled.
>
> Brazil? He twirled a button,
>   Without a glance my way:
> "But, madam, is there nothing else
>   That we can show to-day?"

A large part of the fascination of verse like this is generated by the friction of disappointment on delight. You are charmed with the thought and fretted by the lapses from intelligible expression. The following eight lines, with which the first part of the book closes, are suggestive of the limitation of a genius like Miss Dickinson's:

> The brain within its groove
>   Runs evenly and true;
> But let a splinter swerve,
>   'T were easier for you
>   To put the water back
>   When floods have slit the hills,
> And scooped a turnpike for themselves,
>   And blotted out the mills.

In all my reading I have not found a more interesting book of verse; one with so many beauties almost buried in so many blemishes. The good things in it are like incomparable crystals set in ugly fragments of worthless stone.

82 "Literary Notes." *Chicago Tribune,* January 10, 1891, p. 13. A reprinting; see no. 77.

83 "New Books." *Commonwealth* 30 (January 10, 1891), 8.

A recent volume destined to be much discussed, one which indeed has already called out much comment and all of a favorable character, is the volume of "Poems by Emily Dickinson." This is indeed a most unique production: it is the work of a poet who evidently wrote only because her heart impelled her irresistibly to speak its thoughts; a poet who had no wish for publicity, no desire for fame, and no ambition to sing in accord with other poets. Much of her work in its technique is rude and rough, but in its thought it is original, striking, suggestive, and most poetic. Emily Dickinson lived in Amherst from 1830 until her death four years ago. Though the daughter of a leading lawyer and prominent college official, she was exceedingly retiring in her disposition, and lived virtually the life of a recluse. After her death, her poems were collected by friends who readily perceived their great value, and they now appear in a volume edited by two of her friends, Mabel Loomis Todd and Col. Higginson.

84 "About Big Men." *Yankee Blade,* January 10, 1891, p. [4]. Reprinted: *Oxford* [Mass.] *Midweekly,* February 11, 1891, p. 12.

Emily Dickinson, who has recently died, and whose verses have just been published, was one of the oddest children of literature who has lived since Thoreau. She lived in an interior Massachusetts town. She was a perpetual invalid, and a woman of abnormally retiring disposition. She was far more shy than Hawthorne. She very seldom went beyond her garden fence; never visited her neighbors, and if her friends came to see her she would sit with her back to them and talk. She was supersensitively bashful. Her poetry, in spite of its great defects, is full of thought that sticks to the memory. Her rhymes were as faulty as those of Emerson; but her thoughts were almost as profound. She might have done much more if she had been in touch with the world about her.

85 Emily Ellsworth Fowler Ford. "Eheu! Emily Dickinson." *Springfield Republican,* January 11, 1891, p. 2. Reprinted: *Springfield Weekly Republican,* January 16, 1891, p. 10. Emily Fowler, an Amherst friend of the poet's, moved to Brooklyn when she became Mrs. Gordon L. Ford in 1853. Herself an established author by the nineties, Mrs. Ford understandably stresses the poet's seclusion in this poem, having experienced it during a visit to Amherst in 1882 when Dickinson declined to see her (see *YH,* I, xlvii). The *Republican* was shortly to publish other comment by Mrs. Ford; see no. 98. Her memoir of Dickinson was partially published in the 1894 *Letters;* see no. 420.

> Oh, friend, these sighs from out your solitude
>   But pierce my heart! Social with bird and bee,
>   Loving your tender flowers with ecstacy,
> You shun the eye, the voice, and shy elude
> The loving souls that dare not to intrude
>   Upon your chosen silence. Friend, you thought
>   No life so sweet and fair as hiding brought,
> And beauty is your song, with interlude
> Of outer life which to your soul seems crude,
>   Thoughtless, unfeeling, idle, scant of grace;
>   Nor will you touch a hand, or greet a face, —
> For common daily strife to you is rude,
>   And, shrinking, you in shadow lonely stay
>   Invisible to all, howe'er we pray.

86 Unverified clipping. Todd's scrapbook attribution of this item to the *New York Evening Sun,* January 12, 1891, could not be confirmed in my examination of that and proximate issues of the paper. Its reference to "The Woman," apparently a journal, led to other fruitless research.

Within the past few weeks a thin little volume of poems has been laid on the counters in the book shops. It bears the simple title, "Poems by Emily Dickinson." Just who Emily Dickinson is, or was, nobody appears to know, but here is a book, not of verses, but of short poems of unusual originality and strength — that you perceive at once. There are faults — bad faults — but there are wonderful excellences. The thought is often undisciplined, but it is never hackneyed. The form is often rugged, yet at times there is a felicity of expression, like that of Emerson at his most inspired. There is a compression of thought that amounts almost to repression, and sometimes results in obscurity. But with such faults it is still remarkable poetry, struck out of a soul akin to those of Emerson and Browning. The story of the writer, as it was told by a friend to The Woman yesterday, is one that is full of imaginative interest. Emily Dickinson died about five years ago, a white-haired woman, whom very few persons had ever seen. Her home was in Amherst, Mass. where her family was one of wealth and of rare culture. For many years Miss Dickinson had lived the life of a recluse in the old family home, seeing sometimes for months at a time not even the dearest intimates of the family. There was in this instinct of seclusion no unfriendliness or touch of morbidness. Hers seemed to be simply a spirit that dwelt aloof in nature. Those about the house knew her always the same — sweet, gentle, unobtrusive, shy, slipping softly about, dressed always in white the year through, watching her flowers and happiest with her own thoughts. She wrote — voluminously it was supposed, though nobody ever knew, for she never published a line during her life. After her death upward of a thousand poems were found, all of them unnamed and evidently written for herself alone, out of which Col. Higginson, with the assistance of Miss Todd, selected 115 for publication. The volume containing these has just appeared. As The Woman has said, they are unusual. They are not clever. They are not poems that people will care to pick up as they do society verse, while they wait for the dinner bell or the carriage. Many people will not care to pick them at all, or, picking them up, will not care to read. For these are things that must be read with the brain and not with eye and ear alone — something that the latter-day verse does not always require.

87   "Inquiring Friends." *Christian Union* 43 (January 15, 1891), 88. The Higginson article is item no. 2.

Why does not The Christian Union have something to say about the poems of Emily Dickinson, which are just now receiving so much attention elsewhere?

Because it likes to lead rather than to follow discussion when possible. See The Christian Union for September 25 for a three-column article on this subject, by Thomas Wentworth Higginson, including several of the poems entire.

88   *Life* 17 (January 15, 1891), 36.

It is not in human nature not to regret that the newspaper notices of Emily Dickinson's poems will never meet the eye of the author. Possibly Miss Dickinson may be cognizant of them in the sphere that she now inhabits, but there is only a limited amount of consolation in that, even if you have faith to believe it — because newspaper notices are a fleeting joy, and of the earth mundane, and it isn't likely that the unfettered spirit would take as much comfort in them as an entity would who was still in the flesh. That there should be no living author to enjoy the handsome things that Miss Dickinson's relics have evoked, is a pain-fuller thought to economical natures than even the waste of honest victuals in New York hotels.

89   "Miss Dickinson's Poems." *Boston Evening Transcript,* January 16, 1891, p. 3. A reprinting; see no. 74.

90   Emily Ellsworth Fowler Ford. "Eheu! Emily Dickinson." *Springfield Weekly Republican,* January 16, 1891, p. 10. A reprinting; see no. 85.

91   "Notes." *Cincinnati Commercial Gazette,* January 17, 1891, p. 13.

—Emily Dickinson's poems have gone through two editions already, and Mrs. Todd and Colonel Higginson, her posthumous editors, are contemplating the publication of two more volumes—one of poetry and one of prose—from her pen.

92   "The Record of 1890." *Literary World* 22 (January 17, 1891), 24.

With Tennyson and Lowell silent, and Browning gone, the field of poetry has been left to the minor singers. Mr. Woodberry, indeed, promises much, but Miss Thomas has not greatly increased her fame by The Inverted Torch. Mr. Stoddard, Mrs. Moulton, "Stuart Sterne," and Mr. Sherman have confirmed their reputation, while Emily Dickinson's poems certainly exhibit a rare quality, little of a master of poetic form as she was. The two recent collections of American sonnets manifest the strength of our poets in this sphere.

93   George Pellew. "Ten Years of American Literature." *Critic,* n.s. 16 (January 17, 1891), 29.

In poetry this absence of high excellence is naturally most noticeable. Little has been written that deserves serious consideration. Lowell, in "Heartsease and Rue," his latest volume of verse, has included at least one poem of characteristic beauty—"Endymion,"—and in "Democracy, and Other Addresses" has shown that his force as a prose-writer is still unabated; Holmes has given us a few verses in which his old humor and delicacy of fancy may still be detected; Whittier "At Sundown," has occasionally warmed his old readers by the embers of his old fire; that Stoddard is still vigorous is shown by "The Lion's Cub, With Other Verse"; while W. W. Story from time to time gleans an ever scantier aftermath of verses from his "portfolio." William Winter, the last of the group of old-fashioned literary Bohemians, writes lines of which the somewhat strained pathos falls to-day on deaf ears. Aldrich's hand, in "Wyndham Towers," shows no loss of cunning. There is seriousness, strength and imagination in the two small volumes of Edgar Fawcett. The late Francis Saltus shows art and a peculiar cynicism and a still more peculiar morbid fancy under the inspiration of Baudelaire. Some flavor of the word-coloring of the school of Shelley is preserved by George E. Woodberry. Richard Watson Gilder has added "The Celestial Passion" to his "New Day" and other poems. Many young poets and innumerable poetesses sing gracefully and acceptably of natural beauty, of flowers, trees and stars, like Mrs. Whitney, Mrs. Deland, Edith Thomas and Maurice Thompson, while a note of warmer feeling is struck by Mrs. Moulton, and the late H. B. Carpenter in "Liber Amoris." A more ambitious attempt was made by S. H. Nichols in "Monte Rosa," an epic that won the remarkable reward of a second edition. In the posthumous poems of Mrs.

Jackson ("H. H."), E. R. Sill and Miss Dickinson, there is a special charm due to the impress of a singularly delicate, intelligent but elusive personality, — and in the posthumous volumes of Emma Lazarus the personality revealed, above all in her enthusiastic Jewish songs, is both intense and strong. The condensed, vivid, local humor that gave fame to the early dialect verses of Bret Harte and John Hay now finds expression only in short stories, such as the strange topsy-turvy unreason of the extravaganzas of Frank Stockton, unless the humorous, pathetic verses of James Whitcomb Riley and the ballads of Will Carleton are their modern representative. The tendency in general has been towards *vers de société,* — the light, graceful, well-bred versification of casual fancies and impressions, — like the work, admirable in its kind, of H. C. Bunner, the semi-collegiate verses of Edward Martin and Herbert Morse, and the dainty, Herrick-haunted songs of F. D. Sherman and the best of the younger men, Clinton Scollard. The most important poetry of the decade is, perhaps, to be found in the recently collected poems of the late Sidney Lanier, who occasionally struck rich, exotic harmonies of word and thought more novel and more suggestive than any heard since the death of Poe.

94 "Hail Alma Mater." *Boston Daily Globe,* January 20, 1891, p. 8. This reference to Austin Dickinson and his sister appears at the end of a column describing "the annual banquet and reunion of the Boston-Amherst Alumni Association."

Away over on the end of the table was the treasurer of the college, William Austin Dickinson. Brown hair and brown sidewhiskers made him look like a poet, but he isn't. The poetry is written by his sister Emily Dickinson.

95 John W. Chadwick. "Emily Dickinson." *Unity* 26 (January 22, 1891), 171. This is Chadwick's second review of Dickinson; his first is no. 51. See also his inclusion of her in an anthology, no. 61. "Some keep the Sabbath" appeared in the *Round Table* for March 12, 1864, as printed here except for the substitution of "going" for "getting" in line 11. Poems noted by title may be identified in the Poem Index.

A few weeks ago her name was utterly unknown beyond the circle of her immediate friends and now for some dozen or twenty thousands it is a sign of singular poetic power. I can not overrate the number, because if only two or three thousand volumes have so far been sold, few who have read them can have failed of reading them to others and many must have done as I have — captured with them the ear of every passing friend. This is a sudden fame, but it was won by years of silent and secluded work, and unless those who die have knowledge how "their works do follow them," she does not know that it has come and heaped its laurel on her grave. But let me be a little more explicit for the sake of those who have not yet made the acquaintance of this gifted woman in her remarkable book. It is published by Roberts Brothers, Boston, and it is edited by her friends, Mabel Loomis Todd and T. W. Higginson. The book numbers 152 pages, but it reverses the Latin rule, *non multa, sed multum,* so far as the amount of matter is concerned. There are many pieces — 123 — but many of them are but six or eight lines long, some even less; the shortest, however, filling the page as a good picture fills the wall and has no brother near the throne. In a brief, while yet sufficient introduction, Mr. Higginson gives a few facts and characteristics of the author's life and his impression of the merits of her verse.

She was born in Amherst, Mass., Dec. 10, 1830, and died there May 15, 1886. Her father was a well-known citizen, a lawyer of the town and the treasurer of Amherst College. Once a year he invited the college dons with others, gentlemen and ladies, to his house. At such times Miss Dickinson received the guests with all the ease and affability of one habituated to the social round. In fact these were her annual emergences from a solitude which for many years confined her to her father's house and for many more within the limits of his grounds. Yet she was not an invalid and the lively sympathy with pain manifested in her poems came from no personal experience. Mr. Higginson does not tell us this in his preface and contrary inference will generally be drawn. But a letter from his co-editor, of which I may unblamed, I trust, make so much use, says, "I am sure you will be interested to know that her complete retirement was merely a voluntary seclusion. She was always in perfect health until the last year or two of her life, but she felt that society was in the main uncongenial—as, indeed, how could one of her peculiar genius find it otherwise?—and so she withdrew more and more, holding communication with her many friends at last only by sending them flowers and notes or poems. She was never morbid or melancholy." This last is in complete accordance with the tenor of her verse. Nor could the longest walks abroad have given her a more vivid apprehension of Nature's force and charm, nor the most crowded hours of glorious life a keener sense of its reality, than came to her within her narrow walls and garden's bounds.

Of these one hundred and twenty-three poems, only three or four were published during her lifetime. This must have meant a good deal of stubborn resistance to the advice of friends, for among these were some perfectly competent to appreciate their quality—her present editors not least. Mr. Higginson, though he saw her but twice, corresponded with her for many years. Of the three or four poems published, one I have treasured in my memory for more than twenty years, not knowing whose it was, having read it in the *Round Table* which broke up too soon for some of us who liked it well. I doubt not that many others, when I quote it, will say as Robert Collyer said to me, "Oh, is that her's? I've loved it all these years."—and then resolve that they must know the fountain from which came those few clear drops. Either it read a little differently in the *Round Table* or my memory has begun to play me false. It is called "A Service of Song," and this is how it sings:

> Some keep the Sabbath going to church;
>   I keep it staying at home,
> With a bobolink for a chorister,
>   And an orchard for a dome.
>
> Some keep the Sabbath in surplice;
>   I just wear my wings,
> And instead of tolling the bell for church
>   Our little sexton sings.
>
> God preaches—a noted clergyman—
>   And the sermon is never long;
> So instead of getting to heaven at last,
>   I'm going all along.

The "noted clergyman" of the third stanza is a characteristic note. She has quite a number of these pretty blasphemies, which Thoreau would have gladly owned, which came, perhaps, from sympathetic contact with his mind. There are Emersonian touches here and there, and one feels how greatly he would have enjoyed her verse, so fresh and vital in its substance and so untrammeled in its form. Helen

Hunt Jackson was one of her friends, and we notice a rumor that Miss Dickinson wrote the "Saxe Holm" stories, which have Amherst ear-marks. But this fact would suit H. H. as well, and we do not expect any reversal of the opinion that she wrote the stories in question.

The form of Emily Dickinson's verse is as original as its intrinsic quality. The measures are extremely simple; the rhythm, though it sometimes halts, is sometimes subtle, often fine. To question it, is here and there to be convinced that her deliberate choice was better than our hasty inference. Most singular is her use, abuse, and her disuse of rhyme, with absolute indifference. It is evident that she never blotted a line because it did not rhyme or rhyme well. When there is no rhyme at all the rhythm and the measure often seem enough. The imperfect rhymes are less occasions for delight. The poems are set apart in four books, I. Life, II. Love, III. Nature. IV. Time and Eternity. The quaintest are in the fourth book, the loveliest in the third, the deepest and the strongest in the first and second. The suggestion of William Blake is strongest in the fourth, but it is very general, not in particulars. There is his insight, daring, humorous play with grim realities. In every book there is the same felicity of word and phrase; the same feeling for the values of words and the same novel, sometimes startling, use of them. Sometimes the poem is a riddle hard to guess. At other times it is as simple as "The Book of Martyrs," or "A Book." The former goes—first stanza:—

> Read, sweet, how others strove,
> Till we are stouter;
> What they renounced,
> Till we are less afraid;
> How many times they bore
> The faithful witness,
> Till we are helped,
> As if a kingdom cared.

And this describes what her own book will do for many:—

> He ate and drank the precious words,
>   His spirit grew robust;
> He knew no more that he was poor,
>   Nor that his frame was dust.
> He danced along the dingy ways,
>   And this bequest of wings
> Was but a book. What liberty
>   A loosened spirit brings!

Nothing could be simpler than Book II. ix. "Have you got a brook in your little heart?" and nothing more unique in its extravagance than vi. "If you were coming in the fall." The poems of Nature are poems of the microcosm for the most part, poems of the little creatures and the little flowers. Here is a whole one in four lines:—

> The pedigree of honey
>   Does not concern the bee;
> A clover, any time, to him
>   Is aristocracy.

One on "The Grass" pleases with much besides its "sovereign barns" and the "Purple Clover" comes in for rarest praise, while nothing could be more deliciously absurd than the description of the sunset in "A Day." But this enumeration might go on for an indefinite and too engrossing length. I hear that there were other fish in her sea as good as these that have been caught in the book, and, indeed, the shining scales of one other are just before me as I write. Certainly this and others should be in the next edition and there is a whisper that her letters were quite as good as her poems, and that, if we are good, we shall have some of them, also, before long. Her friends and editors must take the responsibility of deciding whether there is any impiety in permitting such wide enjoyment of what was done so silently and secretly.

96 Mary G. Cutler. "Fulfillment." *Unity* 26 (January 22, 1891), 171.

Within a pure and gentle woman's breast,
Hidden away from every careless eye,
And silent, in deep, proud humility,
Sweet rhythmic thoughts long lay in troubled rest.
Trembling, they longed to leave that quiet nest,
In venturous flight their eager wings to try,
And voice and song the tender melody
Whose sacred mission was so dimly guessed.

Fast crowding days and months and years sped on;
Still closely nestling in that loving breast, —
No lofty height, no wreath of laurel won, —
Life of her life, in love made manifest;
Soul of her love, love true and pure and fair,
The thoughts aye sing in word and deed and prayer.

97 "Editorial." *Unity* 26 (January 22, 1891), 169.

We are glad to print this week Mr. Chadwick's appreciative word of that shy poet soul, Emily Dickinson. How little did this gentle hermit dream that her musings might some day fulfill her desire:

If I can stop one heart from breaking,
I shall not live in vain;
If I can ease one life the aching,
Or cool one pain,
Or help one fainting robin
Unto his nest again,
I shall not live in vain.

We find not so much William Blake in her verses, however, as of Shelley, in short metre, with an occasional suggestion of far-off Omar Khayyán.

98 *Springfield Weekly Republican*, January 23, 1891, p. 9. The "friend" is Emily Ellsworth Fowler Ford, whose poem in tribute to Dickinson was first published January 11, 1891 (no. 85). Maurice Thompson's review in *America* had just appeared (no. 81).

We published a week ago a choice sonnet addressed to the recluse poet, Emily Dickinson, by a schoolmate, townswoman and personal friend. This friend writes to us: —

The reception of her work has been most encouraging for American verse, which has been trifling with metrical forms and adorning with poetic diction poor, thin thoughts—or often dressing pretty dolls very beautifully. These pungent words and rhythms which broke from her soul have life and will give life. She is like some of the minor English bards,—Barnes in simplicity and naturalness, but her dress of thought is far more scholarly,—and Emily Bronte, and Blake with whom she is mentioned. The praises and comprehension of the public have given me great joy as well as surprise, but I think there has been dissatisfaction with much that is published for some little time, and these genuine records of her soul meet a real want.

It is true that there has been a remarkable response to this wonderful spiritual verse of Emily Dickinson, but it has been accompanied by a vexatious display of the current feebleness of vision among professed critics, who complain of the ragged lines and imperfect rhymes,—as if one should complain that every leaf of the rose is not a perfect geometrical figure, or that the rainbow is not definitely bounded by straight chalk marks. Maurice Thompson has much impugned his title to the name of poet by such small mechanical stringency concerning Emily Dickinson.

99   "Literary Notes." *Brooklyn Standard Union*, January 24, 1891, p. 6. It is likely that the letter alluded to here was transmitted to the *Standard Union* by Emily Ellsworth Fowler Ford (see no. 85), though another Brooklyn resident at the time was Ellen E. Dickinson, widow of William Hawley Dickinson, one of the poet's cousins (see no. 360). The letter's author is not known.

Concerning Emily Dickinson, whose posthumous poems are attracting general attention, a recent Amherst (Mass.) letter says: "I wonder that her friends should be willing to give her sayings to the public. Years ago some college student gained her affections; her friends disapproved. She gave up all society—never till the day of her death went out by the front door of the house, and requested that her body be carried through the back door to the cemetery—which was done. She always dressed in white." Miss Dickinson's father was the Hon. Edward Dickinson, one of the last Whig members of Congress from Massachusetts.

100 "Strange Poems." *Christian Advocate* 66 (January 29, 1891), 65. The *Christian Advocate* had quoted Dickinson only once: "How many times these low feet staggered" appeared in its "Home and Young Folks" column Jan. 8, 1891, p. 22. Later in the same year (and under the same heading) it reprinted "Whose are the little beds, I asked" (July 16, p. 468). It gave no other space to Dickinson during the decade.

Harper's for January has a criticism by W. D. Howells on the strange poems of Emily Dickinson. This peculiar woman, of whom we have heard for many years, and scraps of whose poetry we had seen and occasionally quoted in this paper, spent her life mainly in her father's house at Amherst, Mass., seldom passed its doors, and never for many years passed the gates of its grounds. Her poems have just been published. She seemed determined that nothing should appear from her pen while she lived. Mr. Howells says that "if nothing else had come of our American life but this strange poetry, we should feel that in the work of Emily Dickinson New England had made a distinctive addition to the literature of the world, and could not be left out of any record of it." Most of the poems are about Love, Nature, Time, and Eternity. Here are some stanzas:

> The bustle in a house
>   The morning after death,
> Is solemnest of industries
>   Enacted upon earth.

> The sweeping up the heart
>   And putting love away
> We shall not want to use again
>   Until eternity.

This certainly represents a phase of feeling, usually however, transient. Love reacts from it, and often becomes stronger than ever. What follows is noble and inspiring:

> I never saw a moor,
>   I never saw the sea;
> Yet know I how the heather looks,
>   And what a wave must be.

> I never spoke with God,
>   Nor visited in heaven;
> Yet certain am I of the spot
>   As if the chart were given.

And this:

> I shall know why, when time is over,
>   And I have ceased to wonder why;
> Christ will explain each separate anguish
>   In the fair school-room of the sky.

In reading her poems we cannot resist the impression that there is something unhealthy in a life of isolation. Perpetual introspection is the mother of melancholy, and melancholy the half-sister of madness.

101 "Men and Things." *Unity* 26 (January 29, 1891), 178.

It is said that two more volumes, one of prose and one of poetry, by the late Emily Dickinson, are to be brought out.

102 Andrew Lang. "A Literary Causerie." *Speaker* [London] 3 (January 31, 1891), 135–36.

Though few people care for poetry, and though a new poet has to wait long for his laurels in England, in America both singers and the love of song seem much more popular. America has lately lost two great lyrists—lost them before their very names were heard of in our country. One was Miss Emily Dickinson, whose remains Mr. Howells has applauded, and has found to be in themselves a justification of America's literary existence. These poems have reached a third edition: but while the term "edition" now means 100 copies, and now 10,000, this fact tells us very little. Judging Miss Dickinson's work by Mr. Howells' specimens, her muse was *super grammaticum*, and was wholly reckless of rhyme. Here is an example:—

> I died for beauty, but was scarce
> Adjusted in the tomb
> When one who died for truth was lain
> In an adjoining room.
>
> He questioned softly why I failed.
> 'For beauty,' I replied.
> 'And I for truth—the two are one;
> We brethren are,' he said.
>
> And so, as kinsmen met a night,
> We talked between the rooms,
> Until the moss had reached our lips,
> And covered up our names.

Here, of course, "replied" does not rhyme to "said"; it is not even in assonance, any more than "names" and "rooms" are in assonance or in rhyme. Aristotle says that the ultimate Democracy is remarkable for the licence it permits to women and to children. Miss Dickinson, like Mrs. Browning, though she was not learned like Mrs. Browning, took great licence with rhymes. Possibly the poetry of Democracy will abound more and more in these liberties. But then the question will arise, Is it poetry at all? For poetry, too, has its laws, and if they are absolutely neglected, poetry will die. This may be of no great moment, as there is plenty of old poetry in stock, but still one must urge that lawless poetry is skimble-skamble stuff, with no right to exist. As to the piece quoted, Mr. Howells says, "How could any phrase nominate its weird witchery aright?" Perhaps the phrase "nonsense," or "fudge," will do well enough. What does the corpse mean by "failing for beauty"? Did it die because it was not pretty? Or did it die for love of the beauty of some other person? And, if the dead bodies could go on conversing for a considerable time, why did they relapse into silence when the moss "had reached their lips, and covered up their names"? Moss does not, in fact, grow inside graves, and how could any development of moss on the tombstone affect these conversational corpses? A poem may be nonsense and yet may be charming, like Mr. William Morris's "Blue Closet," which has the inconsequence of a dream. But a poem like the poem of the dead bodies is unrhymed nonsense, which would be Heine if it could.

103   "Books in Season." *Publishers' Weekly* 39 (January 31, 1891), 223.

Roberts Brothers will publish February 10 the following: "Petrarch—his life and works," by May Alden Ward (author of a similar work on Dante), a clear and well-written sketch, in which the subject is considered as the precursor of the Renaissance, and as one of the great triumvirate that created the Italian language and inaugurated its literature; a volume of essays by Joseph Henry Allen, entitled "Positive Religion;" and a volume entitled "Power Through Repose," by Annie Payson Call, who treats of such subjects as training for rest, rest in sleep, the body's guidance, training of the mind, etc. They also announce a new edition of the poems of Emily Dickinson, which have been so successful. The price has been reduced to $1.25, and the drab-and-white edition will be discontinued.

104 Alexander Young. "Boston Letter." *Critic,* n.s. 15 (January 31, 1891), 57. The "fourth edition" was printed in a new binding January 24th, priced 25 cents less than the $1.50 charged for the previous printing; see *DB,* p. 8.

In the fourth edition of "Poems," by Emily Dickinson, which the same firm will bring out on the same date, the price has been popularized. The growing demand for these remarkable poems is encouraging for the success of the contemplated volumes of prose and poetry by the same author.

105 "Books and Barbarism." Unverified clipping. Todd's scrapbook attribution of this item to the *Brooklyn Standard Union* for January 31, 1891, could not be confirmed in my search of that and proximate issues of the paper. Yet the byline and dateline of the clipping read: "Correspondence of the Standard Union. Boston, Jan. 30." The Boston contributor may have been Lilian Whiting; see no. 213.

Three editions of the poems of Emily Dickinson, of Amherst, have already been published by Roberts Brothers, and the fourth will be out in a few days. It will be a cheaper edition than the white and gold ones which have been issued thus far, in anticipation of wider popular demand, for the writings of this new poet, who has created a sensation in the literary world, but which she has not lived to see. It will be in the library style of binding, in permanent shape, and will be finely finished. I learn from those who have some knowledge personally of Miss Dickinson, that her authorship of these poems has been a great surprise to them. It is told here regarding her that she was a complete recluse. She did not mingle with the world, and though it was known that she was engaged more or less in literary matters, even to the extent that the Saxe Holm writings were attributed to her, yet those who were familiar with her life had not expected this volume of poems from her pen. The surroundings of her home in Amherst were congenial to her temperament, and it is doubtless true that it was intensified by the air of seclusion which pervaded the grounds of the Hon. Edward Dickinson, her father, even though they were on one of the most frequented streets of the village. Amherst's two colleges draw so many people to the town every year that hundreds pass by this interesting estate. It can easily be described, so that no one can miss it. As the visitor to the town goes from the station of the New London Northern Railroad to the central village, he will pass a high bank on the right, with a white brick house standing at its highest part half hidden in the trees. No other place resembles it, and this short description is enough to enable any stranger to find it. The house is of old pattern. Trees and shrubs fill the grounds. A row of trees stands almost in the middle of the sidewalk in front. The house seems to shrink from public view, and the growth of the town, plus the modern concrete walk on the other side of the street, has tended to leave this modest residence more to one side than before.

The air of seclusion is intensified by the tall and dense hemlock hedge on the line of the adjoining estate, that of Miss Dickinson's brother, Mr. W.A. Dickinson, the treasurer of Amherst College, and it does not seem so strange, after seeing the place, that the author of these poems, which are attracting so many readers, and exciting so many detailed newspaper notices, was given to solitude, and shrank from close contact with the world. Her old house is likely to stand for many years in its present condition. Amherst's growth is not rapid, and, though this house is on a busy street, and almost within a stone's throw of the First Congregational Church, yet the movement of population is not likely to encroach for a generation to the extent of its removal. Back of it are the homes of the college professors, the Tylers, father and son, and the society building of D.K.E.; but the wood-crowned eminence will still keep for years the area of half-forest which brings the mountain wildness close to the centre of the town, and future readers who wish to see the home of Emily Dickinson will doubtless find its essential traits unchanged for a long time.

106   Arlo Bates. "Literary Topics in Boston." *Book Buyer*, n.s. 8 (February 1891), 10. Mention of forthcoming Dickinson volumes appeared in the *Critic* for December 27th (item no. 56). The sticking point seems to have been Lavinia who, as late as March 20th, was still withholding her consent for a second book of her sister's poems (*AB*, 117).

From the supernatural to the poems of the late Emily Dickinson is only a step, so thoroughly were her writings permeated with the feeling for other-worldliness. The popularity of her book has been so great that when this letter gets into print the fourth edition will have left the press. The report that a volume of her prose work and another of her poetry are to be published is at least premature in so far that nothing of the sort has been decided upon.

107   Carrie Blake. "Emily Dickinson." Report of a lecture by Heloise Edwina Hersey at Wheaton Seminary (Norton, Mass.). *Rushlight* 34:4 (February 1891), 56–57. The critic whose literary judgment has momentarily "blundered" is apparently Howells, the subject of Miss Hersey's lecture that followed upon her discussion of Dickinson. The 1890 text of "If I shouldn't be alive" did not set "granite" in italics.

I feel myself in duty bound to be a sort of literary news-bearer to you, so I bring to your notice an almost unknown writer, Miss Emily Dickinson, and a little volume of her poems which appeared two months ago. Partly by dint of advertising, and partly on account of the merit of the poems, the work has attracted much attention. Miss Dickinson lived in Amherst and was known through all the region round as a recluse. For nearly twenty years before her death, she never appeared in public, but before that she did sometimes appear at parties given by the President of Amherst College. Tradition tells us that there was a disappointment in love, her father opposing her marriage with the man she loved. Her work gains interest from this fact.

The one power which English literature ought to give to us is the power to know the good, the tolerable, and the poor. But it does not always give this to us. Every little while, some one whose judgment we have trusted, makes a blunder. For example, Mr. Trowbridge told us he knew he had found a new planet — that he had read some of the most remarkable productions of the age. They were the first two stories by Amélie Rives; but his planet has proved to be a very short-tailed comet.

Now about Miss Dickinson. It is a difficult matter to decide upon her merit, since we cannot tell how she might have written if she had lived a different life. If you dip into this book, I want you to be able to distinguish some things that are very good from others that are very bad. There is no doubt that she had an imagination quite remarkable. Read some of her poems. That this woman should have chosen to write in rhyme is very strange. We should suppose if she had written enough to fill a volume she would somewhere have had a *rhyme*, but seldom does she make one, and then only by accident. This volume is divided into four parts, — Life, Love, Nature, Time and Eternity. The last division is by far the most powerful.

I died for beauty, but was scarce
    Adjusted in the tomb,
When one who died for truth was lain
    In an adjoining room.

He questioned softly why I failed?
    'For beauty,' I replied.
'And I for truth, — the two are one;
    We brethren are,' he said.

And so, as kinsmen met a night,
    We talked between the rooms,
Until the moss had reached our lips,
    And covered up our names.

We shall forgive the woman for rhyming *rooms* with *names*.

Miss Dickinson has a most fatal gift of uniting absurd figures with solemn thoughts. She is fond of trying to represent, in one way or another, the solidity and changelessness of the features after death, and each figure she chooses is a little worse than the others. She is very fond of robins.

If I shouldn't be alive
    When the robins come,
Give the one in red cravat
    A memorial crumb.

If I couldn't thank you,
    Being just asleep,
You will know I'm trying
    With my *granite* lip.

In another place she talks about a *soldered* mouth. Here is another example, it is the first of the poems of *Love*.

Mine by the right of the white election!
    Mine by the royal seal!
Mine by the sign in the scarlet prison
    Bars cannot conceal!

Mine, here in vision and in veto!
    Mine, by the grave's repeal
Titled, confirmed, — delirious charter! —
    Mine, while the ages steal.

"The right of the white election," — I have not the faintest idea what that means. "Mine by the royal seal"! The explanation of the scarlet prison may be the heart, and I had a few moments irreverent enough to think that the "bars" might represent the *ribs!* This is an example of what she can do. Here is poetry run mad. I ought to warn you, however, that most of the critics commend it unreservedly, Howells among the number; but Lang, having great command of the King's English, calls it *balderdash*.

Her lines on the mayflower are full of beauty and poetic genius, and there are in them a few adjectives which are remarkable in their application, — as "pink, small, and punctual." She is very fond of this flower.

But to go back to the poems of time and eternity.

THE CHARIOT.

Because I could not stop for Death,
    He kindly stopped for me;
The carriage held but just ourselves
    And Immortality.

We slowly drove, he knew no haste,
    And I had put away
My labor and my leisure too,
    For his civility.

We passed the school where children played,
    Their lessons scarcely done;
We passed the fields of gazing grain,
    We passed the setting sun.

We paused before a house that seemed
    A swelling of the ground;
The roof was scarcely visible,
    The cornice but a mound.

Since then 'tis centuries; but each
    Feels shorter than the day
I first surmised the horses' heads
    Were toward eternity.

Here is one which reminds us of Hawthorne, mysterious and ghostly. Do not expect any particular point; its interest lies in its impossibility.

THE LONELY HOUSE.

I know some lonely house off the road   [houses
A robber'd like the look of, —
Wooden barred,
And windows hanging low,
Inviting to
A portico,
Where two could creep;
One hand the tools,
The other peep
To make sure all's asleep.
Old-fashioned eyes,
Not easy to surprise!

How orderly the kitchen'd look by night,
With just a clock, —
But they could gag the tick,
And mice won't bark;
And so the walls don't tell,
None will.
A pair of spectacles afar just stir —   [ajar
An almanac's aware.

Was it the mat winked,
Or a nervous star?
The moon slides down the stair
To see who's there.

There's plunder,—where?
Tankard, or spoon,
Ear-ring, or stone,
A watch, some ancient brooch
To match the grandmamma,
Staid sleeping there.

Day rattles, too,
Stealth's slow;
The sun has got as far
As the third sycamore.
Screams chanticleer,
"Who's there?"
And echoes train away,   [trains
Sneer—"Where?"
While the old couple, just astir,
Fancy the sunrise left the door ajar!

108 "Talk About Books." *Chautauquan* 12 (February 1891), 692.

The general principle underlying the famous exclamation of Miles Standish, "If you wish a thing to be well done, you must do it yourself," is not less applicable to poetry than to people. Any poem speaks for itself better than the critic can speak for it. Poems like those of Emily Dickinson especially emphasize this truth. They are indescribable. The reader is disarmed of hostile criticism at the outset. Who could withstand the gentle appeal of the opening lines:

This is my letter to the world,
    That never wrote to me,—
The simple news that Nature told,
    With tender majesty.

Her message is committed
    To hands I cannot see;
For love of her, sweet countrymen,
    Judge tenderly of me!

One is impressed with the marvelous independent peculiarity of the author. The boldness, depth, and strength of her thought fascinate the attention. The surprising, sudden, and irregular turns of expression intoxicate the fancy with a rare suggestiveness. As Mr. Higginson says in the preface, "In many cases these verses seem to the reader like poetry torn up by the roots, with rain, and dew, and earth still clinging to them, giving a freshness and a fragrance not otherwise to be conveyed." The volume already has attracted wide attention, and many of the poems have been quoted. But no lover of poetry will be content with a cursory reading of the book. It is one to be owned, studied, and loved.

109 "The Books of 1890." *Literary News* 12 (February 1891), 48–49. On p. 61 of this issue, where the poet's name is spelled correctly, it is noted that "Miss Dickinson's 'Poems' are already in their fourth edition."

Almost every department, however, contained some book that was widely read, and in several instances made a financial success for the publisher. In fiction the stories of Kipling made a decided sensation; in theology and religion, Mr. Henry B. Alden's "God and His World," a remarkable book for a layman, first published anonymously; "Lux Mundi;" and Rev. Howard MacQueary's "The Evolution of Man and Christianity," excited considerable attention; in biography "The Journal of Marie Bashkirtseff" and "The Autobiography of Joseph Jefferson" stood out, and much money was made on Ward McAllister's twaddle about "Society As I Have Found it." "Lecky's History of England in the Eighteenth Century" was completed and Henry Adams' "History of the United States of America" was well received by competent critics. The sensation of the year among works of travel was Stanley's "In Darkest Africa;" and in works of social and political interest General Booth's "In Darkest England" and Prof. Fiske's "Civil Government in the United States" were widely read. Emily Dickenson's "Poems" have evoked more praise and criticism than almost any book published in their field.

110 William Morton Payne. "Recent Books of Poetry." *Dial* ii (February 1891), 313.

The poems of Miss Emily Dickinson, collected and edited by the care of two friends, stand as far apart from ordinary verse as do the flowers of the Monotropa — by a more than happy thought chosen to decorate the cover — from ordinary woodland blossoms. Colonel Higginson, one of the editors, says: "It is believed that the thoughtful reader will find in these pages a quality more suggestive of the poetry of William Blake than of anything to be elsewhere found, — flashes of wholly original and profound insight into nature and life; words and phrases exhibiting an extraordinary vividness of descriptive and imaginative power, yet often set in a seemingly whimsical or even rugged frame." The suggestion of Blake seems to us very evident, how evident may be judged from the following characteristic example of Miss Dickinson's work:

> I died for beauty, but was scarce
>   Adjusted in the tomb.
> When one who died for Truth was lain
>   In an adjoining room.
>
> He questioned softly why I failed?
>   "For beauty." I replied.
> "And I for truth — the two are one;
>   We brethren are," he said.
>
> And so, as kinsmen met a night,
>   We talked between the rooms,
> Until the moss had reached our lips,
>   And covered up our names."

Such verses certainly justify the quoted characterization. Their form is rugged, but, "when a thought takes one's breath away," as Colonel Higginson observes, merely formal defects do not shock us. We must also find space for the exquisite lines to "Indian Summer":

> These are the days when birds come back,
> A very few, a bird or two,
> To take a backward look.

These are the days when skies put on
The old, old sophistries of June, —
A blue and gold mistake.

Oh, fraud that cannot cheat the bee,
Almost thy plausibility
Induces my belief.

Till ranks of seeds their witness bear,
And softly through the altered air
Hurries a timid leaf.

Oh, sacrament of summer days,
Oh, last communion in the haze,
Permit a child to join.

Thy sacred emblems to partake,
Thy consecrated bread to break,
Taste thine immortal wine!

111 "Editorial Notes." *Independent* 43 (February 5, 1891), 193. Three poems, destined for inclusion in the *Second Series*, were sent to the *Independent* by Mabel Todd: "Went up a year this evening," "I held a Jewel in my fingers," and "God made a little Gentian." For the *Hartford Courant*'s estimate of these poems, see no. 115.

Our column of poetry is notable for three little poems by Emily Dickinson, whose posthumous volume has attracted so much attention, and these verses are of rare quality.

112 "Literary Notes." *Independent* 43 (February 5, 1891), 202.

The volume of "Poems" by the late Emily Dickinson, has gone into the fourth edition, at a popular price.

There seems to be a strange blight on literature, or at least poetic literature, in this country. Why do none of the younger poets grow up? Why do they always remain younger poets? Each publishes his first volume with careful workmanship and much promise between the lines; we expect great things of him; and then — he is never heard of again. What becomes of him? Either he has died untimely, or the publishers have caught him and shut him in a desk at a pittance a week; or he acquires expensive tastes and must humor these, and so the world swallows him; or he marries for money, and then he swallows the world, and so is undone; in short, he either succeeds or fails in life (as it is called), and in either case he is too much absorbed in the process to heed the earlier impulse. By chance the poems on the first page of this paper come from two of these "inheritors of unfulfilled renown." Emily Dickinson's poems form perhaps the most remarkable volume of imaginative literature of the year; and Charles Henry Lüders, died only two weeks ago in Philadelphia, where he was one of a bright set of young literary men. He was hardly more than thirty years of age; loved by his friends as a gentle and winning soul, he had become known to the public through the magazines as one who had the unmistakable gift of wonder-working, the fitful wandering light of inspiration, which seems to elude even its possessors.

113 "Literature of the Day." *Chicago Tribune*, February 7, 1891, p. 12. *Poems,* 1890 used six periods to represent Dickinson's horizontal line dividing her manuscript version of "I'll tell you how the sun rose" into two equal parts.

A second Lady of Shalot is Emily Dickinson. She has not wandered among men, nor even looked upon them from her window, but has only gazed upon their fleeting reflections in her mirror, where she has seen all their emotions, their sorrows, and joys with the clearness and depth, the transparent intensity which mirrors impart to their reflections. These vivid, intense impressions she has written down, not for the public eye, but for her own pleasure, and, now that she is here no more to shrink from the criticism of the outer world, these among the most remarkable productions of the day are offered to us at her sister's instigation, by her two friends, Mabel Loomis Todd and T. W. Higginson, under the simple title "Poems."

What can be said about them? They are beyond the pale of criticism by reason of the proud indifference to opinion and the utter disregard of established rules for poetic composition, which the author shows in every line. But the spirit is there untrammeled by conventionality; daring, probing, showing things forth with a marvelous word power.

Here is one bit that seems as though it must have been lived by the poet. It is called "The Mystery of Pain," and reminds one of W. E. Henley's "Hospital Sketches":

> Pain has an element of blank;
> It cannot recollect
> When it began, or if there were
> A day when it was not.
>
> It has no future but itself,
> Its infinite realms contain
> Its past, enlightened to perceive
> New periods of pain.

Miss Dickinson possessed a power of exquisite imagery, a power of conception as delicate and perfect as anything in English poetry. Among a great deal that is morbid—the morbidness of a self-centered person who lived an entirely secluded life—we come upon little riotous morsels of fancy like the lines beginning, "I taste a liquor never brewed," or the following dainty caprice called "A Day:"

> I'll tell you how the sun rose—
>   A ribbon at a time,
> The steeples swam in amethyst
>   The news like squirrels ran.
>
> The hills untied their bonnets,
>   The bobolinks begun,
> Then said I softly to myself,
>   "That must have been the sun!"
>   . . . . . .
> But how he set, I know not.
>   They seemed a purple stile
> Which little boys and girls
>   Were climbing all the while.

[There

Till when they reached the other side,
   A dominie in gray
Put gently up the evening bars,
   And led the flock away.

114 "Literary Notes." *Boston Beacon* 8 (February 7, 1891), 3.

The "Poems" of Emily Dickinson will shortly appear in a fourth edition, which goes to show that literature of originality and power is not wholly neglected even in these degenerate days.

115 "Bric-a-brac." *Hartford Courant,* February 7, 1891, p. 2. "Emigravit" is the title given "Went up a year this evening." The other two poems published in the *Independent* were "God made a little Gentian" and "I held a Jewel in my fingers" (see no. III).

Emily Dickinson has shown rare genius of a spontaneous but fitful and un-pruned kind in her poetry. At times, however, she runs into obscurantism and infelicity, which is true of the poem "Emigravit" in the current *Independent.* Two others of hers there printed are very beautiful. Miss Dickinson's book of verses has gone into its fourth edition.

116 "Literary Bric-a-Brac." Unverified clipping attributed to the *Boston Budget* for February 8, 1891, in Todd's scrapbook. The item lists volumes published the previous day by Roberts Brothers, noting among them "a fourth edition of the poems of Emily Dickinson."

117 "Literary Notes." *Book Review* I:I (February 10, 1891). Unlocated. Todd's clipping includes the masthead of this first issue of the *Book Review,* but the journal must have been short-lived; no record of its existence survives in standard sources.

Emily Dickinson's publishers announce the fourth edition of her poems, which have met with phenomenal success. The book is plainly bound in cloth, with gilt top. Price, $1.00.

118 Unlocated Roberts Brothers advertisement. The "fourth edition" was announced February 10, 1891. For the full text of the quoted review, see no. 63.

FOURTH EDITION.

"The unique book of the year just ended, and, from the poetical point of view, the most worthy as well as the most uncommon, is the collection of Miss Emily Dickinson's Poems, lately brought out by Roberts Brothers. Compared with the better known verses of the day, or even with most of those which have borne the test applied by generations of English-speaking readers, these posthumous poems are like strange orchids among a mass of gay, sweet-smelling, highly cultivated but not rare or unfamiliar flowers. Considered merely as rhymed and metrical compositions, they are over-full of apparently willful sins against rule and convention; but, like the fantastic blooms to which we have compared them, these deviations from common standards justify themselves by appeal to a law not made for chrysanthemums and roses, not binding in the school-room nor in the editorial rooms of popular magazines," says the Catholic World. Emily Dickinson's Poems, which though published only two months, is already in its 4th edition. Price $1.25. ROBERTS BROTHERS, PUBLISHERS, BOSTON.

119 "An Odd Child of Literature." *Oxford* [Mass.] *Midweekly,* February 11, 1891, p. 12. A reprinting; see item no. 84.

120 Caroline Kirkland. "Emily Dickinson's Poems." *Figaro* 2 (February 12, 1891), 428.

Strange product of heredity, environment and climate are these profound, far-reaching, often unmusical "poems" of Emily Dickinson's. They are instinct with a woman's sensitiveness, and yet are strong with the fearlessness of a man. With sudden flashes of genius she touches the very heart of things and yet at other times her ideas seem distorted and warped. She has created her world. She has not, as the world's great have done, gone outside of herself to study that which lies about her, but has been self-absorbed, self-analyzing. Her very great power, thus concentred, has laid bare many emotions that we all hide deep down in our hearts, thoughts that in the wholesome, breezy rush of living, of everyday existence, we hardly are conscious of thinking until these vivid words light up with flashes here and there that deep, dark undercurrent of life from which arise, almost unbidden, the best and the worst that is in us.

There is, in these poems, a grotesque power of imagery, a startling originality that rivets the attention of the reader. What a strange brain it must have been that conceived the stanza called "Refuge"!

> The clouds their backs together laid,
> The north began to push,   [begun
> The forests galloped till they fell,
> The lightning skipped like mice;
> The thunder crumbled like a stuff —
> How good to be safe in tombs,
> Where Nature's temper cannot reach,
> Nor vengeance ever comes!

"The lightning skipped like mice," what titantic congruity there is in the comparison!

The quaint fancy of the following lines cannot fail to tickle the literary palate:

> Death is a dialogue between
> The spirit and the dust.
> "Dissolve", says Death. The Spirit, "Sir
> I have another trust".
>
> Death doubts it, argues from the ground,
> The Spirit turns away,
> Just laying off, for evidence,
> An overcoat of clay.

Learned disquisitions could be written on this volume of poems, so suggestive, so original and so imperfect, that they are a fit subject for a Boston fad. As much meaning could be got out of them that the author never put in as has been extracted, by clubs and classes, from Browning, Ibsen or Danté. The collection is edited by Mabel Loomis Todd and T. W. Higginson, with a preface by the latter, in which he gives us many interesting points about Emily Dickinson's strange life passed in morbid loneliness. He likens her peculiar, untainted originality to the genius of William Blake. There is much similarity in spirit. Both were abortive geniuses; both were, in a certain way, monsters in the poetic world, but often touch deeper chords then greater than they have sounded.

121 "News and Notes." *Literary World* 22 (February 14, 1891), 62. The following sentence ends a brief paragraph listing books published by Roberts Brothers on February 10th: "They announce a new edition of the poems of Emily Dickinson; the price has been reduced to $1.25, and the drab-and-white edition will be discontinued."

122 "Current Literary Topics." *New York Evening Telegram*, February 20, 1891, p. 2.

The poems of Miss Emily Dickinson, to which Colonel Thomas Wentworth Higginson was one of the first to call the attention of the reading world, are meeting with a large sale and have already gone into the fourth edition. Miss Dickinson was a poet of great originality and force and her untimely death meant a serious loss to American literature.

122A "Descriptive Price-List of New Books." *Book News* 9 (March 1891), 271. The following sentence accompanies routine bibliographical citation of *Poems*, 1890.

This volume of poems, posthumously published and written by an eccentric old maid, have attracted universal attention for their originality, force and spiritual quality.

123 "The Point of View." *Scribner's Magazine* 9 (March 1891), 395–96. *Scribner's* literary authority, and its reviewer's careful judiciousness of tone, combined to made this one of the most admired—and damaging—of Dickinson's early notices. Even the *Nation*, whose own poetry critic was Higginson, recommended it (see next entry).

"When a thought takes your breath away a lesson in grammar is an impertinence," remarks Mr. T. W. Higginson in his sympathetic introduction to the remarkable "Poems" of the late Miss Emily Dickinson, recently published. This is a happy if rhetorical way of restating the familiar contention that in all departments of art substance is more important than form. By this time anything that may be said *ex parte* on either side of this time-honored discussion is sure to seem a platitude. One thinks of Mill's felicitous tabling of the classics *vs.* the sciences question in education by the query: "Should a tailor make coats or trousers?" Or of the settlement, by a recent authority upon etiquette, of the great problem whether, passing each other in the street, the lady or the gentleman should bow first: "They should bow together," he decides. In irresponsible moments, however—that is to say in most moments—one is apt to have a preference due to the domination of his reflective powers by his temperament. And in the presence of these poems of Miss Dickinson I think a temperament of any sensitiveness must feel even an alternation of preferences—being inclined now to deem them, in virtue of their substance, superior to the ordinary restrictions of form, and now to lament the loss involved in a disregard of the advantages of form. Having one's breath taken away is a very agreeable sensation, but it is not the finest sensation of which we are susceptible; and instead of being grateful for it one is very apt, if he be a connoisseur in this kind of sensations, to suffer annoyance at the perversity which is implied in a poet who, though capable of taking one's breath away, nevertheless prefers to do so in arbitrary rather than in artistic fashion. Such a poet, one feels instinctively, should rise above wilfulness, whimsicality, the disposition to challenge and defy.

After all, what do we mean by "importance"? Would it not be fair to say that the term is a relative one to this extent, that as to the importance of any specific thing the contemporary judgment, and that of posterity, are almost sure to be at variance. And is it not true that from the nature of things the contemporary judgment lays most stress on substance, and that the "final" judgment is favorable to form? Substantially speaking, how many historic things of immense contemporary vogue seem insipid to us, whereas scarcely anything of very great formal merit has been allowed to perish. In other words, is there not an element of universality about perfection of form which significance of thought does not possess; or, at any rate, is not perfection more nearly attainable in form than it is in substance? And nothing is so preservative as perfection or any approach to it.

One thing is very certain—neglect of form involves the sacrifice of an element of positive attractiveness as well as offending positively by perverseness and eccentricity. Whether rhyme and rhythm, cadence, purity, flawlessness, melody are essential or not to poetry, the abandonment of the artistic quality which they imply is obviously a loss. "The first indispensable faculty of a singer is ability to sing," exclaims Mr. Swinburne with his usual peremptoriness in his essay on Collins. And all poetry—it may be conceded to him, in spite of the notorious overweighting of his own thought by his musical quality—has at least a lyric element, though, of course, it does not all demand the "lyric cry." Formlessness is the antithesis of art, and so far as poetry is formless it loses that immensely attractive interest which is purely aesthetic. It not merely offends by perversely ignoring the conventionally established though rationally evolved and soundly based rules of the game it purports to play, but in announcing thus, boldly, its independence of any aesthetic, any sensuous, interest, it puts a severe strain on the quality of its own substance—handicaps it in most dangerous fashion instead of giving it that aid and furtherance which the best substance is sure to need. If, as in Miss Dickinson's case, there be occasionally a subtle but essential order in what, superficially, seems chaotic, it may legitimately be maintained that to lay any stress on this is merely to argue against conventionality and not at all in favor of amorphousness. It is simply to assert the elasticity of orchestration and emphasize its range—to exalt the value of new forms over the old. And it is curious to note how prone are all apologists for formlessness, including Mr. Higginson in the present instance, and the admirers of Walt Whitman, *passim*, for example, to insist that what to the convention-steeped sense appears amorphous is in reality the very acme of form. Singularly enough, Mr. Higginson concludes his introduction to these poems by citing a sentence of Mr. Ruskin in favor of "thought" as opposed to "workmanship." Was there ever so striking an example as Mr. Ruskin of what "workmanship" has done even for the most *saugrenu* thought?

124 "Notes." *Nation* 52 (March 5, 1891), 200. A survey of the March issue of *Scribner's* concludes: "We observe also in 'The Point of View' some well-timed and well-weighed remarks on the 'remarkableness' of the literary form of Miss Emily Dickinson's lately discovered muse."

125 Caroline Healey Dall. "Three Books Concerning Women." *Springfield Republican*, March 7, 1891, p. 8. Dall writes for the *Republican* from Washington, D.C., dating this correspondence March 1891. The friend, whose recollection of Dickinson she quotes, has not been identified.

I have been desiring for some time to draw the attention of your readers to three books which especially concern women, but their concerns seem to fill every vacant corner of Washington life this winter, and the time has not come. These books are "Anne Bradstreet and Her Time," "The Poems of Emily Dickinson" and the "Dreams" of Olive Schreiner. . . .

A year or two ago the whole critical world was startled by the publication of the journal of Marie Bashkirtseff and its suggestions. Quite as remarkable a revelation is to be found in the poems of Emily Dickinson. The record is incomplete. We have need to know her personal history. It is impossible not to read between the lines, but we want help to be sure we read accurately. Face to face with life and love, but above all with death and disappointment has this woman come. Nothing of human experience has she scorned, nothing evaded, and so critically has she tested what she has endured that few people will understand what they find in her alembic. Every line challenges much thinking, and many times must this little volume be read ere it can be appreciated. In her own words: —

What then? Why nothing.
Only, your inference therefrom.

It is not so much William Blake as Emerson that she resembled—only nothing in Emerson's experience led him to deal with her subjects. And by "subjects," I do not mean the titles somebody has given to her verses; but what was actually at the root of the impulse which caused them to be written. Frequently in her selection of grim and repulsive images she reminds one of Browning. Think of the experience that went behind lines like these: —

How many times these low feet staggered,
Only the soldered mouth can tell.

*   *   *   *   *

I like a look of agony,
Because I know its true.

And what wonderful power in this: —

The spirit turns away,
Just laying off for evidence
An overcoat of clay!

It is not as poems that these things will be judged but as personal revelations. And what this woman suffered and recorded it becomes other women to understand. I am strongly impressed with the idea that a far finer volume will be compiled some day of this author's poems. Since it was printed I have seen some lovely things in newspaper columns. I supposed they belonged to the volume, but searching I do not find them. "I think," writes one of her friends to me, "that for many years no one but her brother, sister and the maid ever saw her. No one knew her 'well' or at all of late, save by hearsay. Even her old friends were denied. She often sent me word she would see me, because her sister was fond of me, but when the time came and I was there she would send me in a note or a glass of wine or a bit of cake, or a tiny bouquet tied up with a ribbon and her 'love,'— but that was all." The women who have this book in their hands have a good deal to think of.

126   Andrew Lang. "Some American Poets." *Illustrated London News* 98 (March 7, 1891), 307. The *News* was published simultaneously in New York during this period.

I read somewhere, lately, that the Americans possess, at present, more minor poets, and better minor poets, than we can boast in England. The phrase "minor poet" is disliked by minstrels, and here let it be taken to denote merely poets who have not yet a recognised national fame, like Lord Tennyson with us and Mr. Whittier in America. Whether, in the larger and less recognised class, we have not at least as many poets to show as the States is a question of statistics. But it is very probable that the Western singers, whether better than ours or not, are, at all events, different from ours, and therefore, so far, interesting.

The works of four new Transatlantic poets lie beside me. *Place aux dames.* Let us take, first, "Poems" by the late Miss Emily Dickinson. This is certainly a very curious little book. It has already reached its fourth edition, partly, no doubt, because Mr. Howells praised it very highly. I cannot go nearly so far as Mr. Howells, because, if poetry is to exist at all, it really must have form and grammar, and must rhyme when it professes to rhyme. The wisdom of the ages and the nature of man insist on so much. We may be told that Democracy does not care, any more than the Emperor did, for grammar. But even if Democracy overleaps itself and lands in savagery again, I believe that our savage successors will, though unconsciously, make their poems grammatical. Savages do not use bad grammar in their own conversation or in their artless compositions. That is a fault of defective civilizations. Miss Dickinson, who died lately at the age of fifty-six, was a recluse, dwelling in Amherst, a town of Massachusetts. She did not write for publication. Her friends have produced her work. Sometimes it is as bad as this—

> Angels' breathless ballot
> Lingers to record thee;
> Imps in eager caucus
> Raffle for my soul.

This, of course, is mere nonsense. What is a "breathless ballot"? How can a ballot record anything, and how can it "linger" in recording, especially if it is in such a hurry as to be breathless? Indeed, one turns over Miss Dickinson's book with a puzzled feeling that there was poetry in her sub-consciousness, but that it never became explicit. One might as well seek for an air in the notes of a bird as for articulate and sustained poetry here. One piece begins—

> This is the land the sunset washes.
> These are the banks of the Yellow Sea.

And here is rhythm and the large sense of evening air—

> Where it rose, or whither it rushes,
> These are the Western mystery.

Night after night her purple traffic
Strews the landing with opal bales;
Merchantmen poise upon horizons,
Dip and vanish with fairy sails.

The second verse is not very easy to construe, but there was poetry in the writer. This, again, has the true lyrical note—

I never saw a moor,
I never saw the sea,
Yet know I how the heather looks,
And what a wave must be.

There is not much else that can be quoted without bringing in the fantastic, irresponsible note of a poet who was her own audience, and had constructed her own individual "Ars Poetica." The words of Mr. Aldrich in "The Sister's Tragedy" (Macmillan) might have been written about Miss Dickinson—

A twilight poet groping quite alone,
Belated in a sphere where every nest
Is emptied of its music and its wings.

Mr. Aldrich's new poem, of course, cannot be criticised in this brief space. His "Sister's Tragedy" is beautiful and accomplished work, a true tragedy tranquilly told, in a happy use of the heroic couplet. The brief poem to the Laureate is admirable, a charming compliment. That other compliment of imitation, wherein, to my mind, Mr. Aldrich was once over-lavish, is not paid by him to the Laureate in this pleasant volume. He speaks with his own voice; and speaks best, perhaps, when gravest. This is grave, in its way—

A PETITION.

To spring belongs the violet, and the blown
Spice of the roses let the summer own.
Grant me this favour, Muse, all else withhold—
That I may not write verse when I am old.
And yet I pray you, Muse, delay the time;
Be not too ready to deny me rhyme;
And when the hour strikes, as it must, dear Muse,
I beg you very gently break the news.

This is as pretty as if Paulus Silentiarius had written it—Paulus, that pleasing *décadent* of thirteen centuries ago. I am happy in having seen "A Petition" well done into Greek elegiacs. Mr. Aldrich's book also contains a play, in prose, on the French occupation of Spain. But here we only deal with verse, and almost everyone who cares for modern verse will take pleasure in that of Mr. Aldrich.

127   K. W. M. "Some Recent Verse." *Christian At Work* 49 (March 12, 1891), 365.

The dainty volume which contains the verses of Emily Dickinson, is one of the books dated 1891 which will be remembered by readers of contemporary poetry. The preface, by T. W. Higginson, who, with Mabel Loomis Todd, edits the collection, is an admirable introduction. As he well says, "the main quality of these poems is that of extraordinary grasp and insight, uttered with an uneven vigor sometimes exasperating, seemingly wayward, but really unsought and inevitable."

The poems are certainly the expression of an unusually interesting personality. Such lines as:

> Much madness is divinest sense
> To a discerning eye;

> *   *   *   *   *

> And that pale sustenance,
> Despair!

Are flashes of illumined thought. Some of the poems suggest Browning, while others in appreciation of value and smoothly flowing lines are not unlike Wordsworth.

The entire book is tantalizing in its glimpses of extreme beauty and its grave defects. Yet the reader recognizes through all the poems a notably high standard.

128 "Literary Chat." *New York Tribune*, March 15, 1891, p. 14. The *Scribner's* review is no. 123.

There is a wholesome comment in "Scribner" this month on the so-called poems of Emily Dickinson—a protest against their lack of form which is refreshing even though it might well have been stronger. For it is hard to see why there should be any "contention that in all departments of art substance is more important than form." One is no more important than the other; one without the other is makeshift and an imperfection. There is such a thing as poetic thought, doubtless; but when the poetic thinker is incapable of clothing the bones of his thought with the beauty of poetic form he should not consider himself a poet, but should give himself to poetic prose, which is good in its way. It is a pity that Colonel Higginson as a critic should allow himself to say so foolish a thing as "When a thought takes your breath away a lesson in grammar is an impertinence." The reader may forego an "ordered elegance" in his poet; but he asks at least that the breath-taking thoughts shall not be disfigured by rags of grammar, tatters of rhyme and hobbling measures.

What, by the way, does "Fourth Edition" mean on the title page of Miss Dickinson's poems? Four thousand?—or four hundred?—or four times two hundred and fifty? Editions are vague things nowadays.

129 *St. Paul* [Minn.] *Pioneer Press*, March 18, 1891, p. 4.

The poetess Emily Dickinson, the latest addition to the "startling school," appears to be open to the criticism that one side of her Pegasus is on stilts and the other side is lame. There is a good deal of jolt in her meter that does not please all her critics. Lines cut into irregular lengths and connected by a certain amount of jingle are not necessarily poetry.

130 Roberts Brothers' advertisement for 1890 *Poems*, "Sixth edition." *Publishers' Weekly* 39 (March 21, 1891), 412. Routine publication information is accompanied by the following phrase from an anonymous review in the *Boston Herald* (no. 59). No source is given for the quotation. The entire sentence from which these words were taken appears in a similar ad six weeks later (no. 160).

"Such a writer is a literary force."

131 Unlocated clipping placed, in Todd's scrapbook, among reviews published early in April 1891.

The little volume of Poems by the late Emily Dickinson is still the talk of the day among lovers of poetry. The book is now in its fourth edition. Colonel Higginson in his preface tells us something of the personality of the author of these very original verses some of which are almost unique in the language. Miss Dickinson was a recluse by temperament and habit, literally spending years without setting her foot beyond the doorstep, and many more years during which her walks were strictly limited to her father's grounds. She habitually concealed her mind, like her person, from all but a few friends. "For myself," says Mr. Higginson, "although I had corresponded with her for many years, I saw her but twice face to face, and brought away the impression of something as unique and remote as Undine, or Mignon or Thekla." I have not space to record any of these "flashes of wholly original and profound insight into nature and life," verses which will seem to the reader "like poetry torn up by the roots, with rain and dew and earth still clinging to them," but to those who enjoy strong, weird, original verses, containing thoughts that often "take one's breath away," as Mr. Higginson says, this little collection will prove to be a delightful discovery, notwithstanding the ridicule cast upon it in some quarters.

132 *Current Literature* 6 (April 1891), 498–99. An identical article, largely a reprinting of Higginson's preface (no. 10), appeared in an unlocated issue of the *St. Louis Book News.*

The posthumous volume of poems by Emily Dickinson has made her the talk of the town in Boston, and four editions have been called for in six weeks. Thomas Wentworth Higginson says of her in the preface to her poems: "The verses of Emily Dickinson belong emphatically to what Emerson long since called the 'poetry of the portfolio' something produced absolutely without the thought of publication, and solely by way of expression of the writer's own mind. A recluse by temperament and habit, literally spending years without setting her foot beyond the doorstep, Miss Dickinson habitually concealed her mind from all but a very few friends; and it was with great difficulty that she was persuaded to print, during her lifetime, three or four poems. Yet she wrote verses in great abundance; and though curiously indifferent to all conventional rules, had yet a rigorous literary standard of her own, and often altered a word many times to suit an ear which had its own tenacious fastidiousness. Miss Dickinson was born in Amherst, Mass., Dec. 10, 1830, and died there May 15, 1886. Her father, Hon. Edward Dickinson, was the leading lawyer of Amherst, and was treasurer of the well-known college there situated. It was his custom once a year to hold a large reception at his house, attended by all the families connected with the institution and by the leading people of the town. On these occasions his daughter Emily emerged from her wonted retirement and did her part as gracious hostess; nor would any one have known from her manner, I have been told, that this was not a daily occurrence. The annual occasion once past, she withdrew again into her seclusion, and except for a very few friends was as invisible to the world as if she had dwelt in a nunnery. For myself, although I had corresponded with her for many years, I saw her but twice face to face, and brought away the impression of something as unique and remote as Undine or Mignon or Thekla. This selection from her poems is published to meet the desire of her personal friends, and especially of her surviving sister. It is believed that the thoughtful reader will find in these pages a quality more suggestive of the poetry of William Blake than of anything to be elsewhere found—flashes of wholly original and profound insight into nature and life; words and phrases exhibiting an extraordinary vividness of descriptive and imaginative power, yet often set in a seemingly whimsical or even rugged frame. In many cases these verses will seem to the reader like poetry torn up by the roots, with rain and dew and earth still clinging to them, giving a freshness and a fragrance not otherwise to be conveyed. Sometimes we catch glimpses of a lyric strain, sustained perhaps but for a line or two at a time, and making the reader regret its sudden cessation. But the main quality of these poems is that of extraordinary grasp and insight, uttered with an uneven vigor sometimes exasperating, seemingly wayward, but really unsought and inevitable. After all, when a thought takes one's breath away, a lesson on grammar seems an impertinence. As Ruskin wrote in his earlier and better days, 'No weight nor mass nor beauty of execution can outweigh one grain or fragment of thought.'"

133 "A Talk Before the Woman's Club." *Springfield Republican*, April 2, 1891. Unverified. Reprinted: *Amherst Record*, April 8, 1891, p. 8. For Todd's diary entries regarding this talk, see *AB*, pp. 123–24. In Boston some days earlier (March 22), Higginson had given a reading from Dickinson's letters to some twenty of his friends, among them Howells and William Roscoe Thayer (see *AB*, pp. 122–23).

Mrs. Mabel Loomis Todd gave a very interesting talk on the late Emily Dickinson of Amherst, before the woman's club at Mrs. Holland's yesterday afternoon. A large number of the club members with a few invited guests completely filled the parlors, listened for an hour to character sketching, anecdotes and bits of verse illustrating the individuality of Miss Dickinson. Mrs. Todd's acquaintance with the poet began some years before her death, and continued by letters and notes, it developed into a strong attachment on both sides. Many of the false reports circulated in regard to Miss Dickinson's seclusion were pronounced false. Mrs. Todd read some yet unpublished poems that proved that the impression produced by the first volume will be confirmed by the second, which is to appear next autumn, probably. Specimens of Miss Dickinson's handwriting were shown, and the speaker said that in arranging the poet's manuscript after her death very little difficulty was found in classifying the different periods by the handwriting, so marked was the change from time to time. From 1000 to 1200 poems were found among Miss Dickinson's effects after her death. Mrs. Todd is a very pleasant speaker, and the grace and beauty of her expression added much to the interesting material of her talk.

134 "A Talk Before the Woman's Club." *Amherst Record*, April 8, 1891, p. 8. A reprinting; see preceding entry.

135 Mary D. Cutting. "Literature." *Christian Inquirer* 4 (April 9, 1891). Unlocated.

In the January *Forum* of the current year is a most interesting and suggestive article by Prof. Edmund Gosse, entitled, "Is Verse in Danger?" Prof. Gosse having declared us to be passing through a period obviously unfavorable to the development of poetry, considers, with his usual clear purpose, incisive manner, and with occasional gleams of fantastic humor the question, "Will anyone who has anything of importance to communicate be likely in the future to express it through the medium of metrical language?" Is the "imperial tyranny" of poetry to give way to the "democracy of prose?" Concluding or admitting that poetry is eternal in its essence and therefore certain to reassert its sway, Prof. Gosse proceeds to make some predictions concerning the poetry of the future. One of the changes that he indicates is, that, "less effort is likely to be made in the immediate future to give pleasure by the manner of poetry, and more skill will be expended on the subject matter." This prophecy is emphasized by a preceding statement that, "a care for form and a considerable skill in the technical art of verse have been acquired by writers of a lower order and that this sort of perfection (the refinement of exterior mechanism) is no longer the hall-mark of a great master."

The works of both the Brownings confirm this statement and justify the prediction. Those of Mrs. Browning in a lesser degree, but as certainly as those of her husband, whose recognized indifference to form (made the subject of hostile criticism by his foes), finds a righteous defense among his friends. Browning devotees hold that to evolve a thought is a greater thing than to perfect a form, and that the revelation of soul phenomena is infinitely more than beauty of construction. If, then, in the immediate future more attention is to be given to the subject matter of poetry and less to the manner, the true claim to a place among the poets will be the power to stimulate our more serious thinking and to make manifest the more subtle and complex sensations of our human nature.

On such a basis we think such high place would be accorded to Emily Dickinson, whose poems, introduced with a most discriminating preface by Thomas Wentworth Higginson, are now given to the public. These poems, mostly posthumous (only three or four having been published before her death), disclose a singular insight into human nature. Written by a woman whose life was almost nun-like in its seclusion they discover a wonderful apprehension of the impulses, passions and also outward circumstances that control human life. They are the poems of a woman, in that their inspiration is that of subtle feeling rather than philosophic thought, but they startle and surprise by their subtlety and inward grasp. The charge that will be brought against them is their lack of rhyme; their want of finished form. But, as Mr. Higginson says in his preface, "when a thought takes one's breath away a lesson on grammar seems an impertinence;" and while they do fail in form and finish they are not wanting in metrical movement. That is usually original and sustained, so that, borne along by the poetic thought and musical movement, the absence of rhymes is at times almost lost sight of, as, for example, in the following:

The heart asks pleasure first,
And then, excuse from pain;
And then, those little anodynes
That deaden suffering;

And then, to go to sleep;
And then, if it should be
The will of its Inquisitor,
The liberty to die.

We meet again a similar disregard for rhyme with a like observance of rhythmic measure in "The Mystery of Pain:"

> Pain has an element of blank;
> It cannot recollect
> When it began, or if there were
> A day when it was not.
>
> It has no future but itself,
> Its infinite realms contain
> Its past, enlightened to perceive
> New periods of pain.

The poems do not always violate poetical technique, and occasionally there appears a strain of musical rhythm and flow, suggesting the conclusion that its common absence is from choice or perhaps the necessity to sing after unconventional methods.

The poems have been grouped into four classes—Life, Love, Nature, Time and Eternity. In those under Nature may be found some beautiful touches, betraying a living sympathy with animate and inanimate life, joined to a power of exquisite delineation. What delicate discrimination in the following on the bee:

> The pedigree of honey
> Does not concern the bee;
> A clover, any time, to him
> Is aristocracy.

And what a fine laying on of color in the lines entitled "The Sea of Sunset:"

> This is the land the sunset washes
>   These are the banks of the Yellow Sea;
> When it rose, or whither it rushes,
>   These are the western mystery!
>
> Night after night her purple traffic
>   Strews the landing with opal bales;
> Merchantmen poise upon horizons,
>   Dip, and vanish with fairy sails.

Emily Dickinson's readers and admirers will be among those who ask of poetry high seriousness and the delight of a reflex companionship. She is not didactic; she will not teach, but she will stimulate. She is not instructive; she will not inform, but she will suggest. She is not lyric; she will not charm the fancy by the cadence of her verse, but she will stir the heart by its melodic note. Nor will she act as comforter; she will not offer consolation, but she will give a comprehending sympathy.

> The bustle in a house
> The morning after death
> Is solemnest of industries
> Enacted upon earth—
>
> The sweeping up the heart,
> And putting love away
> We shall not want to use again
> Until eternity.

136 "Literature—Notes." *Jewish Messenger* 69 (April 10, 1891), 5.

Emily Dickinson's verses, written for the portfolio rather than the public, are more and more quoted. Their charm consists as much in brevity as in originality.

137 G[ertrude] E[uphemia] Meredith. "The Poems of Emily Dickinson." *Literary World* 22 (April 11, 1891), 128. For other expressions in verse, see index *s.v.* Poems in tribute.

> I hold her volume in my hand,
> With half my mind I snatch its words:
> (The other half enough affords
> For listening and answer bland).
>
> She was a woman, too, it seems,
> Whom life not wholly satisfied;
> She loved: more heartily, she died;
> To die's the keener in her dreams.
>
> And I, who flagged, my zeal renew:
> The trivial's phantom-terrors flee
> This witness of reality.
> I can live more since death's so true.

138 Charles E. L. Wingate. "Boston Letter." *Critic*, n.s. 15 (April 18, 1891), 212. For Wingate's impressions of the Todd-Higginson talk, see no. 161.

There is a society in Boston composed of the alumnae of educational institutions and called the College Club. At a coming meeting an interesting feature will be the reading of several unpublished poems by the late Emily Dickinson, the Amherst recluse whose volume of rugged, thoughtful verse, edited by her friends, Mrs. Mabel Loomis Todd and Col. T. W. Higginson, has just passed into its fifth edition. Mrs. Todd and Col. Higginson are to read the new poems before the Club. They are said to be of the same sort as those already published—entirely free from conventionalities, that is to say, and yet imbued with poetic fervor—literary flowers torn up by the roots, to use Col. Higginson's simile in the preface to her book, fresh and fragrant with the rain and dew and earth. The fifteenth of May will mark the fifth anniversary of Miss Dickinson's death, so that a reading near that date will be appropriate.

139 "A College Club Chat," ca. April 18, 1891. Unlocated newspaper clipping. The Todd-Higginson talk before the Boston College Alumnae Club took place during the afternoon of May 2, before an audience of about two hundred; see no. 153 and *AB*, pp. 126–28.

A spring pleasure which is awaiting the club will be the reading of unpublished verses of the poet, Miss Emily Dickinson, who was unknown during her retiring lifetime, but whose genius was recognized immediately in the book of poems published after her death. Mrs. Mabel Loomis Todd and Col. T. W. Higginson will read the unpublished verses and will give a clever glimpse of that mind which away from society and the influences of the busy world had a wonderful conception of the meaning of passion and of the depths of human nature. Although the rhythm and the form of the poetry are not bound to the laws of poetical expression, the thoughts are so rarely beautiful that there is no doubt that their presentation before the college graduates and their friends will be appreciated.

140   "Miss Dickinson's Poems." *San Jose* [Calif.] *Mercury*, April 19, 1891, p. 7.
Indian pipes, rather than lilies, decorated the cover of *Poems* 1890.

"Poems," by Emily Dickinson, is the title of a handsome duodecimo volume of 152 pages published by Roberts Brothers of Boston. The typographical appearance of the book is excellent, and the cloth covers, illuminated by a dainty group of lilies of the valley stamped in gold, is one of the most attractive bits of work of this kind that has appeared in a long time. Miss Dickinson's poems have been edited by Mabel Loomis Todd and T. W. Higginson, and are prefaced with a short introduction written by Mr. Higginson in which a brief account is given of the life of the authoress. From this we learn that she was the daughter of the Hon. Edward Dickinson of Amherst, Massachusetts, that she was born in 1830, and after having lived the life of a recluse, died in 1886. Mr. Higginson says that her verses belong to what Emerson called the "poetry of the portfolio;" something produced absolutely without the thought of publication and solely by way of expression of the writer's mind. He is of the opinion, too, that in them "the thoughtful reader will find a quality more suggestive of the poetry of William Blake than of anything to be elsewhere found; flashes of wholly original and profound insight into nature and life; words and phrases exhibiting an extraordinary vividness of descriptive and imaginative power, yet often set in a seemingly whimsical or even rugged frame." After this elaborate flourish of trumpets, the reader on turning to the poems will be disappointed. The New England clique have a tendency to overpraise one another, and Miss Dickinson is an extremely New England poetess indeed. She has ideas which may be original but are certainly not novel, and she expresses them in a form of verse which may be novel but is certainly not poetical. The poems are all short and most of them not above ten or fifteen lines long. They read like the first random notes of a poem rather than of the poem itself, and appear to be fleeting ideas jotted down in a hurry with the intention of elaborating them later on. We are told, however, that the author "had a rigorous literary standard of her own and often altered a word many times to suit an ear which had its own tenacious fastidiousness." The reader can form an estimate of the style and mode of sentiment of Miss Dickinson from this specimen of her work, which in length, meter and meaning is a fair example of the whole:

NO TIME.

I had no time to hate because
   The grave would hinder me,
And life was not so ample, I
   Could finish enmity.

Nor had I time to love; but since
   Some industry must be,
The little toil of love I thought
   Was large enough for me.

141   "Literary Notes." *America* 6 (April 23, 1891), 110.

Emily Dickinson's remarkable poems, which are at once beautiful and uncouth, have reached a fifth edition.

142 "Marie Bashkirtseff." *Boston Transcript,* April 25, 1891, p. 9. On Bashkirtseff and Stepniak, see the index. It is likely that Higginson read "I had
been hungry, all the Years," a poem he and Mrs. Todd included among
those published in the *Second Series* (1891).

Mr. Stepniak's lecture on Marie Bashkirtseff was prefaced by Mr. T. W. Higginson in an interesting fashion Friday. He spoke of the extraordinary manner in
which fame came to Marie Bashkirtseff, and drew a comparison between the way
it came to her and has come to Emily Dickinson after death. Colonel Higginson
read an unpublished poem of Miss Dickinson on the hunger for fame and the
possible satisfaction of the hunger coming too late.
    Mr. Stepniak then spoke of the elements of success in Marie Bashkirtseff, pay-
ing a tribute to the Russian woman and the light into which the life of this wonderful girl brings Russian womanhood, although she is essentially French in her
ideas of life, and not Russian. . . .
    Colonel Higginson's introductory speeches at the Stepniak lectures have been
a happy hit.

143 "Notes About Women—Literature." *Woman's Tribune* 8 (April 25, 1891),
135. On this talk before the Springfield, Mass., Woman's Club, see
no. 133.

Over a thousand unpublished poems have been found among the papers of
the late Emily Dickinson of Amherst, Mass.; Mrs. Mabel Loomis Todd recently
made this lamented poet the subject of an interesting address before the Woman's
Club, of Springfield.

144 "Among May Magazines." *Albany Journal,* April 30, 1891, p. 5. This announcement, published widely in newspapers across the country (see
nos. 146, 149, 152), goes on to describe other features of the latest *St.
Nicholas,* a popular children's magazine. The poem is "Will there really
be a morning?"

"St. Nicholas" presents a very tempting table of contents, beginning with an
imaginative poem, "Morning," by the late Emily Dickinson.

145 [Samuel J. Barrows.] "Emily Dickinson's Poems." *Christian Register* 70
(April 30, 1891), 274. This defense of Dickinson's religious propriety was
provoked by the *Register's* publication of "God is a distant—stately
Lover." The poem occasioned indignant letters to the journal's editor,
Barrows, from at least three readers; see *AB,* pp. 124–25. Todd mentioned this episode forty years later in a note appended to the reprinting
of her introduction to the first edition of Dickinson's letters in *Letters
of Emily Dickinson, New and Enlarged Edition,* ed. Mabel Loomis
Todd (N.Y.: Harper, 1931), p. xxx. Her note begins: "Incredible as it now
seems, I had to wage a constant battle throughout all those early years
against charges of [Dickinson's] irreverence." A penciled note following
this clipping in Todd's scrapbook reads, "Barrows."

In our issue of December 18, 1890, we published a review of "Miss Dickinson's
Poems" by Mr. Chadwick. These poems were issued after her death, and edited
by two of her friends, Mabel Loomis Todd and Col. T. W. Higginson. It may be

said without hesitation that this is one of the freshest, most original and suggestive volumes of poetry that has been published in recent years. Miss Dickinson was a recluse. She communed very little with society, but much with nature and with her own mind. She was not made to play a part in the world's great orchestra. She was more like an Aeolian harp through which the wind swept over a delicately attuned nature, sometimes awaking the minor, sometimes the major chord, and now and then striking a dissonant note which only seemed to give more richness and piquancy to the harmony. Her poetry was never made of sustained notes or flowing strains. It was made of little gusts of song, snatches of melody, broken chords, and arpeggios. Her forms of expression were unconventional, not savoring of the auctioneer's catalogue, like those of Walt Whitman, who shovels out of the mine the raw material for poetry, and refuses to smelt, mould, and polish it, but more, as Mr. Higginson reminds us, like the poetry of William Blake than of any to be elsewhere found. "Flashes of wholly original and profound insight into nature and life, words and phrases exhibiting an extraordinary vividness of descriptive and imaginative power, yet often set in a seemingly whimsical or even rugged frame. . . . The main quality of these poems is that of extraordinary grasp and insight, uttered with an uneven vigor, sometimes exasperating, seemingly wayward, but really unsought and inevitable."

A few weeks since we received from Miss Todd a poem by Miss Dickinson not included in the volume, and published it in the *Christian Register*. Those who had read Mr. Chadwick's interesting analysis of the poems were undoubtedly much interested by the additional specimen of her singularly individual style and habit of thought. Others found the poem not easily explicable, and there were a few upon whose ear its strange accents jarred as if flippant and irreverent.

In music there are certain chords whose effect on the ear depends wholly on the way in which they are approached. If approached in one way, they are singularly hard and unmusical; approached in another, they take their place in the flow of melody, and we are conscious of no discord. So the effect upon the ear and the mind of one of Miss Dickinson's poems depends very much upon the way in which it is approached. Those who had read but a score of the fifty "Poems" in the charming little volume bearing this title were already "prepared," as a musician would say, for the discord, and found its resolution in the more finished, restful cadence of some other of her verses. It was but another example of Emerson's "Each and All." To see the beauty of the shell, we must see it on the seashore when we can hear the ocean's surge. To get the message of the flower, we must seek it in its native haunts. Some of Miss Dickinson's poems, but only a few, may be taken out of their setting. Each poem is a fragment; to get the whole impression of this rare, singular life, we must read them together.

Still another thing must be borne in mind. Her verses, as Col. Higginson says, "belong emphatically to what Emerson long since called 'the Poetry of the Portfolio,'—something produced absolutely without the thought of publication, and solely by way of expression of the writer's own mind. Such verses must inevitably forfeit whatever advantage lies in the discipline of public criticism and the enforced conformity to accepted ways. On the other hand, it may often gain something through the habit of freedom and the unconventional utterance of daring thoughts." The words "For the *Christian Register*" over the lines we published were misleading. We are accustomed thus to patent original and unpublished poems in our columns; but the truth was that these verses were not written directly for the *Register*, or any other paper. They were simply the musings of a soul insulated in its own privacy. There is no advertisement of self here, no thought of notoriety, no singing for gold or gain. Such poems cannot be tried by the rules of the school or any conventional canons. Yet they may remind us that the laws of literature and poetic art are not merely conventional and pedantic like those of the old Mastersingers which Wagner satirized in his opera. For daily companionship we may prefer ordinary people of familiar habit and average ability; but now and then what a refreshment to come into contact with a soul of original insight, of rare and marked individuality, with its own peculiar accent, who sees things in fresh relations to life, and who flashes with sudden and brilliant inspiration!

Some of the most exquisite of Miss Dickinson's poems are those which reveal her deep communion with nature. Here is one to the bee, which is as sweet and fragrant as the flower it sips. There is a whole summer in this poem:—

> Like trains of cars on tracks of plush
> I hear the level bee:
> A jar across the flowers goes,
> Their velvet masonry
>
> Withstands until the sweet assault
> Their chivalry consumes,
> While he, victorious, tilts away
> To vanquish other blooms.
>
> His feet are shod with gauze,
> His helmet is of gold,
> His breast a single onyx
> With chrysoprase inlaid.
>
> His labor is a chant,
> His idleness a tune;
> Oh for a bee's experience
> Of clovers and of noon!

Here is another,—

> The pedigree of honey
> Does not concern the bee;
> A clover, any time, to him
> Is aristocracy.

This tender poem shows who her companions were:—

> If I shouldn't be alive
> When the robins come,
> Give the one in red cravat
> A memorial crumb.
>
> If I couldn't thank you,
> Being just asleep,
> You will know I'm trying
> With my granite lip.

Here is a Sabbath-day musing:—

> Some keep the Sabbath going to church:
> I keep it staying at home,
> With a bobolink for a chorister,
> And an orchard for a dome.

> Some keep the Sabbath in surplice:
>   I just wear my wings;
> And, instead of tolling the bell for church,
>   Our little sexton sings.
>
> God preaches, — a noted clergyman, —
>   And the sermon is never long;
> So, instead of getting to heaven at last,
>   I'm going all along!

Would she have liked to commune with God in the presence of other human hearts, or did she write this because she seemed nearer to him when alone? Such privacy with God the soul must seek as Jesus sought it in the mountain. Yet nature is not the only cathedral; and the aspirations, struggles, strivings, defeats, and victories of man himself are what we need to contemplate in sympathetic and fraternal companionship if we would find God in man as we find him in nature. The recluse needs, too, to come sometimes into the busy world, and into "the *assembly* of the saints," as the man of the busy world needs to seek the recluse.

And yet it is clear that she did not wish her life to be lived wholly apart from the life of her kind. How human and how noble the aspiration in these lines! —

> If I can stop one heart from breaking,
>   I shall not live in vain;
> If I can ease one life the aching,
>   Or cool the pain,
> Or help one fainting robin
>   Unto his nest again,
> I shall not live in vain.

The following we have given before, but it is worth quoting again to show the certainty and perfect naturalness of her thought of God: —

> I never saw a moor,
>   I never saw the sea;
> Yet know I how the heather looks,
>   And what a wave must be.
>
> I never spoke with God,
>   Nor visited in heaven;
> Yet certain am I of the spot
>   As if the chart were given.

Here, too, she is looking out in imagination on a tremulous ocean: —

> Whether my bark went down at sea,
>   Whether she met with gales,
> Whether to isles enchanted
>   She bent her docile sails;
>
> By what mystic mooring
>   She is held to-day, —
> This is the errand of the eye
>   Out upon the bay.

There are some verses as enigmatical and mystical as anything in Browning or Emerson. We cannot parse or analyze them, but even these mists of song float in graceful wreaths. Such a soul saw God, nature, and man at first hand, and made its own interpretation, its own alphabet and character. She wrote her own hymn-book and her own ritual; but we should as soon think of charging Emerson with irreverence as of so charging her.

Her poems on death and eternity usher us into the deeper mysteries. Here is one,—a tender psalm of trust:—

Afraid? Of whom am I afraid?
  Not death; for who is he?
The porter of my father's lodge
  As much abaseth me.   [abasheth

Of life? 'Twere odd I fear a thing
  That comprehendeth me
In one or more existences
  At Deity's decree.

Of resurrection? Is the east
  Afraid to trust the morn
With her fastidious forehead?
  As soon impeach my crown!

Emily Dickinson's poems are something more than a dry herbarium of flowers which the literary botanist may study simply to classify and label. They are fresh, fragrant, living flowers, such as do not grow in our gardens or by the wayside, but such as may be found in sheltered nooks of life where the sun has shone and the birds sang.

146 "Literary Mention." *Philadelphia Call*, April 30, 1891, p. 4. Reprinted: *Bismarck* [N. Dak.] *Tribune*, May 3, 1891, p. 2. For similar announcements, some with only slightly different language, see nos. 144, 149, 152.

St. Nicholas for May presents a very tempting table of contents, beginning with an imaginative poem, "Morning," by the late Emily Dickinson, whose work has been so cordially praised by the critics.

147 "New Publications." *Art Amateur* 24 (May 1891), 157.

These poems are, in relation to poetry, what the drawings of Blake are to pictorial art. Violating every canon of the mechanism and rules, they are yet its very essence and spirit. Indeed, one wonders if ordinary finish and care would not have robbed them of some of their peculiar charm; for, without doubt, the entirely original fancies they embody are so eerie and evanescent that to polish them were to lose their native beauty. Like the early wood-cuts of the emblem writers, they deal with great subjects in a way that, grotesque and imperfect though it be, realizes the force of the truth they express. Some of the quaint designs of Allendorf, Cranach or Grün have a fascination wanting in the masterpieces of Italian art; for you feel they were very true and perfectly finished to the artist's own criticism, and expressed absolutely his peculiarly individual view of his subject. This little book has more fantasy and food for imagination than any volume of recent years; and whether as a study of the frank utterances of an untrained poet, or for the pleasure derived from unexpected ways of saying familiar truths, it is piquant and exquisite in its flavor to those satiated with the polished monotony of much of the verse of today.

148 Arlo Bates. "Literary Topics in Boston." *Book Buyer,* n.s. 8 (May 1891),
153. Reprinted: *Christian Inquirer,* June 4, 1891. Bates's claim that Dickinson read her poems to her friends has not elsewhere been corrobo-
rated. For Eugene Field's comment on the poet, see no. 154.

Another volume of the poems of Emily Dickinson is in preparation, and her
editors, by further search among the voluminous papers which she left, have
found material which they consider better than anything to which they had access in compiling the first volume, now in its sixth edition. Eugene Field is not
quite accurate in his statement that none of Miss Dickinson's friends knew that
she wrote verse. The secret was an open one to all her friends, and to the more
intimate of them she read more or less of her writings. Mrs. Jackson, "H. H.," was
constantly urging her to publish a volume during her lifetime. It is a curious and
unanswerable question how much difference there would have been in the success of the book had it been put forward as the work of a living author. Doubtless there would at least have been more criticism on the lack of technique. The
impossibility of altering the author's style removed from the shoulders of the
critics all responsibility in the line of discipline, and left them free to praise.

149 "'St. Nicholas' For the Summer." *Century* 42 (May 1891), among advertising pages. This blurb for the children's magazine, *St. Nicholas* (a publication of the Century Company), constitutes the *Century's* only notice of Dickinson. It was widely reprinted, with the language slightly
changed—see nos. 144, 146, 152. The opening poem is "Will there really
be a morning?"

During the coming summer *St. Nicholas* will continue to march gracefully in
advance of the procession—a kind of May Queen. The number for the month of
flowers opens with a poem by the late Emily Dickinson, whose poems have recently attracted the attention of critics and have been ranked as works of genuine inspiration.

150 "Some Books of Verse." *Overland Monthly* 17, ser. 2 (May 1891), 549–50.
All but the final paragraph draws heavily on Higginson's "Preface"
(no. 10).

Probably no book of the year has created a more profound impression than the
Poems of Emily Dickinson. These as presented are edited by her friends after the
author's death, and contain the literary life record of a recluse who wrote entirely
for her own satisfaction, and without expectation of publication. During her lifetime, with two or three exceptions, she never allowed her poems to go into print,
and as a result never acquired the discipline of criticism, the conventionalizing
quality that comes from consideration of one's work in type. What has attracted
attention is the daring fancy, the wonderful insight, the felicitous characterization, which mark these bits of verse. All are short, and many are mere fragments.
The fact that the author herself does not present them to the public disarms the
criticism that otherwise would object to them as obscure. They are not only enigmatical, but often entirely ungrammatical in construction. But no one can read
them without admiration for their peculiar imaginative strength, and bewilderment at this unexpected originality. There is nothing quite like them in the
language except perhaps the poetry of William Blake, though there is a terseness
and sonorousness about them that is suggestive of Emerson. Unconsciously, in

many of them, Miss Dickinson has fallen into the use of the meters and rhythms which have come down to us in Mother Goose, — the world meters and rhythms which have in them the universal melody that in itself is enduring. The following quotations will serve to illustrate these things better than words.

Presentiment is that long shadow on the lawn,
Indicative that suns go down;
The notice to the startled grass
That darkness is about to pass.

Because I could not stop for Death,
He kindly stopped for me;
The carriage held but just ourselves
And Immortality.

We slowly drove, he knew no haste,
And I had put away
My labor, and my leisure, too,
For his civility.

We passed the school were children played,
Their lessons scarcely done;
We passed the fields of gazing grain,
We passed the setting sun.

We paused before a house that seemed
A swelling of the ground;
The roof was scarcely visible,
The cornice but a mound.

Since then 'tis centuries; but each
Feels shorter than the day
I first surmised the horses' heads   [Were toward
Were turned toward eternity.

I had no time to hate, because
The grave would hinder me,
And life was not so ample I
Could finish enmity.

Nor had I time to love; but since
Some industry must be,
The little toil of love, I thought
Was large enough for me.

The bustle in a house
The morning after death
Is solemnest of industries
Enacted upon earth, —

The sweeping of the heart,   [sweeping up
And putting love away

We shall not want to use again
Until eternity.

These quaint and striking instances might be repeated as many times as there are poems in the book. Not all, however, are satisfactory. Many are merely grotesque or fantastic, and some are absolutely unintelligible in their obscurity. One lays down the book with a feeling of perplexity that is akin to exasperation, that being so good they should not be better. They have true poetic quality in them without doubt, but as a whole are too crude and fragmentary to admit of unqualified endorsement.

151 C. M. Smith. "Emily Dickinson." *Dartmouth Literary Monthly* 5 (May 1891), 339–42. This sympathetic assessment marks an extreme in moralistic interpretation of the poems.

A great disappointment and grief changed the life of Emily Dickinson from one of leadership in society in the New England town where she lived to one of close seclusion. She lived years without leaving the house, and never went beyond her father's grounds from young womanhood to the end of her life. She was born in 1830, and died in 1886. Much of her time was devoted to writing verses, which she left in great abundance. But she was as much a recluse in mind as in person, and allowed but few of these to be printed during her life. Recently a small volume of them has been published. The selections for the volume and its editing were cared for by no less a critic than Thomas Wentworth Higginson, who had some acquaintance with Miss Dickinson. In his preface to the volume he mentions this acquaintance thus: "For myself, although I had corresponded with her for many years, I saw her but twice face to face, and brought away the impression of something as unique and remote as Undine or Mignon or Thekla."

These verses seem to have been written for a pastime and to relieve the pent up feelings of the writer, and with no thought of publication. This tended to a freedom of thought and form that is not found in verses written with some one, as it were, looking over the shoulder. They partake of the familiar, disclosing, first-person spirit of the diary, that is so interesting because it throws down the high bars of the conventional. The only evidence of an idea of publication that is found in her verses is in the following, which opens the volume:

This is my letter to the world
    That never wrote to me;
The simple news that nature told
    With tender majesty.

Her message is committed
    To hands I cannot see;
For love of her, sweet countrymen,
    Judge tenderly of me!

But these may have been, and probably were, the result of a passing mood, and not written with any thought of the place which they here occupy.

"We do not demand rhyme in poetry, nor always metre; but rhythmical beauty is essential." This has been written in a criticism of Walt Whitman's verse, to which Miss Dickinson's may be compared in its utter indifference to all conventional rules. Rhyme is everywhere disregarded; the metre, though far more uniform, is often faulty, but in all the verses there is a rhythmical beauty which shows that the writer had standards of her own, and her work was not carelessly done without thought of perfection. It is said that she often altered a word many times before it suited a literary taste as fastidious as it was exactingly followed. It must be confessed that her selection of words does not always seem the best, and sometimes there is a seemingly puerility of expression. But the worst has been said of them, modest and unpretentious as they are in length, form, and treatment. Often there is a strength and vividness that is wonderful, and a breadth that seems impossible when one considers the life and experience of the writer. They show an imagination of the highest order, and remarkable insight. Who that has been most active in the world, and felt temptation most strongly and knows the constant struggle between good and evil in his breast, can portray it all with more vigor and exactness than she has in these lines?

Soul, wilt thou toss again?
By just such a hazard
Hundreds have lost, indeed,
But tens have won an all.

Angels' breathless ballot
Lingers to record thee;
Imps in eager caucus
Raffle for my soul!

The course of the weak pleasure-seeker, who is without aspiration or hope except to avoid the results of his folly, is swiftly marked, —

The heart asks pleasure first,
And then, excuse from pain;
And then, those little anodynes
That deaden suffering;

And then, to go to sleep;
And then, if it should be
The will of its Inquisitor,
The liberty to die.

The verses all show a faculty for compressing thoughts, and often great thoughts, into small compass: no words are wasted, especially in filling out a line. The line is left incomplete rather than insert a superfluous word. This compactness gives a movement that is rapid and pleasing. Poems depicting nature are among the best. The range of subjects is not so limited as might be expected, but the birds, bees, and butterflies that visited her were welcomed, and made much of in her songs. She was a great lover of flowers, and had many of them to share with her verses her attention, and they, of course, got into the verses. The grass, the shower, the wind are subjects for her faithful, nature-loving pen. But not all her themes were taken from these objects, common to her even in her inland seclusion. Look how she portrays the sea, which she had never beheld:

Glee! the great storm is over!
    Four have recovered the land;
Forty gone down together
    Into the boiling sand.

Ring! for the scant salvation!
    Toll! for the bonnie souls,
Neighbor and friend and bridegroom,
    Spinning upon the shoals.

How they will tell the shipwreck
    When winter shakes the door,
Till the children ask, "But the forty?
    Did they come back no more?"

Then a silence suffuses the story,
    And a softness the teller's eye,
The children no further question;
    And only the waves reply.

Where shall we look for a picture of shipwreck truer than this? And the sea is hard to paint with words, as it is with the brush.

The poems entitled "Time" and "Eternity" touch upon the largest themes. Life, with its aspirations and disappointments, its joys and sorrows, is looked squarely in the face. Here we get glimpses of the heart of the writer as she unconsciously reveals a bit of its sufferings. They are but glimpses, however, for like every sensitive heart, hers was loath to reveal itself. It is a hard thing, too, to make the heart understood. It has a little language of its own, and its nearest neighbor cannot understand it. How rare is the full, free communion of heart and heart! How keenly true are those old words that mount to the lips so often, "The heart knoweth his own bitterness: and a stranger doth not intermeddle with his joy." The untrammelled intercourse of heart with heart seems to be a high privilege reserved for the relations between man and his Maker, who alone knoweth all its thoughts and intents. The thought of death seems often to have been in the mind of this lonely woman, but it left no morbidness. The "secrets of that gloom whereto all go" were pondered again and again, and the hopes of the resurrection and eternity shed a brightness upon them.

We pass from the more stately lines on the vanity of earthly pride and honor—

Safe in their alabaster chambers,
    Untouched by morning and untouched by noon,
Sleep the meek members of the resurrection,—
    Rafter of satin and roof of stone.

Light laughs the breeze in her castle above them;   [castle of sunshine
    Babbles the bee in a stolid ear;
Pipe the sweet birds in ignorant cadence—
    Ah! what sagacity perished here!

Grand go the years in the crescent above them,
    Worlds scoop their arcs, and firmaments row;
Diadems drop, and Doges surrender,
    Soundless as dots on a disk of snow—

to these startlingly real lines that at one touch seem to set every heart-string to vibrating. Where shall we look for eight short lines that tell a greater story?

The bustle in a house,
The morning after death,
Is solemnest of industries
Enacted upon earth.—

The sweeping up the heart,
And putting love away
We shall not want to use again
Until eternity.

The volume of Miss Dickinson's verses is published especially to meet the desire of her friends. But others must find a charm and help in them. They are crude in form, and sometimes even ungrammatical, but when "a thought takes one's breath away," he will not scrutinize very closely its setting.

152 "St. Nicholas for May." *Chillicothe* [Ohio] *News*, May 1, 1891. Unlocated. A reprinting; see no. 146. In the Todd scrapbook, this clipping is accompanied by a handwritten note listing several newspapers "among many others" carrying a description of the May issue of *St. Nicholas*, a children's magazine. They include [all unlocated]: *Houston* [Texas] *Post*, May 3; *Dixon* [Ill.] *Telegraph*, May 7; *York* [Pa.] *Daily*, May 7; *Livonia* [N.Y.] *Gazette*, May 13.

153 "Reminiscences of Emily Dickinson." *Boston Evening Transcript*, May 2, 1891, p. 9. The Todd-Higginson talk was given this day before an audience of two hundred at the Boston College Club. The poet's brother traveled from Amherst to attend (*AB*, pp. 127–28). Some of Mrs. Todd's remarks recorded here prefigure those she would make in her edition of Dickinson's letters; see no. 419. The source of George Washington Cable's opinion is unknown. Since he and Mabel Todd were friends, his comment may derive from a personal conversation or unpublished letter. The "prelude" mentioned in the second paragraph refers to "This is my letter to the World," the opening poem of Dickinson's first volume of verse. Todd included "The show is not the show" and "Unto my books so good to turn" in *Poems* (1891) but "Publication is the auction" did not appear until 1929.

So many strange and unfounded stories have gone abroad concerning the poetess recently discovered to Boston that it was a peculiar privilege to gain admittance to Sleeper Hall this afternoon, where two personal friends of Emily Dickinson were present to speak of her. It was a happy thought of the College Club to invite Mrs. Mabel Loomis Todd and Colonel Higginson to address them on this interesting theme. Mrs. Todd sketched the story of Miss Dickinson's life, and corrected the popular impression that she was always a recluse; that she was an invalid, an irreverent woman, an eccentric person in matters of dress, or a monument to a love-tragedy. As a matter of fact, she had seen society in more than one place, and her nature was a joyous one; but "the show is not the show," she wrote, and this disappointment in the unreality of things, a repugnancy to every sort of sham, coupled with a certain innate shyness, led her to mingle constantly less and less with the world. Life to her looked vast and inexpressibly solemn. Trivialities seemed increasingly despicable. Toward middle age she ceased to leave the house; even her loved garden was deserted for a conservatory. By letters and gifts she kept up her connections with friends: and to children— to whom she loved to play the part of a good fairy, lowering sweet surprises to them from her window—she was always accessible.

She delighted in music and her library.

Unto my books how sweet to turn!   [books so good

runs one of her poems. Much of her time must have been spent in writing, for after her death eight hundred manuscript poems were found, carefully arranged, while fragments of nearly as many more were also discovered. Did she think of a possible publication of them? One of the preludes seems to give a color to this supposition. Then, too, she mentioned papers to be destroyed after her death, and the poems were not among these. On the other hand, there is this from her pen:

> Publication is the auction
> Of the mind of man—

Like Thoreau, said the speaker, Emily Dickinson was "no more lonely than the North Star." Two other sayings she quoted as a comfort to those that are still to seek for an explanation of Miss Dickinson's solitude. This from Emerson: "Now and then a man exquisitely made can live alone." And from Lord Bacon, this: "Whosoever is delighted in solitude is either a Wilde Beast or a God."

In her consideration of the poetical value of this writer's work, Mrs. Todd quite justly said that it is too soon to estimate it fully as yet. But few of her poems have been published. Cable says the greatness of her verse exceeds its beauty; and almost universally her rhyming is condemned. One critic, subtler than the rest, notes in her poetry a rhythm that satisfies a sense more elusive than hearing—a harmony of thought, as it were, rather than of sound. Certainly, form was a secondary consideration with her. Her need of expression was imperative. Her faculty for epigram was wonderful, as the examples given showed. Her most marked peculiarity was her deftness in catching the airiest and most fleeting emotions, and giving them to our vision in a score of words where another would have used a hundred.

Mrs. Todd included many unpublished poems in her address, which aptly illustrated her claims for Miss Dickinson.

Colonel Higginson read letters received from Emily Dickinson, and thus concluded a charming session.

154   Eugene Field. "Sharps and Flats." *Chicago Daily News.* A typewritten transcript of this item, dated May 3, 1891, is on file at the Jones Library, Amherst. Unfortunately, search of Field's well-known column for the *News* was unable to verify this reference to Dickinson in issues of the paper published within a few months of May 1891. Field's disparagement of Higginson's (and Todd's) editing stands alone in the nineties.

Emily Dickinson was a strange creature. None of her friends knew that she wrote verse: the secret did not come out until after her death. She studiously avoided society. In appearance she was not prepossessing, having the stern aspect of the typical New England spinster. One of her peculiarities was to wear white the year around. Her gowns, severely simple, were always white, and she wore her hair in the severe old style, parted in the middle and caught back in a Grecian knot. Miss Dickinson was seldom seen upon the streets, and she was even less frequently to be met at the little social gatherings in the college town in which her life was spent. She was regarded by those who knew her as a strange, if not a weird, creature. This opinion has doubtless been confirmed by the posthumous poetry of hers which has been published, after having been very badly edited by Mr. T. W. Higginson.

155   *Bookseller* [London], no. 402 (May 6, 1891), p. 447. This notice cites Roberts Brothers' "Fifth Edition." It combines lines to arrange the second and third quatrains of "The soul selects her own society" as a single four-line stanza.

It is probable that the reputation which these poems have gained in their own land will be forthcoming here in due time. The editorial preface compares them to Blake. Certainly America, generally sterile in poetical production, has produced nothing so truly poetical as these fugitive thoughts. The author of them, so we are told, led the life of a recluse, yet had an eye for nature and for man of most wondrous insight. Her own nun-like existence is portrayed best in such lines as these on "Exclusion":—

> Unmoved, she notes the chariot's pausing at her low gate:
> Unmoved, an emperor is kneeling upon her mat.
> I've known her from an ample nation choose one;
> Then close the valves of her attention like stone.

156 "Emily Dickinson." *Northampton* [Mass.] *Daily Herald,* May 7, 1891, p. 1. Material following the first three paragraphs of this article derives from the *Boston Evening Transcript,* no. 153.

In Boston, last Saturday afternoon, in Sleeper Hall, Colonel Higginson and Mrs. Mabel Loomis Todd spoke, before the College Club, on the life and literary work of Emily Dickinson, of Amherst, the notable and gifted woman whose eccentric life of utter seclusion for many years before her death two years ago has given rise to much speculation and many fanciful explanations which have been received as facts, but are declared to be untrue by the friends of the lady. Certain it is that Miss Dickinson, when still a young and attractive woman, retired so entirely from the social world that for many years she was never seen outside of her father's house in Amherst, and very rarely seen by any person within the house except the immediate members of the family, save once a year, when, at the annual reception her father (a trustee of the college) gave to the Amherst college students and faculty the recluse appeared and assisted in entertaining the guests with all the ease and grace of an adept in and devotee of social arts. It is said that her repugnance to society and shrinking from the outside world became so intensified that she requested that her body should be carried from the back door of the house when removed for burial, and that the request was complied with.

Tales of thwarted love naturally were invented by gossiping imaginations, and some of Miss Dickinson's poems strongly deepen the impression that there may have been some foundation for the idea. But if her life really had its tragic romance the secret had been so loyally guarded by her friends that the inquisitive public does not yet and probably never will know it as an acknowledged fact.

Of this singular life and richly endowed intellect two of her most appreciative friends, Mr. Higginson and Mrs. Todd, spoke thus, substantially, but most hearers felt that they learned but little more of the real cause which led this woman, whose superior material advantages and intellectual gifts might have so greatly blessed the world in many ways, to so completely yield to a morbid sensitiveness, which very many finely-organized natures would be glad to indulge in a similar manner were it not that such indulgence seems to them supreme selfishness. Ah! how many of us would gladly also shut the door, and forever bolt it, between ourselves and the "empty show" which is not even an honest empty show, and surrounding ourselves with congenial environments,—books, flowers, music, the half-dozen tried and trusted, helpful friends of the heart, which are all that any sensitively earnest soul ever wants or needs—beautifully, peacefully, poetically dream life away, undisturbed and unharassed by the petty perplexities or mammoth illusions of life, the disgusting deceptions, cruel dishonesties, maddening, crushing misapprehensions and tormenting work-a-day cares of the everyday world, which uncongenial elements every actively useful human life must meet, and bravely control and nobly conquer, if human life is to be lived to any really useful purpose.

Mrs. Todd sketched the story of Miss Dickinson's life, and corrected the popular impression that she was always a recluse; that she was an invalid, an irreverent woman, an eccentric person in matters of dress, or a monument to a love-tragedy. As a matter of fact, she had seen society in more than one place, and her nature was a joyous one; but "the show is not the show," she wrote, and this disappointment in the unreality of things, a repugnancy to every sort of sham, coupled with a certain innate shyness, led her to mingle constantly less and less with the world. Life to her looked vast and inexpressibly solemn. Trivialities seemed increasingly despicable. Toward middle age she ceased to leave the house; even her loved garden was deserted for a conservatory. By letters and gifts she kept up her connections with friends; and to children—to whom she loved to play the part of a good fairy, lowering sweet surprises to them from her window—she was always accessible.

She delighted in music and her library.

Unto my books how sweet to turn!   [books so good

runs one of her poems. Much of her time must have been spent in writing, for after her death eight hundred manuscript poems were found, carefully arranged, while fragments of nearly as many more were also discovered. Did she think of a possible publication of them? One of the preludes seems to give a color to this supposition. Then, too, she mentioned papers to be destroyed after her death, and the poems were not among these. On the other hand, there is this from her pen:

Publication is the auction
Of the mind of man—

Like Thoreau, said the speaker, Emily Dickinson was "no more lonely than the North Star." Two other sayings she quoted as a comfort to those that are still to seek for an explanation of Miss Dickinson's solitude. This from Emerson: "Now and then a man exquisitely made can live alone." And from Lord Bacon, this: "Whosoever is delighted in solitude is either a Wilde Beast or a God."

In her consideration of the poetical value of this writer's work, Mrs. Todd quite justly said that it is too soon to estimate it fully as yet. But few of her poems have been published. Cable says the greatness of her verse exceeds its beauty; and almost universally her rhyming is condemned. One critic, subtler than the rest, notes in her poetry a rhythm that satisfies a sense more elusive than hearing—a harmony of thought, as it were, rather than of sound. Certainly, form was a secondary consideration with her. Her need of expression was imperative. Her faculty for epigram was wonderful, as the examples given showed. Her most marked peculiarity was her deftness in catching the airiest and most fleeting emotions, and giving them to our vision in a score of words where another would have used a hundred.

Mrs. Todd included many unpublished poems in her address, which aptly illustrated her claims for Miss Dickinson.

Colonel Higginson read letters received from Emily Dickinson.

157 Joel Benton. "Literary Chat." *Brooklyn Daily Times*, May 9, 1891, p. 7.
Reprinted: *Savannah* [Ga.] *Morning News*, May 11, 1891, p. 2.

Mrs. Mabel Loomis Todd, joint editor with T. W. Higginson of the remarkable book of poems of the late Emily Dickinson, lectured a few days ago at Amherst, Mass., upon the characteristics of this newly discovered poet. She said that Miss Dickinson was not quite the severe recluse that some of the vagrant newspaper reports attempt to make her. Then she had, as those who have read her verses must infer, a very marked individuality. Nearly 1,200 poems were found among the MSS., and out of these a new volume of verse will be made up, which may very likely appear in the coming autumn.

158 "Among the Books." *Epworth Herald* 1 (May 9, 1891), 7.

This volume contains selections from poems which were written with no thought of publication, and so they come to us with that charm of modest worth which is found in wildwood flowers. Living in retirement, a recluse by temperament and habit, Miss Dickinson caught glimpses of the heart of nature, which she described in words that reveal unusual descriptive and imaginative powers. The delicate touches of pathos, the pure love of the beautiful, the clear delineation of mental crises and soul-struggles afford varied beauty to verses which cannot fail to delight and satisfy those who read poetry for the living thought rather than the cold form of meter.

159 "Notes." *Louisville Courier-Journal*, May 9, 1891, p. 7.

Another volume of the poems of Emily Dickinson is in preparation, and her editors, by further search among the voluminous papers which she left, have found material which they consider better than anything to which they had access in compiling the first volume, now in its sixth edition.

160 Roberts Brothers advertisement for 1890 *Poems*, "Sixth edition." *Publishers' Weekly* 39 (May 9, 1891), 668. Routine publication information is accompanied by the following unattributed quotation from an anonymous review in the *Boston Herald* (no. 59). An earlier announcement (no. 130) carried only the first phrase of the quoted sentence.

"Such a writer is a literary force, not only by the direct influence of her work, but, by silencing the frivolous and the trivial, permitted the world to know how true a singer lived in it unknown."

161 Charles E. L. Wingate. "Boston Letter." *Critic*, n.s. 15 (May 9, 1891), 253. This would seem to be a second-hand account, deriving from the *Boston Evening Transcript*'s report, no. 153.

An astonishing statement regarding the literary activity of Emily Dickinson was made by Mrs. Mabel Loomis Todd at the College Club meeting on Saturday. The poet, whose work, published by Roberts Bros., after her death, has now entered upon its sixth edition, must have spent very much of her time in writing, as she left 800 manuscript poems complete, besides fragments of nearly as many more. That she wrote for love of writing is certain, for as one reads her poems he feels that her heart, as well as her thoughts, was in her work; but yet, as Mrs. Todd pointed out, there were indications of a hope of publication expressed both in the preludes and in the fact that, in mentioning the papers to be destroyed after her death, she did not include these poems. Col. T. W. Higginson, whose interesting preface introduces Miss Dickinson's published poems, read to the College Club several letters from the poet, his enjoyable acquaintance with whom was almost entirely by correspondence; while Mrs. Todd corrected certain impressions regarding the author's life. Those ideas, that made of Miss Dickinson a woman eccentrically dressed, an invalid, an irreverent woman, or the victim of a love tragedy, were explained away, and she was shown to have had a strong dislike for the shams and trivialities of life, which united with shyness to keep her confined to her home. Her love of children was illustrated by her lowering of gifts from her windows, while her pleasure in books and in music was marked.

162 Lilian Whiting. "Boston Days." *New Orleans Times-Democrat,* May 10, 1891, p. 11.

Among the various literary festivities of Boston of late have been an Emily Dickinson matinee; a poetic love feast held by the college club, meeting in Jacob Sleeper Hall, of Boston University, when Col. Higginson and Mrs. Mabel Loomis Todd (the editors of the published volume of her poems) were invited to address a select audience. Mrs. Todd, who knew Miss Dickinson well, said that she was not the eccentric recluse which popular belief had accepted, but that in her early life she had seen a good deal of the world. As she grew old she grew more and more disinclined to go out, and delighted herself with music and books. "Life to her looked vast and increasingly solemn," said Mrs. Loomis. "Trivialities seemed increasingly despicable." But Miss Dickinson's life only illustrates the truth that too much solitude and introspection deprives one of estimating the values of life aright. There are trivialities which are despicable, to be sure, but there are more which are of value, and which make up no small part of the significance of existence. It is well to hold in mind that truth stated by Dr. Drummond that a great part of the life of Christ was spent simply in doing kind things.

163 "Literary Foot Notes." *Savannah* [Ga.] *Morning News,* May 11, 1891, p. 2. A reprinting; see no. 157.

164 "Notes." *Congregationalist* 76 (May 14, 1891), 165.

Another volume of poems by the late Emily Dickinson is being prepared for publication. It is seldom that an author gains public favor so suddenly and generally, especially after having died.

165 "Bric-a-brac." *Hartford Courant,* May 16, 1891, p. 3. Reprinted: *Worcester* [Mass.] *Spy,* May 18, 1891, p. 4; *Christian Union* 43 (June 4, 1891), 739; *Boston Evening Transcript,* July 7, 1891.

Mrs. Todd, who assisted Colonel Higginson in editing the poems of Emily Dickinson, recently gave some interesting reminiscences of the recluse-poet. "Toward middle-age," she says, "Miss Dickinson ceased to leave the house; even her loved garden was deserted for a conservatory. By letters and gifts she kept up her connection with friends, and to children, to whom she was always a good fairy, she would lower sweet surprises and gifts from the window." Only a few of the many manuscript poems left by the strange and gifted woman have been published.

166 "Books and Writers." *Worcester* [Mass.] *Spy,* May 18, 1891, p. 4. A reprinting; see no. 165.

167 "Literature—Notes." *Jewish Messenger* 69 (May 22, 1891), 5.

Not every poet is like Emily Dickinson, who left 800 manuscript poems after her death and as many fragments. She was too much of a poet to care for publicity. Her song was unpremeditated art.

168 [Denis Wortman.] "The Reading Room." *Christian Intelligencer* 62 (May 27, 1891), 12. The handwritten authorial attribution in Todd's scrapbook is confirmed in *AB*, p. 58.

Most of our diamonds, opals, emaralds, being polished and set after the best manner of art, how unwontedly one enjoys a handful of them in the rough—only one side cut to show their fineness. What unexpected flashes, what possibilities of beauty; and how rich one feels with that sense of reserved power in them, the sense of a treasure greater than one cares to show! And just such jewels by the handful Miss Dickinson has left us; broken bits of beauty, glimpses of strange glory, samples of endless suggestion! Her friends have not been over-sanguine of their reception; the critics have not been too indulgent. A few of the poems—all very short—perfectly wrought; the most of them apparently handled carelessly, as though to say, "These are nothing to me; wait till I have something worth while." What shall one say of rhyming "tell" with "still," "arm" with "exclaim," "own," with "young," "pearl" with "alcohol"? all which are fair examples of many instances. There is a frequent scorn of traditional rhyme; an *abandon* of expression, with a delightful *abandon* of thought and feeling. And yet you enjoy them all the more for it. You recognize them as mere studies; you exclaim, "Such sketches—then what pictures when finished!" In many you recognize a finish in the very incompleteness, the poetry lying in the subtle, instantaneous insight, and the expression *naive,* yet how dexterous! The book is a basket of seed-thoughts.

169 A[lice] W[ard] B[ailey]. "Living in Four Towns." *Boston Journal.* Unverified. This undated clipping was placed among materials appearing early in June 1890 in Todd's scrapbook. Only the first paragraph of this sketch of Amherst mentions Dickinson and is reprinted here; another account of the town by the same author, giving some attention to the poet's home, is reproduced in its entirety (see no. 176).

I think I may consider myself half a Homer. He was born in seven towns, I am living in four; four Amhersts, seen respectively from the first, second, third and fourth stories of its principal hotel, the Amherst House. From the first floor, where is the office in which I smoke my post-prandial cigar, I see the village life, the town element, the business of the place. From the second, where the dining room is situated, I look away to the colleges, to the pleasant dwellings and the well-kept streets. This is Amherst, the university and the home. Upon the third floor I have a friend, who contends that his room is the best in the house (it isn't, for mine is), and from his windows I got glimpses of Holyoke and Tom, of Toby and Sugarloaf, great soft, furry looking mountains giving one a comfortable, secure feeling as if so many big, affectionate St. Bernards had sprawled out by one's side. There are also Pelham Hills, a wall to the east, and on the west the vague, blue outline of the Berkshires. This is the Amherst of the tourist, the Amherst of picturesque drives, of romantic views and thrilling associations. The fourth Amherst is seen from my own room in the tiptop of the house. This is a sublimated skyey sort of an Amherst, an upper stratum overlooking mountain and valley, and having an intimate acquaintance with the clouds. It might be called the Amherst of the poet, of J. G. Holland and Helen Hunt and Emily Dickinson, for it recalls their visions and bears witness to the faithfulness of their impressions of this Amherst at least. Twice a day—every man is a poet twice a day—at morning and evening I enjoy the rarefied atmosphere of my lofty chamber. The rest of the time I study Amherst from a lower plane, from the shaded streets, where you may hear the squirrel chatter or the blue jay scream, and may see the one pour himself like a drop of red quicksilver along the boughs of the huge elms, or watch the other whetting his beak on a convenient twig.

170   "Poems by Emily Dickinson." *Packer Alumna* 7 (June 1891), 139.

In the town of Amherst amid the hills of Massachusetts, Emily Dickinson was born and lived for fifty-five years, and yet she so carefully hid herself and her genius that it was not until after her death that the world discovered her rare poetical gifts. Seldom going beyond the doorstep of her home, almost never beyond her father's grounds, she showed herself only to a few intimate friends and refused to have her poetry put into print. But since her death in 1886, her poems have been collected and are now given to the public with an introduction by T. W. Higginson.

The first impression upon opening the book is the brevity of all the poems, they seem almost like fragments, yet upon closer inspection we find each contains a complete, yet suggestive thought. Originality, imagination, insight into life and nature, and a certain weird strain are all shown in these remarkable verses which the author has evidently not attempted to trim down to the requirements of rhetoric. Has the writer given us a glimpse of her own nature in the poem called "Exclusion"?

> The soul selects her own society,
>   Then shuts the door;
> On her divine majority
>   Obtrude no more.
>
> Unmoved, she notes the chariot's pausing
>   At her low gate;
> Unmoved, an Emperor is kneeling
>   Upon her mat.
>
> I've known her from an ample nation
>   Choose one;
> Then close the valves of her attention
>   Like stone.

171   Le Roy Phillips. "The Poems of Emily Dickinson." *Amherst Literary Monthly* 6 (June 1891), 90–91. Reprinted: *New England Magazine*, n.s. 5 (November 1891), 311. In the reprinting, two words are capitalized: "Mind" (line 5) and "Nature" (line 9). For other dedicatory verses, see index *s.v.* poems in tribute.

> Her message to a world she never knew
> Reveals the thoughts sweet nature would disclose

To one unmoved by earthly fame, who chose
To toil apart, unknown, and so withdrew;
And, guided by a higher mind, while true
To nature and herself, her spirit rose
To share a sweet companionship with those
Whose hallowed eyes see things beyond our view.
She heard kind nature speaking everywhere
Whose constant voice was soft with melody.
She praised the budding flowers that make earth fair, —
Some tender thought in each she loved to see, —
Or spoke, perchance, of earthly joy and care,
Or talked with Death, her soul's own liberty.

172 Henry Park Schauffler. "Suggestions from the Poems of Emily Dickinson." *Amherst Literary Monthly* 6 (June 1891), 87–90.

Nature, in her kind sternness, has laid down the law that growth necessitates, not only a latent possibility of further development, but also requires a strenuous use and exercise of the material already at hand. Having applied this law to ourselves, and in particular to that essential, characterizing part of man, the mind, and recognizing as we must its boundless capacity for development, we are forced to the conclusion that here no real growth is possible without a healthy and vigorous system of mental calisthenics. Anything, then, that is a stimulus to careful, painstaking, introspective thought we should warmly welcome. Anyone who by skillful suggestiveness can open to us the gate of broader, richer thinking is our best friend. We gladly bow to such a friend, hasten to burn the sweet incense of gratitude, saying with Wordsworth:

And I have felt
A presence that disturbs me with the joy
Of elevated thoughts.

Just such a presence lives in the poems of Emily Dickinson. If called upon to point out the keystone of their power, to solve the secret of their great success in the literary world, the answer would unhesitatingly be, they are intensely thought-provoking. There is little charm in a story, which explains with minutest detail that which should be left for each one's imagination to picture. By nature we are selfish enough to desire some part in the development of a plot, some honor paid us by permission given our own minds to surround the different characters with scenery of our own making. The highest art in music, painting, sculpture, or literature is that which is the most suggestive.

Read a stanza like this on the mystery of pain, and see if it does not set you thinking, see if it does not give that treasured imagination of yours the chance to play back and forth, and play beauty and strength into your thought:

Pain has an element of blank;
It cannot recollect
When it began, or if there were
A day when it was not.

Emily Dickinson brooked no fetters of rhyme or rhythm. The average poet often belittles and perhaps destroys the suggestive power of a verse, by a change of word bringing with it a different shade of meaning; but Miss Dickinson, in her subjection of expression to thought, gains the strength of perfect freedom and the impetus of untrammelled suggestion.

Robertson defines poetry as, "The indirect expression of feelings that cannot be expressed directly." Perhaps the feelings are too deep and strong to find direct expression. Possibly this "indirect expression" means suggestive power, and the maturing in the reader's mind of that thought, which well-formed in the poet-soul, could yet be expressed only in germinal language. Most probable it is, that a woman of keen intellect and clear insight would think those thoughts of nature, life, and death, which could not fail to kindle other minds to corresponding mental activity, and endower poems of hers with the enviable name of thought-provoking verse.

Suggestiveness in thought and expression grows from a tendency to the natural as well as the unnatural things of life: "Glancing from heaven to earth, from earth to heaven." Some one has said that "The deepest truths are the simplest and most common." With this definition Wordsworth's conception of the poet's sphere coincides:

> The common things of sky and earth,
> And hill and valley he has viewed:
> And impulses of deeper birth
> Have come to him in solitude.

What could be more characteristic of Miss Dickinson's writings! All the "impulses of deeper birth" most certainly came to her in solitude; and when she sang of common things, — grass, flowers, birds, the wind, and the ancient hills, — all were graced with a perfect naturalness. This it is that almost startles one into saying: "Why! I have often thought just that very thing myself; how strange that I should never have seen it so expressed before." Note the dainty touch with which she assigns to the grass its pleasure-duty:

> And stir all day to pretty tunes
> The breezes fetch along,
> And hold the sunshine in its lap,
> And bow to everything.

Or: —

> It struck me every day
> The lightning was as new
> As if the cloud that instant slit,
> And let the fire through.

Mark the power of naturalness both in thought and expression. Why, you feel perfectly at home when that thought, clad in its simple, unadorned attire, greets your mind.

Tennyson, drawing the picture of an ideal poet, said of him:

> He saw through life and death, through good and ill,
> He saw through his own soul,
> The marvel of the everlasting will,
> An open scroll
> Before him lay.

To Emily Dickinson, Nature as well as the "Everlasting will," lay as an open scroll; and thanks to her this scroll lies open now to us. She had the rare power of being able to robe subjects like Death and the Grave, in a personality so fitting and so natural, that she almost robbed them of their dreadfulness.

> One dignity delays for all,
>   One mitred afternoon.
> None can avoid this purple,
>   None escape this crown.   [None evade

The query comes, what is there in these poems to foster a higher literary taste? Look closely, and you will see a subtlety of thought like a thread of silver running through them all; so much is implied, so much left just unsaid.

But it would be unfair not to mention what might be called the sterling quality of worth these poems possess. They are like some spicy sweet which whets the taste for stronger diet. Let one who has but little poetry in his soul look carefully into this delightful little volume of poems, and the probability is that his literary taste in general will be quickened; he will turn to his discarded Wordsworth, Tennyson, or Milton with a zest which he could not have before summoned.

173 *Christian Inquirer*, June 4, 1891. Unlocated. A reprinting; see no. 148.

174 "Literary Notes." *Christian Union* 43 (June 4, 1891), 739. A reprinting; see no. 165.

175 "Notes." *Chicago Inter-Ocean*, June 6, 1891, p. 11. Reprinted: *Current Literature* 7 (July 1891), 480.

Miss Emily Dickinson, whose poems have been published only since her death, is said to have left 800 manuscripts of complete poems and fragments of nearly as many more. Her shyness amounted almost to a mania and her later years were spent entirely in her own home, but she loved children and had a habit of lowering gifts to them from her windows.

176 A[lice] W[ard] B[ailey]. "The Home of Emily Dickinson: Some Observations Concerning the Characteristics of Amherst." *Springfield Republican*, June 10, 1891, pp. 2–3. The poet's "not-distant kinswoman" is probably her sister Lavinia. For a similar piece by this author, see no. 169. In both the author adopts a male persona.

It would seem that the admiration for Emily Dickinson's poems is assuming the proportions of a "cult." This morning as I stepped out upon the veranda of the Amherst house, three women of modest appearance but with keen, intellectual faces, inquired of the proprietor which direction they should take to find the home of Emily Dickinson the poet. They had come from a distance to visit the spot and to inquire into the conditions which produced and fostered so singular a genius; — the poet hunter is nothing if not scientific nowadays. Listening to their conversation brought something very like interest to my own breast. I followed their lead, strolled through the beautiful streets, studied curiously the physiognomy of those I met, and asked myself what part of all this belonged to the poet, — hers by appropriation and use? How much of it explains, as far as such things can be explained, the quaintness of diction, the peculiarity of thought, in poems which within a twelvemonth after their first publication are reviewed by the leading magazines, read aloud in fashionable gatherings and discussed with only less awe and acumen than are brought to bear upon the works of Browning himself.

It is hard to describe the charm of Amherst to anyone who has not felt it, the charm of mountain and valley, of wilderness and crowded thoroughfare, of college and country-seat. The most untamed of wildflowers blossom within a half-hour's walk of the imposing new town hall, and under the very eaves of the extensive college libraries may be picked up provincialisms to last a dialect writer a lifetime. The theosophists who contend that every event leaves an impression that their "sensitives" can detect it, should bring one of these delicate human machines to Amherst; but the poor fellow would go mad with the medley of sights and sounds, if at once the palimpsest gave forth all its impressions.

Everything has happened here from the rebellion of Daniel Shays to the composition of these singular poems. Callous mortal that I am, associations twitched my sleeve and jogged my elbow as I sauntered along the streets, asking me what company of merry children racketed in this big square house, until it looks as if it were full to bursting of happy secrets? What love-lorn maiden looked out of that gray dormer window for a lover who came not, and whispered her disappointment to the shaggy old rosebush which still stands on tip-toe at the window-sill waiting for the conclusion of the story? Between those sentinel lilacs how many generations of stalwart men were carried out, "whither they would not?" Ah! who knows? Not we who come and go in the valley, but Holyoke and Tom who have seen it all, and Toby and Sugarloaf and gentle Pelham hills. Perhaps the poet would have said it was the mountains who passed on to her what she undoubtedly knew of the complex and varied life of the place, though the thoughtful, expressive faces which are the rule here, suggest that her townspeople might have told Emily Dickinson much that she died without dreaming of,—but then she would have been a philanthropist instead of a recluse, a novelist instead of a poet. They do not grudge her the choice. There is a fine independence about them which savors of the days when each house had several acres of land around it, and every man had plenty of room in which to flourish his elbows.

Above all, a town is like a tree, having the various rings of its development within the present enfolding bark. Amherst is still a precinct of Hadley somewhere in her heart. The dame's cap towers above the matron's bonnet; Old Hadley street, so long that looking down its double walls of elms to the blue rim of Holyoke, is like looking out to sea between two crags, so wide that it is a good summer afternoon's walk to cross it,—*do* the Hadleyites have a cis-common as the Gauls did a cis-Alpine bond? Only Hadley street still crosses the lives of many people who live in Amherst. Others besides Emily Dickinson have felt the untamed influence which made of her a recluse. "Upon my word," said a certain dear old lady whose home is on one of the least frequented streets, "it does look as if everybody had left town, and *I'm glad of it.*" She settled herself to her knitting with a delicious sense of having her world to herself.

Other tides have fed Amherst, however; other and distant streams of ambitious intellectual and social life. There are men here who study for the world's benefit, who write books to be published, not to be hid away, who perpetrate witticisms and wise sayings to have them repeated, not for the mere satisfaction of having uttered them. One feels the presence of an audience in the background of many quotations referred to a not-distant kinswoman of Miss Dickinson. "Why do people rave over the beauty of daisies? They look to me like hard-boiled eggs cut in two," she says to a college student, and is probably not surprised when the conceit travels far and wide.

Amherst is no less noted for the people who love to talk than it is for those who love to keep silence. The cheering smiles and cordial greetings of one of these are still missed in Amherst streets, though she who dispensed them has been dead several years. "Do tell me who that woman is!" ejaculated a man from out of town who had come in to do business with a citizen of Amherst and who had waited an hour on the corner while Mme ___ chatted on and on as if nothing could stop her. "Do tell me who that woman is. I'd rather have her in the house than a pianner."

How do such influences come into the lives of those who avoid them? Do they travel underground, like subterranean rivers, or are they caught up like mists to fall again in a distant place. Shutting herself away from Amherst as she did, communing only with the mountains, the trees, the birds, the flowers and her few chosen friends, Emily Dickinson was nevertheless the child of Amherst, of its whimsicality and its culture, of its friendliness and its freedom, the child of Amherst when she mused in her garden and asked Pelham hills "What *is* morning?" and when she admitted the children who shared her rare confidence, and when she was borne over the green fields to the cemetery by the men who had been faithful servants in her father's household. And Amherst people claim her now, those who never saw her, and they understand her strange verses as do none who have never lived in Amherst.

"Yes, it is a field which has scarcely been worked at all," said Mr. Chase, the hotel proprietor, when I returned to the veranda and told him what I had learned. "There's a great deal of good material going to waste on these quiet and shady streets. When people first began to come to Amherst, summers, all they thought of was excursions. They went to Whately Glen, and to the Notch, and they climbed Mr. Lincoln and the other mountains. Then came the folks who go crazy over antiques, tall clocks, spindle-legged tables and chairs, blue china and so on. They say Bishop Huntington has a roomful of articles over in Hadley, his summer home, and no one can tell the use of more than half of them. Now you 'literary fellers' are beginning to find out what an amount of your sort of stuff can be found here, and there are pilgrims coming to see where Miss Emily Dickinson lived; that will be the next role Amherst will play. Well she's equal to it. Now look at that and tell me where you can get anything to beat it!?"

The pliant boughs of the elm trees which lined the three streets within our range were swaying in the evening breeze; on Pelham hills the sunset glow was sent back from every cottage window in flashes of dazzling light; a chorus of student voices could be heard singing on the campus, and below us, by twos and fours, groups of youths and maidens were going home from an afternoon game of tennis. It was as gay a picture and in as fair a setting as one could find anywhere.

"But you'd better come in," says Mr. Chase, never quite oblivious of the creature comforts, "we have fresh trout for supper."

177 "The Newly Discovered Poet." *Providence Journal*, June 14, 1891, p. 13.

It would seem late to call attention to Miss Dickinson's poems, of which the first published volume is already in its sixth edition, were it not that one constantly encounters people, reading people, to whom they and their author are wholly unfamiliar even by repute. And because it seems a pity that genius so undoubted, and of so unhackneyed a quality as hers, should remain unknown to even one reader to whom its acquaintance would bring keen pleasure, and because, too, her editors and friends, Colonel Higginson and Mrs. Todd, are preparing a second volume from freshly found material which they pronounce finer than that from which they drew in making up the first, this brief notice is proffered to serve merely as the pointing index finger on a way-board.

Miss Dickinson was a daughter of the Hon. Edward Dickinson, of Amherst, Mass. She passed her life in that town, and died there not long since, yet so great a recluse had she been for many years that Amherst dwellers of the present generation, if they knew of her existence, knew her but as a name. She rarely crossed the threshold of her home to go, even into the homestead grounds, and Colonel Higginson, who met her but twice in a friendship and correspondence of years, says she affected him like some strange, remote presence from a dream world. He adds that she emerged occasionally from her absolute seclusion to play admirably the part of gracious hostess when her father entertained college and other magnates, and she did not deny herself in her retreat to old and close friends, but in most ways this "New England nun" seems to have been far more rigidly cloistered than many a Roman one.

Why did she seclude herself so profoundly? will at once be asked.

Mrs. Todd has stated recently in Boston that her retirement was not due to disappointment in love, but a resident of Amherst expresses surprise at this declaration, and says "it is understood at Amherst, by old residents, that her engagement with a young man of promise was objected to by her father, and that while she yielded to his judgment, she deliberately chose to limit her activities to the homestead in which she was born." He adds: "It will be remembered that at one time Emily Dickinson was credited with the authorship of the Saxe Holm stories. They were written evidently by some one who knew Amherst village of thirty years ago very intimately. While the Saxe Holm stories were in Mrs. Jackson's handwriting, she said more than once that she was not the author. Dr. Holland once said that he was not the possessor of the secret, although the stories appeared in his magazine, and he declared he would be heartily relieved if the mystery were cleared up."

Those who knew her were aware that she wrote much, and Mrs. Jackson, "H. H.," urged her strongly to publish a volume of poems, but vainly. It was due to her sister's wish that one was compiled after her death, and the reception it met, a reception justifying a second volume, proved that sisterly affection had not led astray a sister's apprehension and critical judgment. And more than the quantity is the quality of its welcome to be reckoned; the little book's warmest greeting has been from those whose friendliness and praise any writer and poet would be happy and proud to win. But so little did Miss Dickinson contemplate a public, that a portion of the volume is but nameless fragments, thought-darts of a line or two, while the completed poems — completed in the rendering of her meaning — have titles found for them by the editors.

The poet is dead and the poems were not written for the world, but to utter herself for her own relief, her own need, her own solace; the world's share in them it gets by act of grace, and but one attitude towards them is possible. If the author had made venture of a volume in her lifetime, probably it would have been very different from this posthumous one; if not, it must be owned the critics would have drawn their blades, and they would have had reason. There are carelessnesses and barbarities that are intolerably discordant in the high society in which they are found, and we should resent them hotly, no doubt, were any liberty of caviling ours. But none is possible; it is much as if, without her will or knowledge, we were reading, over this recluse woman's shoulder, the most intimate thoughts of her strong, ardent, melancholy soul as they flashed nakedly into life at the point of her pen in all the freedom of solitude save for her own parental eyes.

Naturally, in such poetry as this—"poetry torn up by the roots, and clung about with earth and rain and dew," as Colonel Higginson expresses it—we come very close to things, and to her who ponders, illuminates them. While one says this or that by way of introduction, or suggestion, it is perhaps more than usually difficult to choose, among these poems, not so definitely one's chief favorites, as those which, within this notice's limits, most adequately render her swift moods, her play of thought and fancy, her impulse, her vigor, her freshness, her unpremeditated grace. But since choose one must, here, first, are some nameless bits:

> The pedigree of honey
>   Does not concern the bee;
> A clover, any time, to him,
>   Is aristocracy.

>   *   *   *   *   *

> Presentiment is that long shadow on the lawn,
> Indicative that suns go down;
> The notice to the startled grass
> That darkness is about to pass.

>   *   *   *   *   *

> A little road not made of man,
>   Enabled of the eye,
> Accessible to thill of bee,
>   Or cart of butterfly.

> If town it have, beyond itself,
>   'Tis that I cannot say;
> I only sigh—no vehicle
>   Bears me along that way.

>   *   *   *   *   *

> Death is a dialogue between
>   The spirit and the dust.
> "Dissolve!" says Death. The Spirit, "Sir,
>   I have another trust."

> Death doubts it, argues from the ground,
>   The Spirit turns away;
> Just laying off, for evidence,
>   An overcoat of clay.

>   *   *   *   *   *

> I had no time to hate, because
>   The grave would hinder me;
> And life was not so ample, I
>   Could finish enmity.

> Nor had I time to love; but since
>   Some industry must be,
> The little toil of love, I thought,
>   Was large enough for me.

And here is one, nameless, that might be entitled "The Old, Old Story:"

> New feet within my garden go;
>> New fingers stir the sod;
> A troubadour upon the elm
>> Betrays the solitude.
>
> New children play upon the green,
>> New weary sleep below;
> And still the pensive spring returns
>> And still the punctual snow.

And one, two, nay three more must end our borrowings. The first is characteristically terse and close-packed:

SUSPENSE.

> Elysium is as far as to
>> The very nearest room,
> If in that room a friend await
>> Felicity or doom.
>
> What fortitude the soul contains,
>> That it can so endure
> The accent of a coming foot,
>> The opening of a door!

In the second we catch the lyric strain with which now and then she too briefly delights us, quits with such tantalizing abruptness:

INDIAN SUMMER.

> These are the days when birds come back,
> A very few, a bird or two
>> To take a backward look.
>
> These are the days when skies put on
> The old, old sophistries of June,
>> A blue and gold mistake.
>
> Oh, fraud that can not cheat the bee,
> Almost thy plausibility
>> Induces my belief.
>
> Till ranks of seeds their witness bear,
> And softly through the altered air
>> Hurries a timid leaf.
>
> Oh, sacrament of summer days,
> Oh, last communion in the haze,
>> Permit a child to join.
>
> Thy sacred emblems to partake,
> Thy consecrated bread to break,
>> Taste thine immortal wine.

And in the last we are reminded, as so often and strongly it happens, that she reminds her readers of William Blake:

THE CHARIOT.

Because I could not stop for Death,
    He kindly stopped for me;
The carriage held but just ourselves
    And Immortality.

We slowly drove, he knew no haste,
    And I had put away
My labor and my leisure, too,
    For his civility.

We passed the school where children played,
    Their lessons scarcely done;
We passed the fields of gazing grain,
    We passed the setting sun.

We paused before a house that seemed
    A swelling of the ground;
The roof was scarcely visible,
    The cornice but a mound.

Since then 'tis centuries; but each
    Feels shorter than the day
I first surmised the horses' heads
    Were toward eternity.

177A "Literary News and Notes." *The Author—Monthly Magazine for Literary Workers* 3:6 (June 15, 1891), 91.

Colonel Thomas Wentworth Higginson is to edit another volume of Emily Dickinson's poems, and is also to have his Nineteenth Century Club address on "The New World and the New Book" published in book form in connection with some kindred papers.

178 "Emily Dickinson's Poems." *Home Journal* 46 (June 24, 1891). Unlocated.

The poems of Emily Dickinson, which have been recently collected, display a striking intellectual power which reminds of Carlyle, of Mrs. Browning, of George Meredith or, as Mr. Higginson points out in his preface, of William Blake. Certain crudities of form and expression are therefore more readily forgiven. There is apparent in her poems no mock sentiment, no light laughing at the death which hovered about her for so many years, but everywhere a serious contemplation of his meaning, a final reluctant surrender to the bitterness of parting with the beauties of a world the natural loveliness of which she so thoroughly appreciated. Every one susceptible of emotion must be moved at the intense pathos with which she recounts her aspirations, conclusions and reflections.

Though the poems bear the imprint of that seclusion from which she so seldom emerged, about them lingers the gracious atmosphere which ever surrounds a gentlewoman. Her impulsiveness and a fine scorn of rigid laws of versification are but signs of her sympathy with present tendencies to seek new forms, and new outlets for universal thought and emotion. By originality, brilliant flashes of insight, and occasional happy expressions, these poems are entitled to definite and permanent place in American literature. They are carefully arranged and edited by her friends, Thomas Wentworth Higginson and Mabel Loomis Todd. A delicate attention to detail is evidenced by the silver Indian pipes upon the soft-toned grayish covers.

179 "Brief Comment: Literary Doings." *Current Literature* 7 (July 1891), 480. A reprinting; see no. 175.

180 "Current Literature." *Boston Evening Transcript,* July 7, 1891. Unverified. A reprinting; see no. 165.

181 "Notes." *Nation* 53 (July 16, 1891), 48. Reprinted: *Chicago Post,* July 17, 1891, p. 4. This report of an Arabic edition gained currency in the nineties, owing perhaps to the *Nation*'s affiliation with Higginson, its regular poetry reviewer. Evidence of the translation remains to be discovered. For Andrew Lang's comment, see no. 126.

The poems of Emily Dickinson, the Amherst recluse, whom Andrew Lang calls "a poet who had constructed her own individual 'Ars Poetica,'" continue in active demand, the eighth American edition being already in preparation. An Arabic translation made in Syria has passed through several editions.

182 "Books, Writers and Readers." *Chicago Post,* July 17, 1891, p. 4. A reprinting; see no. 181.

183 "Notes." *Critic,* n.s. 16 (July 18, 1891), 36. Reprinted: *Christian Union* 44 (July 25, 1891), 195; *Philadelphia Press,* July 25, 1891, p. 11; *Current Literature* 8 (October 1891), 317. This note derives from item no. 181.

Of the poems of Emily Dickinson, "an Arabic translation, made in Syria" is said to have passed through several editions.

184 "New Books and Reprints." *Saturday Review* [London] 72 (July 18, 1891), 94. This notice cites the American edition of the poems, although the first British edition was soon to appear; see no. 188.

Poems, by Emily Dickinson, form a collection of verse more noteworthy for quaintness of phrase and odd unexpectedness of conceits than for the Blake-like quality which Mr. Higginson, a friendly editor, discovers. For example:—

> Belshazzar had a letter—
> He never had but one;
> Belshazzar's correspondent
> Concluded, and begun
> In that immortal copy
> The conscience of us all
> Can read without its glasses
> On revelation's wall.

On the whole, the poetry of Miss Dickinson surprises more often by singularity than charms by *naïveté* and simplicity.

185 *Christian Union* 44 (July 25, 1891), 195. A reprinting; see no. 183.

186 "Literary Notes." *Philadelphia Press*, July 25, 1891, p. 11. A reprinting; see no. 183.

187 "Gossip for Readers of Books." *Kansas City* [Mo.] *Star*, August 1, 1891, p. 4.

Emily Dickinson's poems, which are not well known even in this, her native country, are said to have passed through several editions in the Arabic.

188 "The Library Table." *Globe* [London], August 3, 1891, p. 6. The only nineties English edition of Dickinson's poems followed the fourth American impression of *Poems*, 1890. It was published in London by Osgood, McIlvaine, July 30, 1891.

America was the first home of a little volume of "Poems by Emily Dickinson, edited by two of her friends," and prefaced by one of them. It would be easy to make fun of the lady's rhythmic and rhyming methods, for they are eccentric to a fault; the poems are, indeed, throughout, of the inspired amateur order. It would, however, be a mistake and unfair to involve them all in one general condemnation. While some are simple to fatuousness, others have real freshness and insight, suggesting that if the writer's talent had but been properly trained it might have had results of solid interest and value. As it is, these "Poems" are more of curiosities than anything else, their attractiveness being notably enhanced by the neat and pretty form given to them by their present publishers, Messrs. Osgood, M'Ilvaine, and Co.

188A "Literary Gossip." *Illustrated London News* 99 (August 8, 1891), 182.

Messrs. Osgood, McIlvaine, and Co. have published in a charming little volume the poems of Miss Emily Dickinson, which have made some stir in America. One of the editors, Mr. T. W. Higginson, says rather happily that "in many cases these verses will seem to the reader like poetry torn up by the roots." This description is justified by the entire waywardness of form, which does not always obscure a strange but genuine vein of poetry. On the other hand, the editors would have shown some discretion by omitting verses which have absolutely no claim to consideration. Miss Dickinson published next to nothing in her lifetime, and she would probably have demurred to the publication of lines like these—

> Mirth is the mail of anguish,
> In which it cautious arm,
> Lest anybody spy the blood
> And "you're hurt" exclaim!

189 "The Literary World." *St. James's Gazette* [London], August 8, 1891, p. 12.

One of the first fruits of the American Copyright Act has been a considerable influx of American books. Some of them we are glad to see. We can all welcome Mr. Howells (in spite of his Howellisms) and Miss Wilkins. But why on earth should anybody on this side, or for that matter the other, care for the poems of Miss Emily Dickinson "edited by two of her friends, Mabel Loomis Todd and T. W. Higginson?" Miss Dickinson was the daughter of a New England lawyer, and she seems to have been in no respect different from other spinster ladies of retiring habits. Here is a thrilling passage from Mr. T. W. Higginson's biography of the deceased poetess. "Her father, Hon. Edward Dickinson, was the leading lawyer of Amherst, and was treasurer of the well-known college there situated. It was his custom once a year to hold a large reception at his house, attended by all the families connected with the institution and by the leading people of the town. On these occasions his daughter Emily emerged from her wonted retirement, and did her part as a gracious hostess; nor would any one have known from her manner, I have been told, that this was not a daily occurrence. The annual occasion once past, she withdrew again into her seclusion, and, except for a very few friends, was as invisible to the world as if she had dwelt in a nunnery. For myself, although I had corresponded with her for many years, I saw her but twice face to face, and brought away the impression of something as unique and remote as Undine or Mignon or Thekla."

In her blameless seclusion Miss Emily wrote verses, as other maiden ladies do. They are mostly very bad verses. Here is a specimen:—

> Success is counted sweetest
> By those who ne'er succeed.
> To comprehend a nectar
> Requires sorest need.
>
> Not one of all the purple host
> Who took the flag to-day
> Can tell the definition,
> So clear, of victory.

This, it appears, was published "at the request of 'H. H.,' the author's towns-woman and friend." We wonder if H. H. understands how you "comprehend a nectar," or whether she thinks that "day" and "victory" are good rhymes? Possibly if Miss Dickinson had learned grammar and had known anything of the laws of metre, and had had any thoughts to express or any faculty of expressing them, she might have become quite a decent fifth-rate versifier.

190 "Books and Book Gossip." *Sunday Sun* [London] 1:14 (August 9, 1891), 1.

Messrs. Osgood and McIlvaine have done well to give us an English edition of the poetry of Miss Emily Dickinson. Miss Dickinson's poetry, as most people interested in such matters are already aware, has aroused the vehement admiration and praise of Mr. Howells, and the equally outspoken disapproval and derision of Mr. Andrew Lang. There must be a considerable number of persons who will be glad to have the opportunity to taste and see for themselves on which side they are going to arrange themselves. There is generally at least some stuff in writers or artists of any kind, who awake an equal vigour of appreciation and deprecation.

191 "New Poetry." *Scotsman* [Edinburgh], August 10, 1891, p. 2.

The *Poems* of the late Miss Emily Dickinson are of a kind that baffle criticism. Mr. T. W. Higginson tells us in the preface that they were not written for the public eye; they were the utterances in verse of a woman who, by temperament and habit, was a recluse, and who wrote because she could not help writing. She

In 1891 James Ripley Osgood (1836–1892), a seasoned and well-connected American publisher, joined with a young Princeton graduate, Clarence McIlvaine, to found the new British firm of Osgood, McIlvaine. Though Dickinson's London volume received a mixed reception, it was not widely reviewed and sold poorly. (No. 188)

4 PARK STREET, BOSTON, *September 26*, 1891.

DEAR MADAM: —

Now that every one is asking "Have you read Emily Dickinson's poems?" and "Who was Emily Dickinson?" the paper by Colonel *Thomas Wentworth Higginson* on

"EMILY DICKINSON'S LETTERS,"

in the October Atlantic, will command attention. Such extraordinary letter-writing as Emily Dickinson's has certainly never been seen in print before — interesting precisely because every tradition in letter-writing is absolutely ignored. No one who wishes to gain some idea of the daily life of this interesting woman should miss the paper.

The October number also contains Dr. Holmes's tribute to Lowell.

Yours truly,

HOUGHTON, MIFFLIN & CO.

The Price of THE ATLANTIC is 35 cents.

Mabel Todd's scrapbooks preserve this advertisement for the issue of the *Atlantic* in which Higginson's essay appeared. (No. 221)

MISS DICKINSON'S POEMS.

Mrs. Moulton says, in the "Boston Herald," of the second series: "Perhaps the greatest literary event of last year, at least in Boston, was the publication of the 'Poems' of Emily Dickinson. For myself, I was one of their lovers. Nor was their charm at all the less for me by reason of their utter disregard for poetic technique. It certainly would not do for all of us who write verse to ignore the laws of poetic art; but there was something in Emily Dickinson that transcended art, and made her a law unto herself. The true fire of genius kindled her work. I look up the 'Second Series' of her 'Poems' with half a doubt whether it would justify itself; since it is not always safe to repeat a successful experiment. But I am convinced that it would be a loss to the world had this second volume remained unpublished."

EMILY DICKINSON'S POEMS.

First and Second Series. Edited by T. W. HIGGINSON and MABEL LOOMIS TODD. With a preface by Mrs. Todd and an autograph letter from Helen Jackson to Miss Dickinson. 16mo, cloth, $1.25; white and gold, $1.50 each.

Mailed on receipt of price.

ROBERTS BROTHERS, Boston, 310 The

Item no. 307.

Dickinson's popularity came as a surprise to Thomas Niles (1825–1894), Roberts Brothers' chief editor. Though a friend and a correspondent of Dickinson's, he was at first reluctant to publish her verse. (No. 299)

Roberts Brothers' place of business from 1885 to 1898. (No. 299) spent years without crossing the doorstep of her father, the treasurer of Amherst College, Massachusetts, and the few who met her face to face "brought away the impression of something as unique and remote as Undine, or Mignon, or Thekla." Certainly these lines bear the impress of a strange individuality. They are "poetry taken up by the roots," often with an abrupt, harsh, and spasmodic wrench that destroys any claim they might make to beauty or even to sense. Miss Dickinson had "a rigorous literary standard of her own, and often altered a word many times to suit an ear which had its own tenacious fastidiousness." The product is often like this —

> The clouds their backs together laid,
> The north began to push,   [begun
> The forests galloped till they fell,
> The lightning skipped like mice;
>
> The thunder crumbled like a stuff —
> How good to be in tombs,
> Where nature's temper cannot reach,
> Nor vengeance ever comes.

At the same time, it cannot be denied that there are marvelous flashes of insight into nature and life, all the more remarkable coming from one who saw so little of either face to face; and an almost morbid power of entering into the life of lowly living things, the birds and bees, and the flowers and the grass. There are also snatches of lyrical music, almost always, however, breaking off with some jarring discord. "The Sea of Sunset" and a few others are, in this respect, exceptions.

> This is the land the sunset washes,
>   These are the banks of the Yellow Sea!
> Where it rose, and whither it rushes,
>   These are the Western Mystery!
>
> Night after night her purple traffic
>   Strews the landing with opal bales;
> Merchantmen poise upon horizons,
>   Dip, and vanish with fairy sails.

Mr. Higginson is right in classing these strange fugitive verses with the poetry of William Blake; among other resemblances there is the suggestion of a morbid mental condition or of latent mental disease.

192 "Books of the Week." *Manchester Guardian*, August 11, 1891, p. 7. The phrase from Persius means "poetess of a magpie," implying a lot of chattering.

A good deal has been heard in England about the poems of Miss Emily Dickinson, an American poetess, but by no means one of Persius's *poetridem picae*, inasmuch as she kept aloof from haunt and speech of men and would hardly allow more than one or two of her poems to be published during her by no means short lifetime. But what has been heard of her has for the most part been so tainted and spoilt by the ridiculous and almost incredible overpraise with which some American critics bespatter their country and its works that it was desirable to have the actual works in hand before judging. Messrs. Osgood have published them, or some of them, in a pretty little volume, with a somewhat grandiloquent preface by Mr. T. W. Higginson, and we do not think that any competent critic will deny that they are really remarkable. How far their excessive quaintness is affected and how far natural—how far their flagrant formal defects are the result of wilful study and how far of simple ignorance—it is very hard still to judge without more documents than we have before us. The influence, direct and full, of Emerson is unmistakable by anyone who knows Emerson's verse; but we are not certain of any other. Miss Dickinson's rhymes are so unbelievable ("alcohol" and "pearl," "grave" and "love") that one is inclined to give the benefit of the doubt and suppose a wilful discord and some misleading theory, till one comes across a "tell-tale" like "scimitar" and "saw," which shows a simply vitiated ear. Her metaphorical conceits and Blake-like simplicities (Mr. Higginson thinks them Blake-like) are sometimes extremely striking and sometimes purely nonsensical. This is almost noble:—

> Afraid? Of whom am I afraid?
>   Not Death; for who is he?
> *The porter of my father's lodge*
>   *As much abasheth me.*

And this, we fear, is more than almost drivelling:—

> Grand go the years in the crescent above them;
>   Worlds scoop their arcs, and firmaments row,
> Diadems drop and Doges surrender,
>   Soundless as dots on a disc of snow.

Occasionally she writes like nobody in the world but Mr. Lewis Carroll, though we think his fauna of fancy "do it the more natural":—

> If I could see you in a year,
>   I'd wind the months in balls,
> And put them each in separate drawers,
>   Until their time befalls.
> If only centuries delayed,
>   I'd count them on my hand,
> Subtracting till my fingers dropped
>   Into Van Dieman's Land.

This suggests that the Griffin and the Mock Turtle have been pursuing their education and have been taking a course of seventeenth-century metaphysical poets. To find "lain" used as if it were "laid" is even worse, while that abominable truant Memory *will* think while reading some of the more gushing of the "nature poems" of the outburst of Mr. Verdant Green over the "joll' lill' birds." And yet amid all this conceit and lack of criticism and so forth there are scattered touches which are not mistakable. One has just pished and pshawed at

> Imps in eager caucus
> Raffle for my soul,

when this really charming little piece at once of meaning and music reconciles us:—

> If I can stop one heart from breaking,
>   I shall not live in vain;
> If I can ease one life the aching,
>   Or cool one pain—
> Or help one fainting robin

Into its nest again—   [Unto
I shall not live in vain.

And this, again, is good in the same key and rhythm:—

I had no time to hate, because
    The grave would hinder me,
And life was not so ample I
    Could finish enmity.
Nor had I time to love; but since
    Some industry must be,
The little toil of love, I thought.
    Was large enough for me.

As for the "nature poems," this stanza will at once show their merit and the danger of her style:—

The murmur of the bee   [a bee
A witchcraft yieldeth me.
If any ask me why,
'T were easier to die
Than tell.

But there is no mistake about this, though the blind or careless neglect to complete the form interferes a little with what is otherwise the strong expression of a true thought:—

Pain has an element of blank;
    It cannot recollect
When it began, or if there were
    A day when it was not.
It has no future but itself,
    Its infinite realms contain
Its past enlightened to perceive
    New periods of pain.

193 *"Reviews, etc." Publishers' Circular Weekly and Booksellers' Record of British and Foreign Literature* [London] 55:1311 (August 15, 1891), 178–79.

From *Messrs. James R. Osgood, McIlvaine & Co.*—Reports as to the great poetic ability of Miss Dickinson have occasionally reached these shores, and to the discriminating mind they have not been entirely free from a suspicion of bias. The fact also that Miss Dickinson led so secluded a life, withdrawing herself from all but a very few friends, and never, for many years, even venturing outside of her father's house, imparted additional attraction to her writings, and invested the poetess, if we may so put it, with a species of sentimental halo that was vastly agreeable to the feelings of the romantic. In a way Miss Dickinson is beyond the pale of criticism—just as, during her life-time, she was beyond the pale of human intercourse; and her verses are so unconventional, so untrammelled by any of the ordinary rules that govern the efforts of versifiers, as to make accurate measurement of her ability exceedingly difficult. Some of the poems in this volume strike us as being remarkably soulful; others again are mere nonsense, or have all the appearance of such. The rhymes to our ears are sometimes very dreadful—"sell" and "daffodil," "among" and "belong," and so on. And yet Mr. Higginson, in his not over-judicious preface, tells us that Miss Dickinson had a "rigorous literary standard of her own, and often altered a word many times to suit an ear which had its own tenacious fastidiousness"! Perhaps the most powerful impression with which we rise from a perusal of the book is of the solitary woman pouring out her impassioned thoughts in verse. From whatever cause the seclusion proceeded, there is something pathetic about it.

194 E. R. "Talk About Books." *Queen, The Lady's Newspaper* [London] 90 (August 15, 1891), 253.

"Poems by Emily Dickinson," published by Osgood, McIlvaine, and Co., and edited by "two of her friends," is one of the most remarkable books of verse that has fallen to my hands. It is full of thought of the rarest kind, and of subtlest music, too, although her verse obeys no law. I do not find, as her editor professes to do, any quality in her mind or work recalling William Blake, and should think it rash to father her genius upon any poet we have known. Miss Dickinson's genius as it was self-developed was self-expressed. Perhaps now and again, as we read, we think of Heine's skill, and Heine's strain, and Heine's wounded heart; but we might more safely say there was some deep kinship between these two than that the later poet had in any sense borrowed from the other. Miss Dickinson wrote without thought of readers, just for her heart's satisfaction. During her lifetime she published nothing, and her editors have now found it a difficult task to select from her whole work specimens sufficiently finished for the general ear. It seems as if Miss Dickinson was satisfied to have song in her heart, and cared little into what words it fell. Sometimes she found rhyme, sometimes not. In her unrhymed verse there is no profession of style. We feel simply that rhymes have been left out which crave admission. It is difficult to speak of her work without the help of quotation. Difficult on the other hand, in two or three short pieces, to sufficiently represent it. There are more than a few which I specially wish to make known. Miss Dickinson was born in 1830, and died in 1886. It is hard to believe, considering the range of thought and incident she has traversed, that she lived, as her editor tells us, the life of a recluse.

Her editors are responsible for her titles. I quote here one verse, "The Chrysalis":

> My cocoon tightens, colours tease,
>   I'm feeling for the air;
> A dim capacity for wings
>   Degrades the dress I wear.

That "dim capacity for wings" is far reaching in its application. How many of us trudge the streets, feeling "for the air," and conscious of dim and undeveloped "capacities" of flight. There is deep thought in the lines "Setting Sail":

> Exultation is the going
> Of an inland soul to sea—
> Past the houses, past the headlands,
> Into deep eternity.

> Bred as we among the mountains
> Can the sailor understand
> The divine intoxication
> Of the first league out from land.

The unrhymed lines called "Real" could hardly have been written by one whose life was uneventful:

I like a look of agony
Because I know it's true, &c.

Once again:

I never saw a moor,
I never saw the sea;
Yet know I how the heather looks,
And what a wave must be.

I never spoke with God,
Nor visited in heaven;
Yet am I certain of the spot   [certain am I
As if the chart were given.

195 "Poetry and Verse." *Glasgow Herald,* August 20, 1891, p. 4.

We can readily accept what Mr. T. W. Higginson says in his preface about Emily Dickinson's "Poems." Her verses belong, he thinks, to what Emerson called the "Poetry of the Portfolio." That is to say, "something produced absolutely without the thought of publication, and solely by way of expression of the author's own mind." Yet a selection of the verses is now published, and they undoubtedly reveal a very peculiar character. Born in 1830, Miss Dickinson was the daughter of the Hon. Edward Dickinson, a lawyer who was also treasurer of Amherst College, Massachusetts. Being a recluse by temperament and habit, and seeing little of the outside world, it was perhaps inevitable that Miss Dickinson should write of nature and human nature as if she had seen and known them in dreams and visions rather than by personal experience. After reading her poetry we are not surprised at Mr. Higginson's remark that, having seen this poetess but twice face to face, he "brought away the impression of something as unique and remote as Undine or Mignon or Thekla." These words are singularly appropriate, for the verses contained in the little book might have been the product of one or other of these personalities. It may be, as Mr. Higginson hints, that the reader may find in Miss Dickinson's pages "a quality more suggestive of the poetry of William Blake than of anything to be elsewhere found." It seems to us, however, that, granting a certain imitative air in the quality, and often even in the form of her verses, Miss Dickinson found her master nearer home in the person and poetry of Emerson. She may remind us of Blake, but quite as much, and even more, does she remind us of her illustrious countryman. She seems, in fact, to have been in poetry a female Emerson, and though less intellectually deep and powerful, yet capable now and again of being the vehicle of "flashes of wholly original and profound insight into nature and life," and of "words and phrases exhibiting extraordinary vividness of descriptive and imaginative power." If we concede the applicability of these attributives, yet it must be said that many of Miss Dickinson's best things are "often set in a seemingly whimsical and even rugged frame," as if her brain was played upon alternately by Puck and Ariel. As a consequence, the product is often "like poetry torn up by the roots, with rain and dew and earth still clinging to them, giving a freshness and a fragrance not otherwise to be conveyed." In saying that "the main quality of these poems is that of extraordinary grasp and insight," Mr. Higginson makes a claim that verges on excess, and even trembles on a mere suggestive edge. If we say that Miss Dickinson's muse is as nearly as possible irresponsible, we admit in so many words its veritable, though limited, inspiration. In a certain degree the poetess was "possessed," and was consequently not her own mistress. She could think like an angel; she could only write like a woman, often without rhyme, and occasionally without reason. Sometimes her thought looks deep when it is only a bit of decent commonplace tortured into obscurity. This, however, is clear enough, though quite in her style: —

> Much madness is divinest sense
> To a discerning eye;
> Much sense the starkest madness.
> 'Tis the majority
> In this, as all, prevails.
> Assent, and you are sane;
> Demur, you're straightway dangerous,
> And handled with a chain.

Here again —

> He ate and drank the precious words,
>   His spirit grew robust;
> He knew no more that he was poor,
>   Nor that his frame was dust.
> He danced along the dingy days,
>   And this bequest of wings
> Was but a book. What liberty
>   A loosened spirit brings.

Emerson might have written that. In fact Miss Dickinson is steeped in the Emersonian spirit. Some stanzas on the "May-Flower" are delightful.

> Pink, small, and punctual,
> Aromatic, low,
> Covert in April,
> Candid in May,

> Dear to the moss,
> Known to the knoll,   [by
> Next to the robin
> In every human soul.

> Bold little beauty,
> Bedecked with thee,
> Nature forswears
> Iniquity.   [Antiquity

From the group of pieces on "Time and Eternity" we quote a few lines which show that Miss Dickinson possessed some grasp of the ballad-maker: —

> I died for beauty, but was scarce
>   Adjusted in the tomb,
> When one who died for truth was lain
>   In an adjoining room.

> He questioned softly why I failed?
>   "For beauty," I replied.

"And I for truth—the two are one—
  We brethren are," he cried.   [he said

And so, as kinsmen met at night,   [a night
  We talked between the rooms.
Until the moss had reached our lips,
  And covered up our names.

It will be seen that Miss Dickinson is not finical in rhyme. Substance and sense are her gods, and on the whole they are sufficient, especially when she contrives to make them clear to her readers, which is not to be invariably expected in the case of a transcendentalist poet. As the work of a lady who seldom met the human world face to face, the book is quite unique. Miss Dickinson's case is not, however, one for imitation or admiration, but rather for a degree of lamentation. Had she been capable of mixing with the world and taking part in its ordinary labours, America might have possessed one of the remarkable female poets of modern times.

196 "Books To Read." *Black and White* [London] 2, no. 29 (August 22, 1891), 270.

Mr. Howells, of America, who regularly preaches, in *Harper's Magazine,* a literary gospel, which may be described as one of patriotic provincialism, has lately so far departed from his habitual intolerance of things English as to praise a new English poet in Mr. Watson. English critics have had no need of any unusual tolerance of work from abroad to welcome the good work of a recent American poet, the late Miss Dickinson. Miss Dickinson died nearly six years ago. She was the daughter of the Treasurer of the well-known College of Amherst, in Massachusetts, and at that insignificant little town on the Connecticut River she seems to have lived and died. The College of Amherst was founded seventy years ago for the purpose of educating "poor and pious young men for the ministry." The possibly not over gay surroundings of Amherst did not suffice to draw Miss Dickinson into the whirl of society. Living a life of seclusion, says her biographer, she emerged but once a year to do the honours at an annual general reception given by her father. The guests on these occasions consisted mainly, no doubt, of the "poor and pious young men" of Amherst College, and Miss Dickinson is said to have discharged this annual function with singular grace and charm. Her biographer remarks that he saw the young poetess but twice, face to face, and that he "brought away the impression of something as unique and remote as Undine, or Mignon, or Thekla." This is cautious rather than satisfying, for no one young lady can well resemble all three of these heroines, and the less discreet reader would be glad to learn whether the poetess were tall or short, fair or dark, pretty or plain. She did not write for publication, she was "a poetess of the portfolio," not of the printing press, and it is, perhaps, not fair in her friends now to publish, or in her critics to criticise, what was never meant to see the light. Miss Dickinson was a mystic first, and a poet afterwards: the rhyme and the rhythm are less to her than the idea underlying both. Often her rhymes are imperfect, as "pearl" and "alcohol," "names" and "rooms," and sometimes they are only vowel rhymes, like the *assonant* ones in Spanish poetry, as "smiled" and "denied," "door" and "draw." It is not possible to say whether this is the result of intention, or because the poems were left unfinished; but the editor suggests the first as the explanation. Miss Dickinson is not of the naturalistic school, but a poet who tries to express in her verse those glimpses of the infinite which she herself as a true seer, though of perhaps not very clear or extended vision, enjoyed. She "deals with mysteries which philosophism has not dreamt of," and the naturalist thinks wiser to ignore; and she used poetry as Corot used painting, to suggest rather than to depict. When the noonday sun came out the French painter used to bid his field pupils pack up their pictures and palettes. "Let us go home," he would say, "we can see too much now." So, too, when M. Zola comes out (with apologies to the other luminary) we see too much; we miss the inner truth. That is, perhaps, how Miss Dickinson would have argued; it is, anyhow, on these principles that her verse is constructed:

> I died for beauty, but was scarce
> Adjusted in the tomb,
> When one who died for truth was lain
> In an adjoining room.
>
> He questioned softly why I failed?
> "For beauty," I replied.
> "And I for truth, — the two are one,
> We brethren are," he said.
>
> And so, as kinsmen met anight   [a night
> We talked between the rooms,
> Until the moss had reached our lips
> And covered up our names.

This is but a scanty sample of the work of a nearly forgotten life of deep thought and deep emotion that it is very well not to let wholly die from our memories. There are a hundred exquisitely said things in this little tardy volume.

197   Charles E. L. Wingate. "Boston Letter." *Critic*, n.s. 16 (August 29, 1891), 107.

The new volume of poems by Emily Dickinson is nearly ready for the press. It contains more poems than the first, with many that are quite as striking. These will be under the same editorship as before — that of Mrs. Todd and Col. Higginson. The *Atlantic* has just received from the latter a paper containing an account of his first acquaintance with Miss Dickinson, together with many of her letters, which, I am told, are at least as quaint and original as her poems.

198   "Poetry of the Month." *Literary Opinion* [London] 7:65 (September 1891), 63.

We question very much whether Miss Emily Dickinson's two friends who edit her *Poems* were well advised in publishing them at all. The verses are spontaneous, unconventional, and sometimes are not without a touch of power and charm, but they are uneven, and her knowledge appears scanty and bookish. This is not a matter for surprise when one learns that Miss Dickinson was a "recluse by temperament and habit"; but when poems are published, and a price is put upon their possession, the matter of circumstances in which they were written cannot be taken into consideration. The "Poetry of the Portfolio," such as Miss Dickinson's work really is, should be approached in a sympathetic frame of mind, and, if possible, with some knowledge of the writer; otherwise the reader is unimpressed by the scenes and thoughts that a friend with the inner understanding would find pregnant of meaning and beauty. It is in this way that many of Miss Dickinson's poems must be considered unworthy of the honour of book-covering; but in fairness to her and her editors we must quote the following verses, in which she is perhaps at her best:—

> The bustle in a house
> The morning after death
> Is solemnest of industries
> Enacted upon earth.
>
> The sweeping up the heart,
> And putting love away
> We shall not want to use again
> Until eternity.

199 "Poetry and the Drama." *Review of Reviews* [London] 4 (September 1891), 308.

The preface states that these poems were written with no idea of publication, and were issued after the author's death at the earnest wish of appreciative friends. The quality of the verse is such as to make one wonder on what possible pretext the author's wishes were not observed.

200 "Current Literature." *Tinsley's Magazine* [London], n.s. 5:28 (September 1891), 365–67.

Here in England we are just beginning to make the acquaintance of an American poetess, Miss Emily Dickinson, of whom one has heard much panegyric in American literary circles and literary papers. Messrs. Osgood, McIlvaine, and Co. have just published a dainty little volume of her "Poems," edited by Mabel Loomis Todd and T. W. Higginson. The latter tells us that she was born in Amherst, Massachusetts, December 10th, 1830, and died there May 15th, 1886. Her father was the leading lawyer in his native town, and treasurer of its well-known College. His gifted daughter, it seems, was a recluse by temperament and habit, passing whole years without setting her foot beyond the doorstep, and many more years without emerging from the seclusion of her father's grounds. She concealed her mind also, as well as herself, from all but a very few friends; and it was not without difficulty that, during her life-time, she was persuaded to expose a few of her poems in the nakedness of type. Yet, if one judged only from her poetry, one would suppose that she had studied humanity from an intimate stand-point, and had had her experiences of the rougher side of life. There can be no doubt that she was possessed of a rare and original genius. There can be as little doubt that she was entirely indifferent to that sense of form, harmony, and proportion which distinguishes the greater poets. The book is provoking reading; on this page, an exquisite lyric—a fine thought in appropriate setting; on that, three or four limping, staggering stanzas, without rhythm or cadence. Think of the contrast between the two pieces subjoined:—

> I had no time to hate, because
> The grave would hinder me,
> And life was not so ample I
> Could finish enmity.

Nor had I time to love,—but since
Some industry must be,
The little toil of love, I thought,
Was huge enough for me.   [large

This is in Miss Dickinson's better manner. Of her worse take the following
brief specimen:—

Safe in thin alabaster chambers,   [their
Untouched by morning and untouched by noon.
Sleep the meek members of the resurrection,
Rafter of satin and roof of stone.
        .   .   .   .
Grand go the years in the crescent above them;
Worlds scoop their arcs, and firmaments sow,   [row
Diadems drop and doges surrender,
Soundless as dots on a disc of snow.

I fear that Miss Dickinson wasted a good deal of her genius and most of her
opportunities.

201 "Literary Notes." *Independent* 43 (September 3, 1891), 1321.

A new volume of poems, by the late Emily Dickinson, is nearly ready for the
press. It is, like its forerunner, under the editorship of Col. T. W. Higginson and
Mrs. Todd, and contains a greater number of poems than that remarkable book.

202 "A Poet and Some Others." *Saturday Review* [London] 72 (September 5,
        1891), 279. Following this discussion of Dickinson, the author considers
        four other new books of verse.

The poems of Miss Emily Dickinson (who has hitherto been known to En-
glishmen chiefly if not only by some very injudicious praise of the kind usual with
Mr. Howells) are posthumously published, and from the short preface written by
her sympathetic and friendly editor we learn some interesting facts of her life.
She appears never to have travelled, or, indeed, left the house of her father in
Amherst, Mass., where she led the life of an absolute recluse, and only appeared
in society at a yearly reception given by her father to his friends. We are told that
she wrote verses abundantly, but "absolutely without the thought of publication,
and solely by way of expression of the writer's own mind." The editor prepares
us for the want of form and polish in her poems, but expects us to regard them
as "poetry torn up from the roots, with rain and dew and earth still clinging to
them, giving a freshness and a fragrance not otherwise to be conveyed." A merit
is here implied in their very imperfections as producing the effect of poetry drawn
from an absolutely natural unconventional source. We very much doubt, however, whether this conclusion may be fairly adduced from the uneducated and illiterate character of some of these verses, although we fully recognize in them
the unmistakable touch of a true poet. In these days considerable mastery over
form in poetry is not uncommon, but in our minor poets it is rare indeed to find
much original thought, or a strongly marked individuality. For this reason it is,
perhaps, difficult not to overvalue these qualities, when we find them, as in Miss
Dickinson, separated from any merits of form. We continually see the thoughts
of prose put into verse, but while some of the poems in the present volume can

scarcely be described as in verse at all, they almost all contain a genuinely poetical thought, or image, or feeling. Miss Dickinson's chief characteristics are, first, a faculty for seizing the impression or feelings of the moment, and fixing them with rare force and accuracy; secondly, a vividness of imagery, which impresses the reader as thoroughly unconventional, and shows considerable imaginative power. The following quotation is a fair specimen of some of the most striking poems in the book:—

> Exultation is the going
> Of an inland soul to sea—
> Past the houses, past the headlands,
> Into deep eternity!
>
> Bred as we, among the mountains,
> Can the sailor understand
> The divine intoxication
> Of the first league out from land?

The editor suggests a comparison between the poems of this writer and those of William Blake; but, beyond the fact that they are both quite indifferent to the technical rules of art, the comparison is not very far-reaching. Miss Dickinson possesses little of that lyrical faculty to which Blake owes his reputation; but, on the other hand, she is gifted with a far saner mind. Her poems, however, may be said to be distinctively American in their peculiarities, and occasionally call to mind the verses of Emerson. The editor with his unfailing sympathy tells us that, "though curiously indifferent to all conventional rules," she yet had "a vigorous literary standard of her own, and often altered a word many times to suit an ear which had its own tenacious fastidiousness." Some of the poems, however, seem destitute of any metre whatever, the lines do not scan, the rhymes are arbitrarily thrown in or left out, in accordance with no fixed system, and grammar, and even good taste are sometimes only conspicuous by their absence. But in some of her roughest poems there is still an idea which forces the reader to attend to its meaning, and impress him, in spite of the irritation he may feel at the form. Take, for instance, the little poem on "The Mystery of Pain":—

> Pain has an element of blank;
>   It cannot recollect
> When it began, or if there were
>   A day when it was not.
> It has no future but itself,
>   Its infinite realms contain
> Its past, enlightened to perceive
>   New periods of pain.

These poems for the most part are of a purely reflective character; but a few, such as the two on shipwreck, show considerable descriptive and emotional power. Moreover, though never perfectly finished or satisfactory in form, some of them are conceived in a lyrical way, and are not without music. Take this verse, for instance:—

> Night after night her purple traffic
>   Strews the landing with opal bales;
> Merchantmen poise upon horizons,
>   Dip, and vanish with fairy sails.

In many of the poems there is a deep underlying sense of the mystery of existence, a yearning to set the soul free, and to know the "why" of things. Death is a subject constantly harped upon, either from the point of view of the dying, or of those who watch the departure of others to that "undiscovered country from whose bourn no traveller returns." The writer dwells on the final pomp and ceremony which attends the poor as well as the rich when they leave this world; the equality of death; the sense that the finite ended is the infinite begun; the agonizing and absorbing watchfulness over life that is ebbing, and then the sudden stillness, the "awful leisure," that succeeds when the end has come and the watchers can do no more. There is much that is very striking in these poems, they reveal great depth of feeling, and the tone of them, though melancholy, is not morbid. In some there is a kind of exultation and a concentrated force of expression which is really remarkable:—

> At last to be identified!
> At last, the lamps upon thy side,
> The rest of life to see!
> Past midnight, past the morning star!
> Past sunrise! Ah! what leagues there are
> Between our feet and day!

The little volume contains much to exercise the satire and scorn of critics. The sublime in Miss Dickinson's poems comes sometimes dangerously near to the ridiculous; but any fair-minded reader will, nevertheless, acknowledge that there is something in her poems which cannot be found in the mechanical productions of mere verse-writers, and that the editor is not far wrong when he says that her poetry contains "flashes of wholly original and profound insight into nature and life, words and phrases exhibiting an extraordinary vividness of descriptive and imaginative power, yet often set in a seemingly whimsical, or even rugged, frame."

203 "Literary Notes." *Independent* 43 (September 10, 1891), 1355.

Colonel Higginson has prepared for *The Atlantic* a sketch of the late Emily Dickinson, whose remarkable poems he edited not long since. Many of her letters are to be included in the paper.

204 "Literary Notes." *Christian Union* 44 (September 12, 1891), 503.

The Boston correspondent of the "Critic" states that the new volume of poems by Emily Dickinson is nearly ready for the press. It contains more poems than the first, with many that are quite as striking. These will be under the same editorship as before—that of Mrs. Todd and Colonel Higginson. "Another work," adds this correspondent, "on which the busy Cambridge author is engaged is his address before the Nineteenth Century Club, in New York, last winter, on 'The New World and the New Book.' The lecture is as yet unpublished, and Colonel Higginson, in preparing it for the press, anticipates some comment with disapproval from those who incline to what he regards as the colonial view of American literature. The address will be accompanied by several kindred papers from 'The Independent' and 'The Christian Union.'"

205 "Recent Poetry and Verse." *Graphic* [London] 44 (September 12, 1891), 305.

A certain interest belongs to "Poems by Emily Dickinson," edited by two of her friends, Mabel Loomis Todd and T. W. Higginson. This lady died in 1886, in her fifty-seventh year, and the selection from her poems is published to meet the desire of her personal friends, and especially of her surviving sister. The editors believe that the thoughtful reader will find in these pages a quality more suggestive of the poetry of William Blake than of anything to be elsewhere found. "These verses," they say, "will seem like poetry torn up by the roots, with rain, and dew, and earth still clinging to them, giving a freshness and fragrance not otherwise to be conveyed." This sort of statement may very well mean that the author had not time or ability to throw her thoughts into the most perfect form. As a matter of fact, the verse is not always readily intelligible; still there can be no question that the late Miss Dickinson possessed the poetic temperament and insight into some of the sorrows and mysteries of life. Nevertheless there is a sense of incompleteness about her work as if the thought were dashed off and committed to her portfolio in a hurry. The following quotation is fairly typical of these essays in verse: —

> The heart asks pleasure first,
>   And then, excuse from pain.
> And then, those little anodynes
>   That deaden suffering;
>
> And then, to go to sleep;
>   And then, if it should be
> The will of its Inquisitor,
>   The liberty to die.

206 "Descriptive Summary of the Fall Announcements." *Publishers' Weekly*, 40 (September 19 & 26 [double issue], 1891), 386.

Several volumes of poetry are announced. A second series of "Emily Dickinson's Poems," edited by T. W. Higginson and Mabel Loomis Todd, will be brought out, with a preface by Mrs. Todd and one autograph letter from Mrs. Helen Jackson to Emily Dickinson.

207 Charles E. L. Wingate. "Boston Letter." *Critic*, n.s. 16 (September 19, 1891), 141.

The little that has been made public about the late Emily Dickinson has increased rather than satisfied the desire to know more of her life and aspirations, and for that reason an article which is to appear in the October *Atlantic*, giving an insight into her character, will be read with much interest. She was so strange, so unconventional, so original, that her letters alone pique the imagination, but the connecting text, by Col. T. W. Higginson, explaining the origin of these letters from the poet to himself, makes clearer some of the peculiar expressions.
It is very evident that Miss Dickinson regarded Col. Higginson as the greatest guide and literary friend to whom she could turn, though Col. Higginson's modest retirement of self throughout the article tries to hide this opinion of his pupil. His corrections she accepted as "surgery," but the surgery of a skilful practitioner; while every letter seems to breathe with the thought, "If you but commend my work, I care nothing for the judgment of others." To Col. Higginson's encouragement and advice, therefore, it seems to me, the world may feel indebted

for the impetus which induced this poet to continued exertions. He does not give the letters which he wrote to her and which would prove so valuable to other young writers, but he cannot, of course, eliminate the expression of appreciation in her letters. The correspondence began in 1862, but not till 1870 did Col. Higginson meet his "scholar," as she delighted to sign herself.

In the letters two of the more interesting points to me were Miss Dickinson's allusions to fame and to religion. "If Fame belonged to me," she wrote, "I could not escape her; if she did not, the longest day would pass me on the chase, and the approbation of my dog would forsake me then. My barefoot rank is better." Of religion: — "I have a brother and a sister; my mother does not care for thought, and father is too busy with his briefs to notice what we do. He buys me many books, but begs me not to read them, because he fears they joggle the mind. They are religious, except one, and address an eclipse, every morning, whom they call their 'Father.'" Yet, she often seemed to imply in herself a belief that friends after death exist in another world and can even communicate with their friends in life; while in one letter to the soldier in the field she wrote: — "I trust you may pass the limit of war; and though not reared to prayer, when service is had in church for our arms, I include yourself. . . . I was thinking to-day, as I noticed, that the 'Supernatural' was only the Natural disclosed." Her outer self Miss Dickinson described in these words: — "I am small, like the wren; and my hair is bold, like the chestnut burr; and my eyes, like the sherry in the glass, that the guest leaves"; while her inner self was perhaps best shown in this expression in her conversation: — "If I read a book and it makes my whole body so cold no fire can ever warm me, I know that is poetry. If I feel physically as if the top of my head were taken off, I know that is poetry. These are the only ways I know it."

208   "The Significance of Emily Dickinson." *Hartford Courant,* September 24, 1891, p. 4.

The danger attending a wide cultivation of literature in any country is that a deification of form will result, to the ignoring of the matter which furnishes the *raison d'etre* of any literary creation. This is especially true in the case of poetry, where form plays so important a part. The younger poets of America, the men and women who are to succeed, or have succeeded, the race of elder singers who have made our literature honorable before the nations, are, as a class, better, more careful artists than the giants who preceded them. And their special pitfall is to be found in the substitution of artistic perfection of form, a critical knowledge of meters and *tours de force* of verse for true inspiration and essential nobility and dignity of subject. They will, unless wary, become absorbed in the manner of doing a thing to the neglect of the matter itself. Hence the wording of such a banner as "Art for Art's Sake;" hence, too, a tendency to carve cameos on chestnuts.

Yet how true it is that the intelligent reading world craves originality and beauty before all else, in poetry even as in other fields of literature. A striking example of this is given by the late Emily Dickinson. Less than a year ago a volume of her lyrics appeared, unheralded and with nothing to float it save merit. Edition after edition has been demanded, the verse has already been translated into other tongues and a forthcoming paper by T. W. Higginson in the October *Atlantic* on "Emily Dickinson's Letters" will be one of the most eagerly read of the month and is especially referred to by the editors as an important contribution. And this in the face of the fact that Miss Dickinson's poetry is so utterly lacking in formal excellence as to provoke a frequent smile in the reader. Rhyme is often coolly ignored, the rhythms are defective, the tropes are sometimes grotesque, the poems are not seldom mere fragments or studies rather than the perfected work of a knowing latter-day artist in language. But, to balance this, we get daring, startling originality, great power and felicity of expression, and a serious yet naively poetic treatment of main themes of human life on its subjective side. And so this Amherst recluse, whose death may have brought her immortality in a double sense, jumps into a phenomenal popularity and the public buys her verse, while it lends a deaf ear to the smoothly-turned sonnets of many a bardling whose work, judged as art, is flawless and infinitely superior to Miss Dickinson's.

There is a moral here for our poets, and it is a comfort to feel that the much-abused public somehow senses a good thing when it is proffered and will now and then wake up and notify the literary folk of its wholesome and unquenchable appetite for what has life, and inspiration and reality.

209 "Literary Notes." *Independent* 43 (September 24, 1891), 1421.

A very curious article in the October *Atlantic* is one contributed by Col. T. W. Higginson, who includes a number of letters from Emily Dickinson, letters of the most singular and interesting character, along with such explanatory narrative as is necessary.

210 "Literature." *Boston Daily Traveller,* September 26, 1891, p. 12.

The October Atlantic is an unusually good number, its traditionally high literary standard being fully maintained, and more than the usual number of articles will attract special attention. That by Colonel Thomas Wentworth Higginson, on "Emily Dickinson's Letters," is especially notable, and Colonel Higginson is here at his best.

211 "The Magazines." *Brooklyn Standard-Union,* September 26, 1891, p. 6.
The first two sentences of this notice appeared as well in the *Chicago Inter-Ocean* for the same day, p. 10.

There are three articles in the "Atlantic" for October to which the reader will at once turn. . . . The third contribution which will command attention is the paper by Col. Thomas Wentworth Higginson on "Emily Dickinson's Letters. Such extraordinary letter-writing as Emily Dickinson's has certainly never been seen in print before. Her letters are interesting precisely because every tradition as to what makes a letter interesting is absolutely ignored, and her style is one that would make the eighteenth century letter-writers turn in their graves.

212 "Roberts Brothers." *Literary World* 22 (September 26, 1891), 339.

The demand for Miss Emily Dickinson's "Poems" has been so great that a second series, edited by Thomas Wentworth Higginson and Mabel Loomis Todd, with a preface by Mrs. Todd and an autograph letter from Helen Jackson to Miss Dickinson, will soon be issued.

213 Lilian Whiting. "The Strangely Isolated Life of Emily Dickinson." *Brooklyn Standard-Union,* September 26, 1891, p. 8.

The "Atlantic Monthly" is the pink and pet and pride of the true Bostonian, and its appearance each month marks more or less of a red-letter day; but the October number is one well calculated to incite enthusiasm with its poem by Dr. Holmes on Mr. Lowell, its very notable criticism on Mr. Howells' critical genius, and Col. Higginson's unique sketch of that most unique of characters, Emily Dickinson, whose post-mortem fame is most fitting for one who in life shrank from even signing her name to a letter. The story of this strange and shy lady is not unfamiliar to the general reader. She was born in Amherst, Mass., in December of 1830, and died in that town in May of '86. In this more than half-century of life passed in a country town isolated by nature in its encircling hills, as well as by distance from larger centres, was yet lived a lifetime of the most profoundly introspective existence. Like that delightful mystic, Prof. Amiel, she could have said: "In action I feel myself out of place; my true 'milieu' is contemplation. . . . I seem to myself to be a mere conjurer's apparatus, an instrument of vision and perception, a person without personality, a subject without any determined individuality. . . ." Few of her townspeople ever saw Emily Dickinson, and still fewer had any kind of acquaintance with her. It is said she would sometimes let down notes by a string from her chamber window rather than go down and receive a caller — a method, indeed, that is not without its desirability, and might be imitated with perhaps mutual relief of caller and the called-on. Col. Higginson had a long correspondence with her, but never saw her but twice, "and then," he says, "I brought away an impression as remote as Undine, or Mignon, or Thekla." In his "Atlantic" paper just out, Col. Higginson writes:

"On April 10, 1862, I took from the post office, in Worcester, Mass., where I was then living, the following letter:

"'Mr. Higginson, — Are you too deeply occupied to say if my verse is alive?

"'The mind is so near itself it cannot see distinctly, and I have none to ask.

"'Should you think it breathed, and had you the leisure to tell me, I should feel quick gratitude.

"'If I make the mistake, that you dared to tell me would give me sincerer honor toward you.

"'I enclose my name, asking you, if you please, sir, to tell me what is true?

"'That you will not betray me it is needless to ask, since honor is its own pawn.'

"The letter was postmarked 'Amherst,' and it was in a handwriting so peculiar that it seemed as if the writer might have taken her first lessons by studying the famous fossil bird-tracks in the museum of that college town. Yet it was not in the slightest degree illiterate, but cultivated, quaint and wholly unique. Of punctuation there was little; she used chiefly dashes, and it has been thought better, in printing these letters, as with her poems, to give them the benefit in this respect of the ordinary usages; and so with her habit as to capitalization, as the printers call it, in which she followed the old English and the present German method of thus distinguishing every noun substantive. But the most curious thing about the letter was the total absence of a signature. It proved, however, that she had written her name on a card, and put it under the shelter of a smaller envelope enclosed in the larger; and even this name was written — as if the shy writer wished to recede as far as possible from view — in pencil, not in ink. The name was Emily Dickinson."

Miss Dickinson's poems have a fairly startling insight and vividness, as if with the vision of a clairvoyant she united the vivisective powers of the scientist. She shows, too, an equally startling disregard of poetic laws, to such a degree that the reader will find himself almost pursuing a new language and perhaps speculating curiously as to what results would have been insured had the author subjected herself to careful study of poetic models—had she learned to chip the marble. Yet what profound truth lies in lines like these:

Success is counted sweetest
    By those who ne'er succeed;
To comprehend a nectar
    Requires sorest need.

Not one of all the purple host
    Who took the flag to-day
Can tell the definition,
    So clear, of victory—

As he, defeated, dying,
    On whose forbidden ear
The distant strains of triumph
    Break, agonized and clear.

As a color picture this is exquisite—this "Sea of Sunset":

This is the land the sunset washes,
    These are the banks of the Yellow Sea;
Where it rose or whither it rushes,
    These are the Western mystery!

Night after night her purple traffic
    Strews the landing with opal bales.
Merchantmen poise upon horizons
    Dip, and vanish with fairy sails.

214 This epistolary advertisement appears as an unlocated clipping in Todd's scrapbook.

4 Park Street, Boston, *September* 26, 1891.

Dear Madam:—
    Now that every one is asking "Have you read Emily Dickinson's poems?" and "Who was Emily Dickinson?" the paper by Colonel *Thomas Wentworth Higginson* on

"EMILY DICKINSON'S LETTERS,"

in the October Atlantic, will command attention. Such extraordinary letter-writing as Emily Dickinson's has certainly never been seen in print before—interesting precisely because every tradition in letter-writing is absolutely ignored. No one who wishes to gain some idea of the daily life of this interesting woman should miss the paper.
    The October number also contains Dr. Holmes's tribute to Lowell.
                    Yours truly,
                    HOUGHTON, MIFFLIN & CO.

The Price of THE ATLANTIC is 35 cents.

215 *New York Sunday Herald*, September 27, 1891, p. 31.

In the October *Atlantic* Colonel T. W. Higginson gives the following pen portrait of the late Emily Dickinson, a poet who was scarcely known outside of her own family circle until after she died: —

"A plain, shy little person, the face without a single good feature, but with eyes, as she herself said, 'like the sherry the guest leaves in the glass,' and with smooth bands of reddish chestnut hair. She had a quaint and nunlike look, as if she might be a German canoness of some religious order, whose prescribed garb was white pique, with a blue net worsted shawl. She came toward me with two day lilies, which she put in a childlike way into my hand, saying softly, under her breath, 'These are my introduction,' and adding also under her breath, in childlike fashion, 'Forgive me if I am frightened; I never see strangers and hardly know what I say.' But soon she began to talk and thenceforward continued almost constantly, pausing sometimes to beg that I would talk instead, but readily recommencing when I evaded. There was not a trace of affectation in all this; she seemed to speak absolutely for her own relief and wholly without watching its effect on her hearer."

216 "Books, Authors and Art." *Springfield Sunday Republican*, September 27, 1891, p. 6. Reprinted in the *Weekly Republican*, October 2, 1891, p. 9.

The article on "Emily Dickinson's Letters" which Thomas Wentworth Higginson has contributed to the October *Atlantic* is such a one as no person who, in Thoreau's phrase, lives in his head, can consciously pass by. The letters confirm the impression of the poems, and several poems not before published are included in them; and there is aroused the old controversy as to what poetry is. Any number of professed critics deny the title of poet to Emily Dickinson because she not only did not care about form but seemed quite ignorant of its requirements. She used rhyme, now and then, but not as if it were of any consequence. And the very point at issue is that: is rhyme necessary to rhythmic poetry? is even perfection in rhythm necessary? What is poetry? It is the old question again. Matthew Arnold says it is a criticism of life, — and we must allow that is a circumscribed definition, although with much truth in it. It is also said that it is melodious words in conventional meters. In truth, we are obliged often to recognize poetry in its essence in prose forms, and it is safest to say that the basic quality of poetry is imagination, framed in harmonious movement. This leaves out the didactic schools of Dryden, Pope and Cowper, Pollok, Blair and Young, and yet in the midst of their conventional or mechanical verse, there is ever and anon genuine poetry, so that the definition does not hold. But when the attempt is made by ordinary versifiers of today to limit verse to form, this fact gives us warrant to oppose such a circumscription. In poetry, as in every other form that expresses the human mind, there is something at the heart and in the light that sets it apart. Poetry must have a distinctive quality. In the common acceptation, things are called poetry which are widely separated — these are the poetry of ideas and the poetry of words. The highest poetry blends both, but if we are to choose between ideas and words, there can be no hesitation. The young people who rhyme today in artistic arrangements of words cannot rightly expect to be ranked with those who wrote in rhythm because rhythm helped their expression, and so regarded it as an instrument and not as an object of attainment. When we read strictures on Mrs. Browning's false rhymes, the first impulse is to say, "What fools these critics are!" for what matter if she rhymes "islands" and "silence," when the thought behind these imperfect correspondences of sound is one of profound imagination?

Emily Dickinson was a poet, if a poet ever lived. She was possessed with a continuing inspiration; she was compelled to write; and whatever she did, so far as we learn from the samples published in the volume of poems issued or in Col. Higginson's record of his acquaintance with her, was intensely poetic, though almost invariably faulty in language as well as rhythm and rhyme. But with all these faults her little shallop is worth thousands of cargoes of finished verse, such as the "artists" of this day are turning out in profusion. She is nearer to Sappho than these elegant rhymesters think. The criticism which is showered upon her posthumous verse is very much like that which the same class of critics visit upon Emerson, and yet Emerson remains the most valuable poet, as poet, that America has known. He was seldom certain of form, though he could and did write in perfect form; but when he disregarded the trammels of false prosody, he infinitely transcended others, simply because his spiritual insight rose above all their tests. And if there be any poet to whom Emily Dickinson can be likened, it is Emerson. Channing, too, with all his insufficiencies, has often the same fine frenzy of feeling to which accepted phrases are incompetent. Eugene Field, who is a very clever and witty poet, and often writes a genuine poem, has contested this question with the *Republican* on the grounds indicated; but with all his ingenuity, he cannot reach the strength and beauty of the erratic and unconfinable genius of Emily Dickinson.

No doubt that the recluse woman was scarcely in her right mind, if we accept the standard of ordinary life. Her whole order of living shows that she was exceptional and extraordinary, and nothing, as it seems, could have made her like other people. Col. Higginson's article makes this entirely plain; from this the public may learn what a few have known for many years, that Emily Dickinson was a creature set apart by Nature herself. She appealed to him, in April 1862, for counsel in respect to her verse. Why she should have chosen him for this office of mentor does not appear, — something he had written must have touched her in a peculiar way, so that he became to her suddenly a personage of importance in her life, and she placed him there at once, and made demands upon him frankly, in this way: —

> Are you too deeply occupied to say if my verse is alive? The mind is so near itself it cannot see distinctly, and I have none to ask. Should you think it breathed, and had you the leisure to tell me, I should feel quick gratitude. If I make the mistake, that you dared to tell me would give me sincerer honor toward you. I enclose my name, asking you, if you please, sir, to tell me what is true? That you will not betray me it is needless to ask, since honor is its own pawn.

The singularity of these phrases would have struck anybody as evidence of a nature not only out of the common, but out of balance. It was, says the one addressed, "in a handwriting so peculiar that it seemed as if the writer might have taken her first lessons by studying the famous fossil bird-tracks in the museum of that college town [Amherst]. Yet it was not in the slightest degree illiterate, but cultivated, quaint and wholly unique." With the letter were included four poems, two of which have been used in the volume of her verse printed, and the other two the receiver now presents, one of which we quote: —

The nearest dream recedes unrealized.
>The heaven we chase
>Like the June bee
>Before the schoolboy

        Invites the race,
        Stoops to an easy clover,
    Dips—evades—teases—deploys—
    Then to the royal clouds
        Lifts his light pinnace,
        Heedless of the boy,
    Staring, bewildered, at the mocking sky.

        Homesick for steadfast honey,—
        Ah! the bee flies not
    Which brews that rare variety!   [That brews

The one who reads that, and does not understand how Col. Higginson should
have had at the moment an impression of "a wholly new and original poetic genius," might as well abandon poetry—it is not in him.
    The strange Emily had her little shrewdnesses, too. For it seems that Mr. Hig-
ginson, in the course of the correspondence thus begun, had put certain questions, one of which she answers in this way: "You asked how old I was? I made
no verse, but one or two until this winter, sir." In the same letter she said of her
reading, "For poets, I have Keats and Mr. and Mrs. Browning. For prose, Ruskin,
Sir Thomas Browne and the Revelations. When a little girl, I had a friend who
taught me immortality, but venturing too near, himself, he never returned. Then
I found one more, but he was not contented I be his scholar, so he left the land."
This is a sufficiently mysterious statement. As the correspondence went on,
the singular woman grew friendly, and expatiated in her strange way on herself
and what she did. She wrote, among other things: "I thanked you for your justice, but could not drop the bells whose jingling cooled my tramp. Perhaps the
value seemed better because you told me first. I smile when you suggest that I
delay 'to publish,' that being foreign to my thought as firmament to fin. If fame
belonged to me, I could not escape her; if she did not, the longest day would pass
me on the chase, and the approbation of my dog would forsake me then. My
barefoot rank is better." The ideas in her mind strike through these words like
fire through a pile of brush,—the brush was naught, but the fire shows all. In
this same letter was this remarkable bit of verse:—

        As if I asked a common alms,
            And in my wondering hand,
        A stranger pressed a kingdom,
            And I bewildered stand;
        As if I asked the Orient
            Had it for me a morn,—
        And it should lift its purple dikes
            And shatter me with dawn!

Presently she wrote in answer to a request for her picture, "Could you believe
me without? I had no portrait, now, but am small like the wren; and my hair is
bold, like the chestnut burr; and my eyes, like the sherry in the glass the guest
leaves. Would this do just as well?" It had to do, and Mr. Higginson afterward
visiting her, found the description not inapt. Perhaps no letter given by Col. Higginson exceeds in interest that she wrote him when he was in camp as colonel
of a negro regiment in the South, in which she says: "I should have liked to see
you before you became improbable. War feels to me an oblique place. . . . I found
you were gone by accident, as I find systems are, or seasons of the year, and obtain no cause, but suppose it a treason of progress that dissolves as it goes. . . . Per-

haps death gave me awe for friends, striking sharp and early, for I held them since in a brittle love, of more alarm than peace. I trust you may pass the limit of war, and though not reared to prayer, when service is held in church for our arms, I include yourself. . . . I was thinking today that the supernatural was only the natural disclosed.

> Not Revelation 'tis that waits,
> But our unfurnished eyes.

Should you, before this reaches you, experience immortality, who will inform me of the exchange? Could you with honor avoid death, I entreat you, sir." This letter alone she signed "your Gnome."

Nothing of what Mr. Higginson gives makes clear the spell of Emily Dickinson's verses. Here is one of those she sent him on the Humming Bird: —

> A route of evanescence,
> With a revolving wheel;
> A resonance of emerald,
> A rush of cochineal;
> And every blossom on the bush
> Adjusts its tumbled head, —
> The mail from Tunis, probably —
> An easy morning's ride.

Such verses as these surely remind one of Emerson's Bumble Bee, but much more of passages in his great essay, "Nature."

Perhaps one might say, finding such evident poetic inspiration conjoined with manifestly incomplete expression, that Emily Dickinson was afflicted with almost an aphasia, for no one can well deny that her words are often hard to wrench into appositeness with her very clear thought. Mr. Higginson gives an account of his first and chief personal interview with this mysterious creature, who constantly signed herself "your scholar," and quotes things she said. There is one question that is persistent with any serious minded person: "How do most people live without any thoughts? There are many people in the world, — you must have noticed them in the street, — how do they live? How do they get strength to put on their clothes in the morning?" This saying will pass under the eyes of hundreds who will not understand what this means, or that they themselves are among the people who live without thoughts. This chaotic poet uttered also such an extravaganza as this: "If I read a book, and it makes my whole body so cold no fire can ever warm me, I know that is poetry. These are the only ways I know it. Is there any other way?" But surely the true perception of poetry is not too keenly expressed in these singular phrases. There is a striking passage in a letter about her father's death: "His heart was pure and terrible, and I think no other like it exists. I am glad there is immortality, but would have tested it myself, before entrusting him. Mr. Bowles was with us, with that exception I saw none." Then later she wrote: "Dear friend: I felt it shelter to speak to you. My brother and sister are with Mr. Bowles, who is buried this afternoon. The last song that I heard — that was, since the birds — was 'He leadeth me, he leadeth me; yea, though I walk' — then the voices stopped, the arch was so low." Altogether, this was a strange and wonderful spirit, and her verses are a priceless legacy to a world too full of excellent formalists.

217   "A Recluse Woman of Genius." *Boston Herald,* September 28, 1891, p. 4.

The public learns something more of Emily Dickinson in the October Atlantic Monthly, from an article on her letters, accompanied with copious examples, contributed by Thomas W. Higginson. Miss Dickinson was as much a discovery as was Marie Bashkirtseff, and she was a far more important one, if she had no Mr. Gladstone to direct public attention to her. She was a poet with as distinct an inspiration as was ever conferred, yet not of a character to attract the attention of any but those who could appreciate its subtle character. This remarkable woman was the daughter of that plain and practical country squire, Edward Dickinson, of Amherst, who is remembered as holding state offices, and as once a candidate for Congress in the old Whig party. This daughter lived in ill health very much to herself for many years. It is only lately that the world has been introduced at all to her unique intellect and character. Col. Higginson's article is interesting, yet it does not by any means fully interpret and explain the woman of whom it treats.

218   "October Magazines." *New York World,* September 28, 1891, p. 26.

Thomas Wentworth Higginson writes affectionately and delicately of the poet Emily Dickinson in the *Atlantic* and submits to sympathetic view some private letters from her to himself.

218A   "Notes." *Book News* 10 (October 1891), 77.

Col. T. W. Higginson writes in the *Atlantic Monthly* of Emily Dickinson. The article includes a number of letters from Miss Dickinson to Col. Higginson, and are said to be of a singularly interesting character.

219   "Brief and Critical Comment." *Current Literature* 8 (October 1891), 317; a reprinting; see no. 183.

220   "Brief and Critical Comment." *Current Literature* 8 (October 1891), 319. The source of the quoted review is not the *Pall Mall Budget* but the *St. James's Gazette;* see no. 189. The *Budget* neither reviewed nor mentioned Dickinson in the nineties.

The Pall Mall Budget says, *a' propos* of a review of Emily Dickinson's Poems: "Possibly if Miss Dickinson had learned grammar and had known anything of the laws of metre, and had had any thoughts to express or any faculty of expressing them, she might have become quite a decent fifth-rate versifier."

221   Thomas Wentworth Higginson. "Emily Dickinson's Letters." *Atlantic Monthly* 68 (October 1891), 444–56. As Mrs. Bingham notes, this widely remarked essay "was well timed to arouse interest in the forthcoming Second Series of *Poems*" and "in the possibility of a volume of Emily's letters." Indeed, no other publication event gave Dickinson wider exposure in the nineties. Both Lavinia Dickinson and Mabel Todd wrote to Higginson of their satisfaction with his article, the latter stressing its "great notoriety and popularity, everywhere" (*AB*, pp. 164–66). The essay was republished, slightly revised, in Higginson's *Carlyle's Laugh, and Other Surprises* (Boston: Houghton, Mifflin, 1909), pp. 184–99. The poet's uncle, whom Higginson recalls meeting, was William Dickinson (see Index).

Few events in American literary history have been more curious than the sudden rise of Emily Dickinson into a posthumous fame only more accentuated by the utterly recluse character of her life and by her aversion to even a literary publicity. The lines which form a prelude to the published volume of her poems are the only ones that have yet come to light indicating even a temporary desire to come in contact with the great world of readers; she seems to have had no reference, in all the rest, to anything but her own thought and a few friends. But for her only sister, it is very doubtful if her poems would ever have been printed at all; and when published, they were launched quietly and without any expectation of a wide audience; yet the outcome of it is that six editions of the volume have been sold within six months, a suddenness of success almost without a parallel in American literature.

One result of this glare of publicity has been a constant and earnest demand by her readers for further information in regard to her; and I have decided with much reluctance to give some extracts from her early correspondence with one whom she always persisted in regarding—with very little ground for it—as a literary counselor and confidant.

It seems to be the opinion of those who have examined her accessible correspondence most widely, that no other letters bring us quite so intimately near to the peculiar quality and aroma of her nature; and it has been urged upon me very strongly that her readers have the right to know something more of this gifted and most interesting woman.

On April 16, 1862, I took from the post office in Worcester, Mass., where I was then living, the following letter: —

Mr. Higginson, — Are you too deeply occupied to say if my verse is alive?
The mind is so near itself it cannot see distinctly, and I have none to ask.
Should you think it breathed, and had you the leisure to tell me, I should feel quick gratitude.
If I make the mistake, that you dared to tell me would give me sincerer honor toward you.
I inclose my name, asking you, if you please, sir, to tell me what is true?
That you will not betray me it is needless to ask, since honor is its own pawn.

The letter was postmarked "Amherst," and it was in a handwriting so peculiar that it seemed as if the writer might have taken her first lessons by studying the famous fossil bird-tracks in the museum of that college town. Yet it was not in the slightest degree illiterate, but cultivated, quaint, and wholly unique. Of punctuation there was little; she used chiefly dashes, and it has been thought better, in printing these letters, as with her poems, to give them the benefit in this respect of the ordinary usages; and so with her habit as to capitalization, as the printers call it, in which she followed the Old English and present German method of thus distinguishing every noun substantive. But the most curious thing about the letter was the total absence of a signature. It proved, however, that she had written her name on a card, and put in under the shelter of a smaller envelope inclosed in the larger; and even this name was written—as if the shy writer wished to recede as far as possible from view—in pencil, not in ink. The name was Emily Dickinson. Inclosed with the letter were four poems, two of which have been already printed, — "Safe in their alabaster chambers" and "I'll tell you how the sun rose," together with the two that here follow. The first comprises in its eight lines a truth so searching that it seems a condensed summary of the whole experience of a long life: —

> We play at paste
> Till qualified for pearl;
> Then drop the paste
> And deem ourself a fool.
>
> The shapes, though, were similar
> And our new hands
> Learned gem-tactics,
> Practicing sands.

Then came one which I have always classed among the most exquisite of her productions, with a singular felicity of phrase and an aerial lift that bears the ear upward with the bee it traces: —

> The nearest dream recedes unrealized.
>   The heaven we chase,
>   Like the June bee
>   Before the schoolboy,
>   Invites the race,
>   Stoops to an easy clover,
> Dips — evades — teases — deploys —
> Then to the royal clouds
>   Lifts his light pinnace,
>   Heedless of the boy
> Staring, bewildered, at the mocking sky.
>
>   Homesick for steadfast honey, —
>   Ah! the bee flies not
> Which brews that rare variety.

The impression of a wholly new and original poetic genius was as distinct on my mind at the first reading of these four poems as it is now, after thirty years of further knowledge; and with it came the problem never yet solved, what place ought to be assigned in literature to what is so remarkable, yet so elusive of criticism. The bee himself did not evade the school boy more than she evaded me; and even at this day I still stand somewhat bewildered, like the boy.

Circumstances, however, soon brought me in contact with an uncle of Emily Dickinson, a gentleman not now living; a prominent citizen of Worcester, a man of integrity and character, who shared her abruptness and impulsiveness but certainly not her poetic temperament, from which he was indeed singularly remote. He could tell but little of her, she being evidently an enigma to him, as to me. It is hard to tell what answer was made by me, under these circumstances, to this letter. It is probable that the advisor sought to gain time a little and find out with what strange creature he was dealing. I remember to have ventured on some criticism which she afterwards called "surgery," and on some questions, part of which she evaded, as will be seen, with a naive skill such as the most experienced and worldly coquette might envy. Her second letter (received April 26, 1862), was as follows: —

Mr. Higginson, — Your kindness claimed earlier gratitude, but I was ill, and write today from my pillow.

Thank you for the surgery; it was not so painful as I supposed. I bring you others, as you ask, though they might not differ. While my thought is undressed, I can make the distinction; but when I put them in the gown, they look alike and numb.

You asked how old I was? I made no verse, but one or two, until this winter, sir.

I had a terror since September, I could tell to none; and so I sing, as the boy does of the burying ground, because I am afraid.

You inquire my books. For poets, I have Keats, and Mr. and Mrs. Browning. For prose, Mr. Ruskin, Sir Thomas Browne, and the Revelations. I went to school, but in your manner of the phrase had no education. When a little girl, I had a friend who taught me Immortality; but venturing too near, himself, he never returned. Soon after my tutor died, and for several years my lexicon was my only companion. Then I found one more, but he was not contented I be his scholar, so he left the land.

You ask of my companions. Hills, sir, and the sundown, and a dog large as myself, that my father bought me. They are better than beings because they know, but do not tell; and the noise in the pool at noon excels my piano.

I have a brother and sister; my mother does not care for thought, and father, too busy with his briefs to notice what we do. He buys me many books, but begs me not to read them, because he fears they joggle the mind. They are religious, except me, and address an eclipse, every morning, whom they call their "Father."

But I fear my story fatigues you. I would like to learn. Could you tell me how to grow, or is it unconveyed, like melody or witchcraft?

You speak of Mr. Whitman. I never read his book but was told that it was disgraceful.

I read Miss Prescott's Circumstance, but it followed me in the dark, so I avoided her.

Two editors of journals came to my father's house this winter, and asked me for my mind, and when I asked them "why" they said I was penurious, and they would use it for the world.

I could not weigh myself, myself. My size felt small to me. I read your chapters in the Atlantic, and experienced honor for you. I was sure you would not reject a confiding question.

Is this sir, what you asked me to tell you? Your friend,

E. Dickinson.

It will be seen that she had now drawn a step nearer, signing her name, and as my "friend." It will also be noticed that I had sounded her about certain American authors, then much read; and that she knew how to put her own criticisms in a very trenchant way. With this letter came some more verses, still in the same birdlike script, as for instance the following: —

> Your riches taught me poverty,
>   Myself a millionaire
> In little wealths, as girls could boast,
>   Till, broad as Buenos Ayre,
> You drifted your dominions
>   A different Peru,
> And I esteemed all poverty
>   For life's estate, with you.

Of mines, I little know, myself,
    But just the names of gems,
The colors of the commonest,
    And scarce of diadems
So much that, did I meet the queen
    Her glory I should know;
But this must be a different wealth,
    To miss it, beggars so.

I'm sure, 'tis India, all day,
    To those who look on you
Without a stint, without a blame,
    Might I but be the Jew!
I'm sure it is Golconda
    Beyond my power to deem,
To have a smile for mine, each day,
    How better than a gem!

At least, it solaces to know
    That there exists a gold
Although I prove it just in time
    Its distance to behold;
Its far, far treasure to surmise
    And estimate the pearl
That slipped my simple fingers through
    While just a girl at school!

Here was already manifest that defiance of form, never through carelessness, and never precisely from whim, which so marked her. The slightest change in the order of words—thus, "While yet at school, a girl"—would have given her a rhyme for this last line; but no; she was intent upon her thought, and it would not have satisfied her to make the change. The other poem further showed, what had already been visible, a rare and delicate sympathy with the life of nature:—

A bird came down the walk;
He did not know I saw;
He bit an angle-worm in halves
And ate the fellow raw.

And then he drank a dew
From a convenient grass,
And then hopped sidewise to a wall,   [the wall
To let a beetle pass.

He glanced with rapid eyes
That hurried all around;
They looked like frightened beads, I thought;
He stirred his velvet head

Like one in danger, cautious.
I offered him a crumb,
And he unrolled his feathers
And rowed him softer home

Than oars divide the ocean,
Too silver for a seam—

Or butterflies, off banks of noon,
Leap, plashless as they swim.

It is possible that in a second letter I gave more of distinct praise or encouragement, for her third is in a different mood. This was received June 8, 1862. There is something startling in its opening image; and in the yet stranger phrase that follows, where she apparently uses "mob" in the sense of chaos or bewilderment: —

DEAR FRIEND, — Your letter gave no drunkenness, because I tasted rum before. Domingo comes but once; yet I have had few pleasures so deep as your opinion, and if I tried to thank you, my tears would block my tongue.

My dying tutor told me that he would like to live till I had been a poet, but Death was much of mob as I could master, then. And when, far afterward, a sudden light on orchards, or a new fashion in the wind troubled my attention, I felt a palsy, here, the verses just relieve.

Your second letter surprised me, and for a moment, swung. I had not supposed it. Your first gave no dishonor, because the true are not ashamed. I thanked you for your justice, but could not drop the bells whose jingling cooled my tramp. Perhaps the balm seemed better, because you bled me first. I smile when you suggest that I delay "to publish," that being foreign to my thought as firmament to fin.

If fame belonged to me, I could not escape her; if she did not, the longest day would pass me on the chase, and the approbation of my dog would forsake me then. My barefoot rank is better.

You think my gait "spasmodic." I am in danger, sir. You think me "uncontrolled." I have no tribunal.

Would you have time to be the "friend" you should think I need? I have a little shape: it would not crowd your desk, nor make much racket as the mouse that dents your galleries.

If I might bring you what I do — not so frequent to trouble you — and ask you if I told it clear, 't would be control to me. The sailor cannot see the North, but knows the needle can. The "hand you stretch me in the dark" I put mine in, and turn away. I have no Saxon now: —

As if I asked a common alms,
And in my wondering hand
A stranger pressed a kingdom,
And I, bewildered, stand;
As if I asked the Orient
Had it for me a morn,
And it should lift its purple dikes
And shatter me with dawn!

But, will you be my preceptor, Mr. Higginson?

With this came the poem already published in her volume and entitled Renunciation; and also that beginning "Of all the sounds dispatched abroad," thus fixing approximately the date of those two. I must soon have written to ask her for her picture, that I might form some impression of my enigmatical correspondent. To this came the following reply, in July, 1862: —

Could you believe me without? I had no portrait, now, but am small, like the wren; and my hair is bold, like the chestnut burr; and my eyes, like the sherry in the glass, that the guest leaves. Would this do just as well?

It often alarms father. He says death might occur, and he has moulds of all the rest, but has no mould of me; but I noticed the quick wore off those things, in a few days, and forestall the dishonor. You will think no caprice of me.

You said "Dark." I know the butterfly, and the lizard, and the orchis. Are not those *your* countrymen?

I am happy to be your scholar, and will deserve the kindness I cannot repay.

If you truly consent, I recite now. Will you tell me my fault, frankly as to yourself, for I had rather wince than die. Men do not call the surgeon to commend the bone, but to set it, sir, and fracture within is more critical. And for this, preceptor, I shall bring you obedience, the blossom from my garden, and every gratitude I know.

Perhaps you smile at me. I could not stop for that. My business is circumference. An ignorance, not of customs, but if caught with the dawn, or the sunset see me, myself the only kangaroo among the beauty, sir, if you please, it afflicts me, and I thought that instruction would take it away.

Because you have much business, beside the growth of me, you will appoint, yourself, how often I shall come, without your inconvenience.

And if at any time you regret you received me, or I prove a different fabric to that you supposed, you must banish me.

When I state myself, as the representative of the verse, it does not mean me, but a supposed person.

You are true about the "perfection." Today makes Yesterday mean.

You spoke of Pippa Passes. I never heard anybody speak of Pippa Passes before. You see my posture is benighted.

To thank you baffles me. Are you perfectly powerful? Had I a pleasure you had not, I could delight to bring it.   YOUR SCHOLAR.

This was accompanied by this strong poem, with its breathless conclusion. The title is of my own giving: —

THE SAINTS' REST.

Of tribulation these are they,
    Denoted by the white;
The spangled gowns, a lesser rank
    Of victors designate.

All these did conquer; but the ones
    Who overcame most times,
Wear nothing commoner than snow,
    No ornaments but palms.

"Surrender" is a sort unknown
    On this superior soil;
"Defeat" an outgrown anguish,
    Remembered as the mile

Our panting ancle barely passed
    When night devoured the road;
But we stood whispering in the house,
    And all we said was "Saved!"

[Note by the writer of the verses.] I spelled ankle wrong.

It would seem that at first I tried a little, — a very little — to lead her in the direction of rules and traditions; but I fear it was only perfunctory, and that she interested me more in her — so to speak — unregenerate condition. Still, she recognizes the endeavor. In this case, as will be seen, I called her attention to the fact that while she took pains to correct the spelling of a word, she was utterly careless of greater irregularities. It will be seen by her answer that with her usual naïve adroitness she turns my point:—

DEAR FRIEND,—Are these more orderly? I thank you for the truth.

I had no monarch in my life, and cannot rule myself; and when I try to organize, my little force explodes and leaves me bare and charred.

I think you called me "wayward." Will you help me improve?

I suppose the pride that stops the breath, in the core of woods, is not of ourself.

You say I confess the little mistake, and omit the large. Because I can see orthography; but the ignorance out of sight is my preceptor's charge.

Of "shunning men and women," they talk of hallowed things, aloud, and embarrass my dog. He and I don't object to them, if they'll exist their side. I think Carlo would please you. He is dumb, and brave. I think you would like the chestnut tree I met in my walk. It hit my notice suddenly, and I thought the skies were in blossom.

Then there's a noiseless noise in the orchard that I let persons hear.

You told me in one letter you could not come to see me "now," and I made no answer; not because I had none, but did not think myself the price that you should come so far.

I do not ask so large a pleasure, lest you might deny me.

You say, "Beyond your knowledge." You would not jest with me, because I believe you; but, preceptor, you cannot mean it?

All men say "What" to me, but I thought it a fashion.

When much in the woods, as a little girl, I was told that the snake would bite me, that I might pick a poisonous flower, or goblins kidnap me; but I went along and met no one but angels, who were far shyer of me than I could be of them, so I haven't that confidence in fraud which many exercise.

I shall observe your precept, thought I don't understand it, always.

I marked a line in one verse, because I met it after I made it, and never consciously touch a paint mixed by another person.

I do not let go it, because it is mine. Have you the portrait of Mrs. Browning? Persons sent me three. If you had none, will you have mine?

YOUR SCHOLAR.

A month or two after this I entered the volunteer army of the civil war, and must have written to her during the winter of 1862–3 from South Carolina or Florida, for the following reached me in camp:—

Amherst.

DEAR FRIEND,—I did not deem that planetary forces annulled, but suffered an exchange of territory, or world.

I should have liked to see you before you became improbable. War feels to me an oblique place. Should there be other summers, would you perhaps come?

I found you were gone, by accident, as I find systems are, or seasons of the year, and obtain no cause, but suppose it a treason of progress that dissolves as it goes. Carlo still remained, and I told him

Best gains must have the losses' test,
To constitute them gains.

My shaggy ally assented.

Perhaps death gave me awe for friends, striking sharp and early, for I held them since in a brittle love, of more alarm than peace. I trust you may pass the limit of war; and though not reared to prayer, when service is had in church for our arms, I include yourself. . . . I was thinking today, as I noticed, that the "Supernatural" was only the Natural disclosed.

Not "Revelation" 'tis that waits,
But our unfurnished eyes.

But I fear I detain you. Should you, before this reaches you, experience immortality, who will inform me of the exchange? Could you, with honor, avoid death, I entreat you, sir. It would bereave   YOUR GNOME.

I trust the "Procession of Flowers" was not a premonition.

I cannot explain this extraordinary signature, substituted for the now customary "Your Scholar," unless she imagined her friend to be in some incredible and remote condition, imparting its strangeness to her. Mr. Howells reminds me that Swedenborg somewhere has an image akin to her "oblique place," where he symbolizes evil as simply an oblique angle. With this letter came verses, most refreshing in that clime of jasmines and mocking-birds, on the familiar robin:—

THE ROBIN.

The robin is the one
That interrupts the morn
With hurried, few, express reports
When March is scarcely on.

The robin is the one
That overflows the noon
With her cherubic quantity,
An April but begun.

The robin is the one
That, speechless from her nest,
Submits that home and certainty
And sanctity are best.

In the summer of 1863 I was wounded, and in hospital for a time, during which came this letter in pencil, written from what was practically a hospital for her, though only for weak eyes:—

DEAR FRIEND,—Are you in danger? I did not know that you were hurt. Will you tell me more? Mr. Hawthorne died.

I was ill since September, and since April in Boston for a physician's care. He does not let me go, yet I work in my prison, and make guests for myself.

Carlo did not come, because that he would die in jail; and the mountains I could not hold now, so I brought but the Gods.

I wish to see you more than before I failed. Will you tell me your health? I am surprised and anxious since receiving your note.

The only news I know
Is bulletins all day
From Immortality.

Can you render my pencil? The physician has taken away my pen.

I inclose the address from a letter, lest my figures fail.

Knowledge of your recovery would excel my own.

E. DICKINSON.

Later this arrived:—

DEAR FRIEND,—I think of you so wholly that I cannot resist to write again, to ask if you are safe? Danger is not at first, for then we are unconscious, but in the after, slower days.

Do not try to be saved, but let redemption find you, as it certainly will. Love is its own rescue; for we, at our supremest, are but its trembling emblems.

YOUR SCHOLAR.

These were my earliest letters from Emily Dickinson, in their order. From this time and up to her death (May 15, 1886) we corresponded at varying intervals, she always persistently keeping up this attitude of "Scholar," and assuming on my part a preceptorship which it is almost needless to say did not exist. Always glad to hear her "recite," as she called it, I soon abandoned all attempt to guide in the slightest degree this extraordinary nature, and simply accepted her confidences, giving as much as I could of what might interest her in return.

Sometimes there would be a long pause, on my part, after which would come a plaintive letter, always terse, like this:—

"Did I displease you? But won't you tell me how?"

Or perhaps the announcement of some event, vast to her small sphere, as this:

Amherst.

Carlo died. EMILY DICKINSON.
Would you instruct me now?

Or sometimes there would arrive an exquisite little detached strain, every word a picture, like this:—

THE HUMMING-BIRD.

A route of evanescence
With a revolving wheel;
A resonance of emerald;
A rush of cochineal.
And every blossom on the bush
Adjusts its tumbled head;—
The mail from Tunis, probably,
An easy morning's ride.

Nothing in literature, I am sure, so condenses into a few words that gorgeous atom of life and fire of which she here attempts the description. It is, however, needless to conceal that many of her brilliant fragments were less satisfying. She almost always grasped whatever she sought, but with some fracture of grammar and dictionary on the way. Often, too, she was obscure and sometimes inscrutable; and though obscurity is sometimes, in Coleridge's phrase, a compliment to the reader, yet it is never safe to press this compliment too hard.

Sometimes, on the other hand, her verses found too much favor for her comfort, and she was urged to publish. In such cases I was sometimes put forward as a defense; and the following letter was the fruit of some such occasion:—

DEAR FRIEND,—Thank you for your advice. I shall implicitly follow it.

The one who asked me for the lines I had never seen.

He spoke of "a charity." I refused, but did not inquire. He again earnestly urged, on the ground that in that way I might "aid unfortunate children." The name of "child" was a snare to me, and I hesitated, choosing my most rudimentary, and without criterion.

I inquired of you. You can scarcely estimate the opinion to one utterly guideless. Again thank you.

Your Scholar.

Again came this, on a similar theme:

Dear Friend,—Are you willing to tell me what is right? Mrs. Jackson, of Colorado ["H. H.," her early schoolmate], was with me a few moments this week, and wished me to write for this. [A circular of the "No Name Series" was inclosed.] I told her I was unwilling, and she asked my why? I said I was incapable, and she seemed not to believe me and asked me not to decide for a few days. Meantime, she would write me. She was so sweetly noble, I would regret to estrange her, and if you would be willing to give me a note saying you disapproved it, and thought me unfit, she would believe you. I am sorry to flee so often to my safest friend, but hope he permits me.

In all this time—nearly eight years—we had never met, but she had sent invitations like the following:—

Amherst.

Dear Friend,—Whom my dog understood could not elude others.

I should be so glad to see you, but think it an apparitional pleasure, not to be fulfilled. I am uncertain of Boston.

I had promised to visit my physician for a few days in May, but father objects because he is in the habit of me.

Is it more far to Amherst?

You will find a minute host, but a spacious welcome. . . .

If I still entreat you to teach me, are you much displeased? I will be patient, constant, never reject your knife, and should my slowness goad you, you knew before myself that

> Except the smaller size
> No lives are round.
> These hurry to a sphere
> And show and end.
> The larger slower grow
> And later hang;
> The summers of Hesperides
> Are long.

Afterwards, came this:—

Amherst.

Dear Friend,—A letter always feels to me like immortality because it is the mind alone without corporeal friend. Indebted in our talk to attitude and accent, there seems a spectral power in thought that walks alone. I would like to thank you for your great kindness, but never try to lift the words which I cannot hold.

Should you come to Amherst, I might then succeed, though gratitude is the timid wealth of those who have nothing. I am sure that you speak the truth, because the noble do, but your letters always surprise me.

My life has been too simple and stern to embarrass any. "Seen of Angels," scarcely my responsibility.

It is difficult not to be fictitious in so fair a place, but tests' severe repairs are permitted all.

When a little girl I remember hearing that remarkable passage and preferring the "Power," not knowing at the time that "Kingdom" and "Glory" were included.

You noticed my dwelling alone. To an emigrant, country is idle except it be his own. You speak kindly of seeing me; could it please your convenience to come so far as Amherst, I should be very glad, but I do not cross my father's ground to any house or town.

Of our greatest acts we are ignorant. You were not aware that you saved my life. To thank you in person has been since then one of my few requests. . . . You will excuse each that I say, because no one taught me.

At last, after many postponements, on August 16, 1870, I found myself face to face with my hitherto unseen correspondent. It was at her father's house, one of those large, square, brick mansions so familiar in our older New England towns, surrounded by trees and blossoming shrubs without, and within exquisitely neat, cool, spacious, and fragrant with flowers. After a little delay, I heard an extremely faint and pattering footstep like that of a child, in the hall, and in glided, almost noiselessly, a plain, shy little person, the face without a single good feature, but with eyes, as she herself said, "like the sherry the guest leaves in the glass," and with the smooth bands of reddish chestnut hair. She had a quaint and nun-like look, as if she might be a German canoness of some religious order, whose prescribed garb was white pique, with a blue net worsted shawl. She came toward me with two day-lilies, which she put in a childlike way into my hand, saying softly, under her breath, "These are my introduction," and adding, also under her breath, in childlike fashion, "Forgive me if I am frightened; I never see strangers, and hardly know what I say." But soon she began to talk, and thenceforward continued almost constantly; pausing sometimes to beg that I would talk instead, but readily recommencing when I evaded. There was not a trace of affectation in all this; she seemed to speak absolutely for her own relief, and wholly without watching its effect on her hearer. Led on by me, she told much about her early life, in which her father was always the chief figure, —evidently a man of the old type, *la vieille roche* of Puritanism—a man who, as she said, read on Sunday "lonely and rigorous books;" and who had from childhood inspired her with such awe, that she never learned to tell time by the clock till she was fifteen, simply because he had tried to explain it to her when she was a little child, and she had been afraid to tell him that she did not understand, and also afraid to ask any one else lest he should hear of it. Yet she had never heard him speak a harsh word, and it needed only a glance at his photograph to see how truly the Puritan tradition was preserved in him. He did not wish his children, when little, to read anything but the Bible; and when, one day, her brother brought her home Longfellow's Kavanagh, he put it secretly under the pianoforte cover, made signs to her, and they both afterwards read it. It may have been before this, however, that a student of her father's was amazed to find that she and her brother had never heard of Lydia Maria Child, then much read, and he brought Letters from New York, and hid it in the great bush of old-fashioned tree-box beside the front door. After the first book she thought in ecstasy, "This, then, is a book, and there are more of them." But she did not find so many as she expected, for she afterwards said to me, "When I lost the use of my eyes, it was a comfort to think there were so few real books that I could easily find one to read me all of them." Afterwards, when she regained her eyes, she read Shakespeare, and thought to herself, "Why is any other book needed?"

She went on talking constantly and saying, in the midst of narrative, things quaint and aphoristic. "Is it oblivion or absorption when things pass from our minds?" "Truth is such a rare thing, it is delightful to tell it." "I find ecstacy in living; the mere sense of living is joy enough." When I asked her if she never felt any want of employment, not going off the grounds and rarely seeing a visitor, she answered, "I never thought of conceiving that I could ever have the slightest approach to such a want in all future time;" and then added, after a pause, "I feel that I have not expressed myself strongly enough," although it seemed to me that she had. She told me of her household occupations, that she made all their bread, because her father liked only hers; then saying shyly, "And people must have puddings," this very timidly and suggestively, as if they were meteors or comets. Interspersed with these confidences came phrases so emphasized as to seem the very wantonness of over-statement, as if she had pleased herself with putting into words what the most extravagant might possibly think without saying, as thus: "How do most people live without any thoughts? There are many people in the world,—you must have noticed them in the street,—how do they live? How do they get strength to put on their clothes in the morning?" Or this crowning extravaganza: "If I read a book and it makes my whole body so cold no fire can ever warm me, I know that is poetry. If I feel physically as if the top of my head were taken off, I know that is poetry. These are the only ways I know it. Is there any other way?"

I have tried to describe her just as she was, with the aid of notes taken at the time; but this interview left our relation very much what it was before;—on my side an interest that was strong and even affectionate, but not based on any thorough comprehension; and on her side a hope, always rather baffled, that I should afford some aid in solving her abstruse problem of life.

The impression undoubtedly made on me was that of an excess of tension, and of an abnormal life. Perhaps in time I could have got beyond that somewhat overstrained relation which not my will, but her needs, had forced upon us. Certainly I should have been most glad to bring it down to the level of simple truth and every-day comradeship; but it was not altogether easy. She was much too enigmatical a being for me to solve in an hour's interview, and an instinct told me that the slightest attempt at direct cross-examination would make her withdraw into her shell; I could only sit still and watch, as one does in the woods; I must name my bird without a gun, as recommended by Emerson. Under the necessity I had no opportunity to see that human and humorous side of her which is strongly emphasized by her nearer friends, and which shows itself in her quaint and unique description of a rural burglary, contained in the volume of her poems. Hence, even her letters to me show her mainly on her *exaltée* side; and should a volume of her correspondence ever be printed, it is very desirable that it should contain some of her letters to friends of closer and more familiar intimacy.

After my visit came this letter:—

Enough is so vast a sweetness, I suppose it never occurs, only pathetic counterfeits.

Fabulous to me as the men of the Revelations who "shall not hunger any more." Even the possible has its insoluble particle.

After you went, I took Macbeth and turned to "Birnam Wood." Came twice "To Dunsinane." I thought and went about my work. . . .

The vein cannot thank the artery, but her solemn indebtedness to him, even the stolidest admit, and so of me who try, whose effort leaves no sound.

You ask great questions accidentally. To answer them would be events. I trust that you are safe.

I ask you to forgive me for all the ignorance I had. I find no nomination sweet as your low opinion.

Speak, if but to blame your obedient child.

You told me of Mrs. Lowell's poems. Would you tell me where I could find them, or are they not for sight? An article of yours, too, perhaps the only one you wrote that I never knew. It was about a "Latch." Are you willing to tell me? [Perhaps "A Sketch."]

If I ask too much, you could please refuse. Shortness to live has made me bold.

Abroad is close tonight and I have but to lift my hands to touch the "Heights of Abraham." DICKINSON.

When I said, at parting, that I would come again some time, she replied, "Say, in a long time; that will be nearer. Some time is no time." We met only once again, and I have no express record of the visit. We corresponded for years, at long intervals, her side of the intercourse being, I fear, better sustained; and she sometimes wrote also to my wife, inclosing flowers or fragrant leaves with a verse or two. Once she sent her one of George Eliot's books, I think Middlemarch, and wrote, "I am bringing you a little granite book for you to lean upon." At other times she would send single poems, such as these: —

THE BLUE JAY.

No brigadier throughout the year
So civic as the jay.
A neighbor and a warrior too,
With shrill felicity
Pursuing winds that censure us
A February Day,
The brother of the universe
Was never blown away.
The snow and he are intimate;
I've often seen them play
When heaven looked upon us all
With such severity
I felt apology were due
To an insulted sky
Whose pompous frown was nutriment
To their temerity.
The pillow of this daring head
Is pungent evergreens;
His larder—terse and militant—
Unknown, refreshing things;
His character—a tonic;
His future—a dispute;
Unfair an immortality
That leaves this neighbor out.

THE WHITE HEAT.

Dare you see a soul at the white heat?
    Then crouch within the door;
Red is the fire's common tint,
    But when the vivid ore

Has sated flame's conditions,
Its quivering substance plays
Without a color, but the light
Of unanointed blaze.

Least village boasts its blacksmith,
Whose anvil's even din
Stands symbol for the finer forge
That soundless tugs within.

Refining these impatient ores
With hammer and with blaze,
Until the designated light
Repudiate the forge.

Then came the death of her father, that strong Puritan father who had communicated to her so much of the vigor of his own nature, and who bought her many books, but begged her not to read them. Mr. Edward Dickinson, after service in the national House of Representatives and other public positions, had become a member of the lower house of the Massachusetts legislature. The session was unusually prolonged, and he was making a speech upon some railway question at noon, one very hot day (July 16, 1874), when he became suddenly faint and sat down. The house adjourned, and a friend walked with him to his lodgings at the Tremont House; where he began to pack his bag for home, after sending for a physician, but died within three hours. Soon afterwards, I received the following letter: —

The last afternoon that my father lived, though with no premonition, I preferred to be with him, and invented an absence for mother, Vinnie [her sister] being asleep. He seemed peculiarly pleased, as I oftenest stayed with myself; and remarked, as the afternoon withdrew, he "would like it to not end."

His pleasure almost embarrassed me, and my brother coming, I suggested they walk. Next morning I woke him for the train, and saw him no more.

His heart was pure and terrible, and I think no other like it exists.

I am glad there is immortality, but would have tested it myself, before entrusting him. Mr. Bowles was with us. With that exception, I saw none. I have wished for you, since my father died, and had you an hour unengrossed, it would be almost priceless. Thank you for each kindness. . . .

Later she wrote: —

When I think of my father's lonely life and lonelier death, there is this redress —
Take all away;
The only thing worth larceny
Is left — the immortality.

My earliest friend wrote me the week before he died, "If I live, I will go to Amherst; if I die, I certainly will."

Is your house deeper off?

YOUR SCHOLAR.

A year afterwards came this: —

DEAR FRIEND, — Mother was paralyzed Tuesday, a year from the evening father died. I thought perhaps you would care.

YOUR SCHOLAR.

With this came the following verse, having a curious seventeenth-century flavor:—

> A death-blow is a life-blow to some,
> Who, till they died, did not alive become;
> Who, had they lived, had died, but when
> They died, vitality begun.

And later come this kindred memorial of one of the oldest and most faithful friends of the family, Mr. Samuel Bowles of the Springfield Republican:—

DEAR FRIEND,—I felt it shelter to speak to you.
My brother and sister are with Mr. Bowles, who is buried this afternoon.
The last song that I heard—that was, since the birds—was "He leadeth me, he leadeth me; yea, though I walk"—then the voices stooped, the arch was so low.

After this added bereavement the inward life of the diminished household became only more concentrated, and the world was held farther and farther away. Yet to this period belongs the following letter, written about 1880, which has more of what is commonly called the objective or external quality than any she ever wrote me; and shows how close might have been her observation and her sympathy, had her rare qualities taken a somewhat different channel:—

DEAR FRIEND,—I was touchingly reminded of [a child who had died] this morning by an Indian woman with gay baskets and a dazzling baby, at the kitchen door. Her little boy "once died," she said, death to her dispelling him. I asked her what her baby liked, and she said "to step." The prairie before the door was gay with flowers of hay, and I led her in. She argued with the birds, she leaned on clover walls and they fell, and dropped her. With jargon sweeter than a bell, she grappled buttercups, and they sank together, the buttercups the heaviest. What sweetest use of days! 'T was noting some such scene made Vaughan humbly say, "My days that are at best but dim and hoary." I think it was Vaughan. . . .

And these few fragmentary memorials—closing, like every human biography, with funerals, yet with such as were to Emily Dickinson only the stately introduction to a higher life—may well end with her description of the death of the very summer she so loved.

> As imperceptibly as grief
> The summer lapsed away,
> Too imperceptible at last
> To feel like perfidy.   [To seem
>
> A quietness distilled,
> As twilight long begun,
> Or Nature spending with herself
> Sequestered afternoon.
>
> The dusk drew earlier in,
> The morning foreign shone,
> A courteous yet harrowing grace
> As guest that would be gone.   [guest who
>
> And thus without a wing
> Or service of a keel
> Our summer made her light escape
> Into the Beautiful.

222 "Emily Dickinson." *Readers Union Journal*, [ca. October 1891], pp. 165–
66. Although *The Readers Union Journal* is preserved as a printed
heading over this clipping in Todd's scrapbook, the existence of a periodical by this title has proved impossible to verify.

The publication of a volume of Miss Dickinson's poems during the present
year introduced to the world a new literary character, whom few had even heard
mentioned during her lifetime. Living an utterly excluded life, afflicted with a
morbid sensitiveness which rendered it a seeming impossibility for her to mingle
in society, her posthumous work shows her to have been a poet in a certain
sense. But it is the letters which she wrote to Thomas Wentworth Higginson,
which are reproduced in the October *Atlantic,* that show the effect of living to
one's self too much. The odd expressions, the unique use of words evince a lively
mind, but lacking in a certain knowledge of expression which is only learned by
conversation and not from books.

"On April 16, 1862," says Mr. Higginson, "I took from the post office in Worcester, Mass., where I was then living, the following letter:

'MR. HIGGINSON — Are you too deeply occupied to say if my verse is alive?
The Mind is so near itself it cannot see distinctly, and I have none to ask.

Would you think it breathed, and had you the leisure to tell me, I should feel
quick gratitude.

If I make the mistake, that you dared to tell me would give me sincerer honor
toward you.

I enclose my name, asking you, if you please, sir, to tell me what is true?

That you will not betray me it is needless to ask, since honor is its own pawn.'

"The letter was postmarked 'Amherst,' and it was in handwriting so peculiar
that it seemed as if the writer might have taken her first lessons by studying the
famous fossil bird-tracks in the museum of that college town. Yet it was not in
the slightest degree illiterate, but cultivated, quaint, and wholly unique. Of punctuation there was little; she used chiefly dashes, and it has been thought better,
in printing these letters, as with her poems, to give them the benefit in this respect of the ordinary usages; and so with her habit as to capitalization, as the
printers call it, in which she followed the Old English and present German
method of thus distinguishing every noun substantive. But the most curious thing
about the letter was the total absence of a signature. It proved, however, that she
had written her name on a card, and put it under the shelter of a smaller envelope
inclosed in the larger; and even this name was written — as if the shy writer wished
to recede as far as possible from view — in pencil, not in ink. The name was Emily
Dickinson."

The correspondence thus so queerly begun was continued for a number of
years. With each letter she sent one or more poems, asking the candid opinion
of Mr. Higginson concerning it, or to tell her if it was "alive." One of these was
a bit of observation of nature:

A bird came down the walk;
He did not know I saw;
He bit an angle-worm in halves
And ate the fellow raw.

And then he drank a dew
From a convenient grass,

And then hopped sidewise to a wall,   [the wall
To let a beetle pass.

Another was the dazzling description of "The Humming Bird:"

A route of evanescence
With a revolving wheel;
A resonance of emerald;
A rush of cochineal.
And every blossom on the bush
Adjusts its tumbled head;—
The mail from Tunis, probably,
An easy morning's ride.

Another letter discloses something of her home-life. She says:

You inquire my books. For poets, I have Keats and Mr. and Mrs. Browning. For prose, Mr. Ruskin, Sir Thomas Browne, and the Revelations. I went to school, but in your manner of the phrase had no education. When a little girl, I had a friend who taught me Immortality; but venturing too near, himself, he never returned. Soon after my tutor died, and for several years my lexicon was my only companion. Then I found one more, but he was not contented I be his scholar, so he left the land.
You ask of my companions. Hills, sir, and the sundown, and a dog large as myself, that my father bought me. They are better than beings because they know, but do not tell; and the noise in the pool at noon excels my piano. I have a brother and sister; my mother does not care for thought, and father, too busy with his briefs to notice what we do. He buys me many books, but begs me not to read them, because he fears they joggle the mind. They are religious, except me, and address an eclipse every morning, whom they call their "Father."

After several years of this sort of acquaintance Mr. Higginson visited her at her home in response to repeated quaint invitations like the following:

I should be so glad to see you, but think it an apparitional pleasure, not to be fulfilled. I am uncertain of Boston.
You will find a minute host but a spacious welcome.

Her visitor relates how after many postponements, "I found myself face to face with my hitherto unseen correspondent."

[Here follows a verbatim extract from the *Atlantic* essay, beginning "'I found myself face to face . . .'" and ending, ". . . 'Why is any other book needed'" (no. 221, p. 193). *The Readers Union Journal* silently omits several sentences, resuming its quotation at "She told me of her household occupations . . ." and ending with ". . . her abstruse problem of life" (p. 194).]

223 "Notes." *Brains* 1 (October 1, 1891), 66.

In the October *Atlantic* Colonel T. W. Higginson gives the following pen portrait of the late Emily Dickinson, a poet who was scarcely known outside of her own family circle until after she died:—

"A plain, shy little person, the face without a single good feature, but with eyes, as she herself said, 'like the sherry the guest leaves in the glass,' and with smooth bands of reddish chestnut hair. She had a quaint and nunlike look, as if she might be a German canoness of some religious order, whose prescribed garb was white piqué with a blue net worsted shawl. She came toward me with two day lilies, which she put in a childlike way into my hand, saying softly, under her breath, 'These are my introduction,' and adding also under her breath, in child-like fashion, 'Forgive me, if I am frightened; I never see strangers and hardly know what I say.' But soon she began to talk and thenceforward continued almost constantly, pausing sometimes to beg that I would talk instead, but readily recommencing when I evaded. There was not a trace of affectation in all this; she seemed to speak absolutely for her own relief and wholly without watching its effect on her hearer."

224 "Notes on the October Magazines." *Christian at Work* 50 (October 1, 1891), 441.

A very curious article is one contributed by Colonel T. W. Higginson, who includes a number of letters from Emily Dickinson, letters of the most singular and interesting character, along with such explanatory narrative as is necessary.

225 "Notes." *Nation* 53 (October 1, 1891), 260.

The literary problem which Emily Dickinson presents is partly solved and partly made more complex by the letters of hers printed by Mr. T. W. Higginson in the October *Atlantic,* and by the slight information about her which he gives along with them. They show that her prose expression was of a piece with her poetical, and so that her literary personality was single and sincere, but they leave us almost as much in the dark as ever in regard to the sources of her strange endowment. But they are of remarkable interest in any case, and reveal her as an Emersonian several shades more concise and oracular than Emerson.

226 "Literary." *Northampton* [Mass.] *Daily Hampshire Gazette,* October 2, 1891, p. [4]. Reprinted: *Hampshire Gazette and Northampton Courier,* October 6, 1891, p. 2.

The October ATLANTIC will command special attention from people in this vicinity, inasmuch as it contains Colonel T. W. Higginson's paper on Emily Dickinson's Letters. Emily Dickinson's home was in Amherst, and she has given to the literary world some of the most exquisite poems published. Such extraordinary letter-writing as Emily Dickinson's has certainly never been seen in print before. Her letters are interesting precisely because every tradition as to what makes a letter interesting is absolutely ignored. Col. Higginson writes thus: "Few events in American literary history have been more curious than the sudden rise of Emily Dickinson into a posthumous fame only more accentuated by the utterly recluse character of her life, and by her aversion to even a literary publicity."

227 "The October Magazines." *Commonwealth* 31 (October 3, 1891), 8.

In the Atlantic, Colonel Higginson continues his exploitation—the word is almost unfair—of Emily Dickinson, printing extracts from her letters, full of curious if not always wholesome interest.

228 "The Magazines." *Boston Home Journal,* October 3, 1891, p. 10.

Col. T. W. Higginson's paper, made up principally of letters from Emily Dickinson, whose sudden rise into posthumous fame is something remarkable, has a delightful interest.

229 "Magazines." *Boston Saturday Evening Gazette,* October 3, 1891, p. [4].

"Emily Dickinson's Letters," by Thomas Wentworth Higginson, is a remarkable revelation of a quaint personality that now and then reminds one of Charlotte Brontë and "Jane Eyre." Certainly no more original correspondent has appeared in this generation than was Miss Dickinson as she is represented in this paper.

230 "The Magazines." *Cambridge* [Mass.] *Tribune,* October 3, 1891, p. 2. Reprinted: *Christian Leader* 61 (October 15, 1891), 3–4.

Col. T. W. Higginson has a characteristic paper on "Emily Dickinson's Letters." Such extraordinary letter-writing as Emily Dickinson's has certainly never been seen in print before. Her letters are interesting precisely because every tradition as to what makes a letter interesting is absolutely ignored, and her style is one that would make the eighteenth-century letter-writers turn in their graves. Her life in her family, strange as it was, only partially accounts for the peculiarities displayed both in her character and in her correspondence. No one who wishes to gain some idea of a woman who has of late come so prominently before the public can afford to miss the paper.

231 *Hartford Courant,* October 3, 1891, p. 10. For the *Courant*'s earlier "editorial comment," see no. 208.

A more curious literary article has rarely been published in a magazine than that by Mr. Higginson in the October *Atlantic* on "Emily Dickinson's Letters." We have made some editorial comment on it, but will here further add that Miss Dickinson's prose, as seen in a correspondence with Mr. Higginson stretching over some years, is so remote from common forms of expression, so occult, so erratic and opaque as almost to cast doubts on the writer's sanity. Closer scrutiny, however, will reveal the fact that a sound and wise though utterly unconventional mind is here striving to make itself known through a strangely warped medium of language. The poems embedded in this deposit of prose are characteristic and some of them rarely lovely and original.

232 [Andrew Lang.] "An American Sappho." *London Daily News,* October 3, 1891, pp. 4–5. On Lang as the probable author of this and an earlier *Daily News* notice, see no. 72. In both reviews he directs his criticism as much to the American essayists promoting Dickinson as he does to the poet herself. Here Higginson's *Atlantic* essay (no. 221) bears most of the attack. Reprinted: *Public Opinion* [London] 60 (October 9, 1891), 465–66 and an unlocated *Cambridge* [Mass.] *Tribune*. Excerpt reprinted: *Springfield* [Mass.] *Homestead,* November 7, 1891, p. 5 and *Critic* 17 (January 23, 1892), 61.

Queer, queer are the fortunes of books. Few fates have been stranger than those which attended the poems of the late Miss Emily Dickinson. This lady dwelt remote, in an American village, a maid whom there were few to quote, and very few to read. She shunned society of every kind and only left her manuscript verses "to a little clan," of whom Mr. Higginson was the chief. On her death her poems were published, were enthusiastically welcomed by Mr. Howells, and have passed through six editions in as many months. Mr. Higginson now publishes, in an American magazine, some of Miss Dickinson's letters. She wrote to him, a stranger, long ago, asking if her verse "was alive." It is very much "alive," in the publisher's sense of that word, and this is the curious thing. For Miss Dickinson's verses scorn, almost equally, rhyme, grammar, rhythm, and sense. Most critics get odd poems from strangers, with requests for a candid opinion, which it is highly dangerous to give. For example, what can a man say to an author whose poem "On a Gipsy Child in London" ends thus:

> So we leave her
> So we leave her,
> Far from where her swarthy kinsfolk roam;
> In the Scarlet Fever,
> Scarlet Fever,
> Scarlet Fever Convalescent Home.

But this, at least, though betraying a lack of humour, has rhyme and common sense to recommend it. Miss Dickinson's performances lack both of these desirable qualities. For instance, this was the first of her effusions that greeted Mr. Higginson:

> We play at paste
> Till qualified for pearl,
> Then drop the paste
> And deem ourselves a fool.   [ourself

Here "a foolish girl" would have rhymed, at least, more or less, but no such meretricious charms allured Miss Dickinson. Mr. Higginson at once conceived that the lady had "a wholly new and original poetic genius" and the American literary public seems to agree with him. The critic, greatly daring, asked the lady "how old she was." She replied, evasively, "I made no verse, except one or two, until this winter, sir." Her favourite poets were Keats and Mr. and Mrs. Browning, her prose writers were St. John, Mr. Ruskin, and Sir Thomas Browne. She certainly did not imitate any of these masters. She was emancipated, very. She had an extraordinary knack of avoiding rhymes which appear inevitable, as

> It's far far treasure to surmise
> And estimate the pearl;
> That slipped my simple fingers through,
> When just a girl at school.   [While

Anybody, except Miss Dickinson, would have written "When just at school, a girl." Even Mr. Higginson sees this. She also showed "a rare and delicate sympathy with the life of Nature," thus:

> A bird came down the walk,
> He did not know I saw,
> He bit an angle-worm in two,   [in halves
> And ate the fellow raw.

'Tis true, 'tis very true, the early bird does not usually cook the worm. We have read nothing more touching since the sailor's poem (we alter the adjectives, while retaining their alliteration).

> A blessed little sparrow
> Built in a blessed spout,
> There came a blessed thunderstorm,
> And washed the beggar out.

That sailor, instead of consulting an unfeeling martinet of a captain, should have sent his lyric to Mr. Higginson. Why, anybody could write like Miss Dickinson:

> A trout came from under a stone,
> He never recked of a hook,
> He bit the worm to the bone,
> And I hauled him out of the brook,

is a sporting reminiscence quite as truly poetical as Miss Dickinson's garden romance.

Mr. Higginson liked the angle-worm, and said so. The lady replied, "Dear friend, your letter gave me no drunkenness, because I tasted rum before." She then dropped into poetry:

> As if I asked the Orient
> Had it for me a morn,
> And it should lift its purple dikes,
> And shatter me with dawn.

where there is a rhyme, a cockney one, it is true, but not unfamiliar to Mr. Swinburne. Mr. Higginson now, very naturally, asked for his correspondent's photograph. She told him that her eyes were like heel-taps, "like the sherry in the glass, that the guest leaves": *La fille aux yeux d'or*, in fact. Miss Dickinson's ankle "panted," in a later composition; ankles in real life "will not do so," but Mr. Higginson "thought it all very capital." The critic did, indeed, try to make his pupil write a little less like a born idiot, "but I fear that she interested me more in her—so to speak—unregenerate condition." She now signed herself "Your Gnome," which really was a very appropriate signature for this elf-like poet, but she perplexed Mr. Higginson. Miss Dickinson had Emily Brontë's affection for dogs; her own dog, Carlo, died, and though we may not be able to admire her verses, we may sympathise in a sorrow which she shared with the master of Camp. The humming bird she described as

> A route of evanescence
> With a revolving wheel;
> A resonance of emerald,
> A rush of cochineal.

Mr. Higginson at last met the poet, of whom he gives a very amiable description. She was the daughter of a home intensely Puritan, was much out of keeping with Puritanism, was little read in books, and here, perhaps, is the simple secret of her oddity, and of her charm for those whom she has charmed. She could make a pudding, though she had little sympathy with the luxurious taste which calls for such dainties. To read poetry "made her feel as if the roof of her head was taken off."

It is easy to see the interest of a character like this, but it is really next to impossible to see the merit of poetry like Miss Dickinson's. She had thought a great deal, she did little but think, yet the expression of her thought is immeasurably obscure, broken, unmelodious, and recklessly wilful. Like other very retiring persons, she was often in her correspondence extremely effusive. Her verse, at its very best, has a distant echo of Blake's, though it is highly probable that she never read anything of his. Poetry is a thing of many laws—felt and understood, and sanctioned by the whole experience of humanity, rather than written. Miss Dickinson in her poetry broke every one of the natural and salutary laws of verse. Hers is the very anarchy of the Muses, and perhaps in this anarchy lies the charm which has made her popular in America, and has caused Mr. Howells to say that she alone would serve to justify American literary existence. Fortunately that continent has a much more valid *raison d'être.* Readers of Miss Dickinson's letters will perhaps regret that the lines of this curious, shy, self-conscious, and expansive lady were ever published at all. She seems to have been a kind of unfinished, rudimentary Brontë, and her character is so unusual and interesting, that it is a pity her rhymes should make matter for mirth. Yet it is impossible for most people to avoid laughing at what is, frankly, so laughable. Unless all poets, from the earliest improvisers to the Laureate, have been wrong in their methods, Miss Dickinson cannot possibly have been right in hers. Compared with her, Walt Whitman is a sturdy poetical conservative. Her only merit is an occasional picturesque touch, and a general pathetic kind of yearning and sense of futility. As she says, she is—

> Homesick for steadfast honey—
> Ah! the bee flies not
> Which brews that rare variety.

The expression is mainly remarkable for being odd; the sentiment of *sehnsucht* [longing] is common to most modern rhyme. Probably neither the matter nor the manner is all that attracts Miss Dickinson's admirers, but a sense of the curious, passionate, and thwarted character of the writer, behind the verse, if we can call it verse. "It takes all sorts to make a world," in poetry as in other affairs, and in this world American taste has found a niche for Miss Dickinson. A conservative taste is more likely to suppose that she had a good deal of the poetic character, but that elements absolutely indispensable were somehow left out of her composition. It may be said for her pieces that, at all events, they are genuine, that they were written because she could not help it, and not with an eye on the magazines. It is much to be wished that her admirers will not become her imitators, defying grammar, rhyme, sense, and prosody. Critics who are asked to be candid about such effusions will be wise if they bid the writers "drop the paste and think themselves a fool," as Miss Dickinson puts it, for coming to the festival of the Muses in such scandalous lack of a wedding garment.

233 "Emily Dickinson's Poems." *San Francisco Evening Bulletin,* October 3, 1891, p. 5. This response to Higginson's *Atlantic* essay (no. 221) was followed with a review of *Poems, Second Series* on November 28, 1891; see no. 278. The previous notice alluded to here appeared December 6, 1890, no. 42.

Some months ago a small volume of poems by this author was reviewed in these columns. The opinion was then expressed that a poet of rare genius had appeared in print. There was a striking originality in many of the lines, and an odd capriciousness, amounting at times to a neglect of rhythm. In the last number of the *Atlantic Monthly*, Thomas Wentworth Higginson has a paper devoted principally to the letters of the deceased author, affirming that from first to last the impression made upon his mind was that of "a wholly new and original poetic genius." One of the most felicitous of her poems is the following:

The nearest dream recedes unrealized.
    The heaven we chase,
    Like the June bee
    Before the schoolboy,
    Invites the race.
    Stoops to an easy clover,
Dips—evades—teases—deploys—
Then to the royal clouds
    Lifts his light pinnace,
    Heedless of the boy
Staring, bewildered, at the mocking sky.

    Homesick for steadfast honey,—
    Ah! the bee flies not
Which brews that rare variety.

The last line with no poetic semblance, is only an eccentricity. But the poem as a whole is one of grace and beauty. Was ever a humming-bird better described than in these lines?

A route of evanescence
With a revolving wheel:
A resonance of emerald;
A rush of cochineal.
And every blossom on the bush
Adjusts its tumbled head:
The mail from Tunis, probably,
An easy morning's ride.

The going out of the poet's life is associated with these lines, describing the death of summer:

As imperceptibly as grief
The summer lapsed away,
Too imperceptible at last
To feel like perfidy.

A quietness distilled,
As twilight long begun,
Or Nature spending with herself
Sequestered afternoon.

The dusk drew earlier in,
The morning foreign shown,
A courteous yet harrowing grace
As guest that would be gone.

And thus without a wing,
Or service of a keel
Our summer made her light escape
Into the beautiful.

234   *Light* 4 (October 3, 1891), 107.

The Atlantic Monthly for October is of unusual interest to Worcester readers in that it contains an article by a former Worcester resident, Col. T. W. Higginson and that he refers to people once well known in our midst. The piece in question is "Emily Dickinson's Letters." She was the niece of Mr. William Dickinson, formerly so well known here. It seems that the poet had written to the then "Rev." T. W. Higginson and he was obviously much puzzled by the tenor of these letters. He says: "Circumstances, however, soon brought me in contact with an uncle of Emily Dickinson, a gentleman not now living; a prominent citizen of Worcester, a man of integrity and character, who shared her abruptness and impulsiveness but certainly not her poetic temperament, from which he was indeed singularly remote. He could tell but little of her, she being, evidently, an enigma to him as to me." To readers in this city, this beginning ought to be sufficient to prompt a most absorbing interest in these letters which are curiosities of the rarest type. She incloses to her mentor, for such she obviously rates Mr. Higginson, some of her stanzas and beautiful some of them are. Was ever anything written, prettier than this?

THE HUMMING BIRD.

A route of evanescence
With a revolving wheel
A resonance of emerald;
A rush of cochineal.
And every blossom on the bush
Adjusts its tumbled head: —
The mail from Tunis, probably,
An easy morning's ride.

Her poems have gone through six editions in six months. At last, the mentor meets his pupil and this is the description. "After a little delay, I heard an exceedingly faint and prattling footstep like that of a child in the hall, and in glided almost noiselessly a plain, shy little person, the face without a single good feature, but with eyes, as she herself said, 'like the sherry the guest leaves in the glass' and with smooth bands of reddish chestnut hair. . . . She came toward me with two day lilies which she put in a childlike way into my hand, saying softly, under her breath, 'These are my introduction.'" The description of the father whom the writer knew only from his picture is singularly applicable to his brother, our late Worcester resident. Had the Atlantic only this article, telling of Emily Dickinson, it still would be one of the best numbers of the year.

235   "October Magazines." *Boston Times* 28 (October 4, 1891), 7.

"Emily Dickinson's Letters" is a most fascinating and curious article, Col. Higginson supplying the necessary explanatory narrative. Her letters are interesting . . . [continues to end, same as *Cambridge Tribune*, no. 230].

236   "Current Periodicals." *Providence Sunday Journal,* October 4, 1891, p. 13.

The most conscientious article in the October Atlantic is "Emily Dickinson's Letters," by Thomas Wentworth Higginson. Miss Dickinson was a poet and a recluse. A volume of her poems published after her death won great success, and has made everything relating to her personality a matter of extreme interest. Mr. Higginson includes in his article a number of the poet's letters written to him giving a running commentary that is necessary for their explanation. The letters are as weird and wild as they are interesting.

237 Mary Abbott. "Emily Dickenson's Rare Genius." *Chicago Post,* October 6, 1891, p. 4. [Misspelling of the poet's name continues throughout the article.]

If Emerson were living and Ruskin were not in retirement one can picture the joy with which these two appreciative minds would have reveled in Emily Dickinson's rare genius and nature, complex to simplicity, or simple to complexity, whichever it may seem to the ordinary comprehension. For it is as difficult, perhaps, to gauge the depth of a limpid as that of a troubled stream; and the one may be as easily conceived deeper than it really is as the other more shallow, and vice versa. Emily Dickinson was one of the few—the truly few—who refuse to be known. In view of this fact it is not altogether clear whether her sister should have published her poems posthumously or not, and whether or not her friend Thomas Wentworth Higginson should have given her letters to the world, or to such a proportion of it as read the *Atlantic Monthly*. What the public has a right to demand in these matters I cannot say. If they had known nothing of them, however, they could have demanded nothing. But the poems are public property now and so are the letters; and you may get well into both before you are aware that you are a repository of betrayed confidence, and as such a compounder of felony. It is too late to go back and be neither; so you go on and reap the fruits of your misconduct boldly. I believe there are solid data known in regard to this strange, shy, solitary creature, such as her age and other incidents; but Mr. Higginson, catching the spirit of his subject, has with great delicacy abstained from knowing, or from telling, these vulgar details, and has given us a vague, suggestive and thoroughly artistic picture of the quaint little person with whom he maintained for years so mysterious a friendship.

———————

He first knew of Miss Dickinson's existence in 1862, through the medium of the Worcester postoffice. He found a letter addressed to him from Amherst, in singular, "fossil bird-track" handwriting, and was at once attracted by the originality of the four poems inclosed with it and by the note itself. There were curiously terse and pointed sentences in the letter, such as:

"Are you too deeply occupied to say if my verse is alive?"
"The mind is so near itself it cannot see distinctly."
"That you will not betray me it is needless to ask, since honor is its own pawn."

These alone would have caused any man to discern a genius, but the verses were extraordinarily "alive." Two of them have not yet been printed, and this one Mr. Higginson classes "among the most exquisite of her productions, with singular felicity of phrase and an aerial lift that bears the ear upward with the bee it traces":

The nearest dream recedes unrealized.
    The heaven we chase,
    Like the June bee
    Before the school boy,

Invites the race,
Stoops to an easy clover,
Dips—evades—teases—deploys—
Then to the royal clouds
Lifts his light pinnace,
Heedless of the boy;
   Staring, bewildered, at the mocking sky.

Homesick for steadfast honey—
Ah, the bee flies not
Which brews that rare variety.

Mr. Higginson was, of course, greatly at a loss how to criticise, or, indeed, how to class such singular, "uncriticisable" work as this—so absolutely original, so truly poetic, yet so wanting in conventional form. But he made some attempt at criticism and received her reply: "Thank you for the surgery; it was not so painful as I supposed. I bring you others, as you ask, though they might not differ. While my thought is undressed, I can make the distinction; but when I put them in the gown they look alike and numb. . . . You inquire my books. For poets, I have Keats and Mr. and Mrs. Browning; for prose, Mr. Ruskin, Sir Thomas Browne and the Revelations. I went to school, but in your manner of the phrase had no education. When a little girl, I had a friend who taught me immortality; but venturing too near himself, he never returned." This is not all nor half the letter, but I dare not quote the whole for fear of wanting space with which to eulogize them! One bit more, however; in speaking of the rest of her family: "They are religious, except me, and address an eclipse every morning, whom they call their 'father.'"

What an elusive, baffling and yet bewitching thing is this quicksilver we call genius! How it runs from us, appearing now in one big shining bubble and now in a hundred sparkling, racing gems! How different from what we call attainment, scholarship, talent! It is magic. We admire, honor, revere those other gifts; we even imitate them. But genius we chase and never catch.

One expects to learn, after the beginning of this correspondence, that Miss Dickinson's lines were cast in loneliness, and that she pined somewhere in primeval shades, but on the contrary it was her nature which was lonely, not her estate. She lived in one of those square, old-fashioned redbrick mansions so common in country towns, and her seclusion was entirely voluntary and against the wills of her relations and friends. Mr. Higginson's first visit to her, after eight years of a remarkable correspondence, was most curious, like everything else in connection with this unique character. She had written him when he asked for her photograph: "Could you believe me without? I have no portrait now, but am small, like the wren; and my hair is bold, like the chestnut burr; and my eyes, like the sherry in the glass that the guest leaves. Would this do just as well?" "The house was blossoming with shrubs outside, and within it was exquisitely neat, cool, spacious and fragrant with flowers. . . . I heard an extremely faint and pattering footstep like a child in the hall, and in glided, almost noiselessly, a plain, shy little person, the face without a single good feature, but with eyes, as she herself said, like the sherry the guest leaves in the glass, and with smooth bands of reddish chestnut hair. She had a quaint and nun-like look, as if she might be a German canoness of some religious order whose prescribed garb was white pique, with a blue net worsted shawl. She came toward me with two day lilies"—and she had never heard of Oscar Wilde!—"which she put, in a childlike way, into my hand, saying softly under her breath, 'These are my introduction.' She was without affectation; she was frightened at first because unaccustomed to strangers, but her talk was soon natural and easy and, it is needless to add, strictly original.

"She told me of her household occupations: that she made all their bread, because her father liked hers, 'and people must have puddings'—this very timidly and suggestively, as if they were meteors or comets." But her talk was not much of puddings. She embodied herself in such extravagances as this: "If I read a book and it makes my body so cold no fire can ever warm me, I know that is poetry. If I feel physically as if the top of my head were taken off, I know that is poetry. These are the only ways I know it. Is there any other way?" This from a person posing for an appreciating public would be thought, and would be, no doubt, rank affectation. In this wood-singer, muffling her voice from all but two or three familiar friends, it was rare naturalness. There was a humorous side to her, and a human, but these Higginson never saw, except when he read, for instance, "her quaint and unique description of a rural burglary, contained in the volume of her poems," or when she spoke of puddings. He saw her only twice, and then, as he says, "exaltee;" so that his descriptions must necessarily be of that character: "A full life and correspondence with her own people would give her more completely as she really was, from all points of view, and possibly that will be written."

But it would not be so impressive nor so stimulating. That it is possible to be perfectly untrammeled in literary scope and style; to sing as one breathes; to be modest and uncertain of one's quality; to develop as God made one, like a tree; to preserve one's genius, above all, as it is given—is a discovery above all price. That the embodiment of all this has found fame, even though it be posthumous, is a fortune in itself to us, as otherwise we should not have known that freedom and simplicity and modesty and shyness were compatible with poetic genius; but it means nothing outside of that. Emily Dickinson's success was of the spirit, and was complete when she put her first song into words. Her literary style was unconventional; sometimes she avoided meter and rhyme, because they hampered her thought; her irregularities were often serious. But who could fetter a poetic fire which burns away rules and shoots out in lambent light confessed? Here is a description of the humming bird:

> A route of evanescence
>   With a revolving wheel;
> A resonance of emerald,
>   A rush of cochineal.
> And every blossom on the bush
>   Adjusts its tumbled head;
> The mail from Tunis, probably,
>   An easy morning's ride.

To those who have had the delight of reading Emily Dickinson's published poems Mr. Higginson's reminiscences in the *Atlantic Monthly* will prove a charming and necessary supplement. For those who have not seen them there is a rare poetic treat coming. She died in 1886 and Mr. Higginson quotes her poem on "The Death of Summer" as applicable to her own taking-off.

238 *Amherst Record,* October 7, 1891, p. 3.

In a very interesting paper on Emily Dickinson's Letters in the October *Atlantic,* Col. T. W. Higginson describes a visit to Emily Dickinson. He says: . . . [Here follows a verbatim extract from Higginson's essay, no. 221, beginning "At last after many postponements, . . ." (above p. 193) and ending ". . . her abstruse problem of life" (above, p. 194)].

239 [Denis Wortman.] "Among Some Books." *Christian Intelligencer* 62 (October 7, 1891), 3–4. The author attribution is by hand in Todd's scrapbook. Wortman's earlier review of the 1890 volume may have helped him gain access to Dickinson's manuscripts (see no. 168). Although the phrase, "the most unique poetry I ever read," does not appear among known reviews before this date, Higginson had used "wholly unique" and "wholly new and original" in his *Atlantic* essay (no. 221).

Another book, "Poems," by Emily Dickinson. Two years ago it would have been asked, who is she? Today one must be quite behind the times not to know of her and somewhat of her history. Seven editions of her little book already issued; and a second volume of additional poems already going through the press; and not a few of her readers ready to say with a certain one in whose literary judgment I have more confidence than in my own, "the most unique poetry I ever read." I imagine the word "unique" fits it most expressly. It is altogether different from any other. There is a subtlety, a weirdness, a spontaneousness, a refined delicacy with bold abruptness; it is more spiritual than religious; it is that sort of portraiture which uses but a few lines and you see the whole thought; the intention is not half expressed—the hint is given, and it is taken for granted your wit will catch the rest; it is a study in two senses, a study to the artist who might fill out the picture and make it a more beautiful one for the drawing-room; it is a study to the reader, too, since he must use his brains to make it out; yet when made out, how beautiful!

I spent a forenoon last summer with Miss Dickinson's manuscripts; I hardly dare tell how many—and yet she had so quietly and unobservably wrought—no sound of hammer heard—her own sister, with whom she was intimate as even few sisters are, was unaware of such wealth of treasure till found in a drawer after her death. Some day I hope to tell more of her, of her manner of work and life, and the quality of her verse, and how she was not the recluse some have mistakenly inferred, but a woman of rare intelligence, accomplished and earnest character. Only now I will say to such as love true poetry, quite out of the literary rut, a poetry that has minded the thought and not the phrasing of it, and yet its phrasing is wonderfully apt and striking, get this volume, and look out for the next. Only be brave enough to know the work of a master, sometimes fragmentary, sometimes only partial studies, sometimes fine work most finely done:

> To fight aloud is very brave,
>   But gallanter, I know,
> Who charge within the bosom
>   The cavalry of woe.

> *   *   *   *   *

> If I can stop one heart from breaking,
>   I shall not live in vain;

If I can ease one life the aching,
    Or cool one pain,
Or help one fainting robin
    Unto his nest again,
    I shall not live in vain.

240 Celia Parker Woolley. "Some Published Letters." *Unity* 28 (October 8, 1891), 42.

Colonel Higginson makes a unique contribution to the last number of the *Atlantic Monthly*, in the publication of the letters of Emily Dickinson, the recluse-poet, recently discovered to the world in her own death; the heir to a posthumous fame as pathetic and inspiring as it is individual.

From her life of shy, almost unnatural retirement at Amherst, she ventured far enough out one April day in 1862, to write a letter to Mr. Higginson, soliciting his judgment of some scraps of verse. She asks him to tell her if her "verse is alive;" her own mind is "so near itself it cannot see distinctly." We may imagine this was to the one receiving it one of many letters of a similar tenor from aspiring makers of rhyme, but it is hardly possible they should have been of the peculiar quality of these. We do not wish to fill our space with comment on them, but rather let them speak for themselves as far as we may. There is the same elusive quality in them that appears in Miss Dickinson's poems. They resemble nothing so much as the startled movements of a bird, that suspecting he is in the vicinity of crumbs, hops confidently towards his human observer, then rises suddenly on wings, or flies away, keeping coy distance, with head bent reflectively to one side, and bright, motionless eyes.

Her chosen mentor evidently returned a kindly but not wholly favorable reply to the request received, for in her next letter she thanks him "for the surgery." Note this new way, and best way, of computing age not by years, but by progress attained in the heart's chosen direction. She had been asked, it seems, how old she was and this was her reply: "I made no verse, but one or two, until this winter, sir." To the inquiry about the books she reads, she answers with the names of Keats, the Brownings, in poetry; Ruskin, Thomas Browne and Revelations, in prose. She has had little education, she tells him, in the accepted sense; once when little she had a friend who taught her Immortality; "but, venturing too near, himself, never returned."

Her friends, she tells him are, "hills, sir, and the sundown, and a dog large as myself." They are to her "better than beings because they know, but do not tell." She describes her mother with simple candor as one who "does not care for thought;" her father as "too busy with his briefs to notice what wo do." The next letter she received praised her more distinctly and made her keenly happy, but she is incredulous and amused at his advice to delay publishing; "that being as foreign to my thought as firmament from fin." Later he asks for her picture, but she hopes he can believe her without. She is as small, she tells him, as the wren, with bold hair, like the chestnut burr, — "my eyes like the sherry in the glass the guest leaves." She wishes this new, unknown friend might visit her; she thinks Carlo (the dog) would please him, and that he would like the chestnut tree she met in her walk; which "hit my notice suddenly, and I thought the skies were in blossom." She adds: "Then there's a noiseless noise in the orchard that I let persons hear."

When her friend, the scholar, leaves his books for the camp, and became a soldier, she is proud but very anxious. He seems far removed now, war is "an oblique place." She prays for his safety: "Could you, with honor, avoid death, I entreat you, sir."

It was not until 1870 that he saw her. "She had a quaint and nun-like look as if she might be a German canoness of some religious order, whose prescribed garb was white pique with a blue, worsted shawl." Her talk is made up of the same mixture of poetry, highest wisdom and extravaganza her letters are. She drops such sayings as these into the conversation describing her daily life: "Is it oblivion or absorption when things pass from our minds?" "Truth is such a rare thing, it is delightful to tell it."

The impression made on the visitor extends to the reader of this curious recital, of "an excess of tension, and of an advanced life." Her more intimate friends spoke of her more "human and humorous side," but Mr. Higginson was conscious, he tells us, he saw her only on the "exaltée" side.

Four years later when her father died, she wrote the news of her loss to him with the words: "I am glad there is immortality, but would have tested it myself, before entrusting him." It was sixteen years before she tasted it herself.

We see in the picture here disclosed, a woman, — sprite, or "gnome," as she signed herself in one of her letters, would be the better term of description — of "rare qualities," as her discoverer says, undoubtedly of the genius type, but showing as much of the eccentricity of genius, as its higher qualities. There are sentences in her written and spoken thoughts, that are sweetly profound, mystical and true as the sayings of any sage or seer, others that strike us as sheer, even silly, affectation. The problem of human nature becomes at once more enticing and more discouraging in the study of such a character. Lest the foregoing selections may seem to define a gift of expression more quaint than vigorous, more striking and peculiar than genuinely useful, let the following stanza be placed here as a correction to such "possible" impression:

> A death-blow is a life-blow to some,
> Who, 'till they died, did not alive become;
> Who, had they lived, had died, but when
> They died, vitality begun.

241 "Literary." *Public Opinion* [London] 60 (October 9, 1891), 465–66. A reprinting; see no. 232.

242 "Magazine Notes." *Christian Union* 44 (October 10, 1891), 689. The Higginson essay mentioned here is no. 2.

It was, we believe, in the Christian Union that Colonel Higginson first called attention to the remarkable poems — remarkable almost as much for their defects as for their indications of genius — written by Emily Dickinson. In the current *Atlantic Monthly* he tells the story of his friendship and literary relations with that strange and interesting person, giving many of her letters, which are hardly less unusual in their character than the poems.

243 *Literary World* 22 (October 10, 1891), 360.

According to an "esteemed contemporary," a young lady, not of Boston, but of Newport, has been suggesting a new word that will, of course, "fill a long-felt want." "Speaking of Walt Whitman, Emily Dickinson, and others, whose thoughts are extremely poetical, but whose verses expressing them have little rhythm and less rhyme, she said: 'I don't call such writers poets exactly, and yet they are not, literally speaking, prose writers. There ought to be some other word to describe them—one of Lewis Carroll's "portmanteau" words. Why not call them *Proets?'"* The objection which at once occurs to us is that "Proet" suggests "proem," and the inference would be that the writers so denominated were about to begin to offer the world genuine poetry—in expression as well as in thought. But they never do begin, unfortunately, and so this word would be too complimentary. How would "prosets" do?

244 "Periodicals." *Literary World* 22 (October 10, 1891), 363.

Readers of the *Atlantic Monthly* for October will naturally turn first to Dr. Holmes' affectionate eulogy on James Russell Lowell. But this is one of several contributions having special distinction. Col. Higginson's account of that curious being, Emily Dickinson; . . .

245 *Christian Leader* 61 (October 15, 1891), 3–4. A reprinting of no. 230.

246 [Thomas Wentworth Higginson.] "Recent Poetry." *Nation* 53 (October 15, 1891), 297. Reprinted: *New York Evening Post*, October 17, 1891, p. 7. Higginson contributed other unsigned reviews of Dickinson to the *Nation*; see nos. 28 and 543.

The extract from a letter of the late Mrs. Helen Jackson ("H. H."), prefixed to the second series of Emily Dickinson's poems (Boston: Roberts Bros.), suggests the curious difference in the careers of these two gifted women, both natives of the same small inland town of Massachusetts. They were playmates and schoolmates; both began to write after early girlhood had passed, and for the utterance of deep personal feeling. But the one easily obtained fame, friends, recognition, influence; she had varied social experience; with many sorrows, she obtained much of what was best and most enjoyable in life, and died in the maturity of a conspicuous literary career. The other died absolutely unknown, even by name, beyond her own domestic circle, and yet this nameless woman was at once uplifted into an extraordinary prominence by the simple publication of her poems, after death. Some added light is thrown on this curious transition by the preface contributed to the present volume by Mrs. Todd, but it leaves many questions to be asked. It, however, brings out clearly a point overlooked by many who have discussed Emily Dickinson's poems. Mrs. Todd has recalled attention to the fact that they should be viewed rather as sketches than as finished works. We can never know what changes the author might have made in them had she seriously addressed herself to putting them in print. Up to the point where she left them, her chief solicitude had clearly been with the phrase, not with the verse or the line. She would make many alterations to secure precisely the adjective or substantive she needed; but the minor changes required to perfect a rhyme or to avoid a repetition were sometimes postponed for some moment of leisure, it may be, or in other cases spurned as unimportant. Even her peculiarities of grammar seem like mere short cuts or abbreviations, as when one takes notes in shorthand. We all know that a really fine poem is rarely struck off at a single sitting; there are usually several stages of completion, at any one of which, up to the very last, the work would seem still imperfect if published. The peculiarity is that almost all of Emily Dickinson's compositions are taken at that intermediate stage; and they are, in short, to be viewed as sketches, not works of conscious completeness. With this interpretation, it may fairly be said that those contained in this second series are quite as remarkable as those in the first. Perhaps they are even more remarkable; at any rate, there are more of them.

They are divided into the same four departments, viz, Life, Love, Nature, Time and Eternity. It is to be noticed, however, that the department of love-poems is, in this volume, more scanty than in its predecessor, as if, the author's little tale of experience, in that direction, were soon told. There is no loss of quality, however, even in that department, and in the other directions both quantity and quality are sustained. There is, in the first volume, for instance, no nobler strain of ethics than this (p. 199), which is also full of verbal felicities:

TRIUMPH.

Triumph may be of several kinds.
    There's triumph in the room
When that old Imperator, Death,
    By faith is overcome.

There's a triumph of the finer mind
    When truth, affronted long,
Advances calm to her supreme,
    Her God her only throng.

A triumph when temptation's bribe
    Is slowly handed back,
One eye upon the heaven renounced
    And one upon the rack.

Severer triumph, by himself
    Experienced, who can pass
Acquitted from that naked bar,
    Jehovah's countenance!

Note, for instance, the fineness of touch in the word "slowly" in the third verse, indicating the greatness of the struggle by the fact that even the utmost heroism cannot instantly decide it. A characteristic effect is also produced by employing the strong Roman "Imperator" instead of the cheapened word "Emperor," and thus placing death as a sovereign of sovereigns. In the following verses we have a haunting picture, not easily to be dropped from the mind:

THE FORGOTTEN GRAVE.

After a hundred years
Nobody knows the place, —
Agony, that enacted there,
Motionless as peace.

Weeds triumphant ranged.
Strangers strolled and spelled
At the lone orthography
Of the elder dead.

Winds of summer fields
Recollect the way, —
Instinct picking up the key
Dropped by memory.

The poems on Nature in this volume indicate the same peculiar intimacy always shown by Emily Dickinson; it seems as if she had been in at the very birth of her birds and flowers, as in the following verses (p. 72):

FRINGED GENTIAN.

God made a little gentian;
It tried to be a rose
And failed, and all the summer laughed.
But just before the snows
There came a purple creature
That ravished all the hill;
And summer hid her forehead,
And mockery was still.
The frosts were her condition;
The Tyrian would not come
Until the North evoked it.
"Creator! shall I bloom?"

The editors have put at the beginning of the volume two verses which seem—unlike all the rest— to show some objective aim in the poems; and they close with these four terse lines, which might well suffice for Emily Dickinson's own epitaph:

Lay this laurel on the one
Too intrinsic for renown.
Laurel! veil your deathless tree,—
Him you chasten, that is he!

247 "Magazines and Reviews." *Anti-Jacobin* [London], no. 38 (October 17, 1891), 914. This note concludes a paragraph on the contents of the current *Atlantic Monthly*.

"Emily Dickinson's Letters," edited by Colonel Wentworth Higginson, strike one as exhibiting the "Whitmania" of a lonely, self-educated, extremely proper, but equally unconventional maiden lady.

248 "Literature—Recent Poetry." *New York Evening Post*, October 17, 1891, p. 7; a reprinting of no. 246.

249 MacGregor Jenkins. "A Child's Recollections of Emily Dickinson." *Christian Union* 44 (October 24, 1891), 776–77. Jenkins later published a book-length reminiscence: *Emily Dickinson, Friend and Neighbor* (Boston: Little, Brown, 1930). Although Thomas H. Johnson was apparently unaware of this article when he prepared his 1958 collection of the poet's letters, all of the correspondence published here found its way into his edition. The letter beginning "Atmospherically it was the most beautiful Christmas" appears as no. 682 in *L* 3:684–85. The notes, "'Little Women'" and "Dear Boys" are nos. 717 and 718, 3:704–05. The poet's words recorded in Jenkins's third-to-last paragraph are taken, somewhat rearranged, from her 1877 letter to the author's mother and father, see 2:592–93, letter no. 520.

The comparatively recent publication of a volume of Emily Dickinson's poems has aroused much interest in the character and life of the gifted woman who left so rare a legacy to the reading world. One cannot read these unusual verses without desiring to know more of the unique genius which created them.

It is not the writer's object to describe in detail, were it possible, the life of this voluntary recluse. I was one of a quartet of children admitted to intimacy with "Miss Emily," the intimacy being of much the same sort as that between herself and the birds and flowers. While she avoided seeing grown-up people, she frequently saw us, and it is only of my childish recollections of this remarkable woman that I venture to write.

Miss Emily's home, "The Mansion," was an awe-inspiring place to me as a child. The house itself, dignified, respectable; the trees, almost primeval, overshadowing it; the courtly old-school gentleman, its proprietor, whom I saw daily in my early years, and who, with his stern face and kindly smile and lofty bearing, still remains my ideal of the true New England type of gentleman; the brilliant, mysterious daughter—all helped to invest the place with much that inspired awe.

Among my earliest recollections of "Miss Emily" is that of coming one summer morning through the gate on my way to the barn behind the house in search of my playfellows. As I passed the corner of the house, Miss Emily called me. She was standing on a rug spread for her on the grass, busy with the potted plants which were all about her. I can see her now as I saw her then—a beautiful woman dressed in white, with soft, fiery, brown eyes and a mass of auburn hair. Her voice I can never forget—clear, low-toned, sweet. She talked to me of her flowers, of those she loved best, of her fear lest the bad weather harm them; then, cutting a few choice buds, she bade me take them, with her love, to my mother. The impression the short interview made upon me, a child of five years, I well remember. To have seen "Miss Emily" was an event, and I ran home with a feeling of great importance to carry her message.

I recall her most often among her flowers, in the summer caring for them just outside the door, through which was easy and quick retreat in case of surprise; in the winter working among the plants in the conservatory.

We children knew how dearly she loved not only her flowers, but the trees, the birds, bees, butterflies, and especially the grass and clover blossoms.

One day in early spring, when the snow was still deep on the ground, she called us in to show us "something beautiful." A chrysalis, long watched among the conservatory plants, had burst its bonds, and floating about in the sunshine was a gorgeous butterfly.

I did not understand all she said about it, but it was beautiful to see her delight and to hear her talk.

Every year we played gypsy. We pitched our tent in the pines near the barn. We dressed in fantastic costumes and roved and marauded in true gypsy fashion, with the usual effect upon neighboring pantries. On one occasion our supplies utterly failed. In vain did we appeal to the servants at the Mansion, in vain besiege the pantry window. We were in desperate straits, when unexpected help came. A window overlooking our camp was raised and Miss Emily's well-known voice called softly to us. To our amazement and joy, a basket was slowly lowered to us. It contained dainties dear to our hearts. Such gingerbread, such cookies and cake, no gypsies ever dreamed of! Many times afterwards our pressing needs were supplied by means of that fascinating basket. We adored our unseen deliverer! She was our friend and champion, keenly interested in all our doings.

Christmas and birthdays brought characteristic gifts from Miss Emily to the children—gifts accompanied with notes which made them doubly precious.

Among my cherished possessions are some of these messages—one is addressed to the two little girls of our quartet!

> Little women!
> Which shall it be, geraniums or tulips?
> The butterfly upon the sky, who doesn't know its name,
> And hasn't any tax to pay, and hasn't any home,
> Is just as high as you and I, and higher, I believe—
> So soar away and never sigh, for that's the way to grieve.

Another came with a Christmas basket:

> DEAR BOYS: Please never grow up, which is "far better." Please never "improve"—you are perfect now.   EMILY.

The same Christmas, in response to some slight trifle sent her, came the following:

> DEAR ____: Atmospherically it was the most beautiful Christmas on record. The hens came to the door with Santa Claus, the pussies washed themselves in the open air without chilling their tongues, and Santa Claus—sweet old gentleman!—was even gallanter than usual. Visitors from the chimney were a new dismay, but all of them brought their hands so full and behaved so sweetly, only a churl could have turned them away. And then the ones at the barn were so happy! M____ gave the hens a check for potatoes, each of the cats had a gilt-edged bone, and the horse had new blankets from Boston.
>
> Do you remember dark-eyed Mr. D., [author's footnote: "Mr. Edward Dickinson, her father, who died the June before."] who used to shake your hand when it was so little it had hardly a stem? He, too, had a beautiful gift of roses from a friend away.
>
> It was a lovely Christmas. But what made you remember me? Tell me with a kiss—or is it a secret?   EMILY.

Is not this like her who wished a "memorial crumb" to be given the robins at her death?

In one of her notes I find a bunch of grass tied with a bit of white ribbon. She says: "These are sticks of rowen. They were chopped by bees, and butterflies piled them Saturday afternoons." The time was autumn, for she writes: "The red leaves take the green leaves' place, and the landscape yields. We go to sleep with the peach in our hands and wake with the stone, but the stone is pledge of summers to come."

The relations between this wonderful woman and the children she loved reveal the joyous gentleness of her character as no written words of hers can.

In the memory of one of these children—the youngest of the fortunate four—she lives a revered, inspiring presence. To have known Emily Dickinson even as child might know her is a privilege.

250 "Americans and Their Books." *London Daily News*, October 1891, pp. 4–5. Reprinted: *Critic*, n.s. 18 (July 23, 1892), 48. This essay may have been written by Andrew Lang; see nos. 72 and 232.

American literature is a topic always dear to American critics and the lack of self-consciousness is not a fault with which they can be justly charged. If it is easy to twist the tail of the British Lion, it is not difficult to annoy the American Eagle by tweaking the pinions which supply his poets with quills. At present Mr. Curtis and Mr. Howells are not annoyed, indeed, but put a little on the defensive, by the remarks of Mr. Theodore Watts. The Americans reply in *Harper's Magazine*, and make out a very fair case for themselves. Mr. Watts, according to Mr. Curtis, "denies that we have any literature." If he does, Mr. Watts must keep before him an uncommonly high standard of what literature is. To another observer it might seem that the Americans have plenty of literature, from the very interesting lispings of the earliest New England Muse to Miss Emily Dickinson, the poet who was *super grammaticam*, like the often quoted Emperor. Probably Mr. Curtis has stated Mr. Watts's ideas rather too absolutely. Mr. Watts may mean that America has no great literature, no native Shakespeare, nor Milton, nor Shelley, but it can hardly be supposed that he means more. Mr. Curtis also proves, and it is a pleasing circumstance, that, whatever we may think of American authors, their lives have been highly respectable. "The eccentricities of genius, the recklessness of Grub Street, the lawlessness of Bohemia, . . . all these are unknown in the story of those who are the pride of American letters." It would be cruel to remind Mr. Curtis that, before we have the "eccentricities of genius," we must have genius itself. That line may be left to Mr. Theodore Watts—if, indeed, he is on the war-path. He may, if he pleases, say, "Yes; you have divagations with whisky and the lasses, oh; but where is your Burns? You have no terrible poetic scandals; but where is your Byron, and whom do you regard, at present, as the American Shelley?" Mr. Watts, no doubt, can take care of himself.

But even a critic who has no point to defend will reply to Mr. Curtis, "If you have none of the lawlessness of Bohemia, where do you place Poe?" Probably not among "those who are the pride of American letters." He certainly was not in private life a person to be proud of, but, as an author, he might pardonably excite a certain national complacency. Yet, on the whole, American authors have been highly respectable men. Thoreau was a little odd, and N. P. Willis had his foibles, but Hawthorne, Longfellow, Emerson, Mr. Bancroft, Mr. Prescott, Mr. Lowell, only to mention the dead, were as remarkable as Scott, Wordsworth, and Southey for all the public and private virtues. "They have deprived genius of its plea of self-indulgence, and civic sloth and indifference of a coveted example." This remark is as true about Americans as about many English writers of distinction. But none of those men on either side of the sea were Byrons or Burnses, and "it takes all sorts to make a world." American literary genius has been well paid and well fed. It has never, except in the one exemplary case of Poe, run at all wild. Possibly, while society and morals gain, literature loses a little by this regularity. But we do hope that no young American men of genius will make this a reason for devotion to the flagon, or undisciplined attentions to "The American Girl" or matron.

As to Mr. Howells, he is exercised by English reflections on the want of a national tone in American literature. This is not a cry with which we need sympathize. If a literature is good we really need ask no more of it; excellence suffices. Besides, as Mr. Howells remarks with really astonishing frankness, "for all aesthetic purposes the American people is not a nation, but a condition." The nail, the very obvious nail, was never more firmly knocked on the head. The Americans are English, "not essentially changed . . . and not very different from the English at home, except in their political environment and the vastness of the scale of their development." Exactly; the man stammered more in New York than in Baltimore, "Because it is a bigger place." But he did not on that account alter his ideas, nor, if he were a literary gentleman, his "copy." America is "a bigger place" than England, there are more people in it, there are plenty of aliens, and there are bears and raccoons. But the trout and salmon are the same, and so, essentially, is the literature. Why should it be different?

What do people want the Americans to do? They cannot all be Walt Whitmans, a circumstance which we would be the very last to regret. One vast Walt is enough for a century: some of the Muses, like the unfeeling husband of Mrs. Harris, may even regret this child as "one too many." "Mr. Whitman seems to have exhausted the resources of formlessness," says Mr. Howells—a Daniel come to judgment and saying delightfully the opposite of what we had anticipated. "It is our misfortune rather than our fault," says Mr. Howells, "to have arrived when all the literary forms were invented." But in that misfortune we are all alike partakers. A small but not undistinguished race of men, in a corner of the Levant, invented all literary forms long ago, long before Albion had heard an English word. Epic, lyric, drama, tragedy, comedy, drawing-room play even (as witness Herondas), fable, idyll, pastoral, novel were all invented by the Greeks. If Quintilian or Longinus could live again, he might say to all of us moderns, "Why have you not a national literature?" that is if, before having a national literature, you must invent new literary forms.

251 Franklin Benjamin Sanborn. "The Breakfast Table." *Boston Daily Advertiser,* October 27, 1891, p. 4. The Lang review addressed here is no. 232.

It was venturesome of Col. Higginson to print so much of his very intimate correspondence with Emily Dickinson—and the natural consequence has followed—that the Philistines are laughing at it and at her verses. One of these English Philistines—possibly Andrew Lang, who writes for the London News editorially—has devoted a column in that journal to the subject. Much that he says is indisputable,—for example: "Her verse, at its very best, has a distant echo of Blake's. Poetry is a thing of many laws—felt and understood, and sanctioned by the whole experience of humanity, rather than written. Miss Dickinson in her poetry broke every one of the natural and salutary laws of verse. Hers is the very anarchy of the Muses, and perhaps in this anarchy lies the charm which has made her popular in America, and has caused Mr. Howells to say that she alone would serve to justify American literary existence."

———————

I take exception to the word "anarchy" which is used in England to express all sorts of deviation from custom—highway robbery, mobbing the bishop of London, or refusing to wear a stove-pipe hat. But the irregularity of Miss Dickinson's verse does find more favor here than it could in England. But our Philistine goes on thus: "She seems to have been a kind of unfinished, rudimentary Brontë, and her character is so unusual and interesting, that it is a pity her rhymes should make matter for mirth. Unless all poets, form the earliest improvisers to laureate, have been wrong in their methods, Miss Dickinson cannot possibly have been right in hers. Compared with her, Walt Whitman is a sturdy poetical conservative. Her only merit is an occasional picturesque touch, and a general pathetic kind of yearning and sense of futility."

———————

This is bad enough; but still worse is the parody that he makes, and his allusion to an English versifier, who seems to have lent an "effort" to this critic for the verdict. He says: "Miss Dickinson's verses scorn, almost equally, rhyme, grammar, rhythm, and sense. Most critics get odd poems from strangers, with requests for a candid opinion, which it is highly dangerous to give. For example, what can a man say to an author whose poem "On a Gipsy Child in London" ends thus: —

> So we leave her
> So we leave her,
> Far from where her swarthy kinsfolk roam,
>   In the Scarlet Fever,
>   Scarlet Fever,
> Scarlet Fever Convalescent Home.

But this, at least, though betraying a lack of humor, has rhyme and common sense to recommend it. Miss Dickinson's performances lack both of these desirable qualities." This is mere Philistinism, like that of the English coroner who read Wordsworth's verses in the House of Commons, and made fun of them. Laughter is the easiest and the worst way of dealing with Wordsworth or with any serious poet.

252 "Magazines." *Golden Rule*, n.s. 6 (October 29, 1891), 73.

The *Atlantic*, in which Dr. Holmes's verses appear, is especially marked this month by its biographical articles, two of which are devoted to Sir John Macdonald and to Dollinger, while Colonel Higginson presents in her own letters a picture of Miss Dickinson, whose death has lately emphasized both her poetic genius and the obscurity of her life.

253 "Periodicals." *Unity* 28 (October 29, 1891), 69. Reference is made to a review by Celia Parker Woolley, no. 240.

The most interesting article in the October *Atlantic* is the sketch of Emily Dickinson, by Col. T. W. Higginson and her accompanying letters to himself, as literary mentor. We have spoken of these at length already.

254 This unidentified clipping, ca. Oct.–Nov. 1891, from Higginson's scrapbook [p. 121] reviews Higginson's *Atlantic* essay on Dickinson's letters (no. 221). The first portion of the review is missing.

". . . few real books, that I could easily find one to read me all of them." Afterward, when sufficiently restored to read Shakespeare, she thought to herself, "Why is any other book needed?" She had earlier written to Colonel Higginson: "You inquire my books? For poets, I have Keats, and Mr. and Mrs. Browning. For prose, Mr. Ruskin, Sir Thomas Browne, and the Revelations. I went to school, but in your manner of the phrase had no education. When a little girl, I had a friend who taught me Immortality; but venturing too near, himself, he never returned. . . . My companions: hills, sir, and the sundown, and a dog as large as myself that my father bought me. They are better than beings, because they know, but do not tell."
With this birthright, with this nature, thrust back upon itself — recoil inevitable — life to Emily Dickinson was fraught with peril. But she saw the danger signal in her solitary way. Providentially the road forked, and one stood ready to meet her necessity. For the unique service rendered this woman of genius by a

man of genius, all who love and admire Emily Dickinson thank Thomas Went-worth Higginson.

It is not difficult to see from what he saved her. Mr. Higginson has noted her touch of likeness to William Blake. It seems to me to lie deeper than in any quality of her verse—to reach down to that delicate mainspring of the mind, the more exquisite whose mechanism is the more easily jarred. A certain correspondence in their verse, is symptomatic of a common peril. In her second letter to Mr. Higginson Miss Dickinson wrote: "I had a terror since September I could tell to none: and, so I sing, as the boy does in the burying ground, because I am afraid." Six years later, when her nature was flowering under the sunshine of his appreciation, and the pruning of his criticism, she wrote to him—her "master": "Of our greatest acts we are ignorant. You were not aware that you saved my life. To thank you in person has been since then one of my few requests."

This was granted, and in 1870 occurred Higginson's first interview with the poet. She met her own description: "Small like the wren; and my hair is bold, like the chestnut burr; and my eyes like the sherry in the glass that the guest leaves." Another friend has said of her: "She was not beautiful, yet had many beauties"—a word that suits, too, her intellect.

I have not dwelt upon Emily Dickinson's faults; they speak for themselves, and sometimes with such a din that the virtues cannot be heard. Granted that her poetry is uneven, so rugged of rhyme and rhythm that it jolts the mind like a corduroy road—I prefer it to a flowery bed of ease. Many can lull, but few can awake.

255 Arlo Bates. "Literary Affairs in Boston." *Book Buyer*, n.s. 8 (November 1891), 417.

The publication in the *Atlantic Monthly* of the letters of Emily Dickinson to Colonel Higginson and the announcement of another volume of her poems have conspired to render the interest in this strange personality greater than ever. I wonder that it has occurred to nobody to make a magazine essay by considering the place in American literature of Walt Whitman and Emily Dickinson together. It could be maintained with a proper show of reasonableness that they belong to the same class; or rather that they are both the result of the same tendency in American intellectual life. In both cases we have the cultivation of the suscepti-bility at the expense of the effective. They are both instances of the development of the sentiment and of the feeling so rapidly and so highly that the acquirement of a technique becomes impossible. It is a natural result of the hot-bed system upon which the intellectual development of this country has gone on. When one considers the brief time that has elapsed since Longfellow was the idol of the American public and reflects how he has taken his proper place, one is furnished with a sort of measure for the rapidity of the pace at which we have been going forward. To master the technical side of art, one must have the sensibilities under control, and it is difficult to master form in a society where everything is ripened so rapidly.

It is true that in the case of Miss Dickinson this effect was intensified by the absence of that criticism which would have come from publication; but in the case of Whitman much the same conditions were secured by the assumption that form was of no consequence, or rather that his own idea of form was final. In the case of both we have the melancholy spectacle of a mind gifted with great origi-nality and with genuine imagination missing its best fruition through the fail-ure to handle to the best advantage the art in which it worked.

256 "Gift and Holiday Books." *Current Review* I (November 1891), 7.

Miss Dickinson was a recluse known to a few friends only. Although a prolific writer, excepting two or three poems she permitted nothing to be published while she lived. Her verse has the untrammelled freedom of a mind unacquainted with critics, which sings to satisfy its own cravings, or ease its own burdens. Although somewhat uneven, her poetry shows much originality, and most pleasing imaginative and descriptive powers, and often she catches a most beautiful simile on the wing as it were with a sort of breathless haste as though fearful it would escape. The poems are divided into four parts: "Life," "Love," "Nature" and "Time and Eternity." Here is a charming little quatrain from "Nature:"

> Presentiment is that long shadow on the lawn
> Indicative that suns go down;
> The notice to the startled grass
> That darkness is about to pass.

256A   Nathan Haskell Dole. "Notes from Boston." *Book News* 10 (November 1891), 93. Dole has just made the point that much modern poetry is amenable to musical setting.

Emily Dickinson just missed that quality of music. Listen to this from her new volume of poems soon to be published by Roberts' Brothers:

AT HOME.

> The night was wide, and furnished scant
>   With but a single star,
> That often as a cloud it met
>   Blew itself out for fear.   [out itself

> The wind pursued the little bush,
>   And drove away the leaves
> November left; then clambered up
>   And fretted in the eaves.

> No squirrel went abroad;
>   A dog's belated feet,
> Like intermittent plush were heard
>   Adown the empty street.

So far with the exception of that odd word "plush" it has an almost singing quality, but the next two stanzas, which I refrain from quoting, end in a characteristic puzzle of sense, or nonsense.
Here is another, unnamed:

> The moon is distant from the sea,
>   And yet with amber hands
> She leads him, docile as a boy,
>   Along appointed sands.

> He never misses a decree;   [degree;
>   Obedient to her eye
> He comes just so far toward the town,
>   Just so far goes away.

> Oh, Signor, thine the amber hand,
>   And mine the distant sea,—
> Obedient to the least command
>   Thine eyes impose on me.

This second series of Miss Dickinson's verse will contain a facsimile of her handwriting in a reproduction of one of the poems, also a letter from Helen Hunt Jackson to the author.

257 Le Roy Phillips. "The Poems of Emily Dickinson." *New England Magazine,* n.s. 5 (November 1891), 311. A reprinting of no. 171.

258 "Leading Articles of the Month." *Review of Reviews* [N.Y.] 4 (November 1891), 459. The London *Review of Reviews,* more selective than its New York counterpart in summarizing American magazines, did not notice Higginson's essay.

One does not necessarily need to be a lover of poetry in order to have one's interest aroused in Emily Dickinson. Genius is of itself fascinating even to one who is indifferent to the medium by which it manifests itself. The genius of Emily Dickinson is unquestionable.

Mr. Thomas Wentworth Higginson has done the public a kindness by publishing in the *Atlantic Monthly* some letters which he received from this remarkable woman, and these letters together with his comments constitute incomparably the best literary article of the month. We fondly hope that he may see fit some time to prepare a biography of her.

As she appears in these letters she is so elusive, so mysterious that it is probable that no number of volumes could give a clear conception of her character. Possibly a character like hers can never be understood, but we have, at least, an intuition of some of her peculiarities. Naïve as Marjory Fleming and at the same time as mysteriously unearthly as—say, Thomas De Quincey, she presents a truly unique picture. We confess that we feel more interest in her and her letters than we have heretofore felt in her poetry. The letters are ungrammatical, obscure, quaint in phraseology, and original in every line. Metrical form was so natural to her that she instinctively falls into it, and her letters at times run on for several paragraphs in almost perfect metre.

On April 16, 1862, Mr. Higginson received this letter, which must have astonished him:

> Mr. Higginson:—Are you too deeply occupied to say if my verse is alive?
> The mind is so near itself it cannot see distinctly and I have none to ask.
> Should you think it breathed, and had you the leisure to tell me, I should feel quick gratitude.
> If I make the mistake, that you dared to tell me would give me sincere honor toward you.
> I inclose my name, asking you, if you please, sir, to tell me what is true?
> That you will not betray me it is needless to ask, since honor is its own pawn.

The letter inclosed two poems subjected to Mr. Higginson's criticism, and though he modestly keeps himself in the background, we may be sure that his reply was wise and generous. In Miss Dickinson's next she thanks him for his "surgery," and tells him something of herself. She reads Keats, Mr. and Mrs. Browning, Ruskin, Thomas Browne, and Revelations. Of her father she says that,

"He buys me many books, but begs me not to read them, because he fears they joggle the mind."

The saucy coquetry of her reply to a question which he had asked is worthy of Rosalind. "You asked me how old I was? I made no verse but one or two until this winter, sir."

In a later letter Mr. Higginson requested her to send him her picture. Here is the answer: "Could you believe me without? I had no portrait, now, but am small, like the wren; and my hair is bold like the chestnut burr, and my eyes, like the sherry in the glass, that the guest leaves. Would this do just as well?" When Mr. Higginson saw her he found that it did quite well.

Her father, like the fathers of so many English-speaking men and women of genius, was a stern Puritan. After his death she herself said of him, "His heart was pure and terrible, and I think no other like it exists." She seems to have revolted against the rigor of the household religion. She says in an early letter that the family are all "religious, except me, and address an eclipse every morning whom they call their 'Father.'" Something of her creed seems to have been expressed in the following sweet note written to Mr. Higginson after he had been wounded in battle: "Dear Friend, — I think of you so wholly that I cannot resist to write again to ask if you are safe? Danger is not at first, for then we are unconscious, but in the after, slower days. Do not try to be saved, but let redemption find you as it certainly will. Love is its own rescue; for we at our supremest are but its trembling emblems. — Your Scholar."

She always called herself his "scholar," and there is little doubt that he was the wisest of teachers, stimulating rather than instructing her, for a genius so peculiar as hers could not have suffered much guiding. She said once, "If I read a book and it makes my whole body so cold no fire can ever warm me, I know that is poetry. If I feel physically as if the top of my head were taken off, I know that is poetry. These are the only ways I know it. Is there any other way?" For her, undoubtedly there was not. Imagine teaching Dr. Blair to this free creature! Mr. Higginson was wise in leaving her, as he himself expresses it, in her "unregenerate condition."

But she could never regard him as anything save a preceptor to be revered and honored. She says: "The vein cannot thank the artery, but her solemn indebtedness to him, even the stolidest admit, and so of me, who try, whose effort leaves no sound. You ask great questions accidently. To answer them would be events. I trust that you are safe. I ask you to forgive me for all the ignorance I had. I find no nomination sweet as your low opinion. Speak if but to blame your obedient child."

259 Henry Park Schauffler. "Second Edition of Emily Dickinson's Poems." *Amherst Literary Monthly* 6 (November 1891), 175–82. The following erratum appears in the same number of this journal: "Through a mistake in printing, the title of the first article is incorrect. It should read, 'The Second Series of Emily Dickinson's Poems.' Schauffler's substitution of "noon" for "morn" in his rendition of "The Snake" demonstrates an apparent preference for the first published version of this poem in the *Springfield Republican* (1866) over the 1891 Higginson-Todd attempt to create a rhyme for "corn."

In the careful consideration of any work of art, it is interesting to note the exact method by which that art has reached its state of perfection. Such a knowledge often enhances the actual value of the object in hand. With this additional light former conceptions become too narrow. The point of view is shifted, and contemporaneous with this shifting, the work of art, be it an oratorio, a madonna, or a Paradise Lost, is sure to broaden into nobler dimensions, to gain a higher beauty, and to thrill with a richer, deeper inspiration.

Applying this principle to the study of Emily Dickinson's Poems, it is natural to conclude that careful criticism will in large part depend upon two things, namely, the method and the aim of her work. What was her method? It was simplicity itself, and was withal perfectly natural. A striking thought would come to her mind; instantly it was jotted down, there being but a moment's interruption in the task of the hour. In this manner hundreds of her thoughts were neatly laid away; untold, prosy thoughts, they would have been to other natures, but to her mind, strong in its subtle poetic power, they came as sweet songs, which were all the sweeter because deftly hidden away, in instant readiness to be resung.

There was a "method in her madness" out of which came "divinest sense"; the sense, meaning to others an incomparable style of poetry, too original to be imitated, almost too self-made for classification. Had she permitted her verse to be published, or even were she ambitious in writing poems of some considerable length, — in such a case only, would criticism from the ordinary point of view be justifiable. But knowing her methods, and her perfect singleness of aim, — an aim which might well be called a strong introspective thought-gathering, — the conclusion follows that her work is far above a superficial criticism of form; and that in her poems she has bequeathed to the world a rare legacy of rare thought.

Taking this point of view, special benefit is to be derived from the study of Emily Dickinson's second and larger volume of poems.

Life, Love, Nature, Time and Eternity; these are the four heads under which her poems are fittingly gathered, and in this order perhaps it is best to consider them.

What is her conception of life?

> Surgeons must be very careful
>   When they take the knife!
> Underneath their fine incisions
>   Stirs the culprit, — Life

With such a delicately traced central idea and as she suggests, admitting in its conception and treatment of nothing but the greatest care, — with this as a starting point, or rather as an intensifying background, her thought can be followed through almost every aspect and phase of human experience. In a terse way she pictures life as a ladder, each step leading upward to a higher. Such a life of progress and attainment she seems to consider as the only one worth living:

> We play at paste
> Till qualified for pearl,
> Then drop the paste,
> And deem ourself a fool.

In a most remarkable way, she goes on further to define power, revealing the most able of metaphysicians in clearness and comprehensiveness of definition:

> Power is only pain,
> Stranded, through discipline,
> Till weights will hang.

Nor does she lack aught in her appreciation of the existing relations between rich and poor, between victory and defeat, or between man's ambition and the final realization of his hopes and wishes.

'Tis beggars banquets best define;

But turning from these comparisons, the reader finds her intent upon the more subtle attributes of the human soul. Hope, remorse, anger, patriotism; these all seem to live and breathe out their various lights and shadows under the guiding influence of her magnetic touch.

Note in the following lines her sturdy New England patriotism. Are you not surprised into a deeper reverence, enthused with a stronger love, for the old, battle-scarred red white and blue, warmed with a more brightly burning fire of gratitude towards the minute men, brought so forcibly to mind in that one proud word "Lexington":

> My country need not change her gown,
>   Her triple suit as sweet
> As when t'was cut at Lexington,
>   And first pronounced a fit.

So deeply in earnest is she upon all various phases of life, both in thought and action, so full to teeming over with possible meaning and suggestiveness are all her strongly chosen words, that when the intensity of the strain is for a moment loosened into a pleasantly bantering but yet decided sarcasm, we gladly join with her in a smile at "The preacher," — so typical of that large and ever-growing class of today, our would-be broad thinkers:

> He preached upon 'breadth' till it argued him narrow,
>   The broad are too broad to define;
> And of 'truth' until it proclaimed him a liar, —
>   The truth never flaunted a sign.

Emily Dickinson's insight into life was something remarkable; it was the discernment of a mind absolutely free from conventional habits of thought. She possessed the happy faculty of being able to clear away from before her vision, at one strong sweep, all the underbrush of artifice, the shrubbery of worldly wisdom and the mist of hypocritical cant. She intended to have her sight obscured by no such flimsy veil; such an one as others were content to dimly peer through. As a consequence her sight was keenly piercing, and in setting down what she saw, her intuition borders almost on prophecy. That which is far beyond the ken of common minds has become to her an unquestionable tactility.

In a word, her view of life is clear, strong and wide reaching. She seems so intimate with every passion or tendency of the human heart, that it is a distinguishing mark of her ability, to find that she treats life in no piecemeal fashion, but rather enshrines it as a perfect whole, all of whose various parts, no matter how different in essential characteristics, are linked in closest union by that golden binding-chain of a single purpose, of a common end.

> Each life converges to some centre
> Expressed or still;
> Exists in every human nature
> A goal.

We come now to a most difficult task; that of rightly interpreting Emily Dickinson's love poems. Difficult it is, because as we learn from the preface she had no great love-disappointment. Naturally this question follows—how then could she experience so deeply, and at time almost passionately, that feeling which differs widely in its component parts from the commonly accepted essentials of a living love?

True, she did love, this we must conclude from the power of her poems; but hers was a love, ideal and spirituelle. However an attempt to answer such a question directly, would be but an advertisement of the blindness of him who should essay to make such answer.

We can then only approximate a reply, and in doing so would first of all, lay down as criterion the strong lines of Tennyson:

> Love took up the harp of life; and smote on all the
>   chords with might;
> Smote the chord of self, that, trembling, passed in
>   music out of sight.

The putting aside of self is the heart's only infallible way of possessing in itself the truest devotion and power of love.

Right here lies the distinction. Had Emily Dickinson passed through any usual love experience, there would have been in her love-poems that burning fire which in its intensity consumes all self. On the contrary we find a decided presence and touch of self pervading these poems. Not that she is in the slightest degree selfish, or too highly self-centred, but rather that she is deficient in the common experience of the deepest of all the heart's passions; and therefore, as would be most natural she has assumed a role, which though beautifully skillful in its attractive mechanism, lacks to a certain degree, the perfection of a full experimental development. And yet these verses have a power which cannot fail to inspire the careful reader. They are possessed of a beauty all their own. There is within them a certain satisfaction, as of love freely given by her real self, through an ideal self, to another being.

It is a quality seldom if ever found in other poets, and one which is highly instructive in its bearing upon a careful analysis and further development of the expressions and embodiment in language of the highest of all man's attributes,— God-given love.

And now we pass into the realm of Nature. Here Emily Dickinson is at home. Very few have ever been better adapted as regards their trend of thought and power of word-painting, to give so deep an insight into Nature.

Her life, in large part, was nature's life; and there is found in her interpretation and method of handling this her second life, not only that which kindles our enthusiasm, but also that, by which we are irresistibly drawn into fuller sympathy and closer communion with Nature.

She has two methods of interpretation. One is the simple, heartfelt expression of the companionship derived from every flower, every bee, every nature-sound, and every golden sunset.

She seeks to teach no lesson, but has given herself up entirely to a joyous revelling among the endless beauties of nature. What a richness in this sunset:

> Where ships of purple gently toss,
>   On seas of daffodil,
> Fantastic sailors mingle,
>   And then,—the wharf is still.

Mark her pleasing naïveté in the following lines:

> Frequently the woods are pink,
> Frequently are brown;
> Frequently the woods undress   [hills
> Behind my native town

She was fond of most small creatures, and some indeed were especially her favored pets. The warm spot in her heart for Nature's children can be shown perhaps in antithesis, by her poem on "The Snake."

> I more than once, at noon,   [at morn
> Have passed, I thought, a whip-lash
> Unbraiding in the sun, —
> When, stooping to secure it,
> It wrinkled and was gone.
> Several of Nature's people
> I know and they know me;
> I feel for them a transport
> Of cordiality;
> But never met this fellow,
> Attended or alone,
> Without a tighter breathing,
> And zero at the bone.

But turning to the second way in which she interprets nature, let us first illustrate:

> How happy is the little stone
> That rambles in the road alone,
> And doesn't care about careers
> And exigencies never fears.

Here evidently she draws from Nature a lesson. This she seldom does so clearly, but sometimes in a very subtle manner, the lesson being so much the more readily remembered, when it has once been painstakingly understood.

Nature is gracefully brought into her service, now talking to us lightly, then looking at us solemnly, or preaching a sermon long-to-be-remembered.

Explain it as we may, there is a hidden something in her nature-verse which cannot be defined, which beggars description and evades classification.

Perhaps it is that her understanding of Nature was so much more keen and far-reaching than that of most mortals, that she actually grew into a sort of nature-world, to us a condition full of mystery, but to her a vital reality. Howsoever this may be, we can yet safely say, that her passionate love for Nature forms the polarization from which emanates the magnetism of her nature-verse.

Time and Eternity, the last division, we glance at but briefly. A detailed analysis, or attempted centralization of the poems under this heading, would involve far too much. Each one is a study in itself, a fruitful theme for painstaking consideration. In her wielding of these subjects, fraught with such great uncertainty to mortal minds, she displays a strength of thought scarce conceivable. She is more spirit than woman; holding converse with death; veiling her eyes at no glory of angels; perfectly calm in the face of eternity; nothing of the spirit-world fearful or strange to her. Most naturally and quietly she says:

> Our journey had advanced;
> Our feet were almost come
> To that odd fork in Being's road,
> Eternity by term.

It has been said of De Quincey that "To him words were things." Equally true is this of Emily Dickinson, but perhaps most apparent in her poems on Life and Eternity.

Here she not only treats words as things, but as living things, infusing them with that same vigor and fearlessness which characterizes her own sturdy mind. So it is that her thought, her work, and her life find no more fitting tribute than that expressed in the remarkable lines with which the volume closes:

> Lay this laurel on the one
> Too intrinsic for renown.
> Laurel! Veil your deathless tree, —
> Him you chasten, that is he!

260 Silas Wegg, Jr. [pseud.] *Sylvia's Home Journal* [London] 14:167 (November 1891), 520.

Everybody who reads poetry is talking just now about Emily Dickinson's "Poems," recently published in this country by Osgood, MacIlvaine & Co. Miss Dickinson was an American lady, who lived a strange, secluded life, and wrote a great deal of "Poetry of the Portfolio," as Emerson called the verse which is not intended for publication. After her death, her friends began to talk about her and her work, and one or two verses found their way into print and attracted immediate attention. Her poems have now been collected and published in a volume which Thomas Wentworth Higginson and another friend of Miss Dickinson's have edited. A great deal of nonsense has been written about this book, for some critics have compared it to the work of Blake and Heine, and others have called it "doggerel." The fact is that Miss Dickinson had a very daring and original imagination, a very pretty fancy, and a great deal of poetic power, but was utterly ignorant of poetic art. She dashed down her thoughts, red hot, and just as they came into her mind, and sometimes she expressed herself with rare happiness and sometimes with equal clumsiness. Here is a quaint little specimen of her work: —

> The bustle in a house
>   The morning after death
> Is solemnest of industries
>   Enacted upon earth.
>
> The sweeping up the heart
>   And putting love away,
> We shall not want to use again
>   Until Eternity.

And here is a very pretty little trifle: —

> The bee is not afraid of me,
>   I know the butterfly;
> The pretty people in the woods
>   Receive me cordially.
>
> The brooks laugh louder when I come,
>   The breezes madder play,
> Wherefore, mine eyes, thy silver mists?
>   Wherefore, O summer's day?

This might be set to music very happily. My own special favourite in the volume is the poem called "The Grass." Here is a bit of it: —

The grass so little has to do,
　A sphere of simple green,
With only butterflies to brood
　And bees to entertain.

And stir all day to pretty tunes
　The breezes fetch along.
And hold the sunshine in its lap,
　And bow to everything;

And thread the dews all night, like pearls.
　And make itself so fine,
A duchess were too common
　For such a noticing.

And even when it dies, to pass
　In odours so divine;
As lowly spices gone to sleep,
　Or amulets of pine.

　I think the fancies in this are very pretty, although the last verse is the only one in which there is even an attempt at rhyme.

261　"Literary Comments." *Springfield* [Mass.] *Homestead*, November 7, 1891, p. 5. This item refers to an article presumably by Andrew Lang (no. 232) that was reprinted in an unlocated *Cambridge* [Mass.] *Tribune*.

　A critic in the Cambridge Tribune takes up T. W. Higginson's article on Emily Dickinson's poetry and displays more levity than that subject has called out before. He requotes, but not to admire, from her "Nature" verses:

A bird came down the walk,
He did not know I saw.
He bit an angle-worm in two   [in halves
And ate the fellow raw,

And declares he had read nothing more touching since the sailor's poem (altering the adjectives):

A blessed little sparrow
　Built in a blessed spout.
There came a blessed thunder-storm
　And washed the beggar out.

　This critic does not bow the knee with the crowd to this much worshiped muse, but declares that such verses are the fair sport of the public when offered to the public. He finds it easy to see the interest of such a character as Emily Dickinson's, although next to impossible to see the merit of her poetry, and ends with this rather severe though not ill-natured criticism:

　She had thought a deal, she did little but think, yet the expression of her thought is immeasurably broken, obscure, unmelodious and recklessly willful. Her verse at its best has a distant echo of Blake's, though it is highly probable that she never read a line of his. Poetry is a thing of many laws—felt and understood and sanctioned by the whole experience of humanity, rather than merely written. Miss Dickinson broke nearly every one of the natural and salutary laws of verse. Readers of the letters of this shy, self-conscious and curiously expansive and effusive lady will, perhaps, regret that her lines were ever published at all. She seems to have been a kind of rudimentary Brontë, and her character so unusual and interesing that it is a pity to make mirth of her rhymes. She cannot possibly have been right in her methods, unless all poets, from the earliest improvisers down to Tennyson, have been wrong in theirs. Compared with her, Walt Whitman is a sturdy, poetical conservative. Her only merit is an occasional picturesque touch and a general pathetic kind of yearning and sense of futility.

262 [Charles Goodrich Whiting.] *Springfield Republican*, November 8, 1891, p. 6. Although this notice is not attributed in the Todd scrapbook, its author identifies himself as the writer of an earlier *Republican* piece known to have been Whiting's (see no. 13). The following review was reprinted in part in an undated Todd newspaper clipping having only the handwritten identification "Oregonian," presumably the *Portland Sunday Oregonian*.

The second series of the poems of Emily Dickinson are now issued by Roberts Bros of Boston, with a preface by one of the editors, Mrs. Mabel Loomis Todd of Amherst. There is a letter from "H. H." given at the outset, in which that accomplished woman said:—

> If such a thing should happen as that I should outlive you, I wish you would make me your literary legatee and executor. Surely after you are what is called "dead" you will be willing that the poor ghosts you have left behind should be cheered and pleased by your verses, will you not? You ought to be. I do not think we have a right to withhold from the world a word or a thought any more than a deed which might help a single soul.

But "H. H." died first, and the verses which she desired to edit have found their way to light without her, but perhaps not without her influence. Mrs. Todd says of the finding of Emily's writing by her sister:—

> Most of the poems had been carefully copied on sheets of note-paper, and tied in little fascicles, each of six or eight sheets. While many of them bear evidence of having been thrown off at white heat, still more had received thoughtful revision. There is the frequent addition of rather perplexing footnotes, affording large choice of words and phrases. And in the copies which she sent to friends, sometimes one form, sometimes another, is found to have been used. Without important exception, her friends have generously placed at the disposal of the editors any poems they have received from her, and these have given the obvious advantage of comparison among several renderings of the same verse. To what further rigorous pruning her verses would have been subjected had she published them herself, we cannot know. They should be regarded in many cases as merely the first strong and suggestive sketches of an artist, intended to be embodied at some time in the finished picture.

There are interesting things said of her change of handwriting, which at first a delicate running hand, became gradually more abrupt until each letter stood distinct and separate from its fellows; there was no punctuation save by dashes, and all important words began with capitals; seldom was a piece of verse given a title. Mrs. Todd makes an inapt comparison when she says: "Like Impressionist pictures, or Wagner's rugged music, the very absence of conventional forms challenges attention." The likeness to impressionist art is true enough, but no one who knows anything about modern music, and especially Wagner, should correlate his work with that of impressionists in any art, for he was the extreme opposite of an impressionist, nor did he produce "rugged" music. Wagner was a mighty, comprehensive genius, who produced every detail with relation to a whole, and made that whole; so that his work is never incomplete, but always inclusive. Nothing could be more infelicitous than to liken Emily Dickinson's vivid inspirations, on the ground of the absence of conventional form, to the grand systematic work of Wagner.

The volume before us begins with a facsimile of one of the poems as Emily Dickinson wrote it, at a time while she yet had what might be called a handwriting—later, she only jotted down separate characters. Its contents are divided into these four books; Life, Love, Nature, Time and Eternity. All of these are so keyed on Eternity that no other title would better fit the whole collection. Emily Dickinson could have adopted the words of Hermione, "To me can life be no commodity," for this was her view of life. Mrs. Todd assures us that "she was not an invalid, and she lived in seclusion from no love disappointment." These things may have been so, but there are poems here printed in respect to love that never could have been written without experience; the deepest feeling must have inspired them, and no one can read them without the conviction that Emily Dickinson knew what she was writing about, whether or not her seclusion was due thereto. Such an indication is in this piece:—

> Wild nights! Wild nights!
> Were I with thee,
> Wild nights should be
> Our luxury!
>
> Futile the winds
> To a heart in port,—
> Done with the compass
> Done with the chart.
>
> Rowing in Eden!
> Ah! the sea!
> Might I but moor
> To-night in thee!

Another verse of subtle power has a hint of sarcasm in it, and she entitled it "Choice":—

> Of all the souls that stand create
> I have elected one.
> When sense from spirit files away,
> And subterfuge is done;
>
> When that which is and that which was
> Apart, intrinsic, stand,
> And this brief tragedy of flesh
> Is shifted like a sand;
>
> When figures show their royal front
> And mists are carved away.—

Behold the atom I preferred
To all the lists of clay!

Weighing the give and take of marriage, she wrote thus: —

I gave myself to him,
And took himself for pay.
The solemn contract of a life
Was ratified this way.

The wealth might disappoint,
Myself a poorer prove
Than this great purchaser suspect.
The daily own of Love

Depreciates the vision;
But, till the merchant buy,
Still fable, in the isles of spice,
The subtle cargoes lie.

At least, 'tis mutual risk, —
Some found it mutual gain;
Sweet debt of Life, — each night to owe,
Insolvent, every noon.

———————

We do not find the poems of this volume inferior to those of the first selection, notwithstanding a few things we would have left out. There is more poetic power and beauty in them than in scores of books of the poetry of the day which is far more finished in technic. Here are vital thoughts, life from the very heart, and the finest proof of culture in ideas that transcend convention. What is all that the makers of rondeaux and sonnets, who are now so numerous, can do beside these irregular verses that throb with human and divine life? Criticise till you are gray, ye Zoiluses of dots and predicates and accurate rhymes, you will never know what makes Emily Dickinson a poet, since you do not demand ideas, but neat arrangements of words. Here is a most significant piece of only eight lines: —

This merit hath the worst —
It cannot be again.
When Fate hath taunted last
And thrown her farthest stone   [furthest

The maimed may pause and breathe,
And glance securely round, —
The deer invites no longer
Than it eludes the hound.

And here is another segment of enduring wisdom, which the writer entitled "Time's Lesson" —

Mine enemy is growing old, —
I have at last revenge.
The palate of the hate departs;
If any would avenge, —

Let him be quick, the viand flits,
It is a faded meat.

Anger as soon as fed is dead;
'Tis starving makes it fat.

Emily Dickinson's poems on Nature are singularly enough less natural and unconstrained than those on human problems. To her Nature seems to present itself commonly as a phantasmagoria which she expresses by incompetent human images as where she writes of "Day's Parlor," in such curious phrases as these: —

The happy winds their timbrels took
    The birds, in docile rows,
Arranged themselves around their prince
    (The wind is prince of those).

The orchard sparkled like a Jew, —
    How mighty 'twas, to stay
A guest in this stupendous place,
    The parlor of the day!

Certainly it is by no such incongruous comparisons as these that this strange woman could gain or for a moment hold her place as poet. Yet "The Sun's Wooing" is quite of the same sort, and there is a sort of artificial lightness and triviality over the verses on this theme in the present volume which was not so obtrusive in the corresponding portions of the first selection. Notwithstanding the vivid character of many of her impressions of Nature, Emily Dickinson does not seem to have had any deep sympathy with the wondrous phenomena of the earth and sky, except as they affected her singular spirit. The lines on "The Snake," which we recalled in our earliest notice of her writing as having been printed in the Republican, are here reprinted, and have been changed somewhat, as we remember. Where in the first stanza "sudden" is used, "instant" appeared when the verses were new, and we think the original adjective preferable. But here are the magical lines: —

A narrow fellow in the grass
Occasionally rides;
You may have met him, — did you not,
His notice sudden is.

The grass divides as with a comb,
A spotted shaft is seen;
And then it closes at your feet
And opens further on.

He likes a boggy acre,
A floor too cool for corn.
Yet when a child, and barefoot,
I more than once, at morn,

Have passed, I thought, a whip-lash
Unbraiding in the sun, —
When, stooping to secure it,
It wrinkled, and was gone.

Several of nature's people
I know, and they know me;

I feel for them a transport
Of cordiality;

But never met this fellow,
Attended or alone,
Without a tighter breathing,
And zero at the bone.

But it is in the verses on Time and Eternity that one closes most warmly on the hand of the recluse woman of Amherst, feeling its throbbing pulse in each grasp of her verse, from the initial moment of this selection, when she says:—

Let down the bars, O death!
The tired flocks come in
Whose bleating ceases to repeat,
Whose wandering is done.

Thine is the stillest night,
Thine the securest fold;
Too near thou art for seeking thee,
Too tender to be told.

Here is another wonderfully appealing utterance of that suspense which all have known:—

Morns like these we parted;
Noons like these she rose,
Fluttering first, then firmer,
To her fair repose.

Never did she lisp it,
And 'twas not for me;
She was mute from transport,
I, from agony!

Till the evening nearing,
One the shutters drew—
Quick! a sharper rustling!
And this linnet flew!

This is a poem that must have been written in anticipation of the end:—

I have not told my garden yet,
Lest that should conquer me;
I have not quite the strength now
To break it to the bee.

I will not name it in the street,
For shops would stare, that I
So shy, so very ignorant,
Should have the face to die.

The hillsides must not know it,
Where I have rambled so,
Nor tell the loving forests
The day that I shall go,

Nor lisp it at the table,
Nor heedless by the way

Hint that within the riddle
One will walk to-day!

263 Mabel Loomis Todd. "Preface" to *Poems by Emily Dickinson, Second Series*, edited by T. W. Higginson and Mabel Loomis Todd. Boston: Roberts Brothers, 1891, pp. [3]–8. Published Nov. 9, 1891. An exchange of letters between Todd and Higginson regarding this preface, when it was in a draft stage, are reprinted in *AB*, pp. 148–49, 151–52. The phrase, "irresistible needle-touch," quoted in the first paragraph, derives from an unsigned review by Higginson (no. 28). Near the end of this preface Mrs. Todd quotes from another anonymous reviewer who spoke of Dickinson's "Emersonian self-possession"; see item 78.

The eagerness with which the first volume of Emily Dickinson's poems has been read shows very clearly that all our alleged modern artificiality does not prevent a prompt appreciation of the qualities of directness and simplicity in approaching the greatest themes,—life and love and death. That "irresistible needle-touch," as one of her best critics has called it, piercing at once the very core of a thought, has found a response as wide and sympathetic as it has been unexpected even to those who knew best her compelling power. This second volume, while open to the same criticism as to form with its predecessor, shows also the same shining beauties.

Although Emily Dickinson had been in the habit of sending occasional poems to friends and correspondents, the full extent of her writing was by no means imagined by them. Her friend "H. H." must at least have suspected it, for in a letter dated 5th September, 1884, she wrote:—

My dear Friend,—What portfolios full of verses you must have! It is a cruel wrong to your "day and generation" that you will not give them light.

If such a thing should happen as that I should outlive you, I wish you would make me your literary legatee and executor. Surely after you are what is called "dead" you will be willing that the poor ghosts you have left behind should be cheered and pleased by your verses, will you not? You ought to be. I do not think we have a right to withhold from the world a word or a thought any more than a *deed* which might help a single soul. . . .

Truly yours,
Helen Jackson.

The "portfolios" were found, shortly after Emily Dickinson's death, by her sister and only surviving housemate. Most of the poems had been carefully copied on sheets of note-paper, and tied in little fascicles, each of six or eight sheets. While many of them bear evidence of having been thrown off at white heat, still more had received thoughtful revision. There is the frequent addition of rather perplexing foot-notes, affording large choices of words and phrases. And in the copies which she sent to friends, sometimes one form, sometimes another, is found to have been used. Without important exception, her friends have generously placed at the disposal of the Editors any poems they had received from her; and these have given the obvious advantage of comparison among several renderings of the same verse.

To what further rigorous pruning her verses would have been subjected had she published them herself, we cannot know. They should be regarded in many cases as merely the first strong and suggestive sketches of an artist, intended to be embodied at some time in the finished picture.

Emily Dickinson appears to have written her first poems in the winter of 1862. In a letter to one of the present Editors the April following, she says, "I made no verse, but one or two, until this winter."

The handwriting was at first somewhat like the delicate, running Italian hand of our elder gentlewoman; but as she advanced in breadth of thought, it grew bolder and more abrupt, until in her latest years each letter stood distinct and separate from its fellows. In most of her poems, particularly the later ones, everything by way of punctuation was discarded, except numerous dashes; and all important words began with capitals. The effect of a page of her more recent manuscript is exceedingly quaint and strong. The fac-simile given in the present volume is from one of the earlier transition periods. Although there is nowhere a date, the handwriting makes it possible to arrange the poems with general chronologic accuracy.

As a rule, the verses were without titles; but "A Country Burial," "A Thunder-Storm," "The Humming-Bird," and a few others were named by their author, frequently at the end, —sometimes only in the accompanying note, if sent to a friend.

The variation of readings, with the fact that she often wrote in pencil and not always clearly, have at times thrown a good deal of responsibility upon her Editors. But all interference not absolutely inevitable has been avoided. The very roughness of her own rendering is part of herself, and not lightly to be touched; for it seems in many cases that she intentionally avoided the smoother and more usual rhymes.

Like impressionist pictures, or Wagner's rugged music, the very absence of conventional form challenges attention. In Emily Dickinson's exacting hands, the especial, intrinsic fitness of a particular order of words might not be sacrificed to anything virtually extrinsic; and her verses all show a strange cadence of inner rhythmical music. Lines are always daringly constructed, and the "thought-rhyme" appears frequently, —appealing, indeed, to an unrecognized sense more elusive than hearing.

Emily Dickinson scrutinized everything with clear-eyed frankness. Every subject was proper ground for legitimate study, even the sombre facts of death and burial, and the unknown life beyond. She touches these themes sometimes lightly, sometimes almost humorously, more often with weird and peculiar power; but she is never by any chance frivolous or trivial. And while, as one critic has said, she may exhibit toward God "an Emersonian self-possession," it was because she looked upon all life with a candor as unprejudiced as it is rare.

She had tried society and the world, and found them lacking. She was not an invalid, and she lived in seclusion from no love-disappointment. Her life was the normal blossoming of a nature introspective to a high degree, whose best thought could not exist in pretence.

Storm, wind, the wild March sky, sunsets and dawns; the birds and bees, butterflies and flowers of her garden, with a few trusted human friends, were sufficient companionship. The coming of the first robin was a jubilee beyond crowning of monarch or birthday of pope; the first red leaf hurrying through "the altered air," an epoch. Immortality was close about her; and while never morbid or melancholy, she lived in its presence.

264 "Notes." *Congregationalist and Boston Recorder* 76 (November 12, 1891), 385.

The late Emily Dickinson and Walt Whitman are classed together by some, on the ground that each sacrificed technique in poetry for the sake of expressing sentiment unhampered.

265 "More of Miss Dickinson's Poems." *Boston Beacon* 8 (November 14, 1891), 3. Dickinson's poem entitled "The Test" is "I can wade Grief."

The first series of *Poems by Emily Dickinson* was the literary sensation of last year; and the series now published is sure still further to pique the curiosity of those who have a taste for the unconventional in literature. Emily Dickinson possessed a nature exquisitely sensitive to outward impressions and inner emotions and ideas, and what she felt and thought she set down with almost unexampled candor and with unerring accuracy. Neglectful of technical form, she hit irresistibly on verbal harmonies of her own, and these, when one has learned to appreciate them, are capable of giving unique pleasure. Miss Todd, who with Mr. Higginson edits the present collection, deprecates any disposition to look upon Emily Dickinson as a morbid and erratic recluse. "She had tried society and the world, and found them lacking. She was not an invalid, and she lived in seclusion from no love-disappointment. Her life was the normal blossoming of a nature introspective to a high degree, whose best thought could not exist in pretence." The contents of the book are classified under the headings of life, love, nature, time and eternity. Sometimes, as in "The Test" (p. 30), the expression is involved and even enigmatic; more often, as in "Compensation"—here quoted— the meaning is crystal clear:—

> For each ecstatic instant
> We must an anguish pay
> In keen and quivering ratio
> To the ecstasy.
>
> For each beloved hour
> Sharp pittances of years,
> Bitter contested farthings
> And coffers heaped with tears.

266 "Literary and Trade Notes." *Publishers' Weekly* 40 (November 14, 1891), 750.

Roberts Bros. have just ready "Emily Dickinson's Poems," second series, edited by T. W. Higginson and Mabel Loomis Todd, with a preface by Mrs. Todd and an autograph letter from Helen Jackson to Miss Dickinson; . . . .

267 Unlocated clipping, ca. November 15, 1891. Placed among materials published in mid-November, 1891, in Todd's scrapbook, this item carries there the handwritten heading, "Springfield, Mass. Wednesday." Search of Springfield papers was without success.

The eagerness with which the first volume of Emily Dickinson's poems has been read, augurs well for a second volume of another set of her strange verses which is just issued by her publishers, Roberts Brothers, of Boston. By many readers these poems are considered to be like impressionists' pictures, or Wagner's weird and rugged music, and their very absence of conventional form and melody attracts attention. Despite that lack, the poems are full of strange power and truth, and contain psychical meanings that are delightful to analytical minds, or to those that perceive the interior nature of things. How good this is, for instance:

> I'm nobody! Who are you?
>   Are you nobody, too?
> Then there's a pair of us—don't tell!
>   They'd banish us, you know.
>
> How dreary to be somebody!
>   How public, like a frog
> To tell your name the livelong day
>   To an admiring bog!

And this—

> Faith is a fine invention
>   For gentlemen who see;
> But microscopes are prudent
>   In an emergency!

This also—

> Surgeons must be very careful
>   When they use the knife;   [take the
> Underneath their fine incisions
>   Stirs the culprit—life!

All the other and larger ones are simply crammed with ideas. Each poem is a study, each to be thoroughly enjoyed for its spiritual power, its philosophy, its clear insight. The volume is beautifully printed, bound in olive and gold, and contains a fac-simile of the poem "Renunciation," by the writer in her own handwriting. A letter from Helen Hunt Jackson is printed in the preface, urging the author to publish her poems and affirming that it was a civil wrong not to do so.

268 "Notes." *Nation* 53 (November 19, 1891), 391. For sales estimates of the various Dickinson volumes, see no. 535 and Appendix D.

The first edition of the new volume of Emily Dickinson's "Poems," edited by Mr. Higginson and Mrs. Todd, has been exhausted within four or five days of issue, although it was double the size of the first edition of volume i., published a year ago. This evidences a sudden popularity quite unprecedented, to which praise and censure alike have probably contributed. The publishers, Roberts Brothers, have the second edition of volume ii. ready today.

269 "Poetry." *Philadelphia Press*, November 21, 1891, p. 10.

The American public has been quick to appreciate the beauty of the late Emily Dickinson's poems, a second series of which, edited by her friends T. W. Higginson and Mabel Loomis Todd, has just been issued in a neat volume by Roberts Brothers. It was due alone to the indifference and modesty of Miss Dickinson that hers has been only a posthumous fame, for there breathes in her work the true spirit of poesy. Roughly moulded as it is—intentionally so, as though the author disdained the drudgery of verbal polish—the artist's touch is on it all. Not alone in the subtle sense of the message of March winds, of butterflies, and of flowers, does the beauty of her verses lie, as when she depicts a sunset:—

> Where ships of purple gently toss
>   On seas of daffodil,
> Fantastic sailors mingle
>   And then — the wharf is still.

Throughout her published work there shows steadily that thoughtful criticism of life which Matthew Arnold defined as the mission of poetry. What, she says: —

> What if I say I shall not wait?
> What if I burst the fleshly gate
> And pass, escaped, to Thee?
> What if I file this mortal off,
> See where it hurt me — that's enough —
> And wade in liberty?

> They cannot take us any more —
> Dungeons may call and guns implore;
> Unmeaning now to me,
> As laughter was an hour ago,
> Or laces, or a traveling show,
> Or who died yesterday!

270 "Some Dainty Books." *Publishers' Weekly* 40 (November 21, 1891), 38.
This separately paged number of *Publishers' Weekly* was entitled "The Christmas Bookshelf." Later in the issue under the heading "Other Holiday Gift Books," Dickinson's two volumes are judged to "make dainty volumes bound in white and gold" (pp. 60–61), while her first volume appears among a list of a half-dozen "gems of booklets for gifts" (p. 61).

The numerous prettily published volumes of poems call for mention. Richard Watson Gilder's "Two Worlds" (Century Co.), with an air of exquisite elegance in its white-and-gold dress and its artistic vignettes, is an offering from one of the most famous of the younger band of American poets. "A Handful of Lavender" (Houghton, M.), by Lizette Woodworth Reese, dedicated "to the sweet memory of Sidney Lanier," is a fragrant bouquet of poems of nature in a dainty cover of white and gold and pink cretonne. Nora Perry's "Lyrics and Legends" (Little, B.), in white and green and gold, are the most recent utterance of a most popular and gifted writer. "The Ride of the Lady," by Helen Gray Cone (Houghton, M.) is a tasteful little volume of genuine poetry, and Mrs. Mason's "The Lost Ring" (Houghton, M.) is an attractively gotten-up volume of semi-religious poems. "The High-Top Sweeting," by Elizabeth Akers (Scribner), are charming lyrics enclosed in a crimson cover decorated with silver apples. The second series of Emily Dickinson's Poems (Roberts) will be eagerly welcomed.

271 "Brilliants." *Boston Budget*, November 22, 1891, p. 11. Unattributed in Todd's scrapbook, the author of this notice was probably Lilian Whiting, editor of the *Budget* (see no. 20). Todd's clipping is dated by hand "Nov. 15, 1891," but this review appeared in the next week's issue.

The first volume of those unique, wonderful poems by Emily Dickinson which appeared last year, edited by Col. Higginson and Mrs. Mabel Loomis Todd, thrilled the reading world with a sense of surprise, delight and critical inquiry. Diamonds in the rough they were, but preëminently diamonds and not paste. The second series needs little heralding. The bare announcement of its publication will incite the eager response of thousands of readers in both this country and England. The volume has the same editors as the previous one, and while to the first Col. Higginson contributed the preface, for this volume Mrs. Todd writes it, and these two brief essays by the two editors form together a most valuable and interesting commentary. To these should be added Col. Higginson's paper on Miss Dickinson, biographical and critical, which appeared in the Atlantic Monthly for October, and the reader will then have as complete a criticism as is attainable on these extraordinary creations. Mrs. Todd opens her prefatory notes by saying:

> The eagerness with which the first volume of Emily Dickinson's poems has been read shows very clearly that all our alleged modern artificiality does not prevent a prompt appreciation of the qualities of directness and simplicity in approaching the greatest themes, — life and love and death. That "irresistible needle-touch," as one of her best critics has called it, piercing at once the very core of a thought, has found a response as wide and sympathetic as it has been unexpected, even to those who know best her compelling power.

One reads these poems breathlessly — those stanzas so vital with condensed significance. As this:

> I'm nobody! Who are You?
>   Are you nobody, too?
> Then there's a pair of us — don't tell!
>   They'd banish us, you know.
>
> How dreary to be somebody!
>   How public, like a frog,
> To tell your name the livelong day
>   To an admiring bog!

Or this:

> I found the phrase to every thought
>   I ever had, but one;
> And that defies me — as a hand
>   Did try to chalk the sun.
>
> To races nurtured in the dark;
>   How would your own begin?
> Can blaze be done in cochineal,
>   Or noon in mazarin?

The temptation to quote would last as long as the poems. Mrs. Todd well compares them to impressionist's pictures, and very felicitous is her expression, "All Emily Dickinson's verses show a strange cadence of inner rhythmical music. . . . Every subject was proper ground for legitimate study, even the sombre facts of death and burial and the unknown life beyond. She touches these themes sometimes lightly, sometimes almost humorously, more often with weird and peculiar power; but she is never by any chance frivolous or trivial. . . . Her life was the normal blossoming of a nature introspective in a high degree. . . . Immortality was close about her, and while never morbid or melancholy, she lived in its presence." The publishers have given the volume the same beautiful form of publication as the former, and its fine, heavy paper, generous margins, and cover of palest green with the fleur-de-lis in gold, and a frontispiece giving the fac-simile of Miss Dickinson's manuscript of her famous poem, "Renunciation," make it all in all, a most attractive as well as a most fascinating volume.

272 "Books and Authors." *Boston Sunday Courier* 97 (November 22, 1891), [2].

The great interest which has been excited by the first volume of the posthumous poems of Miss Emily Dickinson has induced her two friends who edited that volume, Colonel T. W. Higginson and Mrs. Mabel Loomis Todd, to prepare a second. It contains between forty and fifty more of the strangely original and equally unconventional poems of this strange author. The same qualities which marked the first volume are to be found in this, although it must be confessed that there are more of the faults and fewer of the virtues than in the other. A stanza like this shows Miss Dickinson at her best, with a keen poetic insight:

> There is a shame of nobleness
>   Confronting sudden pelf,
> A finer shame of ecstasy
>   Convicted of itself.

The workmanship anybody could pick flaws in. There is happy and exuberant fancy, too, in this address to the roses:

> Pigmy seraphs gone astray,
> Velvet people from Vevay,
> Belles from some lost summer day,
> Bees' exclusive coterie.
> Paris could not lay a fold   [the fold
> Belted down with emerald;
> Venus could not show a cheek
> Of a tint so lustrous meek.

And this is better yet, to the humming bird.

> A route of evanescence
> With a revolving wheel;
> A resonance of emerald,
> A rush of cochineal;
> And every blossom on the bush
> Adjusts its tumbled head,
> The mail from Tunis, probably,
> An easy morning's ride.

This in a more serious mood is no less characteristic both in thought and in expression:

> Let down the bars, O Death!
>   The tired flocks come in
> Whose bleating ceases to repeat
>   Whose wandering is done.
>
> Thine is the stillest night,
>   Thine the securest fold;
> Too near thou art for seeking thee
>   Too tender to be told.

And this description of the battlefield is wonderful in its way:

They dropped like flakes, they dropped like stars,
   Like petals of the rose   [from a
When suddenly across the June
   A wind with fingers goes.

They perished in the seamless grass,
   No eye could find the place;
But God in his repealless list   [on his
   Can summon every face.

What a fine and imaginative phrase is "seamless grass!" There are few poets who
might not envy its happy originality.

273 Louise Chandler Moulton. "With the Poets." *Boston Sunday Herald*,
    November 22, 1891, p. 24. Mrs. Moulton, who could speak from a posi-
    tion as securely within the London establishment as that afforded any
    American (see no. 23), alludes here to a livelier English discussion of
    Dickinson than can be discovered in published British comment on the
    poet. The interest she refers to may have been confined to her circle of
    friends and to the literary salon. Her characterization of *The Speaker's*
    "warm praise" seems overgenerous; see nos. 54 and 74. Andrew Lang's
    Speaker review is no. 102. Roberts Brothers drew on Moulton's com-
    ment for some of its advertisements (see nos. 307 and 346).

Perhaps the greatest literary event of last year, at least in Boston, was the publication, by Roberts Bros. of the "Poems" of Emily Dickinson. Nor was interest
in the work by any means confined to Boston, or even to America. The "Speaker"
(London) praised the "Poems" warmly—Andrew Lang satirized them somewhat
cruelly—and discussion was rife about them on the other side of the water as well
as on this. For myself, I was one of their lovers. Nor was their charm at all the
less for me by reason of their utter disregard for poetic technique. It certainly
would not do for all of us who write verses to ignore the laws of poetic art; but
there was something in Emily Dickinson that transcended art, and made her a
law unto herself. The true fire of genius kindled her work. I took up the "Second
Series" of her "Poems" with half a doubt whether it would justify itself; since it
is not always safe to repeat a successful experiment. But I am convinced that it
would be a loss to the world had this second volume remained unpublished.
    The book is edited, as was its predecessor, by Miss Dickinson's two friends,
Col. T. W. Higginson and Mrs. Mabel Loomis Todd. It was Col. Higginson who
wrote the introduction to the first volume; it is Mrs. Todd who discriminately
prefaces the second, and suggests the best possible apology—if any apology had
been needed—for Miss Dickinson's disregard of conventional form. She happily
compares the poems to impressionist pictures, or the rugged compositions of
Wagner. The "thought-rhyme" in them appeals to a sense more elusive than hearing; and the verses all possess a strange cadence of inner rhythmical music. I am
not absolutely sure that the poems in this volume equal those which most impressed me in the first; and yet, if this series had been the first to challenge our
attention with its potent spell of novel and original music, it may be that I should
have been as deeply moved by it as I was by its forerunner. Could one ask, indeed,
for anything lovelier than

MELODIES UNHEARD.

Musicians wrestle everywhere;
All day, among the crowded air,
    I hear the silver strife;
And—waking long before the dawn—
Such transport breaks upon the town
    I think it that "new life"!

It is not bird—it has no nest—
Nor band, in brass and scarlet dressed,
    Nor tambourine, nor man;
It is not hymn from pulpit read—
The morning stars the treble led
    On time's first afternoon!

Some say it is the spheres at play!
Some say that bright majority
    Of vanished dames and men!
Some think it service in the place
Where we, with late, celestial face,
    Please God, shall ascertain!

I turn back a page, and I come upon something that ought to have been written about Robert Browning—perhaps it was written of him, prophetically—for it is *precisely in his spirit:*

I know that he exists
Somewhere, in silence.
He has hid his rare life
From our gross eyes.

'Tis an instant's play,
'Tis a fond ambush,
Just to make bliss
Earn her own surprise!

But should the play
Prove piercing earnest,
Should the glee glaze
In death's stiff stare,

Would not the fun
Look too expensive?
Would not the jest
Have crawled too far?

I am not sure that the poems under the general heading of "Nature" are not the very loveliest in the whole book. Miss Dickinson had resources enough in herself to make solitude—that desperate, last test of the nobility of human souls—endurable. She preferred the companionship of Nature to that of men; and to her finely attuned ear Nature spoke; and she translated for the world utterances unheard by duller neighbors. Read her portrait of

MOTHER NATURE.

Nature, the gentlest mother,
Impatient of no child,
The feeblest or the waywardest —
Her admonition mild

In forest and the hill
By traveller is heard,
Restraining rampant squirrel,
Or too impetuous bird.

How fair her conversation,
A summer afternoon —
Her household, her assembly;
And when the sun goes down

Her voice among the aisles
Incites the timid prayer
Of the minutest cricket,
The most unworthy flower.

When all the children sleep
She turns as long away
As will suffice to light her lamps;
Then, bending from the sky

With infinite affection
And infiniter care
Her golden finger on her lip
Wills silence everywhere.

The wooing of the sun; the robin "interrupting the morning"; the butterfly
coming forth from the cocoon as a lady from her bower; that pigmy seraph gone
astray, the rose; that confiding prodigal, the blissful oriole; the wind that taps
like a tired man; the gossiping leaves; the sunsets, those theatricals of day; the
summer that lapses as imperceptibly as grief — who but Emily Dickinson understands them all? This single "Nature" section of her book is enough to make
good her claim to grateful and immortal remembrance. I have been talking as if
I loved the "Nature" poems best; and now those on "Time and Eternity" entreat
and reproach me. Read this one, written when the poet has heard *her own death
sentence:*

I have not told my garden yet,
Lest that should conquer me;
I have not quite the strength now
To break it to the bee.

I will not name it in the street,
For shops would stare that I,
So shy, so very ignorant,
Should have the face to die.

The hillsides must not know it,
Where I have rambled so,

Nor tell the loving forests
The day that I shall go.

Nor lisp it at the table,
Nor heedless by the way
Hint that within the riddle
One will walk today!

Now you shall read eight lines as mutinous as lines can be to all laws of art—
mad, perhaps, the perfect Lang would consider them—which I venture anyone
but the truest of true poets could have written:

As by the dead we love to sit,
Become so wondrous dear,
As for the lost we grapple.
Though all the rest are here—

In broken mathematics
We estimate our prize,
Vast in its fading ratio
To our penurious eyes!

I turn on and on—I see poems by the score that I want to quote, and must
not. What shall I do? I can only say to all of you who love these specimens that
I have given you, read the whole book, for you cannot afford to miss any of it.
And yet I will cull for you this one more. Ah, can any of you know what it means
to me?

A COUNTRY BURIAL.

Ample make this bed,
Make this bed with awe;
In it wait till judgment break
Excellent and fair.

Be its mattress straight,
Be its pillow round;
Let no sunrise's yellow noise
Interrupt this ground.

No, the "Nature" poems are not the best! Dearest of all are these that go down
into the valley of Death and climb to the heights of Heaven.

274 "Told by Many Authors." *New York Commercial Advertiser,* November 23, 1891, p. 6.

The little volume is edited by two of her friends, T. W. Higginson and Mabel
L. Todd. The latter writes an appreciative preface and quotes a note from Helen
Jackson, in which the latter says to Miss Dickinson: "What portfolios of verses
you must have! It is a cruel wrong to your 'day and generation' that you will not
give them light. If such a thing should happen as that I should outlive you, I
wish you would make me your literary legatee and executor. Surely, after you are
what is called 'dead' you will be willing that the poor ghosts you have left behind should be cheered and pleased by your verses, will you not? You ought to
be. I do not think we have a right to withhold from the world a word or a thought
any more than a deed which might help a single soul." The remainder of the

preface tells how and when the poems came to be. The poems are classified into Life, Love, Nature, Time and Eternity. The envoi is:

> My nosegays are for captives;
>   Dim long expectant eyes,
> Fingers denied the plucking,
>   Patient till Paradise.
> To such, if they should whisper
>   Of morning and the moor,
> They bear no other errand,
>   And I no other prayer.

A facsimile of a few lines in her writing opens the little book.

275 "Emily Dickinson's Second Volume." *Hartford Courant*, November 24, 1891, p. 4.

The appearance of a second series of the poems of Emily Dickinson is a matter of interest to all lovers of poetry. The publication of the book is consequent upon the extraordinary popularity gained by the first volume of Miss Dickinson's verse, which, given to the public only a few months since, ran with great rapidity through a number of editions and was even translated into foreign tongues. The present volume, like the earlier, has been made up and edited by two of Miss Dickinson's friends, Colonel Higginson and Mrs. Mabel Loomis Todd. It is bound and printed with good taste and elegance and made further attractive by a facsimile reproduction of the poem "Renunciation," one of the most notable pieces of verse in the first volume.

In reading this later collection of the poems, one notes many of the same characteristics: the unworldly spirit, the occasional haunting beauty of expression, the deep seriousness, married to an often startling quaintness or homeliness of phrasing, the utter unconventionality, the absence of the technique of the art.

Life, Love, Nature, Time and Eternity are the subjects treated of in the various divisions of the book and it were easy to pick out expressions, lines, passages and even whole poems which show the gifted writer at her best, this being particularly true of a number of the lyrics under the caption "Nature." Such, for example, is the poem "Out of the Morning," "The Juggler of Day," and the untitled piece number forty-five, containing this beautiful closing stanza:—

> And thus, without a wing,
> Or service of a keel,
> Our summer made her light escape
>   Into the beautiful.

The general treatment of the subject Life and of that of Love is on the whole distinctly less happy, although poems may be mentioned in each division which are beautiful in spots, or characteristic and original, *in toto*. Such is the two-stanza lyric, "The Lost Jewel," and, earlier in the book, the bizarre but very striking poem, "The Railway Train."

But it is incumbent upon the sincere but not unbalanced admirers of Emily Dickinson—and we count ourselves one of them—to say that a wrong has been done her in publishing some, yes, many of the poems in this volume. It begets the suspicion that a mercantile motive was behind the making of it and that the judicious editors, who are unquestionably capable of discriminating the good from the bad, were forced to include many indifferent, or even bad verses, in order to bring the book up to the required size. We have no hesitation in saying that it would have been a kindness to the gifted Amherst lady to exclude fully one half the poems herein included. Some of them are worse than sketchy; are incoherent, inchoate, non-parsable and occult to a degree, which leaves the reader in a state, not of poetic stimulation, but of intellectual irritation. A wrong has been done to Miss Dickinson in publishing them. The temptation no doubt was great. This book will go like wild fire and this would be true of whatever it contained; all the more reason why wise conservative censorship should have been exercised.

Comparing the first and second volumes, it must be declared that the later book is inferior; it is the indiscriminating Emily Dickinson cult that decides otherwise.

But it must be remembered that the volume contains well nigh two hundred lyrics, and hence that, as a whole, many brilliant, strong, deep and lovely poems are embraced in it. We can do no better in closing than by quoting one or two such as examples of Emily Dickinson's real claim to the title, poet. Here is the preface poem, which introduces the volume:—

My nosegays are for captives:
    Dim, long expectant eyes,
Fingers denied the plucking,
    Patient till Paradise.
To such, if they should whisper
    Of morning and the moor,
They have no other errand,
    And I, no other prayer.

THE BLUEBIRD.

Before you thought of spring,
    Except as a surmise,
You see, God bless his suddenness,
    A fellow in the skies
Of independent hues,
    A little weather worn,
Inspiriting habiliments
    Of indigo and brown.

With specimens of song,
    As if for you to choose,
Discretion in the interval,
    With gay delays he goes
To some superior tree
    Without a single leaf,
And shouts for joy to nobody
    But his seraphic self!

276 "New Publications." *Boston Saturday Evening Gazette* 89 (November 28, 1891), p. [4].

The second series of *Poems* by Emily Dickinson will undoubtedly attract as much attention as the first. They are instinct with that originality which marks

Miss Dickinson as a poet, and have more genuine inspiration in them than twenty volumes of ordinary modern verse. At the same time, in reading them we cannot help thinking that genius is near akin to madness, for some of her utterances appear incoherent. Miss Dickinson lacked art and sustained power, but she had a wonderful faculty in selecting the right word to express a swift meaning. The present volume is edited by her friends, T. W. Higginson and Mabel Loomis Todd, and the latter furnishes an appreciative preface. The facsimile of Miss Dickinson's poem, "Renunciation," which is a feature of the book, will be eagerly welcomed.

277 "Books and Authors." *Boston Traveller*, November 28, 1891, p. II.

One of the books of the present season is a second series of Emily Dickinson, as was the first series one of the books of last year. That, it will be remembered, was most adversely criticized, and the adverse critics of last year will not change their tone when they examine the present volume, since they will find the same characteristics, the same defects of form which they pointed out last year. Those who were then attracted and won by the poet's simplicity and directness in dealing with the greatest of all themes, love and life and death, will be again attracted and won. In her preface to the present volume, Mrs. Mabel Loomis Todd, who with Colonel Thomas Wentworth Higginson has edited this volume as well as its predecessor, tells some interesting facts concerning the author's work. During her lifetime the poet published little, and the manuscripts left by her were in the nature of a surprise to her friends. "Many of the poems had been carefully copied on sheets of note paper and tied in little fascicles, each of six or eight sheets. While many of them bear evidence of having been thrown off at white heat, still more had received thoughtful revision. There is the frequent addition of rather perplexing foot-notes, affording large choice of words and phrases. And in the copies she sent to her friends, sometimes one form, sometimes another is found to have been used. . . . To what rigorous pruning her verses would have been subjected had she published them herself, we cannot know. They should be regarded in many cases as the first strong and suggestive sketches of an artist, intended to be embodied at some time in the finished picture." We cannot resist the temptation to quote a few of these sketches:

HOPE.

Hope is the thing with feathers
    That perches in the soul,
And sings the tune without the words
    And never stops at all.

And sweetest in the gale is heard,
    And sore must be the storm
That could abash the little bird
    That kept so many warm.

I've heard it in the chilliest land,
    And in the strangest sea;
Yet, never, in extremity
    It asked a crumb of me.

Perhaps revision would have bettered the form, but might this not have been at the expense of strength? One can but be glad that the following was not revised:

THE GOAL.

Each life conveys to some centre,   [converges
Expressed or still;
Exists in every human nature
A goal.

Admitted scarcely to itself, it may be,
Too fair
For credibility's temerity
To dare.

Adored with caution, as a brittle heaven,
To reach,
Were hopeless as the rainbow's raiment
To touch.

Yet persevered toward, surer for the distance;
How high
Unto the saints' slow diligence
The sky.

Ungained, it may be, by a life's low venture,   [by life's
But then,
Eternity enables the endeavoring
Again.

What, again, could breathe sweeter music than this?

MELODIES UNHEARD.

Musicians wrestle everywhere;
All day, among the crowded air,
        I hear the silver strife;
And—waking long before the dawn—
Such transport breaks upon the town
        I think it that "new life"!

It is not bird—it has no nest—
Nor band, in brass and scarlet dressed,
        Nor tambourine, nor man;
It is not hymn from pulpit read—
The morning stars the treble led
        On time's first afternoon!

Some say it is the spheres at play!
Some say that bright majority
        Of vanished dames and men!
Some think it service in the place
Where we, with late, celestial face,
        Please God, shall ascertain!

And is there not a rare, exquisite, subtle charm in these few lines?

As by the dead we love to sit,
Become so wondrous dear,
As for the lost we grapple,
Though all the rest are here—

In broken mathematics
We estimate our prize,
Vast in its fading ratio
To our penurious eyes!

And is not there a wonderful graphic force in this?

REMORSE.

Remorse is memory awake,
  Her companies astir, —
A presence of departed acts
  At window and at door.

It's past set down before the soul,
  And lighted with a match,
Perusal to facilitate
  Of its condemned despatch.   [condensed

Remorse is cureless, — the disease
  Not even God can heal;
For 'tis his institution
  The complement of hell.

Miss Dickinson's poems in this second series, like those in the first, merit reading from beginning to end, — and re-reading. Miss Todd says of her, and in her few terse words she describes the poet: "Her life was the natural blossoming of a nature introspective to a high degree, whose best thoughts could not exist in pretence. Storm, wind, and the wild March sky, sunsets and dawns; the birds and bees, butterflies and flowers of her garden, with a few trusted friends, were sufficient companionship. The coming of the first robin was a jubilee beyond crowning of monarch or birthday of pope; the first red leaf hurrying through 'the altered air,' an epoch. Immortality was close about her; and while never morbid or melancholy, she lived in its presence." The volume is published in the elegant style which Roberts Bros., Boston, give their best works, and these poems are worthy the beautiful setting given them.

278 "Poems by Emily Dickinson." *San Francisco Evening Bulletin,* November 28, 1891, p. 5. The only earlier review is no. 42.

The second series of these poems, edited by T. W. Higginson and Mabel Loomis Todd, appeared some time ago. A copy was at that time reviewed at length. These poems bear the stamp of genius. In thought and construction they are unique. The first series having attracted so much attention, the second was published. The little volume now appears with such artistic taste in the matter of printing and binding as to make it every way suitable for holiday remembrance.

279 J.B.A. "The Home of Emily Dickinson." *Packer Alumna* 7 (December 1891), 143. This record of a visit with Lavinia has been overlooked in modern scholarship. Its author remains a mystery, someone apparently who had known the poet but not her sister. Perhaps the writer had only corresponded with the poet, for the homestead is here described as if seen for the first time. Manifest inaccuracies leave open the possibility that the recollection is imaginary: e.g., Edward Dickinson was not a judge and Lavinia was the younger, not the older sister. If reliable, the article is important for its view of the Dickinson library and garden, for the affection it suggests between Emily and Vinnie, and for its revelation that Lavinia had a hand in constructing the poem fascicles.

"To have known Emily," said the gracious gentlewoman who welcomed us to the Dickinson homestead in Amherst, "is in itself an introduction to me," and in the spirit of one who shows to an appreciative eye his jewel caskets, she showed us the favorite room, the garden, and the handwriting of the poetess, whose posthumous fame has served only to increase, and not to awaken, the belief of her sister in her genius.

The passion of our time for personalities, transmuted by a human interest in those who have taught or exhilarated us, is no unworthy trait, but a seeking for the elusive secret of originality. Accordingly, we gazed with interest on the large, yellow brick house, standing somewhat close to the street, but screened from too curious scrutiny by stately old trees, whose branches waving across the squarely-built house, take off all appearance of angularity.

Within, the calm orderliness of New England housekeeping prevailed. The library, to the right of the main hall, shows in its piles of books escaping from the bookcases which line two sides of the room, the legal bent of its collector, Judge Dickinson, the father of Emily. Here are Webster and Clay and Everett, legal authorities in numbers, but among them, also, the standard writers of fiction and verse of the earlier half of our century. This was the favorite room of the poetess; here she sat and tasted the —

> Precious, mouldering pleasure 'tis
> To meet an antique book
> In just the dress his century wore.

Here, too, she received those of her father's guests whom her somewhat capricious fancy chose from among the many that crowded his receptions. From this window she must often have looked upon the wide-spread landscape, whose foreground is the campus with the tower of the college church peeping above the trees, and whose background is the circling sweep of the Holyoke range.

> The red upon the hill
> Taketh away my will,

we remember she has said.

A bowl of flaming nasturtiums, lighting up the somber gleam of rosewood and walnut, drew us into the garden, to which our hostess devotes much loving care. Here is no formal geometrical arrangement of scentless plants, but a careful carelessness of hollyhocks, honey-suckle, sweet peas and other old-fashioned flowers, dear to sight and smell and memory. On one side of the garden is the lawn with choice trees judiciously placed, and beyond stretches the orchard. Here would be inspiration and delight to look, and linger, and listen all a summer's day. Her descriptions of bee and humming-bird, of "Summer's Armies," of which the armor-bearer, in her estimation, seems the purple clover, shows the keen observation of the poetess, while the very spirit of the passing seasons is embodied in a "Psalm of the Day," "Indian Summer," "Beclouded," and the poem beginning

> There's a certain slant of light,
>   On winter afternoons,
> That oppresses, like the weight
>   Of cathedral tunes.

Inside the house again, our hostess kindly brought out for our inspection the packets of poems that were found, after Miss Emily's death, in a bureau drawer. The writing is angular and individual, but not difficult to read; capitals are used with no sparing hand, while the punctuation is almost limited to the dash. The poems are copied on both sides of the paper, one following directly upon the other, with never an erasure, but here and there a word written above the line, or at the foot of the page, indicating an after-thought of meaning or form. The secret of the hidden poems was known only to one who had been nurse and maid and friend for many years, who, at her bidding, tied the precious parcels with violet or blue or red cord. Helen Hunt Jackson, in a letter which we were permitted to see, urged her friend to enrich the world with her thought, but almost seemed to divine that the "message" would be "committed to hands I cannot see," when she asked that in the event of Miss Dickinson's death before her own, she might be made her "literary legatee."

Miss Dickinson's poems are never conclusively autobiographic; there seemed no sequence of subject or of chronology in the poems of a single packet. She seems ever an elusive personality, this shy spirit, whose fitting emblem is the Indian pipe selected for the design on the cover of the dainty volume of her verse. Her friend's letters show that she possessed altruistic feelings, but from society she shrank deliberately. Yet she was not a morose spirit; so keen was her sense of the ridiculous that in her later days of invalidism the anxious care of the sister dreaded the paroxysm of mirth that overcame her when a funny story was told in her hearing.

They were much to each other, these two, especially after the shock of their father's sudden death, while attending the Legislature, and during the long invalidism of the mother. The affection of the older sister for the younger, petted, gifted one came out strongly in all her conversation. She delighted to tell of Emily's beautiful auburn hair, hazel eyes and delicacy of complexion, revealed more plainly by the white gowns she always wore; of Emily's affectionate clinging to her for practical guidance and of the fame of Emily's poems "delayed till she had ceased to know." The first confirmation of her own belief in the living power of the poems came from a neighbor, who read them as soon as they were published and coming to congratulate her, exclaimed, "O, those poems!" and burst into tears. "Ah!" said her hostess, "we shall have no finer applause than this."

280 *Baltimore News,* ca. December 1891. The newspaper attribution of this undated clipping is by hand in Todd's scrapbook.

It is possible for true poetry to be without verbal polish, and yet not rough, coarse and repellant like Whitman's. The late Emily Dickinson's verses, a second volume of which is just published by Roberts Brothers, is attracting much attention. Here is one verse:

> What if I say I shall not wait?
> What if I burst the fleshly gate
> And pass, escaped, to Thee?
> What if I file this mortal off
> See where it hurt me—that's enough—
> And wade in liberty?
>
> They cannot take us any more—
> Dungeons may call and guns implore;
> Unmeaning now to me,

As laughter was an hour ago,
Or laces, or a traveling show,
Or who died yesterday!

281 *Boston Globe,* ca. December 1891. This clipping is simply dated "1891" in the Todd scrapbook.

The second series of "Poems of Emily Dickinson," edited by T. W. Higginson and Mabel L. Todd, brings fully as characteristic and powerful work as the first series. It has the poet's remarkable insight into nature and life, which, in its secret working and surprising revelations, has mystical power. It represents anew her quaintly halting and broken utterance, as if words were inadequate to express faithfully, or were too feeble to convey at all, together with a kind of natural language of her thought that revealed of itself instantly what she had learned of the spirit of wood and field, and of her soul; it has the same resistless call to sympathy with her in all her seeking.

She looked on nature—

> With just my soul
> Upon the window pane,
> Where others put their eyes,
> Incautious of the sun.

She looked on life—

> Experiment to me
> Is every one I meet.
> If it contained a kernel?   [contain
> The figure of a nut
> Presents upon a tree
> Equally plausibly;
> But meat within is requisite
> To squirrels and to me.

The thought and language are in perfect harmony in "The Humming Bird," which is the best description yet made of the impressions of the moment's show of itself by the bird.

> A route of evanescence,
> With a revolving wheel;
> A resonance of emerald,
> A rush of cochineal;
> And every blossom on the bush
> Adjusts its tumbled head—
> The mail from Tunis, probably,
> An early morning's ride.

The preface contains further facts of Miss Dickinson's private life and work. The poem, "Renunciation," is reproduced in facsimile.

282 "Talk About New Books." *Catholic World* 54 (December 1891), 448.

It would be far from true to say that there are no fine, strange verses in the second series of Emily Dickinson's poems. And yet her friends were certainly wise in their generation when they set forth the best wine from her long-closed cellars first, and whetted the reader's palate with its half-bitter sweetness and faint, unique bouquet. In this new volume the shocks of keen pleasure come less often, and lines that cling to the memory, and pictures that seize and pre-empt some hitherto unsettled corner in the brain, are indefinitely fewer. Still, one comes now and again upon a characteristic blending of sentiment and landscape, some rendering of the inner woman in the largest terms of outward nature, which would identify itself, unnamed, in any collection of poems. This, for example, which is called "The Sun's Wooing":

> The sun just touched the morning;
>   The morning, happy thing,
> Supposed that he had come to dwell,
>   And life would be all spring.
>
> She felt herself supremer—
>   A raised, ethereal thing;
> Henceforth for her what holiday!
>   Meantime her wheeling King
> Trailed slow along the orchards
>   His haughty, spangled hems,
> Leaving a new necessity—
>   The want of diadems!
>
> The morning fluttered, staggered,
>   Felt feebly for her crown—
> Her unanointed forehead
>   Henceforth her only one.

283 *Fall River* [Mass.] *Monitor*, ca. December 1891. The newspaper attribution for this undated clipping is by hand in Todd's scrapbook. The earlier review to which this notice refers is unlocated.

It is but a short time since we called attention in these columns to a collection of poems by the deeply lamented Miss Dickinson. We predicted then great and growing favor for the book, and our predictions have been realized, as it has had a large sale and has met with most cordial commendation both from press and reviews. And all of this, despite the fact that Miss Dickinson is a comparatively unknown writer and the still weightier fact that her verses are not merely those bits of exquisite melody that catch the fancy and haunt the memory with their sweetness: such poetry almost inevitably leaps into quick popularity, but melodious as is much of Miss Dickinson's versification, it is not the chief or the most marked characteristic of her writing. It is the deep thought, the strong originality and the careless, almost rough, envelope, which most powerfully mark her writings; they must be read, pondered over, studied, to ascertain their meaning, their strength and sweetness. Sometimes it is a familiar idea, so quaintly presented, with such power in its unusual presentation, that you feel yourself for the moment, in the presence of an utterly and startlingly unfamiliar thought, and then comes, with sweet, melodious utterance, some wonted scene of daily life, or some phase of Nature's loveliness, of which Miss Dickinson is the most devout and ardent worshipper, to be followed by verse or poem, rich in meaning, but requiring the close attention of the thoughtful brain. The same characteristics mark this new volume of her poems, which were the strength and beauty of the first, and it seems very wonderful that one who wrote so much and so well, should only be generally known after her death: it is as mournful as strange. This has a very interesting introduction from the pen of Mabel Loomis Todd, giving us more and very welcome insight into Miss Dickinson's life and character; it has also an autograph letter of Helen Hunt's to her. The volume is issued in the charmingly tasteful style which characterizes the publications of Roberts Brothers, and is a very dainty little volume.

284 "Book Reviews." *Packer Alumna* 7 (December 1891), 151.

The second series of Emily Dickinson's poems opens with a fac-simile reproduction of "Renunciation," a strong poem printed in the first volume. The poems show the .me characteristics as those previously published. A careful, almost an itemized noting of the details of nature and of life, a child-like questioning of the great facts of human experience, and, at times, a certain whimsicality of treatment coming out in simile or metaphor, that whether it appeals to us individually or not, is original and often very effective. In the poems on Time and Eternity, there is the same Anglo-Saxon imagination, busy with the outward facts of death, and the same yearning for spiritual light that was shown in the earlier published poems, but here it seems faith is oftener attained and generally through the study of nature.

285 *Pittsburgh Post*, ca. December 1891. The newspaper attribution for this undated clipping is by hand in Todd's scrapbook.

The "Poems of Emily Dickinson," "edited by two of her friends," Mrs. Todd and Colonel Higginson, have been issued by Roberts Bros., Boston, in fawn and gold. They are included under the titles "Life," "Love," "Nature," "Time and Eternity." Miss Dickinson was an original thinker, and her verses have been called a "modern argument for eternity." In the introduction Mrs. Todd says: "Emily Dickinson scrutinized everything with clear-eyed frankness. Every subject was proper ground for legitimate study, even the somber facts of death and burial and the unknown life beyond. She touches these themes sometimes lightly, sometimes almost humorously, more often with weird and peculiar power; but she is never by any chance frivolous or trivial."

286 *Portland* [Oregon] *Transcript*, ca. December 1891. The newspaper attribution for this undated clipping is by hand in Todd's scrapbook.

A second volume of the *Poems of Emily Dickinson*, edited by two of her friends, T. W. Higginson and Mabel Loomis Todd, is published by Roberts Brothers, Boston. These poems, like those of the first volume, are of especial interest, not only because of their intrinsic merit, but because they first see the light after the poet's death, having been found carefully copied on note paper and tied in little bundles each of six or eight sheets. It is this remarkable fact that a poet so worthy of the name, should care so little for public recognition, that most of her poems were enjoyed only by herself, that makes them of peculiar interest. They are all short and convey in few, terse words, that do not always constitute the best rhythm, a wonderful breadth of meaning. Since she wrote more for herself than anyone else, one feels that these poems are the overflow in words of her wealth of thought that filled her life completely, and caused its seclusion to be more desirable than the attractions of society, which she had tried and found wanting.

287 *Truth*, ca. December 1891. The periodical attribution for this undated clipping is by hand in Todd's scrapbook.

Roberts Brothers are also the publishers of a second volume of the posthumous poems of Emily Dickinson, the strangely gifted, recluse singer of whose existence and writings Massachusetts became aware only after she had passed on to the immortals, when Colonel Thomas Wentworth Higginson edited and sent out the first collection. This second series shows the same high imaginative qualities, the same delicate, sad and introverted emotional quality, the same imperfect handling of metre and rhythm, the technicalities of her art, yet with a native impulse to harmony often attaining the melody akin to a wild-bird's song. She was the possessor of a true lyrical power which, had she lived, and come out to a broader atmosphere, might have made her one of the world's great singers. The poems as they stand have a curious interest for all thoughtful students of literature.

288 Unidentified clipping, ca. December 1891. This notice is without any identification in Todd's scrapbook.

It is enough to say that a second volume of the poems of Emily Dickinson has appeared. Everybody who read the first volume will want to read the second one, and will be the more deeply impressed with the wonderful and strange genius who produced these bits of versification.

289 "Notes." *Brains* 1 (December 1, 1891), 114.

Two of her friends and admirers, Thomas Wentworth Higginson and Mabel Loomis Todd, have edited a second volume of Emily Dickinson's poems. There is a very enthusiastic, descriptive, and biographical sketch in the way of a preface, giving an idea of this modest little woman, who scanned everything with a clear-eyed frankness. Evidently Miss Dickinson threw a great deal of responsibility upon her editors. She did not write for publication nor for fame, and here at least is one poet who wrote for poetry's sake. As Miss Todd says, "Her life was the normal blossoming of a nature introspective to a high degree, whose best thought could not exist in pretence." There is a striking disregard of conventionality about her writings. There is no attempt to reach effect. They are the musings of a meditative and often melancholy soul, grown half weary of the world.

290 "Emily Dickinson's Poems—Second Series." *Amherst Record*, December 2, 1891, p. 4.

When the first volume of Emily Dickinson's poems was given to the public, it met with such instant and hearty recognition and approval that edition after edition was exhausted. The Second Series of these poems, issued by the publishing house of Roberts Bros., Boston, with a sympathetic and helpful preface by Mabel Loomis Todd, bids fair to more than duplicate the success of the earlier volume. To the ordinary reviewer of books it is a difficult and delicate task to assign to these poems their proper place in literature. To one who understands the word poetry to mean lines smoothly written and smoothly read, conventional rhythm and conventional rhyme, a symmetry of anapest and dactyl, "feet" rhyming with "meet" and "boat" with "float," there will be little poetry in the tangled skeins of thought and emotion, sense and sentiment that are here interwoven. But to the one who gives to the word poetry its truer richer meaning, the soul and not the substance, the spirit that binds together the good in all humanity and joins the beauty of earth to the glory of the heavens, to such an one the poems of Emily Dickinson bring a message and a thought. That message is oft-times quaintly expressed, and the thought is strange, even startling; but it is never commonplace, never irksome. It is as if the genius of the "good gray poet" had found an echo among the Hampshire hills, and yet not an echo, rather an answer. Emily Dickinson read nature as an open book, and what she read she has transcribed for others whose vision is less keen, whose spirit is not so close in touch with the unwritten harmony in forest and glen, mountain and meadow, the opening flowers, the singing birds, the hymn of insects, the drifting clouds, the glories of the sunset, nature's grand symphonic poem that appeals to all that is highest and purest and best in human nature. After one has visited some grand conservatory and feasted the eye on the richest and rarest products of floriculture, has been surfeited with the glory of color and the weight of perfume of the floral aristocracy, it is a relief to turn to the wild rose growing by the wayside hedge, its airy petals tinted with the blush of dawn, its perfume nature's incense. So from the realistic literature of the age, the novels "written with a purpose," the poems metrically correct and unimpeachable as to rhyme, it is a pleasure to turn to the verse of one who wrote without the ever-present fear of critic's condemnation, who made a friend of nature and in her writings has made the beauty of that friendship known to mankind.

291   "Some Holiday Poetry." December 2, 1891. The date and initials which appear to be "A.H.F." are inscribed by hand in the Todd scrapbook.

The eager, loving welcome given to the little volume of poems by Emily Dickinson, and the interest it at once attracted, will not be soon forgotten by the many who are really good readers. A new volume, just published, of poems by the same gifted writer, merits, and is already receiving, the same welcome. The announcement that more of her manuscript had been found, was to be edited by T. W. Higginson and Mabel Loomis Todd, aroused general interest, and Miss Dickinson's friends and admirers are not to be disappointed in the new poems here presented. The same loving insight into nature and man, the same fearless handling of the most solemn things, the same forcible brevity, the same quaint originality, the same odd and irregular expressions are in this second series of poems. The introductory essay is at once critical and sympathetic. "Renunciation," a poem printed in the first volume, is given here in fac-simile.

292   *Westfield* [Mass.] *Times and News-Letter,* December 2, 1891, p. 2. In her diary for Dec. 1, Mrs. Todd writes: "went to Mrs. D. L. Gillett's, & read my paper on Emily Dickinson, also many letters & unpublished poems, to a club of ladies. They were all intensely interested, and I received quite an ovation" [*AB*, p. 188]. At that lecture, Mrs. A. P. Strong, formerly Abiah Root, Dickinson's girlhood friend, came forward to offer her collection of letters for an edition of the poet's correspondence; see *Letters of Emily Dickinson* (1931), pp. xv–xvi.

Through the kindness of Mrs. D. L. Gillett the Tuesday Morning Club were given a rare treat at their regular meeting yesterday morning. Emily Dickinson, the new light in the poetical world, was the topic of the hour. Mrs. Mabel Loomis Todd, wife of Prof. Todd of Amherst College, an acquaintance and friend of this poet, gave a most interesting and delightful talk upon her life and writings illustrating her "illusive personality" as she termed it, by reading many of her characteristic poems yet unpublished, and relating many incidents eminently descriptive of her peculiarities of thought and manner. Specimens of her very singular handwriting were shown, and letters to Samuel Bowles, Dr. Holland, T. W. Higginson, and to her friends of girlhood days were read, all showing a warm heart, bright intellect and a wonderful power of expression. Mrs. Todd's charmingly informal manner lent added grace to her well-chosen words, and awakened in her listeners a sympathetic appreciation.

293 [Robert Bridges.] Droch (pseud.). "Bookishness." *Life* 18 (December 3, 1891), 326.

In the second series of "Poems by Emily Dickinson" there are many pieces to deepen the impression made by the first volume, though there is no new phase of her poetic talent shown. All her mannerisms appeared in the earlier volume, so that this one will be judged less for its eccentricities than its original and permanent beauties.

The reader probably will conclude that it is not her quaint and shy skepticism, her half-worldly cynicism (which she arrived at through no experience of the world, but by an intellectual process) that charms him most. But it is the real poetic quality of beautiful imagery, flashed on you in a word or brief phrase, that gives these verses their fascination. The subjective side of Miss Dickinson's poems as been praised so excessively, that one is apt to overlook the felicity of her descriptive pieces like "The Railway Train," "The Thunder-storm," and "The Snake," in which there is not a trace of introspection; and the most compact of all in this category, "The Humming Bird":

> A route of evanescence
> With a revolving wheel;
> A resonance of emerald,
> A rush of cochineal,
> And every blossom on the bush,
> Adjusts its tumbled head, —
> The mail from Tunis, probably,
> An easy morning's ride.

294 "Some Recent Verse." *Christian At Work* 50 (December 3, 1891), 727.

We also have from the same publisher a second series of the Poems of Emily Dickinson. Here again we strike upon a true and high note. The best attestation of the real value of Emily Dickinson's poems lies in the fact that the first volume of the series, published only a short time ago, has already won its way into a general popularity. Poor and bad fiction may find currency in some quarters, but poor and bad poetry never. Miss Dickinson's verse has been a revelation to the literary world, and the present volume will undoubtedly find many readers.

295 "Our Book Tables." *Philadelphia Public Ledger*, December 4, 1891, p. 6. Roberts Brothers had used John W. Chadwick's phrase "argument for immortality" (no. 51) in its advertising (no. 73).

The "Poems of Emily Dickinson" (first and second series), edited by Mrs. Todd and Colonel Higginson, are issued in neat 16-mo. volumes in the same approved livery of enamelled white and gold. The verses of this original thinker have been called a modern "argument for immortality."

296 "Books and Authors." *Boston Home Journal,* n.s. 5 (December 5, 1891), 10. The earlier review referred to here is no. 16.

There has probably been no new book of poems published the past year which created the interest that did an unpretentious book that was sent out without any heralding, whose author was wholly unknown in the literary world, and who had passed to the higher life with no thought of the posthumous fame that was to come to her. That modest volume, bearing the simple title, "Poems by Emily Dickinson," with its unconventionality, but breathing the genius of the true poet on every page, struck the popular heart at once, and edition after edition was demanded. Nor was the popularity that the poems achieved an ephemeral one; they are of too much intrinsic merit and they have too many delightfully unconventional qualities. They are the outgushings of a heart attuned to the praise of God and to all that is beautiful and lovely in nature, and they find a sure response in the heart universal. The book has taken a cherished place in poetic literature, and it will not lose its hold. The remarkable success of the book has induced the publication of a second series of Emily Dickinson's poems, which has just been issued, the volumes being edited by two of her friends, T. W. Higginson and Mabel Loomis Todd, and containing an appreciative preface by the latter. What we said at the time of the publication of the first series will apply equally to this book. The poems are delightfully unconventional, and never surfeit for want of variety in mood and subject. They are classified under the headings, Life, Love, Nature, Time and Eternity. A fac-simile of Miss Dickinson's "Renunciation" is given in the front of the book.

297 K. B. Oracle. [pseud.] "Letter About Books." *Wave* 7:31 (December 5, 1891), 9. This epistolary column is addressed to "Matilda," as if from one woman to another. The following paragraph appears in the middle of the letter.

Supposing, *en passant,* you look at a volume of poems I have here. They are by Emily Dickinson and are prefaced by a facsimile of her well-known poem "Renunciation." If you can read it you are gifted with a greater endowment of intuition than I dare claim. But for the matter of that, why waste time over hieroglyphics unless one is an Egyptologist, which, heaven forfend. Miss Dickinson is inclined to introspection. Strange as it may appear, she has thoughts, and in her dainty verses you will generally find an idea enshrined. She writes of life, love, nature, time, and eternity, attempts nothing dramatic, and is really Emersonian in her simple verbal method of expression. You will permit the form. For creed and systems she appears to have but little reverence. There's an epigrammatic turn to her mind that is exhibited in the sharp brevity of her briefer poems — neat, clear-cut, and full of insight. Read them as an antidote to the others I have been telling you of.

298 "Weekly Record of New Publications." *Publishers' Weekly* 40 (December 5, 1891), 934. The following paragraph accompanies the routine bibliographical entry for *Poems,* Second Series.

"Life," "Love," "Nature," "Time and Eternity" are the names under which Emily Dickinson's friends have grouped this second series of her notable poems. The eagerness with which the first series was read, guarantees a welcome for these. There is a fac-simile of one of the author's poems, also a preface by Mrs. Todd and an autograph letter from Helen Jackson to Miss Dickinson.

299 Charles E. L. Wingate. "Boston Letter." *Critic*, n.s. 16 (December 5, 1891), 320. For Sanborn on Lang, see no. 251.

I was very much interested to hear from Mr. Niles of Roberts Bros. that their second volume of Emily Dickinson's poems is meeting with a cordial reception. The demand for the book has been remarkably great. In England the poems have not been received with any favor, I am told, and that result one might expect after reading Andrew Lang's severe attack. Frank B. Sanborn, by the way, has characterized that part of Mr. Lang's criticism of Miss Dickinson, wherein he ridicules the poet on the ground of her works lacking rhyme and common sense, as being mere Philistinism, reminding him of the English coroner who read Wordsworth's verses in the House of Commons and made fun of them. Laughter, declares Mr. Sanborn, is the easiest and the worst way of dealing with Wordsworth or with any serious poet. Here in America, and especially here in New England, the poems of Miss Dickinson are now accepted as standards in their own original line.

300 "Books and Bookmen." *Light* 4 (December 5, 1891), 322.

No volume of verse, in many of day, has called forth the interest and admiration that the first series of Emily Dickinson's evoked. Edition after edition was exhausted and still the call came for more. To this second series there are prefixed a fac-simile of "Renunciation," printed in the first volume, and a preface which to a limited extent acquaints us with the writer herself. A remarkable being she was, unquestionably, divinely touched by the spirit of song. There is nothing of the perfectly metered and rhymed verses that conform to the rule of poesy, nor is there any of the strange assemblages that have given to Walt Whitman his fame, but from "I'm nobody! Who are you!" to

> Lay this laurel on the one
> Too intrinsic for renown.
> Laurel! veil your deathless tree,—
> Him you chasten, that is he!

the reader feels that he is dealing with no ordinary poetaster. Condensation is one of the writer's merits. Like Poe she does not believe in the long poem. A stanza, a line, a word present vivid pictures. Like the humming bird which she so vividly describes in the first series, she goes from thought to thought; just a sip here and a dip there, the reader, all the time, admiring the implied thought, the scene just hinted at. An epic would weary her; perhaps it would be an impossibility, but in aptness of expression, she has had few equals. In "Compensation" she says:

> For each ecstatic instant,
> We must an anguish pay
> In keen and quivering rates   [ratio
> To the ecstasy.

One is prompted to quote the whole book, for every thought is a gem but then there would be no temptation to buy and possess the volume, for all favorable book reviews should have a stimulating end in mind. Selection might be made at random with no danger of failure, so here is

THE RAILWAY TRAIN.

I like to see it lap the miles,
And lick the valleys up,
And then stop to feed itself at tanks;
And then prodigious, step

Around a pile of mountains,
And, supercilious, peer
In shanties by the side of roads;
And then a quarry pare

To fit its sides, and crawl between,
Complaining all the while
In horrid, hooting stanza;
Then chase itself down hill,

And neigh like Boanerges;
Then, punctual as a star,
Stop—docile and omnipotent—
At its own stable door.

The arrangement of the collection is under four heads, first Life, then Love, next Nature and finally Time and Eternity, and the progress from the first to the last is admirable. In all there are 166 selections, not much in quantity but more in quality than many a more ambitious array. She has imitated no one, has invaded no one's domain. She found a world, a small one, all her own, and how completely, perfectly has she occupied it!

301 "Poems Fresh From the Press." *Cleveland Sunday Plain Dealer*, December 6, 1891, p. 4.

When Emily Dickinson died in New England not long ago only a very few of her most intimate acquaintances knew that a true poet had passed away. Not a line of her poetry had ever been printed or offered for publication. A few of her nearest friends had from time to time received a few verses apparently dashed off in the heat of the moment, without time having been taken to put them into proper shape. Irregular as they were, fracturing every accepted canon as to poetic form, many of these bits of verse startled and puzzled their recipients. The poetic soul was there but clothed in garments of almost grotesque fashion and sometimes repellent raggedness. After her death there was found in the late residence of Miss Dickinson, where she had lived in secluded life, a large number of poems daintily written on narrow sheets of paper stitched together, many of them bearing marks of revision that showed her methods of composition. Dashed off at fire heat, eager to seize and fasten the thought without much regard to the form, she afterwards endeavored to perfect the lines without weakening the thought. Two of her literary friends, T. W. Higginson and Mabel Loomis Todd, undertook to edit some of the poems and publish them, more as a souvenir of the dead poet that her personal friends would value than with the expectation that the volume would be appreciated by the general public. A larger number than they expected saw the merit of the poems and a second collection has been published in a daintily printed volume by Roberts Brothers. Miss Dickinson's poems are all brief.

They are strong and suggestive sketches, dashes of color that reveal as in a flash the perfect painting never to be finished. Viewed through a lens to discover the details the sketch appears crude, with splotches of color and harsh lines. Nevertheless, the touch of genius is clearly recognizable. Miss Dickinson's lines rhyme or do not rhyme, just as it happens. She evidently gave little thought to the matter when she dashed them off, but, as her editors say, "her verses all show a strange cadence of inner rhythmical music." Charmed by that music and seized by the thought the reader does not discover until upon closer investigation that her lines are daringly constructed and frequently defy all accepted rules of versification. Written by one less richly gifted with poetic inspiration many of the verses would irresistibly produce ridicule instead of commanding respect, if not admiration.

Here is one of the most finished of her poems and its beauty will be felt by everyone who can appreciate genuine poetry. It has a pathetic interest, being evidently written under the consciousness of approaching death and having a suggestion of the old superstition of telling of a death to the bees and the flowers:

> I have not told my garden yet,
>   Lest that should conquer me;
> I have not quite the strength now
>   To break it to the bee.
>
> I will not name it in the street,
>   For shops would stare, that I
> So shy, so very ignorant,
>   Should have the face to die.
>
> The hillsides must not know it,
>   Where I have rambled so,
> Nor tell the loving forests
>   The day that I shall go.
>
> Nor lisp it at the table,
>   Nor heedless by the way
> Hint that within the riddle
>   One will walk today!

As an illustration of a different and more characteristic sytle take this impressionist painting of a storm:

> It sounded as if the streets were running,
>   And then the streets stood still.
> Eclipse was all we could see at the window,
>   And awe was all we could feel.
>
> By and by the boldest stole out of his covert,
>   To see if time was there.
> Nature was in her beryl apron,
>   Mixing fresher air.

There is temptation on nearly every page to quote lines showing at the same time the poetic quality and the carelessness of conventional forms of Miss Dickinson's poetry, but three short specimens must suffice. The first has a touch of sarcasm, almost unique in the collection. It is headed "The Preacher":

> He preached upon "breadth" till it argued him narrow, —
> The broad are too broad to define:

> And of the "truth" until it proclaimed him a liar,—
> The truth never flaunted a sign.
>
> Simplicity fled from his counterfeit presence
> As gold the pyrites would shun.
> What confusion would cover the innocent Jesus
> To meet so enabled a man!

The next embodies a truth paradoxically stated:

> A death-blow is a life-blow to some
> Who, till they died, did not alive become;
> Who, had they lived, had died, but when
> They died, vitality begun.

A sunset is thus fancifully hinted at rather than described:

> Where ships of purple gently toss
> On seas of daffodil,
> Fantastic sailors mingle,
> And then—the wharf is still.

302 *New York World*, December 6, 1891, p. 26.

A second series of the poems of Emily Dickinson, as edited by Thomas Wentworth Higginson and Mabel Loomis Todd, has been issued by Roberts Brothers, of Boston. It is questionable if the admirers of Miss Dickinson's experimental vagaries have done wisely in spreading her posthumous crudities before the public. There are, at least, many alleged poems in the book which a judicious hand should have eliminated from the collection, such, for example, as this:

> I went to heaven.
> 'Twas a small town,
> Lit with a ruby,
> Lathed with down.
> Stiller than the fields
> At the full dew,
> Beautiful as the pictures
> No man drew,
> People like the moth,
> Of mechlin, frames,
> Duties of gossamer,
> And eider names.
> Almost contented
> I could be
> 'Mong such unique
> Society.

It requires more than charity to find in such lines any degree of art suggesting "impressionist pictures" or "Wagner's rugged music." It is true that "the very absence of conventional form challenges attention," but not in the complimentary sense prefatorially implied by the editors. It is not fair to Miss Dickinson, however, to let the above extract stand as a representative poem, and it must be admitted that she has expressed some thoughts of life, of love, and of death which, notwithstanding the "daringly constructed" lines, appeal to a fine sense—to "an unrecognized sense more elusive than hearing." Of such is the following:

I have not told my garden yet,
Lest that should conquer me;
I have not quite the strength now
To break it to the bee.

I will not name it in the street,
For shops would stare, that I,
So shy, so very ignorant,
Should have the face to die,

The hillsides must not know it,
Where I have rambled so,
Nor tell the loving forests
The day that I shall go.

Nor lisp it at the table,
Nor heedless by the way
Hint that within the riddle
One will walk to-day!

To the eye and ear of a poet demanding that attention to *technique* which distinguishes the most perfect verse the liberties taken by Miss Dickinson are simply appalling, such as rhyming "blaze" with "forge," "pay" with "ectasy," "up" with "step," "star" with "door," "me" with "say," and "meet" with "nut."

It is in her more mystical moods that Miss Dickinson pays the least attention to style of construction. Her poems of nature more nearly approach the canonical lines. Here is one of her best:

THE SNAKE.

A narrow fellow in the grass
Occasionally rides;
You may have met him—did you not?
His notice sudden is.

The grass divides as with a comb,
A spotted shaft is seen;
And then it closes at your feet,
And opens further on.

He likes a boggy acre,
A floor to cool for corn.
Yet when a child, and barefoot,
I more than once, at morn,

Have passed, I thought, a whip-lash
Unbraiding in the sun,
When, stooping to secure it,
It wrinkled, and was gone.

Several of nature's people
I know, and they know me;
I feel for them a transport
Of cordiality.

But never met this fellow,
Attended or alone,

Without a tighter breathing,
And zero at the bone.

303 "Recent Publications." *Providence Sunday Journal,* December 6, 1891,
p. 13.

The second series of the poems by Emily Dickinson contain the same marked
features as the first, the same indifference to form, and the same keen and
spiritual insight and extraordinary felicity of language in interpreting thought and
condition.

304 "Book Notes." *Boston Journal,* December 8, 1891, p. 5.

The second volume of "Poems," by Emily Dickinson, edited by two of her
friends, T. W. Higginson and Mabel Loomis Todd, finds the public better prepared
for the appreciation of the works of this clear-eyed eccentric poet than the first
published verse had done. There is no stronger incident in American literature
than the posthumous fame of the recluse who "had tried society and the world,
and found them lacking," and whose quiet introspective life resulted in "portfolios"
of verses found shortly after her death, by her sister and only surviving housemate. The book opens with a copy of the poem "Renunciation" (fac-simile). The
collected poems are merged in the groups of Life, Love, Nature, Time and Eternity. They are marked by originality, both of thought and expression. If the poet's
individuality is sometimes too pronounced there is such freshness with vigor
that the poems offer recompense for study. A sarcasm at the pretenses and frivolities of existence is one of the unexpected characteristics of the verse.

305 Dorothy Lundt. "Library and Foyer." *Boston Evening Transcript,* December 9, 1891, p. 6.

Vengeful authors, burning with the slights put upon them by the publishing
fraternity, would have revelled in the recent *naif* remark of a young authoress,
fresh from her interview with the head of a well-known book house. All innocent
of ironical intent — "Why, you've no idea how surprised I was," quoth she. "He was
so nice and *human,* don't you know; not a bit like a *publisher.*"

The appearance of a second volume of Emily Dickinson's verse sets one wondering afresh what, among all the roughnesses and queernesses and seeming affectations of her style — if she may be said to have a style — is the secret of the
magnetic charm her work undeniably has for the thoughtful reader. A phrase in
the preface to this latest collection gives a very significant hint on the subject,
where her editor says that Miss Dickinson's verses should in many cases be regarded "as merely the first strong and suggestive sketches of an artist, intended
to be embodied at some time in the finished picture." Regarded as such, the verses
take on the charm of the workshop — of the world behind the scenes — which has
such potent attraction for every one to whom art, in any form, genuinely appeals.
We touch the artist in the work in process of creation in his workshop as we never
touch him in the work framed, bound or otherwise completed after its kind, "seen
by us and all the world in circle." The half-finished sketches of an old master, revealing where here a line was contemplated and there a line was erased, have a
subtler fascination for latter-day artists than have all the treasures of the Uffizi.
The first rough draft of a famous tale is a treasure incomparable in its hints of
changed ideals and bettered methods of work. A drama in rehearsal is full of

unique entertainment to the lucky on-looker. Bohemia owes not a little of its flavorsome charm to the fact that it is a world of workshops.

So with Emily Dickinson's verses; their very lack of finish has in it compensation, in added nearness to the singer's personality. And the personality of the artist is an uncannily elusive thing, be his written speech never so frank. It is a thing consciously and sensitively guarded, too, and kept within a magic circle which, if one try to cross, there awaits him a repulse as certain and inexplicable as that of the invisible witch-walls of old legend. Now and then a keen, defiant hint of this finds its way straight and, as it would seem, inadvertently from the artist's self, through the artist's work. Witness this queer bit of verse—the first, appropriately enough, in Miss Dickinson's new volume, with its repelling, as of outpushed palms:

> I'm nobody! who are you?
> Are you nobody, too?
> Then there's a pair of us—
>   Don't tell!
> They'd banish us, you know.
> How dreary to be somebody!
> How public, like a frog:
> To tell your name, the livelong day,
> To an admiring bog!

306 "Our Boston Literary Letter." *Springfield Republican*, December 10, 1891, p. 5.

No greater contrast could well exist than between the fluent, finished, graceful poems of Holmes and the quaint, piercing, often affected verses and metrical ejaculations of Emily Dickinson; in whom what Wordsworth calls "the accomplishment of verse" was so provokingly absent. Provokingly, because we feel that, had she chosen, she might have written good verses as easily as these ragged and baffling rhymes. Great as the contrast is, however, between the diligent doctor, writing good verse for 70 years, and the intermittent, rhapsodical, evasive woman, persistent in nothing but whim and thought, and a kind of evanescent humor,— there is a similarity beneath the surface worth heeding—for in both it is the fancy that is chiefly at work, and wit—that is, the flash of the unexpected—is the most frequent result with both. The Amherst sibyl had a narrow life and a deep-searching observation; Dr. Holmes has had a broad and varied life, over which his eye has wandered with penetration, but without going to the bottom of things often. This second volume of Miss Dickinson's epigrams and fragments is well enough, and is justified by the success of the first one; but it is hardly needful to print more, even if there are others left in the portfolio. Enough has now been given to the world to show what the writer was; more would not deepen the impression, and might tend to efface it.

307 Publisher's advertisement. *Boston Evening Transcript*, December 12, 1891, p. 6. For the full text of Mrs. Moulton's review, see no. 273. The first three and last sentences of this excerpt were printed in large type.

Mrs. Moulton says, in the "Boston Herald," of the second series: "Perhaps the greatest literary event of last year, at least in Boston, was the publication of the 'Poems' of Emily Dickinson. For myself, I was one of their lovers. Nor was their charm at all the less for me by reason of their utter disregard for poetic technique. It certainly would not do for all of us who write verses to ignore the laws of poetic art; but there was something in Emily Dickinson that transcended art, and made her a law unto herself. The true fire of genius kindled her work. I took up the 'Second Series' of her 'Poems' with half a doubt whether it would justify itself; since it is not always safe to repeat a successful experiment. But I am convinced that it would be a loss to the world had this second volume remained unpublished."

308 "New Books." *Boston Evening Transcript*. December 12, 1891, p. 7. *The Lover's Year Book of Poetry: A Collection of Love Poems For Every Day in the Year* compiled by Horace Parker Chandler, was the first in a series of six similar volumes, all published by Roberts Brothers (1891–96). Dickinson's "She rose to his requirement, dropped" (I, 99) was her only poem included in the series.

THE LOVER'S YEAR BOOK OF POETRY

This exquisite little green and white volume is the first volume of "The Lover's Calendar," prepared by Horace Chandler, with an extremely graceful introduction. Here we have a live poem, and a most beautiful one, of every day in the year, and here we find not only all our old favorite poems but a number of dainty fugitive pieces which we noted with pleasure in some daily paper perhaps and now are delighted to have in a more permanent form.

The old English poets are represented generously, especially Shakespeare, and then we come step by step down to our own day and find our best-loved verses by Gilder, or Arlo Bates, or Emily Dickinson have not been omitted from the collection.

"To lovers then, of whatever sex, age, or clime, the pages of this book are dedicated."

We recommend the volumes as unique and specially adapted for holiday purposes.

309 "New Holiday Books." *Cambridge* [Mass.] *Tribune* 14 (December 12, 1891), 1. The *Tribune* did not review *Poems*, 1890. The fourth sentence echoes Andrew Lang's remark from a *London Daily News* editorial reprinted in the *Tribune* (nos. 232 and 261): "She cannot possibly have been right in her methods, unless all poets, from the earliest improvisers down to Tennyson, have been wrong in theirs."

To those who have watched with interest the apotheosis of this gifted woman this second series of the "Poems" of Emily Dickinson must possess a rare interest. The vagueness, the illusory nature of the spirit and the music that marked the first efforts are repeated also here. The same keen spiritual insight, fettered by faults of outer form at once attracts and repels. Unless poets from the beginning of the world have been wrong in valuing form, Emily Dickinson has wilfully, or can it be ignorantly, flung aside a polished weapon. But like young David, with an unpolished pebble from the brook, she has struck straight at the heart of Philistinism and every-day commonplaceness. Here and there a couplet has a rare felicity as

> Hope is the thing with feathers
> That perches in the soul,

but when the stanza concludes with

> And sings the tune without the words
> And never stops at all,

there is a certain painful drop, like that of a wounded bird. The poems on "Compensation" ring true from the heart; "The Martyrs" has a firm and strong touch. Certain of the poems, such as "The Goal," have a strong Goethe-like quality, and the expression of the involved thought is German in its construction. Poem no. 41, beginning:

> To learn the transport by the pain
> As blind men learn the sun,

has a note of genuine passion and heart-felt pain ringing through its pathetic stanzas. One of the most charming and light in touch among the poems under "Love," is "The Letter." After reading that and the earnest poem beginning:

> Your riches taught me poverty,

the reader is led to wonder, despite the editor's positive assertion, whether there be not a tragedy hidden under that verse which depicts so subtly the passions of a human woman-soul.

310 "Today's Literature." *Chicago Tribune*, December 12, 1891, p. 12. The literary editor of the *Tribune*, from the summer of 1891 to September 1892, was Edward J. Harding. The bracketed inserts are the author's own.

This second series of the poems of Emily Dickinson, compiled by her literary administrators, Mr. Thomas Wentworth Higginson and Mrs. Mabel Loomis Todd, will revive public interest in the personality of that remarkable woman. Of her appearance, habits, and tastes, of the few events in her pure and sequestered life, we already knew the little there was to be told. In one of her letters to Mr. Higginson—those quaint, shy effusions, of which the unconventionality is tempered by a certain primness—she says of herself: "I am small, like the wren, and my hair is bold, like the chestnut burr, and my eyes like the sherry in the glass that the guest leaves." Her own language, again, can best describe the timidity and love of solitude that impelled her to a life of almost conventual seclusion. "You ask of my companions. Hills, sir, and the sundown, and a dog large as myself that my father bought me. They are better than [human] beings because they know, but do not tell; and the noise in the pool at noon excels my piano." "[You speak] of shunning men and women. They talk of hallowed things aloud and embarrass my dog. He and I don't object to them if they'll exist their side." "I sing, as the boy does of [in] the burying-ground, because I am afraid." In contrast with these qualities she revealed an arch and playful humor, together with a critical insight of the most thorough-going frankness. To a shyness that shrank at times from the gaze of a flower she united an audacity that assumed to treat with deity on equal terms. A childlike simplicity and directness added a final charm to this most unworldly of souls.

It is this childlike element, we think, that appeals most strongly to the reader of her poems. One occasionally finds the same difficulty in following the irregular hop-step-and-jump of her thought as in attempting to keep pace with the skipping mental gait of an intelligent child. Her wayward and irresponsible fancy describes every sort of abrupt angle and eccentric curve, but naturally and without effort. This naturalness distinguishes her work from that of Quarles and his fellows, whose far-fetched conceits are so lacking in spontaneity. Of the coquetry and self-consciousness that mar the work of so many poets one never sees a trace; she composes with her eye upon her object and seeks to please herself alone. Her wonderful acuteness and her uncompromising naturalism are not the effect of culture, but a part of her childhood's unforfeited inheritance. She has a child's ignorance of the world, a child's imagination and love of color. One smiles at the significance with which she invests the idea of an Earl; to be "Duke of Exeter"—ah, that is a too, too daring flight! How like a child's fancy is this, which describes the "clear shining after rain":

> The boldest stole out of his covert,   [By and by the boldest
>   To see if time was there;
> Nature was in her beryl apron,
>   Mixing fresher air.

One compares her with Emerson, with Scott's "Pet Marjorie," and with Blake, the English painter-poet; but, after all, she is just herself, the solitary example of a floral species as yet unclassified.

Of these characteristics the effect is intensified by the eccentricities of her style. Her verse is often grammatically obscure; she does not hesitate to employ a word in a sense which is foreign to it; the metaphysical quips and fetches in which she indulges are sometimes too fine-spun to be intelligible. Her rhythm, too, is frequently irregular, though never devoid of a certain music; and her numerous false rhymes are unpardonable. Rhymed, unrhymed, and imperfectly rhymed stanzas occur in the same poem, conforming to no rule but that of the writer's caprice. Mrs. Todd speaks of the "thought-rhymes" which appear in her friend's work, "appealing to an unrecognized sense more elusive than hearing." If we understand the term aright, the "thought-rhyme" is as often absent as present in these irregular stanzas; at any rate, one cannot go jumping from word-rhymes to thought-rhymes and back again, all in the same piece. Mrs. Todd should have taken stronger ground. We are willing to condone these technical offenses because the offender is Emily Dickinson. An Emily Dickinson who was willing to conform to rules, to suppress her individuality, and to follow the beaten track, would not have been the Emily Dickinson of our admiration. Her faults were merely the defects of her qualities; her originality and her eccentricity were fostered by the same conditions. "When I try to organize," she says of herself, "my little force explodes and leaves me bare and charred." Her imperfections, then, are the price of her charm, and a price we are only too ready to pay.

Of the quality of these poems it is difficult to give an idea by the aid of selections. Their effect is cumulative; then, too, the emotional element is less conspicuous than the esthetic, the esthetic less so than the intellectual. Her landscape studies are, perhaps, the most pictorially effective, especially the storm scenes. Here is a pretty sketch.

APRIL.

> An altered look about the hills;
> A Tyrian light the village fills;
> A wider sunrise in the dawn;
> A deeper twilight on the lawn;
> A print of a vermilion foot;
> A purple finger on the slope;
> A flippant fly upon the pane;
> A spider at his trade again;

An added strut in chanticleer;
A flower expected everywhere;
An ax shrill ringing in the woods;   [singing
Fern odors on untraveled roads—
All this, and more I cannot tell,
A furtive look you know as well,
And Nicodemus' mystery
Receives its annual reply.

With all the fine sympathy with nature and its teeming life which her poems of this class display, we do not regard them as thoroughly characteristic of the writer's genius. The great mysteries of existence touch her with a keener thrill. What plaintiveness in a cry like this:

Let down the bars, O Death!
The tired flocks come in
Whose bleating ceases to repeat,
Whose wandering is done.

Thine is the stillest night,
Thine the securest fold;
Too near thou art for seeking thee,
Too tender to be told.

Or in this other:

At least to pray is left, is left.
    O Jesus! in the air
I know not which thy chamber is—
    I'm knocking everywhere.
Thou stirrest earthquake in the South,
    And maelstrom in the sea;
Say, Jesus Christ of Nazareth,
    Hast thou no arm for me.

The low key of the ensuing poem is characteristic:

Their height in heaven comforts not,
    Their glory naught to me;
'Twas best imperfect, as it was;
    I'm finite, I can't see.

The house of Supposition,
    The glimmering frontier
That skirts the acres of Perhaps,
    To me shows insecure.

The wealth I had contented me;
    If 'twas a meaner size,
Then I had counted it until
    It pleased my narrow eyes

Better than larger values,
    However true they show;   [their show
This timid life of evidence
    Keeps pleading, "I don't know."

The next is the child of a brighter mood:

> Pompless no life can pass away;
> The lowliest career
> To the same pageant wends its way
> As that exalted here.
> How cordial is the mystery!
> The hospitable pall
> A "this way!" beckons spaciously,
> A miracle for all!

And this has a sweet, sympathetic note:

> To learn the transport by the pain,
> As blind men learn the sun;
> To die of thirst, suspecting
> That brooks in meadows run;
>
> To stay the homesick, homesick feet
> Upon a foreign shore
> Haunted by native lands the while
> And blue, beloved air—
>
> This is the sovereign anguish,
> This, the signal woe!
> These are the patient laureates
> Whose voices, trained below,
>
> Ascend in ceaseless carol,
> Inaudible, indeed,
> To us, the duller scholars
> Of the mysterious bard!

One more quotation, and we have done:

> The nearest dream recedes, unrealized.
> The heaven we chase
> Like the June bee
> Before the schoolboy
> Invites the race;
> Stoops to an easy clover—
> Dips—evades—teases—deploys;
> Then to the royal clouds
> Lifts his light pinnace
> Heedless of the boy
> Staring, bewildered, at the mocking sky.
>
> Homesick for steadfast honey;
> Ah! the bee flies not
> That brews that rare variety.

Artless, imperfect as they are, these verses have a freshness that is only too rare in our self-conscious age.

311 "Emily Dickinson." *Light* 4 (December 12, 1891), 349. The "near relatives" granted a deathbed interview must be the poet's earlier-mentioned Worcester uncle, William Dickinson, and his second wife. The *Chris-*

tian Union reminiscence by MacGregor Jenkins is no. 249. The *Light* reviewed *Poems*, Second Series in the previous week's issue (no. 300).

The second volume of Miss Dickinson's poems is reviewed in another column. As, in the years ago, she was a visitor in this city and still has relatives here, it is not amiss to make some further mention of her. It is true that very little can be added to the pleasant little sketch, given by Colonel Higginson in the Atlantic but even this little may be of interest. Hers was not a personality that admitted of a long biography. Her fame is altogether posthumous. Her girlhood in her Amherst home, presided over by that sternest of Puritans, her father, would probably disclose little that is peculiar. Her education, away from home, was had at Mount Holyoke where she was an intimate friend of Miss Fiske, also an Amherst girl and the famous Helen Hunt Jackson of later years. Another friend in the seminary was Mrs. Simeon Newton of State Street, Worcester. In those days, Mrs. Newton recalls her as a modest, retiring girl, with no indications of poetic ability, yet even then possessing some marked peculiarities.

Whence came this ability to express her thoughts in verse? Not even a Galton could find any reason for it among her paternal ancestors. Metered Psalms would include about all the poetry that they cared for; but when we turn to the Norcrosses, her maternal relatives, we find literary taste and activity that readily accounts for her own devotion. Not that the Dickinsons were not highly intellectual, for her father and brothers have been connected with Amherst from the beginning and her grandfather, a Yale man, was its founder, but prose realities rather than poetic fancies filled their minds. Her uncle, William Dickinson, of this city, was prepared for college but preferred business to school. He sent two sons, however, through college courses. He was himself, always interested in school affairs and was the donor of the bell in the High School tower.

After her death, her sister, Lavinia, to whom she willed her poems, many hundred in number, has with others, as Col. Higginson and Mrs. Todd, made judicious selections for publication. Then it is that her marked peculiarities of manner are the more vividly remembered. After her father's death she would wear white only, and after the dismissal of the Rev. Mr. Jenkins from the Amherst church, she never attended meeting. In a recent Christian Union, a member of this Jenkins family has given a child's recollection of Emily Dickinson. A cousin was an invalid, obliged to be wheeled about in a chair. Emily would never see Cousin H___, but frequently sent bunches of flowers to be tied to the invalid's chair. She was devoted to flowers and to this day, her sister, as far as possible, preserves the grounds and floral display as Emily loved them.

Her last interview with certain near relatives was very peculiar. They had come from a distance and at first she declined a meeting, but later she consented to five minutes conversation each with uncle and aunt in a dark hallway. It was a visit of words only, for vision was impossible. When her father was in Congress, she was in society at the Capitol but afterwards, she almost completely withdrew herself, scarcely appearing save as she and her sister served at the annual lawn parties given by her father at Commencement.

The life, so full of sentiment that no one knew while she lived, must have had a thousand unsatisfied longings. Possibly, in that beyond where she and so many of her kindred are, there may be a fruition unattainable here. Let us hope so.

312 "Poems by Emily Dickinson." *Boston Evening Transcript*, December 15, 1891, p. 6.

In this artificial generation Emily Dickinson's pronounced individuality and intellectual audacity have given her a host of admirers. We take up the second volume of her poems, fearing lest her best bits of verse were culled for the collection published last year. But we have the same crisp epigrammatic style and the same intensity of feeling:

> I noticed people disappeared
> When but a little child;
> Supposed they visited remote
> Or settled regions wild.
>
> Now know I they both visited
> And settled regions wild;
> But did before they died—a fact   [because they
> Denied the little child—   [Withheld

is as typical of Miss Dickinson's style as any two verses included in the poems of last year.

> Surgeons must be very careful
> When they take the knife;
> Underneath their fine incisions
> Stirs the culprit life—

is another specimen of the writer's poetic originality, though perhaps the poem, "Pompless no life can pass away," will appeal to more readers still.

"Summer's Obsequies" is one of the lighter poems, as is also "The Preacher." More serious poems are the bit of didactic verse called "Hunger," and "A Death Blow is a Life Blow to Some." In one poem we find Miss Dickinson saying,

> I found the phrase for every thought
> I ever had but one.

and yet in reading over her poems we think that the opposite of this statement is true. Thoughts came to her more easily than did the phrases in which to express them to others. Her concepts were grand, but her tongue halted often, and her poems are like unfinished sketches and belong to the "Impressionist" school. Only occasionally do we find anything which can claim to be more than suggestive work. And yet as we say this we find ourselves under the spell of the writer's strong personality; we may criticize many of her poems, we may rebel against the malicious uncouthness of many of her rhymes, and we may again and again question the mental soundness of the writer, but we cannot fail to recognize the rugged strength and beauty which underlie much of her poetic work. The spirit of her writings was never the spirit of the dilettante poet. She wrote as the ancient prophets spoke, because something within her prompted it; and we who read with the critic's eye find something deeper than pleasure in this, even as in the former volume of her verses.

313 "Poetry and Fiction." *Boston Post*, December 15, 1891, p. 5.

The first volume of the poems of Emily Dickinson was most eagerly received, but the puzzled world could do no better towards defining them than by accepting the original and poetic definition of Colonel Higginson, that they were "poetry torn up by the roots." The new volume is evidently sprung from the same soil of imagination, but will scarcely meet the same eager reception, if only because it has not the same sharpness of novelty. The curiously bad rhymes are abundant, as before, offset in a way by a spiritual rhythm that knows not rhyme. Several of the pieces had already been printed in the selection from Miss Dickinson's letters which appeared in the Atlantic Monthly and was noticed at length in the *Post,* and the volume is discriminated from its predecessor chiefly by a number of extraordinary and sometimes rather unpleasant love poems. "In the Garden" and "The Snake" are two of a group of beautiful and keenly observing poems of nature and outdoor life.

314 [James Gibbons Huneker.] "The Raconteur." *The Musical Courier* 23 (December 16, 1891), 709. In the *Courier* 29 (December 26, 1894), 22, Huneker reprinted "The Dandelion's pallid tube" and "A Route of Evanescence," describing the latter as a "unique exemplar of verbal felicity." He again quoted her sentence with which he begins this notice in the same journal, 38 (March 29, 1899), 29.

"And the noise in the pool at noon excels my piano."
—Emily Dickinson

"The wretched tinkler called a piano, which tries at the whole orchestra and murders every instrument in the attempt, is like our modern civilization—a tuning and a diminishing of individuals for an insipid harmony."
—George Meredith

The first very Walt Whitman-ish sentence is from Emily Dickinson's letters to Thomas Wentworth Higginson, and it keys exactly my present mood, which is not, gentle reader, cynical indifference to music—*that* mood, praised be Apollo, has gone for ever—but rather a groping after a music more spiritual than is made on the piano, a putting forth imaginative tentacles to feel, taste, touch an art that I fear exists only in the shadowy recesses of my inner consciousness. And yet that same consciousness gives a premonitory quiver when it encounters a rhythmical nature such as Emily Dickinson, who had a delicacy of expression like Chopin's—she was a New England Chopin—a Chopin living in the bleak-soul-unfavorable conditions of the Yankee atmosphere, and her soul, timidly ardent and coy in color, repressed itself within the bounds of a few shyly passionate phrases that are as fragmentary as Sappho's, but nearly as precious. How unlike Marie Bashkirtseff's morbid vanity is the following bit of fluent inquiry:

I'm nobody! Who are you?
    Are you nobody, too?
Then there's a pair of us—don't tell!
    They'd banish us, you know.

How dreary to be somebody!
    How public, like a frog.
To tell your name the livelong day
    To an admiring bog!

315 [Thomas Wentworth Higginson.] "Recent Poetry." *Nation* 53 (Dec. 17, 1891), 468. Higginson here compares Rumanian folk songs (the subject of his review) to Dickinson's "Success is counted sweetest."

They deal with nature and time and eternity with a strange directness, like that of Emily Dickinson: the graves give up their dead; nay the dead soldier lies absorbed in the one yearning hope that they will not put him actually in the grave till he has learned how the fight ended.

316 "Recent Poetry and Verse." *Critic*, n.s. 16 (December 19, 1891), 346. The writer takes particular issue with Higginson's preface to the 1890 edition (no. 10). For a reply to this review, see no. 334.

One year ago a volume of curiously formless poems, revealing an unusual quality of grasp and insight and written by a woman who had spent her life in seclusion, was edited by Col. T. W. Higginson and Mrs. Mabel Loomis Todd, two of the author's friends. It was well received by the reviewers, who recognized the writer's unusualness and originality of thought, and it has since gone through several editions, proving that a great many persons care comparatively little for the form of expression in poetry so long as the thoughts expressed are startling, eccentric and new. The success of that volume has led the editors to prepare another one containing a quantity of the same sort of strange verse in which are to be found the same beauties and same faults as were noticed in its predecessor. There are many things in "Poems Second Series," which, as somebody has said of the former verses, "take away one's breath." But one does not wish to have one's breath taken away entirely. A thought may be striking, but the stroke should not be fatal. After reading two volumes of Miss Dickinson's poems one gets exhausted, and a healthy mind begins to fear paralysis. There is too much of the same thing in them—morbid feeling, jerky and disjointed writing, and occasional faults of grammar. We do not agree with Col. Higginson that in considering these poems, "a lesson on grammar seems an impertinence"; it is their lack of grammatical correctness and their absolute formlessness which keeps them almost outside the pale of poetry. Nevertheless, to those who liked the first book we commend the second, even though it does contain a stanza like this:—

> A few incisive mornings
> A few ascetic eyes,—
> Gone Mr. Bryant's golden-rod
> And Mr. Thomson's sheaves.

It is Mrs. Todd who writes the preface. In it we are told of the author that "she had tried society and the world, and found them lacking. . . . Her life was the normal blossoming of a nature introspective to a high degree, whose best thought could not exist in pretence."

317 "Poems By Emily Dickinson." *Literary World* 22 (December 19, 1891), 486. As if to give it special notice, Mrs. Todd copied the last sentence of this review on another page of her scrapbook.

This second series of poems deepens every impression made by the previous volume of Miss Dickinson's verse. Again we find the hardly human dumbness, the isolated and singular point of view, the neuralgic darts of feeling voiced in words that are sometimes almost inarticulate, sometimes curiously far-fetched— the rhyme, meter, and vocabulary jarring upon the artistic sense. One pities deeply the suffering of such an incommunicative spirit. Some of her strange observations are most keen, as when she names the mushroom

> . . . vegetation's juggler,
> The germ of alibi;

and there is an Emersonian dignity in

SIMPLICITY.

How happy is the little stone
That rambles in the road alone,
And doesn't care about careers,
And exigencies never fears;
Whose coat of elemental brown
A passing universe put on;
And independent as the sun,
Associates or glows alone,
Fulfilling absolute decree
In casual simplicity.

Vivid are the pictures of an imminent thunderstorm:

The wind began to rock the grass   [begun
With threatening tunes and low, . . .
The dust did scoop itself like hands,
And throw away the road. . . .

The wagons quickened on the streets,
The thunder hurried slow;
The lightning showed a yellow beak,
And then a livid claw.

Verses of extraordinary insight occur in the group which refers to Death — in whose shadow the shrinking, strangely muted creature seems to have been more at ease than in the glare of human life. She has acquainted her soul with death that approaches, yet confesses,

I have not told my garden yet
Lest that should conquer me;
I have not quite the strength now
To break it to the bee.

But whatever of fear or of fettered tongue has been hers, a last moment expresses itself in simple music; though even here the ear, as unaccustomed to speech, lapses away from rhyme:

Let down the bars, O Death!
The tired flocks come in
Whose bleating ceases to repeat,
Whose wandering is done.

Thine is the stillest night,
Thine the securest fold;
Too near thou art for seeking thee,
Too tender to be told.

The best criticism of Miss Dickinson's verse is that which has set the wan Indian pipe upon her book as an emblem.

318 Unlocated clipping, December 20, 1891. Todd's scrapbook provides a separately clipped printed date above this notice and a handwritten place of publication, "Boston, Massachusetts." Virginia Terris suggests that Fawcett wrote this letter to Mabel Todd after hearing one of her lectures on ED (*GC*, 27–28). During the decade Fawcett attacked Whitman for disregarding the "merely technical sort of thing," calling him "lawless" and "hysterical."

Mr. Edgar Fawcett, the distinguished poet and romanticist, writing to a friend of Emily Dickinson's poems, makes a critique too fine to be permitted to remain in the oblivion of a private letter:

Mr. Fawcett says: "I meant to speak of Emily Dickinson's poems when I last wrote you. Her work impresses me very much. I sent the first volume of her poems to Swinburne. I was so delighted with it that I mailed him my own marked copy, and I feel sure that he must have enjoyed it. Ah, with all that woman's disdain of rhyme, the posing—can go to school to her. She is an artist to the finger tips, even though her 'loves' may not be in assonance with her 'doves,' and all that merely technical sort of thing. The astonishing part of her work is that we find ourselves loving even its faults and eccentricities. One can imagine her saying some sweet, quaint, novel thing about her publishers and vendors being Death & Co., Number Zero, Valley of the Shadow Villa. The shy but heaven-tinted violets of her verse break forth from every page with a wilding symmetry and fragrance that for a while make one think one's Tennyson a rose too heavily perfumed, or even one's Longfellow a sort of over-cultured exotic. Surely there were never such 'wood-notes' warbled in lovelier and more silvery trebles."

319   Arthur Chamberlain. "The Poems of Emily Dickinson." *Commonwealth* 31 (December 26, 1891), 7.

The second series of Emily Dickinson's poems presumably completes the collection of materials from which her critics and her readers may reconstruct, as best they can, a singular but genuine personality. The material is more ample than might appear at the first glance; for the poems, though short, are not fragmentary, and they are often condensed to a high degree. Many of them, in truth, are fairly epigrammatic in their terseness, and the idea is compressed to such an extent that the author seems to have thought, if the expression may be permitted, in shorthand. Possibly her very marked tendency toward personification may have been an aid in this particular; but, however it may have come about, here are some perfectly adequate and brilliantly vivid descriptions in from four to eight short lines.

If poetry is a criticism of life under the conditions of poetic truth, as Matthew Arnold has affirmed, then these stanzas are surely poetry; and if really great poetry must show high truth and high seriousness, this poetry must rank well up in the scale. The illumination that it throws upon any subject is rather an electric flash than the more general and pervasive daylight, and the short duration as well as the intensity of the gleam aids the sharpness of the impression, which certainly has the effect of veracity and does not lack seriousness, even when the expression is most whimsical.

Indeed, many of the poems seem survivals from the "Fantastic School" so-called, for strange comparisons and singular conceits abound; but they are not idle bits of laborious commonplace fretted into unwholesome prominence; they are rather descriptions of almost scientific exactness. What could describe the quick, silent, sinuous disappearance of a snake more accurately than the line,

It wrinkled, and was gone?

Or the hush of a summer evening better than the concluding lines of "Mother Nature,"

> Her golden finger on her lip,
> Wills silence everywhere?

Or the changes of a sunset sky as do the phrases in "She Sweeps with Many-Colored Brooms," with its "purple ravellings," "amber threads," and the east littered with "duds of emerald?"

It is true that here and there the thought is not as entirely original as is the phrase.

> We play at paste
> Till qualified for pearl,

suggests in its thought Tennyson's "The baby new to earth and sky" and Browning's "Rabbi Ben Ezra," as "Triumph" suggests the latter's "Prospice;" but such thoughts are the common property of humanity.

Although each poem is a genuine whole, the concluding strain often has a lingering cadence that seems to prolong itself indefinitely; the form never brings the reader up with a round turn and a mental jounce; but rather, to use Miss Dickinson's own expression, it seems as though it "bubbled slow away." This is entirely in keeping with her feeling, as expressed in many of the poems, that desire is something more fine than fulfillment — a quality of mind which may explain a certain aloofness, so to say, which seems not unlike the point of view that a ghost might assume in regarding sublunary things, "an Emersonian self-possession" indeed.

The question of form in poetry is a much debated one, and the entirely frank disregard of accurate rhymes in many of these poems is a fair field for criticism. Putting aside the plea that there may be poetical expression apart from rhyme and even from metre as of dubious value at best, it is well to admit that the occasional lapses in rhyme are a drawback to perfection where they occur in these poems; but it is also evident that they are akin to certain omissions in an artist's sketch rather than to any lack of ability. There are hints here and there that Miss Dickinson might easily have gained the mastery of all the intricacies of rhyme, and whatever variations her rhythm may show, its modulations are musical, and the accent is seldom, if ever forced. Very often the form suits the sentiment with an absolute propriety, as in "Called Back"; while in "I know that He Exists" there is an unusual play of rhyme and a rhythm which cheats the ear into a supposition of rhyme where it really does not exist. "The Letter" is a marvel in the way of happy expression of eagerness and coyness at once and is one of the most original, as it is one of the most charming poems in the volume.

Of the four books, "Life," "Love," "Nature," "Time and Eternity," into which this second series is divided, "Love" and "Nature" seem to us the most excellent. "Life" contains the only poem in which the thought seems untrue; for, with all possible respect for Miss Dickinson, "laces" do not "reveal the surge" nor "mists the Apennine." There may be some occult truth in the statement, but it is not evident at least to Philistine eyes. But then, Miss Dickinson was evidently born to be the despair of reviewers.

In the fourth book, "Time and Eternity," there seems to be an inability to realize that anything so good as Heaven can be true; but this, it is probable, is more in effect than in fact, not so much to be taken literally as to be viewed as a strong means of expression for the transcendent charm of immortality. At least, Miss Dickinson is entitled to the benefit of the doubt. "Void" is that veritable "twilight land" in which Mr. Aldrich's "hurrying ghosts met face to face." There are a few pieces of direct and personal pathos—an appeal which is used in the poems rather sparingly; for had it been used more freely, one feels that its keenness might have proved unbearable. In "Summer's Obsequies" there is a mock seriousness that very nearly, if not quite betrays the author into irreverence.

The preface, by Mabel Loomis Todd, is a sympathetic and accurate character-ization of Emily Dickinson's genius, if we may allow her that word, which indeed has often enough been bestowed with far less provocation. Whether it be genius or only talent raised to a very high degree, there is a force and an originality in her work which makes one wonder if, putting aside the differences of training and environment, Emily Dickinson may not in some ways be spiritually akin to Marie Bashkirtseff; and one longs for another Landor to write an "Imaginary Conversation"!

320   "New Books." *Churchman* 64 (December 26, 1891), 851.

That a second series of Emily Dickinson's poems should be demanded not long after the appearance of the first, if it proves nothing else, at least shows that her poetical writings are popular among a certain class. This second volume, like the first, is the tribute of affection in the editorship of two of her friends, who have well done their work of selection and editing.

321   [John White Chadwick.] "Poems of Emily Dickinson." *Christian Regis-ter* 70 (December 31, 1891), 868–69. The reviewer's access to Dickinson manuscripts makes his identity clear; see no. 51.

We have wondered a good deal whether, if this second series had appeared first, it would have made the profound impression made by the first. We hardly think it would. To say that this is the gleaning after the other's reaping would be to differentiate it too widely from that for truth and for the honor it deserves. Pos-sibly, to seem as good as the first series, the second must have been better. It is not that. It is not quite so good. Very likely we shall not feel so sure of this after we have read this over as many times as we have the other. The range of topics and the manner are the same; for the former, Nature and Love and Life and Death; for the latter, a compactness verging on an algebraic notation of ideas, a supreme indifference to rhyme, sometimes a halting rhythm, but often, and for the most part, a rhythm that is full of music and of fire. Out of the great abundance of good things we hardly know which to select for special approbation. Those who do not like snakes and those who do will find No. XXIV., Book III., "The Snake," much to their mind. That on the "Going" of some little one is charged with infinite pathos. That called "Triumph" is perhaps the strongest in the book; and the two following verses are the best of that:—

> There's triumph of the finer mind
> When Truth, affronted long,
> Advances calm to her supreme,
> Her God her only throng.
>
> A triumph when temptation's bribe
> Is slowly handed back,
> One eye upon the heaven renounced,
> And one upon the rack.

One of the quaintest is that beginning, "I went to heaven," XIV., p. 196; but does not the punctuation make it unnecessarily obscure? We do not remember any such obscurity in the original which we were privileged to see. Should it not be

> People like the moth
> Of Mechlin frames?

The one on "Her Small Library" (p. 74) is quite as good as the great one on "A Book" in the first series, and the third stanza has the real "lyrical cry" of which we hear so much. Her various readings, we are told, were many; and in III., one of the rarest, the editors have chosen "pinnance"—

> Lifts his light pinnance—

when they had also "pinnacle" at their command, if a private copy kindly sent to us was correctly written. The former is an inversion of a simile of Pope; the latter would be an easy and characteristic reversion to the original meaning of "pinnacle,"—a little wing or feather. In dozens of poems where the whole is baffling there are lines and phrases of great power and beauty. Mrs. Todd contributes a preface which admits us to a nearer view of her friend's secluded but not morbid or unhappy life than Mr. Higginson's exquisitely beautiful preface to the first series. There is also a fac-simile of one of her poems, and her handwriting was as remarkable as the substance of her work. She had many humorous conceits. We have seen the original of the quaint verses on "The American Flag" (p. 52); and with them she sent a flag of her own making,—three bits of braid, red, white, and blue, pinned together with a thorn! The wonder is her symbol did not get into her song.

322 *Congregationalist* 75 (December 31, 1891), 459.

It is a sad pity when the substance of true poetry is put at a disadvantage by the writer's recklessness in respect to form. The second series of *Poems by Emily Dickinson*, edited by Col. T. W. Higginson and Mabel L. Todd, is as exasperating as the first. Her verses are fragmentary in thought and often clumsy in expression, and they pay small heed to rhyme or meter. Yet they are poetry. There is no denying that honestly. Some of them fairly throb with meaning and take an abiding hold of the mind. It is hard to understand how such a mind as Miss Dickinson's must have been in its native powers can have exhibited the intellectual—we had almost added the moral—defects which the construction of her poems displays. She gave forth irregular flashes of poetic fire while most poets burn with some measure of steadiness for a time. Whether due to incapacity, indifference, eccentricity or excessive modesty, the manner of her poetry is a permanent blemish. That her poems are in larger demand now than at the first has no special significance, but the fact that thoughtful readers seem disposed to read them again and again indicates that some among them are to live, and that means that there is enough true poetry in them to insure their continued life in spite of faults which very justly would doom most writers' poems to oblivion.

323 Anna C[allender] Brackett. *The Technique of Rest.* New York: Harpers, 1892, pp. 25, 117–18. Suggesting we should not be bothered by lapses of memory, the author quotes a portion of Dickinson's conversation with Higginson as recorded in the latter's *Atlantic* essay (no. 221). The "insight" referred to in the opening sentence is "the principle of the spiritual harvest." In her second mention, Brackett argues that positive thinking can triumph over negative circumstances. Her quotation again derives from the Higginson essay.

Those who by daily living have in some degree attained this insight have no reason to be troubled over any failure in memory which advancing age may bring. Emily Dickinson wisely asks, "Is it oblivion *or absorption* when things pass from our minds?" We take out our watch to look at the time in order to decide whether we will follow some course of action. We decide, and put the watch back again, and are perhaps troubled afterwards to find that we cannot remember what the time was. [p. 25]

There is nothing more sure to undermine health than constant gnawing dissatisfaction with one's lot. And that is in your own power to destroy, though you may not be able to alter the circumstances. Emily Dickinson said a wise thing when she wrote, "Do not try to be saved, but let redemption find you, as it certainly will." She might have added, as she surely meant, if you keep in the roads by which it travels. In most cases of nervous exhaustion it is the diseased mind which requires treatment, or has required treatment long before. [pp. 117–18]

324 Thomas Wentworth Higginson. *The New World and the New Book.* Boston: Lee and Shepard, 1892, p. 16. In an address delivered January 15, 1891, Higginson quotes from an unidentified (and still apparently unknown) letter from Dickinson.

. . . we must remember that libraries, galleries, and buildings are all secondary to that great human life of which they are only the secretions or appendages. "My Madonnas"—thus wrote to me that recluse woman of genius, Emily Dickinson— "are the women who pass my house to their work, bearing Saviours in their arms." Words wait on thoughts, thoughts on life; and after these, technical training is an easy thing.

325 [Thomas Bailey Aldrich.] "*In Re* Emily Dickinson." *Atlantic Monthly* 69 (January 1892), 143–44. This essay became the best-known—and perhaps most influential—rejection of Dickinson's poetry to appear in the 1890s. On Aldrich's aesthetic principles, see *CR*, pp. 57–59. Aldrich softened some of his harshest strictures in 1903 when he republished this review (see *CR*, pp. 93–94). Aldrich appears to have before him not the Second Series but the initial 1890 Dickinson volume. He begins by paraphrasing the final words of a notice in the *Saint James's Gazette* (no. 189). The sentence he alludes to was reprinted in America in *Current Literature* for October 1891 (no. 220). Aldrich's language in his final paragraph suggests that he must also have known Andrew Lang's *London Daily News* remark that "Unless all poets, from the earliest improvisers to the Laureate, have been wrong in their methods, Miss Dickinson cannot possibly have been right in hers" (no. 232). Aldrich's essay was praised and partially reprinted by Richard Henry Stoddard, no. 333, and again partially reprinted, no. 339.

The English critic who said of Miss Emily Dickinson that she might have become a fifth-rate poet "if she had only mastered the rudiments of grammar and gone into metrical training for about fifteen years,"—the rather candid English critic who said this somewhat overstated his case. If Miss Dickinson had undergone the austere curriculum indicated, she would, I am sure, have become an admirable lyric poet of the second magnitude. In the first volume of her poetical chaos is a little poem which needs only slight revision in the initial stanza in order to make it worthy of ranking with some of the odd swallow flights in Heine's lyrical *intermezzo*. I have ventured to desecrate this stanza by tossing a rhyme into it, as the other stanzas happened to rhyme, and here print the lyric, hoping the reader will not accuse me of overvaluing it:

I taste a liquor never brewed
In vats upon the Rhine;   [From tankards scooped in pearl
No tankard ever held a draught   [Not all the vats upon the Rhine
Of alcohol like mine.   [Yield such an alcohol

Inebriate of air am I,
And debauchee of dew,
Reeling, through endless summer days,
From inns of molten blue.

When landlords turn the drunken bee
Out of the Foxglove's door,
When butterflies renounce their drams,
I shall but drink the more!

Till seraphs swing their snowy caps   [hats
And saints to windows run,
To see the little tippler
Leaning against the sun!

Certainly those inns of molten blue, and that disreputable honey-gatherer who got himself turned out-of-doors at the sign of the Foxglove, are very taking matters. I know of more important things that interest me less. There are three or four bits of this kind in Miss Dickinson's book; but for the most part the ideas totter and toddle, not having learned to walk. In spite of this, several of the quatrains are curiously touching, they have such a pathetic air of yearning to be poems.

It is plain that Miss Dickinson possessed an extremely unconventional and grotesque fancy. She was deeply tinged by the mysticism of Blake, and strongly influenced by the mannerism of Emerson. The very way she tied her bonnet-strings, preparatory to one of her nunlike walks in her claustral garden, must have been Emersonian. She had much fancy of a queer sort, but only, as it appears to me, intermittent flashes of imagination. I fail to detect in her work any of that profound thought which her editor professes to discover in it. The phenomenal insight, I am inclined to believe, exists only in his partiality; for whenever a woman poet is in question Mr. Higginson always puts on his rose-colored spectacles. This is being chivalrous; but the invariable result is not clear vision. That Miss Dickinson's whimsical memoranda have a certain something which, for want of a more precise name, we term *quality* is not to be denied except by the unconvertible heathen who are not worth conversion. But the incoherence and formlessness of her—I don't know how to designate them—versicles are fatal. Sydney Smith, or some other humorist, mentions a person whose bump of veneration was so inadequately developed as to permit him to damn the equator if he wanted to. This certainly established a precedent for independence; but an eccentric, dreamy, half-educated recluse in an out-of-the-way New England village (or anywhere else) cannot with impunity set at defiance the laws of gravitation and grammar. In his charming preface to Miss Dickinson's collection, Mr. Higginson insidiously remarks: "After all, when a thought takes one's breath away, a lesson on grammar seems an impertinence." But an ungrammatical thought does not, as a general thing, take one's breath away, except in a sense the reverse of flattering. Touching this matter of mere technique Mr. Ruskin has a word to say (it appears that he said it "In his earlier and better days"), and Mr. Higginson quotes it: "No weight, nor mass, nor beauty of execution can outweigh one grain or fragment of thought." This is a proposition to which one would cordially subscribe, if it were not so intemperately stated. A suggestive commentary on Mr. Ruskin's impressive dictum is furnished by the fact that Mr. Ruskin has lately published a volume of the most tedious verse that has been printed in this century. The substance of it is weighty enough, but the workmanship lacks just that touch which distinguishes the artist from the bungler, — the touch of which Mr. Ruskin seems not to have much regarded either in his later or "in his earlier and better days."

If Miss Dickinson's *disjecta membra* are poems, then Shakespeare's prolonged imposition should be exposed without further loss of time, and Lord Tennyson ought to be advised of the error of his ways before it is too late. But I do not hold the situation to be so desperate. Miss Dickinson's versicles have a queerness and a quaintness that have stirred a momentary curiosity in emotional bosoms. Oblivion lingers in the immediate neighborhood.

326 "Volumes of Poems." *Book Buyer* 8 (January 1892), 650.

The second series of *The Poems of Emily Dickinson* will be apt to arouse the same curiosity and interest that the first series did. The characteristics of her verse are well illustrated in this odd bit, which opens the volume with an abruptness that is startling:

> I'm nobody! Who are you?
>   Are you nobody, too?
> Then there's a pair of us—dont' tell!
>   They'd banish us, you know.
>
> How dreary to be somebody!
>   How public, like a frog
> To tell your name the livelong day
>   To an admiring bog!

Despite their unconventional form, the poems possess a weird power and even fascination, arising as much from the boldness and originality of the author's thought as from her directness of phrase. Considered as suggestive sketches to be worked into a more artistic form later, her poems are full of interest. Those in this volume are divided into four groups relating to Life, Love, Nature, and Time and Eternity.

327 "New Poetry." *Boston Herald*, ca. January 1892. Clippings of this review in both Higginson's and Todd's scrapbooks are attributed by hand to the *Herald* and (in Todd only) dated "Jan. '92." Aside from issues for January 1–3, which were unavailable for examination, papers for the month were searched without result. The reviewer in this column goes on to give

Arlo Bates's volume of verse, *The Poet and His Self,* high praise. "The light that never was" derives from Wordsworth's "Elegiac Stanzas Suggested by a Picture of Peele Castle."

Roberts Bros. published during the season before the holidays two volumes of poetry which demand more than a passing notice, though in neither case are they the first appearance of the writers as poets. Miss Dickinson's collection is the second gleaning from her manuscripts, and Mr. Bates gathers up from his portfolio what has accumulated since he last appeared in print. We have the kindest feeling toward these volumes because they stand for genuine merit and the choicest kind of lyrical expression, and they embody the spirit and the purpose of our time, as it finds expression in verse. We need not accept Col. Higginson's estimate of Miss Dickinson's work in order to appreciate it at its proper value, neither need we laud Mr. Bates to the skies as the coming American poet, but we think that in each case we have received from the authors of these volumes contributions which extend our knowledge of the field with which modern poetry deals at its highest and best. Miss Dickinson is less certain than Mr. Bates. Sometimes she is hopelessly intricate in her expressions, and says nothing to the common mortal, but again she is full of light and power. She should be judged by her best, and this is often wonderfully fine. We could pick out from the second series of her poems, again and again, passages and complete pieces which contain glimpses of "the light that never was on sea or land," and yet there is much which means nothing to the reader and must be omitted.

328 "Talk About Books." *Chautauquan* 14 (January 1892), 509–10.

The second series of Poems by Emily Dickinson is welcomely greeted as a continuation of the thought flash-lights which illumined her first volume. In the second she treats her themes in the abrupt, startling way characteristic of her. Life, Love, Nature, and other primal mysteries furnish subjects upon which she throws a sudden gleam as strong as it is momentary. Her verse seems to have occurred to her extempore; sometimes crude but always vivid, scorning elaboration. She runs over rhythm as a horse jumps a hedge, with a bracing if not smooth effect. Candor holds in check her daring, which carries the reader's interest from poem to poem.

329 "Gaining Happiness By Giving It." *Delineator* [London & N.Y.] 39:1 (January 1892), 84. The quoted lines, from Dickinson's "The Bustle in a House," appear too well known among the readers of this women's magazine to require attribution.

When anniversaries are past we are compelled to think of them as psychological problems that no man has understood or, if understanding, has yet explained. They are the set times for squaring accounts with ourselves and for

> —sweeping up the heart,
>   And putting love away.
> We shall not want to use again
>   Until Eternity.

330 *Golden Rule,* ca. January 1892. Identified only by periodical title in Todd's scrapbook. Unverified.

Emily Dickinson's *Poems* have been received with undeserved praise and equally undeserved criticism. They certainly contain qualities that will not allow them to be passed by unnoticed, as both her admirers and her critics admit. There is, indeed, a charm about them, however they transgress the laws of syntax and prosody and sometimes rebel against rhyme and rhythm; and the reader who opens the volume is apt to read every little poem through to the end before he puts the book on the shelf. The dainty verses that preface the volume give one a taste of the quality of the work and an insight into the author's spirit.

> My nosegays are for captives,
>   Dim, long-expectant eyes,
> Fingers denied the plucking,
>   Patient till Paradise.
>
> To such, if they should whisper
>   Of morning and the moor,
> They have no other errand,   [They bear
>   And I no other prayer.

331 "Poetry and the Drama." *Literary News* 13 (January 1892), 29.

"Life," "Love," "Nature," "Time and eternity," are the names under which Emily Dickinson's friends have grouped this second series of her notable poems. The eagerness with which the first series was read, guarantees a welcome for these. There is a fac-simile of one of the author's poems, also a preface by Mrs. Todd and an autograph-letter from Helen Jackson to Miss Dickinson.

332 Andrew Lang. "A Patriotic Critic." *Illustrated London News* 100 (January 2, 1892), 14–15. This review of a collection of Higginson's essays urging American literary independence prompted some characteristic remarks by Lang on Dickinson's grammar. Only the opening of the review and other Dickinson-related passages are reprinted.

The name of Mr. Thomas Wentworth Higginson has hitherto, perhaps, been best known in England as that of the gentleman who edited Miss Dickinson's poems. About these, English critics ventured to say, with insular superciliousness, that poetry really should contain rhyme and reason, and grammar. Miss Dickinson's pieces were written in defiance of this opinion, which is still accepted, on the whole, by the majority of human beings. Mr. Higginson now appears as the author of "The New World and the New Book." . . .

So with Edgar Poe. Tonics are not kept at his store. The establishments of many other poets deal in tonics, excellent draughts, but there are hours when we have "no use for" tonics. To ask Poe for them is like asking Miss Dickinson's works for rhyme or reason.

Mr. Higginson is very severe on the grammar of some English writers, whose grammar is, perhaps, not their forte; but, he accepts Miss Dickinson, whose grammar was conspicuous in the way usually quoted, through the French, from Tacitus. Mr. Higginson has to mention Thales's celebrated "corner" in oil-presses. The original authority from whom he quotes it is—Mr. Hamerton!

But this example of profound scholarship, and these strainings at the gnats of English colloquialisms while swallowing the dromedary of Miss Dickinson's grammar, are not the main points of curiosity in Mr. Higginson's book. . . .

333 Richard Henry Stoddard. "World of Letters." *New York Mail and Express*, January 4, 1892, p. 8. One of the most admired American men of letters of his time, Stoddard here reprints the greater part of Aldrich's essay on Dickinson, adding some prefatory comments and silently adopting Aldrich's recasting of "I taste a liquor never brewed" (no. 325). Hoping to elicit an early, positive response from Stoddard, Roberts Brothers had sent him a pre-publication review copy of Dickinson's first volume of verse; see *AB*, p. 68.

The *Atlantic Monthly* is, if not the last, almost the last, of our periodicals that care enough for literature, pure and simple, to criticize it without fear and without favor, and without regard to the fads of the time—Browningese, Ibsenese, or, to come to the latest, Dickinsonese, which is now a mild epidemic in New England. Miss Dickinson was a Massachusetts woman whose life was passed in reading and writing—in reading earnest, soulful, profound books, which she was unable to digest, and in writing what she mistook for poetry, and what to the irreverent mind sounds like the worst parts of Emerson and Blake.

She died a few years ago, leaving enough unmetrical manuscript to make two volumes, which have since been published under the editorial supervision of Mr. Thomas Wentworth Higginson, and have created a cult in Boston. That they do not share it in the editorial rooms of the *Atlantic Monthly* is evident in the January number, where, in "The Contributors' Club," the posthumous poetry of Miss Dickinson is treated with more seriousness than we have been able to bestow upon it, and than it is really entitled to.

The writer of this criticism begins by quoting the remark of an English critic who is of the opinion that Miss Dickinson might have become a fifth-rate poet "if she had only mastered the rudiments of grammar and gone into metrical training for about fifteen years," after which he proceeds to quote one of her lyrics, which we copy below as a curiosity of literature:

> I taste a liquor never brewed
> In vats upon the Rhine;
> No tankard ever held a draught
> Of alcohol like mine.
>
> Inebriate of air am I,
> And debauchee of dew,
> Reeling, through endless summer days,
> From inns of molten blue.
>
> When landlords turn the drunken bee
> Out of the Foxglove's door,
> When butterflies renounce their drams,
> I shall but drink the more!
>
> Till seraphs swing their snowy caps
> And saints to windows run,
> To see the little tippler
> Leaning against the sun!

But let us see what the *Atlantic* contributor finds to say, for a little verse like this goes, or ought to go, a great way outside of New England. "It is plain," he says, "that Miss Dickinson possessed an extremely unconventional and grotesque fancy." [Taking up Aldrich's review at this point, Stoddard quotes it in full to its end without further comment of his own.]

334   Francis H. Stoddard. "Technique in Emily Dickinson's Poems." *Critic,*
n.s. 17 (January 9, 1892), 24–25. Responding to the *Critic*'s review of
Poems, Second Series (no. 316), the author, a professor of English at the
University of the City of New York (now NYU), is the first to give this
close attention to the "form and tone" of a Dickinson poem.

To the Editors of The Critic:—
   In your issue of Dec. 19 an evidently competent reviewer refers to the first
volume of Miss Dickinson's poems, issued a year ago, as a "volume of curiously
formless poems," and suggests that the fact of the issuance of several editions
proves "that a great many persons care little for the form of expression in poetry
so long as the thoughts expressed are startling, eccentric and new." In the same
review the critic says of the two volumes taken together that "their absolute
formlessness keeps them almost outside the pale of poetry." The thought here
seems to be that real poetry must have perfection of technique, must have metrical and grammatical finish: the poems of Emily Dickinson do not have such
finish; hence these verses are almost out of the pale of poetry. The major prem-
ise here set down has not been attacked of late. The minor one is not so easily
disposed of. For Miss Dickinson's poems may be formless, or they may be worded
to so fine and subtle a device that they seem formless, just as the spectrum of a
far-off star may seem blankness until examined with a lens of especial power. I
wish to examine one poem of Miss Dickinson's, taken almost at random, and
search for the fine lines of the spectrum. For such example I take this poem:—

> I died for beauty, but was scarce
>   Adjusted in the tomb,
> When one who died for truth was lain
>   In an adjoining room.
>
> He questioned, softly, why I failed?
>   For beauty, I replied.
> And I for truth,—the two are one;
>   We brethren are; he said.
>
> And so as kinsman met a night,
>   We talked between the rooms,
>   Until the moss had reached our lips,
> And covered up our names.

   Now the notion here is the notion of the unity of truth and beauty. If harmony with the thought is to prevail in the verse we should expect a closely parallel structure with a figure in dual accent—*i.e.,* based upon two factors. Such
a figure we get:—

> I died' for beauty', but was scarce
>   Adjusted' in the tomb',
> When one who died' for truth' was lain
>   In an adjoin'ing room'.

   Two pairs of lines, each with two accents, the similar words being matched
in pairs—*justed': joining', died': died', tomb': room'. Beauty'* and *truth'* do not perfectly match, of course, because not yet proved to be one in nature. These exact

correspondences would produce mechanical regularity and overprove the proposition by overemphasizing the innate notion of harmony, if care were not taken. So care is taken to contrast the positions of the members of the separate pairs. That is, in the first line, the slurred words *but was scarce* are at the end, while in the corresponding line the slurred words *when one who* are at the beginning. Similarly, the slurred words *in the* in the second line are contrasted in position with the slurred words *in an* in the fourth line.

In the second stanza we have a more perfectly parallel figure, in accord with the development of the notion of harmony between truth and beauty.

> He questioned', softly', why' I failed'?
>> For beauty'; I replied'.
> And I'—for truth'—the two' are one',
>> We brethren' are; he said'.

Almost a formal balancing, but with a suggestion of relief; as, for example, in the harmonic echo of *he questioned*', in the opening line, with *We brethren*', in the closing line, suggesting a recurrence of the first verse motive.

In the last verse comes the deeper verity that though truth and beauty are one spiritually, they can never be at one in this world. So at the close the pattern changes and together with the hint of the attainment of perfect harmony we have a reversion both in form and tone. It is a suggestion of the death reversion which springs the thought to a harmony more subtle and remote.

> And so as kinsmen' met a night',
>> We talked' between the rooms',
>> Until the moss' had reached our lips'
> And covered' up our names'.

The rhyme changes to alliteration which is beginning-rhyme instead of end-rhyme—*night : names.* That is, our earthly names are lost in the endless night of death; ourselves, at one with each other, at one with truth and beauty, entered into the endless day of beauty and truth.

I submit that such art as this may be subtle and medieval, but it is not formlessness.

335 E[lisha] J[ay] Edwards. "Emily Dickinson's Poems." January 12, 1892. Without further identification in Todd's scrapbook, this newspaper clipping carries the dateline "New York, Jan 12" and the heading "Special Correspondence." The suggestion that Dickinson sent her poems to Longfellow is without foundation.

A day or two before Christmas a literary man living in New York being desirous to present to a friend a copy of the poems of Emily Dickinson visited a number of bookstores, and was astonished to find that he could not get a single copy. Asking the reason he was told that the demand for these poems had far exceeded the supply. One bookseller said that he could have sold the entire edition over his counters. Another declared that he had laid in a stock which he thought would last for a year, and he had sold it out within two days. A third said that he had telegraphed the publishers and they had sent back word that the second edition was exhausted as soon as published.

No such experience as this in the case of an unknown poet has been reported in New York City, at least in the present generation. The poems have been fiercely attacked by the critics; they have been called ungrammatical, incoherent and vague, yet they have touched the popular chord, and it looks now as though the sale of them will be something phenomenal.

The great public does not mind if a poem is ungrammatical or is not a well of English undefiled, provided it only touches something in the human heart. When Phoebe Cary wrote the poem beginning "One sweetly solemn thought," she had to endure the attacks of the critics, who pointed out grammatical errors and serious faults of prosody, and these criticisms were undoubtedly well founded; but the critics did not realize that in spite of these technical defects there was a sublime thought in the poem which appealed to the common understanding, and powerfully. The people received it, and it has been translated into every civilized and many savage tongues, and is now sung and read the world over.

Whether that will be the fate of any of Miss Dickinson's poems is a question, but they have certainly attained a phenomenal popularity. The career of this singular being suggests in some respects that of the author of "Jane Eyre." A timid, shrinking, inexperienced girl, living in a lonely hamlet in the west of England — knowing nothing of life excepting those things her intuition taught her and what she gleaned by reading — wrote in secrecy a story and sent it to one after another of declining publishers in London. At last one braver than the others, or wiser, published it, and "Jane Eyre" became famous, its authoress a celebrity, and people marveled that this woman who was almost a child, and who had had no life beyond that of a curate's cottage, could have written that which was destined to remain permanent in English literature.

Miss Dickinson was even more of a recluse than Charlotte Bronte. She passed her whole life in the little college town of Amherst, Mass. Her father was an instructor in the college, but there were many people in that town who, although they knew that Professor Dickinson had a daughter, yet knew it only by public report. They had never seen her. She seldom ventured beyond her father's dooryard, and for months at a time did not leave the house. Her health, though delicate, was not such as to compel such retirement, but she shrank from contact with the world, was of extraordinary timidity, and in many things seemed a mere child.

She found her companions between the covers of her father's books. She knew the heroes of old, and let her imagination rest upon them until they seemed almost real to her. She knew American and English literature as few scholars know them, and she peopled her imagination with the creations of the greatest masters of romance and fiction, and dwelt with them rather than the human beings who were living about her.

Some years ago Miss Dickinson sent a few of her poems to the Cambridge critics and poets. Mr. Longfellow read some of them in manuscript, and so did Thomas Wentworth Higginson. They saw the defects, but they saw the inspiration which compelled the writing of these poems, and they gave the girl encouragement. Mr. Higginson, being inspired by something of curiosity as well as admiration, sought to meet the girl, and he found her a timid recluse, whose strange habit of life could be explained neither by herself nor by her family.

Miss Dickinson died a year or so ago, and then were published the poems which have created something like amazament, a great deal of criticism and an unquestioned popularity. They are the song of a veritable hermit, the pleadings of one whose life had been introspective, and they reveal that strangeness of sentiment which seclusion is sure to produce. But after all the common chord has been struck in some of them, and, if they are not accepted as poems of the first rank, they will always be regarded as curiosities of literature, as have been the forgeries of Chatterton, and in some respects as "Jane Eyre" has ever been esteemed.

336 [Jessie B. Wortman.] "Our Bookshelves." *Christian Intelligencer* 43 (January 13, 1892), 12. The author attribution is by hand in Todd's scrapbook.

A new volume of Emily Dickinson's poems! This arouses much enthusiasm in those favored ones who have already made the acquaintance of that original genius through her first volume and through her letters to Col. Higginson published in the October *Atlantic Monthly*. These poems of the second series have the same startling and shining characteristics which flashed upon us out of the first series. All are short, all unique. No lover of *belles lettres* but would be fascinated by her original, peculiar quality, and would be indebted to her for a new literary sensation. "Simplicity" is rather a typical poem:

How happy is the little stone
That rambles in the road alone,
And doesn't care about careers,
And exigencies never fears;
Whose coat of elemental brown
A passing universe put on;
And independent as the sun,
Associates or glows alone,
Fulfilling absolute decree
In casual simplicity.

337 Ellen Battelle Dietrick. "One-Sided Criticism." *Woman's Journal* 23 (January 16, 1892), 18. This letter to the editor of the *Woman's Journal* replies to Aldrich's essay (no. 325).

Editors Woman's Journal:

It is very much to be hoped, in the interests of good taste and of justice, that a generation of writers will some day arise, a larger proportion of whom can review the intellectual products of a woman without constant reference to her sex. Such an allusion as that in the last *Atlantic* "Contributor's Club" is offensive to the last degree.

Not content with a sweeping condemnation of Emily Dickinson's "incoherence and formlessness" (qualities which are now supposed peculiarly to manifest genius in Walt Whitman), not content with denying her the right of poetic title, with pronouncing her thoughts "ideas which totter and toddle," the critic goes out of his way to accuse Col. Higginson of weak sentimentality in behalf of women in that Col. Higginson professes admiration of Miss Dickinson's writing. Such a fling is more worthy of a school boy than of one who aspires to the dignity of a critic.

Here and there a woman is found guilty of the same lack of justice. This same number of the *Atlantic* contains an article by an individual deeply bent on proving that Harriet Martineau has no claim to literary merit. She has raked forth some half-century old private letters of John Stuart Mill, in which Mill criticises, with the usual severity of his criticism, an article of Miss Martineau's, written for the *Westminster Review*. But, not satisfied with giving Mill's comments verbatim, the editor of the letters informs us, with evident satisfaction, that we may "be quite sure that Mill's criticism would have wounded her to the quick by its reiteration of her weakness in argument, her 'goody' tone, her vain assumption of philosophy, and by the contrasting of her imitation of a masculine style with her *feminine feebleness* of reasoning." The cool assumption that everything good in the world of letters is masculine, and everything weak and feeble feminine, is considerably out of date at the present time.

This Martineau-crushing individual—who rejoices in the formidable cognomen of "C. Marion D. (Robertson) Towers"—explains that the particular reason why we may be so sure of Miss Martineau's mental anguish (had she but known what Mill thought of her) is because "Miss Martineau prided herself on seeing things as men did, and on being admitted by them to a certain equality on account of her mental superiority to her sex." Ambitious but misguided Miss Martineau! How lucky that she was deep in her grave before this revelation of her feminine feebleness of reasoning, her vain presumption in daring to claim equality with men, was exploded like dynamite on a startled world. Let us hope her ghost will not rise and tear its dishevelled tresses.

A curious confirmation of the bias of this writer's mind is further given. Mill declares vehemently of a masculine contributor that his "sentences are not only unscholarly, but absolutely unintelligible, from inattention to ambiguities of small words and of collocation." But the editor of his letters, who has just ground Miss Martineau to powder, has not a syllable of comment on this specimen of "masculine style." It never seems faintly to occur to her that there is considerable "vain assumption of philosophy," and even some "feebleness of reasoning" in the productions of a man who attempts to write a learned article, and produces only absolutely "unintelligible sentences."

It is against this spirit of inappropriate criticism, born of an old prejudice against women writers, that every lover of justice should protest. Emily Dickinson may be an ungrammatical, wild, erratic scribbler, instead of a poet; Harriet Martineau may have been a weak, sentimental, feeble-minded member of the literati. But to drag in the mere question of sex, in criticizing the writings of either, is worse than inane. It is as ill-mannered as it would be, for instance, if one were to pronounce Howells a *masculinely* feeble reasoner, because he is individually feeble in depicting women. Most intelligent women recognize that Howells' seeming inability to comprehend that there is other than one weak, silly type of womankind, is an individual defect, not by any means a characteristic of all masculine portraitures of women. And it is a cause for some congratulation that, as critics, they have not yet fallen into the vulgar error of making outrageous flings at half the race, because many men amongst this half manifest mental incompetency.

Before leaving this subject, it should be said, in justice to the great champion of equal opportunities for women and men, that while the letters now put forth as written by Mill may be indisputably his, any admirer of his would ask for stronger evidence than mere assertion that they are genuine. The man who wrote, "When we further consider that to understand one woman is not necessarily to understand any other women," could scarcely have been a man who would sweepingly charge all women with feeble-mindedness because one magazine article of one woman did not strike him as suitable for a certain occasion. Nor does it seem probable that the Mill who wrote, "Two women, since political economy has been made a science, have known enough of it to write usefully on the subject; of how many of the innumerable men who have written on it during the same time is it possible, with truth, to say more?" could be identical with the man now put forward as pronouncing one of these very women *femininely* feeble in reasoning power.

338 Julia Noyes Stickney. "Literary Correspondence." *Christian Leader* 62 (January 21, 1892), 3. Lavinia Dickinson was at Ipswich Female Seminary 1849–1850.

A book from Roberts Brothers, edited by Col. Higginson and Mary Loomis Todd, now brings to me the elm-shaded heights of Amherst, Mass., and my own acquaintance with the sister of "Emily Dickinson," at Ipswich Seminary, many years ago. The poems of this late popular writer bear such striking originality, that those who study them find in their very want of form a vivid impression resembling Wagner's rugged music.

Emily Dickinson had tried the society of the world and found it lacking, and then she turned to the introspective life, and with a few bold touches she left some etchings which must be looked at long, as the artist gazes at his bit of scenery till it grows into life and meaning. The seventeenth among the short poems is unique to me for its austere pictures of its four phases of life, the last of its great, inevitable and mysterious climax, on earth.

> Triumph may be of several kinds.
>   There's triumph in the room
> When that old Imperator, Death,
>   By faith is overcome.
>
> There's triumph of the finer mind
>   When truth, affronted long,
> Advances calm to her supreme,
>   Her God, her only throng.
>
> A triumph when temptation's bribe
>   Is slowly handed back,
> One eye upon the heaven renounced
>   And one upon the rack,
>
> Severer triumph, by himself
>   Experienced, who can pass
> Acquitted from that naked bar,
>   Jehovah's countenance!

339 "Emily Dickinson." *Boston Saturday Evening Gazette* 80 (January 23, 1892), [1].

A writer in the "Contributors' Club" of the *Atlantic Monthly* criticizes Emily Dickinson's poetry rather sharply as follows:

[Takes up Aldrich's review, no. 325, beginning with the sentence "Miss Dickinson possessed an extremely unconventional and grotesque fancy" and continues its quotation in full to the essay's end.]

340 "Miss Dickinson's Poetry." *Critic*, n.s. 17 (January 23, 1892), 61. A partial reprinting of Andrew Lang's article from the *London Daily News*, no. 232. The excerpt opens at the paragraph beginning "It is easy to see the interest of a character like this," and closes with the sentence in that paragraph, "Her only merit is an occasional picturesque touch, and a general pathetic kind of yearning and sense of futility."

341 "Comment on New Books." *Atlantic Monthly* 69 (February 1892), 277. This guardedly favorable notice in the *Atlantic*'s regular review column was published in the issue immediately following that containing Aldrich's famous attack (no. 325). It has the nature of a quiet rejoinder, particularly as the reviewer turns to Dickinson as offering relief from the "wearying fluency" of Alfred Austin, an English poet not unlike Aldrich in grace and cultivation.

A second series of Poems by Emily Dickinson has been issued, edited, as was the first, by T. W. Higginson and Mabel Loomis Todd. It has an interesting preface by Mrs. Todd and a fac-simile of Miss Dickinson's handwriting. A classification of her verse has been attempted under the headings Life, Love, Nature, Time, and Eternity. What strikes one afresh, as he takes up the book, is his interest in reading, independent of his poetic preferences. The quick contact with another nature, and that a singularly aggressive one, makes reading Miss Dickinson an intellectual excitement. We raise our objections, we rule out poem after poem, yet we keep on reading, never sure but irritation will give way to delight. The lawless is sometimes more interesting than the lawful.

342 "About Authors." *Book Buyer*, n.s. 9 (February 1892), 7. Mrs. Todd refers here to a portrait of the poet as a ten-year-old child by Otis A. Bullard, an itinerant painter. Within the year Todd found the now well-known daguerreotype of Dickinson taken at Mount Holyoke when she was seventeen (see *AB*, pp. 224–26 and *Home*, pp. 519–22) but the earlier portrait continued to be favored by the family. Roberts Brothers furnished it, rather than the daguerreotype, to promote its 1894 edition of the *Letters*; see *Publishers Weekly* 46 (November 17, 1894), p. 79.

In reply to an inquiry as to whether or not there was in existence a photograph of Emily Dickinson from which a portrait could be engraved, Mrs. Mabel Loomis Todd, joint-editor with Colonel T. W. Higginson of the poet's two volumes, wrote as follows from Amherst, Mass.:

"I am sorry to say there is no photograph of Emily Dickinson whatever, and even no known daguerreotype, as she was always strongly disinclined to permit any 'mould' of herself to be made. Nothing later than childhood, or her far-away, earliest girlhood, was ever taken.

"When Colonel Higginson asked for her picture in 1862, she wrote, you remember:

"'Could you believe me without? I had no portrait, now, but am small, like the wren; and my hair is bold, like the chestnut burr; and my eyes, like the sherry in the glass, that the guest leaves. Would this do just as well?'

"Much as I should enjoy seeing an engraving of Emily Dickinson in the *Book Buyer*, that is the only picture of her extant."

343 *Concord* [N.H.] *People and Patriot*, February 1892. The clipping is attributed and dated by hand in Todd's scrapbook. Its author may be the Frances Matilda Abbott of review no. 71. Unverified.

The extraordinary and unexpected success which attended the unheralded publication of the first volume of Emily Dickinson's poems, a year ago, shows that

This portrait of Dickinson at ten years was the only likeness to be published in the nineties. According to Mabel Todd, the poet's brother and sister believed the now famous daguerreotype of Dickinson was lacking "in expression and individuality." (Nos. 342 and 419).

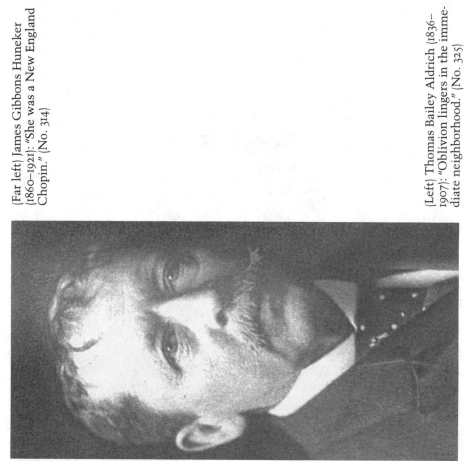

(Far left) James Gibbons Huneker (1860–1921): "She was a New England Chopin." (No. 314)

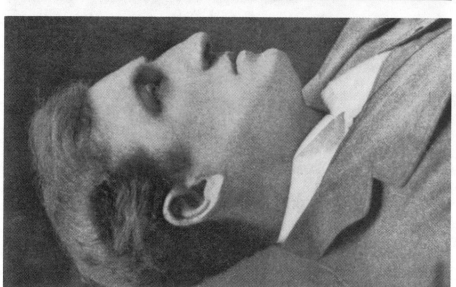

(Left) Thomas Bailey Aldrich (1836–1907): "Oblivion lingers in the immediate neighborhood." (No. 325)

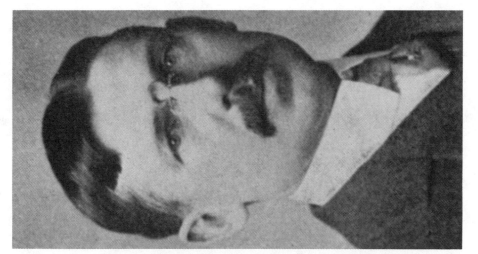

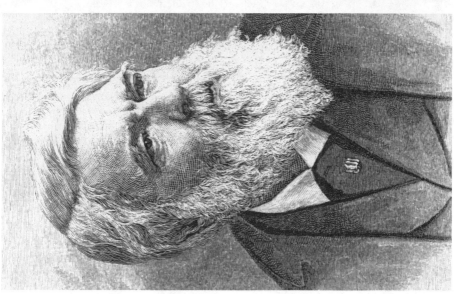

(Right) Richard Henry Stoddard (1825–1903): "Dickinsonese is now a mild epidemic in New England." (No. 333)

(Far right) Mark Anthony DeWolfe Howe (1864–1960): "It would often seem that she was longing for poetic appreciation and sympathy." (No. 398)

Item no. 457. A similar advertisement appeared for the 1894 *Letters* (no. 458).

the world recognizes what is real. This woman lived in Amherst, Mass., a life more secluded than Charlotte Bronte's, and not till after her death was the public allowed to know that hers was a genius so rare that it occupies an absolutely unique place in literature. Her poetry is of the quietest, most unobtrusive sort, but it clings like the five-fingered ampelopsis. It is not poetry at all according to conventional standards. The author has thrown away everything that could interfere with her thought. Rhyme and rhetoric are usually sacrificed, and yet the poetic instinct is always satisfied. However her lines may neglect the form, they accord with the inner soul of harmony. There is no comparison to make between the first and second volumes of her poems; they are all of a piece. Whoever has read one must have the other, and the world will not rest satisfied till every scrap of her writings, letters as well as literature, has been published. For those who have not yet met Emily Dickinson, and there must be many, for she has made her way noiselessly as well as swiftly, we commend the article in the October *Atlantic* by T. W. Higginson, so long her friend and correspondent. In addition to his own just and acute comments, it gives her letters to him, and many selections from this volume of her poems. Though striking, they are not the best, for one cannot get the best of her work without taking the whole.

344 "Rambles Among Books." *Delineator* [London & N.Y.] 39:2 (February 1892), 176.

From the press of Roberts Brothers, Boston, we have received a second volume of the posthumous poems of that strangely gifted and secluded woman, Emily Dickinson. The first selection from the manuscripts left by Miss Dickinson was eagerly read and enthusiastically praised, as it deserved, since little has lately been printed that is finer, stronger or more poetic than her verse. Her thoughts and her expression of them combine to inform the reader that she knew little of the world and held speech with few if any of her kind. That her pen was her only confidante and her soul her only adviser and instructor are facts also quickly realized; and to this sad seclusion she is indebted for one of her several charms that instantly touches the sensitive reader. Had she dwelt in a world of letters her poems would doubtless have borne that indescribable impress and sign manual that is set upon greatness. Perhaps, though, she would have been silent, for she writes—never thinking of future fame—

> How dreary to be somebody!
>   How public like a frog.
> To tell your name the livelong day,
>   To an admiring bog!

She wrote this, as if a prophetic spirit was hovering near and whispering to her of future recognition by a world that she refused to enter.

The sorrowful romance of Emily Dickinson's life—to speak of which would be disloyalty to her delicacy and desire—brought to her what few of her kind and her talents have ever had—leisure to think, to dream, to weep and to write fully what came to her. Now and then, through a very narrow and designedly small circle of friends, a poem found its way from her almost cloistered library into the light of publication, but from these isolated verses no one ever dreamed what a wealth of poetic imaginings she would leave to the world. Less finished and, perhaps, less scholarly are her lines than those of that priestly recluse, Joseph Rous; but the two writers are close kin in many personal characteristics.

345 "Recent Verse. II." *Overland Monthly* 19 (February 1892), 218–19. The earlier review is no. 150.

Six months ago a good deal of space was given to a review of the first series of poems by Emily Dickinson. It is somewhat to be regretted that the praise with which this book was received and its success has led to the publication of another and larger volume of her work. There is in it a too evident desire on the part of the compiler to meet the demand, rather than the higher canons of literary taste. Had this been the first volume to be issued it would have been remarkable and won attention and sympathetic appreciation. Many of the poems are as strong and as striking as any in the first series. But there are a large number that display so patently the worst faults of this unconventional writer—that are so devoid of rhythm and harmony and often so absolutely unintelligible in sense— that the feeling experienced on laying down the book is one of disappointment: the feeling one has in hearing of some littleness or shortcoming in a friend sincerely admired.

But this fault noted, it must be admitted that there is enough in the book to justify a high opinion of the powers of the author. What could be tenderer or more musical than this?

> I should not dare to leave my friend
> Because—because if he should die
> While I was gone, and I—too late—
> Should reach the heart that wanted me;
>
> If I should disappoint the eyes
> That hunted, hunted so, to see,
> And could not bear to shut until
> They "noticed" me—they noticed me;
>
> If I should stab the patient faith
> So sure I'd come—so sure I'd come,
> It listening, listening, went to sleep
> Telling my tardy name,—
>
> My heart would wish it broke before,
> Since breaking then, since breaking then,
> Were useless as next morning's sun,
> Where midnight frosts had lain!

Very simple too but very sweet is "The Battle Field:"

> They dropped like flakes, they dropped like stars,
>   Like petals from a rose,
> While suddenly across the June
>   A wind like fingers goes.   [with fingers
>
> They perished in the seamless grass,—
>   No eye could find the place:
> But God on his repealless list
>   Can summon every face.

Living in practical solitude as she did, her introspection led her to the most vivid realization of the meaning of death and immortality. The consideration of these themes must have become almost a disease with her; for every conceivable phase of them receives attention in her verses. At times her familiar way of treating sacred subjects is almost grotesque; but never are her views morbid or tinged with doubt or fear.

> Let down the bars, O Death!
> The tired flocks come in.
> Whose bleating ceases to repeat,
> Whose wandering is done.

> Thine is the stillest night,
> Thine the securest fold;
> Too near thou art for seeking thee,
> Too tender to be told.

Everything in the book bears the stamp of her unique originality. After all, though, it is not this which makes her work remarkable. It is rather the keen vision, the direct and forcible thought, — and above all her wonderful felicity of expression and characterization.

346 Roberts Brothers' advertisement. "Our Recent Books." *Publishers' Weekly* 41 (February 6, 1892), 270. This entry for *"Emily Dickinson's Poems*, First and Second Series" (here as separate volumes) is preceded by the quoted phrase "Etching Done By Lightning" (see no. 457). The following blurb, from Louise Chandler Moulton's review (no. 273) accompanies routine publication information.

Mrs. MOULTON says: "Perhaps the greatest literary event of last year, at least in Boston, was the publication of the 'Poems' of Emily Dickinson. . . . But I am convinced that it would be a loss to the world had this second volume remained unpublished."

347 C. M. E. "To the Editors of the Critic." *Critic*, n.s. 17 (February 13, 1892), 105. Writing from Vassar College, January 19, 1892, the author responds here to an article by Molly Seawell on "The Absence of the Creative Faculty in Women" which appeared in the *Critic*, November 29, 1891. The December 26 issue of the *Critic* printed several letters of rejoinder to Seawell, one of which read, "Dear Sir: Will you in future direct my "Critic" to Mollie Elliot Seawell? I do not wish to see it any more. Yours respectfully, Miss ____." The same issue also carried a lengthy reply by Sidwell N. Breeze, the "refutation" referred to below. T. W. Higginson added his objections to Seawell in a *Harper's Bazaar* article reprinted in the *Critic* for January 23rd, but he did not mention Dickinson. From London, Andrew Lang took note of the dispute (no. 368).

Perhaps you have wondered how Molly Elliot Seawell's article has affected college girls, or "the women of the coming century." We are not asleep: the *Critic* has kept *some* of us wide awake of late, as we are deeply interested in the Creative Faculty, be it found in men or in women. We recognize the superabundance of this power in men, and wish that it were more evenly distributed. The fact that one subscriber thought Miss Seawell needed information, and contributed her *Critic* as a means of providing it, was laudable — and amusing; but I fear not many of your subscribers will be so unselfish. The refutation in your issue of Dec. 26 eased a few minds, at least. The thing which condemns Miss Seawell's article is its use of the word "never." There is "the germ of" truth in many of her statements, but while acknowledging the supremacy of man in the creative line, we are bound to accept some of the works of women as creations, or else say that nothing has ever been created by anybody. Miss Seawell's "never" sweeps away names that have stood the test of time as well as of contemporary criticism. The fact that men do not dust, sweep and shake rugs is no proof that they cannot do it: it is only too true, indeed, that when they undertake this task, they are wonderfully successful; and that women have been confined to household duties is no proof that they cannot succeed in other vocations.

It is to be hoped that in future women will make up in quality what perhaps is lacking in quantity, in her work. As a beginning, she must cease writing trash. I should like very much, by the way, to read an estimate of Emily Dickinson by M. E. S. I think it would attract considerable attention.

348 Arthur Chamberlain. "Emily Dickinson—Poet and Woman." *Commonwealth* 31 (February 20, 1892), 6–7. In *AB* (p. 196), Millicent Todd Bingham writes: "During this time my mother's talks about Emily were gaining in popularity. On February thirteenth she spoke at The Kensington, Boston, to 'Parlors full' of friends, and on the day following to a smaller group." Mrs. Todd personally invited Mr. Chamberlain to her lecture, perhaps on the strength of his favorable notice of the first volume of poems (no. 319). He reciprocated the kindness by submitting a draft of the following article for her corrections.

Those who heard Mrs. Mabel Loomis Todd's keen, witty and sympathetic exposition of Emily Dickinson's genuine but elusive genius, which she gave last Saturday afternoon in the apartments of Mrs. John Adams Andrews at the Kensington, must have felt that the author was singularly fortunate in her interpreter.

A friendship of several years with Miss Dickinson, supplemented by three years of careful study of her letters and poems with a view to their publication, has given Mrs. Todd that full knowledge and mastery of her subject, which—save for the love that must vivify all knowledge—is the first essential of adequate criticism. As she stood there—an almost girlish figure in her black lace dress whose sole adornment was a small bunch of her favorite jonquils—every tone and gesture revealed not only the intelligent critic but the loving friend.

It appears that several hundred poems by Miss Dickinson remain still unpublished; and that those letters, scraps of which have already been given to the public, may make up a delightful volume of their own. Some of these additional poems, as well as a number of quotations from the letters, were interwoven in that graceful, but all too brief stream of description, elucidation and anecdote, with which Mrs. Todd delighted her audience.

Miss Dickinson, it seems, was not always that absolute recluse which she has been represented. In her early life she accompanied her father on several of his journeys, and her record at school shows her to have been a markedly brilliant pupil. It was only in her later life that she withdrew more and more from general society, retaining for her intimate friends that spirit of companionship which can easily dispense with the "pushing and clawing" which Emerson reprobates—a companionship that annuls time and space and is itself a fore-gleam of eternity.

All the sensational stories of a "woman in white," flitting, ghost-like, about a dimly-lighted house, must give place to the conception of a woman full of life and quick of wit, dressed in common-sense gowns of white flannel, muslin, or piqué, as might best suit the time of year; a life-long friend of children; a lover of flowers and—need it be added?—a successful floriculturist, alike in garden or conservatory; while not without that routine of happy household duties that are a part of the lot of most women.

One of those earlier duties was the setting of the table—and "thereby hangs a tale," illustrative of that quiet humor which was no slight element in the mental make-up of Emily Dickinson.

In putting the plates upon the table, Emily chanced to give her father one with a "nick" in it. It annoyed him, and he requested her never again to place it before him. But "the total depravity of inanimate things" seemed to inspire that plate, and Mr. Dickinson came to the table several times only to find that objectionable piece of china confronting him. At length, losing his patience—and possibly his temper, as well—he spoke more severely to Emily, and wound up by expressing his hope that he should *never* see that plate again! Emily disappeared shortly afterward; but a diligent search found her well away from the house, by a rock in the garden. She held in one hand a fragment or two of the devoted plate, and a hammer was in the other.

She was busily engaged in reducing the plate to an almost impalpable powder—"as a reminder," Mrs. Todd drily suggested, "*not* to put it again upon the table;"—and as Miss Dickinson did not number Mme. Blavatsky among her acquaintances, it is fair to assume that the "smash" was permanent.

A few words regarding the ancestry of Emily Dickinson may not be amiss. She was descended from the best Puritan stock—from men who were leaders in no ignoble enterprises, and from women whose lives were filled with that gracious strength that marked the gentlewoman of the earlier time. That so orchid-like a personality as that of Emily Dickinson's—to quote Mrs. Todd's felicitous epithet—should have come from the stern Calvinistic environment alike of her ancestors and even of her own home is only another illustration of that sweetness which comes out of strength. Calvinism is a somewhat gnarly tree, but its core is as sound as eternal righteousness can make it, and the recent graft of liberal thought bears some wonderfully fine olives. This may explain that real reverence which underlies the most startling of Miss Dickinson's utterances; a reverence which we need no longer question, now that Mrs. Todd has set it forth with that explicit statement of one who speaks with authority. Nor will it be difficult for the discerning mind to discover in that same Calvinistic inheritance the reason for the hatred of cant and sham which is conspicuous in all of Miss Dickinson's writings.

Her letters, it may be said, are fully as original as are her poems; and the punctuation especially in these of later date, recalls that famous chapter "On snakes in Ireland." The earlier ones contain a comma here and there; periods there are generally none. Even in her latest style of penmanship, where each letter enjoys its own isolation, there is little, however, that is illegible. Those who hold that character shows itself in handwriting would find these letters an apt illustration of their theory. One comment by Miss Dickinson should endear her forever to all persons whose belongings—notably well-beloved Mss.—suffer a strange and wide dispersion during the vernal equinox: "'House' is being cleaned—I prefer pestilence."

Miss Dickinson escaped one of the minor miseries of a woman's existence—her dresses were never draped upon her while they were in the process of manufacture. Did she have a "form" for that purpose? Certainly; an excellent one—in the person of her sister. What weary woman will not plead for that sister's canonization?

One more item of information may be added: Emily Dickinson was not the victim of any disappointment in love; that disappointment, if it existed at all in connection with her, was the lot of certain members of the other sex.

It would be hard to imagine anything more satisfactory than the simple, informal, but—or should it be, and?—artistic manner in which Mrs. Todd made her audience acquainted with the real Emily Dickinson.

Among those whose privilege it was to listen to this revelation may be mentioned: Mrs. Langley, Mrs. Henry Wilmarth, Mr. and Mrs. William Lloyd Garrison, Mrs. Louise Chandler Moulton, Mrs. Eben J. Loomis, Mr. and Mrs. Joshua Kendall, Mrs. Mary E. Williams, of Salem, General Francis A. Walker, Miss Grace Chandler, Mr. Nathan Haskell Dole, Mrs. William Eliot Griffis, Mrs. C. A. Coffin, Mrs. D. W. Spooner, and Mr. William R. Strong.

349   Nathan Haskell Dole. "Notes from Boston." *Book News* 10 (March 1892), 307–08. Reprinted: *Book Buyer* 9 (May 1892), 157–58.

Saturday afternoon last Mrs. Mabel Loomis Todd read a very interesting paper in a private parlor, at the Kensington, on the late Emily Dickinson and her poems. Mrs. Todd was one of the comparatively few who were admitted to anything like intimacy with the weird recluse of Amherst. Her friendship began in this way: Mrs. Todd wishing to send Miss Dickinson a little gift, painted a panel with the pale Indian pipe. It happened that this delicate flower was a particular passion with the poetess, and the gift went straight to her heart. This incident explains the appropriate employment of the flower as a decoration of the cover of the first volume of her poems. Indeed the drawing was made from the very panel which always stood in Miss Dickinson's room.

Mrs. Todd exploded the popular notion that Miss Dickinson was always a recluse. When her father was in Congress she spent several winters in Washington, and mingled in gay society, which she enjoyed, though still feeling that she had no real part in it. It was only in the last years of her life that she lived in her own home, somewhat like a dear ghost, seen but scarcely tangible, dwelling among her favorite flowers and in the shadows. She had once played the piano in a most individual manner, but this practice she gave up while still retaining her love for music. She delighted to have her friends sing or play to her at twilight. She herself would not come into the music room, but sat outside in the entry and rewarded the performer, not with praise, nor even with speech, but with some dainty refreshment of cream or cake or with a higher guerdon of a slip of paper with a poem written on the spot during the music.

Mrs. Todd never, in all the years of her acquaintance with her, had a face-to-face conversation about common-place mundane affairs. She dressed always in white, but such was her dislike to being "fitted" that her sister was obliged to act as her model. In spite of the white dresses she was neither morbid nor an invalid, but possessed of a keen sense of humor, which sometimes betrayed itself in grotesque plays upon words and always in the queerest, quaintest turns of expression. Her letters are full of daring originalities, which, if they were not so evidently the coruscations of her individuality, would be affectations. She was always doing odd undreamed of things. Once, when her father desired her presence at church, she stoutly refused. A conflict of wills ensued, such as is possible only in an old New England "orthodox" family. In the end Mr. Dickinson went to church alone. When the family returned home Emily was nowhere to be found. She did not appear at dinner. At last, toward the close of the day, she was discovered sitting in the cellar bulkhead, calmly reading a book, and her only remark was, that she had not cared to discuss the question of going to church and so had retired under-ground.

It happened that once in her service of laying the table she put at her father's place a plate that had a bad nick in it. This annoyed the old gentleman very much and he rather sternly forbade her ever again to let him see that plate. But perverse fate brought it about that twice in succession again the offending plate with the old nick in it, fell to Mr. Dickinson's share, who was very indignant. It did not happen again, for after that last dinner Emily disappeared and was found back of the barn under a big tree with a hammer and a stone between which she was reducing the plate into the most infinitesimal fragments and she remarked that now she hoped she should remember not to put it on the table again.

After her death her sister and her friends were amazed at the immense amount of literary material which she had left behind her. Besides the poems collected in the first volume which is now in its eleventh edition and in the second series which have reached a sale of over five thousand since November, there are at least twelve hundred poems catalogued and no one knows how many more in a mass of notes and manuscripts found among her possessions—enough to make several stout volumes. Mrs. Todd is engaged in preparing and editing a volume of her letters which were written to Dr. and Mrs. Holland, Mr. Samuel Bowles, Colonel Higginson and others of her friends. She was a voluminous letter-writer and these precious documents reveal her personality in a surprising way.

350 "Books and Writers." *Sunday School Times* 34 (March 12, 1892), 172. The English reviewer is Andrew Lang; the quoted review, no. 232.

The two volumes of *Poems by Emily Dickinson* have now been before the public long enough to secure dispassionate criticism by judicious students of nineteenth-century verse. At first they were received with loud acclaim by a small but earnest company of reverential readers, who turned to them as some of the lesser transcendentalists used to bow toward the latest utterer of esoteric inwardness. Now, however, the ablest contemporary English reviewer of verse calls her work "immeasurably obscure, broken, unmelodious, and recklessly wilful," and declares that "in hers is the very anarchy of the Muses; . . . it is a pity her rhymes should make matter for mirth." Between acclaim and contempt, however, there is a place for the middle view that Miss Dickinson's writing is sometimes strong in utterance of original thought, but, though not lacking in poetic ideas, is crude, diffuse, and in no true sense poetry. Art is needed to make pictures out of colors, or poetry out of words.

351 Unlocated clipping, March 24, 1892. This lecture was given in New Britain, Conn., March 23, 1892. See *AB*, pp. 211–212, for a list of some 27 talks Mrs. Todd gave on Dickinson from 1891 to 1898.

The Ladies' Literary Club met with Mrs. Alfred Stanley on Washington Street yesterday afternoon. Mrs. David Todd, wife of Professor Todd of Amherst College, gave a lecture on the "Life and Writings of Emily Dickinson."

352 "I Saw the Sun To-day and Laughed." *Mahogany Tree* 1 (March 26, 1892), 198. The first parody of Dickinson, these untitled lines are signed "E—y D—k—n." For other verses sportively attributed to her, see no. 496.

I saw the sun to-day and laughed,
    Heigh-ho! the jolly sun.
I'm going round you like a shaft
    Shot outward from a gun.

With the great big earth beneath my feet
    I'll race the Planet Mars;
You crack your whip and around will sweep
    To an audience of stars.

353 Hamilton Aïdé. "Poems by Emily Dickinson." *Nineteenth Century* [London] 31 (April 1892), 703–06. This review-article occasioned a post card from Higginson to Todd, April 18, 1892: "You'll find in 19th Century for April 1892 a review of E. D. by Hamilton Aïdé attributing the 1st preface to *Mrs.* T.W.H. I dined with him at Mrs. [Julia Ward] Howe's & he probably took me for a disguised woman!" [*AB*, p. 201]. Aïdé may also have read Higginson's *Atlantic* essay (221) shortly before writing this piece, for his second paragraph echoes the latter's reference to Dickinson's "abstruse problem of life." In the title and throughout this article as originally published in the *Nineteenth Century*, the poet's name was spelled "Dickenson."

An American lady, who nearly missed being the most distinguished poetess her country has yet produced, died in middle age some six years ago. In life she was but little known, and rarely even seen. This aloofness, tinged with eccentricity, and possibly attributable to some early sorrow, characterizes all she wrote. Her scattered verse has only been published since her death; and such fame as Emily Dickinson has achieved as yet is, therefore, posthumous. She avoided publicity in any form; and this indifference to recognition, I take it, accounts for the imperfection of her verse. I cannot subscribe to the idea that her audacious violation of rhyme, her careless obscurity were wilful. I rather incline to the belief that, writing for herself alone, so long as she committed the thought that burned within her to paper, with some assonance which pleased her ear—or even, in some cases, without it—she was satisfied. She would not have been satisfied that these thoughts, clearly the cries wrung from a passionate, suffering soul, should have been given to the world without further polish. Yet we cannot regret the publication of this little volume. The world is richer by some exquisite lines, some beautiful couplets; only in one or two instances by a poem which is complete and perfect. But in all, the possession of Imagination—that rarest of gifts—is conspicuous: Imagination, and a strong individuality, akin to that of no other writer, though at moments there is something that recalls Blake, and, at others, Emily Brontë. The following is a vivid example of her strong conception. One can almost fancy that the writer had before her eyes some grand allegorical design by G. Watts when she sat down, and wrote at white heat:—

THE CHARIOT

Because I could not stop for Death,
    He kindly stopped for me;
The carriage held but just ourselves,
    And Immortality.

We slowly drove, he knew no haste,
    And I had put away

My labor and my leisure, too,
    For his civility.

We passed the school where children played,
    Their lessons scarcely done;
We passed the fields of gazing grain:
    We passed the setting sun.

We paused before a house that seemed
    A swelling of the ground;
The roof was scarcely visible,
    The cornice but a mound.

Since then 'tis centuries; but each
    Feels shorter than the day
I first surmised the horses' heads
    Were toward eternity.

Those five stanzas, though I suppose they cannot be called perfect, inasmuch as the rhymes in the second and fifth must be judged incorrect, have a quality which is rare in poetry of any period. Miss Dickinson's gift of *seeing*, now as in an Apocalyptic vision, now as in a dream of fairyland, is unique among minor minstrels. Her range, it is true, is limited: as though the solitary soul only looked outwardly on certain phases of nature, inwardly on certain insoluble problems of life. But in such exquisite poems as the following—exquisite, in spite of its provoking imperfection—one sees how Imagination with her could descend from its lofty pedestal and pipe and frisk away among the meadows to a fanciful tune of its own.

THE GRASS

The grass so little has to do—
    A sphere of simple green,
With only butterflies to brood,
    And bees to entertain,

And stir all day to pretty tunes
    The breezes fetch along,
And hold the sunshine in its lap,
    And bow to everything;

And thread the dews all night, like pearls,
    And make itself so fine,—
A duchess were too common
    For such a noticing.

And even when it dies, to pass
    In odours so divine,
As lowly spices gone to sleep,
    Or amulets of pine.

And then to dwell in sov'reign barns,
    And dream the days away,—
The grass so little has to do,
    I wish I were the hay!

The blemishes in these stanzas are obvious; and the third one seems to me entirely bad; but one pardons a great deal for the sake of the second (in spite of the careless neglect of rhyme), and the last, which contains two exquisite lines. A common singer would have *seen* no further than the cutting down of the grass, "which to-day is and to-morrow is cast into the oven."

Akin to this, but deeper in feeling, is the nearly perfect little song numbered ix. in the collection labelled 'Love.'

I

Have you got a brook in your little heart,
    Where bashful flowers blow,
And blushing birds go down to drink,
    And shadows tremble so?

II

And nobody knows, so still it flows,
    That any brook is there;
And yet your little draught of life
    Is daily drunken there.

III

Then look out for the little brook in March,
    When the rivers overflow,
And the snows come hurrying from the hills,
    And the bridges often go.

IV

And later, in August it may be,
    When the meadows parching lie,
Beware, lest this little brook of life,
    Some burning noon go dry!

Many of the poems, as a whole, are poor, but in nearly all occurs some original thought struck out in a finely-turned line. In one, which expresses the intense longing to know how a beloved and absent one died, she asks

And was he confident until
    Ill fluttered out in everlasting well?

and she concludes her tender, anxious catechism thus:

Was he afraid or tranquil?
    Might he know
How conscious consciousness could grow,
Till love that was, and love too blest to be
Meet,—and the junction be Eternity?

I could quote many more passages showing the pearls that are strung on pack-thread, alongside common beads, throughout these curious poems. But space will only allow me to transcribe two couplets, which are complete in themselves, and which, as the cry of a suffering soul, not bereft of faith, and struggling for resignation, seem to me wonderfully pathetic, in their passionate, child-like simplicity.

I shall know why, when time is over,
    And I have ceased to wonder why;
Christ will explain each separate anguish,
    In the fair schoolroom of the sky.

He will tell me what Peter promised,
    And I, for wonder at his woe,
I shall forget the drop of anguish
    That scalds me now, that scalds me now.

In the short preface which tells how Miss Dickinson spent years without setting her foot beyond the doorstep of her father's house, Mrs. T. W. Higginson says: "In many cases these verses will seem to the reader like poetry torn up by the roots, with rain and dew and earth still clinging to them, giving a freshness and fragrance not otherwise to be conveyed." That is a very apt image. And yet the last thing that could be said of this volume is that it is "of the earth, earthy."

354 "American." *Bookman* [London] 2:7 (April 1892), 10.

We hear that the late Miss Emily Dickinson left more than a thousand poems and letters behind her, and that the publication of a volume containing the most interesting of them is now being contemplated by her friends. Two volumes of her posthumous poems have already been issued in America, but only one of them (the first) has been published in England. Emily Dickinson must, to say the least of it, have been unusually eccentric. A friend of hers told a correspondent of the *Bookman* that Miss Dickinson always dressed in white, both in winter and summer, and that she would sit outside in the hall to listen to music which was being played, for her especial behoof, in the drawing-room. Her way of being intimate with her friends was to write them frequently, but never or rarely to see them, and at one period of her life she even refused to sit on a chair that someone else had occupied. These are trivial personalities, but they are not uninteresting in view of the theory of mental derangement which has been put forward concerning her.

355 (Mrs.) J. H. Spear. "Emily Dickinson." *Kappa Alpha Theta* 6 (April 1892), 117–19. The 1881 Dickinson letter first published here is reprinted in *L* 3:719–20.

Last year the first volume of Miss Emily Dickinson's poems flashed before the public like a meteor. To all but a cluster of friends around Amherst, the question "who is Miss Dickinson?" was unanswerable. Now many have read her unique poems and are glad to learn of her gentle, beautiful life. As Mr. Higginson said in the preface to the first volume, "Such verse must inevitably forfeit whatever advantage lies in the discipline of public criticism and the enforced conformity to accepted ways," and "when a thought takes one's breath away, a lesson on grammar seems an impertinence."

One cannot criticize, he can only hold his breath and read, thankful that such sweet, grand thoughts have been allowed to be so quaintly and forcibly expressed, and that we are allowed to enjoy them.

We have no *desire* to criticize and it would seem as much out of place as to question the work of the Great Architect in building the irregular outline of the mountains.

Miss Dickinson gave all her poems to her only sister and from the dedication in Vol. I,

This is my message to the world   [letter
That never wrote to me,

It seems as if she looked forward to the possibility of their publication after her death; although during her life she shrank from allowing her inner thoughts thus to come before the public, as she shrank from appearing there herself.

To Miss Lavinia Dickinson we are indebted for the very great pleasure of sharing the treasures. No bit of her sister's own writing has ever been allowed to be desecrated by the printers. All belonging to her has been guarded with most tender and reverential care. The papers have been copied and thus sent to the press. The proof reading has been a great task, for the printers insisted on using conventional forms to clothe thoughts which would lose their greatest charm if expressed by ordinary words and phrases.

Mrs. J. G. Holland was a personal friend of Miss Dickinson, and one of the few who not only saw her often but who knew her intimately. We are indebted to her for most of these reminiscences and also for her kind permission to publish the following letter sent her on the occasion of her daughter's marriage, soon after Dr. Holland's death. This has never been given to the public before:

Sweet Sister:

We were much relieved to know that the dear event had occurred. I feared much for the parting to you to whom parting has come so thickly in the last few days. I knew all would be beautiful, and rejoice it was so.

Few daughters have the Immortality of a Father for a bridal gift. Could there be one more costly!

As we have never ceased to think of you, we will more tenderly now. Confide our happiness to Annie in her happiness.

We hope the unknown Balm may ease the Balm withdrawn. You and Katie, the little Sisters, lose her yet obtain her, for each new width of love largens all the rest.

Mother and Vinnie think and speak, Vinnie hopes to write. Would that Mother could—but the poor hand is idle.

Shall I return to you your last and sweetest word—"But I love you all."

Emily.

She was very fond of Mrs. Browning, whom she is said to have resembled, and spoke of her as one would of a personal friend. Toward George Eliot she had a very different feeling. She said it seemed as if every sentence of hers "had been held up before God and prayed over!" She was very domestic as all will remember who ever tasted her delicious bread and delicate cake. She was in every way a model housekeeper. If fact everything she did at all was done perfectly. She was very fond of her plants and attended them with great care. She was always busy, and writing was only her recreation, yet she left over 12,000 manuscripts. Her hair was auburn and her eyes a soft brown. She always dressed in light colors, often in white, even in winter, and a delicate little round blue cape tied at the throat with a silk cord always hung gracefully over her slender shoulders, even at the large annual receptions given by her father. She never felt entirely happy at these gatherings unless her friend, "the little Sister," would promise to "receive" with them. Often when unable to meet visitors whom she cared for she would send into the parlor some of her own delicious cake, and a dainty remembrance like a single flower of red geranium, with a buttercup and spray of delicate grass, accompanied occasionally by such a little poem as that beginning "I hide myself within my flowers." We cannot copy many of her poems but this is so characteristic we cannot leave it out.

I'm nobody! Who are you?
Are you nobody, too?
Then there's a pair of us—don't tell!
They'd banish us you know.

How dreary to be somebody?
How public, like a frog
To tell your name the livelong day
To an admiring bog!

Could any friend desire sweeter expression of love than this?

Alter? When the hills do;
Falter? When the sun
Question if his glory
Be the only one.   [perfect one.

Surfeit? When the daffodil
Doth of the dew;
Even as herself, O friend!
I will of you!

No fitter ending to these few reminiscences can be found than these words of hers, particularly the last two lines:

Some keep the Sabbath going to church;
I keep it staying at home.
With a bobolink for a chorister
And an orchard for a dome.

Some keep the Sabbath in surplice!
I just wear my wings,
And instead of tolling the bell for church,
Our little sexton sings.

God preaches—a noted clergyman,
And the sermon is never long,
So instead of getting to Heaven *at last,*
I'm going all along!

And no one doubted who knew that beautiful life.

356 "Current Literature." *Spectator* [London] 68 (April 2, 1892), 472. This notice refers to the American (Roberts Brothers) edition of the *Poems,* presumably the more recent 1891 "Second Series."

Yet a third volume of American origin is *Poems,* by Emily Dickinson. There is something of force in these verses, but we can hardly think that it was well to publish them, except, indeed, as a memorial of the deceased author. Looking at them in this aspect, wo do not care to criticise.

357 Louise B. Edwards. "Emily Dickinson." *Housekeeper's Weekly* 3 (April 9, 1892), 2–3. For other discussions of Dickinson in this issue of the *Housekeeper's Weekly,* see the two following entries. Mrs. Todd's remarks on Dickinson quoted here are drawn from a Nathan Haskell Dole article, no. 349.

"I smile when you suggest that I delay 'to publish,' that being as foreign to my thought as firmament to fin. If fame belonged to me, I could not escape her; if she did not, the longest day would pass me on the chase."

So runs a letter from Emily Dickinson to her friend and literary confessor, Thomas Wentworth Higginson. Today, cognizant of the remarkable notice which has been given to her posthumous poems, we can only smile at the utter unconsciousness on the writer's part of the extraordinary success which was to be the portion of the poems which she wrote, as she expressed it, "just to relieve," and without the faintest intention or inclination to give them to the world. In life the shyest and most shrinking creature imaginable, dying, she could not escape the fame which belonged to her, and her poems and herself through them have met criticism and appreciation in literary circles everywhere.

Her literary works are discussed elsewhere in this number of the *Housekeeper's Weekly*, so nothing need be said of them here, save to touch on their remarkable poetical charm, coupled with an equally remarkable disregard for grammar, syntax, and rhythm. Until after her death her family had no idea of the mass of letters, notes, and verses which she left behind her,—enough to make several volumes besides the one issued in November, which has already reached a sale of twelve thousand. It is only from her letters, in which she speaks with a childlike freedom and confidence, that we are given glimpses of the personality of this gifted woman, whose eccentricity was only matched by the rare spirituality and sweetness of her nature. In the *Atlantic Monthly* for October, Col. Higginson gives some interesting extracts from her correspondence with him.

From these she impresses us as a recluse, who, well content to stay in her home in Amherst, with a few choice books and her beloved birds and flowers, held herself aloof from a busy, rushing world with which she had no part. This idea, however, is refuted by Mrs. Mabel Loomis Todd, one of the few privileged ones who were admitted to intimacy with her. Says Mrs. Todd:

"When her father was in Congress she spent several winters in Washington, and mingled in gay society, which she enjoyed, though still feeling that she had no real part in it. It was only in the last years of her life that she lived in her own home, somewhat like a dear ghost, seen but scarcely tangible, dwelling among her favorite flowers and in the shadows."

In her family she hardly seems to have been understood, and little wonder, perhaps. She herself says, with unconscious sarcasm in the latter part of the sentence:

"They are religious, except me, and address an eclipse every morning whom they call their Father."

Mrs. Todd tells of an incident which occurred on one occasion, when, her father wishing her to accompany him to church,—

"A conflict of wills ensued, such as is possible only in an old New England 'orthodox' family. In the end Mr. Dickinson went to church alone. When the family returned home Emily was nowhere to be found. She did not appear at dinner. At last, toward the close of the day, she was discovered sitting in the cellar bulkhead, calmly reading a book, and her only remark was, that she had not cared to discuss the question of going to church and so had retired underground."

But although she excepted herself from the category of the "religious," she had, after all, spiritual insight of the keenest and most delicate. Here is an extract from a letter to Mr. Higginson:

"My life has been too simple and stern to embarrass any. 'Seen of Angels,' scarcely my responsibility."

And another:

"When much in the woods, as a little girl, I was told that the snake would bite me, that I might pick a poisonous flower, or goblins kidnap me; but I went along and met no one but angels, who were far shyer of me than I could be of them, so I haven't that confidence in fraud which many exercise."

In speaking of immortality she has many quaint and felicitous turns of expression. In one of her later letters, written just after the death of her father, she says, with a tinge of pathos:

"I am glad there is immortality, but would have tested it myself before entrusting him."

Her education must have been a curious one. Perhaps she gives the clue to the unusual style of her poems when she says:

"I had no monarch in my life, and cannot rule myself, and when I try to organize, my little force explodes and leaves me bare and charred."

And again,

"You inquire my books. For poets, I have Keats, and Mr. and Mrs. Browning. For prose, Mr. Ruskin, Sir Thomas Browne, and the Revelations. I went to school, but in your manner of the phrase had no education. When a little girl, I had a friend who taught me Immortality, but himself venturing too near, he never returned."

She was at one time an accomplished pianist, but, as she became more and more retiring, gave it up, herself quaintly declaring that "the noise in the pool at noon excels my piano." Mrs. Todd records that,

"She dressed always in white, but such was her dislike to being 'fitted' that her sister was obliged to act as her model. In spite of the white dresses she was neither morbid nor an invalid, but possessed of a keen sense of humor, which sometimes displayed itself in grotesque plays upon words, and always in the queerest, quaintest turns of expression."

Yet with all her oddness, and what Mrs. Whitney terms "other-worldliness," there was no affectation about her, no loftiness. She loved her kind, and wished them well, especially the children, to whom she was so near in heart. Some childish recollections of her are given elsewhere in this issue. When accused of "shunning men and women," she gave it as her reason that "they talk of hallowed things aloud." For her near friends she had a tenacious and anxious affection. In a letter written to Col. Higginson, soon after his enlistment in the army of the Civil War, she says that "although not reared to prayer, when service is had in church for our arms, I include yourself," and adds somewhat sadly:

"Perhaps death gave me awe for friends, striking sharp and early, for I have held them since in a brittle love, of more alarm than peace."

And closes in quaint fashion:

"Could you, with honor, avoid death, I entreat you, sir. It would bereave
YOUR GNOME."

She continued a voluminous correspondence with her few chosen friends, rich in quaint, poetic and epigrammatical phrases, up to the time of her death, in 1886. Death could hold no terrors for one whose hold on this life had so little tenacity. That the limitations of existence wearied her, and that she longed to try her wings, is shown in one brief aphorism of hers:

"Enough is so vast a sweetness, I suppose it never occurs, only pathetic counterfeits."

Without doubt she who "when a little girl was taught immortality," found in that immortality but the verification of her own lines:

> Not Revelation 'tis that waits,
> But our unfurnished eyes.

358　"The Children's Friend." *Housekeeper's Weekly* 3 (April 9, 1892), 5–6.
　　The quoted article by MacGregor Jenkins is no. 249.

In "A Child's Recollections of Emily Dickinson," MacGregor Jenkins, in the *Christian Union*, gives some memory-pictures of his intercourse with the strange, shy, gifted woman, whose unique verses have been recently given to the world, and have aroused so much interest and discussion. Says Mr. Jenkins: "I was one of a quartette of children admitted to intimacy with 'Miss Emily,' the intimacy being of much the same sort as that between herself and the birds and flowers. While she avoided seeing grown-up people, she frequently saw us, and it is only of my childish recollections of this remarkable woman that I venture to write." [Quotation from the Jenkins article continues to its end.]

359　W. M. "Emily Dickinson's Poems." *Housekeeper's Weekly* 3 (April 9, 1892), 4.

Do you never come across things in your reading that you would give worlds to have written? I sometimes do—I suppose they express so beautifully or so completely thoughts of my own, or perhaps call forth thoughts of which I was not before conscious.

Of this nature are some of the poems of Emily Dickinson. Possibly, as has been suggested in these columns, her verses have "little rhythm and less rhyme," but they are so running over with the spirit of poetry that one is hardly conscious of any lack in their outward form. I have been often surprised, on studying the construction of a verse, to find that it contained no rhyme at all. Yet I had not missed it, so beautiful was the thought, so expressive the diction, and so musical the inward rhythm, though the outward might be faulty.

> The grass so little has to do—
> 　A spear of simple green,　　　　　　　　　　[sphere
> With only butterflies to brood,
> 　And bees to entertain,
>
> And stir all day to pretty tunes
> 　The breezes fetch along,
> And hold the sunshine in its lap
> 　And bow to everything;
>
> And thread the dews all night, like pearls,
> 　And make itself so fine,—

> A duchess were too common
>   For such a noticing.
>
> And even when it dies, to pass
>   In odors so divine, —
> As lovely spices gone to sleep,
>   Or amulets of pine,
>
> And then to dwell in sovereign barns,
>   And dream the days away, —
> The grass so little has to do,
>   I wish I were a hay!

Is there no rhythm there? Is it not overflowing with music, and so abounding in the poetry of green coolness and summer zephyrs and warm fragrances that the thought of a mere rhyme sinks quite out of sight? Is it not in this that the force of her verse often lies? The author never sacrifices the thought for the form. She will have the meaning, and just her own particular meaning, at any cost, and the result, in its daring originality, has a directness and an unlooked-for charm that is all its own.

The poems, it is interesting to read, were written with no thought of publication, but, as the preface to the first volume says, "solely by way of expression of the author's own mind." Most of them were unknown, even to her nearest friends, until after her death, when they were found and published by them. This accounts, no doubt, in great part, for her free and unconventional utterance and her bold originality. But, "though curiously indifferent to all conventional rules, she had yet a vigorous literary standard of her own, and often altered a word many times to suit her own tenacious fastidiousness."

That which makes her work the more remarkable, her insight into life and nature the more marvelous, is the fact that she lived for years a recluse, "literally spending years without setting her foot beyond the door-step." Yet her descriptions of nature suggest such close observation, and her sympathy with her moods is so perfect that one is forced to believe that she spoke literal truth when she wrote —

> I never saw a moor,
>   I never saw the sea;
> Yet know I how the heather looks,
>   And what a wave must be.
>
> I never spoke with God,
>   Nor visited in heaven;
> Yet certain am I of the spot
>   As if the chart were given.

She was never married, yet her comprehension of the heights and depths of love was intense, and her thought upon it deep and strong.

> Alter? When the hills do.
>   Falter? When the sun
> Question if his glory
>   Be the perfect one.
>
> Surfeit? When the daffodil
>   Doth of the dew;
> Even as herself, O friend!
>   I will of you!

It would almost seem, when one considers her habit of life, that her wonderful insight must be largely spiritual, a kind of second sight, and only in part, at least, the result of experience and observation. But whatever the source of her power, it is of such a quality that one feels her personality, and feels, too, when he has become familiar with her mind, as though she were an actual friend of his own.

I wish I might quote many more of her poems, but want of space forbids. Suffice it to say that here is one which shows the tender, *human* side of her nature, and which makes one wish she might know how great an inspiration and help to others are the poems she wrought in secret, not knowing they would ever meet other eyes.

> If I can stop one heart from breaking,
>   I shall not live in vain;
> If I can ease one life the aching,
>   Or cool one pain,
> Or help one fainting robin
>   Unto his nest again,
> I shall not live in vain.

360 Ellen E. Dickinson. "Emily Dickinson." *Brooklyn Eagle,* April 28, 1892, p. 4. The author was the widow of William Hawley Dickinson, the "favorite cousin" mentioned in this article. For other reminiscences of the poet by Mrs. Dickinson, see 391 and 495. The snake-inspired poem alluded to here is no doubt "A narrow fellow in the grass."

Emily Dickinson's verses may be called a diary of her life, her thoughts and experiences from day to day, the minor strain running through them all, giving evidence of an early and life lasting grief. Her environments were eminently calculated to give color to her poetic instincts, her birds, her flowers and the charming scenery with which she was surrounded ever awakening new admiration in one who had an abiding and exquisite love and tenderness for the beautiful.

Miss Dickinson was born in Amherst, Mass., and during the fifty-six years of her life, ending May 18, 1886, resided in a quaint old mansion with a flower garden on one side and a shaded lawn on the other, which is one of the most attractive dwellings in this venerable college town. Her father, Edward Dickinson, was a distinguished lawyer and treasurer of Amherst college. Emily, it is said, was considered a very bright and eccentric girl, a gifted conversationalist, her keen repartee and witty sayings being repeated as very clever and unusual. While Mr. Dickinson was in congress she spent two or three seasons in Washington and was noted for her brilliant talk. All the latter years of her life were devoted to a retirement from society, in the seclusion of her Amherst home, very rarely seeing anyone who did not belong to it, save on the occasion of the annual reception given by her family to the college magnates and the best people of the vicinity. At such intervals she was a delightful hostess, had the most perfect savoir faire and graciousness, but after their recurrence at once became a recluse. Her presence, however, pervaded the whole mansion, beautiful flowers arranged by her hands were found in unexpected places, a dainty dessert of her creation was on the dinner table, or the rustle of her garments in a corridor suggested a possible resemblance to angels' wings. Her dress was of blue and white, summer and winter, and of somewhat curious fashion. Her face was beaming with intelligence and most attractive, but she was in no sense of the word beautiful. She was of medium height, and a fair complexion, prominent blue eyes and a wealth of Titian red hair. She came and went in the household, yet was not at all times visible to it, sometimes vanishing, as it were, unexpectedly into adjoining apartments, or appearing from them as unexpectedly, yet never forgetting her appointed tasks as assistant in the daily rounds of domestic labor. With her other accomplishments Emily Dickinson was skilled in cookery. The table whereon she made delicious pies and bread and cakes, stood in front of a window in the kitchen opening on the lawn. Close beside her she kept pencil and paper for record of any passing thought she felt worthy of remembrance. One summer morning while thus occupied she saw a little green snake gliding through the grass toward the window and, laying down her pastry knife, wrote some verses which her strange visitor inspired. It was in the beautiful old fashioned garden that most of her poetical fancies came to her. She loved gardening, the brown earth, the buds, opening blossoms, the butterflies and honey bees and marvel of green leaves; and under her manipulation every growing thing seemed to flourish; indeed, the flowers were sentiment to her and gave her lessons of life and love and questions of the eternal fitness of events. The mountains in the distance, she said, gave her a sense of restfulness and peace at dawn. No effect of nature within her horizon was lost upon her inquiring and wondering gaze and all ministered to her changeful moods. She had a rare sense of humor and could tell a comic story with dramatic appreciation. Music of the better sort, particularly singing, gave her the keenest pleasure. On one occasion a woman guest sang an Italian aria in the drawing room when she supposed she was quite alone. "That is simply divine," said Emily, coming from a corner where she had hidden herself. It is a matter of regret to those who knew and loved this gifted woman that some evidences are not preserved of her witty sayings: those concise sentences which gave so much in their terseness. A servant girl at one time came in the library who had a new and very skimp calico gown. After her departure Emily said: "Mary has a new calico sarcophagus, it seems." A favorite cousin brought his newly wedded wife to visit his relatives. Emily did not appear till in the shades of the autumn evening, when the woman guest was alone in the library. Coming close to her the poetess said: "Why, you look just like a fashion plate in that gold colored dress." The new cousin responded with a brief quotation from Thoreau's writings. Grasping the hands of her visitor in her own and pressing them, Emily said, "From this time we are acquainted."

Mr. Emerson, Colonel Higginson, Dr. J. G. Holland, Mr. Bowles of the Springfield *Republican* and other noted men visited her occasionally. They encouraged her to give her verses to the world at large. To a woman friend who urged her in the same direction she replied, "I could as soon disrobe in public as have my verses printed." Many people were aware that Emily was writing verses every day; that her pen was most prolific in poetical fancies, but few persons were permitted to read them, save her only sister, Miss Lavinia Dickinson, whose admiration for Emily was a kind of worship.

In all the thirty years of Emily Dickinson's retirement from the world she never left her father's grounds but twice, on brief excursions to visit a noted oculist in Boston.

She dreamed dreams in the old mansion and garden, in the changing seasons, the winds, and all nature, till she was allowed to pass on into the immortality from which it seemed she was detained unwillingly so many years. One can forget the criticisms, favorable and the reverse, which have been printed concerning the verses of the poetess of Amherst, and still count her a genius. Of the more

remarkable poems in the volume published by Roberts of Boston is "Renunciation" and "Resurrection." Of the wittiest are the following lines:

> Belshazzar had a letter,
> He never had but one:
> Belshazzar's correspondent
> Concluded and begun.
> In that immortal copy
> The conscience of us all
> Can read without its glasses
> On revelation's wall.

361 [Nathan Haskell Dole]. "Emily Dickinson's Personality." *Book Buyer* 9
  (May 1892), 157–58. Largely a reprinting; see no. 349.

In a recent letter from Boston, published in *Book News*, Nathan Haskell Dole
gave an interesting summary of a paper by Mrs. Mabel Loomis Todd, on the late
Emily Dickinson and her poems.
  "Mrs. Todd," said Mr. Dole, "was one of the comparatively few who were admitted to anything like intimacy with the weird recluse of Amherst. . . ." [The
remainder of the Dole article is reprinted in full, without further comment.]

362 Mary Elwell Storrs. "Emily Dickinson, 1830–1886." *Springfield Sunday
  Republican*, May 22, 1892, p. 2. For other dedicatory verses, see index
  s.v. poems in tribute to Emily Dickinson.

> That face pathetic haunts my days of late;
> All pale, yet crowned with flowers, she sighs and sings;
> Defiant music clashes as it flows,
> Clear notes and tangled fascinate the ear;
> So sings the thrush against the rising storm,
> The caged canary trills and quivers so;
> Ah, warblers sweet, her voice outsings ye all,
> Thrilling and throbbing from a human heart.
>
> Now calm and strong, audacious and severe,
> Now glad and childlike, ringing wild and clear,
> The loud winds blow, the swift grass rustles low:
> Carousing bees, and butterflies, and song
> Of birds, and waving flags and flowers, prolong
> A vivid panorama of delight
> Returning oft upon the inward sight!
>
> Thus rimmed and decked, wise wisdom sets its truths,
> Vying in choices with the Concord seer,
> In epigram, in hived sententiousness.
> The chimes may falter, rhythmic waves pulse on.
>
> And life's supremest hours take form and move:—
> Not heart-throes only, but the very scenes
> Unfold and pass, as in a magic glass,
> Nor Hawthorne's probings open deeper depths;
> The sad strains, swan-like, die in ecstasy
> Of love, of pain, of triumph over grief.

O soul, made white before the great white throne,
Past pain! Dost thou released shrink quivering still,
Laid open, bare, by earth's publicity!
Yet comfort thee! thy great heart's sympathy,
Like shadowing pine, like morning's tearful dew,
Cheers the drear sands, soothes scorching pain to rest!

April, 1891

363 "Mrs. Todd's Lecture on Emily Dickinson." *Amherst Record*, June 8,
1892, p. 3. Another account of Mrs. Todd's Amherst College talk appeared in the same issue of the *Record*; see next entry. On this June 2
talk, which 110 people attended, see also no. 365 and *AB*, pp. 203–05.

A highly intelligent and appreciative audience gathered in Walker Hall last
Wednesday to listen to a lecture by Mrs. Todd on Emily Dickinson and her poems.
    She was introduced to her hearers with most fitting words by Pres't Gates, and
held their delighted attention for an hour and a half. Mrs. Todd has given so much
time to the study of Miss Dickinson's poems, and to their preparation for the
press, that she is a most competent critic of the minutest peculiarities of her
poetry. At the same time she was personally acquainted with the author, and
could show something of the daily life of one who was a hidden and mysterious
being even to her neighbors. Mrs. Todd clothed with flesh and blood a person
whose name had before been to them little more than the name of a spirit.
    The lecturer spoke of the want of rhyme and rhythm in many of the poems,
but regarded them all wonderful for their originality, and found in every poem
some gem of thought or image or expression. Mrs. Todd *read* many of the poems,
and the reading with her peculiar emphasis often brought out beauties which even
those who were familiar with the poems had not seen before.
    The clear and distinct enunciation of the lecturer, her musical voice, and self-
possessed and graceful bearing gave interest to everything that was said and made
the time of the lecture exceedingly pleasant and profitable to all who were
present.

364 [Thomas Power Field.] "An Hour with Emily Dickinson." *Amherst Record*, June 8, 1892, p. 4. The attribution, "Dr. Field," is by hand in Todd's
scrapbook.

An appreciative audience gathered by the courtesy of President Gates, in
Walker Hall, Thursday afternoon last, to listen to Mrs. Todd, while she led their
minds in most interesting communion with the poetic spirit of Emily Dickinson. To those acquainted with the poems of this wonderful woman, Mrs. Todd's
familiar talk was delightful, as she brought out the delicate shades of meaning
which they had not before noticed and appreciated. To those of us who in our busy
life, have time for only those things easily understood, Mrs. Todd gave a feast of
fat things. Surely if time and patient study of an author are essential to the fullest appreciation of an author's poems, Emily Dickinson is fortunate in her compiler. Mrs. Todd has brought a large acquaintance with men and books and withal
a loving sympathy with nature as seen in tree and flower and sunlit cloud to her
delightful task of telling us what Miss Emily Dickinson *thought* in the days of
her solitude. The strange, mystical spirit which held such real communion with
the works of nature in their myriad forms, from the reptile in her garden to the

bird on the bough, has found one who has so deeply drunk of her own spirit, as to be able to unfold to the delight of others, the otherwise hidden meaning couched in many of her lines, and to make it a real pleasure to study her writings.

365 "Notes." *Critic*, n.s. 17 (June 11, 1892), 334. In *AB*, p. 414, Mrs. Bingham notes that in the fall of 1894 Roberts Brothers reprinted this article in full as an advertisement for its forthcoming edition of Dickinson's letters.

"Emily Dickinson," writes a correspondent in Massachusetts, "was the subject of a lecture given at Amherst College, on June 2, by Mrs. Mabel Loomis Todd, her friend and editor. It was practically an introduction of Miss Dickinson to her neighbors, and was extremely interesting in that it showed to Amherst people that she who had been known to them only as a strange character, hiding herself from everybody, and living an isolated and reputedly an erratic life, was really one of the most natural and unaffected of beings. The congruity between herself and her poems seems perfect; and in her letters, from which Mrs. Todd quoted largely, she is exhibited as one of the most delightful of correspondents and friends and wisest of hearthstone philosophers. Man, we are told, 'is a gregarious animal.' There have been exceptions; and Emily Dickinson was, by her very constitution, one of them. And by virtue of fortunate circumstances, which allowed her to live out her bent, her mind bore a rich fruitage of a kind exotic to the world where we are always jostling elbows. It is altogether pleasing to be informed that only the first fruits of the harvest have yet been offered us. She knew the worth of her productions and kept copies of the hundreds of little poems she was constantly sending to her friends (though so guardedly in respect of possible publication that only two were ever printed), and there are enough of them to make several volumes yet; while of her charming letters a great store have been collected from her few but long-time correspondents; and it is safe to predict that when these are published they will be as welcome as the poems have been."

366 "Recent Books of Verse." *Christian Union* 45 (June 18, 1892), 1212. The *Christian Union* routinely welcomed contributions by Higginson, among them his inaugural essay on Dickinson (no. 2). More recently it had published MacGregor Jenkins's childhood reminiscences of the poet (249). In this belated notice, however, the journal appears to distance itself from whole-hearted endorsement of the Amherst recluse. This bellwether review suggests that Higginson and Todd could no longer count on a generally favorable reception for Dickinson in the editorial rooms of the religious and family weeklies.

Every man is to be judged after his kind; and if Miss Emily Dickinson elected — in the most piquant manner imaginable—to be "nobody," a fresh, unconventional, unhampered nobody, why, let us accept her as such, and admire her candid fancy with not too much reference to the great crudities of her work. Her posthumous "Poems," edited by Thomas Wentworth Higginson and Mabel Loomis Todd, are prefaced by an introduction from the pen of the latter, which, many will think, does Miss Dickinson more than justice. The poetess is described as having tried society and the world, and as having found them lacking. "She was not an invalid, and she lived in seclusion from no love disappointment. . . . Immortality was close about her, and, while never morbid or melancholy, she lived in its presence." If her poetry gives a true reflection of herself we can scarcely agree with this last statement. Indeed, one must close his ears here and there to quite an acrid tone toward the world of which she refused to be a part. It must be remembered that if the artist rid herself of certain criticisms by retiring from the standard of others, still the victory is less than when those irksome incumbrances are borne patiently and are triumphed over. To be sure, a "somebody" is more greatly tempted to pretense; but is not the merit finer if he overcome pretense? Nor can we admire entirely the particular form of "Emersonian self-possession" which this author exhibits toward her Master. We do not believe that the poem entitled "A Prayer" was meant to be irreverent, but it comes dangerously near it; nor can we see any compensating advantage gained. It is the eagle who can look Phoebus in the face, but in certain troubled conditions of the atmosphere much lowlier birds may safely apostrophize him. When this is said — and it applies to no considerable part of Miss Dickinson's work — one must also admit the many good things in the "Poems" — their unexpected quality, which renders them so readable, the clever bits one stumbles on here and there, nuggets with the right hue and true ring. There has however, been plenty of work for the editors to refine this metal to a presentable standard.

367 "Americans and Their Books." *Critic*, n.s. 18 (July 23, 1892), 48. Reprinted from *London Daily News*, October 27, 1891 (no. 250).

368 [Andrew Lang.] "The Superior Sex." *Critic* 18 (August 27, 1892), 112. Reprinted from an undated *London Daily News*. When Millie Elliot Seawell and Higginson faced off in the pages of the *Critic* on the issue of whether women possess creativity in the arts, neither mentioned Dickinson. Others, on both sides of the issue, did; see no. 347. Only the opening third of Lang's article is reprinted here.

Miss Mollie Elliot Seawell is a young lady who sticks to her guns. Some months ago she boldly maintained the thesis that women, in art and literature, were no match for men. This she did in an American journal, and some of her sex, with their own noble logic, ceased to subscribe to the paper, while many others wrote refutations. Miss Seawell pulverized them, and retired on her laurels. But, lo! there came forth a champion from the camp of the men, the redoubtable Colonel Higginson, who was, as it were, the Columbus of Miss Emily Dickinson, and discovered a continent of poetry where others had only seen a misty ocean of bad rhymes and bad grammar. The gallant Colonel averred that Miss Seawell had omitted many celebrated ladies from her argument, and spoke of her "outburst against her own sex." The fair Penthesilea of common sense then girt on her armor, and she does battle with the Colonel in the *Critic*. She did not make outbursts against her own sex, she declares; she only put them in their proper place. . . .

369 "Jottings." *Boston Transcript*, September 12, 1892, p. 4.

Emily Dickinson spoke well of autumn in the ordinary sense of rhyme, as well as with that subtle "thought rhyme" of hers:

> The morns are meeker than they were,
>   The nuts are getting brown;
> The berry's cheek is plumper,
>   The rose is out of town.

370 "The Home." "Helps to High Living." *Unity* (Chicago), October 20, 1892, p. 63.

> Sun. ——Itself its sovereign, of itself
>   The soul should stand in awe.
> Mon. ——Defeat whets victory, they say.
> Tues. ——Eternity enables the endeavoring again.
> Wed. ——Learn the transport by the pain
>   As blind men learn the sun.
> Thurs. —He deposes doom,
>   Who hath suffered him.
> Fri. ——The vane a little to the east
>   Scares muslin souls away.
> Sat. ——To comprehend a nectar
>   Requires sorest need.
>
>   —Emily Dickinson.

371 M[ary] B[owen]. "To Emily Dickinson." *Unit* [Grinnell College, Iowa] 5 (October 29, 1892), 53. Reprinted: *Under the Scarlet and Black: Poems Selected from the Undergraduate Publications of Iowa College,* ed. Hervey S. McCowan and Frank F. Everest (Grinnell, Iowa: Herald Publishing Co., 1893), p. 27; *Dial* 15 (July 16, 1893), 43. For other dedicatory verses, see index *s.v.* poems in tribute to Emily Dickinson.

> A harp AEolian, on a lonely sill
> Was placed to feel the subtle wind's soft touch.
> Perhaps its strains were burdened overmuch
>   With nature's sadness and her discords; still,
>   Responsive to its master's touchless thrill,
>   It told the clover's whisper to the breeze,
>   The wordless plaint of wind-swept winter trees
> With melody unknown to human skill.
>   So in the quiet of a life apart
> From other lives, their passions and their pain,
>   The hand of nature touched thy tune'd heart
> And, lo, thou utterest in simple strain
>   A song, too thought-rich for a fettered art,
> Yet bearing ever Nature's sad refrain.

371A C[larke, Helen A.]. "Some Notable American Verse." *Poet-Lore,* 4:11 ([November] 1892), 581. The author here takes up *Poems,* Second Series, among fifteen other recent publications.

Miss Emily Dickinson has more the quality of the bloodroot, delicate, passionate, but with a sting which sends the reader wiser away. Some one has said that her poetry resembles that of William Blake more than that of any other poet; but William Blake does not to our recollection deal in any such terse aphoristic utterances, where truth is nested in subtle suggestion.

> The soul unto itself
> Is an imperial friend
> Or the most agonizing spy
> An enemy could send.

Secure against its own
No treason it can fear;
Itself its sovereign, of itself
The soul should stand in awe.

372 "The Culture That Inspires." November 1892. The date is by hand in
Todd's scrapbook. Unlocated.

It was a noble speech made the other day by Mr. Charles L. Hutchinson at
the dinner to Dr. Harper, the new president of the Chicago University. If a Chicago business man chosen treasurer of the board of trustees of a great university
can make a speech like that there will certainly be a great university established
in Chicago and it will be under the right sort of auspices and influences. Here is
the splendid closing of the speech of this Universalist treasurer of an institution founded by Baptists' money and with a majority of its board of trustees Baptists, too.

[This article prints a dozen paragraphs from Mr. Hutchinson's speech on the importance of "knowledge and culture," ending as follows with Mr. Hutchinson's
concluding remarks:]

"The truth of God is not bound; so Paul affirmed to Timothy.

Can you not hear, even today, the voice of that grand apostle crying down the
ages, 'The truth of God is not bound.' It was not bound to Judaism. It was not
bound to Catholicism. It was not bound to Luther and the Reformation. No sect
and no people of today have a full revelation. Each has a part; but whenever or
wherever a man or a people discover a truth of God an eternal fact, it shall abide.
As a nation we believe that to us has been revealed more than to any other upon
the face of the earth, and that today we in our imperfect way embody in our life
a fuller interpretation of that truth than any other. That truth is revealed by inspiration, and the greatest source of inspiration is education.

Why question its source? Rather believe with the strange genius of Emily
Dickinson:

The pedigree of honey
   Does not concern the bee:
A clover any time to him
   Is aristocracy

See the truth if you will at Unitarian Harvard; seek it at Congregational Yale;
at Princeton under Presbyterian influences; embrace the opportunities offered by
Universalist Tufts; come to the University of Chicago under Baptist dominion.
Whenever and wherever you find that knowledge and culture which develops
the soul as well as the intellect, bid the work and the worker Godspeed.

All honor, then, to any institution that stands for education and enlighten-
ment. Do not hesitate to take the truth of God because it is handed in the name
of the Baptists. Thank God that He has put it into their hearts to offer it and lend
a helping hand.

As a city we are seeking to set before the nation a true ideal. What is that true
ideal? As Canon Farrar says, 'It is duty; it is righteousness; it is the law of Sinai;
it is the law of Christ.'"

373 [Thomas Wentworth Higginson.] "Recent Poetry." *Nation* 55 (December 15, 1892), 453.

Mr. Arlo Bates, who perhaps has never visited Oriental lands himself, yet puts more positive flavor into his "Told in the Gate" (Roberts Bros.) simply because he handles his Eastern properties with a stronger grasp and is less fascinated by the bewitchment of the embroidery. But there is something to be said, after all, for the materials which one's home yields, and Mrs. Julia C. R. Dorr extracts more vigorous verse from the Ethan Allen legends in the Vermont of her childhood ("The Armorer's Errand" in her "Poems," Scribners) than out of the many themes she borrows from foreign lands. This is partly because her natural theme is the daylight, while there are far more gifted poets, like the late Anne Reeve Aldrich ("Songs about Love and Death," Scribners), whose whole existence dwells, like Emily Dickinson's, in the dim twilight, so that it matters not what the chosen theme may be: the subjective quality is all in all. Who would not guess that the following verses, for instance, were by Emily Dickinson herself (p. 128)?

A LITTLE PARABLE.

I made the cross myself whose weight
    Was later laid on me.
This thought is torture as I toil
    Up life's steep Calvary.

To think mine own hands drove the nails!
    I sang a merry song,
And chose the heaviest wood I had
    To build it firm and strong.

If I had guessed — if I had dreamed
    Its weight was meant for me,
I should have made a lighter cross
    To bear up Calvary.

374 *Unity* (Chicago). Unlocated. Attributed to *Unity* by hand and placed among December 1892 clippings in Todd's scrapbook.

Last and most important in the way of poetic contributions of the year is the second volume of Emily Dickinson's poems. Now that she is gone, her friends give to the world what she so scrupulously guarded from it. The weird little poet of death was shy and sore, but tender and responsive. Closer study will discover in her the poet of suffering. She fully appreciated the gospel power of pain. Note this, her "Martyrs" song:

Through the straight pass of suffering
    The martyrs even trod,
Their feet upon temptation,
    Their faces upon God.

A stately, shriven company;
    Convulsion playing round,
Harmless as streaks of meteor
    Upon a planet's bound.

Their faith the everlasting troth;
    Their expectation fair;
The needle to the north degree
    Wades so, through polar air.

375 "Personal." *Home Journal,* December 21, 1892. Unlocated. The member of the poet's family whose letter is quoted would seem to be either Lavinia or Susan.

Miss Stella King gave another reading before the Murray Hill Club last Thursday morning at the house of Mrs. G. C. Clausen, Fifth Avenue. The selections for the most part were in the lighter vein, and fresher than common, and the music was exceptionally good.

The authors discussed were Mary E. Wilkins and Emily Dickinson, with a few selections from Eugene Field. An interesting sketch of Miss Wilkins was followed by the reading of her short story, "Sonny," new to most of those present, and given with Miss King's usual appreciative humor. She then drew a vivid picture of the life and genius of Emily Dickinson, of whom the world knew little until after her death. Timid in body, but daring in thought, she shrank from the public both in person and in print, but she left hundreds of wonderful little poems whose quality astonished even those who lived beside her. In describing her Miss King quoted from a recent letter by a member of her family.

"Emily was wonderful from her birth. She was remarkable in appearance; her skin was as delicate as a peach, her eyes large, brilliant and tender—chestnut eyes, I call them; hair, chestnut, massive, and soft as down. She always had flowers about her and they seemed a part of her. Her devotion to her friends was heavenly; her sympathy for all suffering was almost a marvel. Her nature was buoyant, yet full of pathos. She was very winning in her ways and few who ever met her will forget her charm. Her laugh was the merriest; she had the rarest and keenest wit and her sense of humor knew no bounds. Colonel Higginson spoke of her on the day she left this home as 'Our friend who has just put on immortality, who seemed scarce ever to have taken it off.'" The selections from her poems were listened to with much interest.

The musical part of the programme was given by Mrs. Arthur Dyett, who sang in an exquisite manner the songs, "Little Boy Blue," words by Eugene Field; "Bel Raggio," from Semiramide; Chamanade's "L'Eté," and "Awake my love, from slumber," by Fannie M. Spencer.

376 Mary Bowen. "To Emily Dickinson." *Under the Scarlet and Black: Poems Selected from the Undergraduate Publications of Iowa College,* ed. Hervey S. McCowan and Frank F. Everest. Grinnell, Iowa: Herald Publishing Co., 1893, p. 27. A reprinting of no. 371. For a critical notice of this volume, see no. 378.

377 Florence S. Hoyt. "Intelligent Sociability." *Congregationalist* 78 (March 2, 1893), 337–38.

The new Baptist minister had just come to town. What could they do to make him and his attractive wife, who had left a flourishing Massachusetts church, feel at home in their Chicago suburb? The new superintendent of schools was also beginning a new life for his family in their community. This was the situation as the Congregational minister and his wife "talked it over" in that comfortable hour after the Sabbath evening service.

As a consequence of their deliberations the second Tuesday evening later found gathered in their simple home thirty persons whom they had deemed congenial. The Baptist minister and his wife, Mr. and Mrs. Superintendent of Schools, the teacher of the new department of manual training in the high school and his wife and several of the other high school teachers were among the number.

After a half-hour of introductions and general conversation the host announced that material had been prepared for an Emily Dickinson evening. To each person were distributed two typewritten slips of paper, each slip bearing a half of a poem by Emily Dickinson. Each person was to find and claim the second half to complete the slip in his hand, which bore a title, so in time the company had been well shaken up and each person held one whole poem. All were seated in one room, and one of the ladies gave a short account of the poet's life for the benefit of any one who might not have read the prefaces to the published volumes nor Colonel Higginson's article in the *Atlantic*.

The hostess gave a short critique of the poems and then introduced the reading by:

> This is my letter to the world
> That never wrote to me,
> The simple news that nature told,
> With tender majesty.
>
> Her message is committed
> To hands I cannot see;
> For love of her, sweet countrymen,
> Judge tenderly of me!

The poems were classified under the general subjects of Nature, Heaven, Love and Life, and were necessarily named in order to call for them. To those who were familiar with the poems was given the pleasure of hearing an old friend speak, and to those who did not know Emily Dickinson a new friend was introduced. Two families purchased the two volumes the next day, a more tangible proof of the enjoyment of the evening than the hearty words that were said to the host and hostess or the enthusiasm that was expressed as the guests enjoyed their coffee or chocolate.

I. NATURE.

1. I'll Lend.	9. April.	
2. My Secret.	10. A Summer Shower.	
3. Why.		
4. Autumn.	11. The Bee.	
5. Beclouded.	12. The Snake.	
6. November.		
7. A Day.	13. The Bluebird.	
8. Sea of Sunset.	14. The Oriole.	
	15. The Robin.	
16. The Purple Clover.		
17. The Grass.		
18. The Fringed Gentian.		

II. HEAVEN.   1. Good-by.   2. Going to Heaven.   3. A Service of Song.   4. Faith.

III. LOVE.   1. Faithfulness.   2. The Wife.

IV. LIFE.   1. Notoriety.   2. The Show.   3. Success.   4. Aristocracy.   5. Weighed and Wanting.   6. A Life Worth Living.

After the last guest had gone I heard the minister's wife say: "Well, my dear, you see it is possible to make a real success of a literary evening. I am going to have an evening of sonnets soon. I shall ask each guest to bring a favorite sonnet. A short paper on this form of verse might be read and then the sonnets. Let each guest be provided with ballots on which he can write the names of authors. The one who recognizes the largest number may have a prize, be allowed to write a sonnet or to designate his favorite among all that have been read and to tell why he prefers it."

"That sounds somewhat complicated and you would have to be pretty sure of your company," said the minister, "but since you have made such a success of this evening I will second you in any entertainment you may care to try."

"There is Helen Hunt Jackson, too," said the elated hostess. "How many of her poems would be delightful rendered in this way! Why, I shall wish to be entertaining intelligent people every week."

The busy mind went on planning long after her tired head had touched her pillow, yet the *motif* of all her planning was not mere social success but the spirit of that last read selection:

> If I can stop one heart from breaking,
>   I shall not live in vain.
> If I can ease one life the aching,
>   Or cool one pain,
> Or help one fainting robin
> Unto his nest again,
>   I shall not live in vain.

378 William Morton Payne. "Recent Books of Poetry." *Dial* 15 (July 16, 1893), 43. This review notices a collection of undergraduate verse from Iowa College, now Grinnell College, containing Mary Bowen's "To Emily Dickinson." For the first printing, see no. 371.

One does not expect very much from undergraduate college verse. "Under the Scarlet and Black" is perhaps deserving of a word of mention as the first book of verse that has yet hailed from a Western college, for the collection comes to us from Grinnell, Iowa. The honors of the volume are borne off by Miss Mary Bowen and Miss Bertha Booth (both of this year's class), and, after some hesitation, we select a piece by the former writer—a sonnet "To Emily Dickinson": [The text of the poem follows.]

379 "A Melancholy Fidelity." *New York Commercial Advertiser*, August 23, 1893, p. 5. This explanation for Dickinson's seclusion has no basis in fact; see *Life*, p. 418. Mrs. Bodman was born Grace Herbert Smith.

Emily Dickinson, the Amherst poet, was a woman of few friendships. The few with whom she was intimate seldom saw her, for when they called she invariably insisted upon their being seated in the hall while she conversed with them from over the bannister in the upper hall. It was her custom to correspond by writing with these friends, and her letters were marvels of poetic expression.

Emily Dickinson wore white at all times of the year. In pleasant weather she used to go walking in the garden and in the spacious grounds around her father's residence, and her companion out of doors was a large Newfoundland dog named Carlo. Mrs. Luther W. Bodman of Chicago recalls the time when, as a little girl, she went walking with Miss Dickinson while the huge dog stalked solemnly beside them. "Gracie," said Miss Dickinson, suddenly addressing her child friend, "do you know that I believe that the first to come and greet me when I go to heaven will be this dear, faithful old friend Carlo?"

It is said that Miss Dickinson's eccentricities resulted largely from disappointment in love. While she was still a girl she became deeply interested in a young man who was pursuing his studies in Amherst College. This young man subsequently became an instructor in the college. Mr. Edward Dickinson, Miss Emily's father, disapproved of the intimacy, which gave promise of ending in marriage, and at last (being a somewhat violent man) he preemptorily forbade the young man the house. It is said that at that time Miss Emily told her father that, as he had closed the doors upon her friend, so he had closed the doors upon her, and from that day she so seldom left the house—and, for that matter, so seldom left her room—that she was for thirty years practically as much a recluse as any nun doing penance.

It will be of interest to Chicago people to know that the man identified by Amherst gossips as the object of Emily Dickinson's hopeless yet loyal affection was the late George Howland.

380 Warwick James Price. "The Poetry of Emily Dickinson." *Yale Literary Magazine* 59 (October 1893), 25–27. For the Hamilton Aïdé comment on Dickinson, see no. 353. Other quotations are from Todd (no. 263) and Higginson (no. 10). Neither George William Curtis nor James Russell Lowell are known to have written on Dickinson. The latter died before her first book was issued. Curtis may be confused with Howells, whose review of Dickinson appeared in his "Editor's Study" column for *Harper's Monthly* (no. 64); Curtis contributed another well-known department for the magazine, "The Editor's Easy Chair."

It was John Ruskin who said, "No weight, nor mass, nor beauty of execution, can outweigh one grain or fragment of thought." And the alleged artificiality of modern life offers unconscious witness to this truth in the interest awakened during the past three or four years in the poetry of Emily Dickinson. It is a poetry that offers little or no opportunity for a false devotion; that affords no chance for worship such as has been paid the so-called impressionist school of art or the harmony of Wagnerian music,—which, at best, can be fully appreciated but by a chosen few. The poems to some, indeed, may be wanting in much that is suggestive of true poetry as that word is vulgarly understood, but the careful and sympathetic reader soon discovers the pearls of the writer's thought, though they be strung on pack thread between common beads.

Emily Dickinson, whom Hamilton Aïdé says "narrowly missed being the most distinguished poetess her country has yet produced," was born in Amherst on the twelfth of December, 1830, and died there in May, 1886. Her life was spent partially in study, largely among her only trusted friends—the sunsets, and breezes, the birds and flowers,—and entirely in seclusion. By habit and temperament she was a recluse, spending years of her life without setting foot beyond her father's doorstep, and many more during which the limits of her walks were the garden hedge and walls.

But though this mode of life led, as well it might, to a peculiar expression of her thought, we yet listen in vain for a note of complaint. Life and love was all very fair to her. Nature was her all, and if she "Looked through nature up to nature's God," with what our critic calls an "Emersonian self-possession," it was only because she looked upon everything with a clear-eyed frankness and candor as unprejudiced as it is rare. And this trait in her character stands out boldly in her writings. Every line was the mere expression of her own mind, and her sister, on going through her portfolio after her death, found not one poem bearing any evidence of having been produced with the thought of publication.

Writing in this way she entirely lost whatever advantage lies in public criticism and the more or less enforced conformity to accepted rules and ways, but there was gained a certain unrestrained freedom, an unconventional utterance of daring thought that causes us to praise the intrinsic beauty of her work, and overlook what it may lack of extrinsic beauty. This is the judgment of George William Curtis and Mr. Lowell. They see the vivid descriptive and imaginative power, the flashes of original and profound insight into nature and life, and they regret with us the sudden failing of the lyric strains that came upon us so unexpectedly. And this they do without remark on the rugged and even whimsical framework in which the work is set. "When a thought takes one's breath away, a lesson on grammar is an impertinence." Perhaps Miss Dickinson had some such thought in her mind when she wrote:

> The Pedigree of honey
> Does not concern the bee;
> A clover, anytime, to him
> Is aristocracy.

This quatrain is quite indicative of her quick perception and close observation when abroad. She noticed as much as did Thoreau with this difference, that Thoreau could never have expressed himself with the same felicity. Could Thoreau, for instance, have written of the grass like this:

> And stir all day to pretty tunes
>   The breezes fetch along,
> And hold the sunshine in its lap,
>   And bow to everything:
> And thread the dews all night, like pearls,
>   And make itself so fine;
> And even when it dies, to pass
>   To odors so divine;
> And then to dwell in sov'reign barns,
>   And dream the days away; —

Or could Thoreau have painted the sunset as it glows for us here upon the canvass of this obscure New England poetess:

> There seemed a purple stile
> Which little yellow boys and girls
> Were climbing all the while,
> Till when they reached the other side
> A Dominie in gray
> Put gently up the evening bars,
> And led the flock away.

Surely such sight as this is all too rare among our lesser poets. There is one more poem that demands notice. It has not inaptly been compared to Dr. Smith's "Ode to the Flowers," quoted in full by Longfellow in his *Outre Mer*. It is perhaps the loveliest bit in the portfolio, and surely a most characteristic utterance of one to whom "the coming of the first robin was a jubilee beyond crowning of monarch or birthday of pope; the first red leaf hurrying through 'the altered air' an epoch." She has called it

A SERVICE OF SONG.

Some keep the Sabbath going to church:
  I keep it staying at home
With a bobolink for a chorister,
  And an orchard for a dome.

Some keep the Sabbath in surplice:
  I just wear my wings,
And instead of tolling the bell for church,
  Our little sexton sings.

God preaches—a noted clergyman—
  And the sermon is never long;
So instead of getting to heaven at last,
  I'm going all along.

381 Richard Hovey. "The Technic of Rhyme." *Independent* 45 (October 19, 1893), 1399–1400.

4. Half-rhyme. I propose this name to distinguish rhyming by repetition of those sounds only which follow the accented vowels, the accented vowels themselves varying:

O pale, pale now those rosy lips
  I aft hae kissed sae *fondly!*
And closed for aye the sparkling glance
  That dwelt on me sae *kindly*—Burns

This has always been used to some extent by English poets, but has recently been brought somewhat prominently into notice by the poems of Emily Dickinson, in which it is used very frequently.

382 Edward E. Hale, Jr. "Mr. John Burroughs on Poe." *Dial* 15 (November 1, 1893), 254–55. This letter to the editor of the *Dial* is signed "State University of Iowa, Oct. 20, 1893." It refers to an article on Poe by John Burroughs in the *Dial* 15 (October 16, 1893), 214–15.

Without taking up the cudgels for Poe and trying to think of one real thing made more dear to us by his matchless rhyme, without depreciating our New England poets and hinting that it might have been yet better had they cared a little more for art, one may still feel that all is not for the best in the remarks of Mr. John Burroughs in your last number (unless, perhaps, we at once turn the page and consider some of the questions put by Mrs. Woolley toward the beginning of her communication). It is doubtless true that there are many with whom the purely art value, so-called, is the only thing to consider in a poem or a picture. But the number of such is, on the whole, small. It is quite right to say that with most readers this view is held less and less in sight. We in America, at least, need no incitement to value literature, or anything else, for its practical worth, or for what may seem such. If we need caution, it is on the other side. We do not need to be told that thought is important,—we know it is, and we are always on the lookout for it. But we do need to be told that art or style is of value too, for, as a rule, we are not so much on the lookout for that; or, if we are, we don't know it so well when we see it.

The more we are told by critics we honor (like Mr. John Burroughs) that thought is important and that art counts for less, the more do we fall into the error that thought is all-important and that art counts for nothing, — and then we have poems like Miss Emily Dickinson's, for example.

Now style, or form, or art, or whatever else one may call it, *is* important. And, more to the point, style is difficult. It is difficult to attain, and it is, on the whole, difficult to appreciate. That it is difficult to appreciate good style, may seem a hard saying; one may think that if a thing be done in the best way everybody will recognize it. It is not so. To appreciate style needs training. And this training we in America will not undergo, so long as we are told that art is unimportant.

One great use of the "full-blown professional literary critic" is that he is apt to insist on art for art's sake. And one great good thing in a poet like Poe is that he shows us what art for art's sake can do. There is small danger that we shall go too far with either. There are comparatively few so constituted by nature that they ever could enjoy art for art's sake if they wanted to. There is little danger that we shall go too far in that direction. The important thing is that we go at all. And go some way we must, or literature runs down-hill, and at the bottom we have a horde of writers with plenty of thought perhaps, with plenty of messages for their time, with plenty of feeling for life, and with the highest ethical or sociological aspirations, but no style at all—because they don't know what it is.

Especially here in the West do we need to be constantly reminded of the value of art, to be taught what is style, to be told even (though it isn't so) that form in art is everything. We are not likely to take it too much to heart, and we may learn something from it. I sometimes almost wish that Mr. Oscar Wilde would come out here again. He could hardly get us to be like Gilbert and Ernest and Cyril and Vivian, but he might perhaps prevent us from becoming what we are likely to become if we persist in binding it upon the tablets of our hearts that good poetry is *only* a criticism of life.

383 "Reviews." *Amherst Student* 27 (November 18, 1893), 71. The first printing in which the 1890 *Poems* and the 1891 *Poems, Second Series* were bound together as one volume was published in March 1893. Another printing of the combined edition appeared in May 1893, apparently the volume reviewed here.

The public first made the acquaintance of the late Emily Dickinson in 1890 and the present volume combines the first and second series of her poems. The author lived all her life in Amherst and died here in 1886. Living as she did the life of a recluse and publishing during her life not more than three or four pieces at most, her verse is the undisciplined expression of a strikingly original mind. The poems are very short as a rule, and differ much among themselves some being really musical, while more often they impress themselves chiefly as crisp and vigorous expressions of thought. As to subject they are classified under "Life," "Love," "Nature," and "Time and Eternity." The rare privilege is offered here of making the acquaintance of a true New England mind, unrestricted by formal rules in her verse, and giving imagination full rein. "After all" says Colonel Higginson in the short introduction "when a thought takes one's breath away, a lesson on grammar seems an impertinence." It will be noticed that Mrs. Todd is one of the editors.

384 Daniel Dulany Addison. *Lucy Larcom, Life, Letters, and Diary.* Boston: Houghton, 1894, p. 285. Excerpt from a Larcom letter to Miss Philena Fobes, dated March 14, 1893.

I have seen Emily Dickinson's poems, and enjoy their queer gleaming and shadowy incoherences. It does not seem as if her mind could have been fairly balanced. But her love of nature redeems many faults.

385 K[ate] D[ickinson] S[weetser]. "Emily Dickinson." *Magazine of Poetry* 6 (February 1894), 108, 111. The author is the poet's second cousin. Her biographical note accompanies six Dickinson poems: "If you were coming in the fall," "One dignity delays for all—," "Success is counted sweetest," "Some keep the Sabbath going to church—," "The Soul selects her own society—," and "Belshazzar had a letter—."

Emily Dickinson was born in Amherst, Mass., December 10th, 1830. She was the daughter of Hon. Edward Dickinson, the leading lawyer of that town, as well as treasurer of the college there situated. From her earliest recollections, Miss Dickinson was brought into contact with the most cultured and distinguished society which her native town afforded, and had she so chosen, she might have been the center of a brilliant circle. Mr. Higginson, in his preface to her first volume of poems, says that, although he corresponded with her for years, he saw her but twice face to face, and his was the general experience, for as a poet she recoiled from notice even more than as a woman, and it was with great difficulty that she was persuaded during her lifetime to publish some three or four poems. She was devoted to her father, and once a year, when he gave a reception to the faculty of the college and to the prominent townspeople, she would emerge from her retirement and act the part of hostess as graciously as if it were her daily wont. She was a fine looking woman, and in one of her letters characterized herself as having eyes and hair the color of the dregs in a sherry glass, and after the death of her father it was her custom to dress always in white. She died May 15th, 1886, in the town where she was born, and from which she had been so few times into the outer world. In her room, where she had spent so many secluded hours, were found the manuscripts which have revealed to the world the great heart, the artist soul and the creative mind which made up the sum of her existence and supplied her with a thought-life so rich that it needed little nourishment from outer vitality. Even the one who knew her best, the poet H. H., had no idea of the fertility of her friend's brain nor of the greatness which had so tardy recognition. Technically considered, her work is crude and faulty, if judged by the rigid standards of rhythm and polish to which genius at large is subjected but there is a wildness in her poems, a vividness of imagery, an exultation of free thought which belong alone to a mind in truest communion with nature, untrammeled by the artificial or the conventional. To bring such work to judgment before the merciless critic of form and meter is not only unjust, but is certain death to its greatest charm. Two volumes of the poems have already been published, attracting widespread acknowledgment of her genius, and her letters, which were rich in thought and fancy, are soon to appear.

386 [Thomas Wentworth Higginson.] "Recent Poetry." *Nation* 58 (June 7, 1894), 433. The "blue jay" poem is "No Brigadier throughout the year."

Mr. Hamlin Garland's "Prairie Songs" must carry a little disappointment to those who were struck with the fresh vigor and strong local coloring of his "Main-travelled Roads," and who regret that he — like all the type he represents, like Bret Harte and Joaquin Miller, for instance — apparently made his best mark at first, and shows no power of growth. These poems are full of valuable material, they carry the very flavor of the upturned furrow; yet the trace of Whitman and Miller is on them all, they are often strained and turgid and, so to speak, over-dressed. It is little that Mr. Garland says "fartherest" (p. 163), and says of the snow, "I saw it lay" (p. 162). These things are trifles — Emily Dickinson took far greater liberties with the Queen's or the President's English; but compare her poem on the "Blue Jay" with Mr. Garland's and see which has the vigor and the grip. Mr. Garland even insults this bit of pure American life by one of the worst of Whitmanisms, the interlarding of foreign words, and calls the jay an "emigre," without an accent — whatever that may mean.

387 "Literary Notes." *Independent* 46 (June 14, 1894), 771. Reprinted: *Philadelphia Call*, July 31, 1894, p. 4. These sales figures were later revised downward; see no. 535.

Twelve thousand copies of the first volume of Miss Emily Dickinson's poems have been issued and seven thousand of the second volume. A collection of her letters will soon appear, edited by her friend, Mrs. David P. Todd, of Amherst.

388 "Literary Notes." *Philadelphia Call*, July 31, 1894, p. 4. A reprinting; see preceding entry.

389 M[ark] A[ntony] de Wolfe Howe, Jr. "Literary Affairs in Boston." *Book Buyer* 11 (September 1894), 378.

The regular processes of biography are working themselves out manifestly in more than one instance hereabouts. So many New Englanders worthy of biographies have died within the last few years, that there has been every opportunity to see what happens. First there are the newspaper obituaries, then the magazine articles, then small sporadic books of reminiscence, and finally the authoritative Life and Letters. It is a natural sequence, a sort of evolution in which the number of possible readers survives in the diminishing manner of the fittest. The crowd cannot escape the newspaper eulogies; only the few care and seek seriously for the Life and Letters.

It is not, however, in accordance with this process that the letters of Emily Dickinson are approaching readiness for publication by Roberts Brothers in the autumn.

Miss Dickinson apparently had very few points of resemblance with other people in most respects. There could not, in any event, have been great commotion in the periodical press about the death of a poetess who was not publicly known to have written at all. After the appearance of the first volume of her poems, a magazine did print her correspondence with Mr. Higginson concerning her writings. Aside from this, little has been given out to throw light upon one of the strangest personalities of our time. Nevertheless there must be a large class of readers whose interest in the poems has been seasoned with a natural curiosity concerning the writer. The letters range from 1847 to 1886, and are addressed to various friends. Many bits of verse are interspersed. How much these looked like prose, in the queer half-printed script she often used, all who have seen her manuscript know. For those who have not seen it, facsimiles of the handwriting at three periods are reproduced; and there is one picture of Miss Dickinson herself, and one of her father's house.

390 "Notes in Season." *Publishers' Weekly* 46 (September 1, 1894), 271. For similar routine publication announcements of the *Letters,* see no. 402. This notice was premature, for the *Letters* were not published until November 15. An advertisement for the *Letters* appeared on the facing page.

They [Roberts Brothers] have also just ready "Emily Dickinson's Letters, 1847–1886," edited by Mabel Loomis Todd, with portrait, view of Miss Dickinson's home in Amherst, and three fac-similes of her handwriting; . . .

391 Ellen E. Dickinson. "Emily Dickinson." *Boston Evening Transcript,* September 28, 1894, p. 4. Reprinted: *Chicago Inter-Ocean,* December 1, 1894, p. 16. For other reminiscences by this author, see nos. 360 and 495. When Mrs. Dickinson speaks in paragraph eight of "a lady recently introduced in the family by marriage" she refers to herself. Next to this clipping in Todd's scrapbook is the pencilled note: "She has no right to use Emily's name, with her face black with hatred." Also, "Vinnie'd have killed her, she nearly did in words." These reactions are explained in *AB,* pp. 262–66.

There is so much interest and admiration expressed at the present time for the verses of Emily Dickinson, that something of her life, and environments from one who was familiarly acquainted with her may prove acceptable to general readers. It was understood for years before her death that she wrote verses, that she was a poetess, but had a sensitiveness as to their being read, although her "Effusions" were her companions, and secret delight, through many seasons.

She was best known as a brilliant conversationalist, with a keen sense of humor and of the ridiculous; could tell an anecdote with rare appreciation of its wit in the drollest manner while preserving a perfect serenity of countenance. Indeed her fund of good stories seemed almost inexhaustible. Her home in Amherst, Mass., is a large, old-fashioned residence of generous proportions, of brick, painted white with green blinds, which has not been modernized, but kept in excellent repair. There is a conservatory, or greenhouse, a cupola, and side piazzas, with a lawn dotted with umbrageous trees, and it is altogether an attractive habitation. On one side of the lawn is a large garden, a perfect wilderness of flowers which Emily Dickinson loved, and where she passed much of her time during the summer. Flowers were sentiment to her; they seemed to spring up and blossom at her touch. Here in this lovely old garden she noted every change of nature, and all were beautiful to her; the springtime with its opening buds and leaves, the rich fullness of summer, and the autumnal decay and death of her favorites. She had a passion, too, for wild flowers, and yearly greeted the trailing arbutus when it was brought to her each spring from the neighboring woods with renewed admiration.

The passing vaporous silvery clouds, the brilliant sunshine, the harbingers of storm, the songs of birds, the drone of bees, the flitting of butterflies, all, all, had a loveliness and voice of their own to her which she expressed in the seclusion of her chamber on hundreds of virginal sheets of paper, which are now a record and a heritage to her relatives, and the world at large. And there were many questionings of her heart, and intelligence, which she expressed in no other way, that were doubtless never answered.

It is evident that Miss Dickinson was born with a decided poetical gift, which time and circumstance developed. It is also evident from her poems that a keen and bitter disappointment led her to give the language of her heart in verse. Her poem called "Renunciation" tells its own story.

Her father, the Hon. Edward Dickinson, was in Congress while Emily was a young girl. It is said that she was greatly admired in Washington society for her brilliant talk, quick repartee and exceptional culture. After one or two seasons of this kind of life she returned to Amherst to become a recluse, rarely seeing anyone beyond her immediate family circle, and wearing blue and white garments through the entire year.

At long intervals she emerged from this exclusion to grace the yearly reception given by her family to the faculty and students of Amherst College (her father being the time-honored treasurer) and to the most distinguished residents of the town and its vicinity. Then, she resumed her society manners, and flashed some conversational gem that her hearers were wont to remember and repeat.

While she was witty, she never seemed to have the slightest *malice prepense.* She had "the charm," as the French call it, without being pretty. Her abundant hair was of Venetian red in color, her eyes were light blue, and prominent, her complexion fair. Her hands were beautiful, and she had a way of using them that was very graceful, and she could make anyone love her whom she chose to honor in that way. Music of the better class was an enchantment to her, particularly the human voice, which she listened to in a kind of rapture and revery, forgetting all outward circumstance of time and place.

For thirty odd years Emily Dickinson never left her home and its surroundings, but her gifted friends occasionally sought her there, and whom she received with appreciative pleasure. Of them was Mr. Emerson, Mr. Whittier, Dr. J. G. Holland, Helen Hunt and Colonel Thomas Wentworth Higginson. Thoreau was naturally one of her favorite authors from his love of nature and power of description in that direction. On one occasion when a lady recently introduced in the family by marriage quoted some sentence from Thoreau's writings, Miss Dickinson recognizing it, hastened to press her visitor's hand as she said, "From this time we are acquainted;" and this was the beginning of a friendship that lasted till the death of the poetess.

With all her mental gifts Emily Dickinson was a past mistress in the art of cookery and housekeeping. She made the desserts for the household dinners; delicious confections and bread, and when engaged in these duties had her table and pastry board under a window that faced the lawn, whereon she ever had pencil and paper to jot down any pretty thought that came to her, and from which she evolved verses later. On some such occasion a little green snake made its way through the grass toward the window, which circumstance she commemorated in verse. Her large yellow pet cat lost its long fluffy tail by some accident, which she sent in playful humor by express to the present scribe. There was a pink ribbon tied round this disconnected appendage, with a verse accompanying it that unfortunately is lost.

Her letters like her verses were fragmentary, composed of sentences which had no relative connection; touches of wit, or keen observation, or pathos; and her chirography was peculiar and difficult to read. A volume of her letters written to various friends who have given them to the public, are soon to be published, edited by Mrs. Todd of Amherst.

It is questionable whether Emily Dickinson ever wrote verses or letters supposing they would be printed after her death. She certainly gave no evidence during her life of a desire to have her writings published, refusing when urged to send her verses to different publications. Still she did not destroy them, and it can fairly be supposed that she anticipated her family might give them to the world. There are still sufficient poems unpublished of her writing to fill several volumes of the size already printed.

Of the various criticisms on this author's productions, none seem quite appropriate or just. If her poems are "unfinished" and "devoid of metrical measure," they are unique in their freshness and beauty. If not a positive genius, she approached it, was most unusual in thought and expression, in brief but exquisite songs that thrill the heart with a sensitive longing for further trials of her skill in elusive, tender, dramatic and pathetic verses.

392 "Announcements." *Brookline* [Mass.] *Library Bulletin* 1 (October 1894), 2.

Modern poetry has many readers. In five months Eugene Field (one book) circulated 15 times; J. W. Riley, 15; Emily Dickinson, 17; Francis Thompson, 7.

393 M[ark] A[ntony] de Wolfe Howe, Jr. "Literary Affairs in Boston." *Book Buyer* 11 (October 1894), 425. Howe's previous notice is no. 389. Dickinson sent the holograph of the poem reproduced here to Mrs. Jonathan F. Jenkins, mother of MacGregor Jenkins; see no. 249.

A month ago there was news to tell of the impending publication of Miss Emily Dickinson's letters. Since then it has been my good fortune to look over a number of manuscript letters and bits of verse sent from time to time by her to a family of intimate friends, and one of the little poems, of a characteristic, indefinable charm, I am permitted to send to the *Book Buyer*. It has never been printed before; yet all of its quaintness cannot vanish when it is taken out of the strange script in which it was put upon paper:

> They might not need me—yet they might;
> I'll let my heart be just in sight.
> A smile so small as mine might be
> Precisely their necessity.

394 *Worcester* [Mass.] *Spy*, ca. October 1894. Unlocated. Attributed to the *Spy* by hand in Todd's scrapbook.

Among the fall publications of Messrs. Roberts Bros. are the letters of Emily Dickinson, a treat to those who have already been attracted by the unusual personality which so thoroughly pervades her published poems.

395 G. "A Connecticut Valley Poet." *Springfield* [Mass.] *Homestead* 16 (October 6, 1894), 11. Allusion is made here to a hostile English critic (quoted by Aldrich, no. 325), the poem "Success is counted sweetest" published in *A Masque of Poets* (Boston: Roberts Brothers, 1878), and Higginson's *Atlantic* article on his acquaintance with Dickinson (no. 221).

In 1891, unheralded and unanticipated, a little volume of poems was given to the public with a name on the title page which it had never heard before. The name was Emily Dickinson and the poems were unlike those of any other singer. They were merely snatches, quaintly punctuated, often imperfect as to rhythm or rhyme, wholly unconventional; they were peeps at nature and love and life such as might have come from a stranger to this planet who was wholly unused to the things of earth. An English critic told us on their appearance that Emily Dickinson might have become a fifth-rate poet if she had only mastered the rudiments of grammar and gone into metrical training for about 15 years. If she had undergone his austere curriculum, one of the rarest poets of the century would have been lost to us. She sung as the birds do, without the training of art, and many of her odd snatches of music in words rank with the swallow-flight in Heine's lyrical intermezzo. There is something in her poems which cannot be found in the mechanical productions of mere verse-makers and as Thomas Wentworth Higginson says in his introduction to her little volume, "Her poetry contains flashes of wholly original and profound insight into nature and life, words and phrases exhibiting an extraordinary vividness of descriptive and imaginative power, yet often set in a seemingly whimsical or even rugged frame."

It is said that a true poet sings for his own pleasure, and if that is so, then Emily Dickinson was one of the very few, for only one or two of her verses were given to the public until after her death, and these few were published anonymously.

She was born in Amherst, Mass., in 1830, and died there in 1886, after having passed the life of a perfect recluse. For years she never set her foot over the doorstep of her father's home and made very few acquaintances, living so that the people in the quiet college town almost forgot her existence. There is no hint of what turned her life in upon itself and probably this was its natural evolution or involution from tendencies inherent in the New England or the Puritan spirit.

One of her few friends was Helen Hunt Jackson through whose persuasion Miss Dickinson's first poem was published in a little volume of anonymous verse called *A Masque of Poets.* Another of her friends was Thomas Wentworth Higginson to whom she sent a bit of verse in 1862 asking for his frank criticism of it. He confesses his bewilderment over such rare thought so rarely set in words and speaks of it as the impression of a wholly new and original poetic genius. Her letters to Mr. Higginson are almost as quaint as her poetry and although her correspondents were few, it is with the most eager anticipation that the reading public is awaiting a little volume which will soon be issued of her letters. Here is a quotation from one of them when Mr. Higginson asked for a portrait of her: "I have no portrait, now, but am small like the wren; and my hair is bold like the chestnut burr, my eyes like the sherry in the glass that the guest leaves. Would this do just as well? It often alarms father. He says death might occur and he has molds of all the rest but has no mold of me; but I noticed the quick wore off these things in a few days and forestall the dishonor. You will think no caprice of me."

Here is what Mr. Higginson himself says about her: "At last, one August day in 1870, I found myself face to face with my hitherto unseen correspondent. It was at her father's house, one of those large, square brick mansions so familiar in old New England towns, surrounded by trees and blossoming shrubs, without and within exquisitely neat, cool, spacious and fragrant with flowers. After a little delay I heard an extremely faint and pattering footstep like that of a child and in glided almost noiselessly a plain, shy, little person, the face without a single good feature, but with eyes as she herself said 'like the sherry the guest leaves in the glass' and with smooth bands of reddish chestnut hair. She had a quaint and nunlike look as if she might be a German canoness of some religious order, whose prescribed garb was white pique with a blue net worsted shawl. She came toward me with two day lilies which she put in a childlike way into my hand,

saying softly under her breath, 'These are my introduction,' and adding in childlike fashion, 'Forgive me if I am frightened; I never see strangers and hardly know
what to say.' But soon she began to talk and thenceforward continued almost
constantly."

From 1862 till her death Mr. Higginson was one of her few and steady correspondents and probably her letters to him, with the bits of verse she frequently
sent him, will constitute the bulk of the little volume which will tell in her own
quaint phraseology nearly all that the world will learn of her secluded life. The
story of the poet would be incomplete without adding a few bits of her verse, so
here are some of them. They are all only snatches of song, but in their brevity is
their chief charm, for the thought is indelibly impressed on the reader's mind.
Who could forget this?

> The pedigree of honey
>   Does not concern the bee.
> The clover any time to him
>   Is aristocracy.

In the following poem she shows us that there was no loneliness in her
seclusion:

> Some keep the Sabbath going to church,
>   I keep it staying at home,
> With a bobolink for a chorister
>   And an orchard for a dome.
>
> Some keep the Sabbath in surplice,
>   I just wear my wings,
> And instead of tolling the bell for church
>   Our little sexton sings.
>
> God preaches—a noted clergyman,
>   And the sermon is never long,
> So instead of getting to heaven at last,
>   I'm going all along.

From no one but a descendant of an austere Puritan family such as the Dickinsons were could have come this picture of after death:

> The bustle in a house,
>   The morning after death,
> Is solemnest of industries
>   Enacted upon earth.
>
> The sweeping up the heart
>   And putting love away,
> We shall not want to use again
>   Until eternity.

Readers of The Homestead are not unacquainted with the name of Martha G.
Dickinson, who is a niece of the departed poetess. Her pleasant bits of verse,
which appear frequently in our pages, are often remindful in movement and
thought of the quaintly worded song which greets us in the pages of Emily Dickinson's little volume.

396 "Notes." *Nation* 59 (October 11, 1894), 269.

Roberts Bros. have in hand Prof. Adolf Harnack's "History of Dogma"; the third and fourth volume of Renan's "History of the People of Israel"; the "Letters of Emily Dickinson," 1847 to 1886, edited by Mrs. Mabel Loomis Todd; "Stars and Telescopes," by Prof. David P. Todd and William Lynn; "The Minor Tactics of Chess," by Franklin K. Young and Edwin C. Howell; and Paul Bourget's "A Saint," translated by Miss Wormeley.

397 "Local News." *Amherst Record*, October 24, 1894, p. 4.

Roberts Bros. of Boston will soon issue the "Letters of Emily Dickinson—1847 to 1886," edited by Mrs. Mabel Loomis Todd.

398 [Mark Antony de Wolfe Howe, Jr.] "Emily Dickinson's Letters." *Book Buyer*, n.s. II (November 1894), 485–86. Though this notice is unsigned, the likely author is Howe; see nos. 389, 393. The essay is accompanied by the frontispiece illustrations from the two *Letters* volumes: a retouched photograph of the Bullard oil painting of the poet as a child and a photograph of the Dickinson homestead.

That passionate, tender spirit which was content to expend its great wealth upon a few chosen friends and a more catholic circle of inanimate loves of the woods, fields and gardens, is reflected in all its narrow beauty in the *Letters of Emily Dickinson*. Ethereal in life, just as her poems are, these *Letters* must, in a certain way, be a disappointment to those who were expecting to find in them the tangible solution of her many mysteries. The young girl who had said, "It makes me shiver to hear a great many people talk—they take all the clothes off their souls," would not be likely to reveal to another her own inner life. Most of her letters are strangely impersonal, coming from a recluse whose solitude must largely have been spent in introspection; and yet, while they contain so little of self, they contain still less of the affairs of the great world outside of her home. Indeed, had not one of her Amherst friends been killed in the war, no reader would have learned from her that the rebellion had been raging three years. "My business is love," she writes with very truth. "I found a bird this morning, down—down on a little bush at the foot of the garden. And wherefore sing, I said, since nobody hears? One sob in the throat, one flutter of bosom—'My business is to sing'—and away she rose! How do I know but cherubim, once themselves as patient, listened and applauded her unnoticed hymn?" Why, it might be asked, with the same answer as applicable to her, was she constantly writing verses, jotting down evanescent flashes of thought on margins of newspapers, backs of envelopes or other scraps of paper, tucking the songs secretly away, to be discovered only after her death? Many of the verses which formed parts of letters, having been published in the collection of her poems, have been omitted here, with loss both to the poems and the letters, we believe.

This soulful woman, with her stern self-repression, often suggesting her English namesake, Emily Brontë, possessed, like her, an intensity of love for Nature in her larger aspects as well as her lowliest individual forms, which sometimes seemed to constitute for these two ardent souls the whole world. The events of the day, with Emily Dickinson, were the blooming of a violet, the screeching of some bluejays, or the purpling of the lovely hills about her home in the evening twilight.

How intensely she loved her few friends can only be imagined after reading these impassioned letters written to Dr. and Mrs. Holland, Mr. and Mrs. Samuel

Bowles, her brother Austin, Mrs. Gordon L. Ford and a few others, breathing out lyrical projectiles, in the midst of her prose stanzas, when the thought seemed best suited to verse. In spite of her seclusion, it would often seem that she was longing for poetic appreciation and sympathy—a longing which if felt was suppressed, with many another ungratified desire. Although an undercurrent of sadness thus flows through her life, there nevertheless ripples along quite merrily a sparkling humor, original, as everything she said was sure to be, and quite incompatible with one's preconceived ideas of this spirituelle recluse. "Mrs. ___ gets bigger and rolls down to church like a reverend marble," she writes in one of those charmingly natural, spontaneous letters to her young cousins, which perhaps, more than any others, reveal most of that elusive personality—her real self. If these volumes were to be read simply for the disclosure of her inner life, too sacredly enshrined for even these friends of her lonely soul to gaze upon, they would be a disappointment indeed. Happily, the letters are, for the most part, so refreshingly original and quaint, that while they do dimly shadow forth the isolated individuality of a most interesting woman, they can and will be enjoyed for themselves alone.

399 Unidentified clipping, ca. November 1894. This item is placed among notices dated early in the month in Todd's scrapbook.

Among the volume of letters promised for the coming season are those which contain the epistles of two singular New-Englanders—a man and a woman who were alike in their unlikeness to the rest of the world. The letters of Emily Dickinson are in the press of Roberts Brothers; and Houghton, Mifflin & Co. are bringing out the newly collected familiar letters of Thoreau. These show the hermit of Walden in a homely, kindly and practical light, having very little of the recluse spirit in their pleasant pages. The volume devoted to Miss Dickinson will contain her portrait.

400 Unidentified clipping, ca. November 1894. This item is placed among notices dated early in the month in Todd's scrapbook.

Mrs. Todd, who, with Thomas Wentworth Higginson, edited and published the two volumes of Emily Dickinson's poems, is collecting her letters for the same purpose. These will be most entertaining reading, as her friends say that her individuality and originality are even more pronounced in her prose than in her verse. It is interesting to learn that Miss Dickinson, with all her remarkable intellectual gifts, was also very practical, having been especially skilled in the art of cooking.

401 "Notes." *Nation* 59 (November 1, 1894), 325–26.

Roberts Bros., Boston, will publish November 10 two volumes of Emily Dickinson's *Letters*, edited by Mrs. David P. Todd of Amherst. They comprise all the prose Emily Dickinson is known to have written, and among the well-known persons to whom they are addressed are Col. Higginson, Dr. J. G. Holland, Helen Hunt, Samuel Bowles, and others. The popularity of Miss Dickinson's *Poems*, of which two volumes have so far been published, the first in 1890 and the second in 1891, has been remarkable, more than 12,000 copies having been sold.

402 "Notes in Season." *Publishers' Weekly* 46 (November 3, 1894), 671. [Routine publication announcements similar to this one were carried by newspapers and periodicals across the country. Todd's scrapbooks contain about a dozen of these for the *Letters,* many identical in wording. They are: *Public Opinion,* Nov. 8; *Springfield Republican,* Nov. 10; *Boston Times,* Nov. 11; *Commonwealth,* Nov. 17; *New York Sun,* Nov. 24; *Literary Era,* Dec.; *Chicago Tribune,* Dec. 1; *New York Evening Post,* Dec. 8, 1894. Four are illegible as to source, dated Nov. 9, Nov. 10, Nov. 17, and Nov. 28.]

Roberts Brothers will have ready November 15 "Emily Dickinson's Letters from 1847 to 1886," edited by Mabel Loomis Todd, with a portrait of Miss Dickinson, a view of her home in Amherst, and three fac-similes of her handwriting at different periods of her life; . . .

403 "Literary Notes." *Boston Beacon* 11 (November 10, 1894), 3.

The "Letters of Emily Dickinson," edited by Mrs. Mabel Loomis Todd of Amherst, will be issued in a few days by Roberts Brothers. The labor of preparing them has been very great, and far beyond that usually involved in such work, for none except the very earliest were dated by Emily Dickinson herself, and their chronological succession has been established only by noting the changes in style and handwriting, the postage stamps and postmarks, and by carefully searching out the times when events mentioned in the letters actually occurred. They will fill nearly five hundred pages, and are divided into two volumes, embellished by several fac-similes of the author's strange chirography.

404 "Literary Notes." *Brooklyn Standard Union,* November 10, 1894, p. 5.
A. L. Bridgman, editor of the paper, wrote to "Prof. Todd," Nov. 9, 1894, "I am very glad to publish in the *Standard Union,* to-morrow, your paragraph concerning the 'Dickinson Letters,' . . ." His letter went on to request a review copy. Whether this publication announcement was written by the person addressed in the letter, David Peck Todd, or by his wife, is uncertain. [Letter courtesy of Amherst College Library, ms. To 525].

Emily Dickinson's "Letters," arranged and edited by Mrs. David P. Todd of Amherst, will be published next week in two volumes by Roberts Brothers of Boston, who, three years ago, brought out the volumes of the same author's "Poems," which have met with such extraordinary popularity. Emily Dickinson's "Letters," almost as much as the "Poems," exhibit her elf-like intimacy with Nature; and these volumes are decorated with the design of Indian pipes, the weird flowers of abode and silence, which Mrs. Todd has chosen with peculiar fitness as emblematic of this strange recluse who, for fifteen years, never ventured beyond the door of her father's house.

405 "Notes and News." *Woman's Journal* 25 (November 10, 1894), 357.

Roberts Brothers announce for publication November 15, 1894, *Emily Dickinson's Letters,* edited by Mabel Loomis Todd, with her portrait as a child, and a view of her home in Amherst, and three fac-similes of her handwriting at different periods of her life. . . . Emily Dickinson, it seems, was a constant and voluminous letter-writer; for since the wide popularity of her strange poems, her friends have been anxious to see some of her prose also in print, and letters written between 1845 and 1886 have been collected and arranged by Mrs. Mabel Loomis

Todd, of Amherst, one of the editors of her poems. They will be issued in two volumes by Roberts Brothers on Nov. 15, and the literary public may be sure of a distinctly new sensation. From the girlish letters dated at Mount Holyoke Seminary in its early days, and full of allusions to Miss Lyon, to the epigrammatic sentences comprising her latest notes, Emily Dickinson's own flashing touch is evident. They are written to Colonel Higginson, Mr. Samuel Bowles, Dr. J. G. Holland, "H. H." and other well-known persons.

406 Unidentified newspaper clipping dated by hand November 10 [1894] in Mrs. Todd's scrapbook.

Mrs. David P. Todd of Amherst finished editing Emily Dickinson's "Letters" last month. They will be issued in two volumes by Roberts Brothers next week, embellished not only with several fac-similes of her unique handwriting, but with a print of the old homestead, where Emily Dickinson lived the close life of a recluse for many years, with a reproduction of a portrait as a child, the only one ever taken of this author.

407 "Out and About." *Boston Saturday Evening Gazette* 82 (November 11, 1894), [3].

A reproduction of an old oil portrait of Emily Dickinson, painted in 1838, when she was but a child, will form the frontispiece of the first volume of her "Letters," collected and edited by Mrs. David P. Todd, of Amherst, to be issued by Roberts Brothers, on November 15. This child portrait, originally in a group with her brother and sister, is the only one known to exist of this rare and recluse woman, as she had an unconquerable aversion to seeing herself reproduced in any sort of "mould." The letters are sparkling and original, and can hardly fail to make a sensation as unique as that of her posthumously published "Poems."

408 "Literary Notes." *Christian Register* 73 (November 15, 1894), 751.

"Emily Dickinson's Letters" will be issued November 15 by Roberts Brothers. They are edited by Mrs. Mabel Loomis Todd of Amherst; and they present more completely than anything else has ever done, a picture of the singular life of this gifted recluse. To her solitude was necessary for best thought, and her isolated years were fullest of mental fruitage. Her airy and playful outlook upon the humorous side of life is in curious contrast to her deep, underlying pathos. Together, they make these letters one of the most fascinating books to appear since the sensational revelations of Marie Bashkirtseff.

409 "Literary Items." *Boston Evening Transcript,* November 16, 1894, p. 6. The *Transcript* for the next day carried on p. 6 a Roberts' Brothers advertisement announcing the *Letters* as "out today."

Emily Dickinson's *Letters,* edited by Mrs. David P. Todd of Amherst, appear today. The lovers of the poems of this gifted recluse will find no disappointment in her prose, which continually bubbles over with the dainty humor of her daily life. The letters, no less than the poems, exhibit Emily Dickinson's elf-like intimacy with nature; they speak of pines, of flowers, and autumnal colors, while no sight or sound or incident of nature seems to have eluded her delicate apprehension. The Letters are addressed to Colonel Higginson, Dr. J. G. Holland, Mr.

Samuel Bowles, "H. H.," and many other friends, and the volumes are embellished with a child portrait of Emily Dickinson, fac-similes of her unique handwriting, and a print of the old family mansion.

410 "Book Lore." *Boston Traveller*, November 17, 1894, p. 5.

Roberts Brothers announce a volume of Emily Dickinson's *Letters*, edited by Mabel Loomis Todd, whose appreciative preface contains this characterization: "Emily Dickinson's letters, almost as much as the poems, exhibit her elf-like intimacy with Nature. She sees and apprehends the great mother's processes, and shares the rapture of all created things under the wide sky. The letters speak of flowers, of pines, and autumnal colors; but no natural sight or sound or incident seems to have escaped her delicate apprehension. Bird songs, crickets, frost, and winter winds, even the toad and snake, mushrooms and bats, have an indescribable charm for her, which she in turn brings to us. March, 'that month of proclamation,' was especially dear; and among her still unpublished verses is a characteristic greeting to the windy month. In all its aspects 'Nature' became the unique charm and consolation of her life, and as such she has written of it."

411 "Notes." *Critic*, n.s. 22 (November 17, 1894), 338.

The lovers of Emily Dickinson's poems have been so eager to see some of her prose that a collection of her letters has been made, dating from 1845, when she was but fourteen years old, to 1886, a few days before her death. They have been carefully arranged and edited by Mrs. Mabel Loomis Todd of Amherst, and are issued by Messrs. Roberts Bros. this week. The letters are said to be "even more piquant, brilliant and characteristic than the poems." Many of them are addressed to a number of well-known persons.

412 "Notes." *Literary Digest* 10 (November 17, 1894), 73.

Those who remember the unusual, even startling, but thoroughly fascinating character of Emily Dickinson's letters to Colonel Higginson, published in the *Atlantic Monthly* for October, 1891, will be gratified to learn that all her other available letters are now collected and edited by Mrs. Mabel Loomis Todd, of Amherst. They will be published in two handsome volumes by Roberts Brothers, of Boston, on November 15, the letters to Colonel Higginson forming one of the ten chapters. Beginning in 1845, when Emily Dickinson had but recently passed her fourteenth birthday, the letters fill all the intervening years until her death in 1886, and were written to Samuel Bowles, Dr. J. G. Holland, "H. H.," and other persons of distinction.

413 "News and Notes." *Literary World* 25 (November 17, 1894), 396. Reprinted: *Chicago Tribune*, Dec. 1, 1894.

Messrs. Roberts Brothers published November 15 Emily Dickinson's *Letters*, edited by Mrs. Mabel Loomis Todd, who has so arranged the letters that the growth in style and individuality forms an interesting study; . . .

414 "Literary Notes." *Outlook* 50 (November 17, 1894), 809. The friend is probably Mrs. Todd, as Lawrence Abbott of the *Outlook*, in a letter to

Prof. Todd Nov. 7, 1894, thanks him for information about the forthcoming *Letters*. [Letter courtesy of Amherst College Library, ms. To 369-1].

"Emily Dickinson's Letters," edited by Mrs. Mabel Loomis Todd, of Amherst, are announced for publication by Messrs. Roberts Brothers, of Boston, this week. Even more than her unique poems published three years ago, they exhibit, writes a friend, her sense of nearness to the great Father whom she knew with such directness.

415 "Literary Notes." *Philadelphia Press*, November 17, 1894, p. 11.

The letters of Emily Dickinson, to be issued November 15, by Roberts Bros., of Boston, are no less startling and fascinating than the famous journals of Marie Bashkirtseff. They give a connected picture of the recluse life of this remarkable woman whose poems made so profound a sensation in 1890 and 1891. Yet the sanctities are not invaded, and one cannot but think she would be gratified at this loving collection and arrangement of her unique prose by the hand of her friend, Mrs. Mabel Loomis Todd, of Amherst, Mass.

416 "Other Holiday Gift-Books." *Publishers' Weekly* 46 (double "Christmas Bookshelf" issue, November 17 and 24, 1894), 76. The 1840 portrait of ED as a child by Otis Bullard, reproduced from the *Letters*, appears on p. 79.

The two volumes of "Emily Dickinson's Poems," edited by T. W. Higginson and Mabel Loomis Todd, are now bound in one attractive volume, and quite new and sure of ready purchasers are "The Letters of Emily Dickinson" from 1847–1886 in two volumes, also edited by Mrs. Todd.

417 "Literary Matters." *Springfield* [Mass.] *Homestead*, November 17, 1894, p. 8.

The lovers of Emily Dickinson's poems have, for two or three years, been eager to see some of her prose writing given to the public. The remarkable success and appreciation with which the poems were greeted seemed to make this more desirable; and as she kept no journals or diaries all the prose she is known to have written is contained in the letters she constantly sent her friends. Mrs. Mabel Loomis Todd has collected and edited over 500 of these letters, covering a period between 1845 and 1886, and they will be issued shortly by Roberts Brothers of Boston. The scattered bits of her verse inclosed in these letters add greatly to their charm, and the public may be sure of a new literary sensation in these brilliant volumes. Emily Dickinson's sense of humor and flashing wit are nowhere seen to better advantage than in her letters, while her deep sense of life's pathos adds a note to which every true nature must respond. Nothing more individual and even startling has been published since the singular revelations of Marie Bashkirtseff.

418 Mabel Loomis Todd. "Introductory" to *Letters of Emily Dickinson*, edited by Mabel Loomis Todd. 2 vols. Boston: Roberts Brothers, 1894, pp. [v]–xii. Published November 21, 1894. Some copies appeared with the variant first sentence, "The lovers of Emily Dickinson's poems have been so eager for her prose that her sister has gathered these letters, and committed their preparation to me" [see *AB*, 304–05 and *DB*, 36–37]. See next entry for other material by Mrs. Todd in this volume. Dickinson's poem of "greeting to the windy month" (mentioned below) is "Dear March, come in."

The lovers of Emily Dickinson's poems have been so eager for her prose that her sister asked me to prepare these volumes of her letters.

Emily Dickinson's verses, often but the reflection of a passing mood, do not always completely represent herself, — rarely, indeed, showing the dainty humor, the frolicsome gaiety, which continually bubbled over in her daily life. The somber and even weird outlook upon this world and the next, characteristic of many of the poems, was by no means a prevailing condition of mind; for, while fully apprehending all the tragic elements in life, enthusiasm and bright joyousness were yet her normal qualities, and stimulating moral heights her native dwelling-place. All this may be glimpsed in her letters, no less full of charm, it is believed, to the general reader, than to Emily Dickinson's personal friends. As she kept no journal, the letters are the more interesting because they contain all the prose which she is known to have written.

It was with something almost like dread that I approached the task of arranging these letters, lest the deep revelations of a peculiarly shy inner life might so pervade them that in true loyalty to their writer none could be publicly used. But with few exceptions they have been read and prepared with entire relief from that feeling, and with unshrinking pleasure; the sanctities were not invaded. Emily kept her little reserves, and bared her soul but seldom, even in intimate correspondence. It was not so much that she was always on spiritual guard, as that she sported with her varying moods, and tested them upon her friends with apparent delight in the effect, as airy and playful as it was half unconscious.

So large is the number of letters to each of several correspondents, that it has seemed best to place these sets in separate chapters. The continuity is perhaps more perfectly preserved in this way than by the usual method of mere chronological succession; especially as, in a life singularly uneventful, no marked periods of travel or achievement serve otherwise to classify them. On this plan a certain order has been possible, too; the opening letters in each chapter are always later than the first of the preceding, although the last letters of one reach a date beyond the beginning of the next. The less remarkable writing, of course, fills the first chapters; but even this shows her love of study, of Nature, and a devotion to home almost as intense as in strange Emily Brontë.

Nothing is perhaps more marked than the change of style between the diffuseness of girlhood and the brilliant sententiousness of late middle life, often startlingly unexpected. And yet suggestions of future picturesque and epigrammatic power occasionally flash through the long, youthful correspondence. Lowell once wrote of the first letters of Carlyle, "The man . . . is all there in the earliest of his writing that we have (potentially there, in character wholly there)." It is chiefly for these "potential" promises that Emily Dickinson's girlish letters are included, all the variations in the evolution of a style having hardly less interest for the student of human nature than of literature. Village life, even in a college town, was very democratic in the early days when the first of these letters were written, and they suggest a refreshing atmosphere of homely simplicity.

Unusual difficulties have been encountered in arranging the letters with definite reference to years, as none but the very earliest were dated. The change in handwriting, of which specimens are given in facsimile, was no less noticeable than Emily Dickinson's development in literary style; and this alone has been a general guide. The thoughtfulness of a few correspondents in recording the time of the letters' reception has been a further and most welcome assistance; while occasionally the kind of postage-stamp and the postmark helped to indicate when they were written, although generally the envelopes had not been preserved. But the larger part have been placed by searching out the dates of contemporaneous incidents mentioned, —for instance, numerous births, marriages, and deaths; any epoch in the life of a friend was an event to Emily Dickinson, always noticed by a bit of flashing verse, or a graceful, if mystically expressed, note of comfort or congratulation. If errors are found in assignment to the proper time, it will not be from lack of having interrogated all available sources of information.

In more recent years, dashes instead of punctuation and capitals for all important words, together with the quaint handwriting, give to the actual manuscript an individual fascination quite irresistible. But the coldness of print destroys that elusive charm, so that dashes and capitals have been restored to their conventional use.

In her later years, Emily Dickinson rarely addressed the envelopes: it seemed as if her sensitive nature shrank from the publicity which even her handwriting would undergo, in the observation of indifferent eyes. Various expedients were resorted to, —obliging friends frequently performed this office for her; sometimes a printed newspaper label was pasted upon the envelope; but the actual strokes of her own pencil were, so far as possible, reserved exclusively for friendly eyes.

Emily Dickinson's great disinclination for an exposition of the theology current during her girlhood is matter for small wonder. While her fathers were men of recognized originality and force, they did not question the religious teaching of the time; they were leaders in town and church, even strict and uncompromising in their piety. Reverence for accepted ways and forms, merely as such, seems entirely to have been left out of Emily's constitution. To her, God was not a far-away and dreary Power to be daily addressed, —the great "Eclipse" of which she wrote, —but He was near and familiar and pervasive. Her garden was full of His brightness and glory; the birds sang and the sky glowed because of Him. To shut herself out of the sunshine in a church, dark, chilly, restricted, was rather to shut herself away from Him; almost pathetically she wrote, "I believe the love of God may be taught not to seem like bears."

In essence, no real irreverence mars her poems or her letters. Of malice aforethought, —an intentional irreverence, —she is never once guilty. The old interpretation of the biblical estimate of life was cause to her for gentle, wide-eyed astonishment. No one knew better the phrases which had become cant, and which seemed always to misrepresent the Father Whom she knew with personal directness and without necessity for human intervention. It was a theologically misconceived idea of a "jealous God," for which she had a profound contempt; and the fact that those ideas were still held by the stricter New England people of her day made not the slightest difference in her expression of disapproval. Fearless and daring, she had Biblical quotation at her finger-tips; and even if she sometimes used it in a way which might shock a conventionalist, she had in her heart too profound an adoration for the great, ever-living, and present Father to hold a shadow of real irreverence toward Him, so peculiarly near. No soul in which dwelt not a very noble and actual love and respect for the essentials could have written as she did of real triumph, of truth, of aspiration.

> We never know how high we are,
>   Till we are called to rise;
> And then, if we are true to plan,
>   Our statures touch the skies.

The heroism we recite
  Would be a daily thing
Did not ourselves the cubits warp,
  For fear to be a king.

Must not one who wrote that have had her ever-open shrine, her reverenced tribunal?

The whims and pretenses of society, its forms and unrealities, seemed to her thin and unworthy. Conventionalities, while they amused, exasperated her also; and the little poem beginning,

The show is not the show,
But they that go,

expresses in large measure her attitude toward society, when she lived in the midst of it. Real life, on the other hand, seemed vast and inexpressibly solemn. Petty trivialities had no part in her constitution, and she came to despise them more and more, — so much, indeed, that with her increasing shyness, she gradually gave up all journeys, and finally retired completely from even the simple life of a New England college town.

As has been said of Emily Brontë, "To this natural isolation of spirit we are in a great measure indebted for that passionate love of Nature which gives such a vivid reality and exquisite simplicity to her descriptions." Emily Dickinson's letters, almost as much as the poems, exhibit her elf-like intimacy with Nature. She sees and apprehends the great mother's processes, and shares the rapture of all created things under the wide sky. The letters speak of flowers, of pines and autumnal colors; but no natural sight or sound or incident seems to have escaped her delicate apprehension.

Bird songs, crickets, frost, and winter winds, even the toad and snake, mushrooms and bats, have an indescribable charm for her, which she in turn brings to us. March, "that month of proclamation," was especially dear; and among her still unpublished verses is a characteristic greeting to the windy month. In all its aspects "Nature became the unique charm and consolation of her life, and as such she has written of it."

Warm thanks are due the friends who have generously lent letters for reproduction. That they were friends of Emily Dickinson, and willing to share her words with the larger outside circle, waiting and appreciative, entitles them to the gratitude, not merely of the Editor, but of all who make up the world that Emily "never saw," but to which, nevertheless, she sent a "message."

419 Mabel Loomis Todd. Editorial comment and narrative bridges in *Letters of Emily Dickinson*, edited by Mabel Loomis Todd. 2 vols., Boston: Roberts Brothers, 1894, passim. Published November 21, 1894. This entry reprints Mrs. Todd's interspersed comments of a general nature; those pertaining to the source and background of a particular letter are not given here. Volume and page numbers for the separate remarks are supplied in brackets.

Intellectual brilliancy of an individual type was already at seventeen her distinguishing characteristic, and nothing of the recluse was yet apparent. Traditions of extraordinary compositions still remain; and it is certain that each was an epoch for those who heard, whether teachers or pupils. An old friend and schoolmate of Emily tells me that she was always surrounded by a group of girls at recess, to hear her strange and intensely funny stories, invented upon the spot. [I, 35]

*   *   *   *   *

The new railroad was opened for the first regular trip from Palmer to Amherst, May 9, 1853. Mr. Edward Dickinson wrote on that day, "We have no railroad jubilee till we see whether all moves right, then we shall glorify becomingly." Everything was apparently satisfactory, for the celebration occurred early in June, when more than three hundred New London people visited Amherst. In the following letter from Emily [to her brother Austin, 20 June 1853] are indications of her growing distaste to mingle in a social melee, despite genuine interest in itself and its cause. [I, 115]

*   *   *   *   *

As Emily Dickinson approached middle life, and even before her thirtieth year, it seemed to become more and more impossible for her to mingle in general society; and a growing feeling of shyness, as early as 1862 or 1863, caused her to abstain, sometimes, from seeing the dearest friends who came to the house. In spite of her sympathy with sadness, and her deep apprehension of the tragic element in life, she was not only keenly humorous and witty, as already said, but, while made serious by the insistence of life's pathos, she was yet at heart as ecstatic as a bird. This combination of qualities made her companionship, when she vouchsafed it, peculiarly breezy and stimulating. Such a nature must inevitably know more pain than pleasure.

Passionately devoted to her friends, her happiness in their love and trust was at times almost too intense to bear; and it will already have been seen how disproportionately great pain was caused by even comparatively slight separations. With her, pathos lay very near raillery and badinage, —sadness very near delight.

Whether, in writing her poems, the joy of creating was sufficient, or whether a thought of future and wider recognition ever came, it is certain that during life her friends made her audience. She cared more for appreciation and approval from the few who were dear than for any applause from an impersonal public. She herself writes, "My friends are my estate." [I, 189–90]

*   *   *   *   *

Emily was often besieged by different persons, literary and otherwise, to benefit the world by her "chirrup," but she steadily refused to publish during her lifetime. In all these years she was constantly writing verses; and while, as already apparent, she frequently enclosed poems in letters to friends, the fact that scores in addition were being written every year was her own secret. Her literary methods were also her own, —she must frequently have tossed off, many times daily, the stray thoughts which came to her. The box of "scraps" found by her sister after her death proves this conclusively, as some of Emily's rarest flashes were caught upon the margins of newspapers, backs of envelopes, or whatever bit of paper was nearest at hand, in the midst of other occupations. In the more carefully copied poems are many alterations, but it is a curious fact that not one change has reference to improvement in rhyme or rhythm. Every suggestion for a different word or phrase was in the evident hope that by some one of them the thought might be made clearer, and not in a single instance merely to smooth the form.

Whether Emily Dickinson had any idea that her work would ever be published cannot be known. Except when a friend occasionally 'turned love to larceny' as some one has aptly said, nothing was printed before her death. One of the poems, indeed, begins, —

Publication is the auction
Of the mind of man.

But the Prelude [the poem, "This is my letter to the world"] to the *Poems*, First Series, almost seems to indicate the thought of a possible future public, when she herself should be beyond the reach of the praise or criticism which her writing might call forth. [II, 267–68]

* * * * *

What words could more vividly express the uplift, the expansion, the wider horizon which books bring! To Emily Dickinson, they were always solace and delight, — "frigates" and "coursers" indeed, to her quiet life, taking her over the world and into the infinite spaces, bringing Cathay and Brazil, Cashmere and Teneriffe, into an intimacy as near and familiar as the summer bees and butterflies of her own home noon. Without the help of books even, her nimble fancy leaped intervening leagues as if it commanded the magic carpet of Prince Houssain; but her love for books and indebtedness to them are many times expressed in the poems, both published and unpublished. [II, 273]

* * * * *

In his article upon Emily Dickinson in the *Atlantic Monthly* for October, 1891 [no. 221], Colonel Higginson has already given many of her letters to himself. The rest are here added.

The first one, enclosing four of her now widely known poems for his criticism, was without signature, but accompanied by a card bearing her name. Her wish for an impartial and extrinsic judgment from a stranger may, perhaps, illustrate Mrs. Ford's suggestion that "she was longing for poetic sympathy" [see next entry]. At a time when she was but newly trying her own wings, she must have felt something warmly and essentially human in Colonel Higginson's writing to be thus led to ask his help rather than another's, — an intuition most happily justified. [II, 300]

* * * * *

After these startling letters it was but natural that Mr. Higginson should have asked to see a photograph of his "enigmatical correspondent." But there was none. She had an unconquerable aversion to seeing herself reproduced in any sort of "mould." The frontispiece to the first volume of these Letters is taken from an oil painting of Emily, when she was but eight years old, in a group with her brother and sister. The only other known representation of her face is a daguerreotype made a few years later; but it is entirely unsatisfactory, both in expression and individuality. [II, 304–05]

* * * * *

In the dim and early dawn of a fragrant summer morning soon after, Emily caused a large cluster of sweet-peas to be gathered from her dewy, old-fashioned garden, that they might be put on the very first train to Springfield, taking the freshness of summer itself to her friends [Mr. and Mrs. Samuel Bowles, 1885]. This note accompanied them: —
Dawn and dew my bearers be.

Ever,
Butterfly.

And the old garden still overflows with annual fragrance and color. Its armies of many-hued hyacinths run riot in the spring sunshine, while crocuses and daffodils peer above the fresh grass under the apple trees; a large magnolia holds its pink cups toward the blue sky, and scarlet hawthorn lights a greenly dusky corner.

And then the roses, and the hedges of sweet-peas; the masses of nasturtiums, and the stately procession of hollyhocks, in happy association with huge bushes of lemon verbena! Still later comes the autumn glory, with salvia and brilliant zinnias and marigolds and clustering chrysanthemums, until "ranks of seeds their witness bear," and November folds her brown mantle over sleeping flowers.

This sweet garden, with its whiffs of long ago, needs only borders of box and sun-dial to be the ideally imagined pleasure-spot of vanished generations. And Emily seems its presiding genius; it is instinct with her presence still, though even before her death years had passed since her footsteps pressed its paths, or her fingers gathered its riches. [II, 351–52]

*   *   *   *   *

After her father's death, her retirement from ordinary forms of human intercourse became almost complete; and these notes [to friends] were the sole link still binding her to the world, — and to only such part of the world as might be represented by those for whom she cared.

Emily's prose style had developed its incisiveness, — like her own thought, it went straight to the essence of things; and while still dressed in language sufficiently to pass in conventional places, it had gradually become divested of everything superfluous.

While the meaning of certain phrases has sometimes puzzled those who received the notes, there is invariably an original, sparkling interpretation for every sentence, clear to any soul possessing even slight accord with hers. Because frequently couched in the form of apparently mysterious oracles, the meaning is sometimes looked for too deeply, — often it is singularly obvious. The remarkable character of these notes seems to have increased as she lived farther and farther away from the years when she had seen and conversed with her friends; and her life was full of thought and occupation during these introspective days. It is impossible to conceive that any sense of personal isolation, or real loneliness of spirit, because of the absence of humanity from her daily life, could have oppressed a nature so richly endowed.

Most of us would require some sudden blow, some fierce crisis, to produce such a result, — a hidden and unusual life like hers. And we love to believe striking and theatrical things of our neighbors; it panders to that romantic element latent in the plainest. But Emily Dickinson's method of living was so simple and natural an outcome of her increasingly shy nature, a development so perfectly in the line of her whole constitution that no far-away and dramatic explanation of her quiet life is necessary to those who are capable of apprehending her.

That sentence alone would reveal the key wherein she wrote with regret for her long-time maid Margaret: "I winced at her loss, for I am in the habit of her, and even a new rolling-pin has an embarrassing element."

Emerson somewhere says, "Now and then a man exquisitely made can live alone;" and Lord Bacon puts the thought with even greater force and directness, — "Whosoever is delighted in Solitude is either a Wilde Beast or a God."

To some natures, introspection is a necessity for expression. "Why should I feel lonely?" exclaimed Thoreau, in his temporary isolation at Walden, "Is not our planet in the Milky Way?" He was, indeed, "no more lonely than the North Star," nor, I believe, was Emily Dickinson, although congenial companionship had, in a sense, been very dear to her.

She has herself written:—

> Never for society
> He shall seek in vain
> Who his own acquaintance
> Cultivates; of men
> Wiser men may weary,
> But the man within
> Never knew satiety,—
> Better entertain
> Than could Border Ballad,
> Or Biscayan Hymn;
> Neither introduction
> Need you—unto him.

Georg Ebers once wrote: "Sheep and geese become restless when separated from the flock; the eagle and lion seek isolation,"—a picturesque and perhaps not less strong presentation of a nearly identical thought.

But although invisible for years, even to life-long friends, Emily never denied herself to children. To them she was always accessible, always delightful, and in their eyes a sort of fairy guardian. Stories are yet told of her roguishly lowering baskets of "goodies" out of her window by a string to little ones waiting below. Mr. MacGregor Jenkins, in a sketch of his recollections of Emily Dickinson [see no. 249], has shown this gracious and womanly side of her nature in a very charming way, quoting a number of her notes to himself and his sister, two members of a quartet of children admitted to her intimacy. Many of Emily Dickinson's daintiest verses are for children,—among them The Sleeping Flowers ["'Whose are the little bed,' I asked"] and Out of the Morning ["Will there really be morning?"]. [II, 367–70]

* * * * *

It is hard for many persons to believe, even now, that Emily Dickinson had nothing to do with the Saxe Holm stories, and certainly some of their incidental poetry bears strong evidence of her unique touch. The little mystery of those remarkable tales was so carefully guarded that after a time people lost interest in surmising, and are not content to accept them as they are. The No Name series of Roberts Brothers was now so long a secret, and in the volume of its verse, *A Masque of Poets*, appeared, probably through the efforts of her old friend 'H. H.,' Emily Dickinson's Success ["Success is counted sweetest"], afterward the opening poem in the first of her published volumes. However obtained, it formed the beginning of an occasional and pleasant correspondence between herself and Mr. Niles, always the genial, helpful, and generous friend of writers. She often sent him poems, which, contrary to her usual custom, she had named herself. [II, 415–16]

* * * * *

Music had always charm for Emily Dickinson. Frequently, when I had been singing, or playing upon the piano at her request, a dainty note would come in to me, with a glass of wine, or a rare rose; in one instance a cream whip, with a single line, 'Whom He loveth He chasteneth,'—of which the application might have been taken in various ways.

I can never forget the twilight seclusion of the old drawing-room, the square piano in its corner, the ancient mahogany furniture, and Emily just outside the door, her dress a spot of white in the dim hall. With the waning afternoon, I would play one thing and another, or sing melodies which often sounded too light and modern and sunshiny for surroundings so like a dreamy corner of the past. At first it seemed to me as if a visitor from another world had alighted for a time, wishing, for some inscrutable reason, to be entertained on a foreign planet. Later, it became not only entirely natural, but so much a habit that I should have missed my solitary recitals quite as much as my often invisible auditor.

Other notes to me, having especial reference to particular persons or occasions, are not of sufficient general interest to be given here.

As her unique life drew toward its close, she became, for the last two years, a semi-invalid, — she who had always rejoiced in strength and bravery enough for her own need, and that of all her friends. [II, 433–34]

*   *   *   *   *

This is hardly the place to speak in detail of Emily Dickinson's verses, their electrical quality, or their impressive effect upon the public, four years after her death. They are pervaded by a singular cadence of hidden rhythmical music, which becomes sympathetically familiar upon intimate acquaintance.

Dr. Holmes somewhere says that rhymes "are iron fetters: it is dragging a chain and a ball to march under their encumbrance;" and if in Emily Dickinson's work there is frequently no rhyme where rhyme should be, a subtle something, welcome and satisfying, takes its place. An orchid among every-day, sweet-smelling flowers, strangeness and irregularity seem but to enhance her fascination.

A striking charactristic of her verse is its epigrammatic quality; terseness and vigor predominate, rather than feminine grace and smoothness. Homely experiences which all recognize, but few record, were to her texts for profound generalization. When the unmeaning mass of much modern poetry is compared with Emily Dickinson's swift revelations, the operation suggests comparing distilled water with richest Burgundy. And as such water is no less insipid if served in cutglass flagons, so we cannot care in what kind of bottle has been stored for years the condensed sweetness of tropic suns.

The eighteenth of May, 1886, Emily Dickinson was carried lovingly over the threshold she had not passed beyond in years.

> She went as softly as the dew   [as quiet as
>   From a familiar flower.
> Not like the dew did she return
>   At the accustomed hour.

To the few who gathered, that sunny afternoon, her friend, fellow-poet, and "master" read Emily Brontë's noble Last Lines, with their lofty voicing of an unchangeable belief in the soul's immortality, — "a favorite," as Colonel Higginson so fitly said, "with our friend, who has now put on that Immortality which she seemed never to have laid off."

She had lived in voluntary retirement from outside eyes; and now, in the sweet May sunshine, tender hands bore her through meadows starry with daisies into a silence and seclusion but little deeper. [II, 439–41]

420 E[mily] E[llsworth] F[owler] F[ord]. Untitled reminiscence in *Letters of Emily Dickinson*, ed. Mabel Loomis Todd (2 vols., Boston: Roberts Brothers, 1894), 1:126–32. Although published in abbreviated form in this edition of the letters, Ford's sketch was rendered in full in the 1931 *Letters* (pp. 123–32). See also Mrs. Ford's poem in tribute to Dickinson, no. 85.

My remembrances of my friend Emily Dickinson are many and vivid, and delightful to me personally, yet they are all trifles in themselves, and only interesting to the general public as they cast light on the growth and changes in her soul.

Our parents were friends, and we knew each other from childhood, but she was several years younger, and how and when we drew together I cannot recall, but I think the friendship was based on certain sympathies and mutual admirations of beauty in nature and ideas. She loved the great aspects of nature, and yet was full of interest and affection for its smaller details. We often walked together over the lovely hills of Amherst, and I remember especially two excursions to Mount Norwottock, five miles away, where we found the climbing fern, and came home laden with pink and white trilliums, and later, yellow lady's-slippers. She knew the wood-lore of the region round about, and could name the haunts and the habits of every wild or garden growth within her reach. Her eyes were wide open to nature's sights, and her ears to nature's voices.

My chief recollections of her are connected with these woodland walks, or outdoor excursions with a merry party, perhaps to Sunderland for the "sugaring off" of the maple sap, or to some wild brook in the deeper forest, where the successful fishermen would afterward cook the chowder. She was a free talker about what interested her, yet I cannot remember one personal opinion expressed of her mates, her home, or her habits.

Later we met to discuss books. The *Atlantic Monthly* was a youngster then, and our joy over a new poem by Lowell, Longfellow, and Whittier, our puzzles over Emerson's "If the red slayer think he slays," our laughter at Oliver Wendell Holmes, were full and satisfying. Lowell was especially dear to us, and once I saw a passionate fit of crying brought on, when a tutor of the College, who died while contesting the senatorship for Louisiana,[1] told us from his eight years of seniority, that "Byron had a much better style," and advised us "to leave Lowell, Motherwell and Emerson alone." Like other young creatures, we were ardent partisans. [Ford's footnote identifying the college tutor: [1] The Hon. Henry M. Spofford, Justice of the Supreme Court of Louisiana, a graduate of Amherst College in the Class of 1840, and brother of Mr. Ainsworth R. Spofford, the Librarian of Congress.]

There was a fine circle of young people in Amherst, and we influenced each other strongly. We were in the adoring mood, and I am glad to say that many of those idols of our girlhood have proved themselves golden. The eight girls who composed this group had talent enough for twice their number, and in their respective spheres of mothers, authors or women, have been noteworthy and admirable. Three of them have passed from earth, but the others live in activity and usefulness.

This group started a little paper in the Academy, now the village High School, which was kept up for two years. Emily Dickinson was one of the wits of the school, and a humorist of the "comic column." Fanny Montague often made the head title of the paper—Forest Leaves—in leaves copied from nature, and fantasies of her own pen-work. She is now a wise member of art circles in Baltimore, a manager of the Museum of Art, and the appointed and intelligent critic of the Japanese exhibit at the Exposition in Chicago. Helen Fiske (the "H. H." of later days) did no special work on the paper for various reasons.

This paper was all in script, and was passed around the school, where the contributions were easily recognized from the handwriting, which in Emily's case was very beautiful—small, clear, and finished. Later, though her writing retained its elegance, it became difficult to read. I wish very much I could find a copy of Forest Leaves, but we recklessly gave the numbers away, and the last one I ever saw turned up at the Maplewood Institute in Pittsfield, Massachusetts, where they started a similar paper. Emily's contributions were irresistible, but I cannot recall them. One bit was stolen by a roguish editor for the College paper, where her touch was instantly recognized; and there were two paragraphs in the *Springfield Republican.*

We had a Shakespeare Club—a rare thing in those days,—and one of the tutors proposed to take all the copies of all the members and mark out the questionable passages. This plan was negatived at the first meeting, as far as "the girls" spoke, who said they did not want the strange things emphasized, nor their books spoiled with marks. Finally we told the men to do as they liked—"we shall read everything." I remember the lofty air with which Emily took her departure, saying, "There's nothing wicked in Shakespeare, and if there is I don't want to know it." The men read for perhaps three meetings from their expurgated editions, and then gave up their plan, and the whole text was read out boldly.

There were many little dances, with cake and lemonade at the end, and one year there was a valentine party, where the lines of various authors were arranged to make apparent sense, but absolute nonsense, the play being to guess the names and places of the misappropriated lines.

Emily was part and parcel of all these gatherings, and there were no signs, in her life and character, of the future recluse. As a prophetic hint, she once asked me if it did not make me shiver to hear a great many people talk—they took "all the clothes off their souls"—and we discussed this matter. She mingled freely in all the companies and excursions of the moment, and the evening frolics.

Several of this group had beauty, all had intelligence and character, and others had charm. Emily was not beautiful, yet she had great beauties. Her eyes were lovely auburn, soft and warm, her hair lay in rings of the same color all over her head, and her skin and teeth were fine. At this time she had a demure manner which brightened easily into fun where she felt at home, but among strangers she was rather shy, silent, and even deprecating. She was exquisitely neat and careful in her dress, and always had flowers about her, another pleasant habit of modernity.

I have so many times seen her in the morning at work in her garden where everything throve under her hand, and wandering there at eventide, that she is perpetually associated in my mind with flowers—a flower herself,—especially as for years it was her habit to send me the first buds of the arbutus which we had often hung over together in the woods, joying in its fresh fragrance as the very breath of coming spring.

My busy married life separated me from these friends of my youth, and intercourse with them has not been frequent; but I rejoice that my early years were passed in scenes of beautiful nature, and with these mates of simple life, high cultivation and noble ideals. In Emily as in others, there was a rare combination of fervor and simplicity, with good practical living, great conscience and directness of purpose. She loved with all her might, there was never a touch of the worlding about her, and we all knew and trusted her love.

Dr. Holland once said to me, "Her poems are too ethereal for publication." I replied, "They are beautiful—so concentrated—but they remind me of air-plants that have no roots in earth." "That is true," he said, "a perfect description;" and I think these lyrical ejaculations, these breathed-out projectiles, sharp as lances, would at that time have fallen into idle ears. But gathered in a volume where many could be read at once as her philosophy of life, they explain each other, and so become intelligible and delightful to the public.

The first poem I ever read was the robin chorister ["Some keep the Sabbath going to church"] (published in the first volume) which she gave my husband years ago. I think in spite of her seclusion, she was longing for poetic sympathy, and that some of her later habits of life originated in this suppressed and ungratified desire.

I only wish the interest and delight her poems have aroused could have come early enough in her career to have kept her social and communicative, and at one with her friends. Still, these late tributes to her memory are most welcome to the circle that loved her, even though they are but laurels to lay on her grave.

421 [W. F. Whetcho.] "Letters of Emily Dickinson." *Boston Daily Advertiser*, November 23, 1894, p. 4. The author attribution is by hand in Todd's scrapbook and confirmed in *AB*, p. 316. Whetcho's second and third paragraphs bring together scattered sentences from Mrs. Todd's introduction to the 1894 *Letters* (no. 418). Ellipses are the author's.

The marked favor with which the "Poems of Emily Dickinson" were received when published two or three years since, is certain to be accorded to the two first published volumes of her letters, which have been edited by Mabel L. Todd. These letters cover the period of the life of this remarkable woman from Feb., 1845, just after she had passed her 14th birthday, to May, 1886, just before she forever closed her eyes on the earthly sunshine she loved. They are, for the most part, familiar letters to intimate friends, and, unlike her verses, they reveal the quaint and delicate humor which made her personality so attractive. In depth of feeling and keenness of insight these letters are in expression like her poetry. They show that her prose—and these letters are all the prose she is known to have written—is as full of the essential elements of poetry as is her verse. One of the features which will attract attention and which the editor emphasizes is the revelation of the impression that the theology of her girlhood and early womanhood made upon her painfully sensitive nature. To her God was not a far-away and dreary power to be daily addressed and propitiated. He was not the great "Eclipse," but he was near and familiar and pervasive. "Her garden was full of his brightness and glory, the birds sang and the sky glowed because of Him. To shut herself out of the sunshine in a church, dark, chilly, restricted, was rather to shut herself away from Him; almost pathetically she wrote, 'I believe the love of God may be taught not to seem like bears.'"

When her poems appeared the criticism was made that there was running through them a vein of irreverence, and this criticism will doubtless be made of the letters. She did not indeed have reverence for accepted ways and forms merely as such, but she is not in its real sense guilty of irreverence in either her poems or her letters. The old interpretation of the Biblical estimate of life was simply a cause to her for gentle, wide-eyed astonishment. No one knew better the phrases which had become cant, and which seemed always to misrepresent the father whom she knew with personal directness and without necessity for human intervention. It was a theologically misconceived idea of a "jealous God" for which she had a profound contempt. . . . Fearless and daring, she had Biblical quotation at her finger-tips; and even if she sometimes used it in a way which might shock a conventionalist, she had in her heart too profound an adoration for the great ever-living and present Father to hold a shadow of real irreverence toward Him, so peculiarly near.

Neither had she respect for the whims and pretenses of society, its forms and unrealities. She despised petty trivialities, and so thoroughly so that she finally kept herself aloof from even the simple life of a New England college rural town. Her letters, like her poems, show how she loved nature, how intimate she was with its processes. She found a charm in bird songs, crickets, frost, winter winds, even in the toad, the snake, mushrooms and bat; these were more to her than artificial people. In real life there was something to her grand and solemn.

The girlhood letters are interesting in themselves, and interesting by comparison with those of later years, as indicating growth and development. The editor found a difficulty in arranging the letters chronologically, owing to absence of dates, and so has adopted the plan of arranging the letters to certain friends in chapters. We cannot forbear to quote from some of these, just to give an idea of their quality.

To her friend Mrs. J. G. Holland she wrote in the late summer of 1856:—

"Don't tell, dear Mrs. Holland, but wicked as I am I read my Bible sometimes, and in it as I read today I found a verse like this, where friends should 'go no more out,' and there were 'no tears,' and I wished as I sat down tonight that we were there—not here—and that wonderful world had commenced which makes such promises, and rather than to write you I were by your side, and the 'hundred and forty and four thousand' were chatting pleasantly, yet not disturbing me. . . . If roses had not failed and frosts had never come, and one had not fallen here and there whom I could not waken, there were no need of other heaven than the one here below; and if God had been here this summer and seen the things I have seen, I guess he would think His Paradise superfluous. Don't tell Him, for the world, though, for after all He's said about it I should like to see what He was building for us, with no hammer and no stone and no journeyman either."

After the death of Samuel Bowles, in 1878, she wrote to Mrs. Bowles:—

"Love makes us heavenly without our trying in the least. 'Tis easier than a Saviour—it does not stay on high and call us to its distance; its low 'Come unto me' begins in every place. It makes but one mistake, it tells us it is 'rest'—perhaps its toil is rest, but what we have not known we shall know again, that divine 'again' for which we are all breathless."

In 1880—"David's grieved decision haunted me when a little girl. I hope he has found Absalom. Immortality as a guest is sacred, but when it becomes as with you and us, a member of the family, the tie is more vivid."

In 1874, to one of her cousins—"The loveliest sermon I ever heard was the disappointment of Jesus in Judas. It was told like a mortal story of intimate young men. I suppose we can ever have will be so sad as that. The last 'I never knew you' may resemble it."

After the sudden death of her father in Boston in 1874 this to her cousins is exquisite: "Father does not live with us now—he lives in a new house. Though it was built in an hour it is better than this. He hasn't any garden because he moved after gardens were made, so we take him the best flowers, and if we only knew he knew, perhaps we could stop crying."

To T. W. Higginson in 1862 who had asked about her poetry, how old she was when she began writing her books, etc., she wrote: "I made no verse but one or two till this winter. I had a trouble since September, I could tell to none; and so I sing, as the boy does of the burying ground, because I am afraid. You inquire my books. For poets I have Keats and Mr. and Mrs. Browning. For prose Mr. Ruskin, Sir Thomas Browne and the Revelations. . . . You ask my companions. Hills, sir, and the sunshine and a dog large as myself. . . . I have a brother and sister; my mother does not care for thought, and father, too busy with his briefs to notice what we do. They are religious except me, and address an eclipse every morning whom they call their Father."

Again: "How do most people live without thoughts? There are many people in the world—you must have noticed them in the street,—how do they live? How do they get strength to put on their clothes in the morning?"

"Enough is so vast a sweetness, I suppose it never occurs, only pathetic counterfeits. Fabulous to me as the men of the Revelations who shall not hunger any more. Even the possible has its insoluble particle."

There may be extravagance in these letters, over statement, but there is thought, high, subtle, delicate. These letters will be read, quoted, will find their place in books of selections. They will comfort bereaved ones; they will help, they will stimulate. These two volumes are among the books of the year.

422 "Literary Notes." *Amherst Student* 28 (November 24, 1894), 80.

Mrs. Todd undertook the task of compiling and editing the letters of Miss Dickinson at the urgent request of many friends. She has been engaged in the work about three years as the compilation was more difficult than at first anticipated. The work is in two volumes, tastily bound, of about 250 pages each. The frontispieces are a child portrait of Emily Dickinson and a picture of the old family mansion on Main Street, Amherst. Fac-similes of her writing at different periods in her life are also given. The letters to each correspondent have been arranged in groups, preference being given to this arrangement rather than to chronological order. Among the many people to whom letters are addressed are: Col. T. W. Higginson, Miss Maria Whitney, Professor J. K. Chickering, Dr. and Mrs. J. G. Holland and Mr. and Mrs. Samuel Bowles.

423 [Atherton Brownell.] "A Thought of God." *Boston Home Journal,* n.s. 8 (November 24, 1894), 5. Mr. Brownell wrote Mrs. Todd, Nov. 5, 1894, requesting information for a sketch of Dickinson's life to appear in the *Home Journal* [Amherst College Library, ms. To 507]. His essay draws on her reply and her introduction to the *Letters,* no. 418. The article is illustrated with the child portrait and photograph of the Dickinson homestead that were used as frontispiece illustrations for the *Letters.*

If ever a person truly lived the statement of Mme. Swetchine when she said "Let us shun everything which might tend to efface the primitive lineaments of our individuality. Let us reflect that each one of us is a thought of God," Emily Dickinson was that person.

There is a strange interest attaching to the power of glancing into a soul; of seeing therein the primitive nature which has thus been most justly called "a thought of God." It was this laying bare of a woman's heart which made the diary of Marie Bashkirtseff so eagerly sought, and in Emily Dickinson America had also a glimpse after her death of the heart promptings, the real ego, of a woman, untutored in the ways of the world, living her own life regardless of surroundings and shunning the gaze of the world, refusing to be influenced by it, and hiding herself from its light.

Emily Dickinson has been compared to Emily Brontë, but it is hardly just to speak of her self repression, because she withdrew from the world and lived the life of a hermit in Amherst. Rather did she withdraw from the world that she might give her personality full rein, but, like Emily Brontë she found in Nature all that which to her was a whole world. To her the blooming of a violet, the screeching of some blue jays, or the purpling of the lovely hills about her home in the evening twilight, were the events of the day.

This was a free and honest Nature in the midst of a world of shams, and it is not surprising that we know nothing of her until after her death, when it is remembered that it was she who said, "It makes me shiver to hear a great many people talk—they take all the clothes off their souls." And, this is indicative of her retiring nature as well as of the flashes of wit, which illuminate the correspondence which has been given to the world through Mabel Loomis Todd, and Roberts Brothers, the publishers.

Most of her letters are strangely impersonal, coming from a recluse whose solitude must largely have been spent in introspection; and yet, while they contain so little of self, they contain still less of the affairs of the great world outside of her home. Indeed, had not one of her Amherst friends been killed in the war, no reader would have learned from her that the rebellion had been raging three years. "*My* business is love," she writes with truth. "I found a bird this morning, down—down on a little bush at the foot of the garden. And wherefore sing, I said, since nobody *hears?* One sob in the throat, one flutter of bosom—'My business is to *sing*'—and away she rose! How do I know but cherubim, once themselves as patient, listened and applauded her unnoticed hymn?"

Why, it might be asked, with the same answer as applicable to her, was she constantly writing verses, jotting down evanescent flashes of thought on margins of newspapers, backs of envelopes or other scraps of paper, tucking the songs secretly away, to be discovered only after her death?

How intensely she loved her few friends can only be imagined after reading these impassioned letters written to Dr. and Mrs. Holland, Mr. and Mrs. Samuel Bowles, her brother Austin, Mrs. Gordon L. Ford and a few others, breathing out lyrical projectiles, in the midst of her prose stanzas, when the thought seemed best suited to verse. In spite of her seclusion, it would often seem that she was longing for poetic appreciation and sympathy—a longing which it felt was suppressed, with many another ungratified desire. Although an undercurrent of sadness thus flows through her life, there nevertheless ripples along quite merrily a sparkling humor, original, as everything she said was sure to be, and quite incompatible with one's preconceived ideas of this spirituelle recluse. "Mrs. ____ gets bigger and rolls down to church like a reverend marble," she writes in one of those charmingly natural, spontaneous letters to her young cousins, which perhaps, more than any others, reveal most of that elusive personality—her real self.

Throughout her work of editing the letters, a task occupying three years of time, Mrs. Mabel Loomis Todd is perhaps the best fitted to speak of Emily Dickinson of any person now living. In a letter to the writer she says: "The brilliant epigrammatic power, the startling expressions, and the flashing wit which illuminates almost every page of her writing, have amply repaid the months of hard work."

Mrs. Todd then tells the story of Emily Dickinson, as follows:

"In their way these letters are as remarkable as Marie Bashkirtseff's journals, and while there is not a particle of real irreverence, some of her quaint ways of putting things, and her peculiar and witty use of Biblical quotation may occasionally startle her stricter readers.

"She was born in 1830, her father being a lawyer of wide distinction, and treasurer of Amherst College. She was for a year at Mount Holyoke Seminary, and some of her brightest early writing is dated there. But even then she began to like solitude better than company, as the letters show. She lived among people until she was past twenty, even going to Washington with her father when he was a member of Congress.

"But it is clear to us that she saw people under protest, even then. Gradually she gave up going out, and still more gradually refrained from seeing those who called. Her first verses seem to have been written about 1860, and when her father died, in 1874, her retirement became absolute; she saw no one afterward.

"But she wrote a mass of verses in these years, and almost hundreds of letters, and watched the comings and goings and general fortunes of her friends with unfailing interest. She spent much time in her conservatory, and constantly sent blossoms to all her friends, accompanied by very unusual notes, which became more odd with every year.

"So many of her friends died that her last few years were deeply tinged with sadness. Still she was always bright, always saw the funny side of life to the last, and seemed possessed of an effervescent vitality which could never fail.

"She always dressed in white the year round, but it was not for spectacular effect, it was her fancy only, and there was no theatrically effective love affair which caused her to leave the world. It was a perfectly natural life for one of her shy nature.

"She died in 1886, May 15, and the day after her sister found a drawer completely filled with manuscript poems, in number over a thousand, copied delicately on sheets of note paper, and tied, every six or eight sheets together, in little volumes.

"All her life she refused to publish, although often entreated. But after her death her sister insisted that the poems should be published, and I finally consented to take them in charge. Colonel Higginson wrote the preface to the first volume, the sale being so great that a second was called for, to which I wrote the preface. Now the letters which I have collected through three years are to appear; and they will present a very complete picture of the life and method of mind of this recluse genius."

In her introductory note to the published letters Mrs. Todd writes much more which is of interest, and from which the following is quoted.

"Emily Dickinson's verses, often but the reflection of a passing mood, do not always completely represent herself, — rarely, indeed, showing the dainty humor, the frolicsome gaiety, which continually bubbled over in her daily life. The somber and even weird outlook upon this world and the next, characteristic of many of the poems, was by no means a prevailing condition of mind; for, while fully apprehending all the tragic elements of life, enthusiasm and bright joyousness were yet her normal qualities, and stimulating moral heights her native dwelling place. All this may be glimpsed in her letters, no less full of charm, it is believed, to the general reader, than to Emily Dickinson's personal friends. As she kept no journal, the letters are the more interesting because they contain all the prose which she is known to have written.

"Nothing is perhaps more marked than the change of style between the diffuseness of girlhood and the brilliant sententiousness of late middle life, often startlingly unexpected. And yet suggestions of future picturesque and epigrammatic power occasionally flash through the long, youthful correspondence. Lowell once wrote of the first letter of Carlyle: 'The man . . . is all there in the earliest of his writing that we have (potentially there, in character wholly there).' It is chiefly for those 'potential' promises that Emily Dickinson's girlish letters are included, all the variations in the evolution of a style having hardly less interest for the student of human nature than of literature. Village life, even in a college town, was very democratic in the early days, when the first of these letters were written, and they suggest a refreshing atmosphere of homely simplicity.

"In her later years, Emily Dickinson rarely addressed the envelopes; it seemed as if her sensitive nature shrank from the publicity which even her handwriting would undergo, in the observation of indifferent eyes. Various expedients were resorted to—obliging friends frequently performed this office for her; sometimes a printed newspaper label was pasted upon the envelope; but the actual strokes of her own pencil were, so far as possible, reserved exclusively for friendly eyes.

"Emily Dickinson's great disinclination for an exposition of the theology current during her girlhood is matter for small wonder. While her fathers were men of recognized originality and force, they did not question the religious teaching of the time; they were leaders in town and church, even strict and uncompromising in their piety. Reverence for accepted ways and forms, merely as such, seems entirely to have been left out of Emily's constitution. To her, God was not a faraway and dreary Power to be daily addressed—the great 'Eclipse' of which she wrote—but He was near and familiar and pervasive. Her garden was full of His brightness and glory; the birds sang and the sky glowed because of Him. To shut herself out of the sunshine in a church, dark, chilly, restricted, was rather to shut herself away from Him; almost pathetically she wrote, 'I believe the love of God may be taught not to seem like bears.'

"In essence, no real irreverence mars her poems or her letters. Of malice aforethought—an intentional irreverence—she is never once guilty. The old interpretation of the Biblical estimate of life was cause to her for gentle, wide-eyed astonishment. No one knew better the phrases which had become cant, and which seemed always to misrepresent the Father whom she knew with personal directness and without necessity for human intervention. It was a theologically misconceived idea of a profound contempt; and the fact that those ideas were still held by the stricter New England people of her day made not the slightest difference in her expression of disapproval. Fearless and daring, she had Biblical quotation at her finger-tips; and even if she sometimes used it in a way which might shock a conventionalist, she had in her heart too profound an adoration for the great, ever-living, and present Father to hold a shadow of real irreverence toward him, so peculiarly near. No soul in which dwelt not a very noble and actual love and respect for the essentials could have written as she did of real triumph, of truth, of aspiration.

> We never know how high we are,
>   Till we are called to rise;
> And then, if we are true to plan,
>   Our statures touch the skies.
>
> The heroism we recite
>   Would be a daily thing
> Did not ourselves the cubits warp,
>   For fear to be a king.

Must not one who wrote that have had her ever-open shrine, her reverenced tribunal!

"The whims and pretenses of society, its forms and unrealities, seemed to her thin and unworthy. Conventionalities, while they amused, exasperated her also; and the little poem beginning

The show is not the show,
But they that go,

expresses in large measure her attitude toward society, when she lived in the midst of it. Real life, on the other hand, seemed vast and inexpressibly solemn. Petty trivialities had no part in her constitution, and she came to despise them more and more—so much, indeed, that with her increasing shyness, she gradually gave up all journeys, and finally retired completely from the simple life of a New England college town.

"As has been said of Emily Brontë, 'To this natural isolation of spirit we are in a great measure indebted for that passionate love of Nature which gives such a vivid reality and exquisite simplicity to her descriptions.' Emily Dickinson's letters, almost as much as the poems, exhibit her elf-like intimacy with Nature. She sees and apprehends the great mother's processes, and shares the rapture of all created things under the wide sky. The letters speak of flowers, or pines and autumnal colors; but no natural sight or sound or incident seems to have escaped her delicate apprehension.

"Bird songs, crickets, frost, and winter winds, even the toad and snake, mushrooms and bats, have an indescribable charm for her, which she in turn brings to us. March, 'that month of proclamation,' was especially dear; and among her still unpublished verses is a characteristic greeting to the windy month. In all its aspects 'Nature became the unique charm and consolation of her life, and as such she has written of it.'"

424 "Publications of the Past Week." *New York Times,* November 24, 1894, p. 3.

Roberts Brothers bring out in the pretty volume of small size the "Letters of Emily Dickinson," as edited by Mabel Loomis Todd. They contain a portrait of Miss Dickinson as a child and a view of her home—a beautiful and stately village home of a style current fifty years ago. Strange was the life of this gifted woman, and the strangeness with the reading of these letters passeth not away.

425 "Personals." *Indianapolis Sentinel,* November 25, 1894, p. 12.

A curious story is told of Emily Dickinson, the poetess, whose letters were brought out in Boston last week. Miss Dickinson spent her entire life in Amherst, Mass., and was always particularly shy and retiring. It is customary in the town to entertain the college students certain evenings in the week, and Miss Emily and her sister observed the custom. But while the boys gathered in the front room Miss Emily sat in the back parlor in the dark, and it was there that the boys went to converse with her. There was no affectation about this queer proceeding. The lady was merely timid and ill at ease in company, and felt that she could not converse under the usual conditions. That she was a delightful conversationalist many witnesses bear testimony.

426 "New Publications." *New York Times,* November 25, 1894, sec. 3, p. 23.
Partially reprinted: *Book News* 13 (February 1895), 267–68. Roberts Brothers used part of this review's first sentence in its advertising; see no. 458.

A most remarkable and interesting woman is revealed in this collection of letters, a woman who lived a recluse in the college town of Amherst, and who wrote poetry which was not published till she had been dead a number of years. She was a bright woman, but, being untrained, her thoughts ran to whimsicalities, and her poetry was unlike anything anybody else had written. Her peculiar life, too, had its effect upon her writings. She stayed at home almost constantly, rarely venturing outside the fences which inclosed her father's place. Her pleasure was in her associations with members of her own family, in her correspondence with a few—a very few—persons, with whom she established terms of delightful intimacy, and finally in her communion with nature. She was not soured the least by her life of retirement, but that life developed in her a great many peculiarities which found expression in the letters she wrote, as well as in the little poems which she dashed off on the margins of newspapers and on the backs of envelopes and stowed away in what she called her "scrap" heap.

There is not the slightest doubt that she would have been delighted if some publisher had got possession of her heap of verses in a surreptitious way and put them into a little book done up in blue and gold, according to the prevailing fashion of the day. This is well established in her correspondence with Thomas Wentworth Higginson. The first letter, dated April 16, 1862, is evidence to the point:

Mr. Higginson, are you too deeply occupied to say if my verse is alive? The mind is so near itself it cannot see distinctly, and I have none to ask. Should you think it breathed, and had you the leisure to tell me, I should feel quick gratitude. If I make the mistake, that you dared to tell me would give me sincerer honor toward you. I inclose my name, asking you, if you please, Sir, to tell me what is true. That you will not betray me it is needless to ask, since honor is its own pawn.

Col. Higginson's reply to this letter has not been preserved, but it is evident from Miss Dickinson's next letter to the Colonel that the poetry did not produce the impression that she had hoped it would produce. The Colonel was interested—in fact, his literary curiosity was greatly aroused. He asked for more and for information about the writer. Miss Dickinson gave the information called for and sent on more poems, and of course received a second letter. Replying to this second letter, she wrote, among other things:

Your second letter surprised me, and for a moment swung. I had not supposed it. Your first gave no dishonor, because the true are not ashamed. I thanked you for your justice, but could not drop the bells whose jingling cooled my tramp. Perhaps the balm seemed better because you bled me first. I smile when you suggest that I delay "to publish," that being foreign to my thought as firmament to fin.

If fame belonged to me, I could not escape her; if she did not, the longest day would pass me on the chase, and the approbation of my dog would forsake me then. My barefoot rank is better.

You think my gait "spasmodic." I am in danger, Sir. You think me "uncontrolled." I have no tribunal.

Would you have time to be the "friend" you should think I need? I have a little shape; it would not crowd your desk, nor make as much racket as the mouse that dents your galleries.

If I might bring you what I do—not so frequent to trouble you—and ask you if I told it clear, 'twould be control to me. The sailor cannot see the north, but knows the needle can. The 'hand you stretch me in the dark' I put mine in, and turn away.

This letter shows plain enough that the writer had an ambition to become known as a poet; her disclaimer is of small account as compared with the confession we may read between the lines. She continued her correspondence with Col. Higginson for many years, but it does not appear from anything in this collection of letters that her later poetry seemed to him at all different from that she wrote when she began to be a poet, and the inference is justifiable that the Colonel never saw anything of hers which he thought should be published. She was a "spasmodic" and "uncontrolled" poet to the end.

Dr. Holland, who was another of Miss Dickinson's close friends, also felt that her poems should not be published — at least that they should not be published individually. "The poems are too ethereal for publication," he said. He said this to Mrs. Gordon L. Ford, and her reply as she recalls it was: "They are beautiful — so concentrated; but they remind me of air plants that have no roots in earth." In a sketch of Miss Dickinson, Mrs. Ford says:

I think these lyrical ejaculations, these breathed-out projectiles, sharp as lances, would at that time have fallen into idle ears. But gathered in a volume where many could be read at once as her philosophy of life, they explain each other, and so become intelligible and delightful to the public.

This undoubtedly is true in the main, and yet there are some of Miss Dickinson's verses which can stand by themselves and take judgment on what they are worth without regard to what they reveal of the character and habits of thought of the writer. Of this sort certainly are the following lines sent with flowers to the late Samuel Bowles of the *Springfield Republican:*

If recollecting were forgetting
Then I remember not.
And if forgetting, recollecting,
How near I had forgot!
And if to miss were merry,
And if to mourn were gay,
How very blithe the fingers
That gathered this to-day! [these

We may say the same of these lines, which were sent in lieu of a letter to Mr. and Mrs. Bowles, accompanying a spray of white pine:

A feather from the whippoorwill
That everlasting sings!
Whose galleries are sunrise,
Whose opera the springs,
Whose emerald nest the ages spin
Of mellow, murmuring thread,
Whose beryl egg, what schoolboys hunt
In "recess" overhead!

A considerable portion of the collection is made up of letters in prose and poetry sent to the Bowleses. In these letters we have a striking illustration of a peculiarity of persons of retiring habits. Miss Dickinson was so afraid of the world that at one time she would not direct an envelope that was to go through the mails, and yet in her letters to Mr. and Mrs. Bowles she unveiled her heart and talked to them as freely as she talked to her flowers in some of her verses. So it always is with the recluse; he is sure to unbosom himself to some person or persons. The striking characteristic of Miss Dickinson's letters, aside from the freedom with which she discloses her sentiments and affections, is, if we may borrow Col. Higginson's phraseology, that they were as "spasmodic" and "uncontrolled" as were her poems. Indeed, her letters were apt to be poems in prose. Here, for example, is one which she wrote to Mrs. Bowles in 1858:

Dear Mrs. Bowles: You send sweet messages. Remembrance is more sweet than robins in May orchards. I love to trust that round bright fires, some, braver than I, take my pilgrim name. How are papa, mamma, and the little people? . . .

It storms in Amherst five days—it snows, and then it rains, and then soft fogs like veils hang on all the houses, and then the days turn topaz, like a lady's pin.

Thank you for bright bouquet, and afterward verbena. I made a plant of a little bough of yellow heliotrope which the bouquet bore me, and call it Mary Bowles. It is many days since the Summer day when you came with Mr. Bowles, and before another Summer day it will be many days. My garden is a little knoll with faces under it, and only the pines sing tunes now the birds are absent. I cannot walk to the distant friends on nights piercing as these, so I put both hands on the window pane, and try to think how birds fly, and imitate, and fail, like Mr. "Rasselas." I could make a balloon of a dandelion, but the fields are gone, and only "Professor Lowe" remains to weep with me. If I built my house I should like to call you. I talk of all these things with Carlo, and his eyes grow meaning, and his shaggy feet keep a slower pace. Are you safe to-night? I hope you may be glad. I ask God on my knee to send you much prosperity, few Winter days, and long suns. I have a childish hope to gather all I love together and sit down beside and smile. . . .

Will you come to Amherst? The streets are very cold now, but we will make you warm. But if you never came, perhaps you could write a letter, saying how much you would like to, if it were "God's will." I give good night and daily love to you and Mr. Bowles.

Mrs. Todd, the editor of Miss Dickinson's letters, knew her intimately, and some of the most charming letters in the collection were written to her. Once she painted for Miss Dickinson a group of Indian pipes. In return she received this pretty little note:

Dear Friend: I cannot make an Indian pipe, but please accept a humming bird—

> A route of evanescence,
> With a revolving wheel;
> A resonance of emerald,
> A rush of cochineal;
> And every blossom on the bush
> Adjusts its tumbled head—
> The mail from Tunis, probably,
> An easy morning's ride.

A curious thing about Miss Dickinson is that, although in her later years— that is to say, after she had passed her twenty-fifth year—she shunned society and clung closely to her home, she in her youthful days was full of fun and the life of the centre of schoolgirls in which she moved. At South Hadley, in the brief period allowed the pupils for relaxation, she was always surrounded by young girls, who delighted to listen to her funny stories and bright, off-hand speeches. Not one of those South Hadley girls would have believed a prophet who should have foretold that their much-admired Emily would shut herself up while she still was a young woman and let the world take care of itself. As a girl, she was intellectually brilliant, and only training was needed to make her famous.

The first thought is one of regret that Miss Dickinson did not fulfill the promise of her girlhood and make a literary name for herself, but, perhaps, it is just as well that she developed in a different way. Her life was unique in many respects, and for the sake of getting such a life the world easily could spare a literary light. It may be said, too, that poems and letters such as Miss Dickinson wrote have a literary value in their very strangeness and irregularity. As Mrs. Todd remarks: "If in Emily Dickinson's work there is frequently no rhyme where rhyme should be, a subtle something, welcome and satisfying, takes its place." Mrs. Todd also speaks with reason when characterizing Miss Dickinson's verse. She says it is remarkable for its epigrammatic quality, its terseness and vigor, rather than for feminine grace and smoothness, and adds: "When the unmeaning mass of much modern poetry is compared with Emily Dickinson's swift revelations, the operation suggests comparing distilled water with richest Burgundy. And, as such water is no less insipid if served in cut-glass flagons, so we cannot care in what kind of bottle has been stored for years the condensed sweetness of tropic suns."

427 "Lines Accompanying a Dainty Gift." *Philadelphia Record*, November 26, 1894, p. 7.

Mrs. Mabel Loomis Todd, the editor of "Letters of Emily Dickinson," knew Miss Dickinson, and some of the most charming letters in the collection were written to her. Once she painted for Miss Dickinson a group of Indian pipes. In return she received this pretty little note:

Dear Friend: I cannot make an Indian pipe, but please accept a humming bird—

A route of evanescence,
With a revolving wheel;
A resonance of emerald,
A rush of cochineal;
And every blossom on the bush
Adjusts its tumbled head—
The mail from Tunis, probably,
An easy morning's ride.

428 "Jottings." *Boston Evening Transcript*, November 27, 1894, p. 4.

There are many delicate bits of unrhymed poetry among the letters of Emily Dickinson. Here is one equal to the one beginning "The pedigree of honey does not concern the bee"—

Go not too near a house of rose;
The depredation of a breeze
Or inundation of a dew
Alarm its walls away:
Nor try to tie the butterfly,
Nor climb the bars of ecstasy.
In insecurity to lie
Is joy's insuring quality.

429 "New Publications." *Boston Herald*, November 27, 1894, p. 7. This review is of interest for its stress on Dickinson as an artist of the new
school ("impressionism") and for its recognition of her importance as a
social critic ("a woman who had her own way of doing things, and who
could not be repressed"). Roberts Brothers liked this piece enough to use
it in their advertising as if it bespoke the opinions of both the New
York and Boston *Herald* (no. 458).

Those who have been interested in Emily Dickinson's poems, and the number is very large, have been eager to see her letters, which contain all the prose
she is known to have written. In the poems there was a somber and even weird
outlook upon this world and the next. They were written in a mood which was
unusual, if not really strange, but they expressed the reality of her life, and it is
in their unhackneyed character and strange fervor that they have attracted general attention. These letters have been collected with great difficulty, and it
would seem as if some of them were too trifling for publication, but, inasmuch
as they contain the only record of her life, they will be received with special interest by the large number of persons who are attracted to her poems. Read continuously, they will seem a little tedious, especially in the first volume, which
contains those written in her earlier years, but when she had reached maturity
the pietism and triviality which formerly characterized them passed away. They
express in a remarkable way her thought and feeling and convictions, and they
are written straight out of her life. Mrs. Mabel Loomis Todd, the editor of these
letters, likens Miss Dickinson to Emily Bronte, who was a similar shy, sensitive
and retiring woman. These letters show an elf-like intimacy with nature. They
speak of flowers, of pines and autumnal colors, but no natural sight or sound or
incident escapes her delicate attention. Bird songs, crickets, frosts and winter
birds, even the toad and the snake, mushrooms and bats, have an indescribable
charm for her, which she knows how to utilize. In all its aspects nature became
the unique charm and consummation of her life, and her letters are full of the expression of what she found in it. It was well to publish these letters as a companion to her poetry. They help us to interpret this strangely realistic and impassioned woman. She was eminently a religious person, but she took religion
in her own way. It was not that of the narrow New England village where she
lived, but the language of a free and liberal spirit, who believed that God was
near and familiar and pervasive. She was entirely out of place in the religious
society in which she moved, and, beyond the few friends to whom she was attached, she seldom mingled freely with people, but she was keenly alive to
everything that was going on in outward nature and in the daily life of those with
whom she came in contact. She was a woman who had her own way of doing
things, and who could not be repressed. There is very little biography in these
letters, but throughout they are revelations of her spiritual and emotional life.
In the earliest letters she is a pupil at Mt. Holyoke Female Seminary, where she
was much influenced by Mary Lyon, but after this experience her life was chiefly
passed at Amherst, where she lived until 1886, and where she died as quietly and
gently as she had lived. The letters are a remarkable exhibition of her personality. They relate almost entirely to herself and her contact with nature. It is almost impossible for her to write even a short note without giving a touch of
natural life. She did not come in contact with many people, and her literary associates were chiefly the persons whom she met in that part of the state.
The letters are addressed largely to members of her own family, but quite a

number were written to Dr. and Mrs. J. G. Holland, to Mr. and Mrs. Bowles, to Mr. T. W. Higginson, and to those members of her family who appreciated her position. To them she wrote naturally and spontaneously. The letters are full of her little griefs and troubles and joys, and in the second volume express a range of life which is broader and freer than that of the earlier period. Not one of these letters is written in a conventional style, and everywhere there are bits of expression which throw a great deal of light upon her life. Miss Dickinson had a great gift for taking pains. She saw things truly, and there are passages in these letters where she grasped great truths and saw them on the farther side, but she never held on to them for more than a moment. Her literary methods were her own, and her best things were flashes from her soul. She aimed to reach the exact expression which she wanted to use, and often she dropped into verse in writing a letter. She was an impressionist of the first magnitude, and whatever was unconventional and went straight to its object drew her at once. All the events of life are treated in these pages in a fresh and unconventional way. When it is remembered that they were written out of one of the quietest of homes and that they express the sensitive spiritual and emotional life of a young woman who knew but little of the world beyond herself, and who, when Col. Higginson asked her to give a sketch of her history, communicated one of the most wonderful personal histories that he had ever received, it will be found that a personality is here revealed which has, perhaps, no counterpart in our literary history. These letters have been gathered by her sister, and Mrs. Todd in editing them has only added such connecting links as were necessary. They throw a great deal of light upon her poems, and enable one to understand much of their weird and strange expressions. Music had charms for Emily Dickinson as truly as the garden or the open fields of nature, but flowers and pets were as real to her as her dearest friends. The strange and exceptional life which is here revealed will be studied by the psychologist with quite as much interest as by the person interested in literature, and it will be difficult for many to believe that so strange a personality could exist in a simple New England village and give hardly any sign of itself until death had finally completed her message to the world. All that has been published from her pen has appeared since her death, and these letters practically close the message which she had to deliver. Her life was in many respects a protest against social and religious conditions, and as an impressionist she had a remarkably distinct and impressive career.

430 "Local News. *Amherst Record*, November 28, 1894, p. 4.

The "Letters of Emily Dickinson," edited by Mabel Loomis Todd and published by Roberts Bros. of Boston, has been issued and is now on sale by M. N. Spear. A note received from the publishers states that two days after the book was placed on sale in Boston one-half the first edition had been exhausted.

431 "Among the Holiday Books." *Evangelist* 65 (November 29, 1894), 16.

Those who knew Emily Dickinson can easily imagine how much to her must have been the coming into her later life, her life of long seclusion, of the bright young spirit of her who became her literary executor. Mrs. Todd understands Emily Dickinson—what is there more to say? Perhaps also to add that in not one instance has the editor violated the sanctities of a life singularly reserved, singularly refined and delicate. It would have been easy to have included in these letters something that it would have hurt the writer to have the public read. Such mistakes have been made by editors of wider fame than Mrs. Todd; but she has not made them.

Perhaps her task was the more easy because Emily Dickinson so thoroughly respected her own sanctities. She gave herself fully, exuberantly even, to her friends, as these letters show. They are full of a humorous self-revelation. But they reveal nothing that dignity, self-respect, the sense of human individuality, forbid to make public. Doubtless there were intimate passages in which for beloved eyes the veil of intimate personality was drawn aside, but those passages are not to be found here.

Those who anywhere during the twenty years before Emily Dickinson's death spent a few years less or more in Amherst, knowing of her only as the strange, gifted woman who always wore a white gown and never crossed her own threshold, but not being of the small number admitted to pass the door of that pleasant house on Main Street, were probably not so much surprised when four years ago they read her poems as they now will be at the reading of these letters. For they knew that she was a woman of unusual parts and strong individuality; they knew that it was not the emptiness of her life or a lack of interest in realities that kept her secluded within the four walls of her own house—they were prepared for something strong, original, elusive, like the poetic element in her verses. But the warm affection, the bubbling merriment, the quick humor that glance and beam in these pages are more than they were prepared for. She is still the poet in these letters of hers—responsive, elusive, suggestive, enigmatical often, yet always touching a deep spring in her reader's heart; but here she is "all that and all the rest," the true woman, sister, friend, deeply loving, self-forgetful, alive to all that concerns those whom she loves, a blithe spirit and a pure, soaring most easily in the upper air, yet living always in the sphere where they live who are her friends. There is no narrowness here, though no account is made of outward events, of public, even of literary interests—no narrowness, for her interest in life includes the interests of all whom she cares for. These volumes may not create the sensation which the publication of her poems did, but the poems need the letters, and the letters are worthy of a place beside the poems.

432 *Albany* [N.Y.] *Times*, ca. December 1894. The publication source for this undated clipping is by hand in Todd's scrapbook.

The admirers of Emily Dickinson's poems have been desirous of seeing some of her prose, so the following letters were gathered together by her sister and given to Mabel Loomis Todd, who is the editor of the two volumes. Emily Dickinson spent the greater part of her life in the beautiful old college town, Amherst, Mass. She was a lovely character, gentle and sympathetic, and was admired and loved by all who knew her. Her letters and poems are full of her own peculiar charm.

433 "Notes and Announcements." *Book Reviews* 2 (December 1894), 270. A routine publication announcement for the *Letters*, identical in wording with no. 402, appears on p. 286 of this issue of *Book Reviews*.

Those that remember the interesting character of Emily Dickinson's letters to Colonel Higginson published in the *Atlantic Monthly* for October, 1891, will be gratified to learn that all her other available letters are now collected and edited by Mrs. Mabel Loomis Todd of Amherst. They were published by Roberts Brothers, of Boston, on November 15, the letters to Colonel Higginson forming one of the ten chapters. Beginning in 1845, when Emily Dickinson had but recently passed her fourteenth birthday, the letters fill all the intervening years until her death in 1886, and were written to Samuel Bowles, Dr. J. G. Holland, "H. H.," and other persons of distinction.

434 "Other Holiday Gift Books." *Literary News* 15 (December 1894), 365. This notice is illustrated with the child portrait by Otis Bullard used as the frontispiece for the first volume of the *Letters*.

Letters of Emily Dickinson from 1847 to 1886, in two volumes, forms a fitting complement to "Emily Dickinson's Poems" published in recent years, as they comprise all the prose Emily Dickinson is known to have written, as the latter included all her poetical works. A special interest attaches to this writer's work, as it was not till death had claimed her that the world learned of her unique gifts through her friends Thomas W. Higginson and Mabel Loomis Todd, who compiled and edited her first work. The editor of the "Letters" is again Mabel Loomis Todd, who has produced a volume of unusual interest not only to Miss Dickinson's friends but to the general literary public. With the letters are included a portrait and a view of Miss Dickinson's home in Amherst, and three fac-similes of her handwriting at different periods of her life.

435 "New Publications." *Boston Saturday Evening Gazette* 82 (December 1, 1894), [4].

The Letters of Emily Dickinson, edited by Miss Mabel Loomis Todd, make two very pretty volumes to be sought by all readers of her poems. The first is dated 1845, so that they give the reader an opportunity to study the gradual growth of that peculiarity of expression which is her chief charm. In the second volume, the first draft of a letter and the appended changes made before sending it give decisive evidence that this strangeness of style was deliberate, not spontaneous. This makes the book none the less interesting, and the portrait of the writer and the facsimiles of her manuscript add to its value. The second volume, with its picture of her home, will amaze many a one, for her work gives the impression that she was one who dwelt somewhat remote from the world, and in a house of some quaintness.

436 Ellen E. Dickinson. "Emily Dickinson." *Chicago Inter-Ocean*, December 1, 1894, p. 16. A reprinting; see no. 391.

437 Lilian Whiting. "Life in Boston." *Chicago Inter-Ocean*, December 1, 1894, p. 14.

The "Letters" of Emily Dickinson are apparently making the same felicitous impression on the reading public that her poems have made. They are full of the most unique and original turns of thought; of strange, mysterious depths of life; of tenderness, high courage, and crystal sincerity, not biographical but retrospective. Mrs. Mabel Loomis Todd who, with Colonel Higginson, edited the poems, has collected and edited these letters, an almost herculean task one would imagine. The letters were written to school friends and to her relatives, to Colonel Higginson, Dr. J. G. Holland, Mr. Samuel Bowles, and Mrs. Todd. They are revelations of the unexpected. Miss Dickinson has been compared to Charlotte Bronte in her peculiar isolation of temperament, but she was more unique than Miss

Bronte, and certainly not less tender at heart and full of overflowing sympathy. The letters fill two volumes which the Roberts house bring out in their dainty style, and they can hardly fail to be held as permanent literature. While there is a proportion of the letters given that does not seem essential, yet the very fullness of the selections offers a clearer view of a most peculiar character that may well be studied with interest.

438   "Emily Dickinson's Letters." *Chicago Tribune,* December 1, 1894, p. 10.

Emily Dickinson was a Puritan nun. Born in Amherst, Mass., where she was bred and taught, she early showed an extremely retiring disposition, and at last deepened into a recluse. Her poems, published a short time ago after her death, were irregular in form; indeed, they defied form, and showed an elf-like intimacy with nature. Had Miss Dickinson been born in one of the older countries she would have found her vocation in taking the veil and immuring herself behind a convent's walls. As it was she buried herself in her New England homestead, and left the world as the result of her self-centered life a volume of scrappy poems, some of them startling in their gleams of imaginative power, and the present two volumes of letters which have been collected since her death.

"It was with something almost like dread that I approached the task of arranging these letters," writes Mabel Loomis Todd, who compiles and edits this correspondence, "lest the deep revelations of a peculiarly shy inner life might so pervade them that in true loyalty to their writer none could be publicly used. But with few exceptions they have been read and prepared with entire relief from that feeling, and with unshrinking pleasure; the sanctities were not invaded. Emily kept her little reserves and bared her soul but seldom, even in intimate correspondence. It was not so much that she was always on spiritual guard as that she sported with her varying moods and tested them upon her friends with apparent delight in the effect as airy and playful as it was half unconscious."

The sanctities have certainly not been invaded, nor has anything been revealed of importance. These letters will claim the attention chiefly of those who have tried to understand Miss Dickinson's poems; to the generality of readers they will be simply puzzling. The extent to which Miss Dickinson carried her eccentricity may be imagined from the following paragraph by the editor, who likes to enshroud her subject with a Delphic mystery:

In her later years Emily Dickinson rarely addressed the envelopes; it seemed as if her sensitive nature shrank from the publicity which even her handwriting would undergo in the observation of indifferent eyes. Various expedients were resorted to—obliging friends frequently performed this office for her; sometimes a printed newspaper label was pasted upon the envelope; but the actual strokes of her own pencil were, so far as possible, reserved exclusively for friendly eyes.

Mrs. Gordon L. Ford of Brooklyn, who died recently, furnishes remembrances of Miss Dickinson, having known the poetess in Amherst nearly fifty years ago:

The *Atlantic Monthly* was a youngster then, and our joy over a new poem by Lowell, Longfellow, and Whittier, our puzzles over Emerson's "If the red slayer think he slays," our laughter at Oliver Wendell Holmes, were full and satisfying. Lowell was especially dear to us, and once I saw a passionate fit of crying brought on when a tutor of the college, who dies while contesting the Senatorship for Louisiana, told us from his eight years of seniority that "Byron had a much better style," and advised us "to leave Lowell, Motherwell, and Emerson alone." Like other young creatures, we were ardent partisans. . . .

We had a Shakespeare club—a rare thing in those days—and one of the tutors proposed to take all the copies of all the members and mark out the questionable passages. This plan was negatived at the first meeting, as far as "the girls" spoke, who said they did not want the strange things emphasized, nor their books spoiled with marks. Finally we told the men to do as they liked—"we shall read everything." I remember the lofty air with which Emily took her departure, saying: "There's nothing wicked in Shakespeare, and if there is I don't want to know it." The men read for perhaps three meetings from their expurgated editions, and then gave up their plan, and the whole text was read out boldly.

In her isolation of spirit and in her passionate love of nature Emily Dickinson often reminds one of Emily Bronte, apropos of which is reproduced this little note which, in 1849, Miss Dickinson sent to Mr. Bowdoin, a law student in her father's office. The occasion of sending it was the returning of a copy of "Jane Eyre":

Mr. Bowdoin: If all these leaves were altars and on every one a prayer that Currer Bell might be saved and you were God—would you answer it?

As Emily Dickinson approached middle life, and even before her thirtieth year, according to the present editor, it seemed to become more and more impossible for her to mingle in general society; and a growing feeling of shyness, as early as 1862 or 1863, caused her to abstain sometimes from seeing the dearest friends who came to the house. In spite of her sympathy with sadness and her deep apprehension of the tragic element in life, she was not only keenly humorous and witty, but, while made serious by the insistence of life's pathos, she was yet at heart as ecstatic as a bird. This combination of qualities made her companionship, when she vouchsafed it, peculiarly breezy and stimulating. Such a nature must inevitably know more pain than pleasure. She was warmly devoted to her friends. Whether in writing her poems the joy of creating was sufficient, or whether a thought of future and wider recognition ever came, it is certain that during life her friends made her audience. She cared more for appreciation and approval from the few who were dear than for any applause from an impersonal public. She herself writes, "My friends are my estate."

Among the closest friends of Miss Dickinson were Mr. and Mrs. Bowles (Mr. Bowles of the Springfield Republican, who died in 1878), and to friends like these she inclosed many of her poems. One occasionally catches a note of music. A spray of white pine was inclosed with this note:

A feather from the whippoorwill
That everlasting sings!
Whose galleries are sunrise,
Whose opera the springs,
Whose emerald nest the ages spin
Of mellow, murmuring thread,
Whose beryl egg, what schoolboys hunt
In recess overhead!

The pathos of the following is appreciated. The author says in a letter to her cousins: "Let Emily sing for you because she cannot pray":

It is not dying hurts us so—
'Tis living hurts us more,
But dying is a different way,
A kind, behind the door—

The Southern custom of the bird
That soon as frosts are due
Adopts a better latitude.
We are the birds that stay,
The shiverers round farmers' doors,
For whose reluctant crumb
We stipulate, till pitying snows
Persuade our feathers home.

Miss Dickinson was often besieged by different persons, literary and otherwise, to benefit the world by her "chirrup," but she steadily refused to publish during her life time. In all these years she was constantly writing verses; and while she frequently inclosed poems in letters to friends, the fact that scores in addition were being written every year was her own secret. Her literary methods were also her own—she must frequently have tossed off, many times daily, the stray thought which came to her. The box of "scraps" found by her sister after her death proves this conclusively, as some of Emily's rarest flashes were caught upon the margins of newspapers, backs of envelopes, or whatever bit of paper was nearest at hand, in the midst of other occupations. In the more carefully copied poems are many alterations, but it is a curious fact that not one change has reference to improvement in rhyme or rhythm. Every suggestion for a different word or phrase was in the evident hope that by some one of them the thought might be made clearer, and not in a single instance merely to smooth the form.

This collection of letters makes disjointed reading. One finds, for instance, a paragraph about George Eliot torn from the context of the letter, and it is submitted to the reader as one finds it. The date is December, 1880:

. . . The look of the words (stating the death of George Eliot) as they lay in the print I shall never forget. Not their face in the casket could have had the eternity to me. Now, my George Eliot. The gift of belief which her greatness denied her I trust she receives in the childhood of the kingdom of heaven. As childhood is earth's confiding time perhaps having no childhood she lost her way to the early trust and no later came. Amazing human heart, a syllable can make to quake like jostled tree, what infinite for thee? . . .

In the second volume are Miss Dickinson's letters to Col. Thomas Wentworth Higginson, to whom in the '60s she applied for advice and criticism. (The reader who is curious will find an article on Miss Dickinson by this gentleman in the *Atlantic* for October, 1891.) The letters here published give one glimpses of Miss Dickinson's nature, but they are more often as perplexing to the reader as they must have been to the recipient a quarter of a century ago. The following was written in 1862:

You inquire of my books. For poets I have Keats and Mr. and Mrs. Browning. For prose, Mr. Ruskin, Sir Thomas Browne, and the "Revelations." I went to school, but in your manner of the phrase had no education. When a little girl, I had a friend who taught me Immortality; but venturing too near, himself, he never returned. Soon after my tutor died, and for several years my lexicon was my only companion. Then I found one more, but he was not contented I be his scholar, so he left the land.

You ask of my companions. Hills, sir, and the sundown, and a dog as large as myself that my father bought me. They are better than beings, because they know, but do not tell; and the noise in the pool at noon excels my piano.

I have a brother and sister; my mother does not care for thought, and father too busy with his briefs to notice what we do. He buys me many books, but begs me not to read them, because he fears they joggle the mind. They are religious, except me, and address an eclipse every morning whom they call their "father."

But I fear my story fatigues you. I would like to learn. Could you tell me how to grow, or is it unconveyed, like melody or witchcraft?

Col. Higginson, it appears, asked for a photograph of his enigmatical correspondent. But there was none. She had an aversion to seeing herself in any kind of "mold," as she called it. The frontispiece to the first volume of these letters is taken from an oil painting when she was 8 years old in a group with her brother and sister. This was her answer to Mr. Higginson's question of her age:

[July 1862.]—Could you believe me without? I had no portrait now, but am small like the wren; and my hair is bold, like the chestnut burr; and my eyes like the sherry in the glass that the guest leaves. Would this do just as well?

It often alarms father. He says death might occur, and he has molds of all the rest, but has no mold of me: but I notice the quick wore off those things in a few days, and forestall the dishonor. You will think no caprice of me?

You said "dark." I know the butterfly, and the lizard, and the orchis. Are not those your countrymen?

I am happy to be your scholar, and will deserve the kindness I cannot repay.

In reading letters like the foregoing one feels much as did old Polonius when he went spying after the muttering Prince of Denmark. Only that one feels utterly incompetent to pluck out the heart of Miss Dickinson's mystery. It is hard for many persons to believe, even now, says the compiler of these letters, that Emily Dickinson had nothing to do with the Saxe Holm stories, and certainly some of their incidental poetry bears strong evidence of her unique touch. The little mystery of those remarkable tales was so carefully guarded that after a time people lost interest in surmising and are now content to accept them as they are. The "No Name" series of Roberts Bros. was not so long a secret, and in the volume of its verse, "A Masque of Poets," appeared, probably through the efforts of her old friend "H. H.," Emily Dickinson's "Success," afterward the opening poem in the first of her published volumes.

As her unique life drew towards its close Miss Dickinson became for the last two years a semi-invalid. She died in May, 1886. At her grave her "master" and friend, Col. Higginson, read Emily Bronte's noble "Last Lines," "a favorite," as the speaker said, "with our friend who had now put on that immortality which she seemed never to have laid off."

439 "Roberts' New Books." *Chicago Tribune,* December 1, 1894, p. 11. A Roberts Brothers advertisement listing seventeen titles, most with a few sentences of description. Dickinson's *Letters,* identified as in its "second edition" appears at the head of the column. The descriptive blurb reprints three sentences from Todd's introduction (no. 418). Reprinted in the *Chicago Inter-Ocean,* December 8, 1894, p. 10.

Emily Dickinson's letters almost as much as her poems, exhibit her elf-like intimacy with nature. She sees and apprehends the great mother's processes, and she shares the rapture of all created things under the sky. The letters speak of flowers, of pines, and autumnal colors; but no natural sight or sound or incident seems to have escaped her delicate apprehension.

440 *Chicago Tribune*, December 1, 1894. A reprinting; see no. 413. Unverified. The source and date attribution are by hand in Todd's scrapbook.

441 "The World of New Books." *Philadelphia Press*, December 1, 1894, p. 11.

When the poems of Emily Dickinson were first published there were many who recognized in her brief and fragmentary verses the inspiration of a great genius. The author seemed to be willfully careless of form, negligent of rhythm and meter and capriciously eccentric in regard to all the laws of versification. But her poems so beautifully unfolded to the reader the glory of common sights, they were informed with such enthusiasm for goodness and the highest love that it was impossible to withhold the heart from the spell of their music. Those who have read and loved her poetry will eagerly welcome the collection of the "Letters of Emily Dickinson," as edited by Mabel Loomis Todd and published by Roberts Bros. (Boston). One is hardly prepared for the dainty humor, the frolicsome gaiety, the joyousness which abound in these letters. Notwithstanding the serious nature of her poetical work we find that her heart had for its prevailing condition really bright and healthy happiness. These letters contain all the prose which she is known to have written, and they merit the close reading which we confidently expect for them.

442 "Books and Authors." *Boston Sunday Courier* 100 (December 2, 1894), [2].

The pair of pretty volumes that contain the letters of the self-isolated woman of Amherst, which are a proper companion to her poems, will afford a truly sympathetic pleasure to a great many persons who never knew her before. These letters especially show her subtle acquaintance with Nature and her mysterious ways. They betray her rapture and communicate her spirit. They treat of such subjects as flowers, pines, and the splendors of autumnal foliage; of bird-songs, crickets, frost and winter winds; of toads and snakes, bats and mushrooms. Stormy March is an especially dear month to her; Nature, in fact, was the charm and consolation of her life. These letters of her brooding spirit were collected by the loving pains of Mabel Loomis Todd, and in the present acceptable form of two small duodecimos are given to the world she never knew. She was a solitary, born to the realm of solitude. Those who love Nature in her varied manifestations with one-half the earnestness that she did, will be drawn to these intimate confessions of hers almost as strongly as if she had written them to themselves. There is a maidenly delicacy in their phrasing, and a domestic familiarity in their current thought, that unconsciously kindles a sympathetic contagiousness in the minds of all who read them with receptive feeling.

443 "Emily Dickinson's Letters." *Boston Times*, December 2, 1894. Attribution is by hand in Todd's scrapbook. Unlocated.

The "Letters of Emily Dickinson," edited by Mabel Loomis Todd, in two volumes, fitly follow her poems, and the admirers of this quaint, rare and peculiar New England product will find here more to enchain their attention. The letters have been discriminatingly prepared and carefully arranged and cover years between 1845 and 1886. In several respects they reflect her nature more completely than does her verse, for there is greater scope and freedom possible. The rare inner life is out-shadowed in its many moods, grave and gay, sensitive, responsive, stimulating. Her love for, and sympathy with nature, is especially emphasized, and her perception and comprehension of the methods and processes in the un-speaking world around are wonderful. Delicacy and frankness of statement com-bine to make her style attractive, and one feels in reading these letters that a friend or acquaintance is talking; indeed, their disingenuousness and at the same time keenness of observation and comment are among their chief charms. The letters of this brainy and untrammeled recluse will be ranked among the books of the season to make a permanent impression, and the value of the volume is enhanced by a portrait of Emily when a child, a view of her Amherst home and three fac-similes of her handwriting.

444 Lilian Whiting. "Boston Days." *New Orleans Times-Democrat*, Decem-ber 2, 1894, p. 17.

This autumn is rich in literature, but of all the new books the most unique are the two volumes of Emily Dickinson's letters. Miss Dickinson's poems are well known, and it is not too much to say that they have achieved a permanent place in our literature; her prose, which consisted solely of private letters, was "sampled" by a number of extracts given a few years ago in the *Atlantic Monthly*, and it was found to have a flavor that incited a desire for more. Her elusive per-sonality always suggests that high and lovely nature of Charlotte Bronte. The two had in common the temperamental solitude. Neither were unsympathetic or un-responsive; but were attuned to a different key from that of the usual day and daylight world. In Miss Dickinson's letters there is the same electric touch, the same swift, immediate revelation, as in her verse. Mrs. Mabel Loomis Todd who, with Col. Higginson, edited the poems, collects and edits these two volumes of letters. It must have been an arduous task, and the order, method and discrimi-nating selection of Mrs. Todd cannot be too highly appreciated. In these letters one finds things like these:

"You have the most triumphant face out of paradise, probably because you are there constantly, instead of ultimately."

"Come often, dear friend, but refrain from going."

"Love makes us heavenly without our trying in the least."

Mrs. Todd notes that after the death of Miss Dickinson's father she retired from almost all forms of human intercourse, "and these notes were the sole link still binding her to the world. Her life was full of thought and occupation dur-ing those introspective days," adds Mrs. Todd, "and it is impossible to conceive that any sense of personal isolation, or real loneliness of spirit because of the absence of humanity from her daily life, could have oppressed a nature so richly endowed."

To a friend Miss Dickinson sent this note with flowers: "I hope no bolder lover brought you the first pond lilies. The water is deeper than the land. The swim-mer never stagnates. I shall bring you a handful of lotus next, but do not tell the Nile."

And again: "To see is perhaps never quite the sorcery it is to surmise, though the obligation to enchantment is always binding."

"Would adding to happiness take it away, or is that a pernicious question?"

The volumes of these letters are a kind of gold mine of surprises all the time. They are vital, piquant, unique, effervescent. They are a suggestive fountain to have at hand on one's literary table.

445 "Along the Literary Wayside." *Springfield Sunday Republican*, Decem-ber 2, 1894, p. 11. This review may have been written by Mary Augusta

Jordan. Her name, penciled next to this clipping in Todd's scrapbook, is
followed by a question mark.

The letters of Emily Dickinson, the recluse genius of Amherst, now published,
much further acquaint us with her character than the poems have done, and are
welcome to all who admire and treasure the wonderful revelations of her erratic
verse. It is nevertheless somewhat painful to read these two volumes, which
Roberts Brothers publish, and which Mrs. Mabel Loomis Todd had edited. For
while we have no doubt that Emily Dickinson cherished the hope that her verses
would be given to the world, — knowing, as she must, how precious they were for
the spirit, — and even caring to leave behind her little address of greeting, — it is
certain that she never meant a line of these letters to be printed. Now that they
are between covers, in plain print, which the vulgar may read, we feel that the
shy and elusive creature is intruded upon, and for our part, we are inclined
humbly to beg pardon. To her, there was something that hurt even in dear
human contact at the last, but long before she quite withdrew herself she felt what
she wrote to Col. Higginson: "Of 'shunning men and women,'" — it would seem
that her correspondent had made some remonstrance — "they talk of hallowed
things, aloud, and embarrass my dog. He and I don't object to them, if they'll
exist their side."

This book is in fact a life of Emily Dickinson, for there is nothing more to say
of that than is said here, — except indeed the one thing that might make plain the
determining cause of her seclusion. We are inclined to think there was no one
event on record that can have that rank, but that it was a gradual process in an
unusually sensitive nature, which finding the world too rude, withdrew and dwelt
apart of necessity. Everything that touched her, and especially the griefs of life,
was serious in its effect; the war was felt more intensely than it would seem; the
births of children, one notes, were often deeply affecting to her. She early felt that
the spirit of God had hold of all the issues of life, — she could not dissociate life
from the profoundest feelings; she must have said with Hermione: "To me can
life be no commodity." This we find in the years that made her character, although
the youthful letters abound in gay and joyous feeling, and throughout all the years
there is seldom absent a playful humor, as well as a happy wit. This was consistent with her home life; and her affections were warm and constant, she loved
her friends even with ardor, rejoiced in their joys and solaced their sorrows. To
herself, her way of life never presented itself as unhealthy, it was simply her
own, and as sacredly right as breathing. Nor is there a trace of the morbid in all
the letters.

Mrs. Todd has edited the letters very well, and her introduction well expresses
what she has done, and the singular character she has had the rare fortune to link
her own name with, first by the poems, and now by this even more intimate work.
The letters are given in chapters according to the friends to whom they were sent;
first we have those to a school friend, beginning when Emily Dickinson was 14
and continuing for eight years; then those to her brother, W. A. Dickinson, during about the same time; letters to the late Mrs. Gordon L. Ford of Brooklyn (who
was Emily Fowler of Amherst and a girlhood friend), to Miss Lavinia Dickinson,
her sister, and others, up to 1865, from another chapter; others still are devoted
to Dr. and Mrs. J. G. Holland, Mr. and Mrs. Samuel Bowles, T. W. Higginson. Dur-

ing the last 16 years of her life the number of correspondents multiply. The first impression received from the girl's letters, from 14 up to 22, is simply that of the natural vivacity of an affectionate, intellectual, bright-spirited girl, and indeed there are many girls who write just such letters. She is sometimes funny. Time, she says in one letter, has carried off a friend to Hartford; "I ran after him and got near enough to him to put some salt on his tail, when he fled, and left me to return alone." She was 14 then, and wrote, as any girl might, "I am growing handsome very fast indeed. I expect I shall be the belle of Amherst when I reach my 17th year. I don't doubt that I shall have perfect crowds of admirers at that age. Then how I shall delight to make them await my bidding," etc. A little later she says: "I shall always remain the same old six-pence." She indulges in proper moralizing over neglected duties, misspent time. But the peculiar tendency of her thought peeps out nevertheless here and there, as when she says to her friend A.:—

Won't you read some work upon snakes?—I have a real anxiety for you. I love those little green ones that slide around by your shoes in the grass and make it rustle with their elbows. There is an air of misanthropy about the striped snake that will commend itself to your taste,—there is no monotony about it,—but we will more of this again.

In fact she was a healthy damsel; given, Mrs. Ford tells us, to long walks in the fields and woods; fond of the wild flowers and knowing their haunts; one of the wits of the school, a "humorist of the comic column" in the high school paper. Of her appearance Mrs. Ford wrote:—

"Emily was not beautiful, yet she had great beauties," notes Mrs. Ford. "Her eyes were lovely auburn, soft and warm, her hair lay in rings of the same color all over her head, and her skin and teeth were fine. She had a demure manner which brightened easily into fun where she felt at home; but among strangers she was rather shy, silent and even deprecating. She was exquisitely neat and careful in her dress, and always had flowers about her."

Compare this with what Emily wrote herself to Mr. Higginson when he wanted her photograph:—

Could you believe me without? I had no portrait now, but am small, like the wren; and my hair is bold like the chestnut burr, and my eyes like the sherry in the glass that the guest leaves.

The portrait of the child Emily of eight years, which forms the frontispiece to the first volume does not help one to see either likeness.

———

It is the extreme warmth of her affections which is the strong new impression of the whole succession of letters. One is not prepared by the poems for this constant engagement in the interests of others, the remembrances of days and seasons, the sending of dainty gifts. All the same, even dear personalities jarred upon her brought too near. Col. Higginson has related his only interview with her; as singular is Mrs. Todd's account of playing on the piano for her in the dim parlor,—"Emily just outside the door, her dress a spot of white in the dim hall." Then "a dainty note would come in to me, with a glass of wine, or a rare rose." We have heard a young woman of Amherst relate her experience when she went, by request, to sing for the recluse. Sitting in the dusky room, and singing apparently to no one, the singer grew to feel as if she were assisting at some mysterious and solemn rite. There was in this side of her nature a real sympathy between herself and the mysterious flower of shade and death, the Indian pipe, which Mrs.

Todd has chosen for her device, placing it upon the green cloth covers of these Letters, as on the Poems. Mrs. Todd had painted a panel of these flowers for her, and in the note acknowledging it, she says "That without suspecting it, you should send me the preferred flower of life, seems almost supernatural, and the sweet glee I felt at meeting it I could confide to none." Long before that she had written to children—she wrote charming little letters to children—"That was my 'pipe' you found in the woods." When she wrote the earlier letters, this part of her nature had not developed, and her style was flowing and even diffuse; but it became as startling in prose as in verse; and words often assumed new meanings which are not in the dictionaries.

————————

There is no way so sure to tell our readers what they will find in Emily Dickinson's letters like quoting from them. But in doing this, it is far more in accord with their character to quote bits. In the war, after the death of the son of President Stearns of Amherst college at Newbern, she wrote: "Sorrow seems more general than it did, and not the estate of a few persons, since the war began; and if the anguish of others helped one with one's own, now would be many medicines."

In early spring: Mother went rambling, and came in with a burdock in her shawl, so we knew that the snow has perished from the earth. Noah would have liked mother.

It is true that the unknown is the largest need of the intellect, though for it no one thinks to thank God.

How do most people live without any thoughts? There are many people in the street,—how do they live? How do they get strength to put on their clothes in the morning?

I hope heaven is warm, there are so many barefoot ones. I hope it is near,—the little tourist was so small, I hope it is not so unlike earth that we shall miss the peculiar form—the mold of the bird. "And with what body do they come?" What hour? Run, run, my soul! Illuminate the house. "Body!" then real,—a face and eyes,—to know that it is them! Paul knew the Man that knew the news, He passed through Bethlehem.

They say that God is everywhere, and yet we always think of him as somewhat of a recluse.

How extraordinary that life's large populations contain so few of power to us—and those a vivid species who leave no mode—like Tyrian dye.

I can't thank you any more. You are thoughtful so many times you grieve me always; now the old words are numb, and there aren't any new ones. Brooks are useless in freshet time.

These last quoted words are addressed to the late Samuel Bowles; her letters to him are remarkable even where all are so remarkable, in the last half of her life.

446 "New Books." *Worcester* [Mass.] *Spy*, December 2, 1894, p. 5.

Emily Dickinson's Letters, edited by Mabel Loomis Todd, as is the case with the letters of many other unique personalities, are very slightly interesting as letters, and very deeply interesting as reflecting Emily Dickinson. If one can overcome a sense of incongruity, to use no stronger word, that a life so remote and impregnably shy should be revealed to the public as intimately as a record of letters reveals, one may take an active pleasure in following these fragments of a poet's self-expression. The joyous side of Emily Dickinson's nature, which her poems reflect but little, but which, Mrs. Todd tells us, was characteristically hers, spends itself in her letters, particularly those to her family and nearest friends. Yet, self-sustained as she seems invariably to have been, one gets the impression that an unusual amount of sadness clouded her life; the letters referring to bereavements, her own, and her friends, are disproportionately frequent. The spontaneity of her poetry is emphasized by the peculiar lights, fanciful, tender, grotesque, which her letters constantly throw upon every-day happenings; and by the half metrical force which her prose unconsciously takes on when the thought is especially poetical.

Of most interest are Miss Dickinson's letters to Col. T. W. Higginson, whom, unknown, she sought as literary critic, and whose criticism and friendship justified her intuition.

For terse phrasing, startling suggestiveness, strong feeling restrained by plain words, this series of letters surely stands alone. In one letter she replies in this wise to Mr. Higginson's request for a portrait: "I had no portrait, now, but am small, like the wren, and my hair is bold, like the chestnut burr; and my eyes, like the sherry in the glass that the guest leaves. Would this do just as well?" A child-portrait of Emily Dickinson accompanies the letters. In later years, she would not permit any "mould" of herself.

Mrs. Todd has performed her task of editing, conscientiously and sympathetically, and the completed work is a valuable contribution, humanely considered, wherever it may be placed as literature.

447 "The Emily Dickinson Letters." *Boston Journal*, December 6, 1894, p. 3.

Emily Dickinson was an Amherst woman, very reticent, and, while possessed of no small ability as a writer, so exceedingly modest that none of her writings ever came to a publisher's hands until after her death. It is stated that she would seldom address her own letters, so fearful was she of having her handwriting the property of strange eyes. She wrote many verses of a peculiarly interesting strain, but they were published first by friends after the author was dead. Now two volumes have been published, giving as much as is possible of her life from her letters. The editor is Mabel Loomis Todd. No prose writings of Miss Dickinson's are in print except these letters. Many of these were not dated. Even in those of the earliest date, when the author was barely fourteen, there is much for the student both of human nature and of literature. The life of the retiring girl was very quiet, and her thoughts were all that dared run riot. The letters are often piquant, and generally unique in phrasing and thought.

448 "Emily Dickinson's Letters." *Denver Times*, December 7, 1894, p. 4. Reprinted from an unlocated *Boston Transcript*.

It will certainly prove a revelation to those who have cared for her poetry to learn from the volume of her prose, soon to appear, that Emily Dickinson began life as a humorist. The late Mrs. Ford, of Brooklyn, one of her girlhood friends, describes her as a writer of letters "sparkling with fun, and that is a new phase to the public."

No personality in our later literary history has attracted attention in just the way that Emily Dickinson does. She was unknown until she died. To readers in general her existence and her talent were not to be counted among the interests of forces of our time until after the death of the gentle recluse of Amherst, the lady who lived always in her father's house, a joyous, enthusiastic spirit hidden from the world which now received her "message." Her poetry indicated much of sadness, and what Mrs. Todd, her biographer, calls a "somber and even weird outlook upon this world and the next," but since stimulating moral heights were her native dwelling place, a sustained cheer of spirit was the natural result. Mrs. Todd says that it was with something almost like dread that she approached the task of arranging the letters collected by the sister of Miss Dickinson from various correspondents, lest the revelations of a peculiarly shy inner life might so pervade them that in true loyalty to their writer none could be publicly used. But, with few exceptions, they have been read and prepared with entire relief from that feeling, and with unshrinking pleasure; the sanctities were not invaded. Emily kept her little reserves and bared her soul but seldom, even in intimate correspondence. It was not so much that she was always on spiritual guard as that she sported with her varying moods and tested them upon her friends with apparent delight in the effect as airy and playful as it was half unconscious. The earlier letters show something of the quality of the mind of a child of special ingenuity and delicacy, but they are not particularly prophetic of the charm of phrase in the later letters. The story told for her brother of the family going to Northampton to hear Jenny Lind sing is interesting for more than one reason. It is written on a July Sunday in 1851, and begins by telling how the family, knowing the world to be hollow, started at 6 to drive to the concert, which began at 8, then—

"We had proceeded some steps when one of the beasts showed symptoms; and just by the blacksmith's shop the exercises commenced, consisting of kicking and plunging on the part of the horse, and whips and moral suasion from the gentleman who drove—the horse refused to proceed, and your respected family with much chagrin dismounted, advanced to the hotel, and for a season halted; another horse was procured, we were politely invited to take our seats and proceed, which we refused to do till the animal was warranted. About half through our journey thunder was said to be heard, and a suspicious cloud came traveling up the sky. What words express our horror when rain began to fall, in drops, sheets, cataracts—what fancy conceive of drippings and of drenchings which we met on the way; how the stage and its mourning captives drew up at Warner's hotel; how all of us alighted, and were conducted in—how the rain did not abate—how we walked in silence to the old Edwards church and took our seats in the same— how Jennie came out like a child and sang and sang again—how bouquets fell in showers and the roof was rent with applause—how it thundered outside, and inside with the thunder of God and of men—judge ye which was the loudest; how we all loved Jennie Lind, but not accustomed oft to her manner of singing didn't fancy that so well as we did her. No doubt it was very fine, but take some notes from her Echo, the bird sounds from the Bird song, and some of her curious trills, and I'd rather have a Yankee. Herself and not her music was what we seemed to love—she has an air of exile in her mild blue eyes, and a something sweet and touching in her native accent which charms her many friends. 'Give me my thatched cottage'—as she sang she grew so earnest and seemed half lost in song, and for a transient time I fancied she had found it, and would be seen 'na mair'; and then her foreign accent made her again a wanderer—we will talk about her some time when you come. Father sat all the evening looking mad, and yet so much amused that you would have died a-laughing. . . . It wasn't sarcasm exactly, nor it wasn't disdain; it was infinitely funnier than either of those virtues, as if old Abraham had come to see the show and thought it was all very well, but a little excess of monkey! She took $4,000 for tickets at Northampton, aside from all expenses."

449 "New Publications." *Philadelphia Public Ledger*, December 7, 1894, pp. 15–16.

Transcendentalism should claim Emily Dickinson for its own as her prose and verse alike fulfill the intention with absolute simplicity, and complete independence of the fetters of rhyme. The "Letters" show the same irregularity of expression, and also a singular quality of "hidden music," which become impressive on further acquaintance. The "Letters" are surcharged with original thought, and they are not subject to the slight disadvantage under which the poems labor. Mrs. Mabel Loomis Todd edits the "Letters" for publication. It has been well said by her that if in Emily Dickinson's work there is frequently no rhyme where rhyme should be, a subtle something, welcome and satisfying, takes its place.

The epigrammatic quality of Miss Dickinson's writing is strongly marked. The thought is often vigorous and expressed with terseness, sometimes even in a brusque manner. So it happens that her poetic fancies are wild flowers—no conventional blooms, but at best "garden escapes." For many years Miss Dickinson lived the life of a recluse, and her disinclination for general society was carried to an unusual degree. Her biographer says that in later years Emily Dickinson rarely addressed the envelopes of her letters; it seemed as if her sensitive spirit shrank from the publicity which even her handwriting would undergo in the observation of indifferent eyes. Various expedients were resorted to. Obliging friends sometimes performed this office, and sometimes a printed newspaper label was pasted upon the envelope, but the actual strokes of her own pencil were, so far as possible, reserved for friendly eyes. If it is not good for man to be alone, the same objection applies to feminine desire to retire from the world. The incident shows that the wish to retreat far from the madding crowd can easily be rendered ridiculous when indulged to excess.

But, although invisible for years, even to life-long friends, Emily never denied herself to children. To them she was always accessible, always delightful, and in their eyes a sort of fairy guardian. Stories are yet told of her roguishly lowering baskets of "goodies" out of her window by a string to little ones waiting below. One of her epistles included in this correspondence runs as follows: "Dear Boys: Please never grow up, which is far better. Please never 'improve;' you are perfect now. Emily."

450 Mary Abbott. "Emily Dickinson's Letters." *Chicago Herald*, December 8, 1894, p. 11.

It seemed probable when the poems of Miss Emily Dickinson were brought out a few years ago that we should hear a good deal more of that singular and gifted creature. Her letters, it was said at the time, were withheld from publication by the feeling of her sister, averse to it; but it seems that this objection has been routed, for the letters are now brought out in a book, edited by Mabel Loomis Todd.

Miss Dickinson's letters to Thomas Wentworth Higginson were reproduced in the article written by him for the *Atlantic Monthly* in 1891, possibly others. At any rate that curious correspondence remains in memory—a unique recollection.

The letters, most of them, are uneventful. And, as a rule, it is not only a mistake, but a mean trick to publish private correspondence. As people grow famous they must, if they are not fools, know that, sooner or later, their letters will be put in print. The letters of great persons, after they have come to be great, bear unmistakable evidences of foreordination and predestination. But to take poor little wayside, woodland Emily Dickinson, who really did shun publicity, or, at least, never thought of such a thing, and print her prattlings, is unkind. Mr. Higginson was guilty of a betrayal of confidence when he allowed her description of herself to go into circulation. "I had no portrait now" (why should she say "I had now?" It must have been affectation in an educated girl, and lack of education in New England does not mix up auxiliaries). "I had no portrait now, but am small, like the wren; and my hair is bold, like the chestnut burr; and my eyes, like the sherry in the glass that the guest leaves." This might be the conceited account of herself of a wonderful beauty. And Mr. Higginson described her, when he did see her, as plain and not fulfilling her own exquisite description. The letter in which this portrait occurs, and others, are published twice; the rest of the Higginson correspondence is given for the first time in this book. There was much that was stilted and affected in those letters and here and there a wonderful shower of stars, like the bursting of a rocket. The mind was an exquisite one; far more exquisite than the expression of it, sometimes.

Yet criticism is disarmed now and then wholly and unequivocally. "I never heard anyone speak of the Pippa passes before" is touching in its simple orientalism. And "If I read a book and it makes my whole body so cold no fire can ever warm me I know that is poetry. If I feel physically as if the top of my head were taken off I know that is poetry. These are the only ways I know it. Is there any other way?" is sublimely pathetic. Colonel Higginson calls them the "very wantonness of overstatement." He should not have called them at all. They were bursts of confidence from a shy, darting little thing who had given him her poetic soul privately to look at. It is as if he put it on exhibition in a shop widow.

"I am glad there is immortality, but would have tested it myself before entrusting him" (in writing of her father's death) was also a strictly confidential utterance. There is a feeling all the time of base spying and peeping on the part of the reader.

Miss Dickinson used to write her thoughts voluminously, but always secretly and as if she could not help it. They were found on margins of newspapers, backs of envelopes, and showed her desire to put ideas into words. The poems are full of thought, and it is only right we should have them; the private correspondence should have been sacred; and sparkling and beautiful as some of it is it is not of public interest, although it may satisfy public curiosity. The book is fascinating, and the task of arranging the letters has been done as delicately as possible and by loving hands.

451 H. B. B[lackwell]. "Literary Notices." *Woman's Journal* 25 (December 8, 1894), 387.

The lovers of Emily Dickinson's poems have been so eager for her prose that her sister has gathered these letters and placed them in the hands of the editor. The exquisite child-portrait of little Emily which is the frontispiece, seems a sort of key to the unconscious self-revelations which follow. Although the exact sequence of dates is not always possible, as she had the foible of disregarding dates, yet they give us the gradual unfolding of an exquisite personality, as the child of 1845 gradually becomes the mature woman of 1886. Her earlier letters show genius, but not the oddity which characterizes her later flashing and fragmentary incoherences, which contain revelations of the utmost value and potency. Taken connectedly, they constitute a sort of spiritual autobiography. Her last letter to her cousins, just before she died, was startling in its sententious brevity. It consisted of five words. "Little Cousins, — Called back. Emily."

Was ever human missive more solemn and suggestive? These letters are confidential communications from one of the shyest and sweetest of human beings.

452 "A New England Nun." *Philadelphia Evening Telegraph*, December 5, 1894, p. 2.

One of Miss Wilkins' most pathetic sketches of Bay State character is entitled *A New England Nun*, a careful and undoubtedly faithful study of a village girl, who, remaining unmarried, gradually settled down into the habits of a recluse, and eventually became as exclusively solitary as if committed to self-communings by religious obligations. Such seems to have been the life of Emily Dickinson, whose poems, published since her death, have attracted the enthusiastic interest of a limited circle of cultivated minds. Surviving her immediate family, and never contracting new relations by marriage, Miss Dickinson lived in the homestead in Amherst, Mass., gradually withdrawing from the world, until at last she lost all connection with society save by occasional letters, and apparently lived during her later years the life of a New England Nun, as strictly immured in the loneliness of her home as if confined within conventual walls.

This seclusion was due partly to the circumstances of Miss Dickinson's single life and partly to the extreme sensitiveness of her delicate and spiritual nature, a sensitiveness that eventually developed into morbid aversion to society and finally into eccentricity bordering on insanity. As witnessing the unbalanced state of her mind in this respect, the involuntary testimony given in *Letters of Emily Dickinson*, currently published, is pathetic, even while it excites the impatience with which demonstrations of mental alienation are wont to awaken. She wrote voluminously to her few friends, but could not bear the public exposure of her handwriting on the superscription of a letter—resorting to various devices for giving the necessary address without writing it. She was fond of giving fruit and flowers to those dear to her, and especially to children, but would lower these gifts in a basket from a chamber window while hiding behind the curtain. She delighted in music, but would only listen to a friend's playing for her on condition of being allowed to sit alone in the dark in another room.

That she had a wonderfully bright mind and singularly clear spiritual insight the inspired beauty of her remarkable poems attests, and the same qualities are shown in different degree in her letters. These letters are given as the only examples extant of her prose writings, and they confirm the report made by friends of her rare intellectual powers. Many of them are distinguished by flashes of almost supernatural brilliancy of thought; and many give expression in epigrammatic sentences to spiritual wisdom and truths of profoundest significance. It was in song, however, that she found her highest and happiest expression, and in her correspondence she constantly returns to spontaneous verse as the medium native to her hand. These bits of improvised melody are necessarily fragmentary, and the best of them cannot be appreciated cut out from their environment; but an example or two may be cited in illustration of her unquestionable poetic gift. The following affords a hint as to her mental attitude respecting social intercourse:—

> Never for society
> He shall seek in vain
> Who his own acquaintance
> Cultivates of men
> Wiser men may weary,

But the man within
Never knew satiety, —
Better entertain
Than could Border Ballads,   [Ballad
Or Biscayen Hymn;
Neither introduction
Need you—unto him.

Like all truly poetic souls Miss Dickinson was deeply in love with Nature, and
richly enjoyed all Nature's wealth of beauty with almost painful intensity. She
saw and understood all that goes on in the rural world during the passing year,
and was ready to welcome each season and flower and bird in its turn visiting her
home. Of the robin she sang with a note like his own:—

The robin is a Gabriel
In humble circumstances,
His dress denotes him socially
Of transport's working classes.
He has the punctuality
Of the New England farmer—   [a New
The same oblique integrity,
A vista vastly warmer.
A small but sturdy residence,
A self-denying household,
The guests of perspicacity
Are all that cross his threshold.
As covert as a fugitive,
Cajoling consternation
By ditties to the enemy
And sylvan punctuation.

Of the deep things of life and death she mused continually, and some of her
mystic utterances seem as though they might have come from beyond the veil.
On the passing away of her mother she wrote, evidently with unpremeditated
art:—

To the bright East she flies;
Brothers of paradise
Remit her home,
Without a change of wings,
Or Love's convenient things,
Enticed to come.

Fashioning what she is,
Fathoming what she was,
We deem we dream—
And that dissolves the days
Through which existence strays
Homeless at home.

The two volumes of letters are mines of jewels, among which may be found
gems of priceless lustre. They do not give much biographic information, and indeed there was apparently pathetically little to give, but they add to the poet's production already published a thesaurus of verse of rare quality and permanent
worth.

453 "Weekly Record of New Publications." *Publishers' Weekly* 46 (December 8, 1894), 1002. The following sentence accompanies routine bibliographical citation.

The lovers of Emily Dickinson's poems have been so eager for her prose that her sister has gathered these letters, and committed their preparation to Mabel Loomis Todd, who also furnishes an interesting introduction on Miss Dickinson's personality.

454 [Mary Augusta Jordan.] "Emily Dickinson's Letters." *Nation* 59 (December 13, 1894), 446–47. Reprinted: *New York Evening Post*, December 18, 1894, p. 12. Partially reprinted: *Book Reviews* 2 (January 1895), 321–22.

These letters begin in reasonable conformity to the principles of the polite letter-writer. By degrees date, address, formal structure drop off or are developed away. At all events, the last of the periods into which the editor divides the letters holds only notes, whose structure reminds the reader of sheet-lightning when they are most connected, of nothing in literature when they are disconnected. These letters cannot fail to arouse sharp differences of opinion, but also they cannot fail to arouse interest. They are an important contribution to our collection of human documents. Valued at their lowest as literature, they are suggestive studies in applied Lombroso. At their best, they are brilliant expressions of an unusual and original personality.

They extend from 1845 to the author's death in 1886, and the labor involved in arranging them, mainly from internal evidence, has been simply enormous. It has been a task, too, calling for exceptional powers of interpretation and sympathy. Mrs. Todd's preface suggests the two lines of interest likely to be felt in the letters: they deepen the impression made by Miss Dickinson's poems, and they afford material for the study of an extraordinary style. The style of a recluse is as definite and legitimate an object of investigation as the conditions that make the writer seclude herself; and these letters, in their early stage, show the usual human tendency to commonplaceness. Miss Dickinson defines genius as the ignition of the affections, and the definition seems likely in her case to have been true. Certainly the preternatural compression and point of her literary expression appears to be the revenge exacted by an over-sensitive temperament for its failure to maintain the ordinary social relations.

The contents of the letters show the writer a less sprite-like, more human, being than she seemed in the poems. There is less of the demonic love in her affections, more of the familiar attachment to horse and house, kith and kin. Her enjoyments, too, sometimes fall short of the elevated ecstasy of a metaphysical sunset or of the consolations of death. But her easy acceptance of the terms of life becomes more and more impossible as the letters go on. The pathos of her recurring, short-lived revivals of the effort to live life whole instead of by spasms is extreme. One cannot help wishing that the writer's sense of humor had been more persistently indulged, or, perhaps, less persistently translated into paradox. The epigram and paradox of the later periods are excellent of their kind, and were doubtless a relief to the writer; but we cannot help profanely wondering what would have been the effect on the author's genius if she had reduced the nervous tension now and then by indulging in a genuine bout of gossip. Her attitude is depressingly superior. She does not abuse her neighbors enough to love them temperately. Her life grows more and more interior, until it reminds the reader of Plato's cave dweller who saw life only as it shadowed itself in the mouth of the den. Her family affections and her friendships are passionately strong, her hold on life slight and shifting. The contemporary life of her country, for example, does not interest her except as a source of disturbance to her own emotional condition, or to the wider self that she found in certain aspects of family, neighborhood, and town. The Civil War was apparently unthinkable, and so unspeakable to her. Its record is the slightest possible in her pages, but the reserve is formidable. Things had a tendency to become unthinkable to her. She had little practical skill in what a clever writer calls "the art of taking hold by the small end."

What name will be given to experience of this sort, what estimate made of its expression, is an interesting question. A still more interesting question is what ought to be the name and estimate. Opinion will probably swing between the conviction that these letters are a precious legacy of genius for which we have to thank the scrupulous industry of Mrs. Todd and the generosity of Miss Lavinia Dickinson, and the equally strong feeling that they are the abnormal expression of a woman abnormal to the point of disease, and that their publication by a friend and a sister is not the least abnormal thing about them. But this difference of opinion involves an endless controversy about standards of taste and the legitimate in art. There have been great geniuses who have not been admired by other great geniuses, and whose genius even was denied. There have been numberless little men who could not impress their talent on men as little as themselves. But whatever the total judgment on Emily Dickinson's letters may be, a judicious selection from them must impress any reader; and if some who persevere to the end complain of a monotonous redundancy, others who have been irresistibly drawn along will rejoice that they are not more select and expurgated. The most Philistine of them will enjoy Miss Dickinson's account of herself written to Colonel Higginson in 1862. Her story of her education compares favorably in its way with St. Augustine's, John Stuart Mill's, Mark Pattison's, and J. H. Newman's. Here is a part of it, beginning (p. 301) with the paragraph introduced by "You asked how old I was?" Evading an answer to this question, Miss Dickinson proceeds without a pause:

"I made no verse, but one or two, until this winter, sir.

"I had a terror since September I could tell to none; and so I sing as the boy does of the burying-ground, because I am afraid.

"You inquire my books. For poets, I have Keats and Mr. and Mrs. Browning. For prose, Mr. Ruskin, Sir Thomas Browne, and the *Revelations*. I went to school, but, in your manner of the phrase, had no education. When a little girl, I had a friend who taught me Immortality; but venturing too near, himself, he never returned. Soon after, my tutor died, and for several years my lexicon was my only companion. Then I found one more, but he was not contented I be his scholar, so he left the land.

"You ask of my companions. Hills, sir, and the sundown, and a dog large as myself that my father bought me. They are better than beings, because they know but do not tell; and the noise in the pool at noon excels my piano.

"I have a brother and sister; my mother does not care for thought, and father, too busy with his briefs to notice what we do. He buys me many books, but begs me not to read them, because he fears they joggle the mind. They are religious, except me, and address an eclipse, every morning, whom they call their 'Father.'"

Every one will be conscious of refreshment on opening the second volume, which introduces the letters to her cousins, by far the most spontaneous of all. Elsewhere, in the longer efforts at least, there is a sense of strain and consciousness, not to call it affectation, as if the solitary instance of a rough draft adduced by Mrs. Todd (p. 424) were not the only one. The tendency, however, of Miss Dickinson's prose to fall into the favorite rhythm of her poems is, whenever observable (and it occurs constantly), the best evidence of the naturalness of her Orphic outpourings. It was often pure chance whether she wrote continuously the full width of the line, or chopped up her measures into verse lengths. For example:

"Travel why to Nature, when she dwells with us? Those who lift their hats shall see her, as devout do God" (p. 180).

"Not that he goes—we love him more who led us while he stayed. Beyond earth's trafficking frontier, for what he moved he made" (p. 224). (Should not this, by the way, read: "Who led us—while he stayed—beyond earth's trafficking frontier"?)

"Be but the maid you are to me, and they will love you more" (p. 256).

"A word is dead when it is said, some say. I say it just begins to live that day" (p. 269).

"The competitions of the sky corrodeless ply" (p. 285).

"I work to drive the awe away, yet awe impels the work" (p. 296).

The new bits of poetry presented in these volumes in connection with the letters are mostly of little worth, but there are one or two striking exceptions. Too original and individual, we fear, for Dr. Murray's use are some neologisms and colloquial phraseology of a curious kind; and how so ingrained a New Englander could confound shall and will passes understanding. There is no lack of bright and witty touches throughout; and on occasion, as in the letter relating the death in battle and burial of young Stearns (p. 242), there is a fine and effective coherency. It would be easy to multiply instances of a style whose early promise was considerable, but hardly maintained. These two are from the girl of twenty and twenty-one (pp. 48, 102):

"Oh, I struggled with great temptation, and it cost me much of denial; but I think in the end I conquered—not a glorious victory, where you hear the rolling drum, but a kind of a helpless victory, where triumph would come of itself: faintest music, weary soldiers, not a waving flag, nor a long, loud shout."

Of Professor Park's preaching:

"The students and chapel people all came to our church, and it was very full and still—so still the buzzing of a fly would have boomed like a cannon. And when it was all over, and that wonderful man sat down, people stared at each other, and looked as wan and wild as if they had seen a spirit, and wondered they had not died."

Mrs. Todd's arrangement of the letters by correspondents rather than chronologically was perhaps the best for readability, but the biographical impression is necessarily weakened thereby, especially as so many of these notes relate to the death of friends and kindred. For example, to ascertain that they give no clue to the nature of the "terror since September," 1861, one has to search the whole of volume i. and part of volume ii. By way of compensation there is a good index. As the volumes are consecutively paged, there is a prospect, we suppose, some day of a one-volume edition.

455 "Letters of Emily Dickinson." *Literary World* 25 (December 15, 1894), 445–46.

In the poetry of Emily Dickinson there was a quality so unique and so penetrating as to awaken keen interest in the writer's personality. To this desire for further acquaintance her sister has responded by permitting her letters to be published under the editorship of her appreciative friend, Mrs. Mabel Loomis Todd, who says:

It was with something almost like dread that I approached the task of arranging these letters, lest the deep revelations of a peculiarly shy inner life might so pervade them that in true loyalty to their writer none could be publicly used. But, with few exceptions, they have been read and prepared with entire relief from that feeling and with unshrinking pleasure; the sanctities were not invaded. Emily kept her little reserves, and bared her soul but seldom even in intimate correspondence. It was not so much that she was always on spiritual guard as that she sported with her varying moods and tested them upon her friends with apparent delight in the effect, as airy and playful as it was half unconscious.

Her letters more freely than her verses indicate "the dainty humor, the frolicsome gaiety, which continually bubbled over in her daily life. The somber and even weird outlook upon this world and the next, characteristic of many of the poems, was by no means a prevailing condition of mind; for, while fully apprehending all the tragic elements in life, enthusiasm and bright joyousness were yet her normal qualities and stimulating moral heights her native dwelling place." All this we must believe since her friend so assures us, yet such sensitiveness as clearly was Emily Dickinson's means great capacity for suffering; and the intensity of her attachment to kindred and friends, as well as the seclusion into which she shrank after her earlier years, suggest that she was instinctively protecting herself by love and withdrawal from currents and counter-currents that would sadly have hurt her in their buffeting.

The letters begin soon after the fourteenth birthday. The difference in style between these and later ones is even more marked than usual. Many people in their youth have written as diffusely as Miss Dickinson, but few in maturity have used forms so condensed and incisive. After attending school in her native town of Amherst she spent a year at Mt. Holyoke Seminary. Among her mates she is remembered as a writer of extraordinary compositions and teller of intensely funny stories. At Amherst, as at the seminary, there was "plain living and high thinking." Emily Dickinson always had choice society, and throughout life received from her loyal friendships some of her keenest pleasure, as is shown by her letters to Dr. and Mrs. J. G. Holland, Mr. and Mrs. Samuel Bowles, and many others. Yet she was hardly more than thirty when her growing shyness sometimes prevented her from seeing her dearest friends when they came to her house. "Her happiness in their love and trust was at times almost too intense to bear, . . . and disproportionately great pain was caused by even comparatively slight separations." To the Hollands she wrote: "We talk of you together, then diverge on life, then hide in you again as a safe fold. Don't leave us long, dear friends! You know we're children still, and children fear the dark."

How epigrammatic Miss Dickinson's letters were can easily be guessed by the readers of her poems. At Christmastime she wrote, "God bless the hearts that suppose they are beating and are not, and infold in his infinite tenderness those that do not know they are beating and are." To one friend she paid this tribute, "You have the most triumphant face out of paradise, probably because you are there constantly instead of ultimately." To another she wrote, "Is not the sweet resentment of friends that we are not strong more inspiring even than the strength itself?" Her love for nature was as intimate as that of Emily Brontë—a source of sweet trouble and exquisite consolation. Here is a note of thanks, "In a world too full of beauty for peace I have met nothing more beautiful." A spirit vibrating like hers to the touch of subtle truth and loveliness could by no possibility accept any current ideas which made God a faraway and dreary power:

Her garden was full of His brightness and glory; the birds sang and the sky glowed because of Him. To shut herself out of the sunshine in a church, dark, chilly, restricted, was rather to shut herself away from Him; almost pathetically she wrote, "I believe the love of God may be taught not to seem like bears."

"In essence no real irreverence mars her poems or her letters," but some expressions in each are as startling as those often uttered by children.

Although this writer of a thousand poems refused all invitations to publish—that being "foreign to her thought as firmament to fin"—she showed a wish for competent and impartial judgment by writing to Col. T. W. Higginson, an entire stranger, and asking him, "Are you too deeply occupied to say if my verse is alive?" Selections from this correspondence have been given by Colonel Higginson in the *Atlantic Monthly* of October, 1891. The other letters of the pupil to her "master" are now added. Obviously she could not have chosen a better critic, one who would more fully appreciate her individuality and at the same time suggest whatever might broaden and enrich it. Mrs. Todd says, "It is hard for many persons to believe even now that Emily Dickinson had nothing to do with the Saxe Holm stories, and certainly some of their incidental poetry bears strong evidence of her unique touch."

After her father's death Miss Dickinson's retirement became almost complete, notes being the chief links that bound her to the world. Yet she never denied herself to children, who looked upon her as a kind of fairy guardian. Something elf-like, indeed, there seems to be in the composition of this rare, sequestered nature. New England has produced many original growths to puzzle and fascinate the student of psychology. None is more sure to move recurrent wonder than this recluse of Amherst. To her should be accorded a scrutiny as delicate and keen as that which is given to Jones Very or Emily Brontë or William Blake.

456 "Literature." *Philadelphia Evening Bulletin*, December 15, 1894, p. 4.

The effect upon the reading public of Emily Dickinson's verses was one of those extraordinary phenomena which from time to time puzzle bibliophiles and start literary critics to overhauling accepted standards. She wrote with a rhythmic consciousness which rendered her seeming lack of the musical sense the more remarkable. She gave expression, in words of striking power, to "thronging visions of blossom and bird and blue, beloved air"—of "life, death, and that vast forever" which seem to have been ever floating through her brooding mind. Her verse (we hesitate to call it poetry) was epigrammatic in quality and almost masculine in the vigor of its underlying thought. People knew little of her; she was shy to the verge of monomania; so far did her eccentricity go that she rarely addressed the envelopes in which she sent letters to friends, because of her dislike that anyone should see her handwriting, except the favorites with whom she corresponded. She lived a recluse at Amherst, and there in May, 1886, she was carried to her long rest and the realization of her dreams. That briefly is the story of Emily Dickinson, and when we remember that this singular woman kept no journal and wrote no prose, outside of her correspondence, the value of the volumes now published becomes apparent. We have here letters to Mrs. Strong, W. A. Dickinson, Dr. and Mrs. J. G. Holland, Mr. and Mrs. Samule Bowles, Thomas Wentworth Higginson, Mrs. Helen Hunt Jackson and a few others, arranged not chronologically but in accordance with a system whereby the letters to each correspondent are grouped together—a system which, in the present case, is the most satisfactory that could have been adopted. The first volume, covering school days and young womanhood, does not contain much of interest to the general reader; but in the second volume we find many letters which seem to illume the strange personality of the writer as by a lightning flash. Here is part of a letter written to two friends in March, 1886—only a little while before Miss Dickinson's death:

I scarcely know where to begin, but love is always a safe place. I have twice been very sick, dears, with a little recess of convalescence, then to be more sick, and have lain in my bed since November, many years, for me, stirring as the arbutus does, a pink and russet hope; but that we will leave with our pillow. When your dear hearts are quite convenient, tell us of their contents, the fabric cared for most, not a fondness wanting.

Do you keep musk, as you used to, like Mrs. Morene, of Mexico? Or cassia carnations, so big they split their fringes of berry? Was your winter a tender shelter—perhaps like Keats's bird, "and hops and hops and hops in little journeys?"

Are you reading and well, and the W____s near and warm? When you see Mrs. French and Dan give them a tear from us. . . .

                                                    "Emily."

We get here a glimpse of Emily Dickinson's epistolary style—terse, suggestive, original as her verse.

The last message she wrote was the briefest possible note addressed to her cousins. It was composed of two words, of startling and dramatic import:

Little Cousins: Called back

                                                    "Emily"

Three days later she died.

These letters have been edited with care and judgment and with just enough of commentary to hold them together. The facsimile illustrations add materially to the value of the work.

457 "Emily Dickinson's Poems. First and Second Series." In Todd's scrapbook this unlocated Roberts Brothers advertisement is placed among materials published in mid-December 1894. The review from which these excerpts derive, as numbered in this volume, is supplied in brackets following each quotation. "Etching done by lightning" derives from a letter Mabel Todd received from a woman she described only as "a gifted poetess." Todd transcribed an extract from the letter and placed it at the end of her second scrapbook of Dickinson clippings.

"Etching done by lightning."

EMILY DICKINSON'S POEMS.

First and Second Series.

Edited by

T. W. Higginson and Mabel Loomis Todd.

The second volume contains a preface by Mrs. Todd, and an autograph letter from Helen Jackson to Miss Dickinson.

Mrs. Moulton says: "Perhaps the greatest literary event of last year, at least in Boston, was the publication of the 'Poems' of Emily Dickinson. . . . But I am convinced that it would be a loss to the world had this second volume remained unpublished." [273]

In compass of thought, grasp of feeling, and vigor of epithet, they are simply extraordinary, and strike notes, very often, like those of some deep-toned organ. — —*Nation.* [28]

They bear the stamp of original genius. There is nothing like these poems in the language. In them the witchery of genius throws its charm and its fascination over what without it would strike the eye as bare singularity. — —*Independent.* [44]

Full of a strange magic of meaning so ethereal that one must apprehend rather than comprehend it. — —*Transcript.* [48]

Here surely is the record of a soul that suffered from isolation, and the stress of dumb emotion, and the desire to make itself understood by means of a voice so long unused that the sound was strange even to her own ears. — —*Literary World.* [40]

16mo, cloth, $1.25 each; white and gold, $1.50 each; two volumes in one, $2.00

At all Bookstores. Postpaid, on receipt of price.

ROBERTS BROTHERS, Boston.

458 "Emily Dickinson's Letters." In Todd's scrapbook this unlocated Roberts Brothers advertisement is placed among materials published in mid-December 1894. A full-page facsimile of the poet's handwriting in 1882 accompanies the ad. The review from which these excerpts derive, as numbered in this volume, is supplied in brackets following each quotation. The fourth and seventh passages derive from the same *Boston Herald* review (no. 429).

"A most remarkable and interesting woman."

EMILY DICKINSON'S LETTERS.

Edited with an Introduction and Notes By Mabel Loomis Todd.

With portrait of Miss Dickinson as a child, a view of her home in Amherst, and three facsimiles of her handwriting at different periods of her life.

Emily Dickinson's letters, almost as much as the poems, exhibit her elf-like intimacy with Nature. She sees and apprehends the great mother's processes, and shares the rapture of all created things under the wide sky. The letters speak of flowers, of pines, and autumnal colors; but no natural sight or sound or incident seems to have escaped her delicate apprehension. —*Preface.* [418]

A most remarkable and interesting woman is revealed in this collection of letters. —*New York Times.* [426]

Evanescent flashes of thought, refreshingly original and quaint. — *Book Buyer.* [398]

Written straight out of her life. — *New York Herald.* [429]

No less startling and fascinating than the famous journals of Marie Bashkirtseff. — *Philadelphia Press.* [415]

Even more piquant, brilliant, and characteristic than the poems. — *Critic.* [411]

A personality is here revealed which has, perhaps, no counterpart in our literary history. — *Boston Herald.* [429]

A distinctly new sensation. — *Woman's Journal.* [405]

They will help, they will stimulate. These two volumes are among the books of the year. — *Advertiser.* [421]

2 vols. 16mo. Buckram Cloth. $2.00.

_____

At all Bookstores. Postpaid, on receipt of price.

ROBERTS BROTHERS, Boston.

459 "Literature." *New York Evening Post,* December 18, 1894, p. 12. A reprinting; see no. 454.

460 "Emily Dickinson's Letters." *Amherst Record,* December 19, 1894, p. 4.

To many who had made acquaintance with Emily Dickinson through the charming medium of her poems, the announcement that the latter were to be supplemented by two volumes of letters was warmly welcomed, but mingled with pleasurable anticipation there was a little of anxiety. The publication of Emily Dickinson's poems assumed almost the greatness of an event in American literature; it introduced to the reading public a mind, a character and a soul, with attributes so novel and so remarkable that critics were forced to discard the stereotyped compliments or condemnations passed upon the common productions of common minds. The poems invited and at the same time almost defied criticism, yet in the end they conquered it. They were attacked by language purists, by those who held it sin to violate the strict canons of machine-made verse, and for a time it was an open question whether the poems were to be permitted to take their place as literature or be banished to the *index expurgatorius.* But the reading public was wiser than the critics, it found the shining gold while the critics were hammering away at the surrounding quartz.

But to many who had learned to love the poems the question presented itself: "Can the marvelous fancy, the delicate instinct, the dainty expression that made a charm of verse be tethered in prose without losing something of freedom and natural grace?" "Can Pegasus eat hay without becoming of the common herd?" Natural questions these, but they are bravely and satisfactorily answered in the two volumes of "Emily Dickinson's Letters." The most ardent admirer of the poems can find in the letters nothing to disappoint, nothing to regret. Although the letters are addressed to near and dear friends there is about many of them an impersonal quality that appeals to the reader as if he or she were the person addressed. The public will appreciate them none the less that they were not written for the public eye. It would be a thankless task to use the literary square and compass to estimate, the critical weight and measure to value, these letters. One who reads them solely as a critic will lose much of the pleasure that they possess for the sympathetic reader. The sentences are not all polished, cause and effect are not always placed in proper relations, there are flights of imagination and depths of introspect before which criticism is powerless.

Were we asked to state the greatest charm possessed by these letters we should say it was their likeness to nature. There neither is nor can be anything artificial about them. They are records of thoughts and fancies and intuitions, common perhaps to many but few have been able to record them so that the world could understand. There is nothing common-place about them even when they deal, as many of them do, with common affairs of life. Emily Dickinson looked out upon life through glasses that reflected her inner nature. She saw the world as few have seen it, and it is our fortune that she has given glimpses of her visions to friends who felt that the world would be the wiser and better could it see as she did. She was a child of nature, and in the letters as in the poems shows an intimacy with nature's mysteries that is almost startling. There was, seemingly, nothing so small or insignificant among nature's creations but she took note of it and found in it something to admire. And from nature up to nature's God was but a little step. With the God of the Puritans she had no acquaintance, but with the all-loving Spirit of Truth and Holiness she was in close communion. The letters contain passages that many might deem irreverent, dealing so frankly as they do with the great problems of life and death and immortality, but those who can understand and appreciate their true meaning will recognize in the love for all things good a love and gratitude to the Author of all that is good.

The letters are arranged in chapters, and those addressed to the same person are given in chronological order. In this way it is easier to trace the development and intellectual growth of the writer. Perhaps the most surprising feature of the volumes is found in the character of the letters written while Miss Dickinson was still a school-girl. Even in her earlier years she had great thoughts and inspirations, and the common affairs of life were invested by her with a peculiar charm. She was loyal and devoted to her friends and her family relations were more to her than all the world beside. Even at Mt. Holyoke seminary where she found many new friends and life was a round of pleasure, she was possessed of great longings for her home in Amherst, and was never so satisfied as when within its walls. There is a marked change in style between these earlier letters and those written in the later years of her life. The latter are more brilliant yet we are not prepared to say more interesting. There is a great charm in noting the first essays of genius as in recognizing the fulfillment of its promise.

The reader of these letters owes a debt of gratitude to Mrs. Mabel Loomis Todd, who collected and arranged them for the press. The task was difficult and laborious, but is more than justified in its results. In preparing and presenting to the public the poems and the letters of Emily Dickinson, Mrs. Todd has performed a great service for American literature, none the less deserving of praise in that it has been a labor of love. The volumes are issued from the well-known publishing house of Roberts Bros. of Boston, a guarantee of their excellence from a typographical standpoint. They are attractively bound in green buckram, with lettering and a floral design stamped in gold. The first edition was exhausted almost as soon as issued and a second edition has been printed and is now on the market. The two volumes are neatly boxed and make an attractive holiday gift.

461 "Christmas Books." *Boston Evening Transcript*, December 19, 1894, p. 8.

Emily Dickinson's "Letters" are much sought for by all whom her quaint affecting poetry touched with its delicacy of feeling. The secluded life of the authoress is revealed anew in these "Letters," which are in a pair of pretty volumes suited to the holiday time.

462 "Christmas Books." *Hartford Courant,*" December 21, 1894, p. 6.

Lucy Larcom and Emily Dickinson are among the noteworthy folk sketched by friends or re-introduced by letters to the public.

463 *Chicago Journal,* December 22, 1894, p. 9. There are echoes, in this review, of Mary Augusta Jordan's *Nation* essay (no. 454).

"Letters of Emily Dickinson" edited by Mabel Loomis Todd, is a two-volume puzzle. Its contents remind one of sheet lightning. Now you see light enough to know that there are clouds, and now you don't see even that. These letters of Emily Dickinson's are just the sort of stuff of which cults are made. The abnormal straining after epigrammatic effect in the later letters, their disjointed appearance and illegible chirography, and their almost utter subjectiveness ought to attract the Browning cranks who have tired of the old fad and have not yet found a new one. In fact, this Amherst recluse appears to have been a feminine Amiel trying to express herself in Browningese.

Emily Dickinson, the eccentric character "discovered" some years ago by Colonel T. W. Higginson, was not a normal human being. Her alleged poems, resembling Walt Whitman's in style and Browning's in strain, can not be held up for popular admiration but her character is one full of interest from other standpoints than that of literature. She was afflicted by a nervous supersensitiveness that grew upon her with the years, until in her later life she was a recluse from the world and even from her friends, save for the weird, epigrammatic letters she wrote. These breathe at least a warm love for kin. But she shrank with a pathetic weakness painful to witness from the rude facts of the world, and lived more and more within herself, until, as her biographer says, her friends finally carried her away to the cemetery to rest in a seclusion scarcely greater than that into which she had withdrawn herself. She lived the strange, inner life reflected in Amiel's journal; but, unlike Amiel, she put her often brilliant thought into a prosy verse or a lofty, rhapsodical prose, instead of using the limpid sentences of the Genevan philosopher.

The letters start out in the first volume with quite ordinary epistles that might have been written by any bright girl with thoughts in her head. Gradually they become more fragmentary, disjointed and take on a tone as of a superior being who was too much occupied with her own thoughts even to think of her neighbors. One feels that she did not find enough fault with humanity to love it. The reader, seeking for the occasional gems among the mass of supermundane dross, sighs for just a breath of back-yard gossip to show that it is a woman and not a sprite or an inhabitant of Mars who talks.

It is true that humor once in a long while bubbles out almost naturally. But the flashes of human sympathy are comparatively rare, and seldom go out further than the bounds of her circumscribed world of kindred and child friends. Indeed, after her father's death she denied herself to almost every one save children—to these she was always a sort of fairy guardian.

It was often pure chance whether Emily Dickinson wrote out her lines to the end or broke them off and made some of her style of verse. Here are a few typical prose extracts. The sentences are not from the same letter, but they are scarcely more disjointed than if they were:

"Travel why to Nature, when she dwells with us? Those who lift their hats shall see her as devout do God."
"Not that he goes—we love him more who led us while he stayed. Beyond earth's trafficking frontier, for what he moved he made."
"Be but the maid you are to me, and they will love you more."
"A word is dead when it is said, some say. I say it just begins to live that day."
"The competitions of the sky corrodeless ply."
"I work to drive the awe away, yet awe impels the work."

Emily Dickinson's was a rare hermit nature, useful as a study in human curiosities, but not meriting the literary fuss that has been and will be made over her by minds of a certain cast—those that fall upon their faces before anything they can not understand.

The element that was lacking in Emily Dickinson's character appears to have been the "art of taking hold by the small end." An event like the war simply appalled her and became unthinkable. All through the war we find scarcely a reference to it in her letters. The trouble seemed to be that she saw all its horrors in mass, and, appalled, took refuge in not seeing it at all.

It will probably always remain a problem whether Mrs. Todd and Miss Lavinia Dickinson have shown good or bad taste in publishing these letters—whether they have blessed the world with some embalmed sparks of genius or have simply paraded the infirmities of a character that was abnormal almost to the point of disease.

464 Caroline Healey Dall. "Two Women's Books." *Boston Evening Transcript*, December 22, 1894, p. 16. The other book, treated in a final paragraph, is Mary Putnam Jacobi's *Common Sense*. Although the identity of Mrs. Dall's informant is not known, comparison with Ellen E. Dickinson's reminiscence, no. 391, is suggestive. Both give special attention to the poet's abundant hair, both imply that she became a recluse after meeting her fate in Washington, D.C., and Mrs. Dickinson describes herself as Mrs. Dall does her source, as "relative" and "friend." Mrs. Dall's account of Dickinson's life in this review elicited a spirited letter of correction from Lavinia; see *Life*, I, 152–55.

Never had the literary world encountered a more startling surprise than the first volume of Emily's poems. At first their mystery prevailed—no one could understand. Then their profound thought, hidden in condensed expression, but responsive to a sympathetic search, told to aching heads the whole story. Four years we have waited for these "Letters," hoping to find in their pages a clue to the whole life, and now we are as much at a loss as ever.

The method is, I think, a mistake. With the papers, arranged in separate groups, we get at the history of Emily's friendships. Chronologically arranged they would have told her own.

Fortunate is it to us that her early letters were all printed. In them we find the real Emily—joyous, sportive, a bit priggish, very precocious, and quite willing to encounter the world's gaze. Whence came the sharp distortion that shut her out from society, and finally induced her to cut print from newspapers to label her envelopes? At first she was religious after the fashion of her family. Then came a time when she could write to Higginson, "They worship an eclipse whom they call Father!"

From the first it was evident that the fulcrum upon which her whole being hung was love. The letters to her only brother show an impassioned feeling; her devotion to every member of her immediate family was extreme, and although no one gauged her father's nature more completely, she loved him to the end and could say calmly, "He does as well as he knows how!"

The group of girls to which she belonged contained some remarkable women: Mrs. Ford, then a Miss Fowler, Fanny Montague, Emily herself, and that delightful but most capricious and fanciful creature whose memory is now sacred to us as "H. H." Mrs. Ford, whose knowledge of her could not have been very intimate after 1853, said to Dr. Holland, "Her poems remind me of air plants that have no roots in earth." It could not have been said later when "Renunciation" was written.

If we could have all the letters written in 1854, during and after her visit to Washington, printed chronologically, I think we should be able to read the story. As it is, we have almost none and they are scattered.

Some years ago a relative of Emily's came to see me. Of Emily's personal appearance she gave the same account as Mrs. Ford. Not beautiful, she had great beauties. Her skin and teeth were fine, her eyes soft, and colored, as she herself said, like the last drop of sherry a guest has left in his glass. The color of her hair was the same, and when she gave a lock of it to Mrs. Ford she wrote, "I shall never give you anything again that will be half so full of sunshine as this."

It was so long that it nearly touched the floor, yet clung to her finely shaped head in little rings. "It was in Washington," said her friend to me, "that Emily met her fate. Her father absolutely refused his consent to her marriage for no reason that was ever given." It was probably, as he once said, when she wanted to go away and make a visit, because "he was used to her, and did not wish to part with her!" When such a motive was urged Emily could not resist. She would wait hoping, once, as we see in that pathetic little poem "Almost." The lover came to see her and just missed her. His "soft sauntering step" did not overtake hers. "Hope," she once wrote, had never "asked a crumb of her." It needed no sustenance, so immortal was her love, so elastic her spirit. And this answered until death came. In a few years her friend passed out of sight. I think from various indications that she never knew where his body lay, only he had gone after she had given her heart to him, and before her father would consent to ratify the contract. It was of little use then for him to bring books as a consolation and tell her not to read them!

"There is no frigate like a book," she wrote, "to take us leagues away." And then, "I am constantly more and more astonished that the body contains the spirit; except for over-mastering work it could not be borne."

> Each that we lost takes part of us,
> A crescent still abides.
> Which, like the moon, some turbid night
> Is summoned by the tides.

She began to write poems in 1862, after disappointment had done its worst, for then I think she knew of her lover's death, and from that time lived in company with Death and wrote much of his power and his mystery. "I made my soul familiar with her extremity," one of the first of these poems begins. Follow the story:

> I asked no other thing
> No other was denied;

Then comes "Almost," the pathetic lost opportunity, and finally the magnificent poem of "Renunciation." Then come others calmed by the passage of years. "Mine by the white election," "Bequest," "Proof," and

> Alter when the hills do.
> So we must keep apart,
> You there, I here,
> With just the door ajar
> That oceans are
> And prayer,
> And that pale sustenance, Despair.

Apart from the painful story so revealed and yet half lost in words that are too small for her emotion, we have here and there an exhibition of her most delicate and subtle perceptions. In Salvini she detects the great power of his *throat*, something hitherto unnoticed.

In a hopeful moment she writes "We go to sleep with a peach, and wake with a stone in the hand, a pledge of summons to come."

Here is a dainty note, a reminiscence of her earlier ways. "Sweet Mrs. Nellie comes with the robins. Robins have wings. Mrs. Nellie has wings. A society for the prevention of wings would be a benefit to us all."

How characteristic of Emily is this quotation from Othello! What other woman ever used it so? — "He that is robbed and smiles steals something from the thief," and these last words written of dear H. H.:

> "Helen of Troy will die, Helen of Colorado never.
> My last word to her was 'Dear friend, can you walk?'
> 'Dear friend, I can fly.'
> Her immortal reply."

It is interesting to note the effect of Emily's correspondents upon her. To the Bowleses and almost always to the Hollands she writes with cheerful sanity. Her letters to Mrs. Ford are delicious. Those to Higginson oftentimes hopelessly obscure. It was a wonder that he answered the first. It is a little strange that Mrs. Todd does not seem to know that it is now acknowledged that the "Saxe Holm Stories," "Mercy Philbrick" and "Hetty's Strange History" were all by one author, namely, "H. H." William H. Channing said when these appeared that it was less of a miracle to find them all Helen Hunt's than to imagine that there were two women capable of the verses in each.

I am sorry to say that the binding of these two precious volumes of Emily's letters is very unworthy of the noble nature they reveal.

465 Mary D. Cutting. "Literature." *Christian Inquirer* 7 (December 27, 1894), 7.

Admirers of the poems of Emily Dickinson have looked for the promised volumes of her letters with a somewhat timid, reluctant eagerness. The success of the poems had been phenomenal, but verse needs no setting save the "local habitation and the name" given its "airy nothings" by the "poet's pen," whereas letters, though they are born, and not made, borrow interest and fascination from the life and circumstances that brought them into being. Brilliant and picturesque as are the letters of Fanny Burney, they owe something of their charm to the distinguished people in art, letters and politics that frequented her father's house; to the savory gossip that attaches to a familiar personal story of royalty, and to her own romantic association with the French Revolution. Vivacious, delicate and witty as are the letters of Madame de Sévigné, they receive color and sparkle from her close friendship with Prince de Conti, Marshal Turenne and Fouquet; and even the prince of letter-writers, Horace Walpole, was better acquainted than any man of his day with the English nation, the Court, and the House of Commons.

What, then, could be expected from the letters of a woman, though a poet, living in a quiet college town in voluntary retirement a life of almost nun-like seclusion, literally not crossing the threshold of her father's door the last years of her life. Certainly not the pomp and circumstance of life; certainly not the characterization of people greatly distinguished. But just as certainly there is discovered in these letters of the recluse poet gay humor, terse epigram, quaint originality, and her own unique personality. The epigram of Madame de Sévigné on Cardinal Retz, that he pretended to retire from a world which he saw retiring from him, is little better than Emily Dickinson's "I cannot stop to strut in a world where bells toll;" and few of Fanny Burney's letters are more gayly humorous than one of Emily Dickinson's to Mrs. Dr. Holland, descriptive of a return, after an absence of fifteen years, to the family residence, where Emily was born, and where she died. She says: "I cannot tell you how we moved. I had rather not remember. I believe my 'effects' were brought in a bandbox, and the 'deathless me' on foot not many moments after. I took at the time a memorandum of my several senses, and also of my hat and coat and my best shoes, but it was lost in the melee, and I am out with lanterns looking for myself." How mirthful, yet without malice, are the following gossipy tid-bits: "Did you know about Mrs. J? She fledged her antique wings. 'Tis said that nothing in her life became her like the leaving it." "There is that which is called an 'awakening' in our church, and I know of no choicer ecstasy than to see Mrs. ____ roll out in crape every morning, I suppose to intimidate anti-Christ." "House is being cleaned. I prefer pestilence. That is more classic and less fell."

The letters are never didactic, nor preceptive concerning men, books or events. The late great Civil War is barely referred to. "War seems to me an oblique place;" and yet, where in the literature of that awful struggle is there to be found any incident more vividly, graphically and pathetically outlined than in the following letter:

"DEAR CHILDREN: 'Tis least that I can do to tell you of brave Frazer—killed at Newbern, darlings. His big heart shot away by a Minie ball!

"I had read of those—I didn't think that Frazer would carry one to Eden with him. Just as he fell, in his soldier's cap, with his sword at his side, Frazer rode through Amherst. Classmates to the right of him, and classmates to the left of him, to guard his narrow face. He fell by the side of Professor Clark, his superior officer, lived ten minutes in a soldier's arms, asked twice for water, murmured just 'My God,' and passed! Sanderson, his classmate, made a box of boards in the night, put the brave boy in, covered with a blanket, rowed six miles to reach the boat—so poor Frazer came. They tell that Colonel Clark cried like a little child when he missed his pet, and could hardly resume his post. They loved each other very much. Nobody here could look on Frazer, not even his father. The doctors would not allow it.

"The bed on which he came was enclosed in a large casket, shut entirely, and covered from head to foot with the sweetest flowers. He went to sleep from the village church. Crowds came to tell him good-night, choirs sang to him, pastors told how brave he was—early—soldier heart. And the family bowed their heads, as the reeds the wind shakes.

"So our part in Frazer is done; but you must come next summer, and we will mind ourselves of this young crusader—too brave that he could fear to die. We will play his tunes; may be he can hear them; we will try to comfort his broken-hearted Ella, who, as the clergyman said, 'gave him peculiar confidence'. . . . Austin is stunned completely. Let us love better, children; it's most that is left to do. With love, Emily."

But while there is found in the letters of Emily Dickinson, epigram, wit, humor, the pathos of war, of life, of death, through and through, over and above all is inwrought that supreme love of Nature, that almost startling realization of God and Immortality, that so strongly marks the poems. Like Emerson, she "looked upon Nature as pregnant with Soul;" for her, as for him, the "Spirit moved always upon the face of the waters," while she, with a confidence greater than his, perhaps, sung:

Take all away
The only thing worth larceny
Is left—the Immortality.

Fragments like the lines just quoted constantly indicate her strong faith in this verity: "I believe we shall in some manner be cherished by our Maker; that the One who gave us this remarkable earth has the power still farther to surprise that which he has caused." Beyond that all is silence. "And with what body do they come! Then they *do come*. Rejoice. Run, run, my soul. Illuminate the house."

And as constantly appears the depth of her love for Nature, and the keen instinct that makes glad response to Nature:

"The wind blows gay today, and the jays bark like terriers."
"An approaching spring; the ear of the heart hears bluebirds already, those enthralling signals."
"Yours was my first arbutus. It was a rosy boast. Blossoms belong to the bees, if needs be, by habeas corpus."
"The career of the flowers differs from our own only in inaudibleness."

So on and on almost endlessly. The admirers of Emily Dickinson's verse, then, need have no apprehension that the letters will receive a less phenomenal welcome that was accorded the poems. In both we find, if not the surprises of genius, at least that "inward light" that gives lustre and warmth.

Mrs. Todd is to be congratulated on the editing. It is done with a discrimination and delicacy that place the letters in the best possible setting.

466 [Morton Dexter.] "Literature." *Congregationalist* 79 (December 27, 1894), 973–74. Dexter is identified as the Literary Editor of the *Congregationalist* and author of this review in a letter by the journal's editor, H. A. Bridgman, to David Todd, dated Dec. 27, 1894 [Amherst College Library, ms. Todd 496].

Emily Dickinson's Letters, edited by Mabel L. Todd, fill two small, attractively printed volumes. They will cause different impressions in different readers. All will agree as to their individuality, their usual geniality, their sprightliness, their frequent piquancy of suggestion not less than of expression, and the occasional profundity of thought. Many will see nothing in them but these commendable qualities. It is equally sure that others will find in them an evident artificiality, as though the writer were posing for literary effect, and straining somewhat at times in the effort, and apparently these can point in justification to the rough draft of a letter to Mrs. Jackson. Here a number of words have been substituted for others, as though in an effort to correct the style and into a more peculiar, and even a unique, diction. One or two sentences are simply incoherent. If the existence of this corrected rough draft be proof of the habit of thus revising such familiar letters, the author hardly can be acquitted of some measure of intellectual affectation. Only her surviving intimates can be aware of the truth. But nobody will be to blame for gaining either impression of her from her letters, and it is probable that she deliberately cultivated eccentricity. The letters are collected from those written to a considerable number of friends and touch upon such themes as happened to interest her, largely personal.

467   D[enis] W[ortman]. "Book Reviews." *Public Opinion* 17 (December 27, 1894), 952.

Those readers who have come to love the quaint, mystical poems of Emily Dickinson will be glad to learn something more of her singular personality as it is revealed in the two volumes of her letters which have been collected and edited by her sympathetic friend, Mabel Loomis Todd. This shy, sensitive woman, who has sometimes been called "the weird recluse of Amherst," lived away from the world and within herself to such an extent that even her nearest friends knew her by her letters rather than from conversation and friendly intercourse. Mrs. Todd herself relates that in all the years of her acquaintance with Emily she never had a face-to-face conversation with her about commonplace mundane affairs. She was not always a recluse, for as a young woman she mingled somewhat in gay society, but its conventionalities and frivolities were distasteful to her and she turned naturally to a life with nature and the chosen circle of home friends. Always a home-loving body, her isolation from the world became more pronounced as she grew older, and after the death of her father she finally retired completely from even the simple life of a New England college town, and was seldom seen outside the limits of her garden.

Her intercourse with the outside world was kept up through letters, of which she was a voluminous writer. These are as unconventional as her poems and are characterized by the same boldness and originality of thought, the same odd, quaint turns of expression and startling phrases that would almost seem to be affectations, were not the absolute sincerity and unworldliness of the woman known and recognized by all who knew her. They show a great wealth of affection stored away in her heart which she lavished upon a small circle of devoted friends, and a passionate love for flowers, birds, trees, changing skies—in short, nature in all her aspects. The events recorded in her letters had little to do with the world at large, but she would not fail to speak of the first spring flower that had appeared in her garden, the earliest bird note that foretold the departure of winter, or the particular aspect that March had worn that day. The intense love that she felt for her friends is shown in her letters to Dr. and Mrs. J. G. Holland, Mr. and Mrs. Samuel Bowles, Mrs. Strong, a school friend of early days, her brother Austin and a few other friends and relatives. Sometimes these letters were mere notes, often hardly more than a line, terse, almost epigrammatic in their force and meaning.

This last characteristic is well shown in some of the remarkable things she said to Higginson, whom she asked to be her literary judge and critic. A few may not be out of place, though many of them lose their force when taken out of the peculiar setting in the letters: "Truth, like ancestors' brocades, can stand alone;" "while Shakespeare remains, literature is firm;" "I find ecstasy in living; the mere sense of living is joy enough." Her description of poetry is what Higginson calls a "crowning extravaganza," and small wonder. This is it: "If I read a book and it makes my whole body so cold no fire can ever warm me, I know that it is poetry. If I feel physically as if the top of my head were taken off, I know that is poetry. These are the only ways I know it. Is there any other way?" To a friend who remembered the anniversary of her father's death, "How can one be fatherless who has a father's friend within confiding reach?" Just before her own death she sent this brief message, startling in its prophetic import, "Little cousins — Called back. Emily."

Those who read the letters expecting to find much of an autobiographical nature in them will be disappointed for they tell but little about herself and give now and then only a glimpse of the real inner life of the soul of the woman, but they have in them so much that is original, both in the quality of thought and in expression, that they have an interest peculiarly their own.

468 "The Emily Dickinson Letters." *Hartford Courant,* December 29, 1894, p. 8. In a Jan. 13, 1895, letter to Mrs. Todd, Higginson noted that this review was "probably" written by Richard Burton; see *AB*, p. 316.

As an example of the New England type of character, running to recluse ways, to imaginative mysticism, childlike naivete and literary expression for the expression's sake, Emily Dickinson, the Amherst poet, is well worth study. Further means to a knowledge of her strange yet fascinating personality are furnished by the publication from the Boston house of Roberts Brothers of a two-volume embodiment of her "Letters," edited by her friend, Mrs. Mabel Loomis Todd, wife of the Amherst professor. Since the appearance of these letters, reviewers have made more or less fun of them or waxed indignant at their often slight excuse for being, their puerility of thought or word; and it must be confessed that at times one inclines to sympathize with such strictures. Some of the sentiments and sentences when detached and read carelessly by a public which knows little and cares less for this quiet Massachusetts woman-hermit, seem simply silly and prejudice one against further examination. But those who, knowing her poems, know the rare gifts and qualities of Miss Dickinson will read on and on, finding much to touch, stimulate and delight. Startling unconventionality is here, a love for and acquaintance with nature almost unique, a love for literature coupled with a delicious ignorance of what one ought to read and be glib about; and, underlying everything else, a religiousness, a spirituality of thought and daily life that make this modern American a true companion of Marcus Aurelius, Thomas a-Kempis, Sir Thomas Browne and others who have preferred the things of God. The correspondence is lighted up, too, by playful humor and girlish gaiety and is very far from being monotonously ethereal and high-pitched. Absolute sincerity can be felt even in the most astonishingly odd or original remarks and views. When, for example, she writes to the elder Samuel Bowles of the "Springfield Republican," "Do you think we shall 'see God?' Think of Abraham strolling with Him in genial promenade!" There is no hint of self-conscious smartness, as there would have been had Henry Heine written the words. The felicity of dictum and expression is evidenced in her reply to Colonel Thomas W. Higginson on his request for her photograph: "I had no portrait, now, but am small, like the wren; and my hair is bold, like the chestnut burr; and my eyes like the sherry in the glass the guest leaves. Would this do just as well?" Mr. Higginson, on first making her acquaintance through correspondence and a glimpse of some of her poems in manuscript, inquired about her reading, being curious to know the sources of culture of such a marked literary individuality. She replied: "For poets, I have Keats, and Mr. and Mrs. Browning. For prose, Mr. Ruskin, Sir Thomas Browne and the 'Revelations.' I went to school, but in your manner of phrase had no education. When a little girl, I had a friend who taught me immortality; but venturing too near himself he never returned. . . . You ask of my companions. Hills, sir, and the sundown and a dog large as myself that my father bought me. They are better than beings because they know but do not tell; and the noise in the pool at noon excels my piano." Ever and anon there is a word or thought on the deep things of the spirit flashed forth in a way to enchain the attention and set the soul athrob. Thus to Dr. and Mrs. J. G. Holland she writes: "Dear Hollands: Good night. I can't stay any longer in a world of death. Austin (her brother) is ill of fever. I buried my garden last week; our man, Dick, lost a little girl through the scarlet fever. I thought perhaps you were dead, and not knowing the sexton's address, interrogate the daisies. Ah, dainty, dainty Death! Ah, democratic Death! Grasping the proudest zinnia from my purple garden—then deep to his bosom calling the serf's child." The critic, always a-tiptoe to detect plagiarism, will at once point out in this apostrophe to death the influence of Walt Whitman; and as a matter of fact, Miss Dickinson, on being asked if she knew of him, replied laconically: "I never read his book, but was told that it was disgraceful."

The thoughtful reader will find many reasons for lingering over these unique volumes, this unsophisticated and exceptional nature. Not only will the best of Emily Dickinson's poetry live, but a more condensed presentation of her letters should have permanent interest and value. In many ways she shows herself in them a feminine Thoreau, and the public will find the revelation of so refreshingly genuine, finely endowed and self-dependent a character a welcome experience. Of Emily Dickinson it can be said, as of very few, that she kept herself unspotted from the world.

469 "Among the Books." *Cambridge* [Mass.] *Tribune* 17 (December 29, 1894), 2. The volume noticed here is Hosmer and Gannett's *The Thought of God in Hymns and Poems* (Second Series, 1894).

The same gentle, reverent spirit that breathed throughout the earlier volume of verse by Frederick L. Hosmer and William C. Gannett, the two well-known poet-clergymen, is quite as much in evidence in this one. But there is a difference between the two collections, and to our thinking the later book is the better. The notes seem to be a little more firmly struck, the hold upon expression a little surer, the literary quality somewhat more marked. A very noble chord is sounded in the opening poem: "One Law, One Life, One Love," by Mr. Hosmer; in "The Word of God," by Mr. Gannett, it is heard again and other chords of varying sweetness and power are found blended with it as one reads one poem after another. Neither of the two poets sings with any other voice than his own and yet one of the poems is so sharp a reminder of Emily Dickinson, that one might think it inspired by lines of hers, if the date, 1885, did not place it fully a lustrum before the world had heard that strange haunting voice of hers. It is assuredly worth the quoting.

WE SEE AS WE ARE

The poem hangs on the berry-bush,
    When comes the poet's eye;
The street begins to masquerade,
    When Shakespeare passes by.

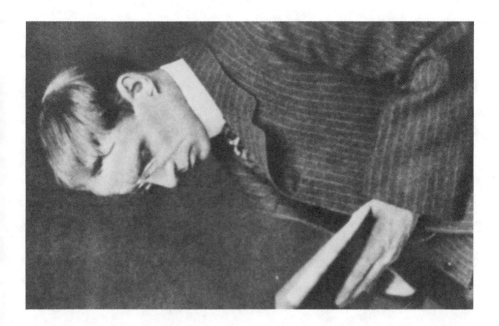

Dickinson's poems and letters reminded reviewers of the sensational,
recently published journals of Marie
Bashkirtseff (1860–1884). (No. 423)

Richard Burton (1861–1940): "Shows
herself a feminine Thoreau." (No.
468)

Bliss Carman (1861–1929): "Illumined and revealed in her poems, the life and character of this original nature make a fit study for the subtlest criticism—such a criticism, indeed, as I know not where they will receive." (No. 557)

Rupert Hughes (1872–1956): "Emily Dickinson and Whitman, with their unbending comradery with God and humanity, are our best realizations of the distinctively American spirit." (No. 553)

John Banister Tabb (1845–1909). Father Tabb's reclusive life and intense, epigrammatic verse provoked several comparisons with Dickinson. (No. 492)

The Christ sees white in Judas' heart,
  He loves his traitor well;
And God, to angel His new Heaven,
  Explores His lowest Hell.

470 "A New England Recluse." *San Francisco Chronicle,* December 30, 1894,
  p. 41.

The "Letters of Emily Dickinson," edited by Mabel Loomis Todd, furnishes
as curious a study of morbid character as the journal of Amiel. A New England
woman of brilliant parts who wrote some verse that will not die voluntarily secluded herself in a little town and lived for many years a singular life. She seemed
to have no sympathy with great events that stirred the world. The Civil War she
refused to think about or discuss. She had several close friends, among whom were
Samuel Bowles and his wife and Helen Hunt Jackson. At 20 she wrote verse that
gave promise of great things, but this promise was never fulfilled. She had a morbid sensitiveness to any notoriety, and she could never be induced to publish any
of her work. The world would have known little more about her than what
Thomas Wentworth Higginson told in an article in the *Atlantic* soon after her
death, had it not been for the careful editing and the publication of these letters.
  More than most volumes of this sort, these contain many epistles which are
of small interest to the public. Yet, probably, the general impression of a unique
character could not have been conveyed so faithfully in any other way as by
printing the outpourings of this emotional nature, held in close check by a cold
New England temperament. A good idea of her peculiar style may be gained from
these extracts from a letter which she wrote to T. W. Higginson in response to
queries in regard to her work and reading:

  I made no verse, but one or two, until this winter, sir.
  I had a terror since September I could tell to none; and so I sing as the boy does
of the burying ground, because I am afraid.
  You inquire my books. For poets, I have Keats and Mr. and Mrs. Browning. For
prose, Mr. Ruskin, Sir Thomas Browne and the Revelations. I went to school, but
in your manner of the phrase had no education. When a little girl, I had a friend
who taught me immortality; but venturing too near, himself, he never returned.
Soon after my tutor died, and for several years my lexicon was my only companion. Then I found one more, but he was not contented I be his scholar, so he left
the land.
  You ask of my companions. Hills, sir, and the sundown, and a dog large as
myself that my father bought me. They are better than beings, because they know
but do not tell; and the noise in the pool at noon excels my piano.
  I have a brother and a sister. My mother does not care for thought and father
is too busy with his briefs to notice what we do. He buys me many books, but
begs me not to read them, because he fears they joggle the mind. They are religious except me, and address an eclipse every morning, whom they call their
"Father."

  Much of Miss Dickinson's prose may be cut up into verse, for, like Black-
more in the descriptive passages of "Lorna Doone," she appears to drop naturally into a strange, Orphic meter. The book has several portraits and facsimiles
of letters.

471 "A Pen-Portrait, by Herself." *Book Buyer*, n.s. II (January 1895), 758. A reprinting of Dickinson's second letter to Higginson, dated April 25, 1862 [*L*, no. 261].

472 E. R. C. "Impressions of Two Hermits. Henry D. Thoreau and Emily Dickinson. Part II." Unlocated clipping, ca. January 1895. Todd's scrapbook contains a pencilled note, "N.Y. Sun (?)" and the article itself carries the dateline "Concluded from Jan. 4." New York papers for likely dates during this month were searched without result. Part I of the article apparently discussed Thoreau.

It is but a few years since any of Miss Dickinson's writings came out; then they were brought to view through the interest of persons whom she had known many years. She had, without the knowledge of many, written in solitude thoughts which she wished to send through the world for years; so that when, after her death, more than a thousand pieces of her verse were found in her desk, it was thought best to reveal her and her thoughts to mankind.

She was a daughter of Edward Dickinson, a lawyer, and at his death a member of the Massachusetts legislature. For a year she attended Mount Holyoke Female Seminary, her letters from which, like her other letters for years from Amherst, are marked by no such brilliancy as characterized those written by her in and after 1862. She lived "among people"—as says her biographer, Mrs. Mabel Loomis Todd, who edits her "Letters," issued by Roberts Brothers from Boston—until she was past 20, even going to Washington with her father when he was a member of Congress; but she gradually withdrew from the world, and when her father died, in 1874, her retirement became absolute.

All her mature life, however, she wrote verses, and letters to friends which included verses; and the most brilliant and original that ever were penned were some of those letters and verses, as we here see. She reminds us of a humming bird of thought; her flights are lofty, and leave a brilliant trail all the way. She says such beautiful, true, and new things, and with such electric force and directness that a defect of manner, as in art, appears of minor consequence. The rose is sometimes irregular, but the verse is far more so—often, indeed, crude in art, and as lame as possible in rhyme. But at her best in thought she is sometimes consummate in art, and the poetic result is a great delight. I can not here supply specimens of her best verse; for them one must read the "Poems" which Col. Thomas Wentworth Higginson and Mrs. Todd have published through Roberts Brothers; I can merely copy a few of the best which appear in the letters, and mix with them some of her best prose passages. You will enjoy, in the book of letters, (which is in two volumes,) the beautiful things which Mrs. Todd tells about her subject in the notes between the letters. Here are the verses and passages:

DEAR COUSIN: Did you know there had been a fire here, and that but for a whim of the wind Austin and Vinnie and Emily would have all been homeless? . . .

We were waked by the ticking of the bells . . . I sprang to the window, and each side of the curtain saw that awful sun. The moon was shining high at the time, and the birds singing like trumpets.

Vinnie came soft as a moccasin: "Don't be afraid, Emily; it is only the Fourth of July." I did not tell that I saw it, for I thought if she felt it best to deceive, it must be that it was.

She took hold of my hand and led me into mother's room. Mother had not waked, and Maggie was sitting by her. I could hear buildings falling, and oil exploding, and people walking and talking gayly, and cannon soft as velvet from parishes that did not know we were burning up. And so much lighter than day was it, that I saw a caterpillar measure a leaf far down in the orchard; and Vinnie kept saying bravely, "It's only the Fourth of July."

It seemed like a theater, or a night in London, or perhaps like chaos. The innocent dew falling as if it thought no evil, . . . and sweet frogs prattling in the pools as if there were no earth.

At seven, people came to tell us that the fire was stopped—stopped by throwing sound houses in as one fills a well.

Mother never waked, and we were all grateful; we knew she would never buy needle and thread at Mr. Cutler's store, and if it were Pompeii nobody could tell her.

Vinnie's "only the Fourth of July" I shall always remember. I think she will tell us so when we die, to keep us from being afraid.

Footlights cannot improve the grave; only immortality.

Forgive me the personality; but I knew, I thought, our peril was yours.

Love for you each.   EMILY.

The slips of the last rose of summer repose in kindred soil, with warring bees for mates. How softly summer shuts, without the creaking of a door, aboard forevermore.

Of George Eliot: The gift of belief which her greatness denied her, I trust she receives in the childhood of the kingdom of heaven. As childhood is earth's confiding time, perhaps having no childhood she lost her way to the early trust, and no later came.

She slipped from our fingers like a flake gathered by the wind, and is now part of the drift called "the infinite."

I cannot tell how eternity seems. It sweeps around me like a sea. . . . Thank you for remembering me. Remembrance—mighty word.

Each that we lose takes part of us;
    A crescent still abides
Which, like the moon some turbid night,
    Is summoned by the tides.

There is no frigate like a book
    To take us lands away,
Nor any coursers like a page
    Of prancing poetry.
This traverse may the poorest take,
    Without oppress of toll,
How frugal is the chariot
    That bears the human soul!   [a human

The most triumphant bird
    I ever knew or met,
Embarked upon a brig today—   [twig
    And till dominion set

> I perish to behold
>   So competent a sight—
> And sang for nothing scrutable
>   But impudent delight;
> Retired and resumed
>   His transitive estate:
> To what delicious accident
>   Does finest glory fit!

Life is a spell so exquisite that everything conspires to break it.

Had we less to say to those we love, perhaps we should say it oftener: but the attempt comes, then the inundation, then it is all over, as is said of the dead.

That we are permanent temporarily, it is warm to know, though we know no more.

When much in the woods, as a little girl, I was told that the snake would bite me, that I might pick a poisonous flower, or goblins kidnap me; but I went along and met no one but angels, who were far shyer of me than I could be of them, so I haven't that confidence in fraud which many exercise.

I was thinking today, as I noticed, that the "supernatural" was only the natural disclosed.

> Not Revelation 'tis that waits,
> But our unfurnished eyes.

To Col. Higginson: Thank you for having been to Amherst. Could you come again, that would be far better, though the finest wish is the futile one.

Of Samuel Bowles: One glance of his would light a world.

Valor in the dark is my Maker's code.

To a friend, with a flower: I send a violet, for L. I should have sent a stem, but was overtaken by snow-drifts. I regret deeply not to add a butterfly, but have lost my hat, which precludes my catching one.

Vesuvius doesn't talk; Aetna doesn't. One of them said a syllable a thousand years ago, and Pompeii heard it and hid forever. She couldn't look the world in the face afterward, I suppose. Bashful Pompeii.

The supper of the heart is when the guest has gone.

473 "New Publications." *Concord* [N.H.] *People and Patriot,* ca. January 1895. Although this notice is dated Jan. 21, 1895, in the clipping file of the Jones Library, Amherst, the date was not a printing day for the paper. Proximate issues were searched without result. It is entirely possible that this review appeared the previous November or December and that its author was Frances Matilda Abbott (see no. 71).

Emily Dickinson died in 1886. Her first volume of poems was published in 1890. Its effect was electrical. Edition after edition was called for. People of poetic temperament found there something new, so real, so creative and yet so still and quiet, that it seemed like the breath of nature. The book did not contain poems so much as the distilled essence of poetry. Absolutely unconventional, often without form, following no external law of rhyme or rhythm, the verses obey an inner law that is all the writer's own. No one who has ever been moved by Emily Dickinson's two volumes of poems will need any introduction to these letters.

Her personality was as unique as her writings. She lived her whole life in Amherst, Mass., where her father was a leading lawyer and treasurer of the college. The first volume contains the only portrait she ever had except a poor daguerreotype. It was painted in a group with her brother and sister when Emily was eight years old. The child's face satisfies the reader's ideal. The second volume has a picture of the fine old New England mansion, screened by a hedge and a tall fence where her life was passed. Though passionately fond of nature and of her garden, and not an invalid, she never crossed the threshold of this house for many years before her death. Her childhood seems not unlike that of any intellectual girl with her fine home environment and the advantages of a college town. She was educated in the old Amherst academy, and spent one year at Mount Holyoke seminary. Mount Holyoke and Emily Dickinson seem the very irony of fate; yet she expresses no dislike to that model institution. On the contrary, she is fond of her teachers, and regrets that she cannot go back another year and graduate. Nothing seems to have hindered but her health. Had that not interfered, what a name would have been added to Mount Holyoke's alumnae list!

It was not till she was in her twenties that she began to exhibit that growing distaste for society which afterwards was to make her such a complete recluse. There is no external happening to account for this, and one would never think of charging her with affectation. Seclusion seems to have been necessary for her development. She could not endure the jar of foreign natures. She possessed the friendship of H. H., Dr. and Mrs. Holland, the Samuel Bowles' family, and was a correspondent, or scholar as she calls herself, of Col. Higginson. Her letters breathe devotion. Her prose is as rare as her poetry, and yet with all her remote unearthliness, she knew how to make bread and took part in other homely household tasks. Her weird genius is beautifully typified by the white Indian pipe or corpse plant, which is found on the covers of all her books.

474 [Mary Augusta Jordan.] "Reviews." *Book Reviews* 2 (January 1895), 321–22. A partial reprinting; see no. 454. The first two-thirds of Jordan's essay is republished here, ending with her sentence, "But whatever the total judgment on Emily Dickinson's letters may be, a judicious selection from them must impress any reader; and if some who persevere to the end complain of a monotonous redundancy, others who have been irresistibly drawn along will rejoice that they are not more select and expurgated."

475 J[ohn] William Lloyd. "Emily Dickinson." *Wind-Harp Songs* (Buffalo: Peter Paul Book Co., 1895), p. 31.

It seems to me you sing a song
That startled every one;
Odd intergrowth of heathen
And New England Puritan.

Your art is like a Japanesque;—
Perspective and detail
Are very independent,
But the picture pleases well.

Suppose a Quaker wood-bird
To throw a parrot wing,
Talk Manx and Hindostanee,
And then go back and sing

Weird bits and beautiful,
A Concord touch or two,
Lyric thought, so stated
As no one else dare do.

476 "The New Books." *Review of Reviews* [N.Y.] 11 (January 1895), 110–11.

The publication of Emily Dickinson's poems a few years ago created no little interest in literary circles. Many intelligent readers cannot "make much out of them," and they are often very distressing to those who have any sense of artistic form. Nevertheless they are poems and notable poems. They stand almost as much alone in our annals of American verse as the productions of Jones Very's peculiar genius. The individuality of Emily Dickinson is an interesting one. As a recluse, a solitary, she left Thoreau far in the shade; by comparison, that much abused walker and hunter after the secret of nature was a man of the world. It is easy to trace Puritan and New England influences in the recluse of Amherst, and she is also distinctly a woman, in her prose as well as in the poems. The letters which Mrs. Todd has edited bear dates from 1845, when the writer was a girl of fourteen, to the time of her death in 1886. Many are to members of her family or more distant relatives and to intimate friends unknown to the general public; but there are a goodly number to Colonel Higginson, whom she called in a characteristic semi-whimsical way "Master;" to J. G. Holland and wife; to Mr. and Mrs. Samuel Bowles. In large measure the letters show the caprice, and mystical, symbolical language of the poems, the curious mingling of heart skepticism with intellectual piety; but they show other sides of the writer's nature, the humorous and the sympathetic in particular, and reveal the development of her mental traits from girlhood onward. *Fac-similes* of her handwriting—as peculiar and "disjointed" as her versification—at different dates are given. A portrait taken early in life and a view of her Amherst (Massachusetts) home—the house which she did not leave for many years before her death—are also of interest.

477 Helen Marshall North. "Emily Dickinson's Letters." *Home Journal* 50 (January 2, 1895), 2.

No fitter emblem could be devised of that shy, sensitive, almost morbid recluse whose poetic fancies were not allowed to wed themselves to print during the author's lifetime than the "Indian Pipes" of the New England woods with which the publisher of the two daintily-bound volumes of Miss Dickinson's letters has decorated the covers. Unique, graceful, delicate, yet not wholly refreshing as flowers, courting the shade, the poet and the flowers experienced their chief happiness in close seclusion among a few loving friends.

The poems of Miss Dickinson have already found their true place in the world of letters and have won many admirers. That a similar welcome will be accorded to her letters may be expected by her friends with some degree of confidence. But we counsel the reader to avoid chronological order as he reads. Let him open delicately to the second volume, or to the later chapters of the first volume, and from some of the joyous, airy fancies of the pen of the mature thinker let him gain his first impressions of the interest with which Miss Dickinson invested her numerous letters of friendship. For, it must be recorded, the initial letters of her early years are commonplace, inane, and characterless to a degree. But, with the later years of youth and beyond, she delights in sparkling for her friends, and her pages gleam with flashes of wit, tender bits of description, and poetic flights which indicate the variety and readiness of her mental processes.

Her fondness for home and family shines out with great strength and sweetness in her numerous letters to her brother in Boston. In her twentieth year she writes to him:

"I would not spend much strength upon those little school-boys; you will need it all for something better and braver after you get away. . . . Duty is black and brown; home is bright and shining, and the spirit and the bride say come, and let him that wandereth 'come,' for 'behold all things are ready.' We are having such lovely weather; the air is sweet and still; now and then a gay leaf falling. The crickets sing all day long; high in a crimson tree a belated bird is singing; a thousand little painters are tingeing hill and dale. . . . How happy if you were here to share these pleasures with us! The fruit should be more sweet, and the dying day more golden; merrier the falling nut if with you we gathered it and hid it down deep in the abyss of basket. . . . I wish you were here, dear Austin; the dust falls on the bureau in your deserted room, and gay frivolous spiders spin away in the corners. I don't go there after dark whenever I can help it, for the twilight seems to pause there, and I am half afraid. . . . I am so happy when I know how soon you are coming, that I put away my sewing and go out in the yard to think. . . . Something seems to whisper 'He is thinking of home this evening,' perhaps because it's evening and the orchestra of winds perform their strange sad music. . . . We are rejoiced that you are coming home. . . . I was sure you would all the while. How very soon it will be now! Why, when I think of it, how near and how happy it is! My heart grows light so fast that I could mount a grasshopper and gallop around the world and not fatigue him any."

The topics discussed in these letters are few, and the brother evidently complained of the ornate rhetoric, for the sister writes on one occasion: "You say that you do not comprehend me, you want a simpler style; gratitude, indeed, for all my fine philosophy! I strove to be exalted, thinking I might reach you, and while I pant and struggle and climb the nearest cloud, you walk out very leisurely in your slippers from Empyrean, and without the slightest notice request me to get down!"

Among the friends to whom many letters were written were Mr. and Mrs. J. G. Holland, Mr. and Mrs. Samuel Bowles, and Mr. T. W. Higginson. The latter was her literary sponsor, and it was to him that she wrote in her thirtieth year, enclosing four poems:

"*Mr. Higginson,* — Are you too deeply occupied to say if my verse is alive? The mind is so near itself it cannot see distinctly, and I have none to ask.

"Should you think it breathed, and you had leisure to tell me, I should feel quick gratitude. . . . I enclose my name, asking you, if you please, sir, to tell me what is true?"

In response to Mr. Higginson's reply, she writes a bit of autobiography which seems almost too personal for public proclamation:

"Thank you for your surgery; it was not so painful as I supposed. I bring you others, as you ask, though they might not differ. While my thought is undressed, I can make the distinction; but, when I put them in the gown, they look alike and numb.

"You asked how old I was? I made no verse, but one or two, until this winter, sir. I had a terror, since September, I could tell to none; and so I sing, as the boy does of the burying-ground, because I am afraid.

"You inquire my books. For poets I have Keats and Mr. and Mrs. Browning. For prose, Mr. Ruskin, Sir Thomas Browne, and Revelations. I went to school, but in your manner of phrase had no education. When a little girl, I had a friend who taught me immortality; but venturing too near, himself, he never returned. . . .

"You ask of my companions. Hills, sir, and the sundown, and a dog as large as myself, that father bought me. They are better than beings, because they know but do not tell, and the noise in the pool at noon excels my piano.

"I have a brother and a sister; my mother does not care for thought, and father, — too busy with his briefs to notice what we do. . . . They are religious except me, and address an eclipse, every morning, whom they call their Father."

And again she writes: "Your second letter surprised me, and, for a moment, swung. . . . I thanked you for your justice, but could not drop the bells whose jingling cooled my tramp. . . . I smile when you suggest that I delay to publish, that being foreign to my thought as firmament to fin. . . . You think my gait 'spasmodic.' I am in danger, sir. You think me 'uncontrolled.' . . . If I might bring you what I do—not so frequent to trouble you—and ask you if I told it clear 'twould be control to me. . . . Have you a portrait of Mrs. Browning? Persons sent me three. If you had none, will you have mine?"

Description of such letters, enigmatic often, and, it must be confessed, akin to that which, in Marie Bashkirtseff, we call affected, is quite impossible. Reading them page by page, one scarcely knows whether he is most pleased or annoyed. The life was a narrow one. In the midst of war-time, her letters betray chiefly a desire to know whether her friend in the ranks is in danger. Looking over many letters of the stirring years, I find but one allusion, other than that inquiring if Colonel Higginson is in danger, to the great events of the day. Her brother is deeply moved by the death of a son of President Stearns, killed in battle, and she writes to a friend simply, "Tell Austin how to get over them." Again, in the spring of 1862, she writes that hearts in Amherst are aching, that "a railroad person rang to bring an evening paper," causing great excitement, not because of special war news, but because her friend Mr. Bowles was expected for a visit.

Many flashes of humor enliven her letters, which, it may be said, are always the letters of a lover, no matter to whom written, and much that is intended for humor seeks its point from some Scriptural allusion or text. "It is a very sober thing to keep my summer in strange towns . . . what, I have not told, but I have found friends in the wilderness. You know Elijah did, and to see the ravens mending my stockings would break a heart long hard. . . . I love to write you . . . it gives my heart a holiday and sets the bells to ringing. If prayers had any answers to them, you were all here tonight, but I seek and I don't find, and knock and it is not opened. Wonder if God is just! Presume He is, however, and 'twas only a blunder of Matthew's. I think mine is the case where, when they ask an egg, they get a scorpion."

After the family-moving, she writes: "I cannot tell you how we moved, I had rather not remember. I believe my effects were brought in a bandbox, and the 'deathless me' on foot, not many moments after. I took, at the time, a memorandum of my several senses, and also of my hat and coat and my best shoes—but it was lost in the melee, and I am out with lanterns, looking for myself. . . . It is a kind of gone-to-Kansas feeling, and, if I sat in a long wagon with my family tied on behind, I should suppose, without doubt, I was a party of emigrants. . . . We shall sit in a parlor 'not made with hands,' unless we are very careful."

The letters to the Bowles family cover a period of twenty-six or twenty-seven years, and are among her happiest, revealing tender interest in the home life of her friends, and sweet remembrance of the child life that blessed it. Her notes of condolence are especially beautiful, whether here or elsewhere in the volumes, and she might be called the mistress of that difficult class of writing. To the Bowles home she writes: "Don't cry, dear Mary. Let us do that for you, because you are too tired now. We don't know how dark it is, but, if you are at sea, perhaps when we say that we are there, you won't be as afraid. The waves are very big, but every one that covers you covers us, too. Dear Mary, you can't see us, but we are close at your side. May we comfort you?"

To Mr. Bowles in Europe she writes a characteristic letter: "You go away . . . and where you go we cannot come . . . but then months have names . . . and each one comes but once a year . . . and though it seems they never could, they sometimes do go by. We hope you are more well than when you lived in America, and that those foreign people are kind and true to you. . . . I have the errand from my heart. . . . I might forget to tell it. Would you please to come home? The long life's years are scant, and fly away, the Bible says, like a told story . . . and I grope fast, with my fingers, for all out of my sight I own, to get it nearer. . . . Should anybody, where you go, talk of Mrs. Browning, you must hear for us, and if you touch her grave, put one hand on the head for me . . . her unmentioned mourner. . . . I tell you, Mr. Bowles, it is a suffering to have a sea . . . no care how blue . . . between your soul and you. . . . A soldier called a morning ago, and asked for a nosegay to take to battle. I suppose he thought we kept an aquarium."

The choicest bits in her letters are those which disclose her love of nature in all her moods, and her close observation of all growing things. Carlo and the kitten are individual; the clouds and the wind, sun and rain, day and night, the orchid and the lizard, bee and butterfly are near and dear friends, never shut out from her loving companionship. Many find in these allusions, so constant in poems and letters, a strong similarity to the pen that traced the Saxe Holm stories, and gather therefrom strong proof of the identity of the two authors. But there is a depth of heart and a richness of life in the stories which the recluse of these letters never knew. Could Emily Dickinson have written "Draxy Miller's Dowry" for example? The deep, undying, changeless love of God, and the almost equally wonderful love of a human lover which inspired two of the best of the Saxe Holm stories, do not appear in Emily Dickinson's writing. She holds her friends in a close clasp, and sends them dainty sentences. We doubt much if the love of self-sacrifice which crowns many of the heroines of the stories were possible to her.

As with the letters of Marie Bashkirtseff, there will be found admirers and critics of these two volumes, but to bring to another a correct judgment of such evanescent expressions is quite like setting a trap to catch a sunbeam. The letters are arranged, not in order of time, but in sections made up of the letters to a single person or group, and this arrangement is somewhat disappointing, since it precludes a just comparison between letters of certain dates, without constant turning of leaves. The editorial work, however, is well done, and the task was not an easy one.

478 "Literature." *Boston Beacon* 12 (January 19, 1895), 3.

The quaint, elusive, mystical nature of a unique woman is piquantly manifested in the *Letters of Emily Dickinson*, collected and edited by Mabel Loomis Todd. These letters, — strange and enigmatic epistles, many of them — range over a period of more than forty years, from 1845 to 1886 and are addressed to perhaps two score different people, among them some relatives; a few intimate friends, like Dr. and Mrs. J. G. Holland, Mr. and Mrs. Samuel Bowles and Colonel T. W. Higginson; and those with whom she incidentally came in intellectual or spiritual contact through the dissemination of her poems. Mrs. Todd has arranged the letters in ten groups, each group chronologically, thinking thereby to preserve better continuity of interest. But as the main object and chief interest of the collection is to elucidate Miss Dickinson's character and development, the plan adopted by Mrs. Todd is open to severe criticism. Instead of having in unbroken order a series of documents illustrating the changing ideals and thoughts of the writer from early youth to maturity, one is presented with disjointed sequences, overlapping each other and in several instances relating to almost identical epochs. Whether read in the order in which they are printed or in a desultory way, the letters certainly possess, however, extraordinary and lasting interest. One gets from these letters, save in a few of those of early date, no trivialities of existence, no conventional utterances concerning human life, but the expression of a wonderful passion for and sympathy with nature, of a deep and tender capacity for friendship, and of that intuition which at times in certain types of mind seems to amount to positive inspiration. Of the more characteristic letters is the following, addressed to Mrs. Bowles and conjecturally dated by the editor, "1863": —

Since I have no sweet flowers to send you, I enclose my heart. A little one, sunburnt, half broken sometimes, yet close as the spaniel to its friends. Your flowers come from heaven, to which, if I should ever go, I will pluck your palms. My words are far away when I attempt to thank you, so take the silver tear instead, from my full eye. You have often remembered me. I have little dominion. Are there not wiser than I, who with curious treasure, could requite your gift?

A page or two further on, announced as sent with flowers, one comes upon this dainty lyric: —

If recollecting were forgetting,
Then I remember not.
And forgetting, recollecting,
How near I had forgot!
And if to miss were merry,
And if to mourn were gay,
How very blithe the fingers
That gather this today!

A child portrait of Emily Dickinson, a view of her home, and fac-similes of three of her letters are given by way of illustrations. The binding of each volume bears on its front cover a picture of that weird woodland plant, the Indian pipe, — a flower that in its ghostly and peculiar beauty may well be taken as typical of Emily Dickinson and of her secluded and almost uncannily fascinating character.

479 "Emily Dickinson's Letters." *New York Tribune,* January 20, 1895, p. 20.

However justly the gentle and elusive personality of Emily Dickinson may have evoked the enthusiastic regard of her friends, we cannot say that the world of letters is greatly enriched by the publication of these two volumes. What is noteworthy in them could have been set forth easily in half the space. The range of ideas if high is narrow; there are repetitions in meaning and even in wording; and some of these halting and seemingly mystical phrases merely express what has been better said in many an ancient maxim and modern epigram. We are aware that in the vicinity of Boston vagueness is sometimes considered the mark of lofty intellect — an Olympian thundering behind the clouds; but the Boston "fad" rarely takes rank as literature.

The school-day letters with which the collection opens are dreary reading.

They are sentimental, somewhat stilted—in fact, girly-girly—and always conventionally reflective in the fashion of the '40's; and the reader cannot but smile at the solemnity with which these trivialities are introduced. Various phrases suggest that the writer was strongly influenced by the books and perhaps by the reported personal peculiarities of the Brontë sisters—and this influence may be traced, indeed, in some of the later epistles. As her school-days receded Miss Dickinson became less platitudinous, and her writings exhibited more and more the poetic apprehension, the touch-and-go pictorial quality, that she was never to lose in after life. Now and then a sentence will go to the heart of a scene or of a sensation like a flash of lightning. We are inclined to doubt, however, whether her neatest strokes were quite unpremeditated. Some of them show a careful carelessness; and the compiler naively notes that in a letter to Mrs. (Helen Hunt) Jackson, found among Miss Dickinson's papers, are many erasures and substitutions giving evidence of painstaking composition. Without implying that there is anything absurd or unworthy in this judicious writing we may say that what is clever and peculiar in these letters is not entirely an unstudied flowering of rare genius. This lady's mind and its outcome, both in prose and poetry, were we believe, more strongly affected by the books she read than her admirers are willing to concede. As there is the Emily Brontë atmosphere in some of her girlish letters, so there is the Emerson note in her later verse.

Mrs. Todd tells us that her friend, though shy in nature and of recluse habit, was keenly humorous, even witty—"at heart as ecstatic as a bird." Of this there are no indications in these letters. There is, indeed, a pretty playfulness concerning bird and beast and flower; but the keen humor and wit must have been manifested in ways not yet revealed to us. The qualities to be found in Miss Dickinson's letters as in her verse are a tender appreciation of Nature as visited in orchard, field and garden; religious, not pious, feeling; an instinctive delight in literature; a deep and true affection for her friends, and a shrinking from approach like that of the mimosa. Sufficient unto her soul, apparently, was the horizon itself established. But the noblest work is not done in a hermit's cave, and a life less centred in self might have found expression in loftier and richer strains than those we owe to this New-England muse.

480 "Out and About." *Worcester* [Mass.] *Spy,* January 24, 1895, p. 4. This account is the fullest record we have of one of Mrs. Todd's lectures. She spoke in Worcester both on Jan. 23rd and again Feb. 25th (see *AB,* p. 325). For a follow-up article, see next entry.

The "tea talk" given Wednesday afternoon in Memorial Hall by Mrs. Charles F. Marble was attended by about 200 women and was a delightful occasion. The talk was by Mrs. Mabel Loomis Todd of Amherst, and was upon the life and work of the late Emily Dickinson, a subject which Mrs. Todd was peculiarly well fitted to speak upon, as she had known the poet in her native town, Amherst, and had edited her letters, and, prior to that, her poems, with the co-operation of Mr. Thomas Wentworth Higginson. The letters appeared just before Christmas of 1894.

"A few years ago, whenever one said anything about Emily Dickinson," began Mrs. Todd, after she had been introduced by Mrs. Marble, "it was necessary to preface your remarks by telling who she was and what she was; now that two volumes of her poems have appeared, and more recently, her letters, the mystic charm of her personality—one of the most interesting in American literature—has been perceived by many, as it manifested itself in prose and verse.

"When Emily Dickinson died, in the spring of 1886, and the waters closed over her uneventful life, she was almost unknown to the world. Only three or four of her poems had been published, and these much against her will. Of all her family, but one member, her sister, Lavinia, survived her, and it was she who, a few days after Emily's death, discovered a bureau drawer full of manuscript poems. No one had imagined that she wrote so much. In all, there were about 1200 poems, written on note paper, collected into bundles of 60 or 70 poems, and tied up with silk or thread; besides which there was a box of "scraps," with between 600 and 700 more poems and fragments, some of them the originals; copies of which she had sent away in letters to friends, as was her wont; others, rough drafts of poems interlined and re-corrected, with lists of words, which had occurred to the author as desirable substitutes for those she had used. It is interesting to note how, when changes were made or planned, they were never for the sake of rhythm or rhyme, but always in the interests of clearness or strength.

"Emily Dickinson's handwriting was always original and strong, especially in the last of its three periods. Beginning in the delicate running Italian style of elder gentlewomen, it became larger and bolder, until at last it resembled an Egyptian hieroglyphic, each letter being created from its fellow.

"When Lavinia Dickinson asked me to look over this drawerful of poems to see if any were fit for publication, the task seemed colossal. The first thing to do in preparing them for publication was to copy them out. Mr. Higginson was adverse to touching them, and said he considered it inadvisable to attempt publication. But when at length they were ready, it was curious to hear the opinions expressed concerning them. It was said that they were of genuine poetic stuff, that they evinced the undoubted touch of genius, but that the public would not take to them, on account of their unconventionality. An edition of 500 copies was the most that should be printed. We had an edition of 500 copies printed, which was exhausted the first month; 2500 copies were sold before Christmas, and before the year was out 11 editions had been issued. Something in them had touched a chord in humanity.

"It is yet too early to judge of the value of Emily Dickinson's work. That she possessed undoubted genius all her critics have agreed, and all but one—John W. Chadwick—have expressed regret at her lack of form. Yet there is the strange cadence of a hidden music underlying her verse, which is like an orchid growing among the ordinary flowers of the field.

"As a woman, Miss Dickinson was quite as original and daring as her poetry. Still the popular imagination which pictures her as a recluse, clad always in white and never stepping outside the house, though based on truth, is due largely to that desire for the sensational and romantic that lurks in every breast. Born of a line remarkable in its men for strong religious convictions, for public spirit and all the civic virtues; in its women for tender, sympathetic womanliness, Emily Dickinson united their strength and tenderness in a character which seems like an exotic, so foreign is it to the parent stem. Unconventional to a degree in all her thinking of nature, life and God; receiving with a gentle, wide-eyed astonishment the old theological truths which had satisfied her parent; studying everything with a clear, unflinching mind, and treating religion often in a light, humorous, or semi-sarcastic vein, she was never trivial or flippant or irreverent.

"As a girl the most remarkable thing about her was her marked intellectual brilliancy. At Amherst Academy and Mount Holyoke Seminary she was among the brightest, and there was then nothing of the recluse about her. Afterwards, with her father, she visited Boston, New York and Philadelphia and saw considerable of society, at the same time finding it rather thin and unsatisfactory.

Returning to Amherst, the dislike of meeting people began, and increased, until she not only would not go out to see them, but did not care to see them in her own home. She had her books, in which she found great solace and delight, and her garden and conservatory, where she always had flowers blooming. She sent many little presents to friends, often some pretty things to eat, for she was a dainty cook. At the same time she began to dress entirely in white, her gowns being of pique, flannel or other material, suitable to the season, and being always fitted to her sister's figure instead of her own. In appearance she was small and graceful, with a delicate complexion, auburn hair and hazel eyes. Her voice was very high and clear, and with a note of surprise or astonishment in it that was most individual.

"Why did Emily Dickinson seclude herself? is often asked, and, as in other cases of the kind, it has been lightly taken for granted that the reason was either disappointment in love or ill health. Now, neither of these holds in the present instance. Save for some trouble with the eyes, Miss Dickinson's health was good until within a year of her death. As for love, she had had many devoted lovers, but there is not the slightest reason to suppose that she ever desired marriage. She was too ethereal, and her ideal of love was too holy for practical married life. No, her dislike of society was simply the outcome of her nature—there was nothing more romantic or more dramatic about it than that. As introspection and meditation became more and more of a necessity to her, all but the congenial few became intolerable to her. Her friends, though dear to her, were not necessary to her; she was no more lonely than is the north star. But to the last she never denied children, and some of her most beautiful poems are about them. She had many resources of pleasure. As a young woman she had played the piano well, and music was always dear to her. Ecstatic as a bird, she rarely became saddened by the pathos of life; but she had a fund of roguishness, wit, and even mischievousness, a fact which has not received the attention from her critics that it should.

"The works of Emily Dickinson have been compared by critics to those of Blake, Heine, Emerson, Shelley, Browning, and the Persian poet, Omar Khaiyam. Did she write for pleasure or for publication? We can never know, but, although loath to publish in her life-time, there is no reason to suppose that she was unwilling to have her poems appear posthumously. At any rate, there were no requests to destroy, as in the case of some other papers. Her verse is remarkable for its terseness and vigor, and an epigrammatic style, which makes it very quotable. It is remarkable, too, in the quality of its first lines, which, in nearly every poem, give promise of a mine of riches to follow. Her prophetic vision and uplift of soul were sublime, and her 'irresistible needle-touch' has pierced to the core of many of the deepest and finest things of life. All her poems are full of a natural, original and impetuous genius. Every-day experiences brought her texts for the most profound generalizations, and the deftness with which she caught vague and fleeting impressions was amazing.

"Although for some years Miss Dickinson and I sustained a warm friendship, in the course of which we exchanged notes and presents, I can recall scarcely one face to face conversation with her. I used often to go to sing to her—she was fond of hearing me—but upon those occasions she would stay out in the hall, which had been darkened for the occasion, and I can see her now, sitting there in her white dress and listening. When it was over, she would send me, by one of the others, a bunch of flowers or a cream-whip, with a note or a little poem, which she had been writing while I was singing."

481 "Out and About." *Worcester* [Mass.] *Spy*, January 25, 1895, p. 4.

The impression made upon one of Mrs. Todd's hearers at the Emily Dickinson lecture, Wednesday, was so strong that as soon as it was over, she made the best of her way to the Public Library—that paradise of the impecunious book-lover—and took out the two volumes of Miss Dickinson's poems. Since then she has read them through twice—not such a formidable task as it may seem—for they are all short, not a single one being as long as "Locksley Hall" or "The Blessed Damozel," and many having only eight short lines. They have been divided by the editors, Mrs. Todd and Col. Higginson, into four groups, "Life," "Love," "Nature," "Time and Eternity," from which it will be seen at a glance how wide was the range of that Amherst girl's thought and how very serious the tendency of her mind.

Some of these poems the writer has copied, believing that those who are not familiar with Miss Dickinson's verse will be interested in reading them, and that her admirers and lovers will not mind seeing them again.

Here are three, printed under the head of "Life":

> I'm nobody! Who are you? Are you nobody, too?
>   Then there's a pair of us—don't tell!
> They'd banish us, you know.
> How dreary to be somebody!
>   How public, like a frog,
> To tell your name the livelong day
>   To an admiring bog!

*   *   *   *   *

> If I can stop one heart from breaking,
>   I shall not live in vain;
> If I can ease one life the aching,
>   Or cool one pain,
> Or help one fainting robin
>   Unto his nest again,
> I shall not live in vain.

THE SHOW.

> The show is not the show,
> But they that go.
> Menagerie to me
> My neighbor be.
> Fair play—
> Both went to see.

*   *   *   *   *

The next, called "A Book," is also placed in the same category. It is one of the most beautiful tributes to literature or the author that we have ever seen.

A BOOK.

> He ate and drank the precious words,
>   His spirit grew robust;
> He knew no more that he was poor,
>   Nor that his frame was dust.

He danced along the dingy days.
   And this bequest of wings
Was but a book. What liberty
   A loosened spirit brings!

   Miss Dickinson's passionate love of nature found expression in many poems, of which two are given here:

OUT OF THE MORNING.

Will there really be a morning?
   Is there such a thing as day?
Could I see it from the mountains
   If I were as tall as they?

Has it feet, like water-lilies?
   Has it feathers, like a bird?
Is it brought from famous countries
   Of which I have never heard?

Oh, some scholar! Oh, some sailor!
   Oh, some wise man from the skies!
Please to tell a little pilgrim
   Where the place called morning lies!

A SERVICE OF SONG.

Some keep the Sabbath going to church;
   I keep it staying at home,
With a bobolink for chorister,
   And an orchard for a dome.

Some keep the Sabbath in surplice;
   I just wear my wings,
And instead of tolling the bell for church,
   Our little sexton sings.

God preaches — a noted clergyman —
   And the sermon is never long;
So, instead of getting to heaven at last,
   I'm going all along.

*   *   *   *   *

   Miss Dickinson's ideas on death and the hereafter are scarcely the thing one would expect to hear at a prayer meeting. Hers was a fearless spirit, that exhibited a truly "Emersonian self-possession" in the presence or thought of its maker, and this feeling extended toward the professional ministers of his word. What scorn, what cutting sarcasm is embodied in the following eight lines! (We can imagine that Amherst had been through a revival.)

THE PREACHER.

He preached upon breadth till it argued him
      narrow, —
   The broad are too broad to define;
And of truth until it proclaimed him a liar —
   The truth never flaunted a sign.

Simplicity fled from his counterfeit presence
  As gold the pyrites would shun.
What confusion would cover the innocent Jesus
  To meet so enabled a man!

         *   *   *   *   *

Several times we find her declining very positively to have anything to do with the conventional heaven of conventional theology.

Is Heaven a physician?
  They say he can heal;   [that he
But medicine posthumous
  Is unavailable.

Is Heaven an exchequer?
  They speak of what we owe;
But that negotiation
  I'm not a party to.

How she regarded the great change, both for herself and in the case of others, the following poems show clearly:

Let down the bars, O Death!
  The tired flocks come in
Whose bleating ceases to repeat,
  Whose wandering is done.

Thine is the stillest night,
  Thine the securest fold;
Too near thou art for seeking Thee,
  Too tender to be told.

         *   *   *   *   *

The bustle in a house
  The morning after death
Is solemnest of industries
  Enacted upon earth, —

The sweeping up the heart,
  And putting love away
We shall not want to use again
  Until eternity.

         *   *   *   *   *

If I shouldn't be alive
  When the robins come,
Give the one in red cravat
  A memorial crumb.

If I couldn't thank you,
  Being just asleep,
You will know I'm trying
  With my granite lip!

         *   *   *   *   *

"I Died for Beauty," notwithstanding its erratic rhymes, is one of her loveliest poems. No power on earth can make "replied" and "said" rhyme, or "rooms" and "names"; but what of that? Neither is the thought new. Yet, as Emily Dickinson handles it, it has all the thrill and fascination of a new discovery.

> I died for beauty, but was scarce
>   Adjusted to the tomb,
> When one who died for truth was lain
>   In an adjoining room.
>
> He questioned softly why I failed?
>   "For beauty," I replied;
> "And I for truth,—the two are one;
>   We brethren are," he said.
>
> And so, as kinsmen met at night,   [a night
>   We talked between the rooms,
> Until the moss had reached our lips
>   And covered up our names.

482 "Notes on New Books." *Philadelphia North American*, January 28, 1895, p. 2. The following constitutes this paper's only notice of Dickinson.

The life of Miss Emily Dickinson was without incident, and the interest of her correspondence lies in the glimpses it affords of a unique personality. Her genius was of the stamp which seeks seclusion and gathers charm from mystery and a posthumous fame. The outdoor world was to her a paradise, with endless revelations of beauty vouchsafed in the yearly round of the season. Her alert mind divined the inmost secrets of the Amherst woods and fields. She knew the habits and the haunts of bird and insect, and all plant forms and with keen delight watched the opening of the spring flowers, and returned home laden with fragrant blossoms. In a garden of her own she passed many a pleasant hour, cultivating a choice array of plants, which bloomed luxuriantly throughout the year. The cordial love of nature and a deep-rooted affection for her home and family may be easily read in Miss Dickinson's letters. They give also numerous specimens of her verse. For their vivacity and ready wit, the reader will be hardly so well prepared as for their quaintness and originality. She was devoted to a small circle of friends, which included Dr. and Mrs. J. G. Holland, Helen Hunt Jackson and Colonel T. W. Higginson.

483 "Emily Dickinson's Letters." *Book News* 13 (February 1895), 267–68. A partial reprinting of no. 426. The omitted middle portion of the *New York Times'* review begins at the sentence "Dr. Holland, who was another of Miss Dickinson's close friends, . . ." and ends with "An easy morning's ride," the last line of the quoted poem, "A route of evanescence."

484 "Literature." *Critic*, n.s. 23 (February 16, 1895), 119.

In publishing the letters of that remarkable woman Emily Dickinson, Mrs. Todd has not merely performed a labor of love, but has given to American literature a unique book. To review Miss Dickinson's letters is like reviewing her poetry: the critic instantly sees that here is something of unquestionable power that may not be labeled off hand with any of the well-worn formulas that fit most books. In the conventional sense of the word, artist is not the term that one thinks of applying to Miss Dickinson. She had the Emersonic habit of trying to express her meaning poignantly and letting the rest go. This trait becomes a confused and irritating abruptness in writers whose meaning is of little worth, in writers of genius it is the startling abruptness of the seer. Men of the one class are ignorant of the value of art, and men of the other class deem their unrestrained utterance more precious than artistic success. But having something to say, and saying it in the way that most perfectly expresses the speaker's personality—this is after all the supreme, though not the only, element of art. Beyond any doubt to Miss Dickinson must be ascribed this cardinal literary virtue. Spontaneity— the birth-right gift of the lyric poet and of woman—was hers also. Poetic spontaneity means not merely the desire to speak, but the need to speak. Miss Dickinson's reluctance to publish (it need only be recalled that her two volumes of poetry are posthumous) and her constant literary activity confirm, if confirmation be needed, her possession of the poetic instinct, which seeks utterance for the sake of utterance, because silence is impossible. "And when," she says, "a sudden light on orchards, or a new fashion in the wind troubled my attention, I felt a palsy, here, the verses just relieve." Herein is the note of every line that she penned— sincerity. Her letters, not a few of which are poems in everything but the conventional typographical arrangement in verses, help to make evident this vital characteristic of her poetry. And they bring to our knowledge the woman as well as the poet.

These letters reveal the inner life of their writer, and the editor accompanies them with a running commentary on such of the outward events of Miss Dickinson's retired existence as give a key to them. It is to be regretted that the comments are so brief, and that Mrs. Todd has not given us the life as well as the letters of her friend. In the early part of the book many will feel disappointed, now and then, after being brought to an interesting point, to find that the next letter bears date of a year or two later. The letters are grouped, all those addressed to one person being printed together. This prevents chronological sequence, but gives an air of unity to each friendship. Some of the earliest are written by the boarding school girl of sixteen to her brother. They show the simplicity of unaffected girlhood, touched here and there by the promise of thoughtful maturity, and sparkling with sunny humor. Girlish jokes are followed, to be sure, by girlish explanations of the same, and the letters are not extraordinarily precocious. But their independence and originality and their spirit of family affection prelude the life that followed, foreshadowing especially the pathetic intensity with which the poet clung to her friends. "Pardon my sanity in a world insane," she wrote, "and love me if you will, for I had rather be loved than to be called a king in earth, or a lord in Heaven." "My friends are my estate. Forgive me, then, the avarice to hoard them." As the years go on, there are flashes of spontaneous phrasing, which become more and more frequent, until to that buoyancy of spirit which so often marks the writing of a shy and sensitive person there is added the radiancy of literary power.

Miss Dickinson's letters lend themselves to quotation, but merely to quote the epigrams with which her pages are strewn would give an unfair idea of her writing. It is the farthest possible remove from the delightfully diffuse correspondence of some of the famous letter writers of her sex, to the condensed, sublimated missives of Emily Dickinson; and for this reason the letters should be quoted in full. Quotation must be confined to a few extracts, however, of those "thoughts like daisies and sentences [that] could hold the bees." A letter written in response to some inquiries from Col. Higginson (she had just sent to him, a stranger, four of her poems for criticism) contains some characteristic sentences: —

"You asked how old I was? I made no verse, but one or two until this winter, sir. . . . You inquire my books. For poets, I have Keats, and Mr. and Mrs. Browning. For prose, Mr. Ruskin, Sir Thomas Browne, and the Revelations. I went to school, but in your manner of the phrase, had no education. When a little girl, I had a friend who taught me immortality; but, venturing too near, himself, he never returned. . . . You ask of my companions. Hills, sir, and the sundown, and a dog, large as myself, that my father bought me. They are better than beings because they know, but do not tell; and the noise in the pool at noon excels my piano."

Without further comment, here are some extracts from very diverse letters: —

"I am glad my little girl is at peace. Peace is a deep place. Some, too faint to push, are assisted by angels." "Men and women, — they talk of hallowed things, aloud, and embarrass my dog." "Home is the definition of God." [On the death of a child.] "'Come unto me' could not alarm those minute feet — how sweet to remember. . . . The little creature must have been priceless — yours and not yours — how hallowed. . . . The little furniture of loss has lips of dirks to stab us. I hope Heaven is warm, there are so many barefoot ones. I hope it is near — the little tourist was so small. I hope it is not so unlike earth that we shall miss the peculiar form — the mould of the bird." "How strange that nature does not knock, and yet does not intrude."

> There is no frigate like a book
>   To take us lands away,
> Nor any coursers like a page
>   Of prancing poetry.

> This traverse may the poorest take
>   Without oppress of toil;   [toll
> How frugal is the chariot
>   That bears the human soul!   [a human

"Mother went rambling, and came in with a burdock on her shawl, so we know that the snow has perished from the earth."

A genuinely heroic spirit is in the noble description of the death in battle and the burial of her young townsman, Frazer Stearns. It is too long to quote, but it is impossible not to refer to it. The dignity of this passage speaks for itself: — "He went to sleep from the village church. Crowds came to tell him good-night, choirs sang to him, pastors told how brave he was — early soldier heart. And the family bowed their heads, as the reeds the wind shakes." The hand that could write such a requiem needs no further praise.

485 "Letters of Emily Dickinson. *Independent* 47 (February 21, 1895), 245.

These volumes have been published as the prose companion to the delightful volumes of Emily Dickinson's poems. They have been collected by her sister, and represent all the prose writing Emily is known to have left behind her. She kept no other journal than is contained in these letters. The first letter was written when she was just past her fourteenth birthday. They are arranged in the separate sets which were addressed to each of her correspondents, and not in the strict sequence of one chronological order. This arrangement, which would not at all answer for a correspondence which dealt more than these letters do with events and the outside world in general, is in this case the best. It brings the letters together in groups where they belong, and connects them by the only continuity they have, that of a continuing personal interest. They make a unique series which for its charm depends to a singular degree on the writer herself. There is not much to be gleaned from them about other people, and not much biographic matter, in the ordinary sense, about herself or her friends. They are vivid and interesting as literary portraiture, and perhaps all the more so for their unconscious absorption in this quiet self-revelation. There is little talk of important outside things in them, nor of those chronic themes of New England homes, politics and theology, nor of literary events, nor of fashion or art, and not much social chit-chat. The one exception is important, the late War. They are full of a charm which is the writer's own, frolicsome, gay, bubbling over with the stream of her own free spirit, and delightful because they cannot be classed anywhere except among the productions of a free spirit, singing its own song and pouring out its own life. She had her own thoughts, we may be sure, on all subjects and could express them, too. Here is a passage from her school life at Mt. Holyoke, written in Valentine week:

"Every night have I looked, and yet in vain, for one of Cupid's messengers. Many of the girls have received very beautiful ones; and I have not quite done hoping for one. Surely my friend Thomas has not lost all his former affection for me! I entreat you to tell him I am pining for a valentine. I am sure I shall not very soon forget last Valentine week, nor any the sooner the fun I had at that time. . . . Monday afternoon Mistress Lyon arose in the hall, and forbade our sending "any of those foolish notes called valentines." But those who were here last year, knowing her opinions, were sufficiently cunning to write and give them into the care of D. during the vacation; so that about 150 were dispatched on Valentine morn, before orders should be put down to the contrary effect. Hearing of this act, Miss Whitman, by and with the advice and consent of the other teachers, with frowning brow, sallied over to the Post Office to ascertain, if possible, the number of the valentines, and worse still, the names of the offenders. Nothing has yet been heard as to the amount of her information, but as D. is a good hand to help the girls, and no one has yet received sentence, we begin to think her mission unsuccessful."

She heard Jenny Lind in the old First Church at Northampton, and wrote:

"*Herself* and not her music was what we seemed to love — she has an air of exile in her mild blue eyes. . . . Father sat all the evening looking *mad,* and yet so much amused you would have *died* a-laughing. . . . It wasn't sarcasm exactly, nor it wasn't disdain, it was infinitely funnier than either of those virtues, as if old Abraham had come to see the show, and thought it was all very well, but a little excess of *monkey!*"

For a Puritan meeting house, she means. He, in his New England way, expressed much the feeling which agitated the same respectable class in England when Jenny Lind sang in Lincoln Cathedral, and was received as guest at the Bishop's palace. The extreme quiet and uneventful evenness of her life at Amherst may be measured by her remark to her sister apropos the excitement of a fire in the village:

"If there must be a fire I'm sorry it couldn't wait until you had got home, *because you seem to enjoy such things very much.*"

The last extract we make from these letters lets us far into the absolute simplicity and purity of Emily Dickinson's character. It is a letter from Mrs. Gordon L. Ford, a daughter of the late Professor Fowler, of Amherst. She writes:

"We had a Shakespeare Club—a rare thing in those days,—and one of the tutors proposed to take all the copies of all the members and mark out the questionable passages. This plan was negatived at the first meeting, as far as 'the girls' spoke, who said they did not want the strange things emphasized, nor their books spoiled with marks. Finally we told the men to do as they liked—'we shall read everything.' I remember the lofty air with which Emily took her departure, saying, 'There's nothing wicked in Shakespeare, and if there is I don't want to know it.' The men read for perhaps three meetings from their expurgated editions, and then gave up their plan, and the whole text was read out boldly."

486 Louis J. Block. "A New England Nun." *Dial* 18 (March 1, 1895), 146–47.

The conscience of New England a half century ago demanded much of its votaries and adherents. The limitations which it set about human intelligence and activity were many and certain. Its intense assurance of its own completeness and rectitude had its incommodities as well as its insights and rewards. To those who could acquiesce in its demands, it opened avenues to spiritual heights whence the outlook was large and superb, though the air might be somewhat thin for the health of daily life. At last, however, the burdens it imposed became too severe for a generation alive to much that was outside of its enclosed space, and the revolt began.

It seems that valuable literatures usually begin with such revolts, and the stronger spirits, after considerable effort and some suffering, throw off the fetters no longer endurable, and rejoice in the larger freedom which they have won. There are always, however, sensitive souls who feel that they must break with the traditions, but cannot find themselves wholly at home in the new and strange. Among the latter must be counted such writers as Emily Dickinson, as well as the Concord recluse, William Ellery Channing, whose poems, when again and properly presented to the world, will doubtless receive a recognition which has thus far been denied them. What has been done for Emily Dickinson will assuredly be done for him, and the result is no more doubtful in his case than it has proved in hers.

Miss Dickinson's letters make an admirable complement to her poems. In her early years she was a copious correspondent, and during her school-days she had a great reputation as a writer of long, and, as we can readily surmise, singularly original composition. The change in her epistolary style, with her growth in years and experience, is worthy of notice. The diffuse and minute letter-writing becomes condensed to a remarkable degree, epigrammatic, and mystical. Her correspondents were many, and include such names as Dr. Holland, Samuel Bowles, Helen Hunt Jackson, and, of course, Mrs. Todd, the devoted editor of these "Letters," and her guide and mentor, Colonel Higginson.

Not quite able to avail herself of the wider scope which the New England revolt was disclosing to her, and incapable of satisfaction with the creeds and moods in which she had been brought up, Emily Dickinson retired into herself, and found solace and serenity in her vivid apprehensions of the truth, and the manifestations of that truth in Nature, which became to her a symbol easily read and transparent to the meaning which it contained. Her correspondence is replete with a gay and delicate humor; the recluse was full of wit and of gentle happiness with her friends. Perhaps she did not take herself and her abandonment of the world with too much seriousness; probably she saw something of its humorous aspect, and would gladly enough have had the strength to share the generous life outside; the effort, doubtless, was too great, and the sympathetic appreciation not sufficiently vigorous and insistent. The letters are free from that strain of morbidness which we sometimes find in her poems, especially in those dealing with the subject of death and its dark accompaniments. Here we have such exquisite passages as this:

"The bed on which he came was enclosed in a large casket, shut entirely, and covered from head to foot with the sweetest flowers. He went to sleep from the village church. Crowds came to tell him good night, choirs sang to him, pastors told how brave he was — early-soldier heart. And the family lowered their heads, as the reeds the wind shakes."

As the introspective habit grew upon her, every incident of a life simple and unvarying in the extreme became touched with an illumination that her thoughts and mood poured forth. "A letter," she says, "always feels to me like immortality, because it is the mind alone without corporeal friend." A burst of severe weather in the spring gives rise to this: "The apple blossoms were slightly disheartened, yesterday, by a snow-storm, but the birds encouraged them all that they could — and how fortunate that the little ones had come to cheer their damask brethren." Here is a letter entire:

"The little package of Ceylon arrived in fragrant safety, and Caliban's 'clust'ring filberds' were not so luscious nor so brown. Honey in March is blissful as inopportune, and to caress the bee a severe temptation, but was not temptation the first zest? We shall seek to be frugal with our sweet possessions, though their enticingness quite leads us astray, and shall endow Austin [Emily Dickinson's brother], as we often do, after a parched day. For how much we thank you. Dear arrears of tenderness we can never repay till the will's great ores are finally sifted; but bullion is better than minted things, for it has no alloy. Thinking of you with fresher love, as the Bible boyishly says, 'New every morning and fresh every evening.'"

The unexpected abounds in these letters, as the reader of the poems will anticipate. "To make even Heaven more heavenly is within the aim of us all." "I shall bring you a handful of Lotus next, but do not tell the Nile." "Not what the stars have done, but what they are to do, is what detains the sky." "Changelessness is Nature's change." She lavishes her verse upon her correspondents.

> Take all away from me
> But leave me ecstasy,
> And I am richer then
> Than all my fellow-men.
> Is it becoming me
> To dwell so wealthily,
> When at my very door
> Are those possessing more,
> In boundless poverty?

Mrs. Todd says: "It is impossible to conceive that any sense of personal isolation, or real loneliness of spirit, because of the absence of humanity from her daily life, could have oppressed a nature so richly endowed." And again: "Emily Dickinson's method of living was so simple and natural an outcome of her increasingly shy nature, a development so perfectly in the line of her whole constitution, that no far-away and dramatic explanation of her quiet life is necessary to those who are capable of apprehending her." Notwithstanding the authoritative source from which this statement comes, many readers will hold a different opinion. No doubt the adjustment of Emily Dickinson to her environment grew in difficulty, and, as often happens in such cases, the effective help was not at hand. The extent of her correspondence, and the character of much of it, indicate how deeply she felt the need and how warmly she would have welcomed the possibility of closer relations with her fellows. The nun and the saint make a figure delicate and unique; but the poet with something real to say to mankind deserves our larger appreciation.

487 Richard Henry Stoddard. "Letters of Emily Dickinson." *New York Mail and Express*, March 2, 1895, p. 20. Dickinson's verse had earlier provoked this critic's "silence" (see headnote to no. 333).

"Letters of Emily Dickinson," edited by Mabel Loomis Todd, is one of those books which, published from time to time, generally make the literary critic pause, in the first place whether he shall say anything about them, or pass them over in silence, and in the next place, provided he makes up his mind to speak of them, what he ought to say, in view of his relation to his readers, and what he can say without seeming to be captious and unkind. Read simply for what they are, we see no good reason why these letters, which fill two volumes, should have been collected and published, and read by the light of what has been assumed respecting the personality of their writer, we still see no reason why they should have been taken from the hands of the persons to whom they were addressed for upward of forty years, and placed in the hands of the public, to whom their assumed personality will not be manifested—at least we think not—by anything in the letters themselves. Miss Dickinson belonged to a class of New England women for whom we entertain a profound personal respect. She was well born, her father being a man of political note in Massachusetts; she was well educated, at Amherst and elsewhere; fond of study and of books, a careful though not, we imagine, a voluminous reader; an affectionate school friend, a good daughter and a gentle sister; averse from society, addicted to her own pursuits and to solitude; with a certain tentative ambition in the direction of literature and in the habit of jotting down her thoughts and fancies in a more or less, usually a less, material form. She wrote many letters, in answer, no doubt, and many more letters, she read, she thought, leading a simple life among her relatives and a meditative life among the scenes she loved, until her uneventful years bore her on through girlhood and through womanhood, until she reached the age of 55, or thereabouts, dying on May 18, 1886. Some years after her death, we forget how many, there grew up a belief on the part of her friends that her literary remains were worthy of publication, and these remains, or such of them as were of a metrical structure, were accordingly published, her "Poems," so called, forming two series, and possibly two volumes, though as to their bookish extent we have no definite recollection. Such, in truth, was the life of Miss Dickinson, who differed in one respect from the kind of New England girl and New England woman of which she was a type, and that was in the disinclination and refusal to print her effusions. It was through no wish of her that they were given to the world, and, judging of their quality from the specimens thereof that appear in these letters of hers, we can see why she was willing that they should perish. She had read too much good literature to overtake them. She differed from the writing sisterhood in her unwillingness to publish her writings, and differed from them still more in a strange inaptitude for learning anything from the books that she read. They may, or may not, have stimulated her mind, but they taught her nothing, for whatever the value, or worthlessness, of her thoughts they were her own—were individual, were original, were unique. If any author was enough to her to be a favorite it was Emerson, and Emerson when he was least the great author that he was—on the dull, obscure and clumsy side of his genius in verse. She stammered, as he sometimes did, and often where, if she had been an apt scholar of her master, he would have spoken plainly. She knew but one man of letters—Mr. T. W. Higginson, who edited, we believe, her posthumous remains, or was instrumental in their publication, and to whom she wrote the only letters in these volumes that are worth reading today. She sent him four of her compositions in verse, asking him to tell her what he thought of them; he answered her letter, and she replied to his inquiries about herself, under the date of April 26, 1862:

Mr. Higginson—Your kindness claimed earlier gratitude, but I was ill, and write today from my pillow.

Thank you for the surgery; it was not so painful as I supposed. I bring you others, as you ask, though they might not differ. While my thought is undressed, I can make the distinction; but when I put them in the gown, they look alike and numb.

You asked how old I was? I made no verse, but one or two, until this winter, sir.

I had a terror since September I could tell to none, and so I sing, as the boy does by the burying ground, because I am afraid.

You inquire my books. For poets I have Keats and Mr. and Mrs. Browning. For prose, Mr. Ruskin, Sir Thomas Browne and the Revelations. I went to school, but, in your meaning of the phrase, had no education. When a little girl I had a friend who taught me Immortality, but venturing too near, himself, he never returned. Soon after my tutor died, and for several years my lexicon was my only companion. Then I found one more, but he was not contented I be his scholar, so he left the land.

You ask of my companions. Hills, sir, and the sundown, and a dog large as myself that my father bought me. They are better than beings because they know and do not tell, and the noise in the pool at noon excels my piano.

I have a brother and sister. My mother does not care for thought, and my father, too busy with his briefs to notice what we do. He buys me many books, but begs me not to read them because he fears they joggle the mind. They are religious except me, and address an eclipse every morning whom they call their "Father."

But I fear my story fatigues you. I would like to learn. Could you tell me how to be good, or is it unconveyed, like melody or witchcraft?

You speak of Mr. Whitman. I never read his book, but was told it was disgraceful.

I read Miss Prescott's "Circumstance," but it followed me in the dark, so I avoided her.

Two editors of journals came to my father's house this winter, and asked me for my mind, and when I asked them why, they said I was penurious, and they would use it for the world.

I could not weigh myself, myself. My size felt small to me. I read your chapters in the "Atlantic," and experienced honor for you. I was sure you would not reject a confiding question.

Is this, sir, what you asked me to tell you?

                                                          Your friend, E. Dickinson.

The Dickinson-Higginson correspondence, or the lady's share of it, fills thirty-one pages of the second volume of those "Letters," and are a justification, if any is needed, for their preservation and publication. They do not read like natural writing, and their cleverness is not expressive for a woman of from 31–53, to whom a ripe intellectual maturity seemed impossible. Clearly Mr. Higginson could do nothing for her. She had other literary friends, however, or rather journalistic friends, one being Mr. Josiah Gilbert Holland, novelist, poet and what not; another Mr. Samuel Bowles, the editor of the Springfield "Republican." The Dickinson-Holland and the Dickinson-Bowles letters are mostly of a personal and domestic character, and as might be inferred are full of kindly feeling and cordiality, but otherwise trivial. They were no doubt pleasant reading in the family circles to which they were addressed, but they are dull reading to the rest of the world, which is quite willing to forget men of the caliber of Mr. Bowles and Mr. Holland, and such like flies in the dubious amber of Miss Dickinson's letters, which have no flavor of literature in them, outside the verses with which they are plentifully besprinkled, and which for the most part are so amazing as to seem like caricatures of poetry in general, and of Emerson in particular, resembling nothing so much as Bayard Taylor's burlesques in the "Echo Club Papers." Here is a lyric out of the Holland letters, the date of which was somewhere in the sixties:

Though my destiny be fustian,
Hers be damask fine —
Though she wear a silver apron,
I, a less divine.

Still, my little gypsy being,
I would far prefer,
Still, my little sunburnt bosom,
To her rosier.

For when frosts their punctual fingers
On her forehead lay,
You and I and Dr. Holland
Bloom eternally.

Roses of a steadfast summer
In a steadfast land,
Where no autumn lifts her pencil,
And no reapers stand.

Here is another, from the Bowles letters, written in 1863:

Nature and God, I neither knew,
But both so well knew me,
They startled, like executors
On an identity.   [Of
Yet neither told, that I could learn;
My secret as secure
As Herschel's private interest,
Or Mercury's affair.

Here is a third in the same letters, dated a little earlier:

So glad are we, a stranger'd deem
'Twas sorry that we were;
For where the holiday should be
There publishes a tear.
Nor how ourselves be justified,
Since grief and joy are done

So similar, an optizan
Could not decide between.

There was, two or three years ago, a Dickinson fad in New England, and there may be still, for ought we know to the contrary, and if there be we shall not combat it, for, as President Lincoln is said to have remarked of some occasion, for people who like this kind of stuff, this is the kind of stuff they like. Speaking for ourselves simply, we prefer something different, and if we must have transcendental verse we prefer it at first hand, as Emerson wrote it in "The Problem," and not as Miss Dickinson tried to write it, without rhyme and without reason.

488 "Books and Authors." *Outlook* 51 (March 23, 1895), 481.

The interest awakened by the publication of Miss Emily Dickinson's verses naturally suggested the publication of her letters, and Mrs. Todd, who has discharged the very responsible function of editor, has shown excellent judgment, discretion, and tact in dealing with the material in her hands. Miss Dickinson's letters, like her verses, are not easily described, and cannot be put readily into any category. They are as individual as was their writer. It is chiefly as a revelation of character that we attach importance to them, and the two volumes of the *Letters of Emily Dickinson* form a contribution to our knowledge of human nature rather than to our literature. They are psychological documents, full of brightness, cleverness, oddity, insight, individuality, with occasional touches of genius; but they lack the sustained power, the soundness of thought, the sanity of view, and the firmness of fiber which make literature. As human documents they are intensely interesting. They reveal a nature of great elevation, intensity, with flashes of striking originality. The quality of these letters is shown by these quotations:

You inquire my books. For poets I have Keats and Mr. and Mrs. Browning. For prose, Mr. Ruskin, Sir Thomas Browne, and the Revelations. I went to school, but, in your manner of the phrase, had no education. When a little girl, I had a friend who taught me Immortality; but venturing too near, himself, he never returned. Soon after, my tutor died, and for several years my lexicon was my only companion. Then I found one more, but he was not contented I be his scholar, so he left the land. . . .

You asked how old I was? I made no verse, but one or two, until this winter, sir. . . . You ask of my companions. Hills, sir, and the sundown, and a dog, large as myself, that my father bought me. They are better than beings, because they know, but do not tell; and the noise in the pool at noon excels my piano. . . .

If I read a book and it makes my whole body so cold no fire can ever warm me, I know that is poetry. If I feel physically as if the top of my head were taken off, I know that is poetry. These are the only ways I know it. Is there any other way? . . .

Enough is so vast a sweetness, I suppose it never occurs, only pathetic counterfeits. . . .

Fabulous to me as the men of the *Revelations* who "shall not hunger any more." Even the possible has its insoluble particle. . . .

Dear One, — "Eye hath not seen nor ear heard." What a recompense! The enthusiasm of God at the reception of his sons! How ecstatic! How infinite! Says the blissful voice, not yet a voice, but a vision, "I will not let thee go, except I bless thee." Emily.

489 Sarah B. Harris. "Emily Dickinson." *Lincoln* [Neb.] *Courier* 10 (April 6, 1895), 3. T. B. Aldrich, rather than George Woodberry, wrote the *Atlantic* review alluded to at the end of this essay (see no. 325).

Living, she avoided all observation. Dead, her volume of poetry reveals her more than her portrait, or daily converse with her, would have done. During her life-time only a few stray poems were published. Since her death in 1886 her poems and her letters have been published by two of her friends, Mabel Loomis Todd and T. W. Higginson.

Strange that one who could not bear to be looked upon should write poetry so subjective. She would not sit for her photograph. She sketches herself in the following:

> I think just how my shape will rise
>> When I shall be forgiven,
> Till hair and eyes and timid head
>> Are out of sight in heaven.

Her father was the leading lawyer of Amherst, Mass. He was also the treasurer of Amherst college. Once a year he gave a reception at his house to the professors and students of the college and to the leading people of the town. "On these occasions" Mr. Higginson says, "his daughter Emily emerged from her wonted retirement and did her part as a gracious hostess; nor would anyone have known from her manner, I have been told, that this was not a daily occurrence. The annual occasion once past, she withdrew again into her seclusion, and, except for a very few friends, was as invisible to the world as if she had dwelt in a nunnery." Her conduct is differently reported by Mr. Howells in the *Atlantic Monthly*, who says that "sometimes when the guests were assembled she withdrew and sat by herself in an adjoining room with her face averted." There were years when she did not go outside her father's house, more years when she did not go outside the grounds. So morbidly afraid of revealing herself that at last she would not address her own letters she still intended her poems to be published the dedication shows:

> This is my letter to the world,
>> That never wrote to me —
> The simple news that Nature told,
>> With tender majesty.
> Her message is committed
>> To hands I cannot see;
> For love of her sweet countrymen,
>> Judge tenderly of me!

Once the public is sure genius is not posing but really wishes to conceal itself it never turns its eyes away from the hiding place. Emily Dickinson would not mingle with her neighbors. She may not have known enough about them to guess that she herself was a subject of comment to them. Her queer ways must have been a boon to the dwellers in a monotonous New England town. "They do say that Em-ly Dickinson has not been out of her front gate for five years." There are great possibilities for the gossips in this opening sentence. She was matinees and federations to Amherst as soon as she got old enough to know what she did not want to do.

Mr. Howells and Mr. Higginson give her high rank among poets. They compare her to Heine and Blake. In the *Atlantic* Mr. Woodberry says she is unworthy the comparison and that oblivion waits for morbid poetry. It may be so. When the first critic in America says so it is probably true. Come to think of it I am glad of it. I go to oblivion myself and we might meet. Her sympathy with nature was constant and close. Her poetry reminds me of Emerson, of Heine, of Thoreau.

THE GRASS.

The grass so little has to do—
　　A sphere of simple green,
With only butterflies to love,   [to brood
　　And bees to entertain,
And stir all day to pretty tunes
　　The breezes fetch along,
And hold the sunshine in its lap
　　And bow to everything;
And thread the dew all night, like pearls,   [dews
　　And make itself so fine—
A duchess were too common
　　For such a noticing.
And even when it dies, to pass
　　In odors so divine,
As lovely spices gone to sleep,
　　Or amulets of pine.
And then to dwell in sovereign barns,
　　And dream the days away—
The grass so little has to do,
　　I wish I were the hay!

490　"Literature." *Christian Register* 74 (April 11, 1895), 234. John White Chadwick, who was still regularly reviewing for the *Christian Register*, is the likely author. Chadwick gave one-sentence mention to Dickinson in two reviews of the poet John Banister Tabb, noting Tabb's greater attention to perfection of form (see *Christian Register* 74 (Jan. 3, 1895), 4 and *Book Buyer* n.s. 13 (May 1896), 226–229.

These are two immensely interesting volumes, and yet one cannot help wondering if they would not have been twice as interesting if there had been half as much. That the bias of friendship should operate with the editor to make a liberal inclusion rather than a rigid exclusion her principle of selection was to be expected, and will not be sternly judged. But a more exclusive habit would have improved the book. The early letters, especially, could have been much condensed without injury, and even with clear gain. They are generally diffuse, and, although bright, not brighter than are written by many girls of the school-going age. They are mainly interesting as indicating the change that came over the spirit of Miss Dickinson's life. Like the two fabled clocks, her handwriting and her style ticked into unison. At first both were continuous, then both became *staccato*, the letters of the writing at last written separately, and the thought coming in more explosive and eccentric spurts as time went on.

These volumes, in their best parts, are not essentially different from the two volumes of verses by which Miss Dickinson is already so well and favorably known. Reading them, we do not know her better: we only know her more. The intellectual quality is the same in either case, but in the books of poems it is more subtle and refined. There, upon the average, we have the best wool of the sheep.

But there are fleeces here as long and white as any parts of her previous volumes. Some of them are in prose, and others are in verse. The criticism has been made upon her poems that they are not poetry, but prose cut up into lines of arbitrary length. The criticism is not well made. To rhyme she was evidently indifferent, but not to rhythm; and something of this—and often it is very fine—is hardly ever wanting. It is much truer that her prose ran into verse than that her verse ran into prose. There are many passages in these letters that are printed as stanzas of poetry. Some of those so printed are better than the least remarkable in the volumes of verse, some of them well up toward the best. But we have also many passages that are printed as prose which are as much verse as any of the parts printed as such. The intellectual and moral and religious characteristics are the same as those which we already knew,—the same brilliancy of phrase; the same daring criticism and approval of the highest powers; the same vivid apprehension of the wonder, beauty, mystery of nature, love, and death.

While there is nothing here to enhance the literary reputation of Miss Dickinson, there is much that helps us to a better knowledge of her personality. It is evident that she was only physically a recluse, that her affections and her sympathies were contracted to no narrow span. She had many friends, and she was always reaching out for more. Col. Higginson was the best conquest that she made, and her letters to him are among the very best. Another thing is plain: that her literary forms, however spontaneous apparently, were not so in reality. They were the result of no mere accident, but of deliberate choice. Different copies of letters, with many changes from one to another, signify that even her letters were written with an artist's hand. Words were no mere counters with her, but the coin of the realm; and she brought it to a rigid test. The outcome of her spiritual experience, in spite of sentences that state the most painful things without reserve, was a vigorous optimism. She goes in and out among the different systems, "pouncing upon her own wherever she finds it." She has heard that Theodore Parker is "poison." "Then I like poison very well," she says. But sometimes she seems as orthodox as any. This is because she could make any creed the symbol of her own thought. "When a god would ride, anything serves him for a chariot." One must attend to what she means as well as to what she says. We should like to quote, but of a hundred things that we have marked we cannot decide upon the best.

491 Mabel Loomis Todd. "Emily Dickinson's Letters." *Bachelor Of Arts* 1 (May 1895), 39–66. This article on the development of Dickinson's letter-writing style was declined by the *Century* in 1894 before being accepted for its inaugural issue by the *Bachelor of Arts*, a little magazine (see *AB*, pp. 279, 280). This article contains two first printings not recorded in the 1955 Johnson variorum: "Dear March—come in" (complete) and "We like March" (partial). Mrs. Todd included the full text of both in her 1896 *Poems*, Third Series.

When Emily Dickinson's strangely compelling poems were first published the critics knew hardly where to place them. It was curiously interesting to read and compare the many notices—to see that, almost without exception, the reviewers agreed in allowing her the possession of undoubted genius, yet also in deploring the fact that she seemed to care so slightly for the form in which her startling little poetic bombs were cast.

Almost everything possible was said of the verses. Poe would have approved the bit of melodrama in her description of "some lonely houses off the road a robber'd like the look of"; Thoreau would have enjoyed some of her "pretty blasphemies"; and she has been compared, not only to William Blake, Heine, and Emerson, but to Browning, Shelley, and to far-off Omar Khayyam, while each of her sudden revelations seems, as one critic remarked, like "a shaft of light sunk instantaneously into the dark abysm" [no. 62]. Yet another wrote that, after all, in reading her incontestable oracles, the lack of rhyme is hardly felt, and to him she really proves that "the adjunct of rhyme is not so necessary to the pleasure of verse as many have believed" [no. 51]. A sentence written two or three years ago by Dr. Holmes, though in another connection, may be quoted as bearing toward the same point. "Rhymes," he says, "are iron fetters; it is dragging a chain and a ball to march under their incumbrance."

By no possibility could any of these poems have been written by any other than Emily Dickinson herself—she has stamped them with unimpeachable evidence of her individual authorship. But they all have—and there are many hundred still unpublished—one curious aspect. In general method of thought and workmanship they are continually similar. There is no advance in style. Many which must have been written as early as 1862 are in no sense less finished or less daring and brilliant than those bearing proof of far later origin, even the last years before her death in 1886. But this is by no means true of her prose.

Since the wide recognition of the poems as unmistakable, if eccentric, works of genius, her sister has wished that Emily's prose writing, quite wholly contained in letters, should be also collected in a volume, and during the last three years this has been in process of accomplishment.

A great many letters have been found, all of them unusual, many more beautiful and striking than the verses; and their publication has seemed the more desirable in that the poems, often but the reflection of a passing mood, do not always truthfully represent herself, rarely, indeed, showing the dainty humor, the frolicsome gaiety, which continually bubbled over in her daily life. The somber and even gruesome outlook upon life, characteristic of many of the verses, was by no means a prevailing condition of mind; for while apprehending to the full all the tragic elements of life, enthusiasm and bright joyousness were yet her normal qualities, and stimulating moral heights her native dwelling place.

All this may be glimpsed, often satisfactorily, in her letters, which progress, in a manner thoroughly normal and strong, from those written with all the diffuseness of early girlhood to the brilliant and sententious epigrams of late middle life. And yet flashes of future picturesque power frequently illuminate the long youthful letters. Lowell once wrote of the letters of Carlyle, "The man . . . is all there in the earliest of his writing that we have (potentially there, in character wholly there)." Emily Dickinson's girlish letters are published chiefly for these "potential" promises. It is hoped that some examples of her changing methods, in letters taken almost at random, will possess interest, all the variations in the evolution of a style having hardly less charm for the student of human nature than of literature.

It was with a certain feeling of dread that I approached these letters to make them ready for the public in a volume, lest the too deep revelations of a peculiarly shy inner life might so pervade them that in truest loyalty none might properly be used. But with few exceptions they have been read and prepared not only with entire relief from that feeling, but with unshrinking pleasure. For Emily kept her little reserves, and bared her soul but seldom. It was not so much that she was always on spiritual guard, as that she sported with her varying moods, testing them upon her friends with an apparent delight in their effect as airy and playful as it was half unconscious.

The earliest of these letters, to a schoolmate, were written when Emily Dickinson had but recently passed her fourteenth birthday. Before the era of outer envelopes, they are quaintly written on large, square sheets of paper, the last page, peculiarly folded and fastened with seals of wax, forming the cover with the address. This early handwriting is almost microscopic, the three large pages entirely filled, and averaging over twenty words to a line. Short extracts only can be given. The first one is dated February 23, 1845.

Old Time wags on pretty much as usual at Amherst, and I know of nothing that has occurred to break the silence; however, the reduction of the postage has excited my risibles somewhat. Only think! We can send a letter before long for five little coppers only, filled with the thoughts and advice of dear friends. But I will not get into a philosophizing strain just yet; there is time enough for that upon another page of this mammoth sheet. . . . Your *beau ideal* D___ I have not seen lately. I presume he was changed into a star some night while gazing at them and placed in the constellation Orion between Bellatrix and Betelgeux. . . . It seems more like smiling May crowned with flowers than cold, Arctic February, wading through snow-drifts. I have heard some sweet little birds sing, but I fear we shall have more cold weather, and their little bills will be frozen up before their songs are finished. . . . Please send me a copy of that romance you were writing at Amherst. I am in a fever to read it. I expect it will be against my Whig feelings.

Already intellectual brilliancy of an individual type was her chief characteristic. She was always original, and her methods of life piquant even then. In early school days she was the best and brightest scholar, both at the old Amherst Academy and at South Hadley Seminary. Traditions of her extraordinary "compositions" still remain, and it is certain that each marked an epoch for those who heard, whether teachers or pupils. One of her schoolmates tells me that she was always surrounded at recess by a group of girls listening to her strange and intensely funny stories, often invented upon the spot.

Emily sometimes alludes in these early letters to the required composition writing—for her no dreaded task.

Another early letter, describing a visit in Boston, is a curious combination of childish delight in the Chinese Museum, and sober reflections upon the improvement of time which might have done credit to a student of Upham's Mental Philosophy.

BOSTON, Sept. 8, 1846.

Father and mother thought a journey would be of service to me, and accordingly I left home for Boston week before last. I had a delightful ride in the cars, and am now getting settled down, if there can be such a state in the city. I am visiting in my aunt's family and am happy.

Happy! did I say? No; not happy, but contented. I have been here a fortnight to-day, and in that time I have both seen and heard a great many wonderful things. Perhaps you might like to know how I have spent the time here. I have been to Mount Auburn, to the Chinese Museum, to Bunker Hill; I have attended two concerts and one Horticultural Exhibition. I have been upon the top of the State House, and almost everywhere that you can imagine. Have you ever been to Mount Auburn? If not, you can form but slight conception of this "city of the Dead." It seems as if nature had formed this spot with a distinct idea in view of its being a resting-place for her children, where, wearied and disappointed, they might stretch themselves beneath the spreading cypress, and close their eyes "calmly as to a night's repose, or flowers at set of sun."

The Chinese Museum is a great curiosity. There is an endless variety of wax figures made to resemble the Chinese, and dressed in their costume. Also articles of Chinese manufacture of an innumerable variety deck the rooms. Two of the Chinese go with this exhibition. One of them is a professor of music in China, and the other is teacher of a writing-school at home. They were both wealthy, and not obliged to labor, but they were also opium-eaters; and fearing to continue the practice lest it destroyed their lives, yet unable to break the rigid chain of habit in their own land, they left their families, and came to this country. They have now entirely overcome the practice. There is something peculiarly interesting to me in this self-denial. The musician played upon two of his instruments, and accompanied them with his voice. It needed great command over my risible faculties to enable me to keep sober as this amateur was performing; yet he was so very polite to give us some of his native music that we could not do otherwise than to express ourselves highly edified with his performances. The writing-master is constantly occupied in writing the names of visitors who request it, upon cards in the Chinese language, for which he charges 12 1/2 cents apiece. He never fails to give his card besides to the persons who wish it. I obtained one of his cards for Viny and myself, and I consider them very precious. . . . Does it seem as though September had come? How swiftly summer has fled and what report has it borne to heaven of misspent time and wasted hours? Eternity only will answer. The ceaseless flight of the seasons is to me a very solemn thought; and yet why do we not strive to make a better improvement of them? With how much emphasis the poet has said, "We take no note of Time but from its loss. 'T were wise in man to give it then a tongue. Pay no moment but in just purchase of its worth, and what its worth ask deathbeds. They can tell. Part with it, as with life, reluctantly." Then we have higher authority than that of man for the improvement of our time. For God has said, "Work while the day lasts, for the night is coming in the which no man can work." Let us strive together to part with time more reluctantly, to watch the pinions of the fleeting moment until they are dim in the distance, and the new-coming moment claims our attention.

A year later her life at South Hadley had begun, and one of her first letters from that famous school has a certain old-time interest:

MT. HOLYOKE SEMINARY,

November 6, 1847.

My Dear A.____ I am really at Mt. Holyoke Seminary, and this is to be my home for a long year. Your affectionate letter was joyfully received, and I wish that this might make you as happy as yours did me. It has been nearly six weeks since I left home, and that is a longer time than I was ever away from home before now. I was very homesick for a few days, and it seemed to me I could not live here. But I am now contented and quite happy, if I can be happy when absent from my dear home and friends. You may laugh at the idea that I cannot be happy when away from home, but you must remember that I have a very dear home and that this is my first trial in the way of absence for any length of time in my life. As you desire it, I will give you a full account of myself since I first left the paternal roof. I came to South Hadley six weeks ago next Thursday. I was much fatigued with the ride, and had a severe cold besides, which prevented me from commencing my examinations until the next day, when I began. I finished them in three days, and found them about what I had anticipated, though the old scholars say they are more strict than they ever have been before. . . . Everything is pleasant and happy here, and I think I could be no happier at any other school away from home. Things seem much more like home than I anticipated, and the teachers are all very kind and affectionate to us. They call on us frequently and urge us to return their calls, and when we do, we always receive a cordial welcome from them. I will tell you my order of time for the day, as you were so kind as to give me yours. At 6 o'clock we all rise. We breakfast at 7. Our study hours begin at 8. At 9 we all meet in Seminary Hall for devotions. At 10 1/4 I recite a review of Ancient History, in connection with which we read Goldsmith and Grimshaw. At 11 I recite a lesson in "Pope's Essay on Man," which is merely transposition. At 12 I practice calisthenics, and at 12 1/4 read until dinner, which is at 12 1/2, and after dinner, from 1 1/2 until 2, I sing in Seminary Hall. From 2 3/4 until 3 3/4 I practice upon the piano. At 3 3/4 I go to sections, where we give in all our accounts for the day, including absence, tardiness, communications, breaking silent study hours, receiving company in our rooms, and ten thousand other things which I will not take time or place to mention. At 4 1/2 we go into Seminary Hall and receive advice from Miss Lyon in the form of a lecture. We have supper at 6, and silent study hours from then until the retiring bell, which rings at 8 3/4, but the tardy bell does not ring until 9 3/4, so that we don't often obey the first warning to retire. Unless we have a good and reasonable excuse for failure upon any of the items that I mentioned above, they are recorded and a black mark stands against our names. As you can easily imagine, we do not like very well to get "exceptions," as they are called scientifically here.

My domestic work is not difficult, and consists in carrying the knives from the first tier of tables at morning and noon, and at night washing and wiping the same quantity of knives. . . . One thing is certain, and that is that Miss Lyon and all the teachers seem to consult our comfort and happiness in everything they do, and you know that is pleasant.

Some of Emily Dickinson's brightest writing during these far away years is contained in letters sent to her brother in Boston and at the Law School in Cambridge. They are, however, largely so personal that but few extracts will be given, one of which is her account of driving from Amherst to Northampton to hear Jenny Lind. The letter was written July 5, 1851, although Emily had already abandoned dating her letters. For those written during the next thirty-five years only approximate dates can be given. The penmanship, which has three distinct periods, is some guide, and the kind of postage stamp used—when the recipient has preserved the envelopes—while the postmark assists somewhat, although at that early time the year was rarely given. The thoughtfulness of a few friends in recording the time of a letter's reception has been a farther and most welcome help to me. But the main reliance in producing proper chronological order has been from searching out the time when events mentioned in the letters occurred. The result of these researches, indeed, into remote and by-gone happenings has been undoubtedly beneficial to the editor, who has become, perforce, unimpeachable authority upon the dates of most of the births, marriages, deaths and fires—in short, upon the general local history of a past generation. The singing of Jenny Lind in Northampton, however, was an event too widely remembered to offer any problems as to its date.

Sunday Afternoon.

I have just come in from church very hot and faded. . . . Our church grows interesting—Zion lifts her head—I overhear remarks signifying Jerusalem. I do not feel at liberty to say any more to-day. . . . I wanted to write you Friday, the night of Jenny Lind, but reaching home past midnight, and my room some time after, encountering several perils starting and on the way, among which a kicking horse, an inexperienced driver, a number of Jove's thunderbolts, and a very terrible rain, are worthy to have record. All of us went—just four; add an absent individual and that will make full five. The concert commenced at eight, but knowing the world was hollow, we thought we'd start at six, and come up with everybody that meant to come up with us. We had proceeded some steps when one of the beasts showed symptoms, and just by the blacksmith's shop exercises commenced, consisting of kicking and plunging on the part of the horse, and whips and moral suasion from the gentleman who drove. The horse refused to proceed, and your respected family, with much chagrin, dismounted, advanced to the hotel, and for a season halted; another horse procured, we were politely invited to take our seats and proceed, which we refused to do till the animal was warranted. About half through our journey thunder was said to be heard, and a suspicious cloud came traveling up the sky. What words express our horror when rain began to fall in drops, sheets, cataracts—what fancy conceive of drippings and of drenchings which we met on the way—how the stage and its mourning captives drew up at Warner's Hotel—how all of us alighted and were conducted in—how the rain did not abate—how we walked in silence to the old Edward's church* [Todd's note: *Evidently a slip of the pen, as Jenny Lind sang in the old First Church on that occasion.] and took our seats in the same—how Jenny came out like a child, and sang and sang again—how bouquets fell in showers, and the roof was rent with applause—how it thundered outside, and inside with the thunder of God and of men—judge ye, which was the loudest—how we all loved Jenny Lind, but not accustomed oft to her manner of singing didn't fancy *that* so well as we did *her.* No doubt it was very fine, but take some notes from her *Echo,* the bird sounds from the *Bird Song,* and some of her curious trills, and I'd rather have a Yankee.

Herself and not her music was what we seemed to love. She has an air of exile in her mild blue eyes, and a something sweet and touching in her native accent which charms her many friends. *Give me my thatched cottage.* As she sang she grew so earnest she seemed half lost in song, and for a transient time I fancied she *had* found it, and would be seen 'na mair'; and then her foreign accent made her again a wanderer. We will talk about her some time when you come.

Another written also to her brother, is postmarked November 17 (1851):

We are thinking most of Thanksgiving than anything else just now—how full will be the circle, less then by none—how the things will smoke—how the board will groan with the thousand savory viands—how when the day is done, lo, the evening cometh, laden with merrie laugh and happy conversation, and then the sleep and the dream each of a knight or "ladie"—how I love to see them, a beautiful company coming down the hill which men call the future, with their hearts full of joy, and their hands with gladness. Thanksgiving, indeed, to a family united once more together before they go away. . . . Don't mind the days—some of them are long ones, but who cares for length when breadth is in store for him?

A still later one is postmarked March 18 (1853):

I presume you remember a story that Vinnie tells of a breach of promise case where the correspondence between the parties consisted of a reply from the girl to one she had never received, but was daily expecting. Well, *I* am writing an answer to a letter I haven't had, so you will see the force of the accompanying anecdote. I have been looking for you ever since dispatching my last, but this is a fickle world, and it's a great source of complacency that 't will all be burned up by and by.

All this time Emily Dickinson lived the usual life of young girls in college towns, during which she wrote a number of characteristic letters to Mrs. J. G. Holland, from which a few extracts follow:

And what I mean is this—I thought of you all last week, until the world grew rounder than it sometimes is, and I broke several dishes.

Monday I solemnly resolved I would be *sensible,* so I wore thick shoes, and thought of Dr. Humphrey and the Moral Law. One glimpse of the *Republican* makes me break things again—I read in it every night.

Who writes those funny accidents, where railroads meet each other unexpectedly, and gentlemen in factories get their heads cut off quite informally? The author, too, relates them in such a sprightly way that they are quite attractive. Vinnie was disappointed to-night that there were not more accidents.

In the spring of 1854 she went with her family to Washington, during her father's term in Congress, although she seemed even then somewhat disinclined to mingle in crowds, particularly away from home. The following letter was written to Mrs. Holland from Philadelphia on the return journey:

We have had many pleasant times, and seen much that is fair and heard much that is wonderful—many sweet ladies and noble gentlemen have taken us by the hand and smiled upon us pleasantly—and the sun shines brighter for our way thus far.

I will not tell you what I saw—the elegance, the grandeur; you will not care to know the value of the diamonds my Lord and Lady wore, but if you haven't been to the sweet Mount Vernon, then I *will* tell you how on one soft spring day we glided down the Potomac in a painted boat, and jumped upon the shore—how hand in hand we stole along up a tangled pathway till we reached the tomb of Gen. George Washington, how we paused beside it, and no one spoke a word, then hand in hand walked on again, not less wise or sad for that marble story; how we went within the door—raised the latch he lifted when he last went home—thank the Ones in Light that he's since passed in through a brighter wicket! Oh, I could spend a long day, if it did not weary you, telling of Mount Vernon—and I will some time if we live and meet again, and God grant we shall!

Later letters to Dr. and Mrs. Holland become even more characteristic. In 1855 the family returned to the old homestead built by Emily Dickinson's grandfather, where, indeed, she was born, but from which they had lived away, in another part of the village, for ten years. The letter following describes the moving "home" again:

I cannot tell you how we moved. I had rather not remember. I believe my "effects" were brought in a bandbox, and the "deathless me," on foot, not many moments after. I took at the time a memorandum of my several senses, and also of my hat and coat, and my best shoes—but it was lost in the *mêlée,* and I am out with lanterns, looking for myself.

Such wits as I reserved, are so badly shattered that repair is useless—and still I can't help laughing at my own catastrophe. I suppose we were going to make a "transit," as heavenly bodies did—but we came budget by budget, as our fellows do, till we fulfilled the pantomime contained in the word "moved." It is a kind of *gone-to-Kansas* feeling, and if I sat in a long wagon, with my family tied behind, I should suppose without doubt I was a party of emigrants!

They say that "home is where the heart is." I think it is where the house is, and the adjacent buildings.

Still later, probably about 1860, came Emily's opinion of friends who do not reply to her letters:

Friday.

DEAR FRIENDS. — I write to you. I receive no letter.

I say "they dignify my trust." I do not disbelieve. I go again. *Cardinals* wouldn't do it. Cockneys wouldn't do it, but I can't *stop* to strut, in a world where bells toll. I hear, through visitor in town, that "Mrs. Holland is not strong." The little peacock in me tells me not to inquire again. Then I remember my tiny friend — how brief she is — how dear she is, and the peacock quite dies away. Now, you need not speak, for perhaps you are weary, and *"Herod"* requires all your thought, but if you are *well* — let Annie draw me a little picture of an erect flower; if you are *ill*, she can hang the flower a little on one side!

Then I shall understand, and you need not stop to write me a letter. Perhaps you laugh at me! Perhaps the whole United States are laughing at me, too! I can't stop for that! *My* business is to love. I found a bird, this morning, down — down — on a little bush at the foot of the garden, and wherefore sing, I said, since nobody *hears?*

One sob in the throat, one flutter of bosom — *"My* business is to *sing"* — and away she rose! How do I know but cherubim, once, themselves, as patient, listened, and applauded her unnoticed hymn?   EMILY.

Who could resist a plea like that, or fail to flood such a correspondent with an epistolary deluge?

Almost equally distasteful with entire silence seem to have been letters written to Emily and her sister jointly, Mrs. Holland receiving this suggestive protest:

SISTER. — A mutual plum is not a plum. I was too respectful to take the pulp and do not like a stone.

Send no union letters. The soul must go by Death alone, so, it must by life, if it is a soul.

If a committee — no matter.

About this time she wrote to Mrs. Holland:

House is being cleaned. I prefer pestilence. That is more classic and less fell.

By middle life it had become quite clear that Emily's best happiness lay in her own home, and in her own soul. Society seemed to her unreal, thin, unworthy. Conventionalities amused while they sickened her.

> The show is not the show,
> But they who go,

expressed in large measure her attitude toward that side of life. Real life, on the other hand, seemed to her very vast and inexpressibly solemn. Petty trivialities had no part in her constitution, and she came to despise them more and more. It was partly owing to this and partly to an innate and constantly increasing shyness which caused her to mingle constantly less with accumulated humanity, to give up her journeys to distant cities, and to retire from even the simple life of a New England college town. But her love for her friends seemed to increase almost in proportion as she had less of their bodily presence, and her letters to and from them formed a large part of her life. She once wrote to Mr. Samuel Bowles:

I hope your cups are full. I hope your vintage is untouched. In such a porcelain life one likes to be sure that all is well, lest one stumble upon one's hopes in a pile of broken crockery.

My friends are my estate.

Forgive me, then, the avarice to hoard them! They tell me those who were poor early have different views of gold. I don't know how that is.

God is not so wary as we, else He would give us no friends, lest we forget Him! The charms of the heaven in the bush are superseded, I fear, by the heaven in the hand, occasionally.

Later she wrote, after Mr. Bowles had returned from Europe, where his health had seemed greatly benefited:

We pray for your new health the prayer that goes not down when they shut the church. We offer you our cups, stintless as to the bee—the lily, her new liquors.

Would you like summer? Taste of ours.

Spices? Buy here.

Ill? We have berries for the parching.

Weary? Furloughs of down.

Perplexed? Estates of violet trouble ne'er looked on.

Captive? We bring reprieve of roses.

Fainting? Flasks of air.

Even for Death a fairy medicine.

But which is it, sir?

With a keen sense of humor, and a nature as ecstatic as a bird's, she was yet made serious by the insistence of life's pathos. The combination of qualities rendered her companionship, when she vouchsafed it, wonderfully breezy and fascinating. But such a soul must inevitably know more pain than pleasure. Passionately devoted to her friends, her happiness was at times almost too intense— and disproportionately large pain, in the earlier years, was caused by even slight separations. With her, pathos lay very near raillery and badinage, pain very near delight.

As early as 1868 or 1870 her prose style was beginning to develop its incisiveness—like her own thought, it went straight to the essence of things, and while still dressed in language sufficiently to allow its passing in conventional places, it was already divested of superfluities. A letter to a cousin in the spring of 1870 suggests the coming simplicity. She had no events, in the usual meaning of the word. Birds and sunshine, a stray breeze, or a passing cloud gave her their own fullness, and made her days great with infinite suggestiveness.

DEAR CHILDREN: I think the blue-birds do their work exactly like me. They dart around just so, with little dodging feet, and look so agitated. I really feel for them, they seem to be so tried. The mud is very deep—up to the wagons' stomachs— arbutus making pink clothes, and everything alive. Even the hens are touched with the things of Bourbon, and make republicans like me feel strangely out of scene. Mother went rambling and came in with a burdock on her shawl, so we know that the snow has perished from the earth.

Noah would have liked mother.

A year or two after, she wrote:

Interview is acres, while the broadest letter feels a bandaged place.

And to the same cousin in 1874:

Spring is a happiness so beautiful, so unique, so unexpected, that I don't know what to do with my heart. I dare not take it, I dare not leave it. What do you advise? Life is a spell so exquisite that everything conspires to break it.

What do I think of *Middlemarch?* What do I think of glory, except that in a few instances this "mortal has already put on immortality." George Eliot is one. The mysteries of human nature surpass the "mysteries of redemption," for the infinite we only suppose, while we see the finite. . . .

I launch Vinnie to-morrow. It will require the combined efforts of Maggie, Providence, and myself, for whatever advances Vinnie makes in nature and art, she has not reduced departure to a science.

But at last an event did come, in the sudden death of her father, and with it a benumbing horror, which almost stopped her own heart from beating, and seemed to undermine the foundations of her world. After a few days she wrote her cousin:

Father does not live with us now—he lives in a new house. Though it was built in an hour, it is better than this. He hasn't any garden, because he moved after gardens were made, so we take him the best flowers, and if we only knew he knew perhaps we could stop crying. . . . The grass begins after Pat has stopped it. Though it is many nights, my mind never comes home.

And afterward to another friend:

Should it be possible for me to speak of my father before I behold him, I shall try to do so to you, whom he always remembered.

When her mind really "came home" again, and the shock was a little in the past, her quaint way of looking at everything came forth once more, and she wrote a cousin who had sent flowers for her father's grave:

I am sure you must have remembered that father had become as little children, or you would never have dared send him a Christmas gift, for you know how he frowned upon Santa Claus and all such prowling gentlemen.

And about the same time: "Nature must be too young to feel, or much too old."

In the night of the fourth of July, 1879, a large fire occurred in Amherst, of which the description went forth to her cousins:

Did you know there had been a fire here, and but for a whim of the wind Vinnie and Emily would have been homeless? But perhaps you saw the *Republican.* We were waked by the ticking of the bells. The bells tick in Amherst to tell the firemen. I sprang to the window, and each side of the curtain saw that awful sun. The moon was shining high at the time and the birds singing like trumpets.

Vinnie came, soft as a moccasin: "Don't be afraid, Emily, it's only the Fourth of July."

I did not tell that I saw it, for I thought if she felt it best to deceive, it must be that it was. She took hold of my hand and let me into mother's room. Mother had not waked. . . . I could hear buildings falling and oil exploding, and people walking and talking gaily, and cannon far and soft as velvet from parishes that did not know that we were burning up.

And so much lighter than day was it that I saw a caterpillar measure a leaf far down in the orchard, and Vinnie kept saying bravely: "It's only the Fourth of July." It seemed like a theater, or a night in London, or perhaps like chaos; the innocent dew falling "as if it thought no evil," and sweet frogs prattling in the pools as if there were no earth. . . . The post office is in the old meeting house where

[Loo] and I went early to avoid the crowd, and—fell asleep with the bumble bees and the Lord God of Elijah.

Vinnie's "It's only Fourth of July" I shall always remember. I think she will tell us so when we die, to keep us from being afraid.

Footlights cannot improve the grave—only immortality.

To the same cousins this sententious paragraph:

God is rather stern with His little ones. "A cup of cold water in My name" is a shivering legacy, February mornings.

After an invalidism of several years, Emily's mother died in the autumn of 1882, of which this remarkable letter was one result:

I hoped to write you before, but mother's dying almost stunned my spirit. I have answered a few inquiries of love, but written little intuitively. She was scarcely the aunt you knew. The great mission of pain had been ratified—cultivated to tenderness by persistent sorrow, so that a larger mother died than had she died before. There was no earthly parting. She slipped from our fingers like a flake gathered by the wind, and is now part of the drift called "the infinite."

We don't know where she is, though so many tell us.

I believe we shall in some manner be cherished by our Maker—that the One who gave us this remarkable earth has the power still farther to surprise that which He has caused. Beyond, all is silence.

Mother was very beautiful when she had died. Seraphs are solemn artists. The illumination that comes but once paused upon her features, and it seemed like hiding a picture to lay her in the ground. But the grass that received my father will suffice his guest—the one he asked at the altar to visit him all his life.

I cannot tell how eternity seems—it sweeps around me like a sea.

But despite the continual pain brought by death, her essentially sunny nature always reasserted itself in time, though toward the end of life the accumulation of losses was almost too much for her loving heart. These years were constantly fertile in some of the strangest and most weird of her verses, as her life drew more and more into itself.

Her great debt to books is constantly dwelt upon both in letters and in many of her poems. An unpublished fragment, inclosed in a letter to a friend, expresses this sense of gratitude in her own quaint way:

> There is no frigate like a book
> To take us lands away,
> Nor any coursers like a page
> Of prancing poetry.
> This traverse may the poorest take
> Without oppress of toll.
> How frugal is the chariot
> That bears a human soul!

Her garden was gradually abandoned for the conservatory, and truly she seemed to have a mysterious friendship with the powers of sun and soil, for always fair were her plants with perennial blossoming.

The secret of her poetic seclusion was neither bodily infirmity, nor love disappointment, incredible as such a statement may seem. Nine-tenths of us, of more every-day mold, would require some sudden blow, some fierce and startling crisis, to produce a hidden and unusual life like hers. And we love to believe strik-

ing and theatrical things of our neighbors. It panders to that romantic element
latent in the plainest of us. But Emily Dickinson's method of living was a simple
and natural outcome of her increasingly shy and introspective nature—a development perfectly in the line of her whole constitution. One sentence alone, written more than thirty years ago, foreshadowed it, was indeed its key. Speaking re-
gretfully of the loss of her long-time maid, Margaret, she said:

> I winced at her loss, for I am in the habit of her, and even a new rolling-pin has
> an embarrassing element.

Congenial companionship was, nevertheless, in a certain sense, very dear to
her, yet I am convinced that she was not lonely in her chosen isolation.

Emerson somewhere says: "Now and then a man exquisitely made can live
alone," and Lord Bacon puts the thought with even greater force and directness—
"Whosoever is delighted in Solitude, is either a Wilde Beast or a God." To some
natures introspection is a necessity for expression. "Why should I feel lonely?" exclaims Thoreau, in his temporary isolation at Walden. "Is not our planet in the
Milky Way?" He was, indeed, "no more lonely than the north star," nor, I believe,
was Emily Dickinson. One of her still unpublished poems begins:

> Never for society
> He shall seek in vain,
> Who his own acquaintance
> Cultivates. . . .

Her intimacy with nature was almost elflike—she saw and apprehended the
great mother's processes, methods; and she shared the rapture of all created things
under the wide sky. March was especially dear. Many of her poems celebrate its
beauties and promises. One especially is such a quaint and personal apostrophe
to his virtues that I cannot refrain from quoting it:

> Dear March, come in!
> How glad I am!
> I looked for you before.
> Put down your hat—
> You must have walked—
> How out of breath you are!
> Dear March, how are you?
> And the rest?
> Did you leave nature well?
> Oh! March, come right upstairs with me—
> I have so much to tell!
>
> I got your letter, and the birds—
> The maples never knew
> That you were coming, I declare,
> How red their faces grew!
> But, March, forgive me—
> And all those hills
> You left for me to hue;
> There was no purple suitable,
> You took it all with you.
>
> Who knocks? That April!
> Lock the door!

I will not be pursued!
He stayed away a year, to call
When I am occupied.
But trifles look so trivial
As soon as you have come,
That blame is just as dear as praise,
And praise as mere as blame.

The closing stanza of another unpublished poem on March reads:

News is he of all the others,
Bold it were to die
With the blue-birds buccaneering
On his British sky.

"What a hazard an accent is!" she wrote in one of her last years. "When I think of the hearts it has scuttled or sunk, I almost fear to lift my hand to so much as a punctuation!"

And to another who had sent her a book — what book, unhappily, we do not know:

DEAR FRIEND: I thank you with wonder. Should you ask me my comprehension of a starlight night, awe were my only reply — and so of the mighty book. It stills, incites, infatuates, blesses and blames in one. Like human affection, we dare not touch it, yet flee — what else remains? . . . How vast is the chastisement of beauty given us by our Maker! A word is inundation when it comes from the sea. Peter took the marine walk at the great risk.

E. DICKINSON.

The comings and goings, the loves and losses of her friends were always remembered by apt and dainty courtesies, the little gifts accompanied by notes often startlingly pertinent. Sometimes but a line — often three or four. With a gift to a young relative on her wedding day came this oriental word:

Will the sweet cousin who is about to make the Etruscan experiment accept a smile which will last a lifetime if ripened in the sun?

In the autumn of 1882 I had wished to send Emily Dickinson some little remembrance, and by a happy thought decided to paint for her a group of those wierd but perfect flowers of shade and silence, the monotropa, or "Indian pipe." She at once sent me the following note:

DEAR FRIEND: That without suspecting it you should send me the preferred flower of life seems almost supernatural, and the sweet glee that I felt at meeting it I could confide to none. I still cherish the clutch with which I bore it from the ground when a wondering child, an unearthly booty; and maturity only enhances mystery, never decreases it.

To duplicate the vision is almost more amazing, for God's unique capacity is too surprising to surprise.

I know not how to thank you. We do not thank the rainbow, though its trophy is a snare. To give delight is hallowed — perhaps the toil of angels, whose avocations are concealed. . . .

With joy,

E. DICKINSON.

When the first volume of poems was ready for publication, five years after her death, and a design was needed for the cover, nothing else seemed so singularly appropriate as these spectral blossoms. The design was cut from the little painting which stood so long in her room. About 1884 she wrote her friend "H. H.," in Colorado:

Who could be ill in March, that month of proclamation? Sleigh-bells and joys contend in my *matinée,* and the North surrenders instead of the South—a reverse of bugles.

Pity me, however; I have finished *Ramona.* Would that, like Shakespeare, it were just published!

One of her last notes was written in the spring of 1886:

I send a violet for L____. I should have sent a stem, but was overtaken by snow-drifts. I regret deeply not to add a butterfly, but have lost my hat, which precludes my catching one.

As examples of her mature style, the later letters might be almost indefinitely multiplied, each with a world of thought in a few lines—a verbal microcosm. But enough have been given to show the trend of her thought, the individual method of her mind, and a use of language which, as a comparison with the earlier letters will show, did not spring full-fledged to its power, but was a distinct evolution, a survival of the fittest in words.

In the quiet of leafy Amherst, in the old family mansion, Emily Dickinson lived and wrote, and here she

> Ascended from our vision
> To countenances new.

In May, 1886, she was borne lovingly over the threshold she had not passed beyond in years.

> She went as softly as the dew   [as quiet
>   From a familiar flower.
> Not like the dew did she return
>   At the accustomed hour.

To the few who gathered that sunny afternoon, her friend, fellow-poet, and "master," read Emily Brontë's "Ode to Immortality." "A favorite," as he so fitly said, "with our friend who has now put on that immortality which she seemed never to have laid off."

She had lived in voluntary retirement from outside eyes, and now, in the sweet May sunshine, tender hands carried her through meadows starry with daisies into a silence and seclusion but little deeper.

492 [Thomas Wentworth Higginson.] "Recent American Poetry." *Nation* 60 (May 23, 1895), 402. Father Tabb was an early admirer of Dickinson; see especially his nineties correspondence in *Letters—Grave and Gay and Other Prose of John Banister Tabb,* ed. Francis E. Litz (Washington, D.C.: Catholic Univ. of America Press, 1950), pp. 61, 62–63, 72, 93, 94, 96, 140. (On the unexpected popularity of both poets, see no. 506.)

The most interesting of the new brood of English poets are unquestionably of Celtic race, and often Catholics: and it is a remarkable fact that the most noticeable recent names on each side of the water are of that same faith—Francis Thompson in England and Father Tabb in America. The former, at least, dwells with a Brotherhood; the latter is a veritable priest, and also a Virginian, although his work is described in foreign newspapers as an emanation of the Puritan and New England muse. The true phenomenon, however, goes deeper than this. Non-Puritan though they be, the verses of this author—"Poems, by John B. Tabb" (Boston: Copeland)—show the most singular analogy here and there with those of the most Puritan and self contained of New England women, Emily Dickinson. There are pages here which might as well have appeared in either of her volumes—the same fine, shy, recluse observation of nature and of men, and the same terse brevity of utterance. Take, for instance, the poem of Father Tabb on "The Humming Bird" (p. 59):

> A flash of harmless lightning,
>   A mist of rainbow dyes.
> The burnished sunbeams brightening
>   From flower to flower he flies;
> While wakes the nodding blossom
>   But just too late to see
> What lip hath touched her bosom
>   And drained her rosary.

Now turn to Emily Dickinson (i., 130):

> A route of evanescence
>   With a revolving wheel;
> A resonance of emerald,
>   A rush of cochineal;
> And every blossom on the bush
>   Adjusts its tumbled head—
> The mail from Tunis, probably,
>   An easy morning's ride.

The woman's characterization is far more terse and vigorous, with more of motion and of color; she does not, like the man, sentimentalize a little bit over the blossom and her wooer, but who can help seeing the analogy? Probably Father Tabb had never heard of Emily Dickinson, nor she of him, when these poems were written; and it would be easy to insist too much on the analogy of mental attitude between the celibate woman and the celibate priest. But note again the resemblance in this bit of fancy, which might have come equally well out of either collection of poems, but is really from Father Tabb's (p. 108):

THE TAX-GATHERER.

> And pray, who are you?
> Said the violet blue
> To the Bee, with surprise
> At his wonderful size,
> To her eyeglass of dew.
>
> "I, madam," quoth he,
> "Am a publican Bee,
> Collecting the tax
> On honey and wax.
> Have you nothing for me?"

There are depths reached by Emily Dickinson, in her strange way, which Father Tabb does not reach; but he touches a far greater variety of interests, and shows constantly the sense of finish and of form on the larger scale, qualities the want of which was so plain in her. There are poems like Herrick or Vaughan in their delicate perfection, pieces of almost flawless chiselling, as, for instance, this (p. 33):

GRIEF SONG.

New grief, new tears; —
  Brief the reign of sorrow;
Clouds that gather with the night
  Scatter on the morrow.

Old grief, old tears; —
  Come and gone together;
Not a fleck upon the sky,
  Telling whence or whither.

Old grief, new tears; —
  Deep to deep is calling;
Life is but a passing cloud
  Whence the rain is falling.

When we add that no recent poet has written with more longing tenderness of woman's love, and with more delicious playful fondness of childhood and infancy, the reader must needs wonder what early joys and sorrows went to the making of this poet.

493 Mary J. Reid. "Julia Dorr and Some of Her Poet Contemporaries." *Midland Monthly* 3 (June 1895), 499–507. In preparing this article the author solicited and received information from both Lavinia Dickinson and Mabel Todd. The following reprinting omits Reid's opening paragraph and other parts of her essay which do not mention Dickinson.

From a host of women poets, I have selected the names of Helen Hunt Jackson, Celia Thaxter, Julia C. R. Dorr, Emily Dickinson, Ina D. Coolbrith, Edith M. Thomas, Louise Imogene Guiney, Harriet Monroe, and that shy, unobtrusive writer of verses, Mary Thacher Higginson, — not because they fully represent our age, but in order to draw attention to a few types which, for the purpose of contrast and comparison, will best exemplify the gentle vivacity with which our women poets have depicted the time. . . .

Emerson and Colonel Higginson have ranked Helen Hunt Jackson ("H. H.") above Augusta Webster, Jean Ingelow and Christina Rossetti. Some half dozen of her poems, as "Down to Sleep," "Gondoliers" and the famous sonnet on "Thought," will doubtless live as long as the "High tide on the Coast of Lincolnshire," or "The Goblin Market." Helen Hunt Jackson had traveled much, was a famous horsewoman, possessed a charming manner, and all her friends record that in conversation she had a ready wit and much natural tact joined to a fresh, original way of looking at life. Personally, she was one of the most popular authors in America. Not only Emerson but hundreds of obscure men and women in farmhouses and factories culled her poems from the newspapers, memorizing them while at work, pasting them in home-made scrap-books or pinning them to the leaves of the family Bible. In San Francisco I once picked up, in a quaint little store on Montgomery street, a pioneer Frenchman's scrap-book. Among French chansons by a local poet named Pierre Cauwet, an ode called "The Lost Galleon," by Frank Bret Harte, — read before the associated alumni of the infant college of California, — and some verses by Ralph Keeler, I found three of Helen

Hunt's poems. Emily Dickinson's opinions of Mrs. Jackson's works are of value as the estimate of a loving friend who never judged a book without having first mastered its contents.

Miss Lavinia Dickinson, Emily's sister, once wrote me:

Emily never knew "H. H." till she was Mrs. Hunt. Major Hunt and herself were a part of a delightful reception at our house. Emily was charmed with them both and their mutual interest began from that event. They met rarely, but on paper "H. H." addressed Emily and urged her in the most earnest way to let the world know of her genius. After she became Mrs. Jackson the visits were repeated and the entreaties continued, but for some shy reason Emily did not seem willing to publish the poems. Emily considered Mrs. Jackson's intellect very rare. I don't remember Emily's opinion of her poems, but my sister often spoke in praise of "Ramona." Helen Hunt Jackson was a brilliant, dashing woman of the world, fearless and brave, while Emily was timid and refined, always shrinking from publicity.

A few critical opinions of "H. H." may be found in Emily Dickinson's letters. To Colonel Higginson Emily wrote:

Mrs. Hunt's poems are stronger than any written by women since Mrs. Browning, with the exception of Mrs. Lewes's. . . . Mrs. Jackson soars to your estimate loftily as a bird.

Emily Dickinson's health was always delicate. As a school-girl her studies at the Mount Holyoke Female Seminary had to be interrupted on account of illness. She early learned that if she wished to accomplish anything as a poet her strength must be husbanded. The world is full of examples of the sacrifices of sisters for talented brothers, Miss Herschel and Miss Wordsworth being but solitary cases plucked from many modern instances; but in all literature there is nothing sweeter than the tacit agreement between Lavinia and Emily Dickinson, whereby the elder sister said in effect (although she may not have put her sacrifice into words), "Live your life as you will, I will be your protector and tower of strength." Emily was her father's idol. Every expressed wish of hers was gratified; rare old books were imported to relieve the monotony of her life,—but even he fretted at her seclusion. At such times Lavinia came to Emily's rescue and argued that since Emily was so tortured by the petty claims of society and, furthermore, felt that she had intellectual work to do which demanded her time, it was better to let her lead the ideal life which she had herself selected.

Emily Dickinson's passion for flowers was even greater than that of Celia Thaxter and Mrs. Dorr. She had Wordsworth's idea so felicitously expressed by Walter Pater, wherein "every natural object seemed to possess more or less of a moral or spiritual life, to be capable of a companionship with man, full of expression, of inexplicable affinities and delicacies of intercourse."

"Emily called Cape Jasmine," wrote Miss Lavinia Dickinson, "the holiest flower that grows. She was in love with every wild flower, and when we were little children we used to spend entire days in the woods hunting for treasures. The most delicate and rare flowers never failed to bloom for Emily, however impossible their rearing was to others."

At the Dickinson homestead the masters of English, French, German and Italian literature were studied until the sisters knew them through and through. Magazines were not excluded, but the books which live for a season never gained admission there. As Emily became more frail, Lavinia spent hours in reading to her. Sometimes it was Shakespeare, the Brownings, Ruskin or the Revelations.

Dante also was a favorite author. Emily was very fond of Miss Lavinia's way of presenting a character to her, and often said: "Vinnie, if ministers knew how to read as you do, they would impress their audience beyond repeal." Emily was herself a most charming reader. It was done with great simplicity and naturalness, with an earnest desire to express the exact conception of the author, without any thought of herself, of the impression her reading was sure to make. All the great masters of literature had a place in her regard, but she loved Lowell, Hawthorne, Shakespeare, the Brownings, the Brontés and George Eliot with a supreme affection.

The poems and letters of Emily Dickinson were not the outcome of a narrow Puritan education, nor of inability to wield the poetical metres easily handled by Mrs. Jackson and Mrs. Dorr, but rather of a prophetic insight. Some subtle instinct taught her that the last thought of the century would be — condensation; that artists would be discovering how small a number of lines might be employed in the delineation of the human figure, novelists would attempt to draw their characters with the few swift strokes of Chaucer, and, above all, poets would strive to render a drama or a whole epoch in two or three stanzas. At the West this thought would seem to have occurred simultaneously to the poets Roswell Martin Field, Charles Edwin Markham, and the late Professor William R. Perkins. Also in Harriet Monroe's "Dedicatory Ode" may be found many lines quite as concise, as:

And the calm Orient wise with many days.

*   *   *   *   *

France, the swift-footed, who with thee
Gazed in the eyes of liberty
And loved the dark no more.

*   *   *   *   *

The challenge of the earth that Adam heard.

*   *   *   *   *

Out of the dark man strives to rise
And struggles inch by inch with toil and tears.

If one would know what gains have been made in vivid characterization and in condensation by our age, contrast De Quincey's celebrated description of Helen Faucit as Antigone with this portrait of Tomaso Salvini by Emily Dickinson:

The brow is that of Deity — the eyes those of the lost, but the power lies in the throat — pleading, sovereign, savage — the panther and the dove.

494   W. S. K. "A Fresh Reading of Emily Dickinson." *Boston Evening Transcript*, July 11, 1895, p. 5.

The fascination of Emily Dickinson's small volumes of posthumous verse has several sources. In what a pretty artless way she personifies the grass and flowers and breezes! Her short-lined stanzas are loaded with meaning — like little pots of honey or vials of attar of roses. Such condensation, such freshness of vision! An old farmhouse is being burglarized; in the dead silence of midnight —

The moon slides down the stair
To see who's there.

Out of forty-four wrecked at sea four only were saved—

> Ring for the scant salvation!
>   Toll for the bonnie souls—
> Neighbor and friend and bridegroom
>   Spinning upon the shoals.

Of wind in pine trees—

> As if some caravan of sound,
> On deserts in the sky,
> Had broken rank,
> Then knit, and passed
> In seamless company.

Of clouds—

> The clouds like listless elephants
> Horizons straggled down.

What delicious freshness (Bunyan-like) of imagery in this couplet:

> Till seraphs swing their snowy hats
> And saints to windows run

(to look down upon earth).

Emily Dickinson's verse has been likened to Blake's. It is a bit like it; but she is unique after all. Her originality is absolute. In the bits of nature poetry I am now going to quote you will find suggestions of no other writer, any more than in Landor's "Pericles and Aspasia" or Emerson's "Humble Bee." Who before has sung so fittingly and prettily of the grass? Only Wordsworth could match it and he has not done so—

> The grass so little has to do
> A sphere of simple green,
> With only butterflies to brood
> And bees to entertain,
>
> And stir all day to pretty tunes
> The breezes fetch along.
> And hold the sunshine in its lap
> And bow to everything.
>
> And thread the dews all night like pearls
> And make itself so fine.

In dealing with the petite and fairy aspects of nature she excels. Did you ever find in your browsings in literature a more delicate conceit than this on the air-line of the bees, the beetle, Puck, Ariel?

> A little road not made of man,
>   Enabled of the eye.
> Accessible to thill of bee
>   Or cart of butterfly.
>
> If town it have beyond itself,
>   'Tis that I cannot say;
> I only sigh—no vehicle
>   Bears me along that way.

Thill of bee! There's condensed imagery for you, one little syllable giving a whole fairy picture of busy bees harnessed to air-wagons and darting in endless lines through the sky, whipped up perhaps, by some elfish wagoner. Then in the second stanza the pantheistic sigh, the longing to be reunited to the absolute, to doff the human and enter into the joyous unconscious again.

Here are lines on the bee worthy to have been incorporated in Emerson's classic "Humble Bee":

> Like trains of cars on tracks of plush
> I hear the level bee,
> A jar across the flower goes, . . .

Here is a picture of a summer shower, apparently followed by an east rain or fog, or else by a clearing-up in the east and hot weather:

> The dust replaced in hoisted roads,
>   The birds jocoser sung,
> The sunshine threw his hat away
>   The orchards spangles hung.

> The breezes brought dejected lutes
>   And bathed them in the glee;
> The east put out a single flag
>   And signed the fête away.

How the first line above condenses the whole sentiment of a long dry spell when it really seems as if all the dust of the roads was "hoisted" and floating in the air.

Not all of Miss Dickinson's verses are great but the gems are scattered pretty thick. Here is a priceless one. The old Greek myth-making spirit that produced the story of Narcissus and a hundred like it in Ovid; Keats; Emerson's "Rhodora"; Savage Landor's lines "To let all flowers live freely . . . in their native place"— all this and more suggested by these exquisite lines:

> So bashful when I spied her.
> So pretty, so ashamed!
> So hidden in her leaflets,
> Lest anybody find;

> So breathless till I passed her,
> So helpless when I turned
> And bore her struggling, blushing,
> Her simple haunts beyond!

But now comes the most marvelous poem of all on Death, a retrospective monologue out of eternity—

> Because I could not stop for Death.
>   He kindly stopped for me;
> The carriage held but just ourselves
>   And Immortality.

> We slowly drove, he knew no haste,
>   And I had put away
> My labor and my leisure too,
>   For his civility.

We passed the school where children played
    Their lessons scarcely done;
We passed the fields of gazing grain,
    We passed the setting sun.

We paused before a house that seemed
    A swelling of the ground;
The roof was scarcely visible,
    The cornice but a mound.

Since then 't is centuries; but each
    Feels shorter than the day
I first surmised the horses' feet
    Were towards eternity.   [toward

Clearly, Death is here regarded (as Landor looked on him) as a benignant and friendly being; the poet was not allowed voluntarily to seek him out, so he kindly waited for her and introduced her to immortality, where a thousand years are as one day. And see what startling effect and freshness her personification of nature has in the phrase "gazing grain." This is a poem to learn by heart. And reading it we mourn that its writer had not lived and longer wrought.

495 Ellen E. Dickinson. "Emily Dickinson: Her Personality and Surroundings in Her Home." *Boston Evening Transcript*, October 12, 1895, p. 15. For other reminiscences by Mrs. Dickinson, see nos. 360, 391. The relative of whom the poet was fond is the author's husband, William Hawley Dickinson, a cousin of the poet's. Errors abound in Mrs. Dickinson's quotation from poems and letters. Her rendering of "The nearest dream," for example, changes its line division, its language and punctuation, and omits the words "Heedless of the boy" which precede "Staring bewildered. . . ."

A few years ago, beyond a limited circle of friends, the name even of Emily Dickinson, the Amherst poetess, had not been heard. Today her poems and letters have been widely read in New England, and in other parts of our country. The elusive, fairy-like trippings of her pen capture the fancy of her readers, and they ask of her personality, experiences and surroundings. Colonel Higginson's account of his acquaintance with her, with extracts from her letters and certain verses which she submitted to his criticism, is the happiest memorial which has been written of this gifted, brilliant and unusual woman; but there remains a closer and more intimate biography to be given to the public. The writings of the author above referred to were greatly admired by Emily Dickinson; they appealed to her fancy and imagination, and desiring his acquaintance she wrote to him and enclosed some verses. Her writing he said "resembled the famous fossil-bird tracks in the Amherst College Museum;" but he read the verses with surprise. There were four poems—"Safe in Thine Alabaster Chamber," "I'll Tell You How the Sun Rose," and the following (with another called "The Robin"):

The nearest dream recedes unrealized,
The heaven we chase like the June bee,
Before the school-boy invites the race,
Stoops to an easy clover,
Dips—evades—teases—deploys,

Then to the royal clouds
Lifts his light pennance   [pinnace
Staring bewildered at the mocking sky.
Homesick for steady honey.   [steadfast
Ah the bee flies not which brews that rare variety.   [that brews

This was in 1862, and from that time until her death in May, 1886, these two gifted people were in correspondence, but did not meet for several years after their paper acquaintance began. She called his criticism "surgery." He naturally inquired when she commenced writing verses, and she replied, "I made no verse but one or two, till this winter," and again, "while my thoughts are undressed I can make the distinction, when put in gown, they are alike, and numb. You inquire what books I read." She wrote in reply, "For poets, I have Keats, and Mr. and Mrs. Browning; for prose, Ruskin and the Revelation; I went to school, but after your manner, had no education; a friend taught me immortality, but venturing too near, never returned. For years my lexicon was my only companion. You ask of my companions. Hills, sir, and the sundown, and a dog as large as myself. I have a brother and a sister. My mother does not care for thought, and father is too busy with his briefs. He buys me many books, but tells me not to read them, he fears they joggle the mind." Miss Dickinson asked Colonel Higginson to be her "preceptor," and he desired her picture. In return, she wrote, "I have no portrait now, but am small like the wren, my hair is bold like the chestnut burr, my eyes like the sherry in the glass that the guest leaves." When he suggested she delay to publish, she replied, "That is as foreign to my thought as firmament to fire." When at length preceptor and pupil met, she held two day lilies in her hand as she entered the room, saying, "This is my introduction."

Later, when he was in the War of the Rebellion, she wrote to him, "Should you before this reaches you experience immortality, who will inform me of the exchange," and again, "Could you with honor avoid death, I entreat you, sir; it would bereave."

The writer is tempted here to quote a few lines from one of "her most exquisite poems," written a few months before her death, on the passing summer —

As imperceptibly as grief,
The summer passed away,   [lapsed
Too imperceptible at last
To feel like perfidy.

A quietness distilled,
As twilight long begun,
Or Nature spending with herself
Sequestered afternoon.

The death of Hon. Edward Dickinson and his wife, the parents of the poetess, left her with her sister alone in the large old-fashioned double-house where she had resided from childhood. As her family affections were very decided, there is no doubt that she felt this bereavement keenly, and that her verses were saddened in consequence.

Her relations with her father were peculiar. She said on one occasion, "I am not very well acquainted with father." She admired and honored him, and endeavored to please him in all ways—made the bread and pastry, because he wished it; but the old Puritan element in his character forbade his outward enjoyment of certain innocent pleasures which her poetic nature delighted in. In her earliest years she was timid in his society, and confessed she could not accurately tell the hour of the day when she was fifteen years of age—because she was afraid to ask him how to accomplish it.

Of comparatively few intimacies which this remarkable woman had, they were generally of an unusual character—authors, poets, travellers, ladies of fashion, men of brilliant education and talk; she entertained in her quaint style, and held them delighted with her wit and quips and turns of conversation. As her "preceptor" said, "she had not a single good feature, but wonderful eyes," and her garments were of blue and white, summer and winter. One of her charms was her spirituelle presence, an influence that pervaded the whole house where she lived and died, and where she glided, so to speak, into the parlor or library, laid a tiny bunch of flowers beside your plate at table, or appeared at the close of a song or sonata, with appreciative intent. Whatever this subtle influence may have been during Emily Dickinson's life, it still remains to a certain degree in the rooms where she lived so many years, and dreamed dreams, as though such a rare and beautiful spirit, though beyond the veil, had left something of her elixir of life and passionate love of Nature. From these windows she greeted the hills in the early dawn, and in her lovely old garden watched her friends, the flowers, the birds, and bees, with whom she held high converse, watched the rise and decline of the sun, admired the silver crescent of the moon, or its full glory; listened to the whispering maples, and remarked the passing seasons. She loved everything within her vision, and cared nothing for the glamour of society, or the affairs of the world. The birth and opening of a flower were more entertaining to her. Her letters were not always written missives. When a relative of whom she was fond, was dying with consumption, she sent a box of trailing arbutus. He understood the message. As children they had gathered the fragrant wood flowers. One and another remembers some remark, some sentence, made by this rare woman worth repeating; for instance, "Some say a word is dead when it is given. I say it begins to live." "A letter always feels like immortality to me, because it is the mind alone without the corporeal friend." "Genius is the ignition of the affections." "Why is any book but Shakespeare needed?" When asked what she considered poetry, she replied, "When I feel physically as if the top of my head was taken off, I know that it is poetry." When her maid wore a new and very narrow gown, she remarked, "___ has a fresh calico sarcophagus." When urged to publish her verses, she said "I would as soon undress in public, as to give my poems to the world."

This remark was in keeping with her naturally shy disposition, and hesitancy to meet strangers, besides the advice of her literary friends, whom she most considered, to "delay publishing." When asked, urged, to write for the "No Name Series," by Helen Hunt, "H. H.," she declined, saying she was "not equal to it," certainly not from lack of ability, but her unwillingness to be criticised by people to whom she was indifferent.

When it is remembered that Miss Dickinson was a recluse, never travelled, beyond her journeys to Washington or Boston, it seems remarkable that she had so true an observation of people and the conduct of life. Her poems were the expression of her inner consciousness. They, as well as her letters, published in two volumes, have been severely criticised, and praised. The poems are unique; if not always metrical, there is a harmony, a dainty measure most fascinating and pleasing, about them. Miss Gordon L. Ford of Brooklyn, deceased, also a poetess, and a woman of rare culture, gave some reminiscences of her early acquaintance with Emily Dickinson in Amherst. She considered her "remarkable" while in school, repeated some of her expressions and opinions, and was certain the poetic inclination was indulged in even at that early date. Dr. and Mrs. J. G. Holland were among Miss Dickinson's warmest friends and admirers; the doctor expressing the opinion that she was "a positive genius" long, long before his death. With her other gifts, she had an appreciation of the comic, and could tell a humorous story with the best. She loved little children and told how a delightful little fellow in her neighborhood, after hearing the Bible account of the infant Samuel, tacked to his usual evening prayer of "God bless my dear mother," etc.: "And the Lord [with a lisp] said Samuel, Samuel, and Samuel said, 'What ma'am?'"

Everyone who reads Emily Dickinson's verse must recognize the minor strain that runs through them all; giving evidence of a bereavement, a secret sorrow, that found solace in quaint songs, and poetical measures, written often in "the wee small hours," or when all about her was hushed in slumber of her heart. How can one regret that she has "laid aside the form," as Spiritualists speak of death, and found herself within the infinite, of which she had so many questionings and longings, for if it was delightful to her to pen her poetical inspirations, how much more satisfactory to exchange the mortal for immortality. The lovers of beautiful verses are indebted to her sister, Miss Lavinia Dickinson, for giving them the effusions of the poetess of Amherst.

496 "Notes." *Chap-Book* 3 (October 15, 1895), 446. These parodies were apparently sent to the *Chap-Book* by Bliss Carman; see the discussion by several hands in *Emily Dickinson Bulletin* (presently *Emily Dickinson Studies*), no. 22 (Second Half, 1973), 207–09. For other spurious attributions, see nos. 352 and 529.

It is not generally known that Emily Dickinson left a far larger number of poems than those already published. Her two volumes, in fact, contain not more than a small percentage of her work. I am permitted to print here for the first time the following characteristic bit of her orphic utterances;

> A clamor in the treetops,
> A scurrying of the wind, —
> The members of the viewless
> With coat-tails out behind.
>
> Excitement in the lobbies
> Of April's house discerned,
> The emptying of portals,
> And winter is adjourned.

It was characteristic of Emily Dickinson to treat solemn subjects in a large familiar manner. She was intimate with the spirit of nature, and had a nodding acquaintance with the deity. This was part of her inheritance from Emerson. There is something almost shocking to our Puritan traditions in the ease with which she addresses herself to sacred themes. The following epigram, though not in her most characteristic manner, illustrates this phase of her genius, quite as well as any of her published verses.

> If God upon the seventh day did rest from all his labors,
> He was either tired of the job or feared to shock the neighbors.
> If not, why didn't he complete the task he set his hand to,
> Instead of leaving us this mess of water he put land to?

497 [Thomas Wentworth Higginson.] "Recent Poetry." *Nation* 61 (October 24, 1895), 296.

It is worth considering wherein lies the charm that attaches, it appears, to "The Black Riders, and Other Lines," by Stephen Crane (Boston: Copeland & Day). It is an attraction which makes young people learn it by heart, carry it into the woods with them, sleep with it under their pillows, and perhaps suggest that it should be buried with them in their early graves. Undoubtedly it offers new sensations: the brevity of its stanzas; its rhymelessness and covert rhythm, as of a condensed Whitman or an amplified Emily Dickinson; a certain modest aggressiveness, stopping short of actual conceit. The power lies largely in the fact that this apparent affectation is not really such, and that there is behind it a vigorous earnestness and a fresh pair of eyes. Even the capitalization of every word seems to imply that the author sought thus to emphasize his "lines"—just as Wordsworth printed "The White Doe of Rylstone," in quarto—to express his sense of their value. A mere experiment will show how much each page loses by being reduced to what printers call "lower-case" type; and yet this result itself seems unsatisfactory because anything which is really good, one might say, could bear to be printed in letters as small as in those microscopic newspapers sent out of Paris under pigeons' wings during the siege. The total effect of the book is that of poetry torn up by the roots—a process always interesting to the botanist, yet bad for the blossoms. As formless, in the ordinary sense, as the productions of Walt Whitman, these "lines" are in other respects the antipodes of his; while Whitman dilutes mercilessly, Crane condenses almost as formidably. He fulfills Joubert's wish, to condense a page into a sentence and a sentence into a word. He grasps his thought as nakedly and simply as Emily Dickinson; gives you a glance at it, or, perhaps, two glances from different points of view, and leaves it there. If it be a paradox, as it commonly is, so much the better for him. Thus (p. 12):

> In a lonely place,
> I encountered a sage
> Who sat, all still,
> Regarding a newspaper.
> He accosted me:
> "Sir, what is this?"
> Then I saw that I was greater,
> Aye, greater than this sage.
>
> I answered him at once,
> "Old, old man, it is the wisdom of the age."
> The sage looked upon me with admiration.

That is all, but it tells its own story, and is the equivalent of many columns. At other times he not merely intimates his own problem, but states it, still tersely (p. 26):

> Behold the grave of a wicked man.
> And near it a stern spirit.
>
> There came a drooping maid with violets,
> But the spirit grasped her arm.
> "No flowers for him," he said.
> The maid wept:
> "Ah, I loved him,"
> But the spirit, grim and frowning,
> "No flowers for him."

> Now this is it.
> If the spirit was just,
> Why did the maid weep?

Again, he gives his protest against superstition (p. 56):

> A man went before a strange God—
> The God of many men, sadly wise.
> And the Deity thundered loudly,
> "Kneel, mortal, and cringe
> And grovel and do homage
> To my particularly sublime Majesty."
> The man fled.
> Then the man went to another God—
> The God of his inner thoughts,
> And this one looked at him
> With soft eyes
> Lit with infinite condescension,
> And said, "My poor child!"

Better, perhaps, than any of these polemics are those "lines" which paint, with a terseness like Emily Dickinson's, some aspect of nature. Since Browning's fine description, in "England in Italy," of the "infinite movement" of a chain of mountains before the traveller, the same thing has not been more vividly put than here (p. 38):

> On the horizon the peaks assembled,
> And, as I looked,
> The march of the mountains began.
> As they marched, they sang,
> "Aye, we come! we come!"

That is all; but it is fine, it tells its own story. If it be asked whether it is also poetry, one can only remember Thoreau's dictum, that no matter how we define poetry, the true poet will presently set the whole definition aside. If it be further asked whether such a book gives promise, the reply must be that experience points the other way. So marked a new departure rarely leads to further growth. Neither Whitman nor Miss Dickinson ever stepped beyond the circle they first drew.

498 [Thomas Wentworth Higginson.] "Recent Poetry." *Nation* 61 (December 12, 1895), 430. Higginson is reviewing a volume of poems by Mrs. Annie Fields.

Helen Jackson and Emily Dickinson are beyond her in passion and originality, but the former of these was often uneven in execution and the latter had no conception of any such quality as evenness.

499 W. Garrett Horder. A biographical note on Dickinson in *The Treasury of American Sacred Song,* edited and selected by W. Garrett Horder (London and New York: Henry Frowde, 1896), p. 354. This popular anthology contained thirteen Dickinson poems. Horder's statement regarding the appearance of her manuscripts, noted by Higginson (no. 564), was corrected in the revised edition of *The Treasury* (London and

New York: Henry Frowde, 1900), p. 368. The two notes are identical except that the phrase in the second sentence, "written in continuous lines like prose" is replaced in 1900 by the words, "which had never seen the light."

Emily Dickinson, b. Amherst, Mass., Dec 10, 1830, d. there, May 13, 1886. Wrote much in verse but only two or three poems printed during life. Occasionally she sent a poem to a friend; great was the surprise to find after her death her portfolio full of poems, written in continuous lines like prose. These were entrusted to Mabel Loomis Todd and Thomas Wentworth Higginson, who issued them in two series (Roberts Brothers). Her verse is bold and unconventional, sometimes faulty, but sometimes well-nigh perfect in form. Her poetry needs to be looked at in the light of her life. I gather from a sketch prefixed to her poems that in her earlier days she mixed much in society, but found it utterly unsatisfying, and then entered on a hermit-like life, even restricting her walks to her father's grounds. Thus her ideas and thoughts were only known to a few close friends. Naturally of an introspective nature, she little needed the ordinary amusements of the world around; her world was within. Storm, wind, the wild March sky, sunsets and dawns, birds, bees, butterflies and flowers, with a few trusted friends, were a sufficient companionship.

499A Charles Dudley Warner (ed.). "Dickinson, Emily." *Biographical Dictionary and Synopsis of Books Ancient and Modern.* Akron, Ohio: Werner, 1896, p. 144. The poet's first book was issued in 1890. For another biographical entry, see no. 567.

An American poet; born in Amherst, Mass., Dec. 10, 1830; died there, May 15, 1886. Living the life of a recluse, she wrote much verse in forms peculiar to herself, but she published almost nothing; although the few pieces that appeared attracted much attention. In 1892 a collection of her poems was issued which received warm praise from competent critics. In all, three volumes of her verse and prose have appeared.

500 J. E. Wetherell. "Preface" to *Later American Poems*, ed. J. E. Wetherell (Toronto: Copp, 1896), pp. iii–iv. This anthology, intended as a "supplementary reading-book for Canadian High Schools," collects poems written after 1860. It reprinted two by Dickinson, "Success is counted sweetest" and "For each ecstatic instant." The following paragraph is from the compiler's brief "Preface."

The editor has taken care to include representations of the work of some writers of exquisite verse at present not widely known in this country. Mr. Sladen's almost exhaustive anthology of "American Poets" published in 1891 (to which the present editor is much indebted) does not contain the names of John B. Tabb, Robert Underwood Johnson, Lizette W. Reese, Gertrude Hall, Harriet Monroe, Bessie Chandler, Stuart Sterne, Elizabeth Akers, Emily Dickenson [sic], Emily Hutchinson, and others included here, who have done remarkable work, or whose poems for the first time have been offered to the public, in very recent years.

501 [Rupert Hughes.] Chelifer (pseud.). "Sappho and Other Princesses of Poetry." *Godey's Magazine* 132 (January 1896), 94–95. Hughes's purpose, in this review of an 1895 translation of Sappho's poems, is to qualify what he feels have been too generous estimates of her work by some critics. Only his paragraphs mentioning Dickinson are reprinted here. Hughes, in his mid-twenties, was soon to publish a notably perceptive review-essay on Dickinson; see no. 553.

Not to oppose to Sappho's supremacy the claims of such lyrists as Jayadeva, David, Pindar, Theokritos, Horace, Petrarca, Heine, Goethe, Hugo, Herrick, Tennyson, and Aldrich, I would venture to submit, for comparison by any un-prejudiced honesty, one hundred and seventy similar fragments from the poetry of her own sex, from the work of Mrs. Browning or Emily Dickinson, yes, from the verse of Christina Rossetti, or the late Anna Reeve Aldrich. Against the superb Ode to Anactoria could be placed, with some show of rivalry, a number of Mrs. Browning's ineffably beautiful "Sonnets from the Portuguese," say that one be-ginning "How do I love thee? Let me count the ways," or "Say over again, and yet once over again, That thou dost love me." Against some bit of Sapphic perfection, like fragment No. 95 —

Γέσπερε, πάνταφέρων, ὄσα φαίνολις ἐσκέδασ᾽ αὔως,
φέρεις οἶν, φὲρεις αἶγα, φέρεις ἄπυ ματέρι παῖδα.

(Of which, by the way, Mr. Wharton's "literal" translation is neither *verbatim* nor *seriatim,* and which should rather be translated somewhat as follows:

Hesper, all things bringing that gleaming daybreak scattered,
Thou bringest the sheep, thou bringest the goat, thou bringest to the
     mother the youngster.)

Against this set some of Emily Dickinson's fervor for Nature, some line like her "Inebriate of air and debauchee of dew."
    Compare, too, the tone of their respective works as a whole. Where Sappho's art, judging from fragments, and from the unanimity of otherwise discordant tra-dition, was spent chiefly on her wild love for fair girls and young men, note the contrasting breadth and depth of Mrs. Browning's song, which could also ring with "The Cry of the Children" and "Casa Guidi Windows," note the large pantheism and fellowship with Nature of Emily Dickinson's fieldward muse.

502 "Three Poems by Emily Dickinson." *Outlook* 53 (January 25, 1896), 141.
    The poems are "This World is not conclusion," "'Tis little I—could care for pearls," and "We learn in the retreating."

Readers of Miss Emily Dickinson's verse and of her letters do not need to be told that she belongs among the writers who cannot be classified. The note of individuality, which is so distinct throughout the entire history of New England, has been nowhere more definitely struck than in her verse and prose. During the latter years of her life she was a recluse, and her thought shows singular insula-tion. She was solitary, but her solitude was populous with thought, imagination, sympathy, kindness, and aspiration. She seemed to owe very little to any liter-ary parentage, although she once said that Keats and the Brownings, Ruskin, Sir Thomas Browne, and Revelation were her books. "I went to school," she writes, "but in the manner of the phrase had no education. When a little girl I had a friend who taught me immortality, but venturing too near, himself, he never re-turned. . . . You ask of my companions. Hills, sir, and the sundown, and a dog large as myself that my father brought me. They are better than beings, because they know but do not tell; and the noise of the pool at noon excels my piano."

Spontaneity, flashes of insight, epigrammatic phrase, are characteristic of Miss Dickinson's prose and verse. She saw things in detached flashes of light. She never took the trouble to co-ordinate the objects of her vision, and they come before us isolated and detached as they came to her. She is often abrupt, sometimes inconsequential, but she has thoughts; and at times these thoughts take on a wonderful felicity of speech. These qualities are admirably illustrated in the three poems by Miss Dickinson here published for the first time. The portrait of Miss Dickinson as a child is reproduced, by permission, from the book "Letters of Emily Dickinson."

503 "Six Books of Verse." *Atlantic Monthly* 77 (February 1896), 271. Commenting on Stephen Crane's *The Black Riders and Other Lines*, the reviewer makes a brief comparison with Dickinson.

The parable form into which many of the fragments are cast gives them half their effectiveness. The audacity of their conception, suggesting a mind not without kinship to Emily Dickinson's, supplies the rest.

504 Sibyl (pseud.). "With Sweet 'Rhyme of Thought.'" *Pacific Commercial Advertiser* [Honolulu], May 23, 1896, p. 3. This talk was given at the home of Sanford B. Dole, President of the Republic of Hawaii.

Friday morning in Mrs. Dole's drawing room Mrs. Mabel Loomis Todd gave an informal talk on Emily Dickinson. This culminated in a most delightful manner the year's discussions of the Modern Novel Club, which after this triumphant session will take a summer vacation.

The members of this club, then, reinforced by their guests, were spellbound by the magnetic charm of the speaker. She has edited all of Miss Dickinson's works that have yet appeared, two volumes of verse and two volumes of her letters, and is engaged upon yet another book of verse. She is a most faithful and sympathetic interpreter of the elusive personality of this strange poetic genius. To her the world is indebted for its whiff of the rare sweet perfume of this sweet exotic. Mrs. Todd has chosen the Indian pipe as a fitting decorative emblem for the covers of the published poems.

The strangely retired life that Emily Dickinson led was not due to blighted affections, Mrs. Todd would have us believe, for she was one of Nature's nuns, who cannot drag so exalted a sentiment as love down into the commonplace of every day. Her lovers, then, were left to adore her, and while her verses speak from the knowledge of love, they show an intellectual coolness rather than the warm nearness of human love. Poor health was never hers, nor does her joyousness permit the theory of deranged or morbid mind. Rather it was excessive shyness in her that led her to shrink from showing her face, her poems, even her handwriting to the world. Towards the last of her life her letters were directed in another's writing. This unparalleled shyness grew upon her, and Mrs. Todd told of visits she made when all she could see of the strange woman was a glimpse of white in a darkened hallway beyond the lighted room where she herself sat and played.

In speaking of these letters, which were never dated, Mrs. Todd suggested some of the difficulties she surmounted in arranging them chronologically. "Friday night" is not strictly specific, nor does "little Maggie died tonight" add to its definiteness when seventeen Maggies in the town were known to have died, four of them Maggie Kellys! At the end of four weeks' determined search for the date of that letter, it was at last learned that a certain little Maggie Kelly had died on Friday night, and the mother was able to supply the missing date of two letters.

In her efforts to determine the dates of other letters she referred to a much ridiculed stamp album, when the letters were not written before stamps came into vogue. She went to newspapers, to town records, to former residents of the town, to old servants and their children. She searched for reports of fires, births, deaths, the first appearance of railroad and water companies, and in short became wiser than the oldest inhabitant.

Emerson's phrase "the poetry of the portfolio," describes Emily Dickinson's work. Twelve hundred poems, some scarcely four lines, were discovered after her death, to the great surprise of her family. These were edited and published at the request of her sister. These poems show lightning flashes of soul and insight into life, an unerring vividness of description and unbounded stretches of imagination. They are original, unformed, often unrhymed, wayward, strange and even fantastic, but they show genius. Flowers, bees and angle-worms they tell of; butterflies and humming-birds, clouds, sun and storm, March and autumn, life, love, death and immortality.

Often did she refer to lists of alternative words, but never from any consideration of rhyme or beauty. Her verse shows the "rhyme of thought," a grace far more subtle and satisfying than mere consonance of words. Her utter inability to grasp the idea of form has crystallized her style, which is original and unique. Often in a first line did she command attention, and flash off, as Thomas Wentworth Higginson says, "a thought that takes our breath away, when a lesson in grammar seems an impertinence."

Many striking incidents of her life were related by Mrs. Todd, many bits of verse were quoted, sparks of verse forged at white heat, and from her letters many epigrammatic sentences. All helped in giving us a better impression of this woman who distilled drops of the essence of things. Many eyes besides the reader's glistened as she read the letter on immortality that Miss Dickinson had written after her mother's death.

Mrs. Todd finished her brilliant characterization of Emily Dickinson, this poet whose verses published after her death have lived in print but five years. The hush that held the company after she ceased to speak was the greatest possible tribute to her magic as a speaker, and to the absorbing interest she had aroused in her poet-friend.

It was remembered that Mrs. Todd and her husband, Professor David Todd, are members of the astronomical party that the yacht Coronet is bearing to Japan. They are running the risk of a great disappointment, in that the precious two minutes and forty seconds of observation may fall in cloudy time; but we will fill their sails with good wishes, however, and may our hopes give them fresh winds and brilliant, starry skies in their desired haven.

504A "Notes and News." *Poet-Lore* 8:6 ([June] 1896), 375–76. The accompanying editorial reply may have been written by Helen A. Clarke (see no. 371A).

EDITORS POET-LORE: Emily Dickinson writes:—

Nature rarer uses yellow
  Than another hue;
Saves she all of that for sunsets,—
  Prodigal of blue,

Spending scarlet like a woman,
  Yellow she affords
Only scantly and selectly,
  Like a lover's words.

Are not the sunsets a part of nature? William Morris writes: "The yellow blossoms which are so common in Nature." Spenser: "Then came the Autumn all in yellow clad." Thomson: "Autumn nodding o'er the yellow plain." Science, in the person of Asa Gray, says: "Of all colors of flowers, white, pale yellow, and yellow are the most common."—'Botanical Text Book,' vol. ii. p. 453.

Having lived in Kansas, the Sunflower State, the lines struck me at once as untrue.   *Ida Ahlborn Weeks.*

Aside from the mere question whether yellow is a predominant color in flowers or not, which is not strictly in point, is it not probable that artists would confirm Emily Dickinson in noticing the relatively infrequent appearance of yellow in the total aspects of outdoor nature, compared with blue, purple, gray, and green, for example?

505 [Thomas Wentworth Higginson.] "Recent Poetry." *Nation* 62 (June 4, 1896), 437, 439. In the earlier excerpt Higginson comments on Christina Rossetti's posthumous *New Poems;* in the latter he addresses the work of an American poet, Caroline Edwards Prentiss.

One of the shorter English poems has a curious flavor of that other recluse woman of genius, Emily Dickinson (p. 183):

THE WAY OF THE WORLD.

A boat that sails upon the sea,
  Sails far and far and far away;
Who sail in her sing songs of glee
  Or watch and pray.

A boat that drifts upon the sea,
  Silent and void to sun and air;
Who sailed in her have ended glee
  And watch and prayer.
    . . . .

The best aspect of "Sunshine and Shadow," by Caroline Edwards Prentiss (Putnams), is in its choice of subjects. These are full of local coloring. "Summer's Calendar," for instance, comprises poems on the ox-eyed daisy, the pond-lily, and the golden-rod; and elsewhere there are verses on violet, anemone, bluet (or Houstonia), buttercup, morning glory, arbutus, wild-rose, Indian pipe (or ghost-flower), and even poison-ivy, which last, we believe, even Emily Dickinson has not included in her weird gallery.

506 "Chronicle and Comment." *Bookman* 3 (August 1896), 498. The University Press, owned by John Wilson and son, was a Cambridge, Mass.,

printing firm serving a number of Boston-area publishers, among them
Copeland and Day and Roberts Brothers. Father Tabb's estimate of
Dickinson, if published in the nineties, has not yet been located,
though it is quite in keeping with comments on her in his correspon-
dence from the period. For those references and for similarities between
Tabb's poems and Dickinson's, see no. 492.

Father Tabb has to be congratulated upon the singular success which has attended the publication of his little book of *Poems* issued a little over a year ago
by Messrs. Copeland and Day. Mr. Wilson, of the University Press, declares that
with one exception never in so short a time have they had to print so many copies
of a first book by an American poet. The exception was Emily Dickinson; and it
is a curious coincidence that Father Tabb should have said recently that "of late
American poets there is none worthy to go down to posterity except Miss Dickinson." This little volume of *Poems* is now in its fifth edition, and another collection will probably be issued by Father Tabb next spring.

507 *Boston Evening Transcript*, August 8, 1896, p. 12.

It has not been generally known that a third volume of the poems of Emily
Dickinson had been prepared by her friend and editor, Mabel Loomis Todd. Mrs.
Todd is now in Japan with her husband, Professor Todd of Amherst, on the astronomical expedition whose members hope to see the total eclipse of the sun
promised today for that longitude. Mrs. Todd has shown an exquisite genius for
selection in her task of presenting the papers left by the dead poet. It is too early
to speak specifically of this third volume which has not yet been published. But
to read every word of it — twice over — in advance of its publication is like entering into the very sanctuary of the rare and delicate spirit who lived as recluse, a
poet and woman unknown until she died, and now most truly known by those
who are appreciative of a reserve that is revealed like an ethereal blossom in her
poetry. Having been allowed by Mrs. Todd to enter into the outer chambers of
knowledge of this poet in the first and second volumes, the door is opened in the
third into an inner, a sacred room, whose air is the very breath of a human spirit.

508 Mabel Loomis Todd. "A Mid-Pacific College." *Outlook* 54 (August 15,
1896), 285. For her second paragraph of an article on Oahu College, Mrs.
Todd draws on a Dickinson poem to describe a volcanic eruption she
had recently witnessed while visiting the Hawaiian Islands. This first
printing of "The reticent volcano keeps" (lacking its middle quatrain) is
not recorded in Johnson's 1955 variorum. The full text was published
two weeks later in *Poems*, Third Series.

In a yet unpublished poem upon the volcano, generically considered, Emily
Dickinson says:

> The reticent volcano keeps
>   His never slumbering plan;
> Confided are his projects pink
>   To no precarious man;
> Admonished by his buckled lips
>   Let every babbler be;
> The only secret people keep
>   Is immortality.

509 Routine publication announcements listing Emily Dickinson's Poems, "Third Series" among Roberts Brothers' books for September were carried by newspapers and periodicals across the country. Those collected in Todd's scrapbooks are: *Chicago Post,* Aug. 22, 1896; *Worcester* [Mass.] *Spy,* Aug. 24, 1896; *Critic,* n.s. 26 (Sept. 12, 1896), 168.

510 "Literary Notes." *New York Tribune,* August 23, 1896, sect. 2, p. 22.

Mrs. Mabel Loomis Todd has a heavy responsibility to answer for. First she printed a collection of poems by her friend, Emily Dickinson. Then we had more poems from the same source and a lot of letters. Now, incredible as it may seem, there is in preparation under Mrs. Todd's editorship, "Emily Dickinson's Poems; Third Series." This is really too much. It seems that "the intellectual activity of Emily Dickinson was so great that a large and characteristic choice is still possible among her literary material"; but while this may have some weight with "the admirers of her peculiar genius" who have asked for "more," we do not think it will appeal to a sober critic. A little of her work is poetic in quality and is colored by a certain amount of originality. But at the best it is minor verse, and the very finest things gathered from her three volumes would not make one book of any thickness.

There is no injustice in thus anticipating the character of the "third series." The first contained much inferior matter, the second was even more disappointing, and it is incredible, we repeat, that Mrs. Todd could have brought together enough good verse to make a new collection. What she has really done, we suspect, has been to collect fragments or even complete poems which belong, as nine-tenths of Emily Dickinson's verses belong, to the sphere of casual, moody writing, to a class of verse which most poets, whether they have genius or not, regard as mere trifles or experiments. Sometimes the genius, the great genius, can afford to print these trifles, once he has made his position secure; but a poet like Emily Dickinson could never safely do any such thing. Her vogue has passed—it was a temporary affair in its highest estate—and now such reputation as she has among minor lyrists is imperilled by the indiscretion of her executors. Poor misunderstood authorship! How it must hunger in its grave to be protected from its friends!

511 Advertisement. "Roberts' New Books." *Publishers' Weekly* 50 (August 29, 1896), 272. *Poems,* Third Series appears among titles listed as "Ready September 1," accompanied by the following sentence drawn from Mrs. Todd's "Preface" to the volume (no. 514). The ad was repeated in *Publishers' Weekly* the next week, p. 292.

The intellectual activity of Emily Dickinson was so great that a large and characteristic choice is still possible among her literary material, and this third volume of her verses is put forth in response to the repeated wish of the admirers of her peculiar genius.

512 Unlocated clipping, ca. September 1896. Placed among notices appearing in late August–early September in Todd's scrapbook. For Holland's estimate of Dickinson, see no. 495.

Why this strenuous effort at a late day to press the claims of Emily Dickinson. The publication of her first volume of poems assured her an honorable place in literature. If she does not sit by Sappho—who sits apart from and above all—she is far removed from the ordinary poetess. Nor does the fact that "Dr. J. G. Holland expressed the opinion that she was a 'positive genius'" fasten the laurel more firmly to her brow.

513 Norman Hapgood. "New York Letter." *Author* [London] 7:4 (September 1, 1896), 81.

Roberts Brothers, of Boston, have in preparation a volume of the poems of Emily Dickinson, the strangely vivid New England spinster, whose poems and letters made a sensation here when they were published under the auspices of Col. T. W. Higginson, who discovered the unknown writer and hailed her as a genius. She then became a decided fad for some time, and the death of the fad seems to have left a steady interest in her work, which is very crude but intelligent and entirely typical of New England feeling away from the centres of population.

514 Mabel Loomis Todd. "Preface" to *Poems by Emily Dickinson*, Third Series, edited by Mabel Loomis Todd. Boston: Roberts Brothers, 1896, pp. [vii]–viii. Published September 1, 1896.

The intellectual activity of Emily Dickinson was so great that a large and characteristic choice is still possible among her literary material, and this third volume of her verses is put forth in response to the repeated wish of the admirers of her peculiar genius.

Much of Emily Dickinson's prose was rhythmic, —even rhymed, though frequently not set apart in lines. Also many verses, written as such, were sent to friends in letters; these were published in 1894, in the volumes of her *Letters*. It has not been necessary, however, to include them in this Series, and all have been omitted, except three or four exceptionally strong ones, as "A Book," and "With Flowers."

There is internal evidence that many of the poems were simply spontaneous flashes of insight, apparently unrelated to outward circumstance. Others, however, had an obvious personal origin; for example, the verses "I had a Guinea golden," which seem to have been sent to some friend travelling in Europe, as a dainty reminder of letter-writing delinquencies. The surroundings in which any of Emily Dickinson's verses are known to have been written usually serve to explain them clearly; but in general the present volume is full of thought needing no interpretation to those who apprehend this scintillating spirit.

515 "Books and Authors." *Boston Sunday Courier* 102 (September 6, 1896), [3].

The works of one whom Fame sought. She sought not after Fame. In her quiet, rural home, the lure of the Muses was more potent than any other outside charm or any other desire of her own. Her great intellectual activity and its incomparable results, the accomplishment of verse, were her whole existence. As a caged thrush sings, so sang she, for the sake of singing and of making beautiful her place in the world, while she might. Her part, her place and experience comprehended a world-joy and knowledge, and "an attainment full and heavenly," that she so well appreciated.

> Few get enough—enough is one;
>   To that ethereal throng
> Have not each one of us the right
>   To stealthily belong?

It was left for the few whose privilege it was to hear her sing in her nun-like seclusion to catch the music and to add to the literature of the True, the Beautiful and the Good, in the preservation of such songs as these. It is true, we liken this singer to the thrush in the cage, because of the calm environment with which she chose to surround her movements. It is equally true that her song is as untutored, as wild, free and lovely as the thrush's song, without a halt, with clear, sure notes, bearing messages ever—the interpretation of the handwriting upon the haloes of humanity and of nature, as she might most pleasingly interpret.

> If the foolish call them 'flowers,'
> Need the wiser tell?
> If the 'savans' classify them,
> It is just as well.
>
> Those who read the Revelations
> Must not criticise
> Those who read the same edition
> With beclouded eyes.
>
> Could we stand with that old Moses,
> Canaan denied,—
> Scan, like him, the stately landscape
> On the other side,—
>
> Doubtless we should deem superfluous
> Many sciences
> Not pursued by learned angels
> In scholastic skies!

We have the third in the series of Miss Dickinson's Poems, as edited by Mabel Todd. They are having an almost phenomenal sale—the substantial recognition of such work by the admiring public everywhere.

516 H. B. B[lackwell]. "Literary Notices." *Woman's Journal* 27 (September 12, 1896), 290. Reference is to *Poems*, Third Series.

There is a curious fascination in the brief, obscure, and somewhat incoherent stanzas of this shy, secluded New England girl. The rhymes are singularly imperfect; sometimes there are no rhymes. The meaning is often only suggested, not expressed. One is often in doubt what the meaning is, or whether there be any. And yet, in almost every stanza there is something that rouses curiosity and enchains attention. The best evidence of genius is that it attracts and stimulates, and Miss Dickinson was a genius.

517 "Among the Books." *Cambridge* [Mass.] *Tribune,* September 12, 1896, p. 2. "Scintillating spirit" is a phrase from Todd's "Preface" (no. 514).

The Poems of Emily Dickinson, third series, are conspicuously a gleaning in an already thoroughly harvested field. The present poems seem almost to say for themselves that they were not considered of sufficient worth and importance to accompany their betters in the other series. This little handful is spread widely to make as much show as possible and to fill a volume even so tiny as this one. Usually only two verses fill a page, sometimes only four lines darken the white expanse of a page. The poems are not as fascinating as previous ones, they do not show the spirit of the writer in strange, even morbid phases, yet always poetically imaginative. These are more conventional and "like everybody else," no puzzling questions put to fate, no moans, no sighs but often a proper kind of piety and echoes of Sunday psalms. Some even are a bit jocose; a curious word to use in connection with the shy, visionary and recluse of the other poems. Emily Dickinson did not bid for fame, not even for popularity. It is perfectly reasonable to suppose that she would have kept these poems back even had she permitted the world to see the others. Hers was a "scintillating spirit" as her friend writes of her. It could not always scintillate with equal brilliancy. None can.

518 "Weekly Record of New Publications." *Publishers' Weekly* 50 (September 12, 1896), 334. Routine publication information precedes the following note.

This third volume of Emily Dickinson's verses is put forth in response to the repeated wish of the admirers of her peculiar genius. It consists of poems often of four lines only on a page grouped under "Life," "Love," "Nature," and "Time and Eternity."

519 Lilian Whiting. "Life in Boston." *Chicago Inter-Ocean*, September 12, 1896, p. 16. Although this review apparently occasioned the warning from the paper's regular reviewer against Dickinson's Boston "cult" (no. 522), Whiting continued her thoughts on Dickinson in her *Inter-Ocean* column two weeks later (no. 531).

Another volume of the poems of Emily Dickinson is a literary event, and while many of the best have appeared in the two preceding volumes, yet the general average of the present collection is sufficiently high to make the reader a debtor to the scholarly care of Mrs. Mabel Loomis Todd, who has edited and arranged them. And there are exceptional lyrics of that rare beauty of thought and spontaneity of insight that so signally characterized Emily Dickinson. As this:

> It might be easier to fail with land in sight
> Than gain my blue peninsula to perish of delight.

And again:

> Who never wanted, maddest joy
> Remains to him unknown;
> The banquet of abstemiousness
> Surpasses that of wine.
> Within its hope, though yet ungrasped,
> Desire's perfect goal,
> No nearer, lest reality
> Should disenthrall thy soul.

Anything more finely epigrammatic than "Lost Faith" one could hardly find:

> To lose one's faith surpasses
> The loss of an estate,
> Because estates can be
> Replenished; faith cannot.

> Inherited with life
> Belief but once can be;
> Annihilate a single clause,
> And being's beggary.

Unique, impressive, strangely fascinating are the often unrhymed poems of this strange, original genius whose insight into the inner springs of life is always marvelous and sometimes appalling. At all events, this collection is one that will create its own demand.

520 "Studies in American Song. A Lyric Strain Through the Epigrammatic Intellectuality of the Verse of Emily Dickinson." *Philadelphia Evening Telegraph*, September 12, 1896, sec. 2, p. 2. This general assessment of Dickinson was followed a week later in the *Telegraph* by a review of the "Third Series" of her poems; see no. 525. The first sentence refers to item no. 507.

A third volume of the verse of Emily Dickinson is to be issued this fall — a volume, we are told that will admit us to the innermost chambers of her being. It is idle to surmise whether this will deepen the appeal made by the two volumes that Mrs. Todd has already given to the world. The reception accorded the first volume was, indeed, remarkable, and it quickly called forth the second. Miss Dickinson's verse was of unique power, whereof, however, epigrammatic intellectuality was a more noticeable element than a strain of pure poetry. That the imaginative glow does suffuse her verse, and that the lyric cry does echo through it, though mayhap at long intervals, will be the purpose of this article to demonstrate. It was, however, probably the singularity of her point of view, the quaintness of her conceits and the rarity of her spiritual atmosphere rather than her true poetical power, that appealed so strongly to the reading public of the day. There was a savor of a something new in these verses; there were certain similarities in the mode of thought to Emerson, and a suggestion of Blake, but there was, too, an indefinable quality possessed by neither of these poets; these verses were original.

Emily Dickinson was a writer of "closet" verse. But three or four of her poems were published during her lifetime, and even these few against her inclination. Her verse was not written to please the public, but to express her individuality. There was no thought of what any critic might say about the children of her fancy, and yet we cannot but believe that she at times cherished a desire that they would be published, for has she not sung

> This is my letter to the world,
> That never wrote to me, —
> The simple news that Nature told,
> With tender majesty.

Most of us would refuse to allow that penultimate line to pass without reservation. What she wrote is undoubtedly "The news that Nature told," but assuredly it was often far from simple; but of this anon. Miss Dickinson sent her verses about among the very small circle of her friends, but these verses were never subjected to that severe criticism without which few litterateurs can improve in their art. None can object to the thoughts of Miss Dickinson's poems, but all can object to her form of expressing these thoughts. It might be argued that the verses retain an originality, a freshness that might have been sacrificed by revision under criticism, but we do not believe that so strong a personality as hers could have been so affected. It might, however, have taught her something of the graces of form, or at least the necessity of grammatical construction when that is needed to express the thought intended. Often one of her incomplete or distorted sentences can be interpreted in several ways. It is not her want of clearness that we are objecting to, for the feeling in and the atmosphere of a poem is oftentimes a compensation for this want of clearness; sometimes, indeed, vagueness is an inevitable condition of a poem.

Emily Dickinson's life was the life of a recluse, and her verse reflects its narrowness. Not that she wrote of but few topics, far from that, for the great things of life—love and joy and sorrow—are often her themes. But for all this, there is ever a sense of confinement in her lines, she is ever yearning for a larger life, yet she would not seek it when it lay easily within her grasp. All that she did experience, however, she felt she had expressed, at least almost all, for she writes

> I found the phrase to every thought
>   I ever had, but one;

What that one is she fails to tell us. Her knowledge of life must have been largely intuitive, for she never lived a broad life, although undoubtedly an intense one. Yet for a recluse her discernment of the struggle for precedence, the agony of failure, the intoxication of success, is indeed remarkable. Nor is this intuitive knowledge of life her only feminine quality—she is intensely feminine in every quality. Her keen intellectual insight seems, too, rather intuitive than the result of studied analysis. She had a peculiar ability at seeing the heart of a problem, and expressing it in a line. This is, perhaps, the most unwonted quality wherewith she was endowed. She sees that

> The heart asks pleasure first
>   And then, excuse from pain;
> And then, those little anodynes
>   That deaden suffering.

And she realizes that often

> Mirth is the mail of anguish,
>   In which it cautious arm,
> Lest anybody spy the blood,
>   And "You're hurt!" exclaim.

How exactly, too, she hits off that peculiar, almost unconscious, state that is experienced during great pain, physical or mental,

> Pain has an element of blank.

Lines in which this power of hers is exhibited might be quoted from almost every other set of verses—indeed, many of these "poems" are merely metrical aphorisms or epigrams. The thought expressed is often, it is true, some familiar Emersonian deliverance, but it is phrased differently, and oftentimes expressed with a succinctness that rivals that of the seer of Concord.

Her femininity is also evidenced in her figures and similes, and leads to that quaintness of conceit and expression that is one of her striking characteristics. She pranks out her views of the great things of life in the terms of the careful housewife and solicitous cultivator of the old-fashioned garden behind the house. She sketches bits of life and Nature she saw from her comfortable New England home—the pomp of village funeral, the joyous whistle of the boy on the street, the importance of the robin on the lawn, the ways of the bee in the flower-bell, the flutter of the fly on the window-pane, the "push" of the wind against the walls of her quiet home. In a fanciful little love-poem she says:—

> If you were coming in the fall,
>   I'd brush the summer by

With half a smile and half a spurn,
    As housewives do a fly.

The same keenness of observation in the little things of everyday life is to be observed in many of her poems of Nature, in "In the Garden," in "The Snake," in "My Cricket," and in "The Snow." Her philosophy of life, in so far as we can follow it in her verse, is Emersonian. She believes firmly in the law of compensation. She holds that

For each ecstatic instant
    We must an anguish pay,
In keen and quivering ratio
    To the ecstasy.

At times she is Wordsworthian in her attitude towards Nature, as in "Mother Nature," but at other times she holds the opposing view, as in "The Oriole's Secret"

The fashion of the ear
Attireth that it hear,
In dun or fair.

Miss Dickinson's fancy is often playful, and sometimes, as in "The Lovers," she writes what is almost vers de societe! Traces of a grim humor, too, she exhibits, and occasionally, as in "The Lonely House," a slight evidence of dramatic power. But none of her attributes that we have mentioned are essentially poetical—they are merely concomitant with poetry. The question is, Has Emily Dickinson the imaginative glow, the lyric cry, and the distinguished diction of the true poet? We hold that she has, though these are not so noticeable as her power of condensed telling utterance. This power, which Father Tabb shares with her, has led to frequent comparison between the two poets. The recluse life of both has forced their attention to similar subjects and sometimes, as in their respective poems on the humming-bird, their similarities are astonishingly close. We think these similarities are rather external, however, than internal. Father Tabb has not her ability to express the kernel of thought in a line, and besides, he is an almost perfect craftsman in verse, which Miss Dickinson is not. Within her narrow range Miss Dickinson is a true poet. She felt and expressed the thrill of spring, the rapture of summer, the regal pain of autumn, the bitterness of winter—the great things of Nature—and the yearning for pleasure, the desire for power, the exaltation of love, the hope of rest in death—the great things of life. All these she felt, we say, but she did not feel them with the glory of intensity that broad poets do. She was capable of no great sweep of imagination; and her lyrical tendency was blighted by her intellectuality; but she has given us some beautiful lyrics, perhaps two-score of them, and among these the choicest are "Summer's Armies," "Psalm of the Day," "The Sea of Sunset," "Indian Summer," "There is a Certain Slant of Light," "The Sun's Wooing," "April," "The Oriole," "The Humming Bird," "Nature Rarer Uses Yellow," "Sunset," "The Juggler of Day," "As Imperceptibly as Grief," and her most perfect poem beginning

I taste a liquor never brewed,
From tankards scooped in pearl;
Not all the vats upon the Rhine
Yield such an alcohol.

There is space to quote no more of it. There is much beauty in it; there is still more in its suggestiveness; as in so much of her verse it is, as she herself puts it,

"Your inference therefrom." But most of all, is Emily Dickinson to be remembered as the bearer of "nosegays—for captives," as the bearer of "an unaccustomed wine" to lips fevered of the struggle with circumstance.

521 "Along the Literary Wayside." *Springfield Republican,* September 13, 1896, p. 13.

It is as wayside poems that the singular and brilliant productions of Emily Dickinson of Amherst will have their place. Only the great and robust productions of the human intellect compel the high road, and insist upon perpetuity. Song is the most immortal utterance of the human mind, the finest gateway of the human soul, yet how much of vivid and heartrending song has been lost in the great scope of our human existence! Every age has contributed to that long list of futile ambitions. And while a few are preserved for immortality among the brightest of songs, who can deeply expect such an exceptional lot? It may seem to us that the exquisite jeweled grace of Emily Dickinson's finest lines ought to persist among the work of this present day so stupid as most of that work is,— so devoid of spirituality and imaginative power. Emily Dickinson was a spiritual diviner, not a daily drudge, and as heaven is higher than earth, her writings are higher than the literary manufacture of the day. But we do not know how much hold her celestial inspirations have on this common earth, where her fellows delve and forge and manipulate and turn out commercial products. The fact that this third series of her poems is published by Roberts Bros. in Mrs. Todd's editorship would indicate that there are still those who desire to buy poetry, in essential packages, from the original fount, with the native qualities intact. We shall see.

This third series of Emily Dickinson's poems does not add anything to the fame of the author. It does not need that anything should be added. The essence of her soul was decanted in that first memorable volume, and its minor currents found their course in the second book; now we would not say that the lees are gathered, for the poetry is much too fine so to describe it, but it is a less exquisite, a less subtle thought that as a rule penetrates these remaining writings of Emily Dickinson. Nevertheless, there are the most pregnant utterances in this new volume; they are not so frequent as in the two preceding collections, but they exceed most of the human utterances of the poets of to-day, who write rather in rhetorical than in emotional expressions. Mrs. Mabel Loomis Todd in her small preface says: "Much of Emily Dickinson's prose was rhythmic,—even rhymed, though frequently not set apart in lines. Also many verses, not written as such, were sent to friends in letters; these were published in 1894, in the volumes of her letters. It has not been necessary to include them in this series."

The volume which we are considering is divided into four books—Life; Love; Nature; Time and Eternity. The division is justified in a measure, but it is also in a measure arbitrary, for the thoughts of so spiritual a creature as Emily Dickinson cannot be strictly labeled. To the simply literary critic, we know well that her poems now, as when the first series appeared, must seem vastly defective in structure, meter, rhyme, stanza, every technic of verse disregarded. But there is a consideration of verse which may be expressed in the one word "magic." When the imagination is involved, technical matters drop into such subordination that they have no right standing, and so it is with Emily Dickinson. There might have been one who could wreak her thoughts into perfect meters, but as it happened, there was only Emily of Amherst, who heard the voice of the Spirit, and answered it and out of her soul spirit responded. The possible incidents of her life, which may have given color to her work are not for us to know, and her editor has kindly refrained from informing us.

Now then we shall proceed to quote for our readers some of the remarkable poems of Emily Dickinson. Is not here a marvelous guide to content? —

> Superiority to fate
>   Is difficult to learn
> 'Tis not conferred by any,
>   But possible to earn,
> A pittance at a time,
>   Until, to our surprise,   [her surprise
> The soul with strict economy
>   Subsists till Paradise.

That is a most significant indication of the necessities of life. Here is another remarkable divination: —

> Hope is a subtle glutton,
>   He feeds upon the air;   [the fair
> And yet, inspected closely,
>   What abstinence is there!
> His is the halcyon table
>   That never seats but one;
> And whatsoever is consumed,
>   The same amounts remain.

The quatrain entitled "A Syllable" is especially remarkable as recalling one of Mrs. Browning's most marvelous sonnets. Emily Dickinson wrote: —

> Could mortal lip divine
>   The undeveloped freight
> Of a delivered syllable
>   'Twould crumble with the weight.

Now Mrs. Browning, a vastly greater poet, in her reach of power is very close to Emily Dickinson in much of her spiritual communing; and it is very interesting to quote here the sonnet of which we have spoken. It is as follows: —

THE SOUL'S EXPRESSION.

> With stammering lips and insufficient sound
> I strive and struggle to deliver right
> That music of my nature, day and night
> With dream and thought and feeling interwound,
> And inly answering all the senses round
> With octaves of a mystic depth and height
> Which step out grandly to the infinite
> From the dark edges of the sensual ground!
> This song of soul I struggle to outbear
> Through portals of the sense, sublime and whole,
> And utter all myself into the air
> But if I did it, — as the thunder-roll
> Breaks its own cloud, my flesh would perish there,
> Before that dread apocalpyse of soul.

Emily Dickinson had wonderful power to set in a small phrase a great truth, as where she said: —

Parting is all we know of heaven,
    And all we need of hell.

That is, the uncertainty is the horror of the end of life. If we knew either the one thing or the other,—whether we should find our friends or be faced by our enemies, it would be at least something settled. But why cannot any one feel sure that, man or woman, he or she shall find the society he belongs to? That is reasonable. Miss Dickinson's verse leads us to another range, that of literature, saying:—

There is no frigate like a book
    To take us lands away,
Nor any coursers like a page
    Of prancing poetry;
This treasure may the poorest take,   [traverse may
    Without oppress of toll;—
How frugal is the chariot
    That bears a human soul!

It is difficult to please the general public in such a problem as that of Emily Dickinson. One cannot strike a partition in transcendental poetry. Either the reader has the insight or has it not; its splendor is lost to the first, and the others have to struggle to understand it,—even fine intellects being troubled to understand Emily Dickinson, because she writes immortal truths in shorthand. Now this little versicle would seem to be transpicuous to any average intellect, yet we have seen those who were puzzled by it. The verses were sent with flowers:—

If recollecting were forgetting,
    Then I remember not;
And if forgetting, recollecting,
    How near I had forgot!
And if to miss were sorry,   [were merry
    And if to mourn were gay,
How very blithe the fingers
    That gathered these to-day!

And here is an analysis of human feeling:

I measure every grief I meet
    With analytic eyes,
I wonder if it weighs like mine,
    Or has an easier size.

I wonder if they bore it long,
    Or did it just begin?
I could not tell the date of mine,
    It feels so old a pain.

I wonder if it hurts to live
    And if they have to try,
And whether, could they choose between,
    They would not rather die.

            *   *   *   *   *

And though I may not guess the kind
    Correctly, yet to me

A piercing comfort it affords
   In passing Calvary,

To note the fashions of the cross
   Of those that stand alone,
Still fascinated to presume
   That none are like my own.   [That some

The representation of "Desire" by Emily Dickinson is simply a fantastic imagination. She writes:—

Who never wanted,—maddest joy
   Remains to him unknown;
The banquet of abstemiousness
   Surpasses that of wine.

Within its hope, though yet ungrasped
   Desire's perfect goal,—
No nearer, lest reality
   Should disenthral thy soul.

Here is a striking improvement of a very commonplace bit of reality:—

Is bliss, then such abyss
I must not put my foot amiss,
For fear I spoil my shoe?

I'd rather suit my foot
Than save my boot;
For yet to buy another pair
Is possible
At any fair.

But bliss is sold just once;
The patent lost,
None buy it any more.

Here is a wonderful quatrain:—

Love is anterior to life,
   Posterior to death,
Initial of creation,
   The exponent of breath.

Perhaps there is no more absolutely betraying verse among all those of Emily Dickinson than that beginning, "He touched me." She had emotions deeper than were ever sounded in the circumstances of her recluse life, and whose accessories we do not need to study. So far as her writings interpret her life, this book contributes several particulars undivined from those that have preceded it. In addition it contains a great many poems of nature which charm deeply the lovers of the earth, and many of them are finely transcendental, as this, for instance:—

Immortal is an ample word
   When what we need is by,
But when it leaves us for a time,
   'Tis a necessity;

Of heaven above the firmest proof
   We fundamental know;

Except for its marauding hand,
   It had been heaven below.

We will add some excellent verses:—

JOY IN DEATH.

If tolling bells I ask the cause,   [bell
   "A soul has gone to God"
I'm answered in a lonesome tone:
   Is heaven then so sad?

That bells should joyful ring to tell
   A soul had gone to heaven.
Would seem to me the proper way
   A good news should be given!

FAREWELL.

Tie the strings to my life, my Lord,
   Then I am ready to go.
Just a look at the horses,—
   Rapid! That will do!

Put me in on the firmest side,
   So I shall never fall.
For we must ride to the judgment,
   And partly it is down hill.   [it's partly

But never I mind the bridges,
   And never I mind the sea.—
Held fast in everlasting race
   By my own choice and thee.

Good-by to the life I used to live,
   And the world I used to know,—
And kiss the hills for me, just once;—
   Now I am ready to go.

522 "Current Literature." *Chicago Inter-Ocean*, September 19, 1896, p. 11. On the same page *Poems*, Third Series, is listed among "Books Received."

The marvel with regard to the genius of Emily Dickinson is not that it was so active, nor that its activity was so veiled in silence during her lifetime, but that it co-existed with so slight a development of the critical faculty. Had she possessed the power of discriminating at all with regard to her own work, she would have left far fewer poems for posthumous publication, but these might have given her undying fame. As it is, we think that when the small cult of her admirers in Boston shall have passed away, the mass of her undigested verses will also lapse into oblivion. The volume before us is the third that has been issued to give her "scribblings" (we call them this because of the evident haste of composition, rather than through an intent to scoff at them) to the world. Such "scrappy" poems are hard to criticise, since they indicate too much poetic thought to be wholly blamed; meanwhile they are generally too unpolished and ragged in form to merit praise. Such verses as:

We outgrow love like other things,
    And put it in the drawer,
Till it an antique fashion shows,
    Like costumes grandsires wore,

and

It's such a little thing to weep,
    So short a thing to sigh;
And yet by trades the size of these
    We men and women die.

may be called diamonds in the rough but such as the following, entitled "Childish Griefs," are worse than nonsense; they are literary crimes:

Softened by time's consummate plush,
    How sleek the woe appears
That threatened childhood's citadel,
    And undermined the years!

Bisected now by bleaker griefs,
    We envy the despair
That devastated childhood's realm,
    So easy to repair.

523 "New Books." *Outlook* 54 (September 19, 1896), 518. There being no poem entitled "Flowers" in the Third Series, the likely reference is to "With Flowers" ("If recollecting were forgetting").

A third series of *Poems* by Emily Dickinson has just been issued, edited by Mabel Loomis Todd. The book includes no less than one hundred and sixty-five short poems. It could hardly be expected that the level reached would be as high as in the previous collections, but it can truly be said that many of these little verses have the same touch of genius united with the same absolute lack of conventional form and method which characterize the best of the poems previously printed. Such, we think, is "Real Riches" (first printed in the *Outlook*), "Flowers," and several others. As usual, there are not a few poems which from ordinary standards one would be very glad to see omitted, but perhaps it is as well that they are included, as they throw light on the strange personality and way of thinking of the author.

524 "New Books and New Editions." *Philadelphia Evening Bulletin*, September 19, 1896, p. 10.

We welcome the third series of the "Poems of Emily Dickinson," edited by Mabel Loomis Todd. There can be no question as to the genius of this New England poet. When she died, her work had just begun to receive a wider recognition than that which had been accorded it by the greatest critics of the day. Her verse was inspired, not made; and, although careless of form, her poetry is never conventional and commonplace. She interpreted the spirit as few have been able to do—flashing upon us the deepest and most enduring truths. The present volume contains several characteristic poems. We shall quote from the poem entitled "A Well":

I.

What mystery pervades a well!
   The water lives so far.
Like neighbor from another world
   Residing in a jar.

II.

The grass does not appear afraid;
   I often wonder he
Can stand so close and look so bold
   At what is dread to me.

III.

Related somehow they may be,
   The edge stands next the sea,   [The sedge
Where he is floorless, yet of fear
   No evidence gives he.

IV.

But nature is a stranger yet;
   The ones that cite her most
Have never passed her haunted house,
   Nor simplified her ghost.

V.

To pity those that know her not
   Is helped by the regret
That those who know her, know her less
   The nearer her they get.

525 "Literature." *Philadelphia Evening Telegraph*, September 19, 1896, sect. 2, p. 2. The *Telegraph* review of the previous week is no. 520.

It was with misgiving that this third volume of selections from the verse of the late Miss Emily Dickinson was opened, misgiving that two readings proved to have been only too well founded. The collection, the editor says, was issued "in response to the repeated wish of the admirers of Miss Dickinson's peculiar genius." It would have perhaps been better to have substituted "friends" for "admirers," for many of the latter felt, from their knowledge of the poet's "peculiar genius" that the publication of further selections from the mass of the manuscripts and letters could not but be fraught with danger to her literary reputation. To her friends this third volume will doubtless be a delight, but the sincere appreciators of Emily Dickinson, the poet, will be compelled to confess that there are few verses in this book up to her highest plane. From each of the former volumes could be culled a score of exquisite poems, but from this volume of 166 so-called poems but seven—"A Book," "Alpine Glow," "Consecration," "Loyalty," "A Light Exists in Spring," "Sunset," and "The Coming of Night." The last of these is one of the very best things of hers that has been given to the world. It must be quoted entire:—

How the old mountains drip with sunset,
   And the brake of dun;
How the hemlocks are tipped in tinsel
   By the wizard sun!

How the old steeples hand the scarlet
    Till the ball is full—
Have I the lip of the flamingo
    That I dare to tell?

Then, how the fire ebbs like billows,
    Touching all the grass
With a departing, sapphire feature,
    As if a Duchess pass!

How a small dusk crawls on the village
    Till the houses blot;
And the odd flambeaux no men carry
    Glimmers on the spot!   [Glimmer

Now it is night in nest and kennel,
    And where was the wood,
Just a dome of abyss is nodding
    Into solitude!

These are the visions babbled Guido;
    Titian never told;
Domenichino dropped the pencil,
    Powerless to unfold.

With the exception of these above named poems there is scarcely anything in this book really worth the publishing. Pithy puttings of quaint conceits there are a plenty, but with few exceptions even these are not so well done as their predecessors of similar character. When this sort of verse was first introduced to the reading public it startled with its originality even when it was not really poetical, but more of it now fails to make the same appeal. Some of it, notably the love-poems, reveal new phases of the woman's personality. Mrs. Todd has told us that Miss Dickinson was not "disappointed in love," but these poems reveal that she thought much of love, and worshipped an ideal lover; some will think she loved a man. Though the poetical value of most of these last garnered verses be not great, they are intensely interesting to students of Miss Dickinson's personality, and there will be to all a feeling of satisfaction that now, at least, they have had access to most of what she wrote. That she is a true poet time will establish, we hold, arguing along the lines followed in an article in these columns just a week ago. But this last volume of verse does little to confirm our belief in the worth of her work.

526 Grace S. Musser. "Emily Dickinson. Letters and Poems of a Lonely New England Woman Who Believed in 'Art for Truth.'" *San Francisco Sunday Call*, September 20, 1896, p. 19. The *Bookman* item is no. 506. Following this review-essay, in the same column, two Dickinson poems are reprinted: "I died for beauty" and "I shall know why, when time is over."

A recent publisher's note to the effect that the large sale of Father Tabb's poems, now in their fifth edition, was paralleled among American poets only by the demand for the posthumous volume of Emily Dickinson, recalls the work of the singular and gifted New England woman. There appears to be an interesting coincidence in this fact, in view of Father Tabb's remark, quoted by the Bookman, that "of late American poets there is none worthy to go down to posterity except Miss Dickinson." Her poems appeared several years ago, four years after their author's death. Her recently published Letters, edited by Mabel Loomis Todd, reveal in part the strange personality of the woman who for years and from her own choice never stepped outside her father's house.

Emily Dickinson was born in Amherst, Mass., in the year 1830. There seems to have been nothing exceptional about her girlhood. Her father was a prosperous man, for years treasurer of Amherst College, and at one time a member of Congress. The pictures of her home show us an attractive colonial house, spacious and dignified, surrounded by spreading elm trees. There were three children— Austin, Emily and Lavinia. Their mother was apparently a sensible and practical New England woman with little time for sentiment. Emily as a young girl appears to have had a happy life. Her education was begun at the village "academy" and "finished" by a year at Mount Holyoke. Her letters at this time are the letters of the average schoolgirl and show no trace of the epigrammatic transcendentalism which marks them later. Neither is there any trace of the shyness which became a passion in her after life. She seems to have joined in the social life of her mates and lived the normal life of the young woman of that time. Her early friend, Mrs. Ford, to whom some of her letters are addressed, prefaces their publication by a short sketch of Emily's girlhood. According to Mrs. Ford she was one of a circle of talented young girls, several of whom became famous in after years. Fanny Montague, the art critic, was one, and another was Helen Fiske, who wrote under the pen name, "H. H.," and whose death in San Francisco a few years ago was a sad loss to American letters. Emily Dickinson, strange to say, was the wit of the group and furnished the funny items for the school paper. The only hint she gave her friend of her future strange aloofness from her fellows was by asking her one day if it did not make her shiver to hear some people talk "as though they took all the clothes off their souls." Not until she is about 20 do we find symptoms of that later malady—if malady be the word for her almost fierce seclusion.

The friend who most helped to form her girlish aspirations was a teacher in the academy, a Mr. Leonard Humphrey, who was a few years older than herself. He was a graduate of Amherst and had showed unusual intellectual ability and penetration. A letter to a friend at this time briefly records his death. His name is only mentioned twice in the course of her whole correspondence and once in a letter to her literary godfather, Mr. Higginson. She says, "My dying tutor told me he would like to live till I had been a poet." This was twelve years after his death! We cannot help wondering whether this was not the key of those minor cadences to which her life was henceforth set. It seems almost a sort of sacrilege to try to pierce that reserve in which she veiled herself. There are souls as tremulous as sensitive plants. A year later in a letter to the same friend she declines a proffered invitation, saying: "I don't go from home unless emergency leads me by the hand, and then I do it obstinately and draw back if I can."

There is no hint as yet of her writing poetry. About this time her brother, Austin, left home and college to take a position in Boston. Her letters to him are delightfully clever, full of wit, with an undercurrent of sadness and loneliness, ostensibly because of his being gone. In these letters we begin to detect the beat of words, the sense of cadence which marks her poetry rather than perfect rhyme or meter. Even in homely sentences one perceives the writer to have that "ear for words" which is somewhat rarer than an ear for music. However, it need not take a verse-maker to write in that manner. This fragment from a letter to her cousin, on the death, in his first battle, of a friend's son, suggests the poet:

"Poor little widow's boy, riding to-night in the mad wind, back to the village burying-ground, where he never dreamed of sleeping. Ah, the dreamless sleep!"

Her letters to her brother detail the family and neighborhood doings, with here and there a suggestion of her growing dislike of meeting people. She mentions a great village fete on the opening of the new railroad. "They all said it was fine, I 'spose' it was. I sat in Professor Tyler's woods and saw the train move off, and then came home for fear somebody would see me or ask me how I did. Dr. Holland was here and called to see us." "Dr. Holland" was J. G. Holland, the well-known author and later the editor of the Century Magazine. A visit to the Hollands' a short time after this was one of the few she ever made. Her letters to them are extremely interesting and show a constantly increasing brilliancy.

The letters to her young cousins in the beginning of the second volume show the womanly and affectionate side of her nature, that had no warp in its attitude toward those she loved.

But by far the most fascinating letters of all are those addressed to Thomas Wentworth Higginson. With her constantly increasing seclusion the necessity for some expression seemed to grow. She made no occupation of writing, but while busy with her house duties or her sewing—for she was pre-eminently a practical, capable New England woman—she would jot down the thoughts that came to her in fragments of verse, writing them often on the margin of newspapers or the backs of old envelopes. There was no system or order in her production and no thought of publication. Any sort of publicity would have been unbearable to the woman, whose shrinking from the eyes of strangers was so great that she resorted to all sorts of devices to avoid addressing her letters in her own hand. Sometimes she used newspaper labels, or if these were not to be had, one of the family performed the office for her. Her penmanship, of which a facsimile is given, seems characteristic of her isolation, each letter standing alone. Writing for herself alone it was not to be expected that her verses should be finished in form. Indeed it is doubtful whether she understood anything of the theory or technique of poetry. But, as one of her critics said: "When a thought takes our breath away, a lesson in grammar seems an impertinence." And though her poems may be fragmentary in form, they are never so in substance. Each contains a distinct thought. As, for example, this:

> Presentiment is that long shadow on the lawn
> Indicative that suns go down;
> The notice to the startled grass
> That darkness is about to pass.

After a time the desire to have some competent authority pass judgment upon her work grew so strong that it led her to do what many with a far less sensitive temperament would have shrunk from doing. She had come to have a great admiration for the work and the critical ability of Mr. Higginson, who was then connected with the Atlantic Monthly, and she wrote him the following letter, inclosing some of her poems:

Mr. Higginson: Are you too deeply occupied to say if my verse is alive?
The mind is so near itself that it cannot see distinctly, and I have none to ask.
Should you think it breathed and had you the leisure to tell me, I should feel quick gratitude.
If I make the mistake, that you dared to tell me would give me sincerer honor toward you.
I inclose my name, asking you, if you please, sir, to tell me what is true?
That you may not betray me it is needless to ask, since honor is its own pawn.

We can imagine how startled and interested Mr. Higginson must have been by the receipt of such a letter. It might have been written by an Emerson or a poet of the Concord school and reminds us that the author was reared in the same mental atmosphere. Mr. Higginson's answers have, unfortunately, not been preserved. It would have been interesting to read the response he made to this singular and powerfully worded appeal for his criticism. We can surmise the gist of his answer by the second letter from Miss Dickinson. She thanks him for his kindness and for his "surgery." He had evidently pointed out that her poems were very irregular in form.

> You asked how old I was? I made no verse but one or two until this winter, sir. . . . You inquire my books. For poets I have Keats and Mr. and Mrs. Browning. For prose Mr. Ruskin, Sir Thomas Browne and the Revelations. . . .

A small company of friends was that, but an excellent one. No wonder Ruskin was her intimate. She was a true disciple of the man who wrote:

> No weight, not mass, nor beauty of execution can outweigh one grain or fragment of thought.

Yet I do not believe that Emily Dickinson was ever consciously defiant of rules. She rather never considered them at all, and sought only to express the thought which grappled her. Sometimes this was done in strikingly homely phraseology, as in the poem:

> Death is a dialogue between
> The spirit and the dust.
> "Dissolve," says Death. The spirit, "Sir,
> I have another trust."
> Death doubts it, argues from the ground.
> The Spirit turns away,
> Just laying off, for evidence,
> An overcoat of clay.

The "overcoat of clay" is stronger and comes more freshly home to the mind than any of the usual phrases, such as the body being a "garment to be laid aside," or the like, which have been said so often that we have mostly lost the feeling out of them. If Emily Dickinson had written to-day, she would have found herself in the full sweep of the art movement, which contends for originality and freshness of expression, at the sacrifice of every art form—instead of the hackneyed, which is powerless to really express.

Her letter goes on:

> I went to school, but, in your manner of the phrase, had no education. When a little girl I had a friend who taught me immortality; but venturing too near himself he never returned.
> You ask of my companions. Hills, sir, and the sundown and a dog large as myself that my father bought me. They are better than beings, because they know but do not tell, and the noise in the pool at noon excels my piano.
> I have a brother and sister. My mother does not care for thought, and father— too busy with his briefs to notice what we do. He buys me many books, but begs me not to read them, because he fears they joggle the mind. They are religious, except me, and address an eclipse every morning, whom they call their father. . . .
> I have had a few pleasures so deep as your opinion, and if I tried to thank you my tears would block my tongue.
> My dying tutor told me that he would like to live till I had been a poet, but

death was as much of a mob as I could master then. And when, far afterward, a sudden light on orchards or a new fashion in the wind troubled my attention I felt a palsy here, the verses just relieve.

If Emily Dickinson had never written any verse these letters would have stamped her a poet. Mr. Howells has said that "if nothing else had come out of our life but this strange poetry we should feel that in the work of Emily Dickinson, America, or New England rather, had made a distinctive addition to the literature of the world, and could not be left out of any record of it."

In this same letter she asks Mr. Higginson if he "has time to be her friend." This was the beginning of a correspondence and of a friendship which lasted over thirty years, until the day of her death, and during all that time Mr. Higginson only saw her face twice. At first he tried to point out her imperfections of rhyme and meters, but he soon ceased, recognizing here a quality beyond all mere form. In one letter he must have told her that her vision was "beyond his knowledge," for she answers, "You say "Beyond your knowledge! You would not jest with me; but, preceptor, you cannot mean it?" Mr. Higginson's interest in the strange genius of his correspondent led him to visit Amherst. He has described his call upon Miss Dickinson in the pages of the Atlantic. Her shyness and aloofness were so great that he felt nearer to her in letters than in conversation. He says that for years she never passed beyond her father's garden, and there were literally years when her foot never crossed her own doorstep. In spite of this fact she is said to have been a gracious and dignified hostess on those occasions, once a year, when her father in his official capacity gave a reception to the faculty and seniors of Amherst College. Mr. Howells, however, records that later in her life she could not even once a year endure this strain, and would often sit in a back room, her face turned from her guests.

Early in life she revolted from the orthodox creed, but she was none the less dominated by her austere Puritan ideals. Strongest among these was an intense craving for sincerity, together with a loathing for cant and social hypocrisy. In her poem called "Real" she has expressed this with daring force:

> I like a look of agony
> Because I know it's true;
> Men do not sham convulsion
> Nor simulate a throe.

> The eyes glaze over, and that is death—   [glaze once
> Impossible to feign;
> The beads upon the forehead,
> By homely anguish strung.

Hamilton Aide reviewed her poems at length in the Nineteenth Century Magazine. He lamented their technical imperfections, saying they were too often "like pearls in packthread," but he did full justice to her power of imagination— her "gift of seeing." That is, after all, the fundamental quality of the poet. Manner is—or should be—accessory to that.

She resembles Emily Bronte in work and in character more nearly than any other woman writer. It seemed fitting that Colonel Higginson should read over her grave the "Last Lines" of her sister poet.

527 "Three Volumes of Verse." *Providence Journal*, September 20, 1896, p. 13. The reviewer may have in mind Andrew Lang's description of a Dickinson poem as "mere maundering" (no. 72).

Miss Mabel Loomis Todd has done the memory of her friend, Emily Dickinson, a poor service, on the other hand, in issuing a "third series" of her alleged poems. While it is true that there was in Miss Dickinson a vein of poetic fancy, the work she actually did was too crude to be regarded as in any way a contribution to literature, and only that queer sort of literary judgment of which we have many examples in these days could so regard it. Witness such stuff as this:

FIRE.

Ashes denote that fire was;
  Respect the grayest pile
For the departed creature's sake
  That hovered there awhile.

Fire exists the first in light,
  And then consolidates—
Only the chemist can disclose
  Into what carbonates.

It is too bad to expose to the cruel gaze of the world these maunderings.

528 "Verse of Emily Dickinson." *New York Times,* September 25, 1896, p. 10.

After the success of the first and second series of Emily Dickinson's verse, this, the third, is presented. In the characteristic volumes of "Letters" published in 1894, the quality of the verse sent the lady's many friends was noticeable, and in the collection now presented may be found two exceptionally strong pieces, "A Book" and "With Flowers." The larger part are exceedingly short, not more than a stanza, but never without a certain strength and elegance of diction. A very strong philosophical bias is evident. Occasionally there is a certain quaintness of thought and peculiarity of rhyme, as the five lines on "The Cocoon":

Drab habitation of whom?
Tabernacle or tomb,
Or dome of worm,
Or porch of gnome,
Or some elf's catacomb?

The poem on Charlotte Brontë's grave is as tender as it is touching, and the final poem on "Eternity" breathes the true spirit of hope and resignation.

529 Mary Abbott. "Emily Dickinson's Poems." *Chicago Times-Herald,* September 26, 1896, p. 9. The fragmentary lines attributed to Dickinson, "God's residence is next to mine, / His furniture is love" are spurious.

Everyone remembers the sensation caused by the first public appearance of Emily Dickinson's letters and verses. These in themselves were extraordinary enough; but prefacing and interspersing them were even more interesting notes and bits of biography by Colonel Thomas Wentworth Higginson, who hardly knew the lady personally until late in her life, but who corresponded intimately with her for years. The flower was born, blushed and died unseen, save by a few favored eyes; and her sequestered life was almost too sacred to lay public hands upon. Her poetry was beautiful in thought, often singular and far-off; the form in which she enveloped it was many times crude and uncouth. There was great interest felt in the new posthumous poet, and great delight was manifested in the character of the verse.

A third series has now appeared; a book of snatches and flashes, rather than of complete embodiments of thought-out or expressed ideas. The series is edited and prefaced by Mabel Loomis Todd, who leaves appreciation to readers, rather than forestalls it by fulsome praise. There are gleams of light, real sunlight, and some pale, cold moonbeams among the scintillations of this remarkable woman's genius. There is never a trace of even poet's passion; and something in every line suggests perhaps now because we are familiar with it, the faded, pathetic life of the New England village recluse.

In these new verses the same "queer" strain is occasionally perceptible; the choice of out-of-the-way words, which do not sound far-fetched or crabbed, like some of Mrs. Browning's, but original or circumlocutory. Again, an ungrammatical construction or strange freak of syntax will give the thought a strained appearance, an ungraceful droop marring the wing-action of a soaring bird.

"Forbidden Fruit," for instance, introduces two unusual phrases. This is it:

> Heaven is what I cannot reach!
> The apple on the tree,
> Provided it do hopeless hang,
> That "heaven" is, to me.
>
> The color on the cruising cloud,
> The interdicted ground
> Behind the hill, the house behind,
> There paradise is found.

The "cruising" cloud and the "interdicted" ground make admirable spots on a not otherwise original landscape drawing. And although color has no palpable predicate and is made to pair with ground—two dissimilar nouns thus falsely represented as nouns of place and referred to by "there"—the effect is excellent and color by poetic license assumes form and distance. It must be glowing imagery, indeed, thus to transfuse attributes. It may be seen how futile the attempt of a mediocre poet would be in similar phrasing to suit his fancy, as: "The color of her hair—there lies my heart." Miss Dickinson is full of transmogrified parts of speech.

At times the grammar sense is shocked beyond repair. This little quatrain is hopelessly marred, in spite of its shy conceit, by the ignoring of common rules. Why did not the editor, by the by, change the number of the auxiliary in the third line?

> Few get enough; enough is all;   [is one
> To that eternal throng
> Have not each one of us the right
> To stealthily belong?

Broken infinitives may be allowed in urgent poetic cases; this is not one.

Such small carpings are swept away, as by magic, when the thunder really rolls in the soul of the poet and reverberates to the upper air.

> When morning comes,
> It is as if a hundred drums
> Did round my pillow roll,
> And shouts fill all my childish sky,

> And bells keep saying, "Victory!"
> From steeples in my soul.

Fragments of exquisite sentiment, just breathed, and no more, abound in the new little book.

> It's such a little thing to weep
> So short a thing to sigh.
>
> *   *   *   *   *
>
> Drowning is not so pitiful
> As the attempt to rise.
>
> *   *   *   *   *
>
> Could mortal lip divine
> The undeveloped freight
> Of a delivered syllable,
> 'Twould crumble with the weight.
>
> *   *   *   *   *
>
> There is no frigate like a book
> To take us lands away.
>
> *   *   *   *   *
>
> How frugal is the chariot
> That bears a human soul.
>
> *   *   *   *   *
>
> God's residence is next to mine,
> His furniture is love.
>
> *   *   *   *   *
>
> Inherited with life,
> Belief but once can be
> Annihilate a simple clause,
> And being's beggary.

These are a few bits taken as one turns over the pages. Satire occasionally steps in and makes a short speech quiet but audible to the audience. As:

> The Maker's cordial visage,
>   However good to see,
> Is shunned, we must admit it,
>   Like an adversity.

And this:

> What soft, cherubic creatures
>   These gentlewomen are!
> One would as soon assault a plush
>   Or violate a star.
>   .   .   .   .
> It's such a common glory,
>   A fisherman's degree!

Redemption, brittle lady,
  Be so ashamed of thee.

This, a part of a reflection on Thanksgiving gorging, is excellent:

Neither patriarch nor pussy,
  I dissect the play;
Seems it, to any hooded thinking,
  Reflex holiday.

Had there been no sharp subtraction
  From the early sum.
Not an acre or a caption
  Where was once a room.

Not a mention, whose small pebble
  Wrinkled any bay—
Unto such, were such assembly,
  'Twere Thanksgiving Day.

This is Swinburnian in construction and reminds one of the involutions in the "Sea-Mew."

Such scenes my heart remembers,
In all as wild Septembers
As this, though life seems other,
Though sweet, than once were mine,

is not unlike:

Unto such, were such assembly,
  'Twere Thanksgiving Day.

The love poems, so-called, are strange—gropings in the dark, unenlightened by the real passion. Fancyings, mutterings, losings, never-findings, these make up the substance of the lady's musings, although now and then comes a really inspired burst out of the cloud. As this:

He touched me, as I live to know   [so I
  That such a day, permitted so,
    I groped upon his breast.
It was a boundless place to me
  And silenced, as the awful sea,
    Puts minor streams to rest.

Vague abstractions are more in the line of Emily Dickinson's loving; as this:

Let me not mar that perfect dream
  By an auroral stain,
But so adjust my daily night
  That it will come again.

A complete poem, by the by. Of nature, the muse sings more freely, naturally, and with greater genius. At sunset she notes:

A sloop of amber slips away
  Upon an ether sea,

> And wrecks in peace a purple tar
>   The son of ecstasy.

"Waiting" should be set to music

> I sing to use the waiting,
>   My bonnet but to tie,
> And shut the door unto my house,
>   No more to do have I.

> Till, his best step approaching,
>   We journey to the day,
> And tell each other how we sang
>   To keep the dark away.

If, as Edgar Poe declared, Shelley's "I Arise From Dreams of Thee" is too short to be considered a poem, then Emily Dickinson has produced nothing worthy of the title, nor near it. Her verse is mostly cut up into tiny bits, being, indeed, as the prefator remarks, "simply spontaneous flashes of insight, apparently unrelated to outward circumstance." Never meant to be laid before any eye but the one to which she singly presented it, each scrap is almost exactly as she jotted it. With so little polishing or preparation the wonder is that there are hundreds of these exquisite gems of fancy, philosophy and pure poetry, susceptible of so little change.

530 "The Third of the Gray Sisters." *Chicago Journal,* September 26, 1896, p. 9.

A third collection of Emily Dickinson's "Poems" has just been issued, edited by Mrs. Mabel Loomis Todd, and published in a form similar to the two preceding volumes, with the symbolical little Indian pipe blossoms nodding on the gray covers. The collection is very much like unto its predecessors, the same words, in different order, expressing in the same metre the same views of life. Nothing is more characteristic of Emily Dickinson than this metre, which she may be said to have appropriated and made her own. Combined with the quaint thought it embodies, it produces the effect of a small gray figure wandering slowly at twilight in a shadowy garden bounded by high walls. The stars, symbolical of the eternal verities, shine down on the quiet figure, but the walls shut out the world about. For this reason the poems classed under the head of "Time and Eternity," have a stronger, clearer ring than those that deal with "Life" and "Love."

The poet's intimacy with "Nature," however, is close, though limited to a narrow range. Altogether, the first impression of Emily Dickinson's writings is repeated and emphasized by this latest comer of the three gray sisters. Few writers have the power of clothing a thought in such simple, vivid speech. There seems almost none of the hindrance of words, for instance, in these lines:

> We never know we go—when we are going;
>   We jest and shut the door;
> Fate following behind us bolts it,
>   And we accost no more.

The thought in the following quatrain is far from new, but its direct utterance strikes the reader with a new force. "Life's Trades" it is called:

It's such a little thing to weep,
　So short a thing to sigh,
And yet by trades the size of these
　We men and women die!

Sometimes, however, incoherence claims Emily for its own, and though the familiar words and metre are there, we search in vain for the illuminating idea. Where, for example, is it in this outburst?

Morning is the place for dew,
　Corn is made at noon,
After-dinner light for flowers,
　Dukes for setting sun!

Was the solitary poet wandering in mental nebula when she penned these words, or was her chirography an inscrutable mystery to her editor, who made what she could out of it?

Her occasional peeps over the wall gave her queer, grim views of the world, as these stanzas, without title or name, testify:

There's been a death in the opposite house
　As lately as today.
I know it by the numb look
　Such houses have alway.

The neighbors rustle in and out,
　The doctor drives away.
A window opens like a pod,
　Abrupt, mechanically;

Somebody flings a mattress out —
　The children hurry by;
They wonder if It died on that —
　I used to when a boy.

The minister goes stiffly in
　As if the house were his,
And he owned all the mourners now
　And little boys besides.

And then the milliner, and the man
　Of the appalling trade,
To take the measure of the house.
　There'll be that dark parade

Of tassels and of coaches soon;
　It's easy as a sign —
The intuition of the news
　In just a country town.

A singular intuition for the grotesque and incongruous lends its piquant flavor to Emily Dickinson's work, and gives it its stamp of originality. This may be accounted for by the peculiar admixture of mysticism and common sense which has occasionally been noted in the New England character. That two such opposite characteristics should abide side by side in a people must often provoke and call up strange mental pictures wherein the every-day prose of Life is transfigured with subtle radiance while the unseen world is imaged in the most common-place objects and events.

It is not probable that another sifting of her manuscripts will give Emily Dickinson's literary executors any more material worthy of publication, so that the time has come for the last word on this strange product of overcivilization — for such, I hold, she was. She stands alone, apart from the other figures of our literature. She was not a part of a literary movement, nor do her poems mark an era. She is therefore a literary freak whose writings may tickle a jaded palate, but can have no permanent influence over a sane mind. Bloodless, disembodied, and unearthly, she represents the final effort of a once rich soil. New England brought forth Emerson, Lowell, Channing, Longfellow, Whittier, and the others of that splendid harvest of intellect, full-bodied, full-blooded, and strong. In a measure, the vitality has now gone out of the land, and in the gathering shade only the pale, sensitive, fragile Indian pipe blossom can push its waxen stem and flower, and Emily Dickinson, anemic, peculiar, burdened with too much genius, and too little flesh and blood, is the result. We must look further west for the next harvest of letters. Meanwhile "requiescat in pace," Emily Dickinson, strange and lonely soul that you were! Your sleep is like that described in your own simple, but forcible lines:

> A long, long sleep, a famous sleep
>   That makes no show for dawn
> A stretch of limb nor stir of lid —   [or stir
>   An independent one.
>
> Was ever idleness like this?
>   Within a hut of stone
> To bask the centuries away
>   Nor once look up for noon?

531   Lilian Whiting. "Life in Boston." *Chicago Inter-Ocean*, September 26, 1896, p. 16. Whiting begins her correspondence to the Chicago paper noting a "new and absorbingly interesting" Roberts Brothers edition of the poems of Johanna Ambrosius. The regular reviewer for the *Inter-Ocean* gave the "Third Series" separate notice (no. 522).

Of all this next week, when these overladen days shall have given me a leisure — denied this week — to lose myself in this new and absorbingly interesting work. In the meantime Emily Dickinson —

> 'Tis little I could care for pearls
>   Who own the ample sea;
> Or brooches, when the Emperor
>   With rubies petteth me.   [pelteth

The poems of Emily Dickinson lend themselves curiously to quotation. Epigrammatic in the extreme, and packed with significance, they haunt the uncanny and impress the imagination. One of those exotic personalities was that of Emily Dickinson, as unique in her own way as Margaret Fuller, though the one was a recluse whose name, even, until her poems were published after her death, was hardly known beyond the limits of her native town, while the other lived in the very heart of the world of letters and events. Miss Dickinson was born in Amherst, Dec. 9, 1830, and died there May 9, 1886. "Except for a very few friends," wrote

Colonel Higginson of her, "she was as invisible to the world as if she had dwelt in a nunnery. For myself, although I had correspondence with her for many years, I saw her but twice face to face, and brought away the impression of something as unique and remote as Undine, or Mignon, or Thekla." The first selection from her poems brought out in 1890, with an introduction from Colonel Higginson, was followed two years later by another, edited and prefaced by Mabel Loomis Todd. Still later Mrs. Todd edited the "Letters" of Miss Dickinson, and now she gives us the third series, and presumably the last, from the poems. Mrs. Todd is both the daughter and the wife of Amherst professors, and has been with her husband this summer in Japan, whence Professor Todd and a party of scientists went to observe the total eclipse of the sun on Aug. 9, and from which expedition they are now daily expected home. It is rather a venture to give the public a third repetition of poetic work so unique as that of Emily Dickinson, and of a quality which must inevitably appeal to the few rather than to the many; but any critical reading of the new volume will prove its justification for existence. One is not sure, indeed, but that some of the strangest and most impressive of all Miss Dickinson's poems are here—as this, which she simply entitles "Parting:"

> My life closed twice before its close;
>   It yet remains to see
> If immortality unveil
>   A third event to me.
>
> So huge, so hopeless to conceive
>   As these that twice befell,
> Parting is all we know of heaven,
>   And all we need of hell.

This quatrain, entitled "Philosophy," is indeed philosophic:

> It might be easier
>   To fail with land in sight
> Than gain my blue peninsula
>   To perish of delight.

And again these intense lines:

> To lose thee sweeter than to gain
>   All other hearts I knew.
> 'Tis true the draught is destitute,   [drought
>   But then I had the dew!

One is tempted on and on into quotations. There are books that are desirable, and a few that are indispensable, and it is perhaps among the latter that the lovers of poetic insight and philosophic thought will come to class the poems of Emily Dickinson. They lack rhyme and rhythm, melody and music. They are uncut gems, but they are genuine ones.

532 "The Literary World." *Boston Daily Advertiser*, September 29, 1896, p. 5.

Emily Dickinson was a woman of rare intellectuality. The thoughts which she expressed in verse are profound, and couched in Emersonian brevity. A third volume of these poems has been compiled by Mabel L. Todd. These are arranged in four divisions, life, love, nature, and time and eternity. They are the thoughts of a moment, caught and embalmed. This on a rose is very pretty:—

A sepal, petal, and a thorn
Upon a common summer's morn,
A flash of dew, a bee or two,
A breeze,
A caper in the trees,
And I'm a rose!

And what a world of sadness is enshrined in these few lines: —

I wonder if the sepulchre
Is not a lonesome way,
When men and boys, and larks and June
Go down the fields to hay!

533 "Emily Dickinson's Poems." *Book News* 15 (October 1896), 56. Reprinted from an unlocated *Hartford Post*.

This will be a welcome book to those who appreciate the peculiar genius of this active intellectual spirit with its scintillating electric flashes of perception, its quaint expressions, and its deep understanding of things we call human. Many of the verses in this volume are brief, mere flashes they seem, done in a second of inspiration and probably never needing the alteration of a word. Only one or two of the pieces in this book have been printed before and the collection thus adds to our acquaintance with the gifted writer as well as increases our wonder at her prodigious accomplishment. Life, love, nature, and time and eternity are the headings under which the verses are grouped, and on almost every page the reader will find words which speak to his own experience, showing him values and purposes never before appreciated, it may be, and supplying, mayhap, some new encouragement, some new point of view. The following lines entitled "Disenchantment," are a good example of the peculiar charm in these lines of the young poet:

It dropped so low in my regard
    I heard it hit the ground,
And go to pieces on the stones
    At bottom of my mind;

Yet blamed the fate that fractured, less
    Than I reviled myself
For entertaining plated wares
    Upon my silver shelf.

534 *Boston Beacon,* ca. October 1896. Unlocated. For follow-up comment in the *Beacon,* see next entry.

The third series of *Poems* by Emily Dickinson, while perhaps not as a whole quite up to the unique standard of the two preceding collections from the same source, contains a great deal that is eminently individual, and should not be overlooked by those who seek for the distinctive flavor in literature. The poems are classified under the headings of "Life," "Love," "Nature," and "Time and Eternity," the first-named division being the more noteworthy, both in quality and scope. Here is a quaint example: —

SUPERIORITY TO FATE.

Superiority to fate
   Is difficult to learn
'T is not conferred by any,
   But possible to earn.

A pittance at a time,
   Until, to her surprise,
The soul with strict Economy,
   Subsists till Paradise.

A note of really profound import is forcibly struck in the following two stanzas; —

PARTING.

My life closed twice before its close,
   It yet remains to see
If immortality unveil
   A third event to me.

So huge, so hopeless to conceive,
   As these that twice befell.
Parting is all we know of heaven,
   And all we need of hell.

To discerning minds, the elusive element of humor which reveals itself now and then in the poems of Emily Dickinson constitutes one of their greatest charms. It appears with delicious shyness in these lines: —

To hang our head ostensibly
   And subsequent to find
That such was not the posture
   Of our immortal mind,

Affords the sly presumption
   That, in so dense a fuzz,
You, too, take cobweb attitudes
   Upon a plane of gauze.

Miss Dickinson rarely falls into another's manner, but could Browning himself have bettered this? —

LOYALTY.

Split the lark and you'll find the music,
   Bulb after bulb, in silver rolled,
Scantily dealt to the summer morning,
   Saved for your ear when lutes be old.

Loose the flood, you shall find it patent,
   Gush after gush, reserved for you;
Scarlet experiment! sceptic Thomas,
   Now do you doubt that your bird is true?   [was true?

Miss Dickinson's poems may be caviar to the general reader, but they are certain to find and hold an audience susceptible to the attractions of an alert and unconventional personality expressing itself without pretence or strenuousness; and that audience may be accounted fit though few.

535 *Boston Beacon,* ca. October 1896. Unlocated. These sales figures, though less than earlier estimates (see no. 387, for example), have been confirmed by recent research (see Appendix D). Joel Myerson's study of Roberts Brothers' records suggests that by this date about 8,700 copies of *Poems* "First Series" had been issued, some 4,500 of the "Second Series" and another 1,000 volumes in which the two series were published together. Sales of the London edition of *Poems* "First Series" could not have exceeded 500 copies. [Roberts Brothers printed 2,500 copies of the *Letters.*] On the sales of Dickinson's volumes, see also Klaus Lubbers (*CR,* 237–38) and Virginia Terris (*GC,* 15–16).

The publishers of Emily Dickinson's "Poems," Messrs. Roberts Brothers, take exception to the *Beacon's* suggestion that Miss Dickinson's verse appeals to a limited, if highly intellectual audience. They think that a sale of 15,000 copies in ten years justifies a more optimistic view of the capacity of the American people for appreciating poetry of such unique quality, and undoubtedly they are right. Very few, if any, poets of late years on this side of the water can be credited with a like degree of popularity, and it is a pleasure, as well as a surprise, to be called upon to record a fact so creditable in every way to the public taste.

536 *Boston Times,* ca. October 1896. Unlocated.

Messrs. Roberts Brothers have published the third series of "Poems by Emily Dickinson," edited by Mabel Loomis Todd. In the preface the editor says that "the intellectual activity of Emily Dickinson was so great that a large and characteristic choice is still possible among her literary material."

Most of the poems show evidence that many of them were "simply spontaneous flashes of insight. The present volume is full of thoughts, needing no interpretation to those who apprehend this scintillating spirit."

There are some one hundred and sixty-five poems in the small volume; most of them are short, many of them only a few lines. For convenience the editor has divided them into different chapters or books, which she designates as "Life," "Love," "Nature," and "Time and Eternity."

The other volumes of the author's poems have made readers familiar with her work, and the present volume needs no praise and certainly no criticism. The publishers have given the book a dainty binding, with paper and letterpress all that could be desired.

537 "Poetry and Drama." *Literary News* 17 (October 1896), 310.

This third volume of Emily Dickinson's verses is put forth in response to the repeated wish of the admirers of her peculiar genius. It consists of poems often of four lines only on a page grouped under "Life," "Love," "Nature," and "Time and Eternity."

538 Talcott Williams. *Book News* 15 (October 1896), 42.

There is a curious New England idea that it is a fine thing to have queer thoughts, whereas in life and letters the simple is the profound. Of this New England idea, Miss Emily Dickinson is the final flower which never quite fruits in anything worth having. The third series of her poems has just appeared, and as the preface frankly says, "is put forth in response to the repeated wish of the admirers of her peculiar genius." Loved, read, and admired by many, it is still true that this is suspiration and not inspiration.

539 "Poetry." *Congregationalist* 81 (October 1, 1896), 488. Reprinted in an unlocated *Light* [Worcester, Mass.].

Mrs. Todd has edited a third selection from the *Poems by Emily Dickinson*. It would be easy by selection of single lines and couplets—as in the other volumes—to show that Miss Dickinson was utterly devoid of the poetic faculty, or that she had remarkable gifts of insight and expression. Some of these orphic sayings are as tantalizing and provoking as the music of a deaf man, who plays a few strong chords and then lets his hand crash carelessly down upon the keys. There is a keen sense of satirical humor, and occasionally the unconventional use of words hits the center like a ball from a rifle. Read this on Disenchantment, and see how little like the ordinary mood was that of this girl:

> It dropped so low in my regard
> I heard it hit the ground,
> And go to pieces on the stones
> At bottom of my mind;
>
> Yet blamed the fate that fractured less
> Than I reviled myself,
> For entertaining plated wares
> Upon my silver shelf.

And, for imagination, read this:

> To make a prairie it takes a clover and one bee—
> One clover, and a bee,
> And revery.
> The revery alone will do
> If bees are few.

Allowing, as we must, that form is a large part of poetry, we cannot agree that most of this is poetry at all, but it is highly poetical here and there. We wish the editor had suppressed a large share of it, which will add nothing to the author's reputation. Nothing more inappropriate as a symbol of Miss Dickinson's original and self-reliant thought could have been selected than the leafless parasitic flower on the cover.

540 "Books and Authors." *Boston Home Journal*, n.s. 10 (October 3, 1896), 12.

Another volume of "POEMS BY EMILY DICKINSON"—the third series—has just been published, edited by Mabel Loomis Todd. The case of Emily Dickinson is a remarkable one in the fact that great fame came to her after her death, whereas in her life she was scarcely known beyond her circle of intimate friends. But that was owing to the fact that while she was a voluminous writer she very rarely allowed a poem to get into print, even in the columns of a newspaper. But the discoveries made after her death showed that she was indeed a worshipper of the Muses, and that her short life had been one happy season of song because her heart must express itself in verse. When the first book of her poems was published it immediately sprang into unexampled popularity, capturing reader and critic; and when her second series was issued a year after, its success proved that Emily

Dickinson's posthumous fame had a solid foundation. It is only necessary for us to say that this third series will share fully in the popularity of its two predecessors. The editor says: "The intellectual activity of Emily Dickinson was so great that a large and characteristic choice is still possible among her literary material, and this third volume of her verses is put forth in response to the repeated wish of the admirers of her peculiar genius."

541 "Emily Dickinson Again." *Chicago Tribune,* October 3, 1896, p. 10. "And if I do, when morning comes," from "I have a king who does not speak," is reprinted with the omission of the stanza's fourth line, "And shouts fill all my childish sky, . . ." The "Third Series" published "I felt a funeral in my brain" without its fifth stanza.

One is rather favorably disappointed, upon the whole, with this third bunch of cullings from the literary flotsam of Emily Dickinson's life. That it is a modestly meager collection speaks well for the editor. Though there are many marks of incompleteness—in fact, some of the brightest bits are chips—yet nothing has been admitted to these pages which does not contain a worthy poetic thought.

From the shortcomings of this third collection it is more than ever apparent that Emily Dickinson's strength was her great intellect rather than her heart—her wealth of strikingly poetic concepts rather than her power to express them. To this fact we owe it that even some of these most incomplete fragments are yet worthy to live in the distinguished company of the author's more finished work.

Emily Dickinson's muse was of the cloistered, contemplative sort. No joyous touch of the light pleasures or follies of life is here, and the poorest verses are those that come nearest attempting it. Nor are the poems on love in this volume at all remarkable. It is only when Miss Dickinson approaches the deep things of life, of death, or, of immortality that she is at her best. But what a diapason then!

> And if I do, when morning comes,
> It is as if a hundred drums
>   Did round my pillow roll
> And bells keep saying, "Victory,"
>   From steeples in my soul.

As with George Meredith, Miss Dickinson's thoughts constantly seem too large for the form into which she crowds them. The result is often occult, but brilliant and epigrammatic when expression is adequate to the thought. One might quote a score of couplets like these:

> Parting is all we know of heaven
> And all we need of hell.

*   *   *   *   *

> You cannot fold a flood
> And put it in a drawer.

*   *   *   *   *

> A snake is summer's treason,
> And guile is where it goes.

*   *   *   *   *

A flower's unobtrusive face
To punctuate the wall.

How could disenchantment be more powerfully portrayed in four lines than in these despite their lack of rhyme:

It dropped so low in my regard
　I heard it hit the ground,
And go to pieces on the stones
　At bottom of my mind.

What poet has ever put the following thought into a richer cameo?

We never know we go—when we are going
　We jest and shut the door:
Fate following behind us bolts it
　And we accost no more.

The two octets, "There is no frigate like a book" and "If recollecting were forgetting," which appeared in the volume of the author's letters, are wisely included in this collection. Among the strongest of the new pieces are "The Inevitable," "The Master," "Trying to Forget," "The Soul's Storm," and the strange poem on "Dying." In the same vein with the last named is this weird piece:

I felt a funeral in my brain,
　And mourners to and fro.
Kept treading, treading, till it seemed
　That sense was breaking through.

And when they all were seated
　A service like a drum,
Kept beating, beating, till I thought
　My mind was going numb.

And then I heard them lift a box,
　And creak across my soul
With those same boots of lead again.
　Then space began to toll.

And all the heavens were a bell.   [As all
　And being but an ear,
And I and silence some strange race.
　Wrecked, solitary here.

Emily Dickinson wrought with the somber things of life, but she was not morbid. Her marble was cold, but even the Parian chips of it bear traces of Greek lines of beauty.

542　"Literary Topics." *Worcester* [Mass.] *Spy*, October 4, 1896, p. 14.

The third series of "Poems of Emily Dickinson," edited by Mabel Loomis Todd, is quite on a par with previous volumes in literary merit. Some of the poems are very beautiful. All are gem-like, and full of fine thought and imagery which is more evident in their abbreviated and sparkling style.

543　[Thomas Wentworth Higginson.] "Recent Poetry." *Nation* 63 (October 8, 1896), 275. Reprinted; see next entry. Partially reprinted: *Literary News*

17 (December 1896), 373. The poem identified as that on p. 200, is "On this wondrous sea."

The junior editor of Emily Dickinson's poems (Mrs. Mabel Loomis Todd) has been induced by the popular interest in previous series to select still a third volume, this being facilitated by the discovery of an unexpected deposit. The curious fame of this author is something unique in literature, being wholly posthumous and achieved without puffing or special effort, and indeed, quite contrary to the expectation of both editors and publishers. No volumes of American poetry, not even the most popular of Longfellow's, have had so wide or so steady a sale. On the other hand, the books met with nothing but vehement hostility and derision on the part of leading English critics, and the sale of the first volume, when reprinted there, did not justify the issue of a second. The sole expressed objection to them, in the English mind, lay in their defects or irregularities of manner; and yet these were not nearly so defiant as those exhibited by Whitman, who has always been more unequivocally accepted in England than at home. There is, however, ample evidence that to a minority, at least, of English readers, Emily Dickinson is very dear. Some consideration is also due to the peculiarly American quality of the landscape, the birds, the flowers, she delineates. What does an Englishman know of the bobolink, the whippoorwill, the Baltimore oriole, even of the American robin or blue-jay? These have hardly been recognized as legitimate stock properties in poetry, either on the part of the London press or that portion of the American which calls itself "cosmopolitan." To use them is still regarded, as when Emerson and Lowell were censured for their use, "a foolish affectation of the familiar." Why not stick to the conventional skylark and nightingale? Yet, as a matter of fact, if we may again draw upon Don Quixote's discourse to the poet, it is better that a Spaniard should write as a Spaniard and a Dutchman as a Dutchman. If Emily Dickinson wishes to say, in her description of a spirit, "'Tis whiter than an Indian pipe" (p. 156), let her say it, although no person born out of her own land may ever have seen that wondrous ghost of a flower (*Monotropa uniflora*, or Indian pipe) which appears on the cover of her volumes, but unhappily in a blaze of gliding that makes it meaningless. Perhaps, in the end, the poet who is truest to his own country may best reach all others. An eminent American librarian, lately visiting England, made it a practice to inquire in the country bookstores what American poet was most in demand with their customers, and was amazed at the discovery that it was usually Whittier.

It is needless to say that Miss Dickinson's poetry achieves its success, in spite of all its flagrant literary faults, by what Ruskin describes as "the perfection and precision of the instantaneous line." She is to be tested, not by her attitude, but by her shot. Does she hit the mark? As a rule she does. Is it a question what a book represents to a human being? This is her answer—only eight lines, but they tell the story (p. 29):

A BOOK.

There is no frigate like a book
    To take us leagues away,
Nor any coursers like a page
    Of prancing poetry.
This traverse may the poorest take
    Without oppress of toll;
How frugal is the chariot
    That bears a human soul!

Again, how many a heart has been vaguely touched in some old and neglected country cemetery by the thought so tersely uttered here (p. 157):

THE MONUMENT.

She laid her docile crescent down,
    And this mechanic stone
Still states, to dates that have forgot,
    The news that she is gone.

So constant to its stolid trust,
    The shaft that never knew.
It shames the constancy that fled
    Before its emblem flew.

The "docile crescent" may be supposed to imply that the life commemorated was immature, and ended while yet expanding.

It is known that Miss Dickinson very rarely gave a title to her poems, and it is to be presumed that in this volume, as in the others, these are supplied by the editor. The fourfold division, "Life," "Love," "Nature," "Time and Eternity," is that preserved in the earlier volumes, and the tolerably equal distribution of the poems into the four departments suggests that this strange, secluded life, seemingly wayward, had in reality a method and balance of its own. It is noticeable, also, that in a few of the poems (as on pp. 79, 200) there is an unexampled regularity of form, beyond anything to be found in the earlier volumes, and perhaps hinting at a growing tendency in her mind. This "Song," for instance (p. 79), surprises the reader, trained to the Dickinsonian muse, with an almost startling commonplaceness of melody. It was apparently sent with a flower:

SONG.

Summer for thee grant I may be
    When summer days are flown!
Thy music still when whippoorwill
    And oriole are done!

For thee to bloom, I'll skip the tomb
    And sow my blossoms o'er;
Pray gather me, Anemone,
    Thy flower forevermore.

544 [Thomas Wentworth Higginson.] "Recent Poetry." *New York Evening Post*, October 10, 1896, p. 14. A reprinting; see preceding entry.

545 "Emily Dickinson's Poems." *New York Commercial Advertiser*, October 10, 1896, p. 14.

Miss Dickinson's work is curious and difficult to class.
If there be such a thing as genius without talent, this she had.
Her work is an improvisation; it is, though not void, without form; it has no comeliness to be desired; it is freighted with thought—sincere, but not original thought; it has every mark of haste, incomplete knowledge of the language, lack of rhythm, and it is sown thick with impossible, distressing rhymes. In fact, Miss Dickinson never learned the fingering of her instrument, as pianists say. She was mastered by words and sounds. She did not know the technique of verse. She never realized that poetry is an art, which must be studied. She is like one who

says "I will compose a symphony," and does not know the elements of music. And so her work has the effect of an earnest, sincere and touching letter written by one who does not know how to spell.

Miss Dickinson had no ear for verse.

Words made no music for her.

Mary Loomis Todd, the editrix of this volume says in her preface: "Much of Emily Dickinson's prose was rhythmic—even rhymed, though frequently not set apart in lines." Between these lines one may find the acknowledgment that Miss Dickinson was not only unfamiliar with the verbal instruments of verse and prose, but that she confused the two—as Dickens occasionally did to his undoing. English prose is an exquisite and perfected instrument. But it must be studied. And in like manner it may be said that the poet who fails to understand that English verse is an art, exquisite and elaborate, fails at the outset.

In reading Miss Dickinson's quatrains one must accept "skies" as an adequate rhyme for "sciences," "enough" and "life" must pair in kindred sound; "begin" and "pain" must be sib in sound. Granting all this and much more, one may find a pleasure in reading these improvised quatrains on life, love, destiny and other topics in which Miss Dickinson was interested. At times her thought—being an improvisation—is cryptic in a degree, and her metaphors, being unforseen are irreconcilable. Here is a typical verse:

> Finite to fail, but infinite to venture,
>   For the one ship that struts the shore
> Many's the gallant, overwhelmed creature
>   Nodding in navies evermore.

Surely this is but undigested thought, not worth poring over. Again, these stanzas called "Saturday Afternoon":

> From all the jails the boys and girls
>   Ecstatically leap—
> Beloved, only afternoon
>   That prison doesn't keep.
>
> They storm the earth and stun the air,
>   A mob of solid bliss.
> Alas! that frowns could lie in wait
>   For such a foe as this.

Merely because this is dark it is not, therefore, sublime. Because a plain matter is put in obscure words it is not, therefore, poetry. What is difficult to understand displays a lack of art in writing. Here, for instance:

> To hang our head ostensibly
>   And subsequent to find
> That such was not the posture
>   Of our immortal mind
>
> Affords the sly presumption
>   That, in so dense a fuzz
> You, too, take cobweb attitudes
>   Upon a plane of gauze.

There is much more of this verse; some of it even woefuller. Her "Farewell to Life," the most conspicuous poem in the book, is an example both of her defects and that note of sincerity, which lends some charm to her work. It reads:

Tie the strings to my life, O Lord,   [my Lord,
   Then I am ready to go!
Just a look at the horses—
   Rapid! That will do!

Put me on the firmest side,   [in on
   So I shall never fall;
For we must ride to the Judgment,
   And its partly down hill.

But I never mind the bridges   [never I
   And I never mind the sea;   [never I
Held fast in everlasting race
   By my own choice and me.   [and thee.

Goodby to the life I used to live
   And the world I used to know;
And kiss the hills for me, just once;
   Now, I am ready to go.

In many ways Miss Dickinson reminds the verse-reader of Adah Isaacs Menken. She has the same turbulent rush of half-formed thoughts, the same inability to express them in terms of poetry.

She was a genius—who failed because she did not have talent.

546 "Short Notes of New Books." *San Francisco Chronicle*, October 11, 1896, p. 4.

A third volume of "Poems by Emily Dickinson" has just been issued. The most of the poetic screeds are from four to eight lines each in length, and all of them embrace some single fancy more or less quaint. The central thought of most of them is pleasing, but few are either profound or highly poetic. The collection is edited by Mabel Loomis Todd, who claims that she is not responsible for structural defects, as it was deemed advisable to print the dead woman's poems without amendment.

547 *Stationer* (N.Y.), October 15, 1896. Unlocated. Mrs. Todd's scrapbook identification of this item, as cited, is puzzling since standard directories do not list a periodical by this title. The New York *American-Stationer* was searched without result. There were 59 separately numbered poems in "Time and Eternity," the final section of *Poems*, Third Series, but 166 in the volume overall.

Poems by Emily Dickinson—Third Series are edited by Mabel Loomis Todd, who says in her preface: "The intellectual activity of Emily Dickinson was so great that a large and characteristic choice is still possible among her literary material. . . . The surroundings in which any of Emily Dickinson's verses are known to have been written usually serve to explain them clearly; but in general the present volume is full of thoughts needing no interpretation to those who apprehend this scintillating spirit." The sixty poems in the volume are classified into four "books," which the editor has named respectively Life, Love, Nature, and Time and Eternity.

548 "Briefer Notice." *Public Opinion* 21 (October 22, 1896), 537. Mrs. Todd's scrapbook citation indicates that this notice also appeared in an unidentified issue of the *Boston Budget*.

Very brief lyrics (the average containing only two or three short four-line stanzas), musically flowing, but with not infrequent bad rhymes—the thoughts, for the most part, not so remarkable for depth or originality or weight as for a certain happiness, piquancy, and at times brilliancy of expression—such are these latest gleaned kernels from Emily Dickinson's threshing-floor. In all the four groups or divisions of the volume—"Life," "Love," "Nature," "Time and Eternity"—there are not a few subtle and truly beautiful touches and turns of expression. Few lovers of dainty (and yet sometimes profoundly illuminating) conceits could turn these fair, large-spaced pages without chancing here and there upon some bit of thought or fancy that must give them pause, and pleasure.

549 "Literary Notes." *Brooklyn Standard-Union*, October 24, 1896, p. 5.

"Poems by Emily Dickinson," third series, edited by Mabel Loomis Todd, is published by Roberts Brothers, Boston. There are about 160 poems in all, and many of them are very sweet. The book is beautifully bound.

550 "Literature." *Independent* 48 (October 29, 1896), 1463.

Say what the critic will against the literary defects so grievously obvious in these poems, there can be no escape from the fascination of Miss Dickinson's strange genius. Poetry is not to be measured by any man's thumb; its superficies may defy every critical gauge, while its contents outshine the queen's jewels. Emily Dickinson was a poet whose limitations of thought and whose constricted organ of expression intensified to a singular degree the peculiarities of her intellectual and emotional conceits. Her verses have the form and effect of brilliant aberrations; they tantalize, they annoy, they surprise and they delight us.

551 "The Third Series of Emily Dickinson's Poems." *Literary World* 27 (October 31, 1896), 361.

Emily Dickinson's especial literary niche is already settled, and the third series of her poems will do nothing to alter the judgment which has already been passed. Those who have cared for her poems will find the same qualities of attraction in this as in the two earlier volumes, and those who have disliked the first and second series will find the same elements of ridicule in the third.

In this volume, as in the two former ones, on one page is the utterance of a penetrating philosopher, and on the next a puerility beside which Mother Goose appears profound. A curious example of these contrasts is found on pages 160 and 161. On page 160 we find a really beautiful little quatrain on a grave:

> Where every bird is bold to go,
>   And bees abashless play,
> The foreigner before he knocks
>   Must thrust the tears away.

On the opposite page, on the same subject, we read the following solemn nonsense:

The grave my little cottage is,
  Where, keeping house for thee,
I make my parlor orderly,
  And lay the marble tea

For two divided briefly,
  A cycle, it may be,
Till everlasting life unite
  In strong society.

Miss Todd has arranged her selection of Miss Dickinson's poems under four heads—Life, Love, Nature, Time and Eternity. The first and the last headings are far the best, and Nature is the poorest.

Some of Miss Dickinson's best and many of her poorest poems are included in this series. Her grim humor is her most endearing quality, and few specimens in her earlier volumes equaled a little poem on "Remembrance:"

Remembrance has a rear and front—
  'Tis something like a house;
It has a garret, also,
  For refuse and the mouse,
Besides the deepest cellar
  That ever mason hewed:
Look to it, by its fathoms
  Ourselves be not pursued.

There is also a Voltaire's sneer in the poem on "Drowning," which ends:

The Maker's cordial visage,
  However good to see,
Is shunned, we must admit it,
  Like an adversity.

As an example of a more genial mood, we like especially "A Book:"

There is no frigate like a book
  To take us lands away,
Nor any coursers like a page
  Of prancing poetry.
This traverse may the poorest take
  Without oppress of toll;
How frugal is the chariot
  That bears a human soul.

For pathos we cannot recall any of Miss Dickinson's poems which surpassed "Parting:"

My life closed twice before its close;
  It yet remains to see
If Immortality unveil
  A third event to me,
So huge, so hopeless to conceive,
  As these that twice befell.
Parting is all we know of heaven,
  And all we need of hell.

These are of Miss Dickinson's best work, but when we come to such lines as,

> Morning is the place for dew,
>   Corn is made at noon,
> After-dinner light for flowers,
>   Dukes for setting sun,

we feel ready to join the scoffers. Ridiculous as the poem just quoted is, there is another yet more absurd and incomprehensible:

> The dying need but little, dear—
>   A glass of water's all,
> A flower's unobtrusive face
>   To punctuate the wall.
> A face, perhaps, a friend's regret,   [A fan,
>   And certainly that one
> No color in the rainbow
>   Perceives that you are gone.

What the last four lines mean we should like to ask the "Society of Psychical Research;" we feel sure that nobody else could explain them.

We recommend this book only to those who have liked its predecessors.

552 *Church* 2 (November 1896), 44. This reviewer, like an earlier one (no. 547), mistakes the number of poems in the book's final section ("Time and Eternity") for that of the entire volume.

A third series of fifty-nine characteristic flashes of verse by Emily Dickinson serves to intensify the impression of inexhaustible supply, which is a part of the charm. Possessing a certain flavor of studied effect, they are yet known to be spontaneous outbursts. Carrying an air of coquetry, they are yet discovered to be artlessness itself. What is at first taken to be quaintness is seen to be only obviousness, and the surprising turn is in reality the commonplace sequence. The only reason why everybody is not "queer" is because you do not know him. No one contends that Emily Dickinson should have a very high place on Parnassus, but many readers of verse are glad to listen to just her way of saying things, and to overlook a certain vexing of their critical sensibilities, for the sake of the charm of indirect directness that pervades the verses. The verses at their best have also an indefinable charm of will-o' the wisp-ness, leading you to feel that the poet is just about to reach a higher height of solid greatness, and will attain next time, and making it impossible for you not to turn the page to see.

553 [Rupert Hughes.] Chelifer (pseud.). "The Ideas of Emily Dickinson." *Godey's Magazine* 133 (November 1896), 541–43. This essay reviews the letters and all three editions of the poems.

Form is the etiquette of art. There is, of course, a quality of form dictated entirely by aesthetic considerations of symmetry, of antistrophe and contrast. But herein is much room for individuality. When I insist, however, that the iron conventions I have grown fond of through bias and custom shall be the Procrustes' bed of your inspiration, and you comply with my outrageous insolence and satrapy, then Form degenerates into bald ceremonial. Some artists are fitted more for court than for the fields, indeed; but not all.

As of everything else in this inabsolute world, there are amendments to the declaration of artistic independence. These, decency will insist on and accept. If you cage your muse in a sonnet, for instance, she should disport herself within its narrow walls and not use her ethereal powers to make excursions through the bars whenever she is cramped for space. If you will write a sonnet, why not write a real sonnet, and not bend it further than its considerable flexibility permits? If you are unwilling to write a real rondeau, why dub your hybrid a rondeau at all? Why not as well write five-lined things and proclaim them quatrains?

So much for the cage-birds that flourish best between the golden wires of form. But what of the larks that die there and only prosper in the loose, flinging themselves in transports at heaven? It is enough for the critic to pick flaws in the rule-compliance of those that subscribe to, and aim at, orthodoxy. But the outlaws, the Robins Goodfellow, must be permitted to go their ways. Your inability to enjoy anything but what conforms gladly to your own pet prejudices, only argues you narrow and in need of mental travel; it is no indictment at all of those whose love and need of liberty is beyond our comprehension. This is not artistic Anarchy, but artistic Democracy. You have been living in an Oriental despotism.

The appearance of a new volume of Emily Dickinson's poems recalls the struggle between the Conservatives and the Liberals at the advent of her first volume. The good Tories simply dismissed her as hopelessly out of the pale — or pail? — of propriety. "But note her ideas!" protested the Liberals. "Bosh! they are mere oddity at best, and utterly spoiled by bad rhymes, by incredible looseness of form! She is not worth serious consideration," and so they dismissed her — from their own minds only. The more fools they!

Form is a perennial delight, but it is not the only delight in art, and it is not the highest delight. The Idea is surely a weightier matter.

Of all fatuities the attempt to rank the great men of the world in exact order of precedence is the vainest. Yet the mind cannot keep from a certain general valuation of its favorites. Every author loses vastly by translation of course, but if he has much of anything at bottom of his exquisite personal magnetism that something will transpire in a good translation. Now, if one could imagine a new language as flexible as the perfect fluid scientists imagine, and if all the aristocracy of literature were translated literally into this new language, the loss to each author being practically the same, it could be left out of account. Then the world's writers would stand before the critic indeed, divested of charms that are stale in their own language but beautiful and new to a foreigner; divested of little tricks of speech of much charm and more trickery; divested of the favoritism of partisanship, of provincialism, of traditional acceptance, of personal character, of many incrustations that make a fundamental comparative criticism almost impossible. Now we should see who had the ideas and who only borrowed them and disguised them into a show of originality; and who had misused them with deceiving art. Under this fierce search-light many a literary idol would grow garish. Such a test would be unfair to those whose happiness in presentation amounts to genius and delights the world. But it would set apart the thinkers from the — not the goats exactly, but something less noble than the thinkers. For to be a thinker is a great thing as well as a courageous.

In this universal translation the charms of form would be quite cancelled, except, possibly, the logical thought-form of the Hebrews. But the worth of ideas would be enhanced beyond the hurt of the scoffing formalist.

In such a test Emily Dickinson would lose little. The startling originality and the captivating individuality of her ideas would set her high among the great thinkers of the world. She did not co-ordinate her thoughts into a philosophy, but she struck out thoughts in a shower of sparks. And ideas are the hard things to get.

She and Walt Whitman and Poe are this nation's most original contributions to the world's poetry. Poe was typical only of Poe. But Emily Dickinson and Whitman, with their unbending comradery with God and humanity, are our best realizations of the distinctively American spirit. Emily Dickinson seems never to have known Walt Whitman's work (the only reference in her letters being this: "I never read his book, but was told that it was disgraceful."!); yet the two poets are closely related in many ways, and she would doubtless have been an ardent admirer of his, had New-England prudery not warned her against considering him.

Among poetesses I should, without timidity, place her above Mrs. Browning, and therefore above all the other poetesses we know: of Sappho we have too little besides her fame. Though Emily Dickinson is a grievous sinner against rhyme and metre there is such a rush and fire to her measures that she is really more lyrical than the sedater Mrs. Browning. It is the gushing outburst of an improvisatory bird, careless of Richterian theories of eight measures to the period, careless of everything but of voicing itself just as it feels.

Her indifference to correct rhyme is a sore trial to the reader at first, but afterward it takes on a positive charm. Its independence is so breezy, almost reckless. Then, too, the suggestion—the "thought-rime," it has been called—soon grows even pleasant to the ear. Examples of her misrhymes, like "grave-love, sound-bond, time-lamb, noon-stone, near-hair, lawn-down, rooms-names," and harder ones like, "morn-again, renown-spurn, death-earth," are not so jarring in the context and under the predominating spell of the idea as when set apart. Her rhymes are like the recurrence to the sea of a swallow that dips again and again in its flight, but swoops only to the spray of the waves and does not quite touch them. Besides there are many lyrics that are technically quite flawless (v. Series I., pp. 110, 17, 18, 25, 27, 37–43 *et passim*). [See editor's note, below.] Others have only one or two false rhymes like this (which is typical of her in many ways, her courage, her grammatic looseness, her quaintness, her homeliness, the depth of her sympathies):

'TROUBLED ABOUT MANY THINGS.'

How many times these low feet staggered,
   Only the soldered mouth can tell;
Try! can you stir the awful rivet?
   Try! can you lift the hasps of steel?

Stroke the cool forehead, hot so often,
   Lift, if you can, the listless hair;
Handle the adamantine fingers
   Never a thimble more shall wear.

Buzz the dull flies on the chamber windows;
   Brave shines the sun through the freckled pane;
Fearless the cobweb swings from the ceiling—
   Indolent housewife in daisies lain!

Her letters show her to have been fond of Browning, and his influence is patent in much of her work; in the intimate conversational and ejaculatory tone; the unwillingness to polish overmuch; the suggestive effect of pointing out, with an exclamation or a query, some vista for the reader to explore for himself. Like

Browning she is equally unafraid of short, sharp words and of polysyllabic monsters. Her niceness with words of Latin origin is remarkable.

Very striking is the audacious homeliness of many of her tropes, homeliness being an apt word because they bring the idea home. In many of these she is very modern, sometimes even scientific.

Dogmatic Dr. Johnson objected to a poet speaking of grass as a "carpet," saying that Nature should be used to dignify common life, while every day figures for Nature robbed her of dignity. This is based not only on a false idea of dignity, but of poetry also, as the artist is more concerned in suggesting his visions vividly than in making them lofty. The right poet is he that finds and proves everyday life beautiful, poetical; rather than he whose Pegasus is a pair of stilts. But to many eyes distance alone lends poetry to anything, and for these Emily Dickinson has much that is torment — this for instance:

> Like trains of cars on tracks of plush,
> I hear the level bee.

They will not see through false rhyme and plain metaphor and loose grammar the utter nobility of such verse as this:

> The bustle in a house
> The morning after death
> Is solemnest of industries
> Enacted upon earth —
>
> The sweeping up the heart,
> And putting love away
> We shall not want to use again
> Until eternity.

But even these orthodox worthies will find much that is irresistible; delicious quibbles and conceits and frenzies that will take on authority if one will only call them Elizabethan. Who could resist such characteristic hilarity in Nature as this?

> Inebriate of air am I,
> And debauchee of dew.
> Reeling, through endless summer days,
> From inns of molten blue.
>
> When landlords turn the drunken bee
> Out of the foxglove's door,
> When butterflies renounce their drams,
> I shall but drink the more!
>
> Till seraphs swing their snowy hats,
> And saints to windows run,
> To see the little tippler
> Leaning against the sun!

Indeed her attitude to Nature is almost unique. She was truly a part of it, a madcap elf in real life. The sole-fire that women like Sappho and Mrs. Browning spent chiefly on personal love, she turned full upon Nature and private matters of Life and Death. She wrote only about five bits of verse before her thirty-second year, and seems never to have had a real love-affair. She accepted only a few friends, and the shyness that kept her from allowing her verse to be published increased with the years. Her life had the obscurity, if not the hard poverty, of the recently discovered "German Sappho," Johanna Ambrosius, than who she is a far more original thinker. Her poems were as a rule hardly more than fleeting words scribbled down hastily and just as her quaint whims came.

The oddity of these whims goes deeper than amusing affectation; the vividness of some of them is simply dumfounding. Thus speaking of the quick coming and going of the mushroom, "the elf of plants," she calls it "the germ of alibi!" She speaks of that "best disgrace a brave man feels, acknowledged of the brave," as "a shame of nobleness" and "a finer shame of ecstasy Convicted of itself." But to quote these new things that are such true things so keenly caught and fixed, would be to reprint almost her whole works.

Her "Letters" make up her only prose contribution to posterity. In them were contained many of her best verses written on the spur of the correspondence. They are packed with the same startling ideas, the same endless enthusiasms. The moon "rides like a girl through a topaz town." Salvini's picture brings this: "The brow is that of Deity—the eyes, those of the lost, but the power lies in the throat—pleading, sovereign, savage—the panther and the dove! Each, how innocent!"

Her letters are hilariously happy at times and they abound in oddities like:

> Peter put up the sunshine,
>   Pattie arrange the stars,
> Tell Luna tea is waiting,
>   And call your brother Mars.

and there are gems of more weight like:

> Though my destiny be fustian,
>   Hers be damask fine—
> Though she wear a silver apron,
>   I, a less divine;
>
> Still, my little gypsy being,
>   I would far prefer.
> Still my little sunburnt bosom,
>   To her rosier.

Her outlook upon Death (and Walt Whitman's also) is so calm, so nonchalant; her pride so near Yankee brag; her seriousness so close to Yankee humor; so fond of every-day things, in short, so bigly democratic, that I feel in the poetry of both of them something markedly American, something majestic that belongs especially over here in our United States. Than these two poets no poet has ever written noblier of death. Than Whitman no one has loved the sea and night better. Than Emily Dickinson no poet has written better of the fields and noon.

The womanliness of her verse, the femininity, even the housewifeliness of much of it is notable. Through it all runs an archness of humor and a rapture in life, in simple things, in the nobility of death. She is the supreme lyrist of every-day life. She surely is, or must become, literature.

[Editor's note. Poems cited in this essay only by page number are as follows: p. 110, "Delayed till she had ceased to know"; p. 17 "Glee! the great storm is over"; p. 18, "If I can stop one heart from breaking"; p. 25, "I asked no other thing"; p. 27, "Some things that fly there be"; p. 37, "'Twas such a little, little boat"; p. 38, "Whether my bark went down at sea"; p. 39, "Belshazzar had a letter"; p. 40, "The brain within its groove"; pp. 41–42, blank pages; p. 43, "Mine by the right of royal election."

554 Norman Hapgood. "New York Letter." *Author* [London] 7:6 (November 2, 1896), 123.

Still another volume of Emily Dickenson's [sic] poems is just out, by Roberts Brothers, resulting from a new discovery of posthumous poems. The demand is steadier and larger for these poems than for those of any other American, even Longfellow. As was especially emphasized by the English critics, her form is most remarkable for its defects, and probably it would be hard for a foreigner to see how much delicate local flavour there is both in her abstract thought, which has the essence of New Englandism in it, and in her descriptions and allusions.

555 "Tatlings." *Daily Tatler* I (November II, 1896), 5.

Of course Miss Emily Dickinson's poems are old-fashioned. They have an early put-away-in-lavender effect, which is their greatest charm. Even now the great, quaintly furnished rooms of the Dickinson homestead and the methodical, well-behaved garden are a most appropriate setting to her memory; and her sister, Miss Lavinia Dickinson, devotes her life to keeping the memory and the garden green. One of the poems in the third series, however, is distinctly modern in conception and style:

> To make a prairie it takes a clover,
> And one bee, —
> One clover, and a bee,
> And revery,
> The revery alone will do
> If bees are few.

556 "For Lovers of Poetry. Poems by Emily Dickinson." *Golden Rule* n.s. II (November 19, 1896), 160.

From the papers left behind her by this strange, flame-spirited hermit of a woman, a third series of her remarkable poems has been made up. They are all very short, but full of matter. What a picture is this: —

> How still the bells in steeples stand
>   Till, swollen with the sky,
> They leap upon their silver feet
>   In frantic melody!

And what brave philosophy in this characteristic bit called "Disenchantment": —

> It dropped so low in my regard
>   I heard it hit the ground,
> And go to pieces on the stones
>   At bottom of my mind;
>
> Yet blamed the fate that fractured less
>   Than I reviled myself

> For entertaining plated wares
> Upon my silver shelf.

These poems vibrate in every line with thought and feeling, like heart-beats felt through the darkness.

557 Bliss Carman. "A Note on Emily Dickinson." *Boston Evening Transcript*, November 21, 1896, p. 15. Himself a poet in revolt against the vitiated academic verse of his time, Carman here offers a revaluation of Dickinson that is sympathetic to her irregularities. The New York journal in whose editorial rooms he first heard of her was the *Independent* — its managing editor William Hayes Ward (see the latter's review of the 1890 *Poems*, no. 44). Carman's allusion to the University Press printing order for Dickinson's first volume seems to derive from the *Bookman* note, no. 506.

Pending the coming in of [Kipling's] "The Seven Seas," it is safe to say that the publication of a new volume of poems by Emily Dickinson is the literary event of the season. Six years ago when her first book was given to the public, it ran through several editions, achieving a larger sale, I believe, than any other first volume ever printed at the University Press, and that is saying a good deal, when one recalls the distinguished works that have issued from that excellent printing shop. Its author's name was entirely unknown, and she herself already passed beyond the confusion of renown; yet so distinctive was her note, so spiritual and intense and absolutely sincere, that she sprang at once into a posthumous fame, unadulterated and almost splendid. It was one more tribute to the New England ideal, the American interest in mortality, the bent for transcendentalism inherited from Emerson; and, by the way, it was at the same time another evidence of the alertness of the American reading public, and its sensitiveness to excellent originality. For while there was novelty in the verse of Emily Dickinson, there was nothing sensational, hardly anything strange; no peculiarity on which a cult could batten. Those who admired her verse must admire it for its poetry alone.

I have just said that there is nothing sensational in Emily Dickinson's poetry; and yet there was, in a small way, a genuine sensation in the editorial rooms of one of the oldest journals in New York when our chief, with that tireless and impetuous enthusiasm of his, came rushing in with his bright discovery — like a whirl of October leaves. He is one of the two American editors who have the superfluous faculty of knowing poetry when they see it; he had fallen upon the immortal maid's first book, and the slumbering poet in him was awake. Nothing would suffice but we must share his youthful elation, listen to the strains of this original and accredited singer. The heat of New York, the routine of an office, the jaded mind of a reviewer, the vitiated habit of the professional manuscript-taster — it was not easy to shake off these at once; we were somewhat cold, perhaps, and a little skeptical of the chief's discovery. Still, we must listen. Hear this —

> Belshazzar had a letter —
> He never had but one;
> Belshazzar's correspondent
> Concluded and begun
> In that immortal copy
> The conscience of us all

Can read without its glasses
On revelation's wall.

Why, yes, certainly that is original enough. But can your wonderful prodigy turn off another verse like it?
"Can she? To be sure! Listen again!"

I taste a liquor never brewed,
    From tankards scooped in pearl;
Not all the vats upon the Rhine
    Yield such an alcohol!

Inebriate of air am I,
    And debauchee of dew,
Reeling, through endless summer days,
    From inns of molten blue.

When landlords turn the drunken bee
    Out of the foxglove's door,
When butterflies renounce their drams,
    I shall but drink the more!

Till seraphs swing their snowy hats,
    And saints to windows run,
To see the little tippler
    Leaning against the sun.

Well, we are convinced, indeed. There can be no doubt of the genuineness of this writer. Such work is fresh from the mint; not immediately current without some scrutiny; yet stamped plainly enough with the hall-mark of genius. We could but give unqualified assent; put the new book on the old shelf at once, with its peers, the acknowledged classics of American literature.

Following this first venture, there has been a second collection of poems, two volumes of letters and now this third book of verse. And allowing one's judgment time to cool, I must say the conviction remains that Emily Dickinson's contribution to English poetry (or American poetry, if you prefer to say so) is by far the most important made by any woman west of the Atlantic. It is so by reason of its thought, its piquancy, its untarnished expression. She borrowed from no one; she was never commonplace; always imaginative and stimulating; and finally, the region of her brooding was that sequestered domain where our profoundest convictions have origin, and whence we trace the Puritan strain within us.

For this New England woman was a type of her race. A life-long recluse, musing on the mysteries of life and death, she yet had that stability of character, that strong sanity of mind, which could hold out against the perils of seclusion, unshaken by solitude, undethroned by doubt. The very fibre of New England must have been there, founded of granite, nourished by an exhilarating air. We are permitted, through Colonel Higginson's introduction to the first series of poems, the merest glimpse into the story of her life in that beautiful college town in the lovely valley of the Connecticut. We imagine her in the old-fashioned house with its stately decency, its air of breeding and reserve, set a little back from the street, ambushed behind a generous hedge, and flanked by an ample garden on the side — a garden full of roses and tall elms and the scent of new-mown hay. There among her own, she chose an unaustere and voluntary monasticism for her daily course, far indeed removed from the average life of our towns, yet not so untypical of that strain of Puritan blood which besets us all. It would never, I feel sure, occur to anyone with the least insight into the New England character, or the remotest inheritance of the New England conscience (with its capacity for abstemiousness, its instinct for being always aloof and restrained, rather than social and blithe), to think of Emily Dickinson as peculiar, or her mode of life as queer. Somewhat strange as the record of it may show to foreign eyes, it was natural enough in its own time and place, though sufficiently unusual to claim something of distinction even of itself. Illumined and revealed in her poems, the life and character of this original nature make a fit study for the subtlest criticism — such a criticism, indeed, as I know not where they will receive. And all the while, as we speak of Emily Dickinson's secluded life, and her individual habit of isolation, her parsimony in friendship and human intercourse, I have a conviction that we should guard against the fancy that she was tinged with any shadow of sadness, or any touch of misanthropy or gloom. It seems rather that she must have had the sunniest of dispositions, as she certainly had the most sensitive and exquisite organization. It was not that the persons or affections of her fellows seemed to her superfluous or harsh or unnecessary, but rather that in one so finely organized as she must have been, the event of meeting another was too exquisite and portentous to be borne. For there are some natures so shy and quick, so undulled by the life of the senses, that they never quite acquire the easy part of the world. You will hear of them shunning the most delightful acquaintance, turning a corner sharply to avoid an encounter, hesitating at the very threshold of welcome, out of some dim inherited, instinctive dread of casual intercourse. They are like timorous elusive spirits, gone astray, perhaps, and landed on the rough planet Earth by a slight mischance; and when they are compelled by circumstance to share in the world's work, their part in it is likely to be an unhappy one. Theirs is the bent for solitude, the custom of silence. And once that fleeing sense of self-protection arises within them, the chances are they will indulge it to the end. And fortunate, indeed, it is, if that end be not disaster. But in Emily Dickinson's case, the stray health of genius came to the support of this hermit's instinct, and preserved her to the end of life sweet and blithe and contented in that innocent nun-like existence in which she chose to be immured. Her own room served her for native land, and in the painted garden beyond her windowsill was foreign travel enough for her. For that frugal soul, the universe of experience was bounded by the blue hills of a New England valley.

It was, of course, part of the inheritance of such a woman to have the religious sense strongly marked. She came of a race that never was at ease in Zion, yet never was content out of sight of the promised land. It best suited their strenuous and warlike nature always to be looking down on the delectable Canaan from the Pisgah of their own unworthiness. Yet, however severe a face life wore to them, and unlovely as their asperity often was, they were still making, though unwittingly, for the liberation of humanity. They were laying a substructure of honesty and seriousness, on which their intellectual inheritors might build, whether in art or politics. And their occupation with religion, with the affairs of the inward life and all its needs, has left an impress on ourselves, given us a trend from which we swerve in vain. And on every page of Emily Dickinson's poetry this ethical tendency, this awful environment of spirituality, is evident. Meditations of Psyche in the House of Clay; epigrams of an immortal guest, left behind on the chamber wall on the eve of silent departure, these brief lyrics seem:

> This world is not conclusion;
>   A sequel stands beyond,
> Invisible as music,
>   But positive as sound.

It beckons and it baffles;
    Philosophies don't know,
And through a riddle, at the last,
    Sagacity must go.

To guess it puzzles scholars;
    To gain it, men have shown
Contempt of generations,
    And crucifixion known.

That is an orphic utterance, no doubt; and such is all of this poet's work. She is, like Emerson, a companion for solitude, a stimulating comrade in the arduous intellectual ways. A symbolist of the symbolists, she is with them a reviver and establisher of the religious sentiment. Full of skepticism and the gentle irony of formal unbelief, putting aside the accepted and narrowing creed, she brings us, as Emerson did, face to face with new objects of worship. In their guidance we come a step nearer the great veil. For it is quite true that he who was hailed as a skeptic and destroyer in his early career, was in reality a prophet and a founder.

And it was inevitable, too, that one so much at home in spiritual matters should be deeply versed in nature—should be on intimate terms of friendship with all Nature's creatures.

Not that her knowledge of them was wide; it could hardly be that. But her sympathy with them was deep. She had ever a word of interpretation for the humblest of the mute dwellers in her garden world, clover or bee or blade. Often in these verses on the natural world there is a touch of whimsical humor that shows her character in very delightful color; as, for instance, in the lines on cobwebs:

The spider as an artist
    Has never been employed,
Though his surpassing merit
    Is freely certified

By every broom and Bridget
    Throughout a Christian land.
Neglected son of genius,
    I take thee by the hand.

There is a touch of intimacy, of fellowship, of kinship with all creation, which is so characteristic of modern poetry, and which is to become characteristic of modern religion. It is the tolerant, gay, debonair note of blameless joy which has been banished so long from the world, coming back to claim its own again. The same chord is struck, though struck much more richly and with added significance in Miss Gertrude Hall's poem "To a Weed."

Did I say that Emily Dickinson's contribution to poetry was more important than that of any other woman in America? Perhaps it is. Yet it has its faults, so hard a thing is perfection in any art, and so perfect the balance of fine qualities necessary to attain it. For while this poet was so eminent in wit, so keen in epigram, so rare and startling in phrase, the extended laborious architecture of an impressive poetic creation was beyond her. So that one has to keep her at hand as a stimulus and refreshment rather than as a solace. She must not be read long at a sitting. She will not bear that sort of treatment any more than Mr. Swinburne will; and for the very opposite reason. In Swinburne there is such a richness of sound, and often such a paucity of thought that one's even mental poise is sadly strained in trying to keep an equilibrium. He is like those garrulous persons, enamored of their own voice, who talk one to death so pleasingly. While in Emily Dickinson there is a lack of sensuousness, just as there was in Emerson. So that, like him, she never could have risen into the first rank of poets. And it was a sure critical instinct that led her never to venture beyond the range where her success was sure.

There is one thing to be remembered in considering her poetry, if we are to allow ourselves the full enjoyment of it; and that is her peculiar rhymes. As Colonel Higginson well remarks, "Though curiously indifferent to all conventional rules, she had a rigorous literary standard of her own, and often altered a word many times to suit an ear which had its own tenacious fastidiousness."

It is usual in verse to call those sounds perfect rhymes in which the final consonants (if there be any) and the final vowels are identical, but the consonants preceding these final vowels, different. So that we call "hand" and "land" perfect rhymes. But this is only a conventional custom among poets. It is consonant with laws of poetry, of course; but it is not in itself a law. It is merely one means at the writer's disposal for marking off his lines for the reader's ear. And when Emily Dickinson chose to use in her own work another slightly different convention, she was at perfect liberty to do so. She violated no law of poetry. The laws of art are as inviolable as the laws of nature.

> Who never wanted—maddest joy
>   Remains to him unknown;
> The banquet of abstemiousness
>   Surpasses that of wine.

"Wine" and "unknown" are not perfect rhymes. No more are "ground" and "mind," "done" and "man"; yet they serve to mark her lines for her reader quite well. Why? Because she has made a new rule for herself, and has followed it carefully. It is simply this—that the final vowels need not be identical; only the final consonants need be identical. The vowels may vary. It is wrong to say that she disregarded any law here. The question is rather: Did her new usage tend to beautiful results? For my part I confess that I like that falling rhyme very much. There is a haunting gypsy accent about it, quite in keeping with the tenor of that wilding music. What a strange and gnomelike presence lurks in all her lines!

558   "Other Holiday Gift Books." *Publishers' Weekly* 50 (November 28, 1896), 84. [Separately paged "Christmas Bookshelf" number.] The "Third Series" is noted earlier in this issue as "among volumes of verse suitable for gift books" (p. 50).

Among the other poems of the year are "Emily Dickinson's Poems: third series," in which Mabel Loomis Todd has gathered those waifs and strays of Miss Dickinson's original genius that were not included in the two preceding volumes.

559   "Among the Newest Books." *Delineator* [N.Y., London, Toronto] 48:6 (December 1896), 815.

To Miss Dickinson's seclusion, her almost solitary life, we owe many a beautiful thought which she confided to her pen rather than to a human companion. These relics of a lonely life—lonely by choice—come to a reading world as bequeathments—gifts from a dear, dead woman whose stay here should have been rich in health and gladness, but was not. Pain and sorrow were hers, and we have their fruits. Her verse lacks musical deftness, a fact proved by these gleanings—a third gathering from the field of her unpublished verse. But while reading them and musing afterward with a finger between the leaves, one feels the cool sweetness of the dew, hears the music of the rain, and sees the tall grass sway in the meadows. It is not quite true to say that Miss Dickinson lived alone. She had the companionship of her books and they were more to her than to those for whom sentient society is a necessity. She could truly say:

> There is no frigate like a book,
>   To take us lands away;
> Nor any courser like a page
>   Of prancing poetry.
> This traverse may the poorest take
>   Without oppress of toil   [toll
> How frugal is the chariot
>   That bears a human soul!

To die meant to her to know all things—to be wherever thought could fly. Her poems infect her readers with this ecstatic aspiration for knowledge, and give them inkling of the gladness that must have been hers after she sobbed herself to sleep.

560 Harry Lyman Koopman. "Emily Dickinson." *Brown Magazine* 8 (December 1896), 82–92. Though himself half-reluctant to give it up, Koopman's essay marks the end of the notion that Dickinson's poetry "defies criticism." He appears to take for granted that the Amherst poet has attained sufficient importance to warrant specifically academic study. His approach relies on the currently popular theory of Hippolyte Taine (race, milieu, and moment), giving primary attention to the relation between literature and life. His discussion of "heredity, sex, solitude, and books" anticipates Frederick Lewis Pattee's claim, in the latter's preface to *Foundations of English Literature* (1899) that literature is the "merely natural results of previous conditions." The author of the reminiscence of Dickinson quoted by Koopman has not been identified, but Joseph K. Chickering fits his description well.

> It's all I have to bring to-day,
>   This, and my heart beside,
> This, and my heart, and all the fields,
>   And all the meadows wide.
> Be sure you count,—should I forget,
>   Some one the sum could tell,—
> This, and my heart, and all the bees
>   Which in the clover dwell.

A third volume of the poems of Emily Dickinson, of which these are the opening lines, places the world under renewed obligation to that rare and striking genius, as also in no slight degree to the loyal devotion which has so patiently and skillfully served its unique executorship. Without waiting for any final decision, if such can ever be given, in regard to the excellence or faultiness of Emily Dickinson's peculiar style, we may even now venture the judgment that her name will henceforth hold a place in any list of the great woman writers of the world, and in any list of the great poets of her own country. Yet it was her lot to produce the works of her genius not only in literary obscurity, but also in a personal seclusion greater, perhaps, than has surrounded any writer of distinction in all the annals of literature.

The story of Emily Dickinson's life reads more like a creation of Hawthorne's necromantic fancy than a veritable life-record. Born in 1830, the turning point of the century, and dying in 1886, she passed a life longer in duration than Shakespeare's, yet one that, measured by its dealings with the world, shrinks to the span of a young girl's. The publicity of village neighborhoods has accustomed us to regard the realization of solitude in the midst of society as a mode of life possible only in great cities. Yet Emily Dickinson, we are told, spent her days in the college town of Amherst, forming occasional friendships, and constantly sending delicacies to the sick, while the recipients of her bounty, who first and last represent nearly every household in town, and even many of her friends, were as ignorant of her personal appearance, except from hearsay, as of the hidden face of the moon.

On the day following Emily Dickinson's death, an appreciative testimonial to her character and genius appeared in the *Springfield Republican* [see App. A]; but few readers of that obituary could have imagined that after five years her name would suddenly become famous through the publication of one and another volume of her poetry; though they might have surmised that her verse, once discovered by the world, would meet with something of the ready and heartfelt admiration which it has encountered. Published materials for a judgment of her life and character, outside of her writings themselves, are unfortunately few. They consist of the notice, before-mentioned, in the *Springfield Republican* for May 16, 1886; the prefaces to the volumes of her poetry; "A child's recollections of Emily Dickinson," by McGregor Jenkins, in the *Christian Union* for October 24, 1891, which may be said to have revealed to the world at large her unique personality. Mention should also be made of a highly appreciative review of her poetry by Mr. Howells, which appeared in *Harper's Magazine* for January, 1891, and also of a notice of her letters, by a writer in the *Nation* for December 13, 1894. But it is from her letters themselves—published in two volumes, in Boston, in 1894—that we are able to construct the clearest account of her life and character, though our knowledge of her still remains fragmentary and tantalizing in the highest degree. Where so little is known, every addition to our knowledge becomes of importance, and, therefore, lovers of Emily Dickinson will welcome the following brief reminiscences, here printed for the first time, which are communicated by one who, though counted among her correspondents, if not her intimate friends, had yet, during years of residence in the same town, seen her but once in life,—a mere glimpse caught at one of her father's annual receptions.

"My acquaintance with Emily Dickinson began some years after her father's death. She came to know me as an occasional caller at the house, and ere long, some special marks of attention were shown,—I say special, perhaps it were better to say customary marks to those whom she learned of through the medium of her sister. A few moments after the latter entered the room, the most timid of knocks would be heard on the door leading into the hall. The sister would disappear, and, after being gone an unconscionably long time, would return, generally with a large silver salver, upon which would be laid an exquisite blossom, a charlotte russe, a bit of cake and a glass of wine,—something dainty and, if possible, something in the preparation of which she herself had borne a part. The gift would sometimes be accompanied by a brief, unsigned note. There seemed to be little one could do in return. Indeed, I do not think she cared for anything but a simple word of appreciation; and when fruit, or flower, or note, was sent to one's house, I, at least found it difficult to couch my acknowledgments in any language that would not seem, to the lady invisible, rude and commonplace. During the later years she was always promising to see me. I dare not say how many times her sister has returned with the message, 'I think Emily will see you next time, but she is not feeling quite equal to it this afternoon.' For the dread of seeing a new, albeit friendly, face, I suppose none of us can imagine. Her sister once said to me, at the time of her mother's funeral, 'Emily will not come down stairs; the sight of so many people would kill her.'—And I am not sure that it would not have brought her perilously near the limit of her powers."

With all that is weird and wayward in the genius of Emily Dickinson, its utterances, when submitted to the tests of criticism, yield much whose existence can be accounted for, and, in fact, no greater proportion than is wont with poets "of the incommunicable lightning" of their own minds. That portion, indeed, defies criticism. It will not be explained, and must be taken as an original fact. Among the qualities of Emily Dickinson that come under this class are certainly: her directness of sight and insight; the immediateness of her relation to nature and life and their problems; the brevity of her visions, corresponding to their intensity; her brilliancy of coloring; her pungency and piquancy of expression; her disregard or defiance of the accepted rules of prosody,—leading her to prefer irregular verse forms, and, generally to substitute for verse a crisp, rhythmic prose marked by occasional rhymes and more frequent assonance and alliteration,—and, lastly, a recurrent use of language that simply conveys no meaning to the reader, in which the thought slips out of the plane of his understanding, to appear anon with apparently unbroken continuity, though, for a space, he had not been able to follow it. With these obscure passages study is of little avail. If they are obscure at first they are apt to remain so. The following poem may serve as a specimen of her oddest manner:

> The zeroes taught us phosphorus—
> We learned to like the fire
> By playing glaciers when a boy,
> And tinder guessed by power
>
> Of opposite to balance odd,
> If white, a red must be!
> Paralysis, our primer dumb
> Unto vitality.

Of course, at this point, her genius draws perilously near to the line which divides great wits from madness; a proximity which is betrayed also by her handwriting, which, in its later style, is as odd and eery, not to say uncanny, as sanity ever produced. Her revolt against verse-traditions connects her with some of the greatest names of our century, throughout which a similar mutiny has continued; whether the result has been more intricate harmonies, as with Shelley, Poe, and Swinburne, or a tendency to break down the distinction between poetry and prose, as in the case with Carlyle, Whitman, and Miss Dickinson herself. But though this revolt did not begin with her, its results in her verse are wholly original and unique. It would be obviously unfair to let the poem last quoted stand as representative of Miss Dickinson's manner. Beside it may well be placed such a seventeenth-century gem as the following from her last volume:

LOVE'S HUMILITY.

> My worthiness is all my doubt,
> His merit all my fear.

> Contrasting which, my qualities
>   Do lowlier appear;
>
> Lest I should insufficient prove
>   For his beloved need,
> The chiefest apprehension
>   Within my loving creed.
>
> So I, the undivine abode
>   Of his elect content,
> Conform my soul as 'twere a church
>   Unto her sacrament.

In considering the elements of Emily Dickinson's poetry that can be referred to conditions apart from her inmost individuality, we discern four distinct modifying influences, namely: heredity, sex, solitude, and books.

The influence of heredity upon her life and writings is strongly marked, and is manifest in the same recoil from puritanism that appears in Emerson and Thoreau; a recoil from sternness and grimness into beauty, a recoil from authority into intellectual freedom; yet in neither direction is the transition complete. Hence the intensity of the utterance, the rapturous delight in nature's beauty, and that beating against the barriers of thought, which is so different from the calmness of escape and freedom. The principle of atavism, or the continual reappearance of ancestral traits, is well known; but the far-reaching scope of the principle is not so generally understood. Anthropologists tell us that the shape of skull common to the cave-dwellers has never wholly ceased to reappear among civilized men. Similarly, our brutal and brute ancestors stretch their mortmain down through hundreds of thousands of years and hold us back in our progress. "There's the respect that makes calamity of so long life;" and the reformer who ignores it is doomed to a bitter undeception in his dreams of an early millennium. There is that, however, in the character of Emily Dickinson, as of all rare, sweet shrinking souls, who appear from time to time among us, that suggests the presence and activity in life of a principle the opposite of atavism. Its name would properly be adnepotism, or heredity by anticipation. According to this principle, qualities that are to prevail in the future appear sporadically years, and often ages, before they become dominant. Thus, beautiful souls that, like Hamlet, find the world out of joint, are only the scattered forerunners of a race to whose better world we, with our undeveloped or calloused sympathies, would be as ill adapted as its present unfortunate representatives are to that which we compose.

The position of woman in literature is destined to become increasingly prominent as the race advances; but the peculiar character of her contribution to thought and expression has not yet been fully manifested. Woman is at once more conservative and more lawless than man; more abandoned both to love and to hate; more intense in imagination and sympathy, but narrower; capable of an apparently intellectual enthusiasm that really springs from the affections, and incapable, except in the strongest, of a degree of spiritual self-dependence that is common to the average of men. These are some of the characteristics of woman that are beginning to make their impression upon literature, and some of them help to account for traits in the poetry of Emily Dickinson that would otherwise seem to be purely individual. It is to the expression of love in her poetry that we naturally turn for peculiarly feminine qualities, and we find them richly manifested. One of her most charming, if not most impassioned, love poems is the following:

The way I read a letter's this:
    'Tis first I lock the door,
And push it with my fingers next
    For transport it be sure.

And then I go the furthest off
    To counteract a knock;
Then draw my little letter forth
    And softly pick its lock.

Then, glancing narrow at the wall,
    And narrow at the floor,
For firm conviction of a mouse
    Not exorcised before,

Peruse how infinite I am
    To—no one that you know!
And sigh for lack of heaven,—but not
    The heaven the creeds bestow.

The effect of solitude upon her poetry, or, more exactly, of her voluntary withdrawal to the inmost circle of home life, is observable in two directions. The fireside became again for her the *focus* of the universe; and the primal facts of life,—birth, death, burial, love, marriage, work, play, pain, joy, duty, sacrifice, freedom, strength, weakness, defeat, victory,—take on in her poetry an epic grandeur. Her relation to nature is of an intimate kind, a comradeship, but it is something of a child's intimacy. The grand co-ordinating conceptions of society and of the universe, in which poet-philosophers dip their wings to mount upward, seem never to have been revealed to her. Doubtless, also, to her seclusion, must be ascribed much of what is oddest and queerest in her poetry. Had her disposition permitted her to seek a general audience, to breathe the common literary atmosphere, to meet a wide instead of a narrowly restricted circle of intelligent people, and, above all, to mingle freely with common humanity, the unconscious influence of such broader acquaintance with life would have given art where now we find in her writing too often only the impulse to expression. As an instance of her sheer power, the violence that takes the heaven of poetry by storm, may be quoted:

THE MASTER.

He fumbles at your spirit
    As players at the keys
Before they drop full music on;
    He stuns you by degrees,

Prepares your brittle substance
    For the ethereal blow,
By fainter hammers, further heard,
    Then nearer, then so slow

Your breath has time to straighten,
    Your brain to bubble cool,—
Deals one imperial thunderbolt
    That scalps your naked soul.

The man of one book, unless he has unusual independence of mind, is likely to be intellectually only the reflection of that book. Miss Dickinson's books seem not to have been many. We know that she read the Bible, Sir Thomas Browne, Keats, Ruskin, George Eliot, and the Brownings; and that she once referred to Shakespeare as rendering all other books needless. The influence of some of these writers is clearly traceable in her poetry, though Shakespeare can hardly be said to exert an influence other than as nature does; the nearest prototypes of her manner being found in the Brownings. But great similarity to Emerson's style can likewise be discerned in her work, while between her poems and Thoreau's there are passages that are almost interchangeable. Comparison has also been made between her poetry and that of Blake. How much of these resemblances is due to unconscious imitation it would be hard to pronounce. Critics are apt to overlook the potency of like causes to produce like results in the work of independent artists. As to direct borrowing, we have her statement that she would "never consciously touch a paint mixed by another person." After all deductions have been made, her style cannot be called imitative or even greatly influenced by her reading.

Her choice of subjects appears to have been determined chiefly by the narrowness of her horizon. Death and the hereafter occupy what would seem to most a disproportionate space; and in the treatment of these themes she displays the greatest strength of her art and the greatest weakness of her philosophy. She was a free thinker, but a free thinker on puritanic premises. Hence the grotesque familiarity of her anthropomorphism, which loses by its crudity more than it gains through vividness. The poet's theology has no right to be an anachronism. Mrs. Browning's man-like God is a worthier conception than Miss Dickinson's; but how immeasurably both fall below the pantheism of Wordsworth and Shelley, with its majestic imagining of the eternal mind, or of the spirit of the universe, which is love, or love made visible as beauty! It is sometimes asserted that the decay of mythology and mythological conceptions of the universe involves and has produced injury to poetry. If poetry were restricted and peculiar to the childhood of the race, like sign-language and belief in miracles, we might suspect truth in the assertion. But, as poetry is one of the fine arts, which are the varied expression of the soul's joy at the harmony it finds between the outer world and itself, there is no reason to suppose, unless progress develops dissonance instead of increased harmony, that poetry will fail to improve with every moral and intellectual advance of mankind. Certainly the foregoing comparison tends to show that the highest truth still remains the highest poetry.

> I died for beauty, but was scarce
> Adjusted in the tomb,
> When one who died for truth was laid   [lain
> In an adjoining room.
>
> He questioned softly why I failed.
> "For beauty," I replied.
> "And I for truth, — the two are one;
> We brethren are," he said.
>
> And so, as kinsmen met a-night,
> We talked between the rooms,
> Until the moss had reached our lips,
> And covered up our names.

SETTING SAIL.

> Exultation is the going
> Of an inland soul to sea —

Past the houses, past the headlands,
Into deep eternity.

Bred as we, among the mountains,
Can the sailor understand
The divine intoxication
Of the first league out from land?

A more familiar and still more characteristic treatment of eternal themes is embodied in her poem entitled:

OLD-FASHIONED.

Arcturus is his other name,—
I'd rather call him star!
It's so unkind of science
To go and interfere!

I pull a flower from the woods,—
A monster with a glass
Computes the stamens in a breath,
And has her in a class.

Whereas I took a butterfly
Aforetime in my hat,
He sits erect in cabinets,
The clover-bells forgot.

What once was heaven, is zenith now.
Where I proposed to go
When time's brief masquerade was done
Is mapped and charted too!

What if the poles should frisk about
And stand upon their heads!
I hope I'm ready for the worst,
Whatever prank betides!

Perhaps the kingdom of Heaven's changed!
I hope the children there
Won't be new-fashioned when I come,
And laugh at me and stare!

I hope the father in the skies
Will lift his little girl,—
Old-fashioned, naughty, everything,—
Over the stile of pearl!

The poems of Emily Dickinson were not written for publication, and, to some extent as a result of this, are marked by absolute honesty. Her verse is a genuine expression, not a dressing up or concealment of thought. That her art suffered as well as gained by this confessional character of her writing cannot be questioned. But the total result of her unique life and song is a voice new to literature, which, though it may never reach the ears of all, will for a time be gladly heard of many, and is not likely, until genuineness of feeling and utterance becomes common-place, ever to be wholly without listeners. To her unknown public, present and to come, she has made her own touching appeal:

This is my letter to the world
   That never wrote to me, —
The simple truth that Nature told,
   With tender majesty.

Her message is committed
   To hands I cannot see;
For love of her, sweet countrymen,
   Judge tenderly of me!

561 "Holiday Gift Books." *Literary News* 17 (December 1896), 373. Higginson's *Nation* review is no. 543.

The third series of poems by this author of curious and wholly posthumous fame has been selected from an unexpected deposit. "It is needless to say," says the Nation, "that Miss Dickinson's poetry achieves its success, in spite of all its flagrant literary faults, by what Ruskin describes as 'the perfection and precision of the instantaneous line.' She is to be tested, not by her attitude, but by her shot. Does she hit the mark? As a rule she does. Is it a question what a book represents to a human being? This is her answer—only eight lines, but they tell the story (p. 29):

A BOOK.

There is no frigate like a book
   To take us leagues away,
Nor any coursers like a page
   Of prancing poetry.
This traverse may the poorest take
   Without oppress of toll;
How frugal is the chariot
   That bears a human soul!"

562 [Julia Whiting.] Van Der Dater (pseud.). "Some Recent Publications." *Bradley: His Book* 2 (December 1896), 66. Mrs. Todd's "Preface" (no. 514) does not mention a fourth series, but she was indeed collecting and copying poems for subsequent volumes; see *AB*, 397.

That there should be a third volume of Emily Dickinson's poems, is more pleasure than the public expected, it having been supposed that all of consequence had been already printed. But it seems there are yet more, Mrs. M. L. Todd in the preface announcing a fourth collection. The present volume, which is marked by the same charm that distinguished its predecessors, is published by Roberts Brothers, who also print the American edition of the "Poems of Johanna Ambrosius," the peasant poet of Germany. The contrast in form and sentiment is as sharp as the difference in the lives of these two, one born of generations of culture, with ease and independence, the other a peasant and toiling like a beast of the fields.

563 "For Today." *Boston Evening Transcript*, December 10, 1896, p. 6. The quotation is from Mrs. Ford's recollection of Dickinson in *Letters* (1894), I, 131–32 (see no. 420).

Dec. 10, 1830, Emily Dickinson was born. Mrs. Gordon L. Ford writes in the first volume of "Emily Dickinson's Letters," edited by Mabel Loomis Todd: "Dr. Holland once said to me, 'Her poems are too ethereal for publication.' I replied, 'They are beautiful—so concentrated—but they remind me of air-plants that have no roots in earth.' 'That is true,' he said, 'a perfect description'; and I think these lyrical ejaculations, these breathed-out projectiles, sharp as lances, would at that time have fallen into idle ears. But gathered in a volume where many could be read at once as her philosophy of life, they explain each other, and so became intelligible and delightful to the public."

564 [Thomas Wentworth Higginson.] "Recent Poetry." *Nation* 63 (December 10, 1896), 442. Reviewing *The Treasury of American Sacred Song*, Higginson here corrects its editor's error regarding Dickinson's manuscripts (see no. 499).

Again, it is not correctly stated (p. 354) that Emily Dickinson's manuscript poems "were written in continuous lines, like prose"; this having rarely, though occasionally, happened. The mistake perhaps grew out of the fact that she frequently, in her letters, passed abruptly from prose to verse, but always marking the distinction in the lines.

565 *New York Times Saturday Review of Books and Art*, December 12, 1896, p. 7.

Mabel Loomis Todd edits the third series of the "Poems of Emily Dickinson." The editor says, "There is internal evidence that many of the poems were simply spontaneous flashes of insight, apparently unrelated to outward circumstances."

566 "Recent Poetry." *Home Journal* 51 (December 30, 1896), 2.

The third series of Emily Dickinson's "Poems," edited by Mabel Loomis Todd, brings more fruit from a very peculiar tree. That Miss Dickinson was earnest in being so unique is undoubted, and the wonder is that, with all her unique ways she did not produce more discord and more unpoetic poetry. There is a strain of sorrow mingled with another strain of doubt in her written nature, and there is even a sacrilegious tone at times which reminds one of the old familiarity of the Cromwellian days,—the familiarity of man with religious expressions which to-day are shunned even in the licensed language of poetry. This third series confirms her position in the poetic world—among the "peculiars."

567 Oscar Fay Adams (ed.). "Dickinson, Emily." *A Dictionary of American Authors*. Boston & New York: Houghton, Mifflin, 1897, p. 98. This biographical entry remained unchanged in revised editions of the *Dictionary* that appeared as late as 1905.

Dickinson, Emily. *Ms.*, 1830–1886. A poet whose entire life was passed in Amherst, Massachusetts, in great seclusion, and who rarely published any of her work. Since her death attention has been drawn to the strikingly original nature of her poetry by the publication of three volumes of Poems, selected from her manuscripts. They display an utter disregard of technique as well as an almost startling originality of conception. *See Letters of, 1847–1886, edited by Mrs. Todd. Rob.*

568 Thomas Wentworth Higginson. "The Prejudice in Favor of Retiracy" in *Book and Heart: Essays on Literature and Life* (N.Y.: Harper, 1897), pp. 206–11. First published in 1896 in an unidentified periodical, this essay discusses the writer's need for privacy. Its next to last paragraph (pp. 209–10) is reprinted here.

If a greater personal shyness exists among literary persons than in any other occupation, it probably comes from the fact that the author, and especially the poet, feels more detached from his work, when done, than is the case with anybody else. His work comes to him as something outside of himself, and, when it is done, his ordinary life is but the nest from which that bird of fancy has flown. Why then should he dwell upon it, or give its precise measurements? The poem comes to him; he cannot sit down and make it by an effort of will. It is strange to him that the word "poet" should mean "maker," when his experience is that the poem, even if a poor one, makes itself. Its production also affords a relief; and this explains the many cases where—as, in America, with Emily Dickinson and Francis Saltus—one may spend a whole lifetime in making verses, and yet let almost nothing be published until after death. This explains also why their own works often seem to authors so remote and worthless; they feel as an apple-tree might feel, if it were human, towards a barrel of its own apples of last season. When to all this is added a woman's lingering tradition of the seclusion due to her sex, it is not strange if authors of that sex hide themselves under initials or feigned names, and decline to publish autobiographies.

569 Frederic Lawrence Knowles. "Notes." *The Golden Treasury of American Songs and Lyrics*. Boston: L.C. Page & Co., 1897, p. 309. This anthology, reprinted in 1898 and 1899, carried the following comment on Dickinson's "The Battle-field" ("They dropped like flakes"). The 1897 and 1898 volumes paired her poem with Bryant's "The Battle-field." Knowles, in his 1899 "new revised edition," removed Dickinson's poem (keeping the Bryant) but forgot to delete his note on it (also p. 309).

The Battle-field. — Miss Dickinson has much of the witchcraft and subtlety of William Blake. Many verses of the shy recluse, whom Mr. Higginson so happily has introduced to the world, are not only daring and unconventional, but recklessly defiant of form. But, as her editor has well said, "When a thought takes one's breath away, a lesson on grammar seems an impertinence." Emily Dickinson had more than a message, more than the charm of unexpectedness, more than the gift of phrase,—she had (and of how many Americans can this be said?) an intense imagination.

570 [Julia Whiting.] Van Der Dater (pseud.). "Some Current Literature." *Bradley: His Book* 2 (January 1897), 108–10. Only comments on Dickinson, in this omnibus review, are reprinted here. Eight pages later, in an unpaged section of the magazine, there is reproduced, in red and black ink, without comment, what appears to be the title page to the 1896 *Poems*. It is not an accurate facsimile, differing from the original in type face and text. For Whiting's earlier notice of *Poems*, "Third Series," see no. 562.

In one of his joyless moods, William Hazlitt declares, "There are only three pleasures in life pure and lasting, and all derived from inanimate things; books, pictures, and the face of nature. While we remember anything we cannot forget them. As long as we have a wish for pleasure we may find it there, for it depends only on our love for them, and not on theirs for us. The enjoyment is purely ideal."

The more genial Lamb adds, "I must confess that I dedicate no inconsiderable portion of my time to other people's thoughts. I dream my life away in others' speculations; I love to lose myself in other men's minds. When I am not walking I am reading. I cannot sit and think. Books think for me." And in the recently published volume of Emily Dickinson's poems she confirms the essayist, in these whimsical lines:

> There is no frigate like a book
>> To take us lands away,
> Nor any courser like a page
>> Of prancing poetry.
> This traverse may the poorest take
>> Without oppress of toil;   [toll
> How frugal is the chariot
>> That bears a human soul!

So "frugal" that only inclination any longer makes the un-read man.

Books of verse that either in elegance of outward guise or sentiment reward the buyer, are the just-published poems of H. C. Bunner, the genial and beloved humorist; "Field Flowers," that collection which is gotten up as a memorial to the poet, Eugene Field; and the third series of Emily Dickinson's verse. . . .

It is a far cry from the exponent of the free and careless joy of life [Eugene Field] to the cultivated product of New England ancestry, Emily Dickinson, whose muse was as audacious as it was original. She was not without reverence; but she feared absolutely nothing, and never consulted convention's "ought nots" when she had somewhat to say, but rather set them joyfully at defiance. The message was of consequence; its form should be as she chose. In everything she writes she expresses herself; there is nothing outside, nothing impersonal. She does not speak in the voice of the world or any atom in it. She is a true egoist, without being in the least egotistical.

There is a curious attraction about her verses that leads the reader on and on to ever new surprises. Now it is a caprice; now a thought as deep as life itself. These differing moods are best exhibited in the following lines. And first to quote from one of her nature poems:

> Could I but ride indefinite
>> As doth the meadow bee
> And visit only where I liked
>> And no man visit me,
>
> And flirt all day with buttercups
>> And marry whom I may
> And dwell a little everywhere,
>> Or better, run away
>
> With no police to follow
>> Or chase me if I do,
> Till I should jump peninsulars
>> To get away from you, —
>
> I said, but just to be a bee
>> Upon a raft of air,
> And row in nowhere all day long,

> And anchor off the bar, —
> What liberty! So captives deem
> Who tight in dungeons are.

There is a curious and unexpected note of sadness in the closing lines, of which the joyous and care-free opening gives no warning. All possible melancholy is conveyed in the lines called "Parting:"

> My life closed twice before its close;
> It yet remains to see
> If Immortality unveil
> A third event to me
>
> So huge, so hopeless to conceive
> As these which twice befell;   [that twice
> Parting is all we know of heaven
> And all we need of hell.

Yet this is followed by an incitement to effort full of courage and hope. She says:

> We never know how high we are
> Till we are called to rise:
> And then, if we are true to plan,
> Our statures touch the skies.

Into what a different world is the reader transported who lays down Emily Dickinson's verse to take up that of Johanna Ambrosius, peasant-poet of Germany. The American woman, with her inheritance of Puritan liberty of thought and action, her personal freedom and ease of life, is in sharp contrast with the peasant, laboring like the beast in the fields, abjectly poor, with the humility of her station, and the patience born of privation and toil.

571 E.R.C. "Emily Dickinson: Notes on Her Personality and Her Latest Poems." Unlocated clipping, late January, early February, 1897. Todd's scrapbook copy carries a clipping service attribution to the *New York Sun* for February 1, 1897, but search of the paper proved fruitless.

A third series of "Poems by Emily Dickinson" is published by Roberts Brothers, Boston. These poems have their profound admirers, and it is doubtless true that they vary in the degree of their intelligibility. Since Browning at least there has been no comprehensive objection to a poem that is not readily understood, and it occurs to us that "Wedded" in this collection is susceptible of study:

> A solemn thing it was, I said,
> A woman white to be,
> And wear, if God should count me fit,
> Her hallowed mystery.
>
> A timid thing to drop a life
> Into the purple well,
> Too plummetless that it come back
> Eternity until.

The mere circumstance that it might also be a solemn thing a woman black to be is doubtless not to be considered as militating in any measure against the main proposition here advanced. The poem called "The Tulip" will possibly appeal in a superior manner to certain intelligences:

> She slept beneath a tree
> Remembered but by me.
> I touched her cradle mute;
> She recognized the foot,
> Put on her carmine suit—
>   And see!

A variation of possible rhetorical figure is specifically implied in "Dawn":

> Not knowing when the dawn will come
>   I open every door;
> Or has it feathers like a bird,
>   Or billows like a shore?

In "March" it occurs to us that the reader has a right to be agitated by the strength and variety of suggestion, and we should not wish to be understood as speaking at all otherwise than quite respectfully of "March":

> We like March, his shoes are purple.
>   He is new and high;
> Makes he mud for dog and peddler,
>   Makes he forest dry;
> Knows the adder's tongue his coming,
>   And begets her spot.
> Stands the sun so close and mighty
>   That our minds are hot.
> News is he of all the others;
>   Bold it were to die
> With the bluebirds buccaneering
>   On his British sky.

For humor we have always had a weakness, and we feel that we are fitted to appreciate the chief sentiment in "Cobwebs," though it is just a trifle difficult to conceive of a poet and a lady greeting a spider in exactly the way specified:

> The spider as an artist
>   Has never been employed,
> Though his surpassing merit
>   Is freely certified
>
> By every broom and Bridget
>   Throughout a Christian land.
> Neglected son of genius,
>   I take thee by the hand.

"The Wind" is mysterious, as in realism it should be. One quite feels the sense of its inevitable passing, and its hopeless inexplicability:

> It's like the light—
>   A fashionless delight
> It's like the bee,
>   A dateless melody.

It's like the woods,
    Private like breeze,
Phraseless, yet it stirs
    The proudest trees.

It's like the morning,
    Best when it's done —
The everlasting clocks
    Chime noon.

The sentiment expressed in "A Snake" is entirely comprehensible:

Sweet is the swamp with its secrets,
    Until we meet a snake;
'Tis then we sigh for houses,
    And our departure take
At that enthralling gallop
    That only childhood knows.
A snake is summer's treason,
    And guile is where it goes.

It is worthy of notice, perhaps, that this poem might equally well have concerned itself with a mouse.

572 William Morton Payne. "Recent Poetry." *Dial* 22 (February 1, 1897), 90.

The daring and the distinction, the production of strong effects by simple
means, that characterize Emily Dickinson's poetry need no setting-forth at this
late day. Take these versicles for examples:

My life closed twice before its close;
    It yet remains to see
If immortality unveil
    A third event to me,

So huge, so hopeless to conceive,
    As these that twice befell.
Parting is all we know of heaven,
    And all we need of hell.

A reader who knew Miss Dickinson's work at all would place them instantly, so
unmistakably did she stamp herself upon her least experiment in verse. We make
the quotation from a "third series" of her poems, edited, like the others, by her
friend, Mrs. Mabel Loomis Todd.

573 "Talk About Books." *Chatauquan* 24 (March 1897), 750.

A radiant, scintillant spirit was Emily Dickinson, whose tender, luminous
thoughts were continually falling in pearls from her lips. Many of these spontaneous outbursts of her rare genius are given in "Poems, Third Series"—a dainty
volume instinct with the lovely personality of its author.

574 Clarence Griffin Child. "Poems by Emily Dickinson." *Citizen* 3 (May
    1897), 61–62.

The issue of a third volume of poems by Emily Dickinson, following upon the publication of her letters, proves how genuine were the interest and admiration with which her poems were at first received. This interest and admiration, were not, in fact, of a nature to be merely transitory. The poems possessed intrinsic poetic worth. The story of their writer—a shy and reserved woman, whose life was passed in the seclusion of a village home—gave them further point and significance; there could be, it seemed, in these days of facile rhyming for pleasure or profit, verse truly a necessary part of the life of the writer—written, moreover, with no desire or expectation that it would ever meet with publicity or ever even be read, save by one or two friends whose intimacy was assurance of perfect understanding and sympathy. There were also special and unusual qualities in this verse—a combination of strength and technical immaturity, of creative energy and incompleteness of form—that gave it exceptional character. So definite was the impression of the vigor of its creative impulse, of the reality of its inspiration, so marked often also what may be termed somewhat harshly the rudeness of its form, that much of it seemed to the reader poetry, as it were, in the making, the creative forces being arrested in action midway. This is what Mr. Higginson felt when he said that here "flashes of wholly original and profound insight into nature and life" are found set in a "whimsical and even rugged frame." It was this which suggested to him the image, for which lovers of Emily Dickinson may well thank him, that her verses seem to the reader like "poetry torn up by the roots with rain and dew and earth still clinging to them, giving a freshness and a fragrance not otherwise to be conveyed." This ruggedness was due simply to the fact that the writer's strength lay in her phrases, and that these were preserved even at loss of metric smoothness; to satisfy lesser considerations was impossible without doing violence to that element of expression in which her strength chiefly consisted. At all events, the impression of the true inspirational character of the poems remained. This impression was undoubtedly in the main a correct one. Emily Dickinson was gnomic in her utterances like Emerson, with all which that implies: conventions of form were not infrequently sacrificed, consciously or unconsciously, for the preservation of what was essential, what was of higher worth.

The present volume is opened with doubts, which are not allayed by the editor's assurance that the intellectual activity of Emily Dickinson was so great that a "large and characteristic choice was still possible among her literary material." A third series implies a third selection—the fear is only natural that the effect created by the previous volumes might not be sustained, and the admiration and love they excited be chilled by dilution. For other reasons, its publication must in any case be welcomed; it is not too much to say that the psychologic interest alone of the poems previously published would justify it, whatever the quality of those now added. To take an analogous case, Lanier may have suffered from the publication of the entire body of his verse, much of which he had not revised, and much of which he might not have chosen to reprint at all; but the student is glad to have all his verse, good or bad, for the reason that he was a theorist and an experimentalist in verse structure. Similarly, if the reader divine in Emily Dickinson's verse an unusual quality, if it seem to afford evidence of the processes involved in poetic creation—such evidences as might have been welcomed by a scholar like Werner, who has made so interesting a study of the nature of lyrical conception—this and any further additions to her published verse must be welcomed. But this leads to the conclusion that Mrs. Todd should have published all that it was possible to publish, in place of making three successive, and, according to her own account, more or less arbitrary selections. It cannot fail to pique one's interest to read the statement in the preface that "much of Emily Dickinson's prose was rhythmic, even rhymed, though frequently not set apart in lines."

Fortunately her admirers, however, jealous of her reputation or their own allegiance, will find no cause to regret the new volume. It would be too much to say that it equals, as a whole, the first or the second series. But there is the same vigor, brevity, pith, startling felicity of pregnant phrase, novel applications of familiar words audacious but compelling acceptance. There is the same intuition of the greatness symbolized in littleness, of austere verities imaged by paradox in the homely incidents of the daily round and common task. There is the same passionate love of Nature, the same realism in description characteristic of the true mystic. Many of the poems have a peculiar lightness and grace. Where poems are at once so brief and so striking, the temptation to quote is irresistible. The following are not cited as being worthier than others, but simply in the hope that they may be adequate in illustration: —

A ROSE.

A sepal, petal, and a thorn
Upon a common summer's morn,
A flash of dew, a bee or two,
   A breeze,
    A caper in the trees, —
And I'm a rose!

A BOOK.

There is no frigate like a book
   To take us lands away,
Nor any coursers like a page
   Of prancing poetry.
This traverse may the poorest take
   Without oppress of toll;
How frugal is the chariot
   That bears a human soul!

575 "Recent Verse." *Overland Monthly* 30 (August 1897), 190. "To make a prairie" is reprinted without its second line: "One clover and a bee, . . ."

In reading the third volume made up from the unpublished poems by Emily Dickinson room will be found for speculation as to what the principle of selection was which governed the choice of the poems published in the other two books. There is no falling away in the originality and strength of the selections in this later book, and at the same time there is a lyric quality, a carefulness of finish, and completeness of poetic quality, not found in the earlier volumes. It would seem that the editors were so struck by the startling directness of her thought, the vivid and original way of looking at things, that they determined to publish only those verses which illustrated these qualities. The impression of the author given by the first books was that she was not so much a writer of poetry as one who had poetic thoughts, but without the power of giving them full expression. This third volume will go far toward removing the impression. The poems are much more sane and comprehensible, and many of them have the swing and go of real melody. They do this, however, without losing strength. What could be more terse and to the point than these: —

It dropped so low in my regard
I heard it hit the ground,
And go to pieces on the stones
At bottom of my mind.

*   *   *   *   *

He fumbles at your spirit
    As players at the keys
Before they drop full music on;
    He stuns you by degrees.

*   *   *   *   *

To make a prairie it takes a clover and one bee, —
    And revery.
And revery alone will do
    If bees are few.

The morbid tendency of her mind is as evident in this as in the preceding books. Death, especially in its homelier and more intimate phases, seems to have an uncontrollable fascination for her, and she writes about it continually and with most uncanny effect. Her avoidance of men and women seems to have brought her in her solitude close to nature, the animals and the birds. They are her intimate friends, and she speaks of them with the knowledge that comes from actual observation.

High from the earth I heard a bird;
    He trod upon the trees
As he esteemed them trifles,
    And then he spied a breeze,
And situated softly
    Upon a pile of wind
Which in a perturbation
    Nature had left behind.
A joyous-going fellow
    I gathered from his talk,
Which both of benediction
    And badinage partook,
Without apparent burden,
    I learned in leafy wood
He was the faithful father
    Of a dependent brood,
And this untoward transport
    His remedy for care, —
A contrast to our respites.
    How different we are!

576 "For Today." *Boston Evening Transcript*, December 10, 1897, p. 6. Higginson's preface is no. 10. For the *Transcript*'s earlier birthday observance, see no. 563.

Dec. 10, 1830. Emily Dickinson was born. In the preface to the first volume of her poems, Thomas Wentworth Higginson says: "It is believed that the thoughtful reader will find in these pages a quality more suggestive of the poetry of William Blake than of anything to be elsewhere found—flashes of wholly original and profound insight into Nature and life; words and phrases exhibiting an extraordinary vividness of descriptive and imaginative power, yet often set in a seemingly whimsical or even rugged frame. . . . In many cases these verses will seem to the reader like poetry torn up by the roots, with rain and dew and earth still clinging to them, giving a freshness and a fragrance not otherwise to be conveyed. . . . When a thought takes one's breath away, a lesson on grammar seems an impertinence. As Ruskin wrote in his earlier and better days. 'No weight, nor mass, nor beauty of execution can outweigh one grain or fragment of thought.'"

577 [Thomas Wentworth Higginson.] "Recent American Poetry." *Nation* 65 (December 16, 1897), 481. Higginson had compared Father Tabb with Dickinson in an earlier *Nation* review (no. 492).

"Lyrics," by John B. Tabb (Copeland), is handicapped by the multiplicity and extreme brevity of the poems, and a certain general similarity of tone to those preceding; but there is scarcely one of the small pages that does not contain a thought, and hardly a thought without a gem of originality. The curious resemblance to Emily Dickinson still continues; thus, the following might have come from either of them (p. 97):

INDIAN SUMMER.

No more the battle of the chase
    The phantom tribes pursue,
But each in its accustomed place
    The autumn hails anew:
And still from solemn councils met
    On every hill and plain.
The smoke of many a calumet
    Ascends to Heaven again.

Or this (p. 28):

LIVERY.

Old-fashioned raiment suits the Tree:
    Tho' flouting winds are fain
To strip the foliage, presently
    He patterns it again;
Fastidious of chivalry,
    Rejecting as in scorn
All other than the panoply
    His ancestors had worn.

578 Katharine Lee Bates. *American Literature* (New York: Macmillan, 1898), pp. 178–79. This volume, by the author of "America the Beautiful," is a literary history. Reprinted 1900, 1904, 1905. The other "Amherst woman" Bates discusses as a writer is Helen Hunt Jackson.

From another Amherst woman, EMILY DICKINSON, an elfish recluse in her father's house and garden, have been wafted to the world a few showers of sibylline leaves more curious than anything else in our minor poetry. In demure and dashing strokes her letters vividly paint that typical New England household, the father "pure and terrible," who "never played," the mother who did not "care for thought," but, as life went on, "achieved in sweetness what she lost in strength," the brother and sister, the pets and flowers, and Irish Maggie "warm and wild and mighty." Safely cloistered in this environment, the shy little poet loved no words so well as *gallant* and *martial* and posed as roguish rebel against the traditional solemnities of Puritanism.

> A smile suffused Jehovah's face;
> The cherubim withdrew;
> Grave saints stole out to look at me,
> And showed their dimples, too.
>
> I left the place with all my might,—
> My prayer away I threw;
> The quiet ages picked it up,
> And Judgment twinkled, too.

579 James Fullarton Muirhead. *The Land of Contrasts: A Briton's View of His American Kin* (Boston: Lamson, Wolff, 1898; London: John Lane, 1898), pp. 178–86. This travel book (by the author of the American Baedeker) devotes a section to literature, giving extensive treatment to James, Howells, and Dickinson. Most reviewers of this volume did not comment on Muirhead's treatment of Dickinson, but see no. 582. Muirhead refers here to the phrase "thought-rhyme" used in Todd's "Preface" to *Poems*, Second Series (no. 263) and to a comment on Whitman and Dickinson made in Higginson's anonymous *Nation* review of Stephen Crane (no. 497). That review appeared Oct. 24, rather than Oct. 10, 1895.

My next example of the American in literature is, I think, to the full as national a type as Mr. Howells, though her Americanism is shown rather in subjective character than in objective theme. Miss Emily Dickinson is still a name so unfamiliar to English readers that I may be pardoned a few lines of biographical explanation. She was born in 1830, the daughter of the leading lawyer of Amherst, a small and quiet town of New England, delightfully situated on a hill, looking out over the undulating woods of the Connecticut valley. It is a little larger than the English Marlborough, and like it owes its distinctive tone to the presence of an important educational institute, Amherst College being one of the best known and worthiest of the smaller American colleges. In this quiet little spot Miss Dickinson spent the whole of her life, and even to its limited society she was almost as invisible as a cloistered nun except for her appearances at an annual reception given by her father to the dignitaries of the town and college. There was no definite reason either in her physical or mental health for this life of extraordinary seclusion; it seems to have been simply the natural outcome of a singularly introspective temperament. She rarely showed or spoke of her poems to any but one or two intimate friends; only three or four were published during her lifetime; and it was with considerable surprise that her relatives found, on her death in 1886, a large mass of poetical remains, finished and unfinished. A considerable selection from them has been published in three little volumes, edited with tender appreciation by two of her friends, Mrs. Mabel Loomis Todd and Col. T. W. Higginson.

Her poems are all in lyrical form—if the word form may be applied to her utter disregard of all metrical conventions. Her lines are rugged and her expressions wayward to an extraordinary degree, but "her verses all show a strange cadence of inner rhythmical music," and the "thought-rhymes" which she often substitutes for the more regular assonances appeal "to an unrecognised sense more elusive than hearing" (Mrs. Todd). In this curious divergence from established rules of verse Miss Dickinson may be likened to Walt Whitman, whom she differs from in every other particular, and notably in her pithiness as opposed to his diffuseness; but with her we feel in the strongest way that her mode is natural and unsought, utterly free from affectation, posing, or self-consciousness.

Colonel Higginson rightly finds her nearest analogue in William Blake; but this "nearest" is far from identity. While tenderly feminine in her sympathy for suffering, her love of nature, her loyalty to her friends, she is in expression the most unfeminine of poets. The usual feminine impulsiveness and full expression of emotion is replaced in her by an extraordinary condensation of phrase and feeling. In her letters we find the eternal womanly in her yearning love for her friends, her brooding anxiety and sympathy for the few lives closely intertwined with her own. In her poems, however, one is rather impressed with the deep well of poetic insight and feeling from which she draws, but never unreservedly. In spite of frequent strange exaggeration of phrase one is always conscious of a fund of reserve force. The subjects of her poems are few, but the piercing delicacy and depth of vision with which she turned from death and eternity to nature and to love make us feel the presence of that rare thing, genius. Hers is a wonderful instance of the way in which genius can dispense with experience; she sees more by pure intuition than others distil from the serried facts of an eventful life. Perhaps, in one of her own phrases, she is "too intrinsic for renown," but she has appealed strongly to a surprisingly large band of readers in the United States, and it seems to me will always hold her audience. Those who admit Miss Dickinson's talent, but deny it to be poetry, may be referred to Thoreau's saying that no definition of poetry can be given which the true poet will not somewhere sometime brush aside. It is a new departure, and the writer in the *Nation* (Oct. 10, 1895) is probably right when he says: "So marked a new departure rarely leads to further growth. Neither Whitman nor Miss Dickinson ever stepped beyond the circle they first drew."

It is difficult to select quite adequate samples of Miss Dickinson's art, but perhaps the following little poems will give some idea of her naked simplicity, terseness, oddness,—of her method, in short, if we can apply that word to anything so spontaneous and unconscious:

> I'm nobody! Who are you?
> Are you nobody, too?
> Then there's a pair of us. Don't tell!
> They'd banish us, you know.

> How dreary to be somebody!
> How public, like a frog,
> To tell your name the livelong day
> To an admiring bog!

*   *   *   *   *

I taste a liquor never brewed,
From tankards scooped in pearl;
Not all the vats upon the Rhine
Yield such an alcohol!

Inebriate of air am I,
And debauchee of dew,
Reeling, through endless summer days,
From inns of molten blue.

When landlords turn the drunken bee
Out of the foxglove's door,
When butterflies renounce their drams,
I shall but drink the more!

Till seraphs swing their snowy hats,
And saints to windows run,
To see the little tippler
Leaning against the sun!

      *   *   *   *   *

But how he set I know not.
There seemed a purple stile
Which little yellow boys and girls
Were climbing all the while,

Till when they reached the other side,
A dominie in grey
Put gently up the evening bars,
And led the flock away.

      *   *   *   *   *

He preached upon "breadth" till it argued him narrow—
The broad are too broad to define;
And of "truth" until it proclaimed him a liar—
The truth never flaunted a sign.
Simplicity fled from his counterfeit presence
As gold the pyrites would shun.
What confusion would cover the innocent Jesus
To meet so enabled a man!

The "so *enabled* a man" is a very characteristic Dickinson phrase. So, too, are these:

He put the belt around my life—
I heard the buckle snap.

      *   *   *   *   *

Unfitted by an instant's grace
For the contented beggar's face
I wore an hour ago.

      *   *   *   *   *

Just his sigh, accented,
Had been legible to me.

*   *   *   *   *

The bustle in a house
The morning after death
Is solemnest of industries
Enacted upon earth —
The sweeping up the heart,
And putting love away
We shall not want to use again
Until eternity.

Her interest in all the familiar sights and sounds of a village garden is evident through all her verses. Her illustrations are not recondite, literary, or conventional; she finds them at her own door. The robin, the buttercup, the maple, furnish what she needs. The bee, in particular, seems to have had a peculiar fascination for her, and hums through all her poems. She had even a kindly word for that "neglected son of genius," the spider. Her love of children is equally evident, and no one has ever better caught the spirit of

SATURDAY AFTERNOON.

From all the jails the boys and girls
    Ecstatically leap,
Beloved, only afternoon
    That prison doesn't keep.

They storm the earth and stun the air,
    A mob of solid bliss.
Alas! that frowns could lie in wait
    For such a foe as this!

The bold extravagance of her diction (which is not, however, mere extravagance) and her ultra-American familiarity with the forces of nature may be illustrated by such stanzas as:

What if the poles should frisk about
    And stand upon their heads!
I hope I'm ready for the worst,
    Whatever prank betides.

*   *   *   *   *

If I could see you in a year,
    I'd wind the months in balls,
And put them each in separate drawers
    Until their time befalls. . . .

If certain, when this life was out,
    That yours and mine should be,
I'd toss it yonder like a rind,
    And taste eternity.

For her the lightnings "skip like mice," the thunder "crumbles like a stuff." What a critic has called her "Emersonian self-possession" towards God may be seen in the little poem on the last page of her first volume, where she addresses the Deity as "burglar, banker, father." There is, however, no flippancy in this, no conscious irreverence; Miss Dickinson is not "orthodox," but she is genuinely spiritual and religious. Inspired by its truly American and *"actuel"* freedom, her muse does not fear to sing of such modern and mechanical phenomena as the railway train, which she loves to see "lap the miles and lick the valleys up," while she is fascinated by the contrast between its prodigious force and the way in which it stops, "docile and omnipotent, at its own stable door." But even she can hardly bring the smoking locomotive into such pathetic relations with nature as the "little brig," whose "white foot tripped, then dropped from sight," leaving "the ocean's heart too smooth, too blue, to break for you."

Her poems on death and the beyond, on time and eternity, are full of her peculiar note. Death is the "one dignity" that "delays for all;" the meanest brow is so ennobled by the majesty of death that "almost a powdered footman might dare to touch it now," and yet no beggar would accept "the *éclat* of death, had he the power to spurn." "The quiet nonchalance of death" is a resting-place which has no terrors for her; death "abashed" her no more than "the porter of her father's lodge." Death's chariot also holds Immortality. The setting sail for "deep eternity" brings a "divine intoxication" such as the "inland soul" feels on its "first league out from land." Though she "never spoke with God, nor visited in heaven," she is "as certain of the spot as if the chart were given." "In heaven somehow, it will be even, some new equation given." "Christ will explain each separate anguish in the fair schoolroom of the sky."

> A death-blow is a life-blow to some
> Who, till they died, did not alive become;
> Who, had they lived, had died, but when
> They died, vitality begun.

The reader who has had the patience to accompany me through these pages devoted to Miss Dickinson will surely own, whether in scoff or praise, the essentially American nature of her muse. Her defects are easily paralleled in the annals of English literature; but only in the liberal atmosphere of the New World, comparatively unshadowed by trammels of authority and standards of taste, could they have co-existed with so much of the highest quality.

580 A. von E. "For the Women's Section: Emily Dickinson, Part I." *Der Westen*, June 12, 1898, sec. 3, p. 1. For Part II, see next entry. Both parts are entirely in German. This appreciative essay is the first discussion of Dickinson in a language other than English.

Human character and ability can be nurtured in solitude, but without some experience in the outside world, no talent can escape a certain onesidedness and limitation. Modern life, however, is not conducive to solitary development, especially not the American way of life with its relentless drive for renewal and change. It captures the strong and devours the weak before they have time to mature. In this environment even exceptional individuals find themselves drifting in the stream of fashion and adopting the values of the day. Without wishing it or knowing why, they become mere representatives of a class. Only when they find enough strength to escape to a little island can they discover and retain their true selves, their only real possession. Of those few who were able to keep their identity—Thoreau and Whitman are among them—there is only one American woman poet.

About eight years ago when the publishing house of Roberts Brothers in Boston issued a volume simply entitled Poems by Emily Dickinson, it is likely that few of those who bought the book knew who its author was or that she had been dead for several years. Some may have been attracted by the book's modest and simple binding. Its gray-green cover was stamped in gilt with the drawing of an Indian Pipe, a strangely delicate plant that grows from rotted tree roots and sends forth stems, blossoms, and leaves—all pale as death. This flower of stillness, shadows, and secrecy was the poet's favorite and its choice as the decoration for a volume of poems which were never intended for publication showed a rare understanding, on the part of her publishers, of Emily Dickinson's individuality. Then the notices appeared. No reviewer knew what to do with these poems. Critics were embarrassed, as they commonly are, when they cannot classify a given work. Her poems did not belong to any school. For the critics, literary history needs to be susceptible of neat and orderly labeling, as in a pharmacy. The reviewers admitted the poet's genius but deplored her carelessness about what they regarded as the proper "form" of poetry. Next they asked themselves to whom she could be compared—a question that helps the literary critic in a tight place—but on that point as well, all attempts failed. They attempted to compare her to Poe, Blake, Emerson, Browning, Shelley, even Heine and Omar Khayyam, but in vain. If she seemed similar at first, further inquiry showed that she was not. Each of her poems, one of her most perceptive critics remarked, resembles a flash of lightning that falls for a second into a precipice. Another even admitted that the absence of rhythm in her oracular statements is hardly missed. Born in Amherst, which has long held an old school tradition, having ties with Concord and Boston (the American Weimar), Emily Dickinson remained largely untouched by these influences as she developed her absolute individuality.

Two volumes of letters were assembled by her sister, who was encouraged by the incredible success of the poems to publish Emily Dickinson's prose as well. These letters suggest a wealth of inner thoughts and emotions, a fundamentally austere personality, a heart longing for love, and a strangely philosophical spirit, one which seemed indifferent to conventional ideas of right and wrong and disinclined to make severe moral judgments. Although the poems are dated after her thirtieth birthday, the letters go back to her school-days. More than once, in reading them, I recalled Richard Le Gallienne's words, "Why do women not publish their letters as men collect their scattered essays? No writings in the world are more direct or convincing than the letters of a really intelligent woman." But Emily Dickinson's letters are not only of biographical interest for those who wish to enter the personal life of the poet; they are of literary importance in themselves. Her letters are a rare example of epigrammatic brevity and force.

About Emily Dickinson's life there is little to be said. She was the daughter of Edward Dickinson, a leading lawyer of Amherst who was later a Member of Congress. Born in 1830 (she died in 1886), Emily Dickinson was educated at Amherst Academy and the well-known Mr. Holyoke Seminary. At both institutions there are still those who remember her unusual compositions and the curious, mostly humorous, stories she used to tell her classmates in free hours. From her earliest youth she had an ability to make friends and to keep them. In a letter in which the then fifteen-year old girl describes a visit to Boston, we find this passage: "I am visiting my aunt's family, and am happy. Happy! did I say? No; not happy, but contented." She always spoke well of her life at the Seminary (where everyone was required to participate in housework), even though this was her first long separation from her parents. She fought courageously against homesickness and she didn't once mention the school's strict discipline.

In another letter, written some years later, she describes her impression of

Jenny Lind. Hearing her for the first time at a Northampton church, Emily Dickinson was impressed more by her personality than her singing. She also found her foreign accent extremely affecting and lovely. In 1854, when she was with her father in Washington, she wrote to Mrs. J. G. Holland: "We have had many pleasant times, and seen much that is fair, and heard much that is wonderful—many sweet ladies and noble gentlemen have taken us by the hand and smiled upon us pleasantly—and the sun shines brighter for our way thus far. I will not tell you what I saw—the elegance, the grandeur; you will not care to know the value of the diamonds my Lord and Lady wore, but if you haven't been to the sweet Mount Vernon, then I will tell you how on one soft spring day we glided down the Potomac in a painted boat, and jumped upon the shore—how hand in hand we stole up a tangled pathway till we reached the tomb of General George Washington, how we paused beside it, and no one spoke a word, then hand in hand, walked on again."

Even at this time Emily Dickinson showed an obvious reluctance to associate with important persons, while at the same time growing closer to her friends. Once she hinted [to the Hollands] that they didn't write often enough: "My business is to love. I found a bird, this morning, down—down—on a little bush at the foot of the garden, and wherefore sing, I said, since nobody hears? One sob in the throat, one flutter of bosom—'My business is to sing'—and away she rose! How do I know but cherubim, once, themselves, as patient, listened, and applauded her unnoticed hymn?" When Mrs. Holland once wrote a letter to both sisters, Emily protested: "A mutual plum is not a plum. I was too respectful to take the pulp and do not like a stone."

The older she grew, the more closely she associated with her friends, while disengaging increasingly from society. She found the great world false, superficial, and unworthy. She was appalled by its limitations even as she made fun of them. "Real life," on the other hand, seemed immeasurably attractive. She was almost dogmatically solemn about it. The less she met with her friends, the more intense grew her correspondence. Once she wrote to Samuel Bowles: "I hope your cups are full. I hope your vintage is untouched. In such a porcelain life one likes to be sure that all is well lest one stumble upon one's hopes in a pile of broken crockery. My friends are my estate. Forgive me then the avarice to hoard them! They tell me those who were poor early have different views of gold. I don't know how that is. God is not so wary as we, else He would give us no friends, lest we forget Him! The charms of heaven in the bush are superseded, I fear, by the heaven in the hand, occasionally." Elsewhere she said, "A personal meeting is like a field, but a letter is only a narrow patch of ground." And on another occasion she writes: "Spring is a happiness so beautiful, so unique, so unexpected, that I don't know what to do with my heart. I dare not take it, I dare not leave it—what do you advise? Life is a spell so exquisite that everything conspires to break it."

The death of her father touched Emily Dickinson deeply. Out of love for him she sometimes overcame her averson to society. Once a year, when he held a reception in his house, she welcomed his guests and no one who saw her on those occasions would have suspected that she normally lived the life of a recluse. When she also lost her mother several years later, she wrote in her mystical manner: "I cannot tell how Eternity seems. It sweeps around me like a sea." From that time on, she never left her home. Her books and flowers composed her world. Even her friend Mabel Loomis Todd, who with Thomas Wentworth Higginson, edited her poems, saw her only twice. Mrs. Todd, knowing of Emily Dickinson's love for Indian Pipes, once sent her a drawing of the curious flower. In her note of thanks, the poet wrote, among other things, "I still cherish the clutch with which I bore it from the ground when a wondering child, an unearthly booty, and maturity only enhances mystery, never decreases it." In spite of her solitude, Emily Dickinson kept her joy in nature in spring. She especially loved March: "Who could be ill in March, that month of proclamation?" she wrote to her friend, the poet "H. H."— Helen Hunt Jackson. In one of her last letters, written in the spring of the year of her death, we find, "I send a violet for L___l. The stem was broken by snow. I'm sorry not to be able to send a butterfly."

A curious character, this woman, who avoided the stream of the world, in which she could easily have stayed afloat, taking refuge instead in her parents' house, where she was born and where she died. Who can say if her talents would have unfolded in the same way had she lived more fully in the ordinary world? Who knows what led her to seek solitude? Emily Dickinson belongs among those whose innermost thoughts and feelings are confided only to the darkness, and perhaps not revealed even to it.

581 A. von E. "For the Women's Section: Emily Dickinson, Part II." *Der Westen,* June 19, 1898, sect. 3, p. 1. The second part of a two-part article; see preceding entry. The four verses quoted here constitute the earliest known translation of Dickinson's poems.

If it is even possible to compare this American poet of such extreme individuality with any other writer, it would be Annette von Droste-Hülshoff. Both women came from old and well-to-do families; both had, in accordance with their time and social status, been given a good education; both lived almost exclusively among the upper class; both, for no apparent reason, gradually withdrew from society, never marrying. To both, nature was not only a changing scenic panorama, but a presence they could address as if it were human. In their poetry, other differences aside, both refused to sacrifice ideas to form. Helvin Schucking, who at first deplored the obscurity and roughness of his friend's poetry, later admitted that these features contributed to the characteristic manner of her work. The same qualities are evident in Emily Dickinson.

In one respect, however, these two poets went their separate ways from the beginning. Whereas the German poet thought of publishing her poems as early as her youth, and later gave considerable thought to choosing the best genre for her work (prose, lyric or epic poetry), the American poet, bird-like, sang spontaneously and for herself alone. She followed her urge for self-expression without regard to those modes which were aesthetically proper at the time, and with little thought for making her ideas fully clear to others. But it was exactly this quality of her poems which produced their strange magic. She developed her own philosophy, religion, moral code, and aesthetics. The literary establishment could hardly be expected to understand, much less appreciate, this indifference to conventional wisdom. To the extent that she realized her originality, Emily Dickinson must have experienced that tyranny of the majority noted by foreign visitors to this country and even deplored recently by such "impartial" Americans as Moncure D. Conway. Something of this feeling seems evident in these heretical lines:

> Much Madness is divinest sense
> To a discerning eye;
> Much sense the starkest madness.
> 'Tis the majority

In this, as all, prevails.
Assent, and you are sane;
Demur,—you're straightway dangerous,
And handled with a chain.

Nevertheless, Emily Dickinson's roughness and heterodoxy does not reduce the beauty of her poetry, taken as a whole. Various as it is in its form and ideas, her work is impossible to criticize from any single point of view. One can only say that it consists of fragments. But is there any *weltanschauung* that is not fragmentary? And how can poetry like hers be anything else, for she seeks above all to articulate impressions, moods, and transitory feelings.

At any rate, it is astonishing how well the poet, in her solitude, could view the world with such penetration and objectivity—and without any sign of pessimism. Instead, one finds in her work an acceptance of fate:

The heart asks pleasure first,
And then, excuse from pain;
And then, those little anodynes
That deaden suffering;

And then, to go to sleep;
And then, if it should be
The will of its Inquisitor,
The liberty to die.

However, Emily Dickinson was not one of those who live among the dead while still alive, longing for release from this world. Rather, she had a strong sense of vocation. Her life work was to be a friend—counseling, consoling, and helping others. Her poetry became the unusual means for fulfilling this purpose. Thus she sings:

If I can stop one heart from breaking,
I shall not live in vain;
If I can ease one life the aching,
Or cool one pain,
Or help one fainting robin
Unto his nest again,
I shall not live in vain.

The experience of love is the fountain of all genuine art; it is impossible to imagine a true poet who does not ultimately derive his inspiration from this source. Of course, to say this does not mean that poems must have an erotic content or even that the absence of love lyrics suggests a poet who didn't have any "experiences," especially in the case of writers like Annette von Droste-Hülshoff and Emily Dickinson, who have lived apart from the world. Both were too reticent to express their personal feelings directly in their work. Nevertheless, in spite of contrary claims by biographers of Droste-Hülshoff and statements that Emily Dickinson had never been in love, both left poems behind which can only be called love songs, though these lyrics did not adhere to conventional forms. Emily Dickinson, who in general was much more personal in her work, even wrote a great number of such poems, and they rank among her best. As an indication of her reticent, yet loving and kindly character, here is a poem entitled "Exclusion":

The soul selects her own society,
Then shuts the door;

On her divine majority
Obtrude no more.

Unmoved, she notes the chariots pausing
At her low gate;
Unmoved, an emperor is kneeling
Upon her mat.

I've known her from an ample nation
Choose one;
Then close the valves of her attention
Like stone.

Among Emily Dickinson's most charming poems are those which originate in her deep and intimate understanding of nature. In one ["Some keep the Sabbath going to church"] she described celebrating Sunday in an orchard with birds for a chorus. There, she said, God himself delivers the sermon and it is never too lengthy. So instead of reaching heaven at the end, she is going all the time. A rain shower, a clover blossom, a bee, a butterfly's cocoon, a daffodil, a gust of wind, a slant of light falling into a room, a leaf of grass, all these things have something to tell her and she has something to say about them. Her images and metaphors are drawn from this world and there are only a few modern women poets whose language is capable of evoking such striking and mysterious pictures. Nothing in nature is so unimportant that it cannot be used to express the truths of life. Neither didactic nor artificial, these lyrics are like nature herself. Is the rock less beautiful for being uneven or the lightning for being jagged? Like the external world itself, these verses taken from nature are sometimes coarse-grained and hard, but not for that reason less appealing. She could not have expressed herself differently. Emily Dickinson had to write as she did to become what she is: the most original woman poet that America has yet produced.

582 "Christmas Books." *Chicago Post,* November 26, 1898, p. 18. The following paragraph is drawn from a review of James Fullarton Muirhead's *The Land of Contrasts* (1898); see no. 579.

"Some Literary Straws" constitutes a chapter which is certainly ingenious, if not instructive. Only three straws are mentioned conspicuously by Mr. Muirhead, and they are Mr. Howells, Miss Emily Dickinson, and Amelie Rives. We may easily understand why Mr. Howells should claim and hold attention, but exactly why Emily Dickinson should be singled out as a distinctively American product we are truly puzzled to explain. With all deference to Miss Dickinson's poetic talents, she was hardly so dazzling a light as to be honored above three score of men and women who have figured and are still figuring in American literature, and we must be pardoned for an expression of skepticism if we fail to see the exploited "likeness to Walt Whitman" in even a remote degree. After a long and enthusiastic notice of the shy little singer of the New England village it is almost amusing to read that "other names that suggest themselves are those of Miss Jewett, Mrs. Elizabeth Phelps Ward, T. B. Aldrich, Thomas Nelson Page, Hamlin Garland, G. W. Cable," and so on. After this summary disposition of these agreeable persons the chapter "fittingly closes" with "passages taken from the tragedy written by Miss Amelie Rives." The fitting conclusion makes us quite forget Mr. Muirhead's sorrowful recognition of the far-reaching influence of—Miss Laura Jean Libbey.

583 Martha Gilbert Dickinson (afterwards Bianchi). "Beneath the Hills; To
E. D." in *Within the Hedge* (New York: Doubleday & McClure, 1899),
pp. 119–27. This and another poem (see next entry), published in her first
book of verse, were written by the poet's niece in tribute to her aunt.
For mention of these two poems, see Higginson's review, no. 590. *Poet-Lore* (11 [1899], 621) described Martha Dickinson's verses as "dainty and
thoughtful, her diction poetic without being forced."

From the unshadowed Autumn afternoon
  The dawn-enraptured dead have turned away;
Absence alone companions me, as with
  The dwellers of forgetfulness I stray.

This same forsaken calm my spirit wrapped
  When fixed in death's absorbed intent you lay;
So unresponsive to my love I knew
  Your soul was with your dreams not with your clay!

If one should find his need a phraseless prayer,
  Standing alone, — an exile set apart —
Perhaps that unknown God would comprehend
  Who chose the symbol of a broken heart.

Strange, that a cross should be love's troth!
    But no,
  Love is redemption if a love divine
Lift love above the myrtle and the bay,
  Sharing its immortality with mine.

Since death first found man out no hour is sure!
  Too easy lies the path unto his door,
Which trodden once, — betrayed security
  Like some disturbèd bird will trust no more.

From those far mansions of inheritance
  Upon the childhood of to-day shall we, —
Maturer grown — cast back a hallowed thought,
  And pity Love as Love was wont to be?

My mind is but a battle-field whereon
  Insurgent thoughts do war, repressed in vain;
Fierce clamoring for reason's overthrow,
  Till dreams renew the bivouac of pain!

If I be dreaming overlong the dream!
  I sicken for the waking! Round my head
The Spring's renascent wonders glorify
  An unfamiliar world — when life is dead.

The wistful South wind for a fonder clime
  Searches and shivers; swift estranged the joy
Of lone communings, solitary ways —
  The pensive vagrancy of youth's employ.

Yet, — yet love has no end! When halting feet
  Distrust their guide, are there not steady wings

To find the harbor of those phantom sails,
    That seek no more the coast of mortal Springs?

How many centuries have eager strode,
    Only to pause at this same narrow gate;
Whose moss-grown hinge ne'er turns for baffled touch,
    Whose portal wears no light for those who wait?

God-haunted tenant of the fleshly frame,
    Cry out against the ignorance of dust!
Until some wrestling prisoner prevail
    To break these earthly bars of life and lust!

The same old burden ages younger hearts,
    The tragic problem wearies childish wills;
While old beginnings press to unreached ends,
    Beneath the calm endurance of the hills.

All passed, all gone their restless, vital way,
    Both those who heard and they who spoke the while;
Those by bereavement torn and those swift seized—
    Who joyed not in the milestone but the mile.

Those who remember are remembered soon;
    Perished as vaguely as the smoke which stands
For friendly cheer and ruddy hearth to-night—
    To-morrow black or lit by alien hands!

Labor and hunger here lie down to sleep—
    Swept is the dwelling, void of hope or fear;
Vanished the tyranny of human aims,
    Darkened the moon of man's reflected sphere.

And yet your proud identity remains,
    Discreet and lowly neighborhood of God;
What mother mourns a universal babe?
    What lover stoops to kiss a common sod?

I will not have thee different in death!
    Be vestured dim in shadow drapery,
Or rugged comrade of the wholesome light—
    Thou art love's own,—and love will follow thee!

How strange that it could stranger seem to meet
    Thee now! That life would reel and mystify
To see thy mounted figure gallant spurn
    Our upland pastures,—left behind to die!

Though Spring all-henceward of thy waking fail,
    Oh hardier brother of the brier-rose,—
Drawing her russet curtains round thy bed,
    The Fall is pillow for thy sure repose.

Where I have watched the ferns go down the year
    In green, and clamber back in brown,—the bloom
Leap in the coppice,—trickle through the dell,
    And sink into November's cloister gloom.

The sedgey roadsides and the wooded slopes
　Do all preserve their sudden loneliness;
Thy season wonders,—unassuaged; each day
　The golden courage of the sun is less.

Thy homeless accents cry to me,—deep though
　Thy tranquil body lie within the shoal
Between these hillocks low of bowing grass—
　Thy soul hath resting place within my soul.

The fact of death is life's fermenting wine;
　Before the dizzy majesty of chance
Love quickens all her offices,—each pulse
　Spurred apprehensive of the final glance.

Pleasure and youth may wander at their will,
　Fame's cold achievement let each laurel fall,
The birth cry of eternity nor hastes
　Nor fails! Death,—death the heritage of all!

Oh world take back thy bribe of certainty!
　All man has fully known is dead or done;
Only the unseen way sufficeth us—
　To know in part infinity begun.

The will that listeth in the seeking wind
　Eludes the craving tongue of prophecy,
The spirit's mating and release are hid—
　The sea hath for her creed,—a mystery!

Ye champions of reticence! Who tent
　Among the spangled cohorts of the dew,
Ye unregretful pioneers of peace—
　No countersign for human hearts have you?

Now must my lone and living purpose pace
　Once more the open shore of stern resolve;
Shake off the passive musing of the dead,
　And 'mid the rival stress of men resolve.

Down Hope's green path to them "who overcome,"
　The pledge of deathless compensation lies;
I take the chance! And with the evening star
　Turn soft away to earn my paradise!

584　Martha Gilbert Dickinson. "Her Grave" in *Within the Hedge* (New York: Doubleday & McClure, 1899), p. 109.

Since each spot where we parted upon earth is dear,
And since our bravest, fondest parting met us here—
I bring the changing flowers that her grave be dressed
As fits the chamber last by her possessed.
Finite can follow infinite but to this stile;
Good-night then, Love—a blessed afterwhile!

585 "Why Was She a Recluse? Two Portland People Talk About Emily Dickinson. *Portland Sunday Oregonian,* March 19, 1899, p. 22. The two reminiscences are by Mrs. Thomas L. Eliot (nee Henrietta Robins Mack) and William L. Brewster. The Mack family purchased half the Dickinson homestead in 1833 and the entire house in 1840. In 1855 it was sold back to the Dickinsons by Mrs. Eliot's father, Samuel Mack. Shortly after his death eleven years later, Henrietta Mack's mother, Rebecca, visited the Dickinson sisters in Amherst. Comment by Mrs. Todd and a selection of the poet's letters, comprising the final section of this article, are drawn from the 1894 *Letters* (Todd's remarks are pp. 368–70); see no. 419.

Portland people will be interested in learning that Emily Dickinson, the New England poet, was warmly attached to the family of a Portland woman, Mrs. Thomas L. Eliot. Mrs. Eliot, indeed, was born in the old colonial house that is now the Dickinson place in Amherst, Mass. Her grandfather bought the house from the Dickinsons about 70 years ago, and 30 years later her father sold it back again to them. A close friendship existed between the two families, both Emily and Lavinia, her sister, conceiving, as children, a romantic devotion for Mrs. Eliot's father and mother. As this incidentally reached the ears of a reporter of The Oregonian, Mrs. Eliot was sought for further information on the subject. She said:

"I am afraid I cannot tell you anything of interest, since my father moved West when I was only two years old, so that I knew Emily Dickinson only during my visits at Amherst when I was a child.

"Edward Dickinson, their father, was a Puritan of Puritans in his ways, very reserved and undemonstrative. When I went East 8 years ago, I had a long talk with Lavinia, who said of him: 'My father would have died for either of us, but he would never let us know it. He never kissed either of us goodnight in his life.' She told me, moreover, that one of the most charming memories of her own and Emily's childhood was the children's parties my mother used to give them.

"Emily, as I remember her, had beautiful auburn hair, but she was not pretty, and was never attractive to me as a child. She was about 15 years older than I. She was very shrinking and sensitive in disposition, and this finally led her to seclude herself entirely from society; she never went beyond her family garden, so morbid did she grow, and out of tune with the world. When my father died, 32 years ago, my mother went East. Emily, at that time, saw no one, and talked to no one, but so romantic had been her attachment for my parents, that she insisted upon meeting my mother, who accordingly went to her home to see her. After being shown into a room that adjoined Emily's, she was seated next to a door which stood ajar, on the other side of which was Emily, and thus the conversation was carried on without either seeing the other's face.

"As for her verses, although there was the ethereal quintessence of poetry in her lines, they were disjointed and erratic, for she would suddenly lose all sense of rhythm and rhyme and drop into prose.

"Lavinia, who was nearly the same age as Emily, is now the sole surviving member of the family. She was also very talented, somewhat eccentric, and like her sister, remained unmarried. She was especially brilliant in conversation, quick at repartee, more attractive in appearance than Emily, and passionately fond of flowers.

"I remember when I visited in Amherst just before my marriage Emily had already entered upon her retired life, seeing no one, and never going outside the family garden; but Lavinia came to see me and brought me the most beautiful flowers. She seemed to have a personal affection for these, speaking to each flower individually as she lifted it from the basket, caressing it as though she hated to part with it, and all this was done so simply and spontaneously as to be absolutely free from affectation.

"Their mother before them was eccentric; she was a very dainty, exquisitely neat housekeeper, so much so, indeed, that her neatness rather oppressed those around her."

William L. Brewster, of this city, who entered Amherst college in 1886, two or three months after Emily Dickinson's death, was acquainted with the Dickinson family. He says that no one at that time in Amherst had any idea of the real value of the little poems that she had been in the habit of sending to friends in return for small gifts of fruit and flowers. No one had yet discovered the touch of genius in her work. The two sisters had lived alone in the big New England house, with only a servant for companion. They were very fond of cooking and enjoyed good living; most of their time, however, was spent in the fine old garden which covered several acres of ground and contained many choice flowers and noble elm trees. They had no close neighbors except their brother, who lived in the adjoining house, but even this they never visited. This brother, who has but recently died, was a lawyer of much ability and influence in the town, treasurer of Amherst College, and invariably elected moderator of the town meeting. He was a man of keen wit, brusque and autocratic, rather than lovable, but entertaining in conversation, with a fund of good stories always at his command. The Dickinson family had for generations back been respected as the aristocrats of the place, and the eccentricities of the two sisters were therefore passed over as simply part of a general "queerness" peculiar to the family. In Mr. Brewster's opinion, however, both were slightly tinged with insanity.

The sympathetic friends of Emily Dickinson who collected her letters and poems after her death were not of this opinion. Neither did they consider this seclusion the result of any absorbing grief. Mrs. Mabel Loomis Todd loyally explains it as follows:

"Most of us would require some sudden blow, some fierce crisis, to produce such a result—a hidden and unusual life like hers. And we love to believe striking and theatrical things of our neighbors; it panders to that romantic element latent in the plainest. But Emily Dickinson's method of living was so simple and natural an outcome of her increasingly shy nature, a development so perfectly in the line with her whole constitution that no far-away life is necessary to those who are capable of apprehending her.

"That sentence alone would reveal the key, wherein she wrote with regret for her long-time maid Margaret: 'I winced at her loss, for I am in the habit of her, and even a new rolling pin has an embarrassing element.' Emerson somewhere says, 'Now and then a man exquisitely made can live alone,' and Lord Bacon puts the thought with even greater force and directness: 'Whosoever is delighted in solitude is either a wilde beaste or a God.' To some natures introspection is a necessity for expression. 'Why should I feel lonely?' exclaimed Thoreau, in his temporary isolation at Walden. 'Is not our planet in the Milky Way?' He was indeed 'no more lonely than the North Star' nor was Emily Dickinson, although congenial companionship had in a sense been very dear to her. George Ebers once wrote: 'Sheep and geese become restless when separated from the flock: the eagle and lion seek isolation'—a picturesque and perhaps not less strong presentation of a nearly identical thought.

"But although invisible for years, even to lifelong friends, Emily Dickinson never denied herself to children. To them she was always accessible, always delightful, and in their eyes a sort of fairy guardian. Stories are yet told of her roguishly lowering baskets of goodies out of her window by a string to the little ones waiting below. Mr. MacGregor Jenkins, in a sketch of his recollections of Emily Dickinson, has shown this gracious and womanly side of her nature in a very charming way, quoting a number of notes to himself and his sister, two members of a quartet of children admitted to her intimacy." These notes and the others that follow to older friends, all selected haphazard, are certainly not morbid, but breathe the dainty humor, joyous freshness of soul, mingling with weird mysticism that made up the prevailing tone of her letters—the only link that bound her to the world:

Happy "Did" and Mac,—We can offer you nothing so charming as your own hearts, which we would seek to possess, had we the requisite wiles. [*L*, no. 482]

Dear Boys—Please never grow up, which is far better. Please never "improve." You are perfect now.   EMILY. [*L*, no. 717]

Little Women—Which shall it be, geraniums or tulips?
The butterfly upon the sky, who doesn't know its name,
And hasn't any tax to pay, and hasn't any home,
Is just as high as you and I, and higher, I believe—
So soar away and never sigh, for that's the way to grieve.
[*L*, no. 482]

(Christmas, 1874.)
Atmospherically, it was the most beautiful Christmas on record. The hens came to the door with Santa Claus, the pussies washed themselves in the open air without chilling their tongues, and Santa Claus—sweet old gentleman—was even gallanter than usual. Visitors from the chimney were a new dismay, but all of them brought their hands so full and behaved so sweetly, only a churl could have turned them away. And then the ones at the barn were so happy! Maggie gave the hens a check for potatoes, each of the cats had a gilt-edged bone, and the horse had new blankets from Boston.

Do you remember dark-eyed Mr. Dickinson, who used to shake your hand when it was so little it had hardly a stem? He, too, had a beautiful gift of roses from a friend away. It was a lovely Christmas. But what made you remember me? Tell me with a kiss—or is it a secret?   EMILY. [*L*, no. 682]

To a niece of her father's who had sent some roses for his grave, she wrote, December 1874:

I am sure you must have remembered that father had "become as little children," or you would never have dared send him a Christmas gift, for you know how he frowned upon Santa Claus, and all such prowling gentlemen. [*L*, no. 425]

Accompanying a box of delicious chocolate caramels sent a friend at New Year's with the receipt. The "Vinnie" referred to is, of course, her sister:

Vinnie says the dear friend would like the rule. We have no statutes here, but each does as it will, which is the sweetest jurisprudence.

With it, I enclose Love's "remainder biscuit," somewhat scorched, perhaps, in baking, but "Love's oven is warm." Forgive the base proportions.

Again receive the love which comes without aspect, and without herald goes.
EMILY. [L, no. 545]

Autumn, 1880. To her maid ill with typhoid fever at her own home:

The missing Maggie is much mourned. All are very naughty, and I am naughtiest of all. The pussies dine on sherry now, and hummingbird cutlets.

The invalid hen took dinner with me, but a hen like Dr. T____'s horse soon drove her away. I am very busy picking up stems and stamens as the hollyhocks leave their clothes around. What shall I send my weary Maggie? Pillows, or fresh brooks? HER GRIEVED MISTRESS. [L, no. 771]

As her strange life drew toward its close, she became for the last two years a semi-invalid—she who always rejoiced in strength and bravery for her own need and that of her friends. Even to the last, however, she brightened the old house with her airy, yet forceful and brilliant personality, for even ill she was a pervasive presence.

March, 1886, one of her last letters written a few weeks before her death:

I scarcely know where to begin, but love is always a safe place. I have twice been very sick, dears, with a little recess of convalescence, then to be more sick, and have lain in my bed ever since November, many years for me, stirring as the arbutus does, a pink and russet hope; but that we will leave with our pillow. When your dear hearts are quite convenient, tell us of their contents, the fabric cared for most, not a fondness wanting.

Do you keep musk, as you used to, like Mrs. Morene of Mexico? Or cassia carnations so big they split their fringes of berry? Was your winter a tender shelter—perhaps like Keats's bird "and hops and hops in little journeys."

Are you reading and well, and the W____s near and warm? When you see Mrs. French and Dan give them a tear from us. [L, no. 1034]

Among her last verses is the following, enclosed in a letter to Helen Hunt Jackson:

> Take all away from me
> But leave me ecstasy,
> And I am richer then
> Than all my fellow-men.
> Is it becoming me
> To dwell so wealthily,
> When at my very door
> Are those possessing more,
> In boundless poverty? [L, no. 976]

586 "In Book Land." *Newport Daily News*, May 16, 1899, p. 3. The two writers alluded to in the opening sentence are Arthur Hugh Clough and Edward Rowland Sill.

Linked to these two retiring great is another; linked by death, by genius, by simplicity and humility. Emily Dickinson would have refused even the resurrection of her thoughts could she have ordered it so. They were herself; epitomes of her woodland shyness, of her evasive personality, her nimble wit, and alert and almost infallible intuition—and herself she screened from acquaintance. Yet had unending hermitage awaited the verses which she scattered in lavish wastefulness, how poorer had been American letters.

Here is the third volume of these rescued poems; as artless, as daring, as competent, as were the two former issues. And yet we miss and grumble at the loss of other verses, sent roving in letters to the friends who were her service of love. The sentient phrase, the exhaustless vitality of every clear-cut word, making each verse a very precipitate of thought, urge the reading. The words sink into the memory almost unconsciously; they are so inevitable one wonders at ordinary cumbrous usage. One can well believe that she

> found the phrase to every thought
> I ever had but one.

For so various are her wisdoms and so unerring her word-choosing that one feels she must also have shared the reader's satisfaction in the propriety of every one. The charm of her individuality, veiled as it is, lurks in every line, in every quip and twist of expression, as in the poem, where hoping in dreams of night to peep into mysteries hid from day-blinded eyes, she says:

> And if I do, when morning comes,
> It is as if a hundred drums
>   Did round my pillow roll,
> And shouts fill all my childish sky,
> And bells keep saying "victory"
>   From steeples in my soul.
>
> And if I don't, the little bird,
> Within the orchard is not heard,
>   And I omit to pray,
> "Father, thy will be done" today,
> For my will goes the other way,
>   And it were perjury!

And the sympathetic little glimpse of childhood joys called "Saturday Afternoon:"

> From all the jails the boys and girls
>   Ecstatically leap—
> Beloved, only afternoon
>   That prison doesn't keep.
>
> They storm the earth and stun the air,
>   A mob of solid bliss.
> Alas! that frowns could lie in wait
>   For such a foe as this.

Her appalling fearlessness of expression is an unfailing delight. In her hand the English language becomes a live and supple thing, pregnant with unguessed values. Yet her poetic work was but as the chips thrown off from the master's ideal, for her greatest worth was the pervasive, piquant, loving, friendly, heart which remains in many memories unfading.

Little, Brown & Co. have taken over the publication of Miss Dickinson's poems from the firm of Roberts Bros.

587 Bliss Carman. "Bliss Carman's Marginal Notes." *Chicago Post,* July 15, 1899, p. 7. Carman is discussing the modernity of William Blake.

Any contemporary reader, with his ear attuned to the cadence of the opening lines from "Woodnotes"—

> For this present, hard
> Is the fortune of the bard,
>   Born out of time;
> All his accomplishment,
> From Nature's utmost treasure spent,
>   Boots not him.

—might easily attribute the following verse to Emerson:

> Hear the voice of the bard,
>   Who present, past and future sees;
> Whose ears have heard
> The Holy Word,
>   That walked among the ancient trees.

But it is not Emerson's, it is not American, it does not belong to this century at all. It is the opening stanza of William Blake's "Songs of Experience," engraved by him in 1794. And the close of the same poem,

> The starry floor.
> The watery shore,
> Are given thee till the break of day.

Surely one would not call that the typical note of the eighteenth century in poetry; it might almost be called typical of the close of the nineteenth.
And again in one of the "Songs of Innocence,"

> Can I see another's woe,
> And not sorrow in it, too?
> Can I see another's grief,
> And not seek for kind relief?

> Can I see a falling tear,
> And not feel my sorrow's share?
> Can a father see his child
> Weep, nor be with sorrow filled?

Here, it is true, there is very little of our modern manner. Yet there is a trick of rhyme which one of the greatest of American poets used to the extent of a mannerism. Yes, more than a mannerism. For Emily Dickinson's peculiar scheme of rhyme was handled with such mastery, with such an exquisite ear for cadence, as to become in her hands a new and original stop in the great organ of English versification. Possibly she got her first hint of it from the English mystic, Blake, the father of modern English symbolism. While Emerson, we may be sure, must have been more than slightly influenced by that mighty visionist.

588 "Three Recent Women Poets." *Chicago Post,* July 15, 1899, p. 5. A review of Martha Gilbert Dickinson's volume of verse, *Within the Hedge* (New York: Doubleday & McClure, 1899); see nos. 583, 584. Martha Dickinson was the poet's niece.

A cousin of Emily Dickinson, she has gone quite to the other extreme in writing her verses. Where one was original, regardless of technique and satisfied if she had something to say without thinking of how to say it, the other is conventional, subservient to the poetical fashions of the day, rather confused in ideas.

589 Susan Hayes Ward. "A Decade of Poetry, 1889–1899." *Independent* 51 (September 28, 1899), 2610. The authors referred to in the first sentence of this excerpt are Julian Hawthorne, Edgar Fawcett, James Whitcomb Riley, and Hamlin Garland. "Spring's Orchestra" is Dickinson's "The saddest noise, the sweetest noise," first published in the *Independent* 50 (June 2, 1898), 705.

More gifted by nature than any of these was Emily Dickinson, the shy poet on whose posthumous volumes the frail bloom of the Indian pipe is stamped as a fitting emblem of her and her work. Thanks are due to the near friends and relatives who have aided in rescuing from scattered correspondence these shoots of verse, which, compact as springtime buds, enfold the leafage, blossom and fruit of poesy's rounded year. But that the rhyme is for her unusually perfect," "Spring's Orchestra" (June 2d, 1898) would be an excellent example of Miss Dickinson's wayward, elusive, captivating style, the despair of critics, the delight of poets.

590 [Thomas Wentworth Higginson.] "Recent Poetry." *Nation* 69 (November 16, 1899), 377. See nos. 583, 584 for the two poems in tribute to her aunt published by Martha Gilbert Dickinson in her volume reviewed here.

In the volume "Within the Hedge," by Martha Gilbert Dickinson (Doubleday), there is sometimes a resemblance to the poems of her aunt Emily so striking that one wonders whether to call it heredity or imitation, as in the following (p. 106):

WRECKED.

No one dreamed of a wreck that night,
  A hundred miles from sea;
The moon hung high her signal light
  Above the lilac tree.

The tides of youth were hardly turned,
  There was no warning frown
On Heaven's face — while undiscerned
  An out-bound heart went down!

Oh sweet old-fashioned garden balms —
  A hundred miles from sea.
How treacherous thy Summer calms!
  Mirage of memory.

It is curious to observe, however, that there are glimpses of Emily Dickinson which show themselves from page to page, even in the poetry of English women. Thus, Winifred Lucas, in her "Fugitives" (John Lane), has many short poems, some of which are as Dickinsonian as this (p. 22):

LOVE HEROIC.

Companioned on the path you chose,
You go the way
A hero goes.
His words you say,
Your deeds he does.
Though in your love to heaven he rose,
The way he knows
Immortal in your life to stay.

There is, however, in the poems of Miss Martha Dickinson a greater evenness of structure and greater variety of subject extending even so far as a poem called "Nooning," describing almost too realistically the street laborers at dinner. One of the most thoughtful and earnest poems is that which closes the book, and is addressed evidently to her aunt. But one of the most condensed and powerful, still recalling Emily Dickinson by its manner, is this brief memorial (p. 109):

HER GRAVE.

Since each spot where we parted upon earth is dear,
And since our bravest, fondest parting met us here—
I bring the changing flowers that her grave be dressed
As fits the chamber last by her possessed.
Finite can follow infinite but to this stile;
Good night then, Love—a blessed afterwhile!

591 J[oseph] K. C[hickering]. "The Late Lavinia Dickinson: Friend's Admiring Tribute to a Unique Personality." *Springfield Weekly Republican*, November 30, 1899, p. 5. From this essay on the poet's sister, who died August 31, 1899, only passages mentioning Emily Dickinson are reprinted here. The full text is available in Millicent Todd Bingham's *Home*, pp. 490–92.

Her conversational and literary gifts would have been more highly appreciated and more widely known, but for the extraordinary powers of her famous sister. I do not know whether this ever occurred to her, but I do know that I never met a human being so absolutely absorbed in admiration of another as was this woman in admiration of her sister. Those who never heard her read one of Emily's poems, or a tribute from some new worshiper at her shrine, missed a rare and uplifting experience. I should add that this enthusiastic devotion to one member of the family circle extended in turn to every other. . . . She was not given to analyzing her spiritual condition. She seemed less conscious of her duties toward her Creator than toward the creatures of his hand. I think she could have adopted as her own her sister's fine lines:—

Afraid? Of whom am I afraid?
Not death; for who is he?
The porter of my father's lodge
As much abasheth me.

Of life? 'Twere odd I fear a thing
That comprehendeth me
In one or more existences
At Deity's decree.

Of Resurrection? Is the east
Afraid to trust the morn
With her fastidious forehead?
As soon impeach my crown!

Appendixes

Indexes

APPENDIX A
Emily Dickinson's Obituary

[Susan Gilbert Dickinson.] "Miss Emily Dickinson of Amherst." *Springfield Republican*, May 18, 1886, p. 4. Reprinted: "Miss Emily Dickinson." *Amherst Record*, May 19, 1886, p. 4. Partially reprinted: *YH*, II, 472–74. For discussion of Helen Hunt Jackson and the "No Name Series," see Sewall, *Life*, 581–83.

The death of Miss Emily Dickinson, daughter of the late Edward Dickinson, at Amherst on Saturday, makes another sad inroad on the small circle so long occupying the old family mansion. It was for a long generation overlooked by death, and one passing in and out there thought of old-fashioned times, when parents and children grew up and passed maturity together, in lives of singular uneventfulness unmarked by sad or joyous crises. Very few in the village, except among the older inhabitants, knew Miss Emily personally, although the facts of her seclusion and intellectual brilliancy were familiar Amherst traditions. There are many houses among all classes into which treasures of fruit and flowers and ambrosial dishes for the sick and well were constantly sent, that will forever miss those evidences of her unselfish consideration, and mourn afresh that she screened herself from close acquaintance. As she passed on in life, her sensitive nature shrank from much personal contact with the world, and more and more turned to her own large wealth of individual resources for companionship, sitting thenceforth, as some one said of her, "in the light of her own fire." Not disappointed with the world, not an invalid until within the past two years, not from any lack of sympathy, not because she was insufficient for any mental work or social career—her endowments being so exceptional—but the "mesh of her soul," as Browning calls the body, was too rare, and the sacred quiet of her own home proved the fit atmosphere for her worth and work. All that must be inviolate. One can only speak of "duties beautifully done"; of her gentle tillage of the rare flowers filling her conservatory, into which, as into the heavenly Paradise, entered nothing that could defile, and which was ever abloom in frost or sunshine, so well she knew her chemistries; of her tenderness to all in the home circle; her gentlewoman's grace and courtesy to all who served in house and grounds; her quick and rich response to all who rejoiced or suffered at home, or among her wide circle of friends the world over. This side of her nature was to her the real entity in which she rested, so simple and strong was her instinct that a woman's hearthstone is her shrine. Her talk and her writings were like no one's else, and although she never published a line, now and then some enthusiastic literary friend would turn love to larceny, and cause a few verses surreptitiously obtained to be printed. Thus, and through other natural ways, many saw and admired her verses, and in consequence frequently notable persons paid her visits, hoping to overcome the protest of her own nature and gain a promise of occasional contributions, at least, to various magazines. She withstood even the fascinations of Mrs. Helen Jackson, who earnestly sought her co-operation in a novel of the No Name series, although one little poem somehow strayed into the volume of verse which appeared in that series. Her pages would ill have fitted even so attractive a story as "Mercy Philbrick's Choice," unwilling though a large part of the literary public were to believe that she had no part in it. "Her wagon was hitched to a star,"—and who could ride or write with such a voyager? A Damascus blade gleaming and glancing in the sun was her wit. Her swift poetic rapture was like the long glistening note of a bird one hears in the June woods at high noon, but can never see. Like a magician she caught the shadowy apparitions of her brain and tossed them in startling picturesqueness to her friends, who, charmed with their simplicity and homeliness as well as profundity, fretted that she had so easily made palpable the tantalizing fancies forever eluding their bungling, fettered grasp. So intimate and passionate was her love of Nature, she seemed herself a part of the high March sky, the summer day and bird-call. Keen and eclectic in her literary tastes, she sifted libraries to Shakespeare and Browning; quick as the lightning in her intuitions and analyses, she seized the kernel instantly, almost impatient of the fewest words, by which she must make her revelation. To her, life was rich and all aglow with God and immortality. With no creed, no formulated faith, hardly knowing the names of dogmas, she walked this life with the gentleness and reverence of old saints, with the firm step of martyrs who sing while they suffer. How better note the flight of this "soul of fire in a shell of pearl" than by her own words?—

> Morns like these, we parted;
> Noons like these, she rose;
> Fluttering first, then firmer,
> To her fair repose.

APPENDIX B
Diaries and Letters of the Nineties Not Published Until the Twentieth Century

FOR full citation of abbreviated titles, see p. 2. Unpublished correspondence of Mrs. Todd relating to her editing of Dickinson is held by the Amherst College Library; the Bieneke Library, Yale University, owns her diary. Richard B. Sewall's *Life of Emily Dickinson* (1974), containing quotations from nineteenth-century diaries and correspondence relating to the poet, has not been analyzed for inclusion here. The exception is Sewall's reprinting of a lengthy reminiscence by Clara Newman Turner (see below).

Alden, Henry M.; see *W. D. Howells: Selected Letters*, ed. Robert C. Leitz (Boston: Twayne, 1980), 3:301, n.3.
Barrows, Samuel; see *AB*, 125; *CR*, 30.
Bates, Arlo; see *AB*, 52–53.
Bowles, Samuel; see *AB*, 251–53, 261–62.
Brownell, William Crary; see Robert Burlingame, *Of Making Many Books* (N.Y.: Scribner's, 1946), 272.
Buffum, Vryling Wilder; see *AB*, 369–70.
Burlingame, Edward L.; see *AB*, 59; Roger Burlingame, *Of Making Many Books* (N.Y.: Scribner's, 1946), 273–74.
Chadwick, John W.; see *AB*, 73, 93–94.
Chickering, Joseph K.; see *AB*, 298.
Cowan, Perez D.; see *AB*, 140, 259, 260.
Currier, Annie Dickinson; see *AB*, 244–45.
Dickinson, Ellen E.; see *AB*, 263, 264–65.
Dickinson, Lavinia; see *AB*, passim.
Dickinson, Susan H.; see *AB*, 86–87, 92, 114–15, 116–18; "Two Generations of Amherst Society" in *Essays on Amherst's History* (Amherst, Mass.: The Vista Trust, 1978), 168–88.
Dickinson, William Austin; see *AB*, 66, 288, 295–96, 300–01.
Dole, Nathan Haskell; see *AB*, 313.
Donald, E. Winchester; see *AB*, 76–77, 314–15.
Elson, A.W.; see *AB*, 272.
Emerson, Forrest F.; see *AB*, 260–61.
Fiske, D.T.; see *AB*, 253.
Fletcher, William I.; see *AB*, 204–05, 306–07.
Flynt, Mrs. William N.; see *AB*, 133.

Ford, Emily Ellsworth Fowler; see Emily Dickinson's *Letters*, ed. Mabel Loomis Todd (New and Enlarged Edition, N.Y.: Harper, 1931), 123–32; *AB*, 241, 242.

Fuller, Gardner; see *AB*, 198, 200.

Gould, George H.; see *AB*, 245–55.

Hale, Edward E.; see *AB*, 254, 255.

Hanks, Annie D.; see *AB*, 178.

Hardy, E.D.; see *AB*, 118–19, 171, 280, 292, 300, 312, 313.

Hickley, Katharine; see *AB*, 184–85.

Higginson, Thomas Wentworth; see *AB*, passim; *Letters and Journals of Thomas Wentworth Higginson, 1846–1906*, ed. Mary Thacher Higginson (Boston: Houghton Mifflin, 1921), 231–32.

Holahan, Martha Eileen; see *AB*, 180–81.

Holland, Elizabeth C.; see *AB*, 193.

Holley, H.W.; see *AB*, 179–80.

Howells, William Dean; see *AB*, 202, 310; *Mark Twain—Howells Letters: The Correspondence of Samuel L. Clemens and William Dean Howells*, ed. Henry Nash Smith and William M. Gibson (Cambridge, Mass.: Harvard Univ. Press, 1960), 2:681; *W. D. Howells: Selected Letters*, ed. Robert C. Leitz (Boston: Twayne, 1980), 3:295–96.

Huntington, (Bishop) Frederick Dan; see *AB*, 197; *YH*, 2:479.

Jackson, Helen Banfield; see *AB*, 240.

Jackson, William S.; see *AB*, 153.

James, Alice; see *Alice James, Her Brothers, Her Journal*, ed. Anna Robeson Burr (New York: Dodd, Mead, 1934), 248–49.

Kellogg, Anna M.; see *AB*, 206.

Kimball, Benjamin; see *AB*, 119–20.

Markham, Edwin; see Genevieve B. Earle, "'Some Watcher of the Skies,'" *The Book Collector's Packet* 3 (March 1939), 11–12.

Montague, Charles C.; see *AB*, 262.

Niles, Thomas; see *AB*, passim.

Norcross, Frances L.; see *AB*, 142, 147, 148, 238–39, 249, 250, 282–84.

Osgood, James R.; see *CR*, 94.

Prevost, A. M.; see *AB*, 184–85.

Rossetti, Christina; see *CR*, 30.

Sanborn, Franklin Benjamin; see *AB*, 293–94.

Speake, Mrs. H. C.; see *AB*, 177.

Stedman, Edmund Clarence; see *Life and Letters of Edmund Clarence Stedman*, ed. Laura Stedman and George M. Gould (New York: Moffat, Yard, 1910), 2: 472–73.

Strong, Abiah P.; see *AB*, 207–09.

Tabb, John Banister; see *AB*, 315–16; *Letters—Grave and Gay and Other Prose of John Banister Tabb*, ed. Francis E. Litz (Washington, D.C.: Catholic Univ. of America Press, 1950), 61, 62–63, 72, 93, 94, 96, 140; *John Bannister Tabb on Emily Dickinson* (New York: Seven Gables Bookshop, 1950), 7 unnumbered pages.

Thayer, William Roscoe; see *AB*, 123; *CR*, 34.

Todd, David Peck; see *AB*, 306.

Todd, Mabel Loomis; see *AB*, 401–05, passim; *YH*, 2:483.

Turner, Clara Newman; see *YH* 1:136; 2:67–68, 141–42, 226, 383–84, 481; Sewall, *Life*, 265–92.

Ward, Samuel G.; see *Letters* (1931), xxii; *AB*, 169–70; *CR*, 33.

Ward, William Hayes; see *AB*, 112–13, 116.

Whitney, Maria; see *AB*, 257–59.

APPENDIX C
Apparently Erroneous Citations
of Nineties Reviews

T H E following citations, deriving from Todd's scrapbooks and from Virginia Terris's 1973 dissertation, "Emily Dickinson and the Genteel Critics," have proved impossible to verify. The arrangement is chronological.

Brooklyn Commercial Advertiser, Jan. 6, 1891, p. 4. *GC*, 378, but not Todd's scrapbooks. There is no publication record of a newspaper with this title for this date. This entry may derive from a *New York Commercial Advertiser* item (no. 78) reflecting the same date and page.

Brooklyn Standard Union, Jan. 6, 1891. *GC*, 378, but not Todd's scrapbooks. Search of this paper and the *Brooklyn Eagle* for this date proved fruitless.

Chicago Evening Post, Feb. 1, 1891. *GC*, 378, but not Todd's scrapbooks. No *Post* was published on this day and a search of proximate issues yielded nothing. This entry may derive from the *Post* item (no. 70) for Jan. 2, 1891.

Boston Evening Transcript, Oct. 14, 1891. *GC*, 378, but not in Todd's scrapbooks.

Joseph M. Pratt. "To Hearing Ears." *Springfield Republican*, Nov. 8, 1891, p. 6. *GC*, 375. This poem has nothing to do with Dickinson, although it appears on the same page as no. 262.

Literary World, Dec. 6, 1891. *GC*, 380. There being no issue for this date, the entry seems to reflect a misprint for an item appearing in the same journal Dec. 6, 1890 (no. 40).

"The Literary Wayside." *Springfield Republican*, Dec. 10, 1891. *GC*, 381. Searched without result. An item appearing on this date might well be a birthday remembrance, but only the *Boston Evening Transcript*, later in the decade, carried such notices for Dickinson.

New York Evening Sun, Dec. 12, 1891. *GC*, 381. The paper for this date, and for Jan. 12, 1892, as cited in *AB*, 407, was searched to no effect. This entry may derive from Todd's clipping dated Jan. 12, 1891 (no. 86).

"Poems by Emily Dickinson." *Boston Sunday Herald*, Dec. 18, 1891, p. 6. *GC*, 382. No number issued on this date. The nearest issues were searched without result.

Cincinnati Commercial Gazette, Dec. 17, 1891. *GC*, 378. Searched without result.

New York Daily Tatler 1 (Nov. 11, 1894), 4–5. *GC*, 384. Probably a misprint for the *Tatler* item two years later (no. 555).

Woman's Journal, Dec. 15, 1894. Reported in Todd's scrapbook. This and proximate issues of the *Woman's Journal* were searched without result. The citation derives from a penciled note near Todd's clipping of a notice the *Letters* had received in the Dec. 8th issue of the *Journal,* indicating that she had been given to believe that another review had appeared there a week later.

"Letters of Emily Dickinson." *New York Commercial Advertiser,* Dec. 27, 1894. GC, 380. Searched unsuccessfully.

"Emily Dickinson." *Boston Evening Transcript.* Oct. 15, 1895. GC, 379. Searched without result.

Chicago Tribune, June 11, 1896. GC, 378. Searched without result.

Critic, Sept. 5, 1896. Todd's scrapbooks. Searched without result.

America, Sept. 10, 1896. Todd's scrapbooks. This journal ceased in 1891.

Christian Union, Sept. 12, 1896. Todd's scrapbooks. The journal title had changed to the *Outlook* by this date. Searched without result.

Philadelphia Ledger, Sept. 12, 1896. Todd's scrapbooks. Searched without result.

Springfield Union, ca. Sept. 13, 1896. Todd's scrapbooks. Searched without result.

New York Times, Sept. 19, 1896. Todd's scrapbooks. Evidently the mistaken date for a review appearing several days later (no. 528).

Zion's Herald, Oct. 8, 1896. GC, 384. Issues for several months either side of this date searched without result.

San Francisco Bulletin, Dec. 6, 1896. GC, 383. Nearest issues searched without result. Probably a misprint for a *Bulletin* item appearing this day six years earlier (no. 42).

APPENDIX D
Sales of Dickinson Volumes in the Nineties

THESE figures derive from information provided in Joel Myerson's *Emily Dickinson: A Descriptive Bibliography* (Pittsburgh, Pa.: University of Pittsburgh Press, 1984), *passim.*

	Myerson Item No.	Printing Date	Printing Order	Cumulative Sales by Volume	Total Sales
Poems, First Series					
(Boston, 1890)	a.	8 Oct. 90	500	500	
	b.	11 Dec. 90	500	1,000	
	c.	? Dec. 90	[500]	1,500	
	d.	23 Dec. 90	500	2,000	
	e.	24 Jan. 91	500	2,500	
	f.	8 Feb. 91	500	3,000	
	g.	14 Mar. 91	500	3,500	
	h.	11 Jul. 91	500	4,000	
	i.	20 Oct. 91	500	4,500	
	j.	9 Nov. 91	1,000	5,500	
	k.	24 Dec. 91	1,000	6,500	
	l.	3 Sep. 92	500	7,000	
	m.	14 Mar. 93	280	7,280	
	n.	? Mar. 93	[280]	7,560	
	o.	? May 93	500	8,060	
	p.	? Nov. 93	[280]	8,340	
	q.	18 Dec. 94	280	8,620	
	r.	7 Feb. 96	280	8,900	
	s.	22 Mar. 97	280	9,180	
	t.	? Jun. 98	[280]	9,460	9,460
Poems, First Series					
(London, 1891)		? Aug. 91	[500]	9,960	9,960
Poems, Second Series					
(Boston, 1891)	a.	21 Oct. 91	960	960	
	b.	14 Nov. 91	1,000	1,960	

	Myerson Item No.	Printing Date	Printing Order	Cumulative Sales by Volume	Total Sales
	c.	3 Dec. 91	1,000	2,960	
	d.	22 Dec. 91	500	3,460	
	e.	28 Dec. 91	1,000	4,460	
	f.	[Dec. 92]	500	4,960	
	g.	? Mar. 93	[280]	5,240	
	h.	? May 93	500	5,740	
	i.	? Dec. 94	280	6,020	
	j.	9 Oct. 96	280	6,300	
	k.	[Dec. 97]	280	6,580	15,480*
Letters of Emily Dickinson (Boston, 1894)	a.	? Nov. 94	1,000	1,000	
	b.	? Dec. 94	1,500	2,500	17,980
Poems, Third Series (Boston, 1896)	a.	8 Apr. 96	1,000	1,000	
	b.	21 Sep. 96	1,000	2,000	19,980
Summaries for the Decade					
	First Series:				
	American editions			8,280	
	British edition			500	8,780
	Second Series			5,520	14,300
	Combined First & Second			1,060	15,360
	Third Series			2,000	17,360
	Letters			2,500	19,860

*Represents separate titles published, counting once those printings in which the First and Second Series were bound together.

Divisions.	1889	1890	No. of new books made in the U. S.	No. of new editions made in the U. S.	No. of new books imported.	No. of new editions imported.
			Analysis of manufacture and importation in 1890.			
Fiction	942	1118	935	105	57	21
Theology and Religion	363	467	304	46	109	8
Law	410	458	425	26	7	..
Juvenile	388	408	209	15	184	..
Education and Language	319	399	240	18	131	10
Biography, Memoirs	178	218	113	14	79	12
Literary, History and Miscellany	144	183	104	19	50	10
Political and Social Science	157	183	151	4	26	2
Poetry and the Drama	171	168	118	8	42	..
Description, Travel	139	162	86	22	49	5
History	110	153	95	20	36	2
Fine Art and Illustrated Books	171	135	85	8	42	..
Useful Arts	129	133	78	12	31	12
Medical Science, Hygiene	157	117	80	21	14	2
Physical and Mathematical Science	96	93	52	6	34	1
Sports and Amusements	43	82	46	7	24	5
Humor and Satire	25	42	35	..	7	..
Domestic and Rural	44	29	20	.	7	2
Mental and Moral Philosophy	28	11	4	2	4	1
	4014	4559	3180	353	933	93
						4559

Book production statistics for the United States, *Publishers' Weekly*, 24 January 1891.

DIVISIONS.	1889.		1890.	
	New Books.	New Editions.	New Books.	New Editions.
Theology, Sermons, Biblical, etc.	630	134	555	153
Educational, Classical and Philological	557	124	561	88
Juvenile Works and Tales	418	93	443	95
Novels, Tales and other Fiction	1040	364	881	323
Law, Jurisprudence, etc.	66	40	40	39
Political and Social Economy, Trade and Commerce	110	16	87	22
Art, Sciences and Illustrated Works	112	34	54	19
Voyages, Travels, Geographical Research . . .	203	57	188	69
History, Biography, etc.	310	114	294	97
Poetry and the Drama	133	54	114	74
Year Books and Serials in Volumes	342	4	318	1
Medicine, Surgery, etc.	133	49	143	50
Belles-Lettres, Essays, Monographs, etc. . . .	157	183	171	191
Miscellaneous, including Pamphlets, not Sermons	483	107	511	100
	4694	1373	4414	1321
		4694		4414
		6067		5735

Book production statistics for Great Britain, *Publishers' Weekly,* 24 January 1891.

APPENDIX E
Reviews of the 1905
London Reissue of Poems (1890)

I N January 1905, carrying the imprint of Methuen & Co., Dickinson's first volume of poems made a second appearance in London. Apparently unaware of the 1891 Osgood, McIlvaine edition, Methuen promoted its new title with the following explanation:

> This is the first issue in England of a very remarkable volume of poems. Miss Dickinson is a highly spiritual and mystical writer, and her poems have some of the flavour of William Blake.

Joel Myerson describes this publication as an "American printing for English sale," for its paper matches that used for American reprintings of the 1890 *Poems* by Little, Brown, from whom Methuen probably purchased the sheets (*DB*, 15). There were two Methuen imprints, the first carrying the year 1904, the second, 1905. Methuen had briefly announced the book for November 1904, but there is no evidence of publication until the volume was brought back into its advertisements as ready for sale January 20, 1905. The last known Methuen listing to carry the title appeared March 15. Dickinson's *Poems* appears in about half of Methuen's advertisements during these two months.

Few British critics noticed this belated appearance of the American poet. Methuen may have been frugal with its review copies, for most dailies and weeklies carrying "books received" columns do not cite the book. Where its publication was so acknowledged, as in such weeklies as the *Spectator*, the *Academy*, the *Saturday Review*, and *Outlook*, there was no further mention. The five reviewers who do comment on the volume appear to treat Dickinson as virtually unknown in England and do not dispute Methuen's claim to be introducing her to British readers. They were alerted to the poet's success in America, however, because the 1904 Methuen issue carried a copyright page with the words "Seventeenth Edition," an identification identical with that of the 1904 Little, Brown reprinting of *Poems* (1890).

Methuen reports that sales and other records of this volume are missing.

E1   [T. P. O'Connor?] "T. P.'s Bookshelf." "A Book of Verse." *T.P.'s Weekly* [London], 5 (January 20, 1905), 107.

I have been glancing through a little volume of "Poems" by Emily Dickinson, poems which have a curious charm. The writer is much better known in

America, where she was born and died, than over here. She was a recluse, hardly ever leaving her father's house; yet in her solitude she learnt a certain wisdom concerning the things of the world. In construction her verse is faulty, often almost ugly; yet it is never without some definite thought. Take "The Secret":

> Some things that fly there be —
> Birds, hours, the bumble-bee:
> Of these no elegy.
>
> Some things that stay there be —
> Grief, hills, eternity:
> Nor this behooveth me.
>
> There are that resting, rise.
> Can I expound the skies?
> How still the riddle lies!

And here is charming fancy called "Autumn":

> The morns are meeker than they were.
> The nuts are getting brown;
> The berry's cheek is plumper,
> The rose is out of town.
>
> The maple wears a gayer scarf,
> The field a scarlet gown.
> Lest I should be old-fashioned,
> I'll put a trinket on.

Such work as this has, at least, a note of its own.

E2   "New Books." *The Manchester Guardian,* January 27, 1905, p. 5. The *Guardian* had more to say in 1891; see no. 192.

The place of Emily Dickinson among poets is not yet definitely fixed, but the fact that a seventeenth edition of her POEMS has appeared shows that in spite of her disregard of form her thoughts appeal to the modern consciousness. Colonel Higginson compares Emily Dickinson to William Blake, but beyond originality they have little in common. This quality may secure remembrance, for some of her work will pass into the common inheritance. Her verse "If I can stop one heart from breaking" may find a place side by side with Blake's "Little lamb, who made thee?" in the anthologies of the future.

E3   "Poetry, Verse, and Drama." *Glasgow Herald,* February 6, 1905, p. 5. The *Herald* also reviewed Dickinson in 1891; see no. 195.

One is more than startled to find a volume bearing the imprint "seventeenth edition," whose author has hitherto been unknown. From the brief preface we gather that the authoress, a native of Massachusetts, died on May 15, 1886, at the age of 56, and that her poems were the fruit of long years of seclusion. The preface draws not unjustly a comparison between her work and that of Blake. There is here the same elements of intellectual and emotional surprise, as of a revealing light suddenly flashed on one's inward vision, so that almost unconsciously one reads again to renew the miracle. Blake's singular purity of phrase is likewise present, an absolute simplicity which is either the crowning attain-

ment of a highly finished art or the faithful record of a wonderfully true insight
into life and nature. Almost necessarily we incline to the latter opinion, for
whether there be highly developed art at work or not, the vision, the spiritual
insight, is undoubted. But while all is spiritual, there is no abstraction; it is
luminous with the reality of life itself. Where every other page contains some
pregnant thought or phrase choice quotation is difficult, but the following,
with its imperfect rhymes yet satisfying rhythm, is characteristic: —

> To fight aloud is very brave,
>   But gallanter, I know,
> Who charge within the bosom,
>   The cavalry of woe.
>
> Who win, and nations do not see,
>   Who fall, and none observe,
> Whose dying eyes no country
>   Regards with patriot love.
>
> We trust in plumed procession,
>   For such the angels go,
> Rank after rank, with even feet
>   And uniforms of snow.

The book is one to dip into again and again, for the striking originality of the
little poems brings something refreshing with it at each venture.

E4   "Recent Verse." *Athenaeum* [London], No. 4036 (March 4, 1905), pp.
269–70. The *Athenaeum* did not review the 1891 London edition.

In editing Miss Dickinson's *Poems*, Mr. T. W. Higginson claims for them
"a quality more suggestive of the poetry of William Blake than of anything to
be elsewhere found." This faith is justified to a point, but one might add that
the influence of Browning is very marked, as witness the poem entitled 'The
Lonely House.' Where else does this echo come from?

> Day rattles, too,
>   Stealth's slow;
> The sun has got as far
> As the third sycamore.
>   Screams chanticleer,
>   "Who's there?"
> And echoes, trains away,
>   Sneer—"Where?"
> While the old couple, just astir,
> Fancy the sunrise left the door ajar!

Mr. Higginson very justly describes these verses as "poetry of the portfolio";
they were, he tells us, produced absolutely without thought of publication, and
the author was only induced to publish a few in her lifetime. The result is, as
the editor remarks, that though the verses gain sometimes "through the habit
of freedom and the unconventional utterance of daring thoughts," they lose "whatever advantage lies in the discipline of public criticism and the enforced conformity to accepted ways."
Miss Dickinson was born in 1830, and died in 1886, and this book has found

considerable favour in America since her death. It is not likely to secure a great vogue in this country, but certainly those who are genuinely interested in poetry will like to possess this specimen of the genuine thing. Miss Dickinson was absolutely indifferent to form and rule. She used rhyme when it came handy, and she ruthlessly abandoned it when it did not. She fell back on assonance, and often very indifferent assonance. Blake had far more form than she; yet is not this like Blake?

> Apparently with no surprise
> To any happy flower,
> The frost beheads it at its play
> In accidental power.
> The bland assassin passes on,   [blond
> The sun proceeds unmoved
> To measure off another day
> For an approving God.

Indeed, one feels at times disposed to echo Miss Dickinson's verses: —

> Much madness is divinest sense
> To a discerning eye;
> Much sense the starkest madness.

Does divine sense, then, lie in such madness as this? —

> I asked no other thing,
> No other was denied.
> I offered Being for it;
> The mighty merchant smiled.

> Brazil? He twirled a button,
> Without a glance my way:
> "But, madam, is there nothing else
> That we can show to-day?"

Yet while one is being brought up by these inexplicable eccentricities one comes upon such a lyrical gem as

> New feet within my garden go,
> New fingers stir the sod;
> A troubadour upon the elm
> Betrays the solitude.

> New children play upon the green,
> New weary sleep below;
> And still the pensive spring returns,
> And still the punctual snow!

Miss Dickinson rushed at her meanings blindly and recklessly. Very often she reached them, and expressed them often in her uncouth mannerisms, and sometimes with sweetness and dignity. But, as often as not, her wild career merely issues in vagueness, in helplessness, in a mist in which she gropes hopelessly after a lost and intangible significance. How simple and how real she can be is seen in such verses as 'The First Lesson'; how *bizarre* and how much divorced from equable emotion is visible in a poem which, nevertheless, clings to the reluctant memory:

I died for beauty, but was scarce
  Adjusted in the tomb,
When one who died for truth was lain
  In an adjoining room.

He questioned softly why I failed?
  "For beauty," I replied.
"And I for truth,—the two are one;
  We brethren are," he said.

And so, as kinsmen met a night,
  We talked between the rooms,
Until the moss had reached our lips,
  And covered up our names.

E5 "The Library." *The Queen* [London] 17 (June 1905), 967. The *Queen's* earlier review is no. 194.

The *Poems* of Emily Dickinson bear out the contention of their able editor, Mr. Thomas Wentworth Higginson, so long the literary dictator of Boston. Col. Higginson, whose taste in *belles lettres* has much distinction, claims that "in these pages a thoughtful reader will find a quality more suggestive of the poetry of William Blake than of anything to be elsewhere found—flashes of wholly original and profound insight into nature and life, words and phrases exhibiting an extraordinary vividness of descriptive and imaginative power, yet often set in a seemingly whimsical or even rugged frame." Here are examples:

The bee is not afraid of me,
I know the butterfly;
The pretty people in the woods
Receive me cordially.

The brooks laugh louder when I come,
The breezes madder play.
Wherefore, mine eyes, thy silver mists?
Wherefore, O summer's day?

This is a whole poem, and so is:

If I can stop one heart from breaking,
I shall not live in vain;
If I can ease one life the aching,
Or cool one pain,
Or help one fainting robin
Unto his nest again,
I shall not live in vain.

I do not quote these as the best examples of Miss Dickinson's poems. She has quite a Blakish originality. All lovers of poetry should read the volume, though at her worst Miss Dickinson would have made even Wordsworth laugh.

Index and Finding List

T H I S listing indexes and provides brief explanatory notation for authors and periodicals, and for persons, titles, subjects, and possibly obscure references in the foregoing documents. Citations refer to item rather than page numbers.

Among subjects treated, for example, is "incisiveness" as a feature of Dickinson's style. Another is "bindings" of the nineties volumes as a matter of interest to reviewers. As it would lead to unwieldy entries, no attempt has been made to collect all references to each Dickinson volume issued during the decade. However, the following publication dates may help those interested in the reception of a particular book: *Poems* [First Series], Nov. 12, 1890; *Poems*, English edition, July 30, 1891; *Poems*, "Second Series," Nov. 9, 1891; *Letters of Emily Dickinson*, Nov. 21, 1894; *Poems*, "Third Series," Sept. 1, 1896.

Other deliberate omissions include review titles, cursory mention of Thomas Wentworth Higginson or Mabel Loomis Todd as editors of the nineties' volumes (though discussions of their editing or of their writing about Dickinson are indexed), identification of Roberts Brothers as Dickinson's publisher, summary mention of the poet's themes by general category (e.g., death, life, nature, eternity) and routine references to members of Dickinson's family, to Amherst as her place of residence and to Boston as her place of publication. It should be mentioned that circulation figures for periodicals and newspapers are based on the not always reliable estimates provided in annual newspaper directories of the period.

Blair, Hugh (1718–1800), mentioned, 258

Blair, Robert (1699–1746), mentioned, 216

Blake, Carrie, reports lecture on ED, 107

Blake, William (1757–1827), compared to ED, 2, 3, 10, 12, 13, 15, 16, 17, 20, 28, 33, 44, 45, 49, 51, 52, 54, 64, 71, 72, 78, 95, 97, 110, 120, 125, 132, 140, 145, 150, 155, 177, 178, 184, 191, 192, 194, 195, 202, 205, 232, 251, 254, 260, 310, 325, 333, 353, 371A, 455, 480, 489, 491, 494, 560, 569, 576, 579, 580, 587, App. E2, E3, E4; Blake's drawings compared to ED, 147

Blatvatsky, Mme. Helena Petrovna (1831–1891; spiritualist and theosophist), mentioned, 348

Block, Louis James (1851–1927; Chicago poet, playwright, high school principal; pub. *Dramatic Sketches and Poems*, 1891), as author, 49

Bloede, Gertrude (1845–1905; Am. poet; pseud. "Stuart Sterne"), mentioned, 92, 500

Bodman, Mrs. Luther W. *See* Smith, Grace Herbert

Boker, George Henry (1823–1890; Am. playwright and poet), mentioned, 32

Book Buyer (N.Y.; pub. by Scribner's, this 60-page monthly had, by the nineties, become more than a company paper; 7,500 circ.), items pub. in, 31, 32, 106, 148, 255, 326, 342, 361, 389, 393, 398, 471

Book News (Phila.; monthly trade journal pub. by John Wanamaker's book department; 8,500 circ.), items pub. in, 39, 62A, 122A, 218A, 256A, 349, 483, 533, 538

Book Review (weekly devoted to current literature that apparently ceased soon after its inaugural issue; place of pub. unknown), item pub. in, 117

Book Reviews (N.Y.; monthly trade journal pub. by Macmillan beginning in 1893; no circ. data), items pub. in, 433, 474

Bookman (London book trade monthly, 1891–1934), item pub. in, 354

Bookman (N.Y.; a 100-page monthly literary review that began its distinguished career in 1895 with a circ. of about 2,250), item pub. in, 506; mentioned, 526, 557

books, ED's love of. *See* reading, ED's

Bookseller (London trade weekly), item pub. in, 155

Booth, Bertha, brief mention, 378

Booth, William (1829–1912; British clergyman and author; founder of the Salvation Army), mentioned, 109

Boston Beacon (woman's society and literary weekly; 5,000 circ.), items pub. in, 45, 114, 265, 403, 478, 534, 535

Boston Budget (woman's society and literary weekly, edited by Lilian Whiting *q.v.*; 4,000 circ.), items pub. in, 20, 58, 116, 271, 548

Boston Courier. See Boston Sunday Courier

Boston Daily Advertiser (14,000 circ.), items pub. in, 50, 69, 251, 421, 532

Boston Daily Globe (130,000 circ.), items pub. in, 94, 281. *See also Boston Sunday Globe*

Boston Daily Traveller (20,000 circ.), items pub. in, 17, 210, 277, 410

Boston Evening Transcript (a sedate daily with a largely upper-class readership, the *Transcript* carried the most influential review columns of the Boston papers; 13,000 circ.), items pub. in, 4, 5, 48, 89, 153, 180, 305, 307, 308, 312, 369, 391, 409, 428, 448, 461, 464, 494, 495, 507, 557, 563, 576

Boston Gazette. See Boston Saturday Evening Gazette

Boston Globe. See Boston Daily Globe and *Boston Sunday Globe*

Boston Herald (daily; 120,000 circ.), 59, 217, 327, 429. *See also Boston Sunday Herald*

North, Helen Marshall (ed. of *The Mary Lyon Year Book*, 1895), as author, 477

Northampton Daily Hampshire Gazette (Northampton, Mass.; 1,000 circ.), item pub. in, 226

Northampton Daily Herald (Northampton, Mass.; 2,000 circ.), item pub. in, 156

obituary, ED's, reprinted, App. A; mentioned, 560

obscurity of ED's poems, 86, 95, 115, 145, 150, 231, 265, 276, 530, 560, 571. *See also* Emerson, ED compared to

O'Connor, Thomas Power (1848–1929; Member of Parliament and editor of *T.P.'s Weekly*, *q.v.*), as possible author, App. E1

Omar Khayyam, compared to ED, 97, 480, 491, 580

Oracle, K. B. (pseud.), as author, 297

originality, ED's [a selective listing], 2, 3, 10, 19, 20, 21, 22, 44, 48, 78, 83, 120, 140, 208, 259, 272, 353, 560, 572, 580

Osgood, James Ripley (1836–1892; London publisher of ED's poems), App. B

Othello, ED's reference to, 464

Ottima (character in Robert Browning's verse-drama, "Pippa Passes"), mentioned, 74

Out of the Heart, Poems For Lovers Young and Old, 61

Outlook (N.Y.; previously *Christian Union* [*q.v.*]; religious weekly noted for its literary contributions), items pub. in, 488, 502, 508, 523

Overland Monthly (San Francisco; the *Atlantic Monthly* of the West; 7,500 circ.), items pub. in, 150, 345, 575

Ovid, mentioned, 494

Oxford Midweekly (Oxford, Mass.; 300 circ.), item pub. in, 119

Pacific Commercial Advertiser (Honolulu), item pub. in, 504

Packard, Clara Sanford. *See* Newton, Mrs. Simeon

Packer Alumna (pub. by Packer Collegiate Institute, Brooklyn, N.Y.), items pub. in, 170, 279, 284

Page, Thomas Nelson (1853–1922; Am. diplomat, author), mentioned, 582

Pall Mall Budget (illustrated London weekly affiliated with the independent Liberal daily *Pall Mall Gazette*; ed. Charles Morley; "cultivated a lighter vein of gossipy interest" than the *Graphic*, the *Illustrated London News*, or *Black and White*), item pub. in, 220

Park, Edwards Amasa (1808–1900; professor at Andover Theological Seminary; one of the most noted preachers in the Congregational church), mentioned by ED, 454

Parker, Theodore, (1810–1860; Unitarian clergyman, author), mentioned by ED, 490

Parkman, Francis (1823–1893; Am. historian), mentioned, 57

parodies of ED's poems, 352, 496, 529

Parsons, George Frederic (1840–1893; affiliated with the *New York Tribune*), sent a review copy of 1890 *Poems*, 77

Pater, Walter (1839–1894), mentioned, 493

Patmore, Coventry (1823–1896; English poet), compared to ED, 63

patriotism, ED's, 2, 259

Pattison, Mark (1813–1884; English literary historian; his *Memoirs* pub. 1883), mentioned, 454

Payne, William Morton (1858–1919; literary editor and leading critic for the Chicago *Dial*), as author, 110, 378, 572

rhythm, ED's use of, 7, 44, 51, 62, 78, 129, 135, 145, 256A, 263, 273, 419, 490, 529

Richter, Jean Paul (1763–1825; German satirist, philosopher; pub. *Introduction to Aesthetics*, 1805), mentioned, 553

riddle, ED's use of. *See* obscurity

Riley, James Whitcomb (1849–1916; "Hoosier poet" known for his dialect verse), compared to ED, 589; mentioned, 93, 392

Rives, Amelie [Princess Troubetzkoy], (1863–1945; popular Am. novelist and playwright), mentioned, 107, 582

Robertson, Thomas William (1829–1871; English actor, dramatist), mentioned, 172

Robin Goodfellow (a merry domestic sprite, also known as Puck), mentioned, 553

Roche, James Jeffrey (1847–1908; Am. poet and journalist, later ambassador to Switzerland; assumed editorship of *The Pilot* [*q.v.*] in 1890), as author, 41; at Mrs. Moulton's, 30

Rollins, Alice [Marland] Wellington (1847–1897; poet, novelist, critic), as possible author, 46

Root, Abiah Palmer, later Mrs. Samuel W. Strong (b. 1830; ED's girlhood friend and correspondent), ED's friendship with, 467; App. B, *s.v.* Strong, Abiah P.

Rossetti, Christina Georgina (1830–1894; English Pre-Raphaelite poet known for religious lyrics marked by intensity and mysticism), compared to ED, 505; like Blake in terseness, 54; mentioned, 32, 493, 501; App. B

Rossetti, Dante Gabriel (1828–1882; English poet and painter), mentioned, 481

Round Table (N.Y.; weekly review founded in 1863 by ED's cousin Henry Sweetser and his cousin Charles Sweetser), the 1864 publication of ED's "Some keep the Sabbath going to church" in the *Round Table* mentioned, 51, 95

Rous, Joseph, ED compared to, 344

Rushlight (student literary publication of Wheaton Seminary, now Wheaton College, Norton, Mass.), item pub. in, 107

Ruskin, John (1819–1900), ED's reading of, 493, 560; mentioned by ED in letter to Higginson, 216, 221, 232, 237, 240, 254, 258, 357, 438, 454, 468, 477, 484, 487, 488, 495, 502, 526; mentioned, 2, 10, 19, 20, 123, 132, 237, 325, 380, 543, 561, 576

St. Augustine (354–430), mentioned, 454

St. James's Gazette (London evening "Clubland" paper representing "cultured, critical, and essentially modern Toryism with a faint democratic flavour"; ed. Sidney J. Low; no circ. data), items pub. in, 189, 220

St. Joseph Daily News (St. Joseph, Mo.; daily; 6,500 circ.), item pub. in, 19

St. Louis Book News, item pub. in, 132

St. Nicholas (N.Y.; distinguished and flourishing monthly juvenile magazine ed. by Mary Mapes Dodge in the nineties; 60,000 circ.), on ED poem first published in, 144, 146, 149, 152

St. Paul Pioneer Press (St. Paul, Minn.; daily; 21,500 circ.), item pub. in, 129

Saltus, Francis (1849–1889; Am. poet; pub. *Honey and Gall*, 1873), compared to ED, 568; mentioned, 93

Salvini, Tommaso (1829–1916; Italian tragedian), mentioned by ED, 464, 493, 553

San Francisco Call. See San Francisco Morning Call

San Francisco Chronicle (daily; 50,000 circ.), items pub. in, 470, 546

San Francisco Evening Bulletin (17,000 circ.), items pub. in, 42, 233, 278

San Francisco Morning Call (48,000 circ.), item pub. in, 526

San Francisco Wave. See Wave

San Jose Mercury (San Jose, Calif.; daily; 8,500 circ.), item pub. in, 140

Sanborn, Franklin Benjamin (1831–1917; antiquarian, author, contributing editor to the *Springfield Republican* in nineties), as author, 251; mentioned, 299; App. B

Sappho (flourished 600 B.C.), compared to ED, 216, 314, 501, 512, 553

Saturday Review (Liberal London weekly with strong literary interests), items pub. in, 184, 202

Savannah Morning News (Savannah, Ga.; 5,000 circ.), item pub. in, 163

Saxe Holm. *See* Holm, Saxe

Schauffler, Henry Park (b. 1870), as author, 172, 259

Schiller, Johann Christoph Friedrich von (1759–1805). *See* Thekla

Schreiner, Olive Emilie Albertina (1855?–1920), mentioned, 125

Scollard, Clinton (1860–1932), mentioned, 93

Scotsman (Edinburgh daily; 50,000 circ. in 1877), item pub. in, 191

Scott, Sir Walter (1771–1832), compared to ED, 310; mentioned, 79, 250

Scribner's Magazine (N.Y.; leading literary monthly; ed. by Edward L. Burlingame in the nineties; 120,000 circ.), item pub. in, 123; ED review noted, 124, 128; on pub. of ED poem in, 1

Scudder, Horace Elisha (1838–1902; author and editor of *Atlantic Monthly* 1890–1898; twice declined ED poems submitted to that journal by Mrs. Todd), as possible author, 62

Seawell, Molly Elliot (1860–1916; Am. novelist), as subject, 347, 368

seclusion, ED's 2, 3, 6, 7, 10, 13, 17, 78, 84, 86, 99, 100, 105, 133, 145, 153, 156, 193, 221, 237, 249, 262, 263, 335, 348, 349, 418, 419, 420, 423, 426, 439, 445, 449, 452, 480, 491, 526, 557, 560, 568, 579, 585, App. A

Sevigné, Marquise de (nee Marie de Rabutin-Chantal, 1626–1696; French letter writer), compared to ED, 465

Shakespeare, William (1564–1616), ED's reading of, 221, 254, 493, 560, App. A; mentioned by ED, 467; character from *Winter's Tale* compared to ED, 262, 445; Shakespeare Club, 420, 438, 485; mentioned, 72, 250, 308, 325, 560. *See also* *Hamlet*; *Othello*

Shays, Daniel (1747–1825), mentioned, 176

Shelley, Percy Bysshe (1792–1822), ED compared to, 97, 480, 491, 560, 580; mentioned, 250, 529

Sherman, Frank Dempster (1860–1916; pub. *Lyrics for a Lute*, 1890), mentioned, 92, 93

Sibyl (pseud.), as author, 504

Sill, Edward Rowland (1841–1887; Am. poet and essayist), compared to ED, 586; mentioned, 93

Smith, C. M., as author, 151

Smith, Dr. Elihu Hubbard (1771–1798; Am. poet, editor, playwright; member of "Hartford Wits"), compared to ED, 380

Smith, Grace Herbert, reminiscence of ED by, 379

Smith, Sydney (1771–1845; London clergyman and wit), mentioned, 325

society, ED's attitude toward, 418, 429. *See also* seclusion

South Hadley, Mass. *See* Mt. Holyoke Seminary

Southey, Robert (1774–1843), mentioned, 250

Spasmodic School. *See* Fantastic School

Speake, Mrs. H. C., App. B

Ward, William Hayes (1835–1916; Congregational clergyman, superintending editor of the *Independent* in the early nineties, editor thereafter [1896–1914]; graduate of Amherst College and friend of Lavinia Dickinson; *see also AB*, pp. 68, 112–20), as author, 44; mentioned, 557; App. B.

Ware, Annie (character in the "Saxe Holm" story, "Whose Wife Was She?"), mentioned, 79

Warner, Charles Dudley (1829–1900; biographer, editor, novelist), as editor, 499A

Washington, George (1732–1799), ED recounts visiting grave, 491, 580

Watson, Sir [John] William (1858–1935; English poet), mentioned, 196

Watts, George Frederic (1817–1904; English painter), mentioned, 353

Watts-Dunton, Walter Theodore (1832–1914; British literary critic), mentioned, 250

Wave, A Weekly for Those in the Swim (San Francisco literary and society paper), item pub. in, 297

Webster, Augusta [Mrs.] (1840–1894; English poet whose dramatic verse was often compared to Robert Browning's), mentioned, 493

Webster, Daniel (1782–1852), legal volumes observed in ED home, 279

Weeks, Ida Ahlborn, letter to editor answered, 504A

Wegg, Silas (pseud.), as author, 260

Wellesley College, a principal of, App. B

Werner, Zacharias (1768–1823; German dramatist and preacher), mentioned, 574

Westen. See Der Westen

Westfield Times and Newsletter (Westfield, Mass.; weekly; 1,400 circ.), item pub. in, 292

Wetherell, James Elgin (1851–1940; Canadian anthologist), as author, 500

Whetcho, W. F. (literary editor of *Boston Daily Advertiser*), as author, 421

Whistler, James Abbott McNeill (1834–1903), mentioned, 64

Whiting, Charles Goodrich (1842–1910; critic, poet, literary editor of the *Springfield Republican* 1874–1910), as author, 13, 262

Whiting, Julia (sister of Charles Goodrich Whiting; pseud. "Van Der Dater"), as author, 562, 570

Whiting, Lilian (1847–1942; journalist, poet, and spiritualist philosopher; editor of *Boston Budget* 1890–1893; her three volumes of essays, *The World Beautiful* [1894–1896], ran through fourteen editions; "she looked at the world through large blue eyes which described the best in everything"), as author, 20, 24, 30, 45, 105, 162, 213, 271, 437, 444, 519, 531

Whitman, Walt (1819–1892), compared to ED, 145, 151, 232, 251, 255, 264, 280, 290, 300, 314, 337, 340, 463, 468, 497, 553 [2 places], 560, 579, 580, 582; mentioned by ED in letter to Higginson, 221; mentioned, 72, 123, 243, 250, 386

Whitney, Adeline Dutton Train (1824–1906; New England poet and novelist), mentioned, 93, 357

Whitney, Maria (1830–1910); ED's friend; teacher of French and German in Smith College), recipient of ED letters, 422; App. B

Whittier, John Greenleaf (1807–1892), alleged to have visited ED, 391; ED's reading of, 420, 438; mentioned, 93, 126, 530, 543

Wilde, Oscar (1856–1900), mentioned, 237, 382

Wilkins, Mary E. *See* Freeman, Mary Wilkins

Williams, Mary E., at ED lecture, 348

Williams, Talcott (1849–1928; editor, journalist; wrote for *Book News* 1889–1909), as author, 538

Willis, Nathaniel Parker (1806–1867; popular Am. poet, journalist, playwright), mentioned, 250

Wilmarth, Mrs. Henry, at ED lecture, 348

Wingate, Charles E[dgar] L[ewis] (1861–1944; succeeded Alexander Young as special Boston correspondent of the *Critic*, 1891), as author, 138, 161, 197, 207, 299

Winter, William (1836–1917; historian, essayist, poet, longtime drama critic for the *New York Tribune*; friend of T. B. Aldrich), mentioned, 93

Woman, The (a column? periodical?), mentioned, 86

womanhood, theme of in ED's poetry, 44, 64, 78, 125, 337, 560; App. A. *See also* femininity

Women's Club [Springfield, Mass.], lecture on ED at, 143

Woman's Journal (Boston weekly pub. by National American Woman Suffrage Association; ed. Lucy Stone and Henry B. Blackwell 1873–1909; 4,500 circ.), items pub. in, 35, 337, 405, 451, 516

Woman's Tribune (Washington, D. C.; woman suffrage weekly, ed. Clara Berwick Colby; 6,500 circ.), item pub. in, 143

Woodberry, George Edward (1855–1930; Mass. critic, poet, professor), mentioned, 27, 92, 93, 489

Woolley, Celia Parker (1848–1918; Am. novelist), as author, 240; mentioned, 382

Woolsey, Sarah Chauncey (1835–1905; Am. poet; pseud. "Susan Coolidge"; friend of Helen Hunt Jackson), as author, 57

Worcester Light. See Light

Worcester Spy (Worcester, Mass.; daily; 7,500 circ.), items pub. in, 166, 394, 480, 481, 509, 542

Wordsworth, William (1770–1850), compared to ED, 127, 493, 494, 497, 560; like Blake in terseness, 54; relation to sister, 493; mentioned, 172, 250, 251, 299, 306, 327

World's Desire, The (novel by H. Rider Haggard and Andrew Lang, 1890), mentioned, 23

Wortman, Denis (1835–1922; Amherst College graduate, clergyman), as author, 168, 250, 467

Wortman, Jessie B., as author, 336

Writer (Boston; literary monthly ed. by William H. Hills; 5,000 circ.), item pub. in, 34

Yale Literary Magazine (New Haven, Conn.; ed. and pub. by students of Yale College; 600 circ.), item pub. in, 380

Yankee Blade (Boston; inexpensive family weekly of fiction and miscellany; ed. Sam Walter Foss; expired 1894; 110,000 circ.), item pub. in, 84

York Daily (York, N.Y.), item pub. in, 152

Young, Alexander (1836–1891; journalist, historian; special Boston correspondent for the *Critic*), as author, 1, 3, 39, 56, 104

Young, Edward (1683–1765), mentioned, 216

Young, Franklin K., as co-author of a book on chess, 396

Youth's Companion (Boston; leading children's weekly that published a number of ED's poems. Edited in the nineties by Daniel Sharp Ford, Hezekiah Butterworth, and Edward Stanwood. 480,000 circ.). *See* Phillips, Le Roy

Zoilus (Greek rhetorician of the 4th cent. B.C.), mentioned, 262

Zola, Emile (1840–1902), mentioned, 196

Index to Poems

POEMS are listed alphabetically by first line, with cross references to and from titles some of the poems had been given in the nineties. In searching a review for discussion of "Because I could not stop for death," for example, it is a convenience to know that the poem may be referred to merely as "The Chariot." To distinguish them from first lines, titles are given in quotation marks. In a few cases, two titles appear, reflecting a title change made between periodical and book publication of a poem.

The nineties volume in which a poem appeared follows its first line: the first 1890 edition was retrospectively termed "First Series" ("1stS"); the 1891 volume was published as *Poems*, "Second Series" ("2ndS"); the 1896 edition became "Third Series" ("3rdS"). In evaluating the degree of attention a poem evoked during the nineties, it should be considered whether it was among those poems not published until 1896, when interest in Dickinson had markedly declined. The abbreviation "Ltrs." is used for those poems which received publication in the 1894 edition of the poet's correspondence. No volume designation following the first line means that the poem appeared during the decade in a periodical only. References to the poems are cited according to the following scheme: "a)" precedes those reviews which quote the poem, partially or in full, and provide more than a sentence or two of discussion; "b)" indicates quotation of the poem but little or no discussion; "c)" designates cursory mention only—no more than a line or two of quotation, if any, and no significant discussion. Note that all poems published in the nineties are listed here in the belief that the critical sensibility of the period reveals itself in the poems it passed over almost as tellingly as in those it noticed.

I stepped from plank to plank ("Experiences"), 3rdS

I taste a liquor never brewed, 1stS, a) 13, 44, 72, 81, 325; b) 7, 47, 64, 74, 494, 553, 557, 579; c) 113, 501

I think just how my shape will rise, 2ndS, b) 489

I think the hemlock likes to stand ("The Hemlock"), 1stS, c) 63

I took my power in my hand ("The Duel"), 2ndS

I went to heaven, 2ndS, a) 321; b) 302

I went to thank her, 1stS

I wish I knew that woman's name, 3rdS

I wonder if the sepulchre. *See* I'm sorry for the dead, today

I worked for chaff, and earning wheat, 3rdS

I years had been from home ("Returning"), 2ndS

If anybody's friend be dead, 2ndS

If I can stop one heart from breaking, 1stS, b) 19, 26, 43, 47, 97, 145, 192, 239, 359, 377, 481, 581, App. E5; c) 553

If I may have it when it's dead, 3rdS

If I should die, 2ndS

If I shouldn't be alive, 1stS, b) 46, 107, 145, 481

If recollecting were forgetting ("With Flowers"), Ltrs., 3rdS, b) 426, 478, 521; c) 514, 523, 528, 541

If the foolish, call them "flowers," 3rdS, b) 515

If tolling bell I ask the cause. *See* Of tolling bell I ask the cause

If you were coming in the fall, 1stS, a) 192; b) 385 [headnote], 579; c) 95

I'll tell you how the sun rose ("A Day"), 1stS, b) 13, 63, 113, 380, 579; c) 95, 221, 495

I'm ceded, I stopped being theirs ("Love's Baptism"), 1stS, 44

I'm nobody! Who are you ("Nobody"), 2ndS, b) 267, 271, 305, 314, 326, 344, 355, 481, 579; c) 300

I'm sorry for the dead, today, 3rdS, b) 532

I'm wife I've finished that ("Apocalypse"), 1stS, b) 27

Immortal is an ample word, 3rdS, b) 521

"Immortality." *See* It is an honorable thought

"In a Library." *See* A precious, mouldering pleasure 'tis

In lands I never saw, they say, 2ndS

"In Shadow." *See* I dreaded that first robin so

"In the Garden." *See* A bird came down the walk

"In Vain." *See* I cannot live with you

"Indian Summer." *See* These are the days when birds come back

"Invisible." *See* From us she wandered now a year

Is bliss, then, such abyss, 3rdS, b) 521

Is heaven a physician, 2ndS, b) 481

It can't be summer, that got through, 2ndS

It dropped so low in my regard ("Disenchantment"), 3rdS, b) 533, 539, 541, 556, 575

It is an honorable thought ("Immortality"), 3rdS

It is not dying hurts us so. *See* 'Tis not that dying hurts us so